Digital Copyright and the Consumer Revolution

Hands off My iPod

Matthew Rimmer

Australian Research Council Future Fellow
Associate Professor, The Australian National University College of Law
Associate Director, ACIPA

Edward Elgar
Cheltenham, UK • Northampton, MA, USA

Published by
Edward Elgar Publishing Limited
The Lypiatts
15 Lansdown Road
Cheltenham
Glos GL50 2JA
UK

Edward Elgar Publishing, Inc.
William Pratt House
9 Dewey Court
Northampton
Massachusetts 01060
USA

Paperback edition 2011

A catalogue record for this book
is available from the British Library

Library of Congress Cataloguing in Publication Data

Rimmer, Matthew.
Digital copyright and the consumer revolution : hands off my iPod / by Matthew Rimmer.
p. cm.
Includes bibliographical references and index.
1. Copyright and electronic data processing—United States. 2. Copyright and electronic data processing. I. Title.
KF3030.1.R56 2007
346.7304′82—dc22
2006034676

ISBN 978 1 84542 948 5 (cased)
ISBN 978 0 85793 371 3 (paperback)

Printed and bound by MPG Books Group, UK

Digital Copyright and the Consumer Revo

Contents

Preface

> The iPod has consumed my life like few things before it. (Dylan Jones, *iPod, Therefore I Am: Thinking Inside the White Box*)

A late adopter of new technology, I received an iPod Shuffle, a hot ticket item, as a Christmas present in December 2005. Travelling across the Pacific from Australia to Canada on New Year's Eve, I listened to one hundred and twenty songs drawn from my musical library. The personal soundtrack to my life included the psychedelic music of Pink Floyd and David Bowie; the agitprop pub rock of Midnight Oil, Hunters & Collectors, and the Cruel Sea; the Antipodean storytelling of singer–songwriters, David Bridie, Paul Kelly and Neil Finn; and the keening of country divas, Kasey Chambers, the Dixie Chicks and KD Lang. I was impressed that the MP3 player allowed me to engage in the 'space-shifting' of my musical collection, and the 'time-shifting' of Internet broadcasts.

As an intellectual property academic, I was also intrigued by the implications of the iPod for copyright law. Apple Computers encouraged its customers to 'rip, mix, burn', yet warned them, 'Don't Steal Music.' The one device could contain copyright works bought from the iTunes music store, copies of vinyl recordings and compact discs from home computers, as well as digital music circulated, without permission, on the Internet and peer to peer networks. It struck me that the 'white box' deserved greater critical scrutiny and examination. There was a need to better explain the complex relationship between copyright law, new digital technologies and consumer behaviour.

My interest in copyright law is a longstanding one. It has been fostered by a number of academic mentors and teachers. I owe much to Professor Peter Drahos for kindling my interest in intellectual property at the Australian National University. I am indebted to my old doctoral supervisor, Professor Kathy Bowrey of the University of Technology Sydney for her enthusiasm, guidance and inspiration. I am grateful to Professor Jill McKeough of the University of Technology Sydney for providing sensible advice, calm support and dry wit. I have also been indebted to Professor Brad Sherman from the University of Queensland for his camaraderie and patronage.

This book has been written while I have been based at the Australian National University College of Law. I have been fortified by the support and the trust of the Dean, Professor Michael Coper, and the Head of School, Professor Stephen Bottomley, and his predecessor, the late great, Professor Phillipa Weeks. I have learnt much from my academic colleagues and students alike. This book has been immeasurably improved by the help and assistance of a number of enthusiastic and dedicated research assistants and Summer Research Scholars, including Katrina Gunn, Ishtiaque Omar, Elsa Gilchrist, Jessica Graham, Christine Henry and Paul Clarke.

I am grateful for the help and support of everyone at Edward Elgar Publishing, including Luke Adams, Edward Elgar, Nep Elverd, Kate Emmins, Emma Gribbon, and Caroline McLin.

This book has been enriched by my associations with a number of organizations. I am an associate director of the research centre, the Australian Centre for Intellectual Property in Agriculture (ACIPA), which is based at the Australian National University, the Griffith University and the University of Queensland. I am grateful for the help and support of all the researchers and administrators who have worked under its banner. I have also had fruitful discussions with members of the 'Unlocking IP' group based at the University of New South Wales, and the Centre for Governance of Knowledge and Development at RegNet. I am a member of the Copyright and Intellectual Property Advisory Group of the Australian Library and Information Association (ALIA). This affiliation has heightened my appreciation of the wonderful work of librarians, archivists and information managers. I am also a director of the Australian Digital Alliance (ADA), an advocacy group, which represents the copyright interests of libraries, educational institutions and technology developers. This lobby group has sharpened my understanding of the abrasive politics of copyright law.

This book was nurtured and cultivated during visits to cold, progressive countries. I am grateful for the productive dialogues that I had in Canada with Professor Michael Geist and Marcus Bornfreund of the University of Ottawa, Professor Margaret Ann Wilkinson of the University of Western Ontario and Professor Myra Tawfik of the University of Windsor. I am also thankful for the exchanges that I had in Scandinavia with Eva Hemmungs Wirten of Uppsala University, Mathias Klang of Göteburg University and Lee Davis of the Copenhagen Business School. I am also obliged for the support of a number of academics from other institutions, including Dr Kirsten Anker of McGill University, Dr Livio Dobrez of the Australian National University, Associate Professor Andrew Kenyon of the University of Melbourne, Dr Dianne Nicol of the University of Tasmania and Professor Carolyn Sappideen of the University of Western Sydney. I also appreciate the insights and wisdom of Chris Creswell of the Attorney General's Department.

As always, I rely upon the kindness of friends, especially Kevin Boreham and Edwin Ho, Helen and James Chisholm, Janine Lapworth, Dr Simone Murray, Dr Kristin Natalier and Al King, Daniel Neidle, Dr Mark Nolan, Tanya Richards-Pugh and Ivan Sun. I am thankful for the magnanimous commitment to education shown by my parents, Professor Peter Rimmer and Dr Susan Rimmer. I am also fortunate to have the insights of my artistic siblings, Joe Rimmer and Rachel Rimmer. I hope that my two children, Marina Rimmer and Joshua Rimmer, will understand the importance of reading public domain, 'Winnie the Pooh', instead of Disney's copyrighted versions. I am also grateful to Joane Ford for the gift of language.

Finally, I wish to thank my wife (and sometime iPod widow), Susan Harris Rimmer, for her generous love, commitment, empathy and eternal patience.

M.R.

Preface to this edition

Published in 2007, *Digital Copyright and the Consumer Revolution: Hands off My iPod* was prophetic about the growing rebellion by citizens and consumers against digital copyright laws.

The efforts to challenge the constitutionality of the copyright term extension have faltered – with Lawrence Golan struggling in an appeal.[1] Orphan works continue to be a great policy problem without any immediate solution.

Following on from its success with the iPod, Apple has released the iPhone and the iPad to great fanfare. In addition to making premium, digital rights management-free music available on iTunes, the company has also brokered a deal to put the back catalogue of The Beatles on its electronic store. Apple has also expanded the range of its services to include a wide variety of television series, movies, computer applications, and eBooks. There has been much debate, though, as to whether Apple has been creating 'tethered appliances' rather than an open, inter-operable system.[2]

Peer-to-peer networks continue to cause consternation for copyright owners with further litigation against The Pirate Bay, Limewire, and versions of BitTorrent.[3] Nonetheless, new versions of the sites have arisen such as the Limewire Pirate Edition. Lawsuits against individual users of peer-to-peer networks remain controversial – with Jammie Thomas-Rasset becoming a martyr figure.[4]

From being an alternative, avant-garde practice, mash-ups have become a staple of mainstream entertainment. There has also been a new publishing genre of literary mash-ups – most famously of all, *Pride and Prejudice and Zombies*. Shepard Fairey has been entangled in legal conflict with his artistic mash-up of Barack Obama.[5] The DJ, Girl Talk, has become a celebrity for his musical mash-ups. His work was featured in Brett Gaylor's documentary, *RiP!: A Remix Manifesto*.[6] The hit television series, *Glee*, has further popularized the genre of mash-ups.

Consumers have lobbied for a further amelioration of the strictures of technological protection measures. In July 2010, the United States Copyright Office recognized a number of new exceptions to the technological protection measures regime.[7] The exemptions related to noncommercial remixes of videos; 'jailbreaking' iPods and iPhones; unlocking cell phones; computer programs and security testing; computer programs protected by dongles; and allowing users to enable the read-aloud function of eBooks.

There has been much conflict over copyright law and intermediaries with litigation in Australia in *Roadshow Films Pty Ltd* v. *iiNet Limited*;[8] a push in various countries for a '3-strikes' rule for repeat infringers by copyright owners; and debate over Internet liability in the *Anti-Counterfeiting Trade Agreement* 2010.

The search engine Google has been embroiled in mega-litigation with an array of rivals and competitors. The company has reached a settlement with authors and publishers over Google Book Search.[9] However, there has been disquiet about the implications of the settlement for competition, innovation, and access to knowledge. Google has set up Google eBookstore to provide access to eBooks to read on the web, and on devices such as Android, iPod touch, iPhones, iPads, Sony's Reader and Barnes & Noble's Nook. Google is also planning to move into the music marketplace with Google Music mooted. As predicted, Google won its appeal against Perfect 10 in respect of the Google Images case.[10] At first instance, Google and YouTube defeated Viacom International, on the grounds that they were sheltered by the safe harbour for Internet intermediaries.[11] The matter is under appeal. Google and YouTube also continue to face a class action from various parties including the British Football Premier League, musical publishers, and helicopter journalist, Robert Tur.[12] Google has also earned the ire of the media mogul, Rupert Murdoch, who has accused the news aggregator of 'kleptomania'.

In the last several years, a number of social networking sites and platforms have risen to prominence. Flickr has been involved in an interesting conflict with a girl, Alison Chang, objecting to Virgin Mobile Australia using Creative Commons-licensed pictures of her in advertising campaigns.[13] Aaron Sorkin's film, *The Social Network*, brilliantly dramatized the conflicts between Mark Zuckerberg and the Winklevoss Twins over the ownership of the site, Facebook. Twitter has been embroiled in controversy over mainstream news services exploiting the work of freelance photographers using TwitPic.[14] The online encyclopaedia, Wikipedia, has adopted Creative Commons licences as its default setting. The whistleblowing site, Wikileaks, has been hugely influential, with its diffusion of diplomatic cables and war logs of the United States military involvement in Afghanistan and Iraq. The site raises fundamental questions of intellectual property law, media law, national security law, and constitutional protections of freedom of speech, and freedom of the press.

2011

NOTES

1. *Golan* v. *Holder* 609 F. 3d 1076 (2010).
2. Zittrain, Jonathan (2008), *The Future of the Internet and How to Stop It*, New Haven and London: Yale University Press and Penguin Books.
3. *Arista Records LLC* v. *Lime Group LLC* 715 F. Supp. 2d 481 (SDNY, 2010).
4. *Capitol Records* v. *Jammie Thomas-Rasset* 2010 WL 291763.
5. *Fairey* v. *Associated Press* 09-01123 (AKH) United States District Court, SDNY (2009).
6. Gaylor, Brett (2009), *RiP!: A Remix Manifesto*, Eyesteel Film.
7. Library of Congress (2010), 'Exemption to Prohibition on Circumvention of Copyright Protection Systems for Access Control Technologies', *Federal Register*, **75**(143), 43825, 27 July 2010.
8. *Roadshow Films Pty Ltd* v. *iiNet Limited* (No. 3) [2010] FCA 24 (4 February 2010).
9. *The Authors' Guild Inc. and the Association of American Publishers* v. *Google Inc* Case No. 05 CV 8136-JES (2008), http://www.googlebooksettlement.com/.
10. *Perfect 10 Inc.* v. *Amazon.com Inc. and Google Inc.* 487 F.3d 701 (2007).
11. *Viacom International* v. *YouTube* 718 F. Supp. 2d 514 (S.D.N.Y. 2010).
12. *The Football Association Premier League Limited et al.* v. *YouTube, Inc. et al.*, Amended Class Action Complaint, 07 Civ. 3582 (LLS), United States District Court, SDNY.
13. *Chang v. Virgin Mobile USA, LLC*, 2009 WL 111570 (N.D.Tex. January 16, 2009).
14. *Agence France Presse* v. *Morel* (2010) United States District Court, SDNY, Trial Proceedings, http://www.bjp-online.com/digital_assets/1811/AFP_v_Morel.pdf.

Introduction

> The songs on our iPods, the television shows we capture on TiVo, the music videos in our new portable video players, the movies we watch in our DVD collections – we believe that these digital slices of media also belong to us in a real sense. (J.D. Lasica, *Darknet*[1])

In the landmark *Sony Betamax* case in 1984, the Supreme Court of the United States held that consumers' home copying of television programmes on video cassette recorders (VCR) was a fair use of copyright works.[2] Accordingly, the Bench ruled that the manufacturer of a VCR was not liable for the secondary copyright infringement, because the technology was capable of substantial non-infringing uses. The judgment has been hailed as 'the Magna Carta and the Declaration of Independence rolled into one' for consumers and technology innovators.[3] The ruling has been lauded by consumers as a boon not only for 'the makers of not just VCRs, but also every other technology capable of being used for infringement (e.g., photocopiers, personal computers, Cisco routers, CD burners, and Apple's iPod)'.[4] At the same time, the decision has been derided as an unwarranted incursion into the economic rights of copyright industries. Jack Valenti of the Motion Picture Association of America famously compared the VCR to 'the Boston strangler'.[5] Others wondered whether the significance of the decision had eroded over time, especially in light of digital technologies.[6]

In 2005, the Supreme Court of the United States had an opportunity to revisit the *Sony Betamax* decision, and consider the rights of consumers in respect of digital copyright. The nine judges considered whether the peer-to-peer networks, Grokster and Streamcast, were liable for secondary copyright infringement because the users of the systems traded copyrighted music and films, without authorization.[7] Awaiting judgment, competing protestors squared off against one another on the steps of the Supreme Court of the United States. On one side, consumer activists marched with placards warning, 'Save Betamax', 'Hands off my iPod', 'Don't Touch my TiVo', and 'Don't Put Home Recording on Pause'.[8] Similarly, supporters of technology developers and entrepreneurs held up banners, proclaiming 'Don't Stop Innovation', 'Pro America Innovation', and 'Pro America, Pro Innovation, Pro Betamax'.[9] On the other side, the supporters of copyright industries held up opposing placards. Some invoked a natural rights theory of copyright law, protesting to a higher authority, 'Thou Shalt Not Steal – God'.[10] Others relied upon the image of romantic authorship, with guitar-wielding musicians seeking sympathy for the plight of starving artists, 'Feed a Musician Today – Download Legally' and 'Don't Steal My Future'.[11] This lively, theatrical display – 'Rent-a-Crowd', if you are cynically inclined – was well organized by the competing interests. Once the verdict was handed down, the various lawyers, business leaders and spin-doctors descended from on high to the steps of the Supreme Court of the United States. A variety of partisan views were delivered on the nature and the significance of the decision in *Grokster*. A media scrum packed into the arena, and listened intently.

This protest was symbolic of a larger concern about the impact of copyright law upon consumers. There has been a growing consumer movement in opposition to the strictures imposed by the copyright industries. A number of NGOs, civil society groups, research centres and legal clinics have been at the vanguard of this movement. The Home Recording Rights Coalition has sought to 'protect your right to buy and use audio and video recorders players, and PCs'.[12] The Electronic Frontier Foundation (EFF) has been a significant advocate for consumer rights in respect of copyright law. The organization bills itself in these terms:

> From the Internet to the iPod, technologies are transforming our society and empowering us as speakers, citizens, creators, and consumers. When our freedoms in the networked world come under attack, the Electronic Frontier Foundation (EFF) is the first line of defense. EFF broke new ground when it was founded in 1990 – well before the Internet was on most people's radar – and continues to confront cutting-edge issues defending free speech, privacy, innovation, and consumer rights today. From the beginning, EFF has championed the public interest in every critical battle affecting digital rights.[13]

Political action groups like the American Civil Liberties Union, which previously had been concerned only with online privacy or censorship, have begun to take an active interest in intellectual property policy.[14] Downhill Battle launched a campaign of civil disobedience in respect of DJ Danger Mouse's mash-up, *The Grey Album*, a musical composition which spliced together The Beatles' *White Album* and Jay-Z's *The Black Album*. The Swarthmore Coalition for the Digital Commons has protested about copyright owners demanding that Internet Service Providers take down and remove politically sensitive copyright works.[15] Ralph Nader's organization, the Consumer Project on Technology (CP Tech), has shown a keen interest in intellectual property, access to knowledge and international law.[16] A number of advocacy and research centres have been established, such as the Creative Commons,[17] the Center for the Study of the Public Domain[18] and Public Knowledge.[19] Legal clinics, like the Stanford Law Center for Internet and the Society,[20] and the Samuelson Law, Technology, and Public Policy Clinic,[21] have also played an important role in representing the interests of consumers in both *amicus curiae* briefs and policy deliberations.

A number of companies who form part of the new economy have championed the cause of consumers. The Consumer Electronics Association has promoted a broad reading of the defence of fair use in a range of contexts. The technology industry has traditionally been a strong advocate of consumer rights and the defence of fair use, and resisted the entreaties of the copyright industries. J.D. Lasica wonders whether such support has been undermined by recent developments, such as media consolidation, government mandates and technology convergence.[22] Internet Service Providers, such as Verizon and Charter Communications, have sought to protect the anonymity and privacy of consumers from subpoenas sought by copyright owners. Search engines have obtained increasing prominence in the digital economy. In order to support its digitization projects, Google has become a champion of the copyright interests of libraries, archives and educational institutions. The behemoth of the computer industry, IBM, has defended open source software in legal battles with the SCO Group. The entrepreneur, James Wales, has funded the development of the online encyclopaedia, *Wikipedia*. There has also been a growing sensitivity amongst government regulators about the impact of copyright law upon competition in a knowledge-based economy.

A number of academics and scholars have become engaged intellectuals, and provided policy support to the cause of copyright law reform. David Bollier comments:

> One of the engines of the new politics of copyright law has been a new generation of legal scholars, academic centers, and policy-oriented legal clinics that are collectively forging a new public-spirited vision. While there is no single, coordinated agenda, legal scholars are collaborating closely on a wide range of research, litigation, and policy advocacy projects. Among the many topics that legal scholarship is addressing are the economic dynamics of commons versus markets, alternative business models for music distribution, the 'geography' of the public domain, and the tensions between the Internet and copyright and trademark law.[23]

There has been a concerted intellectual effort to reconceptualize the role of the consumer in copyright law. There have been three strands to this literature. First, the scholars of new historicism have sought to recast consumers as citizens, commoners and social actors. Second, the practitioners of cultural studies have emphasized that copyright users can be bricoleurs, creators and political activists. Third, the theorists of law and technology have stressed the need to focus upon the ability of consumers to manipulate and adapt technology.

I. CITIZENS, COMMONERS AND GLEANERS

There have been a number of histories, which have focused upon the role of authorship and ownership in copyright law.[24] Most recently, academics and intellectuals have taken a new interest in the larger social objectives of copyright regulation in early historical debates.[25] Ronan Deazley has commented: 'In allocating the right to exclusively publish a given literary work, the eighteenth-century parliamentarians were not concerned primarily with the rights of the individual, but acted in the furtherance of these much broader social goals.'[26]

The first modern copyright statute (the *Statute of Anne* 1710 (UK)) was enacted in the United Kingdom. The preamble stated that this legislation was 'An Act for the Encouragement of Learning, by vesting the Copies of printed Books in the Authors or Purchasers of such Copies, during the Times therein mentioned'. A number of features of this statute served the interests of the larger public. The temporal limitation upon copyright duration ensured that works would fall into the public domain. The restriction upon copyright term also encouraged greater competition. The formal requirements of registration enabled users to locate the owners of copyright works. The requirement for books to be deposited in university libraries ensured that there was public access to copyrighted works. There was much litigation involving the booksellers of England and Scotland over whether the *Statute of Anne* 1710 (UK) extinguished common law rights in respect of copyright.[27] The House of Lords eventually established in *Donaldson* v. *Beckett* that copyright law was a 'creature of statute', in which rights and responsibilities were determined by legislation.[28]

A number of writers, including James Boyle,[29] Lawrence Lessig,[30] David Bollier[31] and Peter Drahos,[32] have proposed reforming copyright law to recover the intellectual commons. They draw parallels between the current expansion of copyright law in the new millennium and the Enclosure of common lands in England that took place between the fifteenth and nineteenth centuries.[33] The co-founder of Public Knowledge, David Bollier has written about the importance of reclaiming the commons:

> The commons is an important concept because it can help us develop a new vision of law and politics. It offers a new vocabulary for talking about roles,

> behaviours, and relationships that cannot be adequately captured by market theory and copyright law. It gets us beyond market-speak in which everyone must be either a producer or a consumer, each with prescribed economic roles, and instead describes a cultural ecology, in which people may play a variety of roles – citizen, creator, collaborator, community member.[34]

Bollier complains: 'Current applications of ordinary citizens as consumers of intellectual property, not as sentient human beings who have their own creative urges and needs to use the artefacts of their culture, including perhaps trademarked Disney characters, to comment upon their life and times.'[35] He concludes: 'If the law is going to recover the public respect that its champions say it deserves, its most zealous champions will need to surrender their imperial ambitions and learn to respect the cultural commons as an equal.'[36]

The language of the 'commons' has had some success in mobilizing the public into activism in copyright law. It has been particularly attractive to libraries, cultural institutions and copyright users. However, some academic commentators have expressed concerns regarding the academic discourse about the 'commons'. The astute Swedish scholar, Eva Hemmungs Wirten, has expressed some scholarly reservations about this discourse of the 'public domain'.[37] She notes: 'Definitions of the public domain are many and confusing, as are indeed the penumbra of rights and uses that come with the territory in question.'[38] Wirten comments that the concepts of the 'public domain', 'creativity' and 'freedom' deserve greater scrutiny and self-reflection. She observed that such terms have a distinct genealogy and history:

> The public domain, and to an even larger degree the commons, operate with and can be approached from a number of perspectives that all somehow relate to place and space, be they primarily natural or virtual, tangible or symbolic. And as new as the concerns of our contemporary digital environment are, the impetus behind the formation of the Electronic Frontier Foundation and the Creative Commons are not that different from what prompted the launch of the Commons Preservation Society in Britain in 1865. Rural, urban, or digital, land is still essential to the way we think about the public domain.[39]

Wirten observed: 'The ongoing copyright wars have resulted in a polarization of debate and ways of thinking that sometimes hide the complexities of the problem at hand.'[40] She concludes that 'a more constructive way to approach the private/public matrix is to envision them not as static opposites, but as constituents of a field in constant flux'.[41] Wirten has suggested that it would be productive to think of copyright users as 'gleaners' who have rights to gather and use cultural material from the commons.[42]

In a mapping exercise, Pamela Samuelson identified 13 distinct conceptions of the 'public domain'. She has argued that there is a need to embrace a vision of multiple public domains:

> Accepting the existence of multiple public domains allows context-sensitive meanings of 'public domain' to evolve. It also contributes to a richer understanding of the contents of public domains, social values these information resources serve, persons and communities who care about public domains, the legal and institutional structures available to preserve them, threats that some public domains face, and strategies for responding to these threats.[43]

Samuelson suggests that such an approach will help broaden awareness about public domains and public domain values: 'When scholars, such as Professors Benkler, Birnhack, Boyle, and Lessig, speak about a wide range of free uses of information resources as a public domain that members of the public should be able to enjoy, they speak in a language accessible to the public, appealing to shared values of the American free speech culture.'[44]

However, the discourse of the 'commons' has not translated into substantial law reform, partly because the terminology suffers from vagueness and uncertainty. It has been open to attack and ridicule from copyright owners. For instance, Scott Martin, the vice-president of intellectual property at Paramount Pictures Corporation, is scathing of the mythology of the public domain.[45] He complains: 'Among the opponents of term extension there has been a tendency to misstate the impact of term extension on the public domain and to rely on slogans and myths in attempting to elevate the value of the public domain over the value of copyrights.'[46] The correspondent from the American Open Technology Consortium considers the metaphorical dimensions of the debate over the copyright term: ' "The Commons" and "the public domain" might be legitimate concepts with deep and relevant histories, but they're too arcane for most of us.'[47] This comment reflects an anxiety about the place of history in contemporary law, as well as insecurity in reading and applying jurisprudence. These fears feed the conservatism of the law, and encourage a minimal positive elaboration of its ends and purposes.

II. BRICOLEURS, PARODISTS AND AMATEURS

Strongly influenced by post-modern ideas about authorship and creativity, media and cultural scholars have argued that creativity in the arts and technology are best served by a culture of sharing, and loose legal controls.[48]

In *The Cultural Life of Intellectual Properties*, Rosemary Coombe provides a map of intellectual property, which is situated in the United States and Canada. She observed that signs of intellectual property are pervasive in ordinary life – copyright symbols, trademarks and celebrity images are omnipresent.[49] She emphasized that intellectual property is not just a product of formal legislation, cases and policy documents: it is a part of everyday life and experience. Coombe develops a post-modern theory of consumption in the course of her text:

> In conditions of postmodernity, cultural consumption is increasingly understood as an active use rather than a passive dependence upon dominant forms of signification. As Micel de Certeau and Paul Willis argue, consumption is always a form of production and people continually engage in cultural practices of bricolage – resignifying media meanings, consumer objects, urban spaces, and cultural texts in order to adapt them to their own interests and make them fulfil their own purposes. The consumer is seen as actively reworking everything from the design of the shopping mall and the rhetoric of the romance to mass-marketed toy culture in the articulation of alternative meanings and identities. Commodified signs become cultural resources with which new social and political realities are forged.[50]

Such scholarship has envisaged consumers as 'bricoleurs', who create and fashion new cultural productions from tinkering with pre-existing copyright works.

The theorists of cultural studies have celebrated post-modern artists who engage in the copying, quotation and remixing of copyright works.[51] They have lionized the artistic accomplishments of literary parodists, appropriation artists, culture-jammers, digital samplers, performance artists, guerrilla broadcasters and open source programmers. In *Darknet*, J.D. Lasica considers the tensions between the mass media of the industrial age and the personal media from the information age. He observed that creators have long borrowed from the copyright works of others:

> Borrowing from earlier works has always been a time-honored and accepted part of the creative tradition. Every painter learns by emulating the masters. Every musician acquires her own voice and style by first imitating those who came before. Fledgling filmmakers imitate the oeuvre of a Spielberg, Kubrick, Kurosawa, or Cassavetes. The fandom phenomenon celebrates pop culture by appropriating it: young adults publish comic-book fanzines that borrow copyrighted images; on Internet fan fiction sites, viewers write episodes that add new story lines for characters from more than five hundred television shows; amateur video buffs have created more than four hundred homemade versions of Star Wars and circulated them online. Every night, dance club DJs and MCs digitally splice together bootleg remixes of Top Forty hits in remarkable new ways.[52]

Lasica concludes, with the quotation: 'Using the omnipresent sea of symbols, images, sounds and texts as source of material, millions of people are laying claim to their cultural inheritance.'[53] He adds: 'Call it postmodern, call it open source, call it rip/mix/burn, the upshot is a culture transformed.'[54]

The Internet and the development of new technologies, such as blogs, fanzines and content sharing sites, has enabled millions of citizens not only to consume cultural content, but also to engage in self-expression and creative play. Dan Hunter and Gregory Lastowka have discussed the rise of 'amateurs' who create cultural work without financial or proprietary motives.[55] The pair comment that, traditionally, consumers were conceived of as mere objects of the imperial power of copyright law: 'The citizenry, in the view of copyright's shareholders, are merely passive beneficiaries of copyright's regime, and are described as "readers," "viewers," and/or "consumers" of content, the product that copyright specialists create.'[56] In grandiloquent terms, the authors observe that this paradigm is under threat from recent technological and cultural developments:

> Like the Roman Empire before it, copyright finds itself today under threat from its borders. The former subjects of copyright are increasingly aware that they are being taxed by copyright, but they have only a vague notion of how allegiance to copyright benefits them. This change in the status quo is largely attributable to the fact that copyright's formerly passive consumer is increasingly an active participant in content-production processes. The average citizen now feels copyright law intruding on her personal information practices.[57]

The two contend: 'Instead of a model of content that proposes manufacturers and consumers, we want to look at the creation of content as a feature of human expressive activity.'[58] The pair have used the phrase, 'amateur-to-amateur', to describe the social phenomenon of popular information creation and free distribution. Hunter and Lastowka comment: 'The big shift to amateurisation in content promises vast potential in people's ability to express themselves and in the social benefits that flow from a vast new corpus of amateur content.'[59] They conclude: 'It would be a tremendous shame if we failed to recognize the opportunity of amateur content and continued to assume that the protection of copyright industries was the only way to guarantee the production of valuable cultural expression.'[60]

III. CONSUMERS, USERS AND ADDICTS

The law and technology movement has been interested in the engagement of consumers with the Internet and new digital technologies of reproduction and distribution.[61]

In her classic text, *Digital Copyright*, Jessica Litman provides a history of the industry lobbying and the political wrangling behind the passage of digital copyright laws through the United States Congress, and the development of the WIPO Internet Treaties in the World Intellectual Property Organization.[62] The resulting legislation has little to say explicitly about the role of the users of copyright works. She highlighted 'the paucity of language speaking to the behaviour of individuals who are consuming rather than exploiting copyright material'.[63] Litman comments that digital copyright laws should be recast to take into account the position of consumers of copyright works:

> If the overwhelming majority of actors regulated by the copyright law are ordinary end users, it makes no sense to insist that each of them retain copyright counsel in order to fit herself within niches created to suit businesses and institutions, nor is it wise to draw the lines where the representatives of today's current stakeholders insist they would prefer to draw them. Extending the prescriptions and proscriptions of the current copyright law to govern the everyday acts of non-commercial, noninstitutional users is a fundamental change. To do so without effecting a drastic shift in the copyright balance will require a comparably fundamental change in the copyright statutory scheme. If we are to devise a copyright law that meets the public's needs, we might most profitably abandon the copyright law's traditional reliance on reproduction, and refashion our measure of unlawful use to better incorporate the public's understanding of the copyright bargain.[64]

Litman is hopeful that copyright industries would be amendable to drafting laws that would be respected amongst the wider public: 'If a law is bad enough, even its proponents might be willing to abandon it in favour of a different law that seems more legitimate to the people it is intended to command.'[65] There is a need to simplify and demystify digital copyright laws, so that they are accessible and comprehensible to the consumers.

In his magnum opus, *The Wealth of Networks*, Yochai Benkler has argued that there has been a fundamental shift away from 'passive' consumers to 'active' users, as a response to the emergence of new technologies and market configurations.[66] He comments upon the change in tastes: 'The industrial information economy specialized in producing finished goods, like movies or music, to be consumed passively, and well-behaved appliances, like televisions, whose use was fully specified at the factory door.'[67] By contrast, Benkler notes: 'The emerging businesses of the networked information economy are focusing on serving the demand of active users for platforms and tools that are much more loosely designed, late-binding – that is, optimized only at the moment of use and not in advance'.[68] Benkler observed: 'To some of the incumbents of the industrial information economy, the pressure from social production is experienced as pure threat.'[69] He postulated that the tension between the 'old' and 'new economy' has been the source of much legal conflict: 'It is the clash between these incumbents and the new practices that was most widely reported in the media in the first five years of the twenty-first century, and that has driven much of policy-making, legislation, and litigation in this area.'[70]

Joseph Liu has argued that 'copyright law currently conceives of consumers in one of two ways, either as passive consumers of copyrighted works or as active authors in their own right'.[71] He contended: 'This binary conception of the consumer, however, is incomplete, as it neglects important and complex consumer interests in autonomy, communication, and creative self-expression.'[72] Liu stressed that 'in determining whether new kinds of uses (such as those enabled by new technology like MP3 players, TiVo, ad-stripping software, and web browsers) constitute fair use, courts should give some weight to these more complex consumer interests in autonomy, communication, and self-expression'.[73] Moreover, he suggested that 'members of Congress also need to be conscious that, in their attempts to bolster copyright law for purposes of reducing infringement, their activities may have an undesirable impact on these more complicated consumer interests'.[74]

In a thoughtful piece of scholarship, Julie Cohen from Georgetown University has expressed discomfort about the term 'user': she notes that the phrase 'manages simultaneously to connote both more active involvement in the processes of culture and a residual aura of addiction that may be entirely appropriate to the age of the iPod, the XBox, and the blogosphere'.[75] She contends that academic scholarship has developed a fanciful and unrealistic typology of 'users' of copyright works:

> In broad brush, scholarly efforts to cast the user have produced three fully-fledged candidates, each more unrealistic than the last: the economic user, who enters the market with a given set of tastes in search of the best deal; the 'post-modern' user, who exercises limited and vaguely oppositional agency in a world in which all meaning is uncertain and all knowledge relative; and the romantic user, whose life is an endless cycle of sophisticated debates about current events, discerning quests for the most freedom-enhancing media technologies, and home production of high-quality music, movies, and open-source software.[76]

Instead of such figures, Cohen seeks to present a new character, 'the situated user'. She observes: 'The situated user engages cultural goods and artifacts found within the context of her culture through a variety of activities ranging from consumption to creative play.'[77] Cohen concludes: 'This model of the situated user suggests that the success of a system of copyright depends on both the extent to which its rules permit individuals to engage in creative play and the extent to which they enable contextual play, or degrees of freedom, within the system of culture more generally.'[78]

Some commentators are somewhat more saturnine about consumer behaviour. Jane Ginsburg claimed that copyright law has obtained a bad reputation, because of consumer and corporate greed.[79] She observed: 'Copyright owners, generally perceived to be large, impersonal and unlovable corporations (the human creators and interpreters – authors and performers – albeit often initial copyright owners, tend to vanish from polemical view), have eyed enhanced prospects for global earnings in an increasingly international copyright market.'[80] She noted that such entities 'have urged and obtained ever more protective legislation that extends the term of copyright and interferes with the development and dissemination of consumer-friendly copying technologies'.[81] Ginsburg observed: 'Consumers, for their part, have exhibited an increasing rapacity in acquiring and "sharing" unauthorized copies of music, and more recently, motion pictures.'[82] She noted that 'some of the general public senses as illegitimate any law, or more particularly, any enforcement that gets in the way of what people can do with their own equipment in their own homes (or dorm rooms)'.[83]

Rebecca Tushnet has demurred that the totality of the concerns represented by the public interest are not necessarily captured by an end-consumer analysis.[84] She has contended: 'In bringing consumers' interests into the analysis, we should not forget that intermediate institutions like schools and libraries are major markets for copyright owners, and therefore, major sources of copyright works for many consumers.'[85] Tushnet stressed that 'these intermediaries often serve to mitigate the strict wealth discrimination imposed by the direct market for copyrighted works, allowing people to read and to watch far more copyrighted works than they could pay for themselves'.[86]

Outline

This book considers battles over digital copyright over the past five years against the backdrop of wider trends and developments in the field. The geographical locus of this study is United States copyright law. This study will consider the impact of the *Sonny Bono Copyright Term Extension Act* 1998 (US) (the *Sonny Bono Act*) and the *Digital Millennium Copyright Act* 1998 (US) (the *DMCA*), and various law reform proposals. There is also a sustained analysis of United States technology, jurisprudence and culture. This book draws comparisons with other key jurisdictions, such as Australia,[87] the United Kingdom,[88] the European Union[89] and Canada.[90] This study examines the progressive adoption of United States standards in Australian digital copyright law, through the *Copyright Amendment (Digital Agenda) Act* 2000 (Cth), the *Australia-United States Free Trade Agreement* 2004, and the *Copyright Amendment Act* 2006 (Cth).[91] This book draws parallels with policy developments in the European Union, such as the *European Community Copyright Term Directive* and the *European Community Information Society Directive*.[92] There are cross-references to equivalent litigation in the European Union, including discussion of litigation against peer-to-peer networks in the Netherlands and Sweden; English jurisprudence on digital sampling; court cases over Internet intermediaries in Ireland, Germany and Belgium; consumer actions over personal copying levies in France; litigation over the use of Creative Commons licences in the Netherlands and Spain; and the development of the BBC Creative Archive. Another useful point of reference is Canada, a crossing point for English, Continental and United States influences on the development of copyright jurisprudence. Interestingly, the Canadian Parliament has declined to follow the international trend towards copyright term extension, and has yet to implement digital copyright laws, with *Bill* C-60 lapsing.[93] There is also a discussion of how the Brazilian Government has become a champion of Creative Commons licences and open source projects.

This book explores the growing resistance and opposition by consumers to digital copyright in the United States. This study will make a unique practical and theoretical contribution to the debate over digital copyright law by reconceptualizing the role of the user in copyright jurisprudence. Julie Cohen has observed that the failure to consider adequately the role of the user in copyright jurisprudence has resulted in unfortunate consequences for theory, policy and law:

> Copyright doctrine, however, is characterized by the absence of the user. As copyright moves into the digital age, this absence has begun to matter profoundly . . . [T]he absence of the user has consequences that reach far beyond debates about the legality of private copying, or about the proper scope of user-oriented exemptions such as the fair use and first sale doctrines. The user's absence produces a domino effect that ripples through the structure of copyright law, shaping both its unquestioned rules and its thorniest dilemmas. The resulting imbalance – empty space where one cornerstone of a well-balanced copyright edifice should be – makes for bad theory, bad policy, and bad law.[94]

This inquiry seeks to redress this lamentable void in copyright jurisprudence. It aims to provide a sense of the heterogenous interests represented by consumers in copyright law. It is worth acknowledging that the term, 'consumer', is a capacious one, covering a range of characters. Helpfully, Breyer J of the Supreme Court of the United States notes that the potential users of copyright works covers 'not only movie buffs and aging jazz fans, but also historians, scholars, teachers, writers, artists, database operators, and researchers of all kinds'.[95] It is also important to recognize that consumers are not just mere 'culture vultures', engaged in the mindless, passive, bovine consumption of new artistic forms and technologies. The users of copyright works are engaged in a multitude of activities, including political expression, cultural transformation and technological tinkering. Moreover, the relationship of consumers to the dictates of copyright law is also a complex one, ranging from obedience to resistance and opposition to indifference and ignorance.

This book does not consider copyright law merely as a formal set of rules and principles, which is autonomous from other regimes of legal regulation. Instead, it is sensitive to the broader social context of copyright law.[96] Fiona Macmillan has commented that copyright law is a melting-pot for a wide range of influences:

> As the most flexible of the intellectual property rights, copyright is subject to constant pressure to adapt in order to respond to a variety of social, cultural, economic and political demands. These demands are sometimes generated by new developments and sometimes by new perceptions and approaches to older issues. There is, for example, a widespread perception that new information and communication technologies have generated serious problems for the integrity of the copyright regime that surpass previous technological challenges . . . At the same time, economic and political developments, especially those promoting regional and global market liberalisation, have generated pressure for harmonisation and conformity amongst historically diverse copyright systems.[97]

Accordingly, this study focuses upon the intersection between copyright law and various other disciplinary approaches, highlighting the points of synergy and dissonance. It is grounded upon an appreciation of the history of copyright law, emphasizing that the current debates over digital copyright echo earlier controversies about the appearance of new technologies. It considers the constitutional validity of the new digital copyright laws, in terms both of the limits of governmental power, and of the impact upon the freedom of political expression. This inquiry is also conscious of the influence of the law and economics movement. It explores the growing influence of competition law, and consumer protection law, in the design and regulation of copyright law. This book acknowledges the powerful discourse of international harmonization. It considers the criss-crossing web of multilateral agreements, regional agreements and bilateral agreements. It notes the influence of international forums, such as the World Trade Organization and the World Intellectual Property Organization.

This book adopts the methodology of analysing the cultural politics of copyright disputes. It looks at the intersection of power, culture and technology. As James Boyle observes, there is a need to focus upon the politics of intellectual property:

> Like most property regimes, our intellectual property regime will be contentious, in distributional, ideological and efficiency terms. It will have effects on market power, economic concentration and social structure. Yet, right now, we have no politics of intellectual property – in the way that we have a politics of the environment or of tax reform. We lack a conceptual map of issues, a rough working model of costs and benefits and a functioning coalition-politics of groups unified by common interest perceived in apparently diverse situations.[98]

The methodology is one of looking at the law creatively: that is to try and identify the social, economic and legal relations that copyright law produces. It seeks to bring to life the real complexity and messiness of the law, as it negotiates the battle over the copyright term and engages with conflicting views and cultures. The spirit of the inquiry is to uncover the disciplinary power of the court and the jurisprudential mechanisms for its exercise. It seeks to analyse what arguments are explicitly acknowledged by the court, and what policy matters are overlooked and ignored. This investigation also highlights the role of *amicus curiae* in bringing policy concerns to the attention of the judiciary. The motivation is that of understanding how copyright law has managed its 'representativeness' and the practical implications of the mismanagement of social diversity. In addition to the formal legal process, a number of academics, lobbyists, journalists and commentators have been kibitzing and barracking from the sidelines. This inquiry evaluates the role of public intellectuals in the debate over copyright theory, policy and law making.[99]

The narrative of this book is bounded by a particular time-frame. The chronology has a distinctive arc. The first chapters recount the early historical debates over copyright term extension, and the initial grappling by judges with 'time-shifting' technologies in the 1980s. There is scene setting in terms of recounting the legislative passage of the *Sonny Bono Act* and the *DMCA*. The bulk of the book is squarely focused upon trends and developments in digital copyright law in the new millennium. In particular, there is a consideration of how the law seeks to accommodate and regulate new technologies, such as electronic publishing ventures, consumer electronics devices like iPods and personal video recorders, games consoles such as the Sony Playstation II, peer-to-peer networks, Internet service providers, the multiple functions of search engines such as Google, and open content, such as *Wikipedia*. The conclusion looks forward to future trends in respect of digital copyright and consumers' rights.

Chapter 1 explores the copyright term extension wrought by the *Sonny Bono Act*. It considers the constitutional challenge by the electronic publisher, Eric Eldritch, to the validity of the *Sonny Bono Act*. In *Eldred* v. *Ashcroft*, the Supreme Court of the United States held by a majority of seven to two that the *Sonny Bono Act* was within the constitutional power of the United States Congress, and not in violation of the First Amendment.[100] This chapter evaluates the litigation in terms of policy debate in a number of discourses: history, intellectual property law, constitutional law and freedom of speech, cultural heritage, economics and competition policy, and international trade. It argues that the extension of the copyright term will inhibit the dissemination of cultural works through the use of new technologies, such as Eric Eldred's Eldritch Press and Project Gutenberg. This chapter concludes that there is a need to resist the attempts of copyright owners to establish the *Sonny Bono Act* as an international model for other jurisdictions.

Chapter 2 considers the push to reform copyright law in order to protect and safeguard consumer rights in the digital millennium. It explores the significance of the Supreme Court of the United States decision in the *Sony Betamax* case, which recognized that consumers were protected by the defence of fair use when they used the Betamax VCR recorder to copy television broadcasts to watch at a later time ('time-shifting').[101] This chapter considers the application of the *Sony Betamax* rule in a number of other contexts: in respect of Replay TV, Clearplay, TiVo, Streamvision and the Slingbox. This chapter also studies the application of the *Sony Betamax* decision in relation to a number of new technologies, such as MP3 players, music lockers, the iPod and podcasting, and satellite radio. Such devices and services enable consumers to store content, such as music and films, in a digital format ('space-shifting').

Chapter 3 considers litigation brought by record companies and motion picture studios against peer-to-peer networks, such as Grokster, Kazaa and BitTorrent.[102] It compares and contrasts the regulatory approaches of key jurisdictions, such as the United States, Australia and the European Union. This chapter dissects the Supreme Court of the United States' ruling in the case of *Grokster* that the peer-to-peer networks, Grokster and Streamcast, had induced copyright infringement.[103] It considers the Federal Court of Australia decision in *Universal Music Australia Pty Ltd* v. *Sharman License Holdings Ltd* (*Kazaa*)[104] that the operators of Kazaa had authorized copyright infringement. Finally, this chapter considers the legal implications of the software, BitTorrent. It explores the legal action taken against BitTorrent websites such as TorrentSpy, eDonkey, Razorback2 and Niteshadow.com. Moreover, it focuses upon the raids upon the Swedish website, The Pirate Bay.

Chapter 4 explores the challenges posed to copyright law through the practice of audio and audio-visual mash-ups. In the field of digital sampling, disk jockeys have shown a recent enthusiasm for 'mash-ups' – new compositions created by combining the rhythm tracks of one song and the vocal track of another. Most famously of all, DJ Danger Mouse remixed the vocals from Jay-Z's *The Black Album* and The Beatles' *White Album* and called his creation *The Grey Album*. In response to cease-and-desist notices, Downhill Battle organized Grey Tuesday, an online protest, in which hundreds of web-sites posted copies of *The Grey Album*. *The Grey Album* poses a number of difficult issues regarding copyright law and digital sampling. It is difficult to conceive of a mash-up consisting of a *de minimis* use, given that it depends upon the extensive use of multiple copyright works. There has been much debate as to whether the defence of fair use should extend beyond transformative uses such as parodies to embrace mash-ups. In addition, there has been discussion about the need to expand compulsory licensing provisions to include not only covers of musical works, but mash-ups. The practice of audio and audio-visual mash-ups could also come into conflict with the provision of moral rights in respect of attribution and integrity in such jurisdictions as Australia, Canada, the United Kingdom and the European Union.

Chapter 5 considers the development of special protections for technological protection measures (TPMs), such as passwords, watermarks, copy-protection, encryption, and access codes, under the *DMCA*. It highlights the impact of digital rights management systems on freedom of speech, access to information, competition law and privacy. This chapter focuses, in particular, upon the so-called 'civil war' within the Sony group of companies. Although Sony Electronics was the champion of consumers' rights in the *Sony Betamax* decision, the Sony content companies have undermined such privileges through the extensive use of digital rights management systems. First of all, it considers the landmark decision of the High Court of Australia on copyright law and TPMs in the matter of *Stevens* v. *Kabushiki Kaisha Sony Computer Entertainment*.[105] The decision is of considerable importance because this is the first time that a superior court in the world has had an opportunity to rule upon so-called 'para-copyright'. Second, this chapter considers the controversy over the Sony BMG rookit software. A number of class actions were launched against the multinational company, because its digital rights management system in respect of sound recordings compromised the privacy and security of the home computers of its consumers.[106] The twin controversies highlight the impact of TPMs upon access to information, competition in the marketplace and consumer privacy.

Chapter 6 considers the increasing litigation by copyright owners against intermediaries of various sorts. In response to subpoenas by copyright

owners under the *DMCA*, th…
Communications, h…
their subscrib…
Diebold Inc.,
publishing doc…
electronic voting machines.[108] Moreover, copyright owners have also brought legal action against a number of alternative pressure points, including Internet search engines, financial institutions and users of peer-to-peer networks. The music industry has sought to take legal action against venture capitalists in order to deprive peer-to-peer networks of capital. In the past few years, the record industry has filed civil lawsuits against hundreds of individuals identified through the subpoena process. The record companies targeted users who were distributing substantial amounts of copyrighted music on peer-to-peer networks, including Kazaa, Grokster, IMesh, Gnutella and Blubster. There has been much legal wrangling over whether such end-users infringe copyright owners' economic rights of distribution.[109] There has been much litigation as to whether the end-users of peer-to-peer networks have any available defences to such charges of copyright infringement, such as the defence of fair use or the doctrine of innocent infringement.[110] In light of such controversies, academics, stakeholders and policy makers have debated the merits of establishing a personal copying levy.

Chapter 7 explores the legal issues surrounding copyright law and Internet search engines. In September and October 2005, the Authors Guild and the Association of American Publishers filed lawsuits in the United States, alleging that the Google Book Search program had infringed copyright in literary works through its unauthorized scanning and copying of books.[111] In response, Google argued that it had not infringed the copyright of the authors or booksellers. The search engine has also attracted other lawsuits. The Agence France-Presse and other press agencies have alleged that Google News infringed on its copyright because it included photographs, stories and news headlines on Google News without permission.[112] The Californian pornography company, Perfect 10, has also filed a lawsuit against Google, claiming that the reproduction of its images infringes the company's copyright, trade marks and publicity rights.[113] There has also been litigation over the Internet search engine participating in web archiving and caching with Google Cache.[114] Google has also grappled with copyright issues associated with Internet videos – both with Google Video and YouTube.

Chapter 8 charts the emergence of the Creative Commons, a movement which relies upon contract law in order to put authors' works into the public domain. It considers illustrative creative endeavours, such as free and open source computer programming, the digital photography site Flickr, digital sampling and mash-ups, the remixable film *Sanctuary*, the BBC Creative Archive, the Public Library of Science and the online encyclopaedia, *Wikipedia*. This chapter highlights the backlash against the Creative Commons from vested interest groups, including copyright industries, copyright collecting societies and industrial unions. Such grievances are summed up by a critic from *Forbes Magazine* who claimed that the Creative Commons comprised 'a ragtag bunch of gleaners who claim that copying is "creativity" because they can't create anything without directly reusing copyrighted material'.[115]

The volume's Conclusion applauds the development of a Declaration of Innovation Independence, a manifesto for the reform of digital copyright laws in light of consumer interests.[116] It also endorses the push to institute a development agenda within the World Trade Organization and the World Intellectual Property Organization, with the proposed Access to Knowledge Treaty (the *A2K Treaty*).[117]

NOTES

1. Lasica, J.D. (2005), *Darknet: Hollywood's War against the Digital Generation*, Hoboken, NJ: John Wiley & Sons, p. 16.
2. *Sony Corporation of America* v. *Universal City Studios Inc*. 464 US 417 (1984) (the *Sony Betamax* case).
3. Home Recording Rights Coalition (2005), 'HRRC Urges Passage of Betamax Codification: Bill Would Promote User Freedom under DMCA', http://www.hrrc.org/news/PressRelease041405.html, 14 April.
4. EFF, http://www.eff.org/legal/cases/betamax/.
5. Valenti, J. (1982), 'Home Recording of Copyrighted Works', Subcommittee on Courts, Civil Liberties, and the Administration of Justice, the Committee on the Judiciary, House of Representatives, http://cryptome.org/hrcw-hear.htm, 12 April.
6. Litman, J. (2005), 'The Sony Paradox', *Case Western Reserve Law Review*, **55**, 917–61 at 960.
7. *Metro-Goldwyn-Mayer Studios Inc*. v. *Grokster, Ltd*. 125 S.Ct. 2764 (2005) ('*Grokster*').
8. McCullagh, Declan (2005), 'Protestors Outside Grokster Supreme Court Arguments: "Hands Off my iPod" Fileswapping Photo', http://www.mccullagh.org/photo/1ds2-5/hands-off-my-ipod-flie-swapping, March.
9. McCullagh, Declan (2005), 'Don't Touch my TiVo Sign Outside Supreme Court During Grokster Peer-to-Peer Case', http://www.mccullagh.org/photo/1ds2-5/dont-touch-my-tivo, March.
10. McCullagh, Declan (2005), 'Protestors Outside Grokster Supreme Court Arguments: "Feed a Musician – Download Legally" ', http://www.mccullagh.org/photo/1ds2-5/feed-a-musician-music-piracy, March.
11. Ibid.
12. The Home Recording Rights Coalition, http://www.hrrc.org/.
13. The Electronic Frontier Foundation, http://www.eff.org/.
14. The American Civil Liberties Union, http://www.aclu.org/.
15. The Swarthmore Coalition for the Digital Commons, http://scdc.sccs.swarthmore.edu/oldhome.php.

16. The Consumer Project on Technology, http://www.cptech.org/.
17. The Creative Commons, http://creativecommons.org/.
18. The Center for the Study of the Public Domain, http://www.law.duke.edu/cspd/.
19. Public Knowledge, http://www.publicknowledge.org/.
20. The Stanford Law Center for Internet and Society, http://cyberlaw.stanford.edu/.
21. Samuelson Law, Technology, and Public Policy Clinic, http://www.law.berkeley.edu/clinics/samuelson/.
22. Lasica, J.D. (2005), *Darknet: Hollywood's War against the Digital Generation*, Hoboken, NJ: John Wiley & Sons Inc., p. 26.
23. Bollier, David (2005), *Brand Name Bullies: The Quest to Own and Control Culture*, Hoboken, NJ: John Wiley & Sons Inc.
24. Patterson, L. Ray (1968), *Copyright in Historical Perspective*, Nashville: Vandebilt University Press; Darnton, Robert (1982), *The Literary Underground of the Old Regime*, Cambridge, Mass.: Harvard University Press; Darnton, Robert (1990), *The Kiss of Lamourette: Reflections in Cultural History*, New York and London: W.W. Norton and Company; Rose, Mark (1993), *Authors And Owners: The Invention Of Copyright*, Cambridge: Harvard University Press; Woodmansee, Martha (1994), *The Author, Art, And The Market: Rereading The History Of Aesthetics*, New York: Columbia University Press; Woodmansee, Martha and Peter Jaszi (eds) (1994), *The Construction Of Authorship: Textual Appropriation In Law And Literature*, Durham, London: Duke University Press; Darnton, Robert (1995), *The Forbidden Best-Sellers of Pre-Revolutionary France*, New York and London: W.W. Norton and Company; Sherman, Brad and Alain Strowel (eds) (1994), *Of Authors And Origins: Essays On Copyright Law*, Oxford: Clarendon Press; Seville, Catherine (1999), *Literary Copyright Reform in Early Victorian England: The Framing of the 1842 Copyright Act*, Cambridge: Cambridge University Press; and Groom, Nick (2002), *The Forger's Shadow: How Forgery Changed The Course Of Literature*, London: Picador.
25. Sherman, Brad and Lionel Bently (1999), *The Making Of Modern Intellectual Property Law: The British Experience 1760-1911*, Cambridge: Cambridge University Press.
26. Deazley, Ronan (2004), *On the Origin of the Right to Copy: Charting the Movement of Copyright in Eighteenth Century Britain*, Oxford: Hart Publishing, p. 226.
27. *Millar* v. *Kincaid* (1759) 98 ER 210; *Tonson* v. *Collins* (1761) 96 ER 169; and *Millar* v. *Taylor* (1769) 4 Burr. 2303; 98 ER 201.
28. *Donaldson* v. *Beckett* (1774) 4 Burr 2408; 98 ER 257.
29. Boyle, James (1996), *Shamans, Software, and Spleens: Law and the Construction of the Information Society*, Cambridge: Harvard University Press; Boyle, J. (1997), 'Foucault in Cyberspace: Surveillance, Sovereignty, and Hardwired Censors', *University of Cincinnati Law Review*, **66**(1), 177–205; Boyle, J. (1997), 'A Politics of Intellectual Property: Environmentalism for the Net', *Duke Law Journal*, **47**, 87–116; and Boyle, J. (2003), 'The Second Enclosure Movement and the Construction of the Public Domain', *Law and Contemporary Problems*, **66**, 33–74.
30. Lessig, Lawrence (1999), *Code And Other Laws Of Cyberspace*, New York: Basic Books; Lessig, Lawrence (2001), *The Future Of Ideas: The Fate Of The Commons In A Connected World*, New York: Random House; and Lessig, Lawrence (2004), *Free Culture: How Big Media Uses Technology And Law To Lock Down Culture And Control Creativity*, New York: Penguin.
31. Bollier, David (2002), *Silent Theft: The Private Plunder of Our Common Wealth*, New York: Routledge; and Bollier, David (2005), *Brand Name Bullies: The Quest to Own and Control Culture*, Hoboken, NJ: John Wiley & Sons Inc.
32. Drahos, Peter (1996), *A Philosophy Of Intellectual Property*, Aldershot: Dartmouth Publishing Company; Braithwaite, John and Peter Drahos (2000), *Global Business Regulation*, Cambridge: Cambridge University Press; and Drahos, Peter and John Braithwaite (2002), *Information Feudalism: Who Owns The Knowledge Economy?*, London: Earthscan Productions.
33. Boyle, J. (2003), 'The Second Enclosure Movement and the Construction of the Public Domain', *Law and Contemporary Problems*, **66**, 33–74.

34. Bollier, David (2005), *Brand Name Bullies: The Quest to Own and Control Culture*, Hoboken, NJ: John Wiley & Sons Inc., pp. 251–2.
35. Ibid., p. 252.
36. Ibid., p. 253.
37. Wirten, E.H. (2006), 'Out of Sight and Out of Mind: On the Cultural Hegemony of Intellectual Property (Critique)', *Cultural Studies*, **20**(2–3), 282–91. See also Wirten, Eva Hemmungs (2003), *No Trespassing: Authorship, Intellectual Property Rights, And The Boundaries Of Globalization*, Toronto: University of Toronto Press; and Wirten, Eva Hemmungs (2008), *Terms of Use: Negotiating the Jungle of Intellectual Commons*, Toronto: University of Toronto Press.
38. Wirten, E.H. (2006), ibid., 283.
39. Wirten, E.H. (2006), ibid., 288.
40. Wirten, E.H. (2006), ibid., 282.
41. Wirten, E.H. (2006), ibid., 282.
42. For a historical discussion of gleaners, see Murota, T. (2004), 'History and Current State of the Commons in England and Wales: John S. Mill at a Turning Point', Research Center for Social Common Capital, Doshisha University.
43. Samuelson, P. (2006), 'Enriching Discourse on Public Domain', *Duke Law Journal*, **55**, 783–4.
44. Ibid., 824–6.
45. Martin, S. (2002), 'The Mythology of the Public Domain: Exploring the Myths Behind Attacks on the Duration of Copyright Protection', *Loyola of Los Angeles Law Review*, **36**, 253–321.
46. Ibid., at 265.
47. American Open Technology Consortium (2003), 'Going Deep', http://www. aotc. info/archives/2003_01.html, 20 January.
48. Edelman, Bernard (1979), *Ownership of the Image: Elements for a Marxist Theory of Law*, London: Routledge; Gaines, Jane (1992), *Contested Culture: The Image, the Voice and the Law*, London: British Film Industry Publishing; Frow, John (1997), *Time and Commodity Culture: Essays in Cultural Theory and Postmodernity*, Oxford: Oxford University Press; and Jones, Dylan (2005), *iPod, Therefore I Am: Thinking Inside the White Box*, London and New York: Bloomsbury.
49. Coombe, Rosemary (1998), *The Cultural Life Of Intellectual Properties*, Durham, NC: Duke University Press.
50. Ibid., p. 104.
51. Klein, Naomi (2000), *No Logo: Taking Aim At The Brand Bullies*, London: Harper Collins; Vaidhyanathan, Siva (2001), *Copyrights And Copywrongs: The Rise Of Intellectual Property And How It Threatens Creativity*, New York: New York University Press; Vaidhyanathan, Siva (2004), *The Anarchist in the Library: How the Clash Between Freedom and Control is Hacking the Real World and Crashing the System*, New York: Basic Books; McLeod, Kembrew (2005), *Freedom of Expression(R): Overzealous Copyright Bozos and Other Enemies of Creativity*, New York: Doubleday; Demers, Joanna (2006), *Steal This Music: How Intellectual Property Law Affects Musical Creativity*, Athens and London: The University of Georgia Press; and Katyal, S. (2006), 'Performance, Property, and the Slashing of Gender in Fan Fiction', *American University of Gender, Social Policy and the Law*, **14**, 461–518.
52. Lasica, J.D. (2005), *Darknet: Hollywood's War Against the Digital Generation*, Hoboken, NJ: John Wiley & Sons Inc., pp. 15–16.
53. Ibid., p. 16.
54. Ibid., p. 16.
55. Hunter, D. and G. Lastowka (2004), 'Amateur-to-Amateur', *William and Mary Law Review*, **46**, 951–1030.
56. Ibid., 953.
57. Ibid., 953–4.
58. Ibid., 955.
59. Ibid., 1029.

60. Ibid., 1029.
61. Shulman, Seth (1999), *Owning the Future*, Boston and New York: Houghton Mifflin Company; Geist, Michael (ed.) (2005), *In The Public Interest: The Future of Canadian Copyright Law*, Toronto: Irwin Law; Gantz, John and Jack Rochester (2005), *Pirates of the Digital Millennium: How the Intellectual Property Wars Damage Our Personal Freedoms, Our Jobs, and the World Economy*, Upper Saddle River, NJ: Prentice-Hall/Financial Times; Bowrey, Kathy (2005), *Law and Internet Cultures*, Cambridge: Cambridge University Press; Klang, Mathias (2006), *Disruptive Technologies: Effects of Technology Regulation on Democracy*, doctoral dissertation, University of Göteborg; Goldsmith, Jack and Tim Wu (2006), *Who Controls the Internet?: Illusions of a Borderless World*, Oxford: Oxford University Press; and Zittrain, J. (2006) 'The Generative Internet', *Harvard Law Review*, **119**, 1974–2040.
62. Litman, Jessica (2001), *Digital Copyright*, Prometheus: Humanity Books.
63. Ibid., p. 71.
64. Ibid., pp. 185–6.
65. Ibid., p. 195.
66. Benkler, Yochai (2006), *The Wealth of Networks: How Social Production Transforms Markets and Freedom*, New Haven and London: Yale University Press, http://www.benkler.org/Benkler_Wealth_Of_Networks.pdf; Benkler builds upon his earlier work here: Benkler, Y. (2000), 'From Consumers to Users: Shifting the Deeper Structures of Regulation Toward Sustainable Commons and User Access', *Federal Communications Law Journal*, **52**, 561–79.
67. Benkler, Y. (2006), ibid., 126.
68. Benkler, Y. (2006), ibid., 126.
69. Benkler, Y. (2006), ibid., 126.
70. Benkler, Y. (2006), ibid., 126.
71. Liu, J. (2003), 'Copyright Law's Theory of the Consumer', *Boston College Law Review*, **44**(2), 397–438 at 397.
72. Ibid., 397.
73. Ibid., 428.
74. Ibid., 428.
75. Cohen, J. (2005), 'The Place of the User in Copyright Law', *Fordham Law Review*, **74**, 347–374 at 347.
76. Ibid., 348.
77. Ibid., 348.
78. Ibid., 348.
79. Ginsburg, J. (2002), 'How Copyright Got A Bad Name For Itself', *Columbia Journal of Law and the Arts*, **26**(1), 61–73.
80. Ibid., 62.
81. Ibid., 62.
82. Ibid., 62.
83. Ibid., 62.
84. Tushnet, R. (2006), 'My Library: Copyright and the Role of Institutions in a Peer-to-Peer World', *The University of California Los Angeles Law Review*, **53**, 978–1029.
85. Ibid., 981.
86. Ibid., 981.
87. For summaries of Australian copyright law, see McKeough, Jill, Kathy Bowrey and Philip Griffith (2003), *Intellectual Property: Commentary and Materials*, 3rd edn, Sydney: Law Book Co; McKeough, Jill, Andrew Stewart and Philip Griffith (2004), *Intellectual Property in Australia*, 3rd edn, Sydney: LexisNexis Butterworths; and McKeough, Jill, Kathy Bowrey and Philip Griffith (2007), *Intellectual Property: Commentary and Materials*, 4th edn, Sydney: Law Book Co.
88. For surveys of United Kingdom copyright law, see Cornish, William and David Llewelyn (2003), *Intellectual Property: Patents, Copyright, Trade Marks and Allied Rights*, 5th edn, London: Sweet & Maxwell; Bently, Lionel and Brad Sherman (2004), *Intellectual Property*, 2nd edn, Oxford: Oxford University Press; and Burrell, Robert

and Allison Coleman (2005), *Copyright Exceptions: The Digital Impact*, Cambridge: Cambridge University Press.

89. For a discussion of European digital copyright law, see Hugenholtz, Bernt (ed.) (1996), *The Future of Copyright in a Digital Environment*, The Hague: Kluwer Law International; European Consumer Law Group (2005), *Copyright Law and Consumer Protection*, Institute of Information Law, the University of Amsterdam, http://www.ivir.nl/publications/other/copyrightlawconsumerprotection.pdf; Hugenholtz, Bernt and Lucie Guilbault (eds) (2006), *The Future of the Public Domain – Identifying the Commons in Information Law*, The Hague: Kluwer Law International.
90. For reviews of Canadian copyright law, see Vaver, David (2000), *Copyright Law*, Toronto: Irwin Law Inc; Gervais, Daniel and Elizabeth Judge (2005), *Intellectual Property: The Law in Canada*, Toronto: Thomson Carswell; and Geist, Michael (ed.) (2005), *In The Public Interest: The Future of Canadian Copyright Law*, Toronto: Irwin Law Inc.
91. *Copyright Amendment (Digital Agenda) Act* 2000 (Cth).
92. *EC Copyright Term Directive*, Council Directive 93/98/EEC of 29 October 1993 harmonizing the term of protection of copyright and certain related rights. *Official Journal* L 290, 24/11/1993 P. 0009 – 0013; and *EC Information Society Directive*, Council Directive 2001/29/EC of 22 May 2001 on the harmonization of certain aspects of copyright and related rights in the information society.
93. *Lucy Maud Montgomery Copyright Term Extension Bill* 2003 (Bill C-36); and *An Act to Amend the Copyright Act* 2005 (C-60).
94. Cohen, J. (2005) 'The Place of the User in Copyright Law', *Fordham Law Review*, **74**, 347–74 at 347–8.
95. *Eldred* v. *Ashcroft* 123 S. Ct. 769 at 805 (2003).
96. For a discussion of key trends and developments in copyright law, see Macmillan, Fiona (ed.) (2005), *New Directions in Copyright Law, Volume 1*, Cheltenham, UK and Northampton, MA, USA: Edward Elgar; Macmillan, Fiona (ed.) (2006), *New Directions in Copyright Law, Volume 2*, Cheltenham, UK and Northampton, MA, USA: Edward Elgar; and Macmillan, Fiona and Kathy Bowrey (eds) (2006), *New Directions in Copyright Law, Volume 3*, Cheltenham, UK and Northampton, MA, USA: Edward Elgar.
97. Macmillan, Fiona (ed.) (2005), *New Directions in Copyright Law, Volume 1*, Cheltenham, UK and Northampton, MA, USA: Edward Elgar, p. ix.
98. Boyle, J. (1997), 'A Politics Of Intellectual Property: Environmentalism For The Net', *Duke Law Journal*, **47** (1), 87–116.
99. Said, Edward (1994), *Representations of the Intellectual: the 1993 Reith Lectures*, New York: Pantheon Books.
100. *Eldred* v. *Ashcroft* 123 S. Ct. 769 (2003).
101. *Sony Corporation of America* v. *Universal City Studios Inc.* 464 US 417 (1984).
102. Boyle, J. (1997), 'Foucault in Cyberspace: Surveillance, Sovereignty, and Hardwired Censors', *University of Cincinnati Law Review*, **66**(1), 177.
103. *Metro-Goldwyn-Mayer Studios Inc.* v. *Grokster, Ltd.* 125 S. Ct. 2764 (2005).
104. *Universal Music Australia Pty Ltd.* v. *Sharman License Holdings Ltd.* [2005] FCA 1242; (2005) 220 ALR 1.
105. *Stevens* v. *Kabushiki Kaisha Sony Computer Entertainment* (2005) 221 ALR 448.
106. *In re Sony BMG CD Technologies Litigation* No 1:05-cv-09575 (NRB) (US District Court for the Southern District of New York, 2005).
107. *Verizon Internet Services* v. *RIAA* 351 F. 3d 1229 (DC Cir 2003); and *In re Charter Communications*, 393 F.3d 771 (8th Cir. 2005).
108. *Online Policy Group* et al. v. *Diebold Inc.* 337 F. Supp. 2d 1195 (2004).
109. *Elektra Entertainment Group* v. *Barker* No. 05 CV 7340 (SDNY, filed Feb. 24, 2006).
110. *BMG et al.* v. *Cecilia Gonzalez* WL 106592 (N.D.Ill.) (2005).
111. *The Authors' Guild* v. *Google Inc* Case No. 05 CV 8136-JES (2005), http://www.boingboing.net/images/AuthorsGuildGoogleComplaint1.pdf; and *McGraw-Hill Companies et al.* v. *Google Inc.* Case No. 05 CV 8881-JES (2005), http://www.publishers.org/press/pdf/40%20McGraw-Hill%20v.%20Google.pdf.

112. *Agence France Presse* v. *Google Inc.*, D.D.C., No. 05-00546 (2005), http://blog.searchenginewatch.com/blog/050321-175410.
113. *Perfect 10 Inc.* v. *Google Inc.*, 16 F.Supp.2d 828 (2006).
114. *Field* v. *Google Inc.* 412 F.Supp.2d 1106, D.Nev. (2006); and *Parker* v. *Google, Inc.* 422 F.Supp.2d 492 (2006).
115. Manes, S. (2004), 'Let's Have Less of Lessig', *Forbes Magazine*, 4 February.
116. Consumer Electronics Association (2005), 'CEA Announces Declaration of Innovation Independence: Presents Six Principles to Guide Intellectual Property Debate', Arlington, Virginia, 16 March.
117. *Draft Treaty on Access to Knowledge* (A2K Treaty), http://www.cptech.org/a2k/consolidatedtext-may9.pdf.

1. The dead poets society: the copyright term and the public domain

> The words of a dead man/are modified in the guts of the living. (W.H. Auden, *In Memory of W.B. Yeats*[1])

The *Sonny Bono Copyright Term Extension Act* 1998 (US) (the *Sonny Bono Act*) was literally a 'Mickey Mouse Bill'. The 1998 statute was the result of intense lobbying by a group of powerful corporate copyright holders, most visibly the Walt Disney Company, which faced the imminent expiration of copyrights on Mickey Mouse and its other famous cartoon characters.[2] The legislation extended the term of copyright protection for copyright works from the life of the author plus 50 years to the life of the author plus 70 years, in line with the European Union. It also extended the term of copyright protection for works made for hire, and existing works, to at least 95 years. Thus Mickey Mouse, a work for hire first copyrighted in 1928, will now pass into the public domain in 2023, instead of 2003 under the previous law.

Sonny Bono, from the 1970s pop group and variety show Sonny and Cher, believed that copyright should be extended, if not made perpetual. As a Florida Senator he introduced the legislation. However, the politician died in a skiing accident before the legislation came to pass. The tragic irony is that the legislation he sponsored was intended to provide a longer term of copyright protection to benefit the estate of deceased copyright owners. In the consideration of the bill, Sonny's widow, Mary Bono, provided this elegy, which was in part a memorial and in part a polemic:

> Copyright term extension is a very fitting memorial for Sonny. This is not only because of his experience as a pioneer in the music and television industries. The most important reason for me was that he was a legislator who understood the delicate balance of the constitutional interests at stake . . . Actually, Sonny wanted the term of copyright protection to last forever. I am informed by staff that such a change would violate the Constitution. I invite all of you to work with me to strengthen our copyright laws in all of the ways available to us. As you know, there is also Jack Valenti's proposal for term to last forever less one day. Perhaps the Committee may look at that next Congress.[3]

In life and even in death, Sonny Bono served as an ideal figurehead for a number of copyright industries. He was able to lend credence to the pretence that the main beneficiaries of the legislation were artists and musicians, rather than the multinational media companies who distributed and transmitted copyright works.

Eric Eldred, the electronic publisher of Eldritch Press, was concerned that the *Sonny Bono Act* would prevent him from publishing books that had been previously in the public domain. He was particularly aggrieved that the poems of Robert Frost would remain in copyright. Like W.H. Auden, the publisher believed that 'the words of a dead man/are modified in the guts of the living'.[4] With the help of Stanford law professor Lawrence Lessig, Eldred decided to launch a legal action against the constitutional validity of the *Sonny Bono Act*. First of all, he argued that the extension of the copyright term went beyond the scope of the Copyright Power under the United States Constitution. That clause provides that 'Congress shall have Power . . . To promote the Progress of Science and Useful Arts by securing for Limited Times to Authors and Inventors the exclusive right to their respective Writings and Discoveries.' Second, the electronic publisher maintained that the legislation violated the freedom of speech guaranteed under the First Amendment.[5]

The petitioner Eldred was supported by nine additional plaintiffs: organizations which provided public access to songs, books and films.[6] He was also bolstered by a number of amicus curiae submissions by historians, intellectual property academics, economists, cultural institutions, various copyright users and members of the new economy.[7] For the respondents, there were a number of amicus curiae, including members of Congress, copyright owners and professional organizations, as well as intellectual property lawyers and academics.[8]

The legal challenge by Eldred against the *Sonny Bono Act* was pursued all the way up to the Supreme Court of the United States. In the United States District Court of Columbia, Green J brusquely dismissed the argument that the *Sonny Bono Act* was unconstitutional.[9] In the Court of Appeals for the District of Columbia, the majority of the circuit judges were more circumspect in finding the *Sonny Bono Act* was constitutional.[10] Sentelle J dissented. Finally, the Supreme Court of the United States in *Eldred* v. *Ashcroft*[11] rejected a constitutional challenge to the validity of the *Sonny Bono Act* by a majority of seven to two.[12] In the leading judgment, Ginsburg J opined that Congress had the authority under the Copyright Clause to extend the term of copyright protection.[13] She maintained that the monopolies granted by copyright law were compatible with the freedom of speech and said a successful constitutional challenge could render all past copyright extensions similarly vulnerable. Breyer and Stevens JJ strongly dissented against the ruling.

This chapter is largely sympathetic to the valiant attempt of Eldred to overturn the extension of the copyright term. However, it expresses a number of reservations about the conservative reliance on the first principles of constitutional law and first amendment concerns to secure the information commons.[14] Historically, the evidence is mixed as to whether the tradition of copyright law has been wholly supportive of the freedom and liberty of copyright users. There has also been a strong counter-tendency towards using copyright law for the purposes of private censorship. The relationship between copyright law and freedom of speech has been quite a contingent one. The development of the internal doctrines of copyright law has largely been forged in remedying specific allegations of infringement. Concern for encroachment on private rights has muddled an elaboration of the precise place of copyright law in the more publicly centred doctrines of constitutional law and freedom of speech. Moreover, there is a strong thread in the freedom of speech discourse in the United States about the marketplace for ideas, which is deeply grounded in the commodification of cultural works. In philosophical terms freedom of speech arguments could be said to be as much about reconciling the conditions for speech with economic concerns about monopolies and competition policy, as about the political priority of free speech trumping private economic interests per se. Furthermore, the abstract arguments about freedom of speech have held little sway in recent negotiations directing the future global development of copyright law. In these circumstances too much dependence upon constitutional law as chief protector of the public domain is troublesome.

This chapter instead advocates a critical theory of copyright law, which highlights the gap between the symbolic significance of legislation and its instrumental effects in terms of economic impact and cultural costs. It demands a greater scrutiny of the politics and the rhetoric of Congress, the judiciary and the public domain. This chapter claims that the case of *Eldred* v. *Ashcroft* offers a lens through which a disciplinary pattern can be discerned. Section one considers the historical debate about the extension of the copyright term. It explores the constitutional challenge to the *Sonny Bono Act*. Section two examines First Amendment issues relating to freedom of speech. It discusses the interaction between copyright doctrine and constitutional law. Section three investigates the idea that copyright law serves to protect the public domain and preserve cultural heritage. Section four analyses the debate over the economic effects of the extension of the copyright term. Section five reflects upon the discussion of the copyright term in the light of harmonization and international trade. Section six evaluates concerns about the impact of the decision upon the validity of the *Copyright Act* 1976 (US) and the debate over 'perpetual copyright'. The conclusion considers the implications of the decision for legislatures, courts and the public.

I. 'A BOUNTY TO GENIUS AND LEARNING': THE HISTORY OF THE COPYRIGHT CLAUSE

The copyright term has been a perennial subject of contention between copyright owners, and copyright users.

Three distinguished historians, Mark Rose, Tyler Ochoa and Edward Walterscheid, made submissions in the Supreme Court case of *Eldred* v. *Ashcroft*.[15] The historians considered the English antecedents, such as the *Statute of Monopolies* 1624 (UK), the *Statute of Anne* 1710 (UK) and *Donaldson* v. *Beckett*.[16] They cite an anonymous pamphleteer protesting against the legislative push by booksellers to extend the copyright term for literary property in 1735:

> I see no Reason for granting a further Term now, which will not hold as well for granting it again and again, as often as the Old ones Expire; so that should this Bill pass, it will in Effect be establishing a perpetual Monopoly, a Thing deservedly odious in the Eye of the Law; it will be a great Cramp to Trade, a Discouragement to Learning, no Benefit to Authors, but a general Tax on the Publick; and all this only to increase the private Gain of the Booksellers.[17]

The historians also investigated the meaning of the Patent and Copyright Clause of the United States and considered statutory and judicial interpretation of the Clause. The historians submitted that the Framers feared that publishers in America would achieve the same power over learning that they held in England. They therefore crafted the Copyright Clause so as to 'prevent the formation of oppressive monopolies'.[18]

In the majority judgment, Ginsburg J maintains that the approach of the United States to the copyright clause departed from the tradition of the United Kingdom.[19] Her Honour draws upon the work of Thomas Nachbar, arguing that the histories in the amicus brief are mythologies, modern projections back onto the past decisions of the Framers:

> [I]n 1798 the fledging republic had more than 200 publishers, printers, and booksellers spread through New York, Boston, Philadelphia, Baltimore, and Charleston, and they were intensely competitive. The few efforts actually undertaken to form trade organizations among publishers in the early 19th century failed almost as soon as they began . . . Contrary to the Eldred petitioners' claims, the Framers did not write the Copyright Clause in order to prevent publishers from exercising control over speech.[20]

This article is a polemic which claims that the historians are as mistaken in their condemnation of modern congresses as they are in their romanticization of past ones. Ginsburg J is ambivalent towards the contested historical sources: on the one hand, she cites the accounts of Mark Rose and L. Ray Patterson with approval; and on the other, she departs from their conclusions that were put forward in the amicus curiae.

Ginsburg J emphasizes that '[t]he economic philosophy behind the [Copyright] [C]lause . . . is the conviction that encouragement of individual effort by personal gain is the best way to advance public welfare through the talents of authors and inventors'.[21] Accordingly, 'copyright law *celebrates* the profit motive, recognizing that the incentive to profit from the exploitation of copyrights will redound to the public benefit by resulting in the proliferation of knowledge'.[22] In her view, 'The profit motive is the engine that ensures the progress of science'.[23] Her Honour argues that Stevens J's characterization of reward to the author as 'a secondary consideration' of copyright law understates the relationship between such rewards and the 'Progress of Science'.[24] She argues that Breyer J's assertion that 'copyright statutes must serve public, not private, ends' misses the mark.[25] The two ends are not mutually exclusive; copyright law serves public ends by providing individuals with an incentive to pursue private ones.[26]

Ginsburg J envisions the history of copyright law in the United States as a process of gentle evolution and progress: 'History reveals an unbroken congressional practice of granting to authors of works with existing copyrights the benefit of term extensions so that all under copyright protection will be governed even-handedly under the same regime.'[27] Her Honour found it significant that early Congresses extended the duration of numerous individual patents as well as copyrights. As early as *McClurg* v. *Kingsland*,[28] the court made it plain that the Intellectual Property Clause permits Congress to amplify an existing patent's terms. Ginsburg J concludes: 'The [*Sonny Bono Act*] follows this historical practice by keeping the duration provisions of the [*Copyright Act* 1976 (US)] largely in place and simply adding 20 years to each of them. Guided by text, history, and precedent, we cannot agree with petitioners' submission that extending the duration of existing copyrights is categorically beyond Congress' authority under the Copyright Clause.'[29]

In his dissenting judgment, Breyer J contended that historical sources support the view that the Copyright Clause serves the primary purpose of promoting the public good. He claimed that this view of the Copyright Clause was supported by the writings of Madison,[30] the environment in which the Framers wrote the Clause, and in the history of the Clause's English antecedent, the *Statute of Anne* 1710 (UK).[31] His Honour essentially upholds the contention of the petitioners that the Copyright Clause sought to prohibit an indefinite and endless power to extend existing terms: 'Against the background of these concerns over corruption, and over the concentration of power in the hands of publishers, this Court should apply a meaning of "limited Times" that would achieve the Framers' purpose.'[32]

Breyer J alludes to Lord Macaulay's famous parliamentary discussion of the extension of Talfourd's copyright legislation in 1841, in which he said that 'copyright is a tax on readers for the purpose of giving a bounty to writers'.[33] He analyses the constitutional objectives that are served by the Intellectual Property Clause. Breyer J stresses that the Constitution itself describes the basic Clause objective as one of 'promot[ing] the Progress of Science', to promote knowledge and learning.[34] He observed:

> The Clause exists not to 'provide a special private benefit', but to stimulate artistic creativity for the general public good . . . The 'reward' is a means, not an end. And that is why the copyright term is limited. It is limited so that its beneficiaries – the public – 'will not be permanently deprived of the fruits of an artist's labors.'[35]

Breyer J notes that '[C]opyright law . . . makes reward to the owner a secondary consideration'.[36] He emphasizes that copyright is 'intended to increase and not to impede the harvest of knowledge'.[37]

In his judgment, Stevens J focuses extensively on statutory and judicial interpretation of the Intellectual Property Clause. His Honour considers the history of the Intellectual Property Clause and the extensions of both the patent and copyright terms. Stevens J questions the adequacy of the historical analysis provided in the majority judgment: 'A more complete and comprehensive look at the history of congressional action under the Copyright/Patent Clause demonstrates that history, in this case, does not provide the "volume of logic", necessary to sustain the *Sonny Bono Act's* constitutionality.'[38] Stevens J observes: 'The fact that the Court has not previously passed upon the constitutionality of retroactive copyright extensions does not insulate the present extension from constitutional challenge.'[39] Stevens J maintains: 'Judicial opinions relied upon by the majority interpreting legislative enactments have either been implicitly overruled or do not support the proposition claimed.'[40] His Honour concludes: 'If Congress may not expand the scope of a patent monopoly, it also may not extend the life of copyright beyond its expiration date.'[41] The judgment is interesting: it provides both an understanding of the diversity and significance of history and an awareness of its limits.

So to what extent are historical arguments influential? There was little consensus amongst judges about the history of copyright law. The accounts provided of the development of copyright law were largely self-serving. As Kathy Bowrey has observed elsewhere: 'In reading about copyright's history it soon becomes apparent that various writers are so engrossed in their own experiences that they can only meaningfully engage with others who come to the subject from a similar point of view.'[42] The majority judgment dismissed the amicus curiae judgment of leading historians of intellectual property. They instead preferred a highly selective and politicized reading of the past. Breyer J is willing to draw together a range of historical arguments to support his argument that 'limited places' did confine the copyright term. However, it might be difficult to recast such enlightenment ideals in modern terms of digital access. For his part, Stevens J harbours doubts as to the relative significance of such matters.[43] Such partial responses might give rise to pessimism about whether a consideration of history at all is worthwhile in such debates.

Nonetheless, it is arguable that history does have an important role to play in understanding copyright law reform. As Paul Edward Geller comments, there is a need to draw hypotheses from history to frame the future development of copyright law: 'Facing both backward and forward, we are tempted to interpret history to anticipate or to influence the future.'[44] What is needed, though, is a better appreciation of the history of copyright law in all its complexity and confusion.

II. 'GOODBYE TO ALL THAT': CONSTITUTIONAL LAW AND THE FIRST AMENDMENT

Peter Jaszi has made the interesting point that he felt as though his testimony to Congress opposing the implementation of the *Sonny Bono Act* could not be heard.[45] He observed:

> In the current climate, it is no longer sufficient to derive indirect arguments for the preservation of the public domain from constitutional first principles, as it were . . . Too often, defenders of the public domain have been overcomplacent in shaping their arguments, imagining that they do not have to make the case for the importance of the informational commons because it is somehow constitutionally secured. Today, defenders of the public domain can no longer rely on arguments cast in an essentially negative form: that some proposed piece of legislation, which will impoverish the public domain in order to contribute to the economic well-being of the U.S. information and entertainment industries, does not measure up to an abstract standard of constitutional justification because it fails to motivate the creation (or distribution) of particular new works.[46]

Peter Jaszi believed that his constitutionally grounded discourse fell on deaf ears, because he felt Congress had become attuned instead to international trade considerations rather than constitutional considerations. He deduces from his experience that discourse about the public good may have been eclipsed by the focus on industry and trade.

Nonetheless, Eldred and Lessig went ahead and brought a constitutional challenge against the validity of the *Sonny Bono Act*. Such arguments caused great ructions in the Supreme Court of the United States. For the majority, Ginsburg J argued that Congress had the authority under the Copyright Clause to extend the term of copyright protection. She maintained that the monopolies granted by copyright law were compatible with the freedom of speech interests guarded by the First Amendment. In a strong dissent, Breyer and Stevens JJ maintained that Congress had gone beyond the scope of its constitutional power under the Copyright Clause. They argued that the practical impact of the legislation would jeopardize the freedom of speech interests protected under the First Amendment.

In the leading majority judgment, Ginsburg J engaged in a defence of judicial quietism: 'Rather than subjecting Congress' legislative choices in the copyright area to heightened judicial scrutiny, we have stressed that "it is not our role to alter the delicate balance Congress has labored to achieve".'[47] Elaborating upon academic arguments about the role of the judiciary,[48] Ginsburg J concluded:

> As we read the Framers' instruction, the Copyright Clause empowers Congress to determine the intellectual property regimes that, overall, in that body's judgment, will serve the ends of the Clause. Beneath the facade of their inventive constitutional interpretation, petitioners forcefully urge that Congress pursued very bad policy in prescribing the [*Sonny Bono Act's*] long terms. The wisdom of Congress' action, however, is not within our province to second guess. Satisfied that the legislation before us remains inside the domain the Constitution assigns to the First Branch, we affirm the judgment of the Court of Appeals.[49]

Ginsburg J was critical of the decision of Breyer J to import policy arguments: 'Moving beyond the bounds of the parties' presentations, and with abundant policy arguments but precious little support from precedent, he would condemn Congress' entire product as irrational.'[50] However, the conservative members of the Supreme Court of the United States were accused of being inconsistent in their interpretation of constitutional powers, taking a strong role in determining the ambit of its commerce power, but deferring to Congress in respect of the Copyright Clause.[51]

In any case, Ginsburg J claimed that the limited monopolies provided by copyright law were compatible with the free speech principles protected under the First Amendment:

> The Copyright Clause and First Amendment were adopted close in time. This proximity indicates that, in the Framers' view, copyright's limited monopolies

> are compatible with free speech principles. Indeed, copyright's purpose is to *promote* the creation and publication of free expression.[52]

Her Honour maintained that a number of judicial doctrines in copyright law contain accommodations of free speech interests protected by the First Amendment. In particular, she mentioned the idea/expression distinction, the defence of fair use, and the exceptions for cultural institutions.

First, Ginsburg J argued that copyright law contained built-in First Amendment accommodations, most notably the distinction between ideas and expression, under which only the latter is eligible for copyright protection. She recalled that in *Harper & Row*, the Supreme Court of the United States observed that this 'idea/expression dichotomy strike[s] a definitional balance between the First Amendment and the Copyright Act by permitting free communication of facts while still protecting an author's expression'.[53] She maintained that the idea/expression doctrine facilitated marketplace competition so that new works are not restrained by rights to old ones. Ginsburg J also reiterated the decision on originality in *Feist*, in which the Supreme Court held that facts in a copyrighted work become instantly available for public exploitation at the moment of publication.[54] She recapitulated academic Melville Nimmer's argument that copyright law and free speech were mutually compatible.[55]

However, this shibboleth is becoming increasingly dated and questioned. Ginsburg J failed to allude to the widespread scepticism about the adequacy of the doctrine. The problem is that the distinction between ideas and expression is difficult if not impossible to draw. This difficulty has only been compounded in the digital era, in which copyright works can be easily reduced to a digital form. As Peter Drahos observes: 'An American realist-inspired approach might conclude that the distinction is used by individual judges to mask highly personal value judgments that are themselves influenced by a host of non-legal factors.'[56] Peter Jaszi suggests that 'courts tend to downplay the fundamental contradiction in the goals of the copyright system by emphasizing the so-called idea/expression dichotomy'.[57] As a result of its uncertain and indeterminate nature, the judicial doctrine provides scant protection for freedom of speech interests.

Second, Ginsburg J contended that the defence of fair use allows the public to use not only facts and ideas contained in a copyrighted work, but also expression itself in certain circumstances. Quoting the decision in *Harper & Row*,[58] her Honour observed that the fair use defence affords considerable 'latitude for scholarship and comment'.[59] Citing *Campbell* v. *Acuff-Rose Music, Inc*,[60] her Honour stresses that even parody is capable of fair use.[61]

In dissent, Breyer J provided the rejoinder:

> The majority also invokes the 'fair use' exception, and it notes that copyright law itself is restricted to protection of a work's expression, not its substantive content. Neither the exception nor the restriction, however, would necessarily help those who wish to obtain from electronic databases material that is not there – say, teachers wishing their students to see albums of Depression Era photographs, to read the recorded words of those who actually lived under slavery, or to contrast, say, Gary Cooper's heroic portrayal of Sergeant York with filmed reality from the battlefield of Verdun. Such harm, and more, will occur despite the 1998 Act's exemptions and despite the other 'First Amendment safeguards' in which the majority places its trust.[62]

A number of reservations could be raised about the defence of fair use being employed as a bulwark against private censorship. The defence of fair use has been frequently read down, so that it does not deal with free speech interests. In particular, the case of *Rogers* v. *Koons* established that the defence of fair use did not extend beyond parody to political criticism or social commentary.[63] Furthermore, the defence of fair use has been undermined by the operation of private contracts, and provisions in the *Digital Millennium Copyright Act* 1998 (US), which provide for special protection for technological protection measures. As a result, it would be fair to say that the defence of fair use provides protection of free speech interests, only in quite limited speech contexts.

Third, Ginsburg J maintained that the legislation supplemented these traditional First Amendment safeguards with special exceptions for cultural institutions. Notably, it allows libraries, archives and similar institutions to 'reproduce' and 'distribute, display, or perform in facsimile or digital form' copies of certain published works 'during the last 20 years of any term of copyright . . . for purposes of preservation, scholarship, or research'.[64]

In dissent, Breyer J argued that the special exemptions for libraries and archives are subject to a number of important restrictions. This exemption applied only where the copy is made for the special listed purposes; it simply permits a library to make 'a copy' for those purposes; it covers only 'published' works not 'subject to normal commercial exploitation' and not obtainable, apparently not even as a used copy, at a 'reasonable price'; and it insists that the library assure itself through 'reasonable investigation' that these conditions have been met. Breyer J despaired: 'What database proprietor can rely on so limited an exemption – particularly when the phrase "reasonable investigation" is so open-ended and particularly if the database has commercial, as well as non-commercial, aspects?'[65]

The case of *Eldred* v. *Ashcroft* demonstrates that there is a need for the judiciary to be vigilant to ensure that copyright law reforms do not have an adverse impact upon freedom of political expression and communication. In his dissent, Breyer J addressed the concern of his colleagues that 'our holding in this case not inhibit the broad decision-making leeway that the Copyright Clause grants Congress'.[66] His Honour maintained that the Supreme Court of the United States was perfectly entitled to rule that the statute in question was unconstitutional:

> We cannot avoid the need to examine the statute carefully by saying that 'Congress has not altered the traditional contours of copyright protection,' for the sentence points to the question, rather than the answer. Nor should we avoid that examination here. That degree of judicial vigilance – at the far outer boundaries of the Clause – is warranted if we are to avoid the monopolies and consequent restrictions of expression that the Clause, read consistently with the First Amendment, seeks to preclude. And that vigilance is all the more necessary in a new Century that will see intellectual property rights and the forms of expression that underlie them play an ever more important role in the Nation's economy and the lives of its citizens.[67]

Stevens J also emphasized that there was a need for greater judicial scrutiny of Congress in this field: 'Fairly read, the Court has stated that Congress' actions under the Copyright/Patent Clause are, for all intents and purposes, judicially unreviewable. That result cannot be squared with the basic tenets of our constitutional structure.'[68] He recalled the trenchant words of Marshall CJ: 'It is emphatically the province and duty of the judicial department to say what the law is.'[69] It should not be taken for granted that copyright law is compatible with freedom of speech.

The Supreme Court of the United States was deeply divided by the constitutional challenge against the validity of the *Sonny Bono Act*. The judgments did not only differ in the readings of historical precedent, but also in terms of approaches to copyright law doctrine and constitutional law. There were divergences in judicial approach to the review of government legislation and policy making. Such disparities are most apparent in the context of policy arguments about cultural heritage, economic and competition policy and international trade.

III. 'INTELLECTUAL PURGATORY': THE COPYRIGHT TERM AND CULTURAL HERITAGE

In addition to concerns about freedom of speech, there were a number of amicus curiae submissions which argued that the *Sonny Bono Act* would have a deleterious effect on cultural heritage and new technologies.[70]

Ginsburg J maintained that the legislation would promote the dissemination of American cultural works. She noted that Congress heard testimony from a number of prominent artists who each expressed the belief that the copyright system's assurance of fair compensation for themselves and their heirs was an incentive to create. Her Honour was blithely unconcerned by reports that Congress was heavily lobbied by multinational entertainment corporations, such as Disney, Time-Warner and BMG. This judgment supports a particular vision of copyright law as an instrument for promoting trade in the cultural output that comes within its purview.[71] Her Honour agreed with the Court of Appeals that 'in an era of multinational publishers and instantaneous electronic transmission, harmonization in this regard has obvious practical benefits'.[72] Ginsburg J also maintained that longer terms would encourage copyright holders to invest in the restoration and public distribution of their works. She cited discussion in Congress that the term extension would provide 'copyright owners generally with the incentive to restore older works and further disseminate them to the public'.[73] Ginsburg J was chary about addressing the practical consequences of the copyright term extension. She did not engage with the amicus curiae briefs of cultural, educational and collecting institutions, which detail the impact of transaction costs and clearance fees.

In his dissenting judgment, Breyer J discussed the serious cultural costs of the copyright term extension:

> This statute will cause serious expression-related harm. It will likely restrict traditional dissemination of copyrighted works. It will likely inhibit new forms of dissemination through the use of new technology. It threatens to interfere with efforts to preserve our Nation's historical and cultural heritage and efforts to use that heritage, say, to educate our Nation's children. It is easy to understand how the statute might benefit the private financial interests of corporations or heirs who own existing copyrights. But I cannot find any constitutionally legitimate, copyright-related way in which the statute will benefit the public. Indeed, in respect to existing works, the serious public harm and the virtually nonexistent public benefit could not be more clear.[74]

The judge emphasized that the statute imposes two kinds of public expression-related costs. First of all, Breyer J argued that the present statute would primarily benefit the holders of existing copyrights, and impose higher royalties than may be necessary to evoke creation of the relevant work. He commented that the 20 extra years of copyright protection would result in the transfer of a substantial sum of royalties to copyright owners. The copyright term extension would enable entertainment companies to engage in the commodification of cultural works, amassing large holdings of copyright works and exploiting them over a long duration.[75] It would mean that new technological means of disseminating old works would be closed to competition.

Second, Breyer J was concerned that copyright extension imposed an onerous requirement upon all potential users of copyrighted works to obtain permission from the copyright owners:

> The potential users of such works include not only movie buffs and aging jazz fans, but also historians, scholars, teachers, writers, artists, database operators, and researchers of all kinds – those who want to make the past accessible for their own use or for that of others. The permissions requirement can inhibit their ability to accomplish that task. Indeed, in an age where computer-accessible databases promise to facilitate research and learning, the permissions requirement can stand as a significant obstacle to realization of that technological hope.[76]

Breyer J elaborated that there are a number of costs associated with the requirement to obtain permission from the copyright owner. First of all, it may prove expensive to track down or contract with the copyright holder. Second, the holder may prove impossible to find. In other words, there may be an 'orphan' copyright work. Third, the holder when found may deny permission either outright or through misinformed efforts to bargain. In fact, the Congressional Research Service has found that the cost of seeking permission 'can be prohibitive'.[77]

The legislation will have a severe impact upon cultural institutions such as libraries, galleries and orchestras. It will interfere with the activities of electronic publishers of public domain works such as Eldred's Eldritch Press, the Internet Archive and Project Gutenberg. In his dissenting judgment, Breyer J observes:

> Similarly, the costs of obtaining permission, now perhaps ranging in the millions of dollars, will multiply as the number of holders of affected copyrights increases from several hundred thousand to several million. The costs to the users of nonprofit databases, now numbering in the low millions, will multiply as the use of those computer-assisted databases becomes more prevalent. And the qualitative costs to education, learning, and research will multiply as our children become ever more dependent for the content of their knowledge upon computer-accessible databases – thereby condemning that which is not so accessible, say, the cultural content of early 20th-century history, to a kind of intellectual purgatory from which it will not easily emerge.[78]

Thus, the American Association of Law Libraries points out that the clearance process associated with creating an electronic archive, Documenting the American South, 'consumed approximately a dozen man-hours' per work.[79] The College Art Association says that the costs of obtaining permission for use of single images, short excerpts, and other short works can become prohibitively high.[80] The National Writers Union provides similar examples.[81] Petitioners point to music fees that may prevent youth or community orchestras, or church choirs, from performing early 20th-century music.[82] Copyright extension caused abandonment of plans to sell sheet music of Maurice Ravel's *Alborada Del Gracioso*.[83] Furthermore electronic libraries such as the Internet Archive, Prelinger Archives and Project Gutenberg will find it difficult to provide digital access to historical texts, audio-visual works, and literary works, which are subject to the control of copyright owners.

In their dissenting judgments, Breyer and Stevens JJ doubt whether the copyright term extension will promote the useful arts by providing incentives to restore old movies. They are instead sympathetic to the claims of amicus curiae for the appellants that the legislation will result in a greater number of 'orphaned' films. These are films that cannot be restored and distributed by the copyright owners because the owners cannot be identified. The American Film Heritage Association argued that film makers and new authors who produce historical film documentaries will lose a great deal of valuable public domain footage through copyright extension: 'Films from the 1920s could contain as much as 75% of motion picture works no longer owned by anyone, with no traceable lineage, called Orphan works.'[84] Similarly, Michael Agee and Hal Roach Studios, restorers of fragile and classic film and television productions, such as the entire Laurel and Hardy 'talking' body of work, made a submission to the court.[85] They complained the *Sonny Bono Act* would frustrate the process of film preservation and restoration and impede commercial and non-commercial attempts to give access to the nation's film heritage.

The legislation will ensure that copyright estates – keepers of the flame – will have greater control over the economic exploitation and artistic integrity of a range of classic artistic and cultural works.[86] As one wit noted, the case creates a 'dead poets society'.[87] The decision will mean that literary works such as Robert Frost's *New Hampshire* poems, Margaret Mitchell's *Gone With the Wind*,[88] H.G. Wells' *The Shape of Things to Come*[89] and James Joyce's *Ulysses*[90] will remain in private hands for a longer time. There will also be greater conflict over the ownership of children's literature. For instance, in 2002, the Great Ormond Street Hospital refused to let the Canadian children's novelist J. Emily Somma publish the novel *After the Rain: A New Adventure for Peter Pan* in the United States and the European Union, because it claimed copyright over the original Peter Pan play by J.M. Barrie.[91] Copyright estates will be able to control the interpretation of dramatic works, as well. For example, the Beckett estate will be able to prolong its strict interpretation of *Waiting for Godot*.[92] The judgment will also harm the public performance of musical works. Music fees may prevent orchestras from performing early twentieth-century music, such as George Gershwin and Aaron Copland, as well as works of great foreign composers such as Igor Stravinsky, Jean Sibelius, Maurice Ravel and Sergei Rachmaninov.[93]

The Estate of the Irish novelist, James Joyce, has been particularly aggressive in policing his revived copyrights.[94] The 'keepers of the flame' have relied upon threats of legal action to discourage the production of derivative works based upon the canonical texts of the novelist. The Estate has also jealously guarded the reputation of the author by vetoing the use of his work in various scholarly productions.[95] Most radically of all, the grandson Stephen Joyce threatened to take legal action to prevent the staging of 'Rejoyce Dublin 2004', a festival celebrating the centenary of Bloomsday. In response, the Irish Parliament rushed through emergency legislation, entitled the *Copyright and Related Rights (Amendment) Act* 2004 (Ireland) to safeguard the celebrations. The legislation clarified that a person could place literary and artistic works on public exhibition, without breaching the copyright vested in such cultural works.

In Australia, similar concerns were expressed about the impact of copyright term extension upon cultural heritage in the debate over the *Australia–United States Free Trade Agreement* 2004 (*AUSFTA*).[96] The copyright officer of the Australian Libraries and Information Association, Colette Ormonde, commented:

> The outcome is bad for libraries. It is bad for students. It is bad for researchers. It is bad for all information users. We have agreed to a very restrictive US copyright regime with no clear dispute mechanism . . . it will cause huge problems. People who have been using information that is in the public domain will suddenly have to pay for it.[97]

The executive director of the Australian Vice-Chancellors' Committee, John Mullarvey, said that Australian universities currently paid $20 million a year in copyright fees and adding 20 years to the period of copyright protection would add to that sum.[98]

Screensound Australia, the National Screen and Sound Archive, is the national audiovisual archive. A number of significant films – protected under copyright law as a series of photographs – were due to come into the public domain, including *Jedda*, *Robbery Under Arms* and *Summer of the Seventeenth Doll*. In addition, a number of significant sound recordings were due to fall into the public domain, including the compositions of Percy Grainger, Alfred Hill, Eugene Goossens and Varney Monk. The organization will be particularly affected by the extension of the copyright term.

The Australian Broadcasting Corporation (ABC) was concerned about the effect of the copyright term extension on a special Digital Conversion Project.[99] The Archives and Library Services section was working with

Technology and Distribution to implement the project which would convert 120 000 hours of analog television and audio archived programming to digital online and hardcopy formats, using special purpose funding. They had hoped: '70 Years of Radio History and 47 Years of Television History to be Digitised by the Australian Broadcasting Corporation'.[100] However, the extension of the copyright term will jeopardize such important initiatives.

The international trend towards the extension of the copyright term will no doubt have a significant cultural and economic impact upon libraries, archives and cultural institutions, as well as educational and research organizations.

IV. 'RHAPSODY IN BLUE': ECONOMIC JAZZ AND COMPETITION POLICY

It is extraordinary that the law and economics movement[101] had so little influence in the debate over the extension of the copyright term. Given the central economic role of intellectual property rights,[102] one would have thought that economic analysis would be germane to the analysis of the duration of copyright law. Strangely, economic considerations did not come to the fore in the legislative debate over the *Sonny Bono Act*. There was little empirical work performed as to the relative economic costs and benefits of the legislation.[103] Nonetheless, Congress went ahead and implemented the statute. This is remarkable given that modern democracies are so commonly accused of being driven by the dictates of economic rationalism. There is a need to explain how Congress could decide to implement such a decision in light of the economic evidence.

There was a greater emphasis upon economics in the constitutional challenge to the *Sonny Bono Act*, yet the majority judgment written by Ginsburg J was largely scornful of the amicus curiae submissions by economists. The dissenting Stevens J briefly mentioned economic arguments. His colleague, Breyer J, was the only one to deploy economic arguments to any great effect.

A group of 17 economists including five Nobel Laureates made an amicus curiae submission.[104] In a keynote address, Lawrence Lessig observed:

> In our case, in *Eldred v. Ashcroft*, we have this brief filed by 17 economists, including Milton Friedman, James Buchanan, Ronald Coase, Ken Arrow, you know, lunatics, right? Left-wing liberals, right? Friedman said he'd only join if the word 'no-brainer' existed in the brief somewhere, like this was a complete no-brainer for him. This is not about left and right. This is about right and wrong. That's what this battle is.[105]

The amicus curiae submission made a number of circumspect points about the economic effect of the legislation. First, the longer term for new works provides only a marginal increase in anticipated compensation for an author. Second, the term extension for existing works makes no significant contribution to an author's economic incentive to create, since in this case the additional compensation was granted after the relevant investment had been made. Third, the legislation extends the period during which a copyright holder determines the quantity produced of a work, and thus increases the inefficiency from above-cost pricing, that is, by lengthening its duration. Finally, the legislation extends the period during which a copyright holder determines the production of derivative works, which affects the creation of new works that are built, in part, out of materials from existing works.

As a matter of constitutional interpretation, Ginsburg J thought it unlikely that the Founding Fathers would conceive of the debate over copyright duration in terms of economic outcomes:

> Justice Breyer several times places the Founding Fathers on his side. It is doubtful, however, that those architects of our Nation, in framing the 'limited Times' prescription, thought in terms of the calculator rather than the calendar.[106]

As a part of wider discourse about judicial activism, Ginsburg J maintained that it was the proper role of Congress, rather than the courts, to be engaged in a discussion about the economic consequences of legislation: 'Calibrating rational economic incentives, however, like "fashion[ing] . . . new rules [in light of] new technology", is a task primarily for Congress, not the courts.'[107] Her Honour noted that Congress heard testimony supporting the copyright term extension from a number of prominent and successful artists, such as Quincy Jones, Bob Dylan, Carlos Santana and Don Henley. It is striking that her Honour preferred to accept anecdotal evidence (rather than systematic evidence) about the economic impact of the *Sonny Bono Act*.

In dissent, Breyer J argued that the statute's extension of copyright protection could not be justified by the traditional economic rationale of copyright law. His Honour observed that the extension would not act as an economic spur encouraging authors to create new works. Drawing extensively upon the evidence of the amicus curiae, Breyer J contended that the commercial life of a copyright work would have been exhausted by that time: 'No potential author can reasonably believe that he has more than a tiny chance of writing a classic that will survive commercially long enough for the copyright extension to matter.'[108] His Honour asked the rhetorical question, 'What potential Shakespeare, Wharton, or Hemingway would be moved by such a sum?'[109] His point was that the incentive theory of copyright law provided no support for the extension of the copyright term.

The law and economics movement has been marginally more influential in other jurisdictions, which have given greater weight to concerns about economic efficiency and competition policy. In 2000, the Australian Intellectual Property and Competition Review considered whether it was appropriate to extend the term of copyright extension to the same duration as the United States and the European Union.[110] The Committee specifically sought from the Australian Copyright Council evidence that an extension would confer benefits in excess of the costs it would impose. No such evidence was provided. Consequently, the Committee recommended that the current term should not be extended.[111] It also recommended that no extension of the copyright term should be introduced in future without a prior thorough and independent review of the resulting costs and benefits.[112]

Paying little heed to such advice, the Australian Federal Government agreed to extend the copyright term as part of the *AUSFTA*. The Government argued that the decision would boost Australia's competitiveness by giving it access to the United States economy. The chief Australian negotiator, Stephen Deady, told the Senate Estimates Committee that the Australian economy would receive an economic boost from the copyright term extension:

> One of the numbers I have seen is that between 1996 and 2000 Australia's exports in this area – IP type areas, copyright industries – grew faster than the national economy, with an average growth rate of about 5.7 per cent. Exports grew by around nine per cent. So there are certainly some advantages in this area of copyright extension.[113]

However, Deady confessed to the Senate Estimates Committee that the Government had not engaged in any economic research of its own into the impact of the copyright term extension. He told the Senate that he had not perused the Australian Intellectual Property and Competition Review, or the amicus brief of the economists in *Eldred* v. *Ashcroft*. Deady ignored the obvious point that Australia was a net importer of copyright works, and would continue to be so with the United States. Any marginal gains by Australian exporters should be weighed against the costs associated with those imports.

Subsequently, the Australian Government commissioned the Centre for International Economics to undertake economic analysis of the impact of the *AUSFTA*, taking into account the outcomes of the final negotiated package.[114] The Centre maintained that the impact of the copyright term extension would be negligible:

> Extending the copyright term does not seem likely to provide additional incentives to create new works, but may in some cases impose costs on consumers. In many cases the increased cost faced by consumers is not likely to be significant. This is because the demand for most creative works is likely to become very small, if not non-existent, well before the current copyright term expires. However, it is not possible to derive any indication of the magnitude of the costs that may stem from the restriction of new works being produced from existing works.[115]

This analysis of the intellectual property chapter was implausible on legal, economic and political grounds. The Centre failed to contextualize the major changes that have taken place and failed to grapple with some of the main economic studies that have been done in relation to copyright term extension and patent term extension. The Centre neglected to undertake an analysis of the magnitude of the costs even though it has been possible in the past to quantify the costs and benefits associated with making changes to intellectual property. Finally, the Centre failed to provide a political rationalization for such a stance. It seems strange to assume that the United States Trade Representative would put such time, energy and political capital into the copyright term extension, if its impact would be only negligible.

Dr Phillipa Dee was also commissioned by the Senate Select Committee to provide an independent economic analysis of the impacts of the *AUSFTA*.[116] She noted: 'The intellectual property (IP) rights chapter is precedent setting in many respects.'[117] Dee denied that it was impossible to quantify the effects of the copyright term extension. Drawing upon data from the Australian Bureau of Statistics, Dee calculated: 'According to this calculation, Australia's net royalty payments could be up to $88 million higher per year as a result of extending the term of copyright. And the discounted present value of the cost to Australia of extending the copyright term is about $700 million'.[118] In response, the Australian Government asserted that the costs of extending the term of copyright estimated in Dee's report were overstated, because the economic life of most copyright material is short. Dee replied: 'My estimation used the same assumptions as were used in the CIE/DFAT report to estimate the gains from extending the term of copyright.'[119] She noted: 'If the costs are overstated, then so too are the benefits.'[120] The economist concluded unequivocally: 'The fact remains that this provision is not in Australia's economic interests.'[121]

There is a need for governments contemplating an alteration of the copyright term to be properly informed about the benefits and costs of such legislative changes. Independent committees like the Australian Intellectual Property and Competition Review Committee are best placed to undertake such research because of their expertise in the field of copyright law. Such organizations are also better insulated against the insidious influence of corporate lobbying. Sam Ricketson has observed that policy development in this field needs to be based upon sound empirical evidence: 'What is required, therefore, are national and international studies that seek to ascertain, on a factual basis, the appropriate term for copyright protection, a kind of cost/benefit approach that seeks to evaluate the public and private costs and benefits of different terms of protection.'[122] Furthermore, the scope of such studies should not be limited to the issue of the extension of copyright term. Thus, even if there are practical benefits that flow from the adoption of a general minimum term of protection, there should be some investigation as to whether the term of protection should be shortened.

V. 'A COMPELLING ENTICEMENT': INTERNATIONAL TRADE AND HARMONIZATION

In congressional hearings into the extension of the copyright term, committee members were of the consensus that the goal of copyright law was to improve the competitive position of companies that have significant investments in inventories of copyright works.[123] Jack Valenti of the Motion Picture Association of America in 1995 observed: 'Copyright term extension has a simple but compelling enticement: it is very much in America's economic interests.'[124] He added that 'whatever can be done ought to be done to amplify America's export dexterity in the global arena'.[125]

In 1995, the European Union extended the copyright term for its member states to the life of the author plus 70 years. The change was a consequence of a Directive of the European Commission in 1993,[126] which required member states to increase their basic term of protection. Ostensibly, the purpose of the Directive was to harmonize the laws of European Union members, as national laws ranged from between life plus 50 years to life plus 70 years. However, as one commentator observes:

> Rather than shifting down to the Berne standard, the Directive has gravitated to the term adopted under German law. It seems that this was done with limited substantive debate of the costs and benefits involved in adopting a longer term of protection.[127]

There is some academic comment that such a harmonization of the copyright term was only accomplished in the European Union after intensive lobbying from copyright owners.[128]

There was a lackadaisical attitude to the extension of the copyright term in the European Union. In the light of heated debates over the copyright term in the past, Sherman and Bently were puzzled that there was so little policy discussion about the adoption of the European Community

Copyright Term Directive in the United Kingdom.[129] They speculated upon the reasons for this lack of controversy, concluding: 'It is rare, in the twentieth century, that we can debate issues and reach conclusions according only to our own perceptions of policy; usually the most pressing concern is whether our laws comply with international norms already reached by interest-group lobbying.'[130] An article from that period by Silke von Lewinski gives a sense of this blasé spirit.[131] She discusses the extension of the copyright term in the European Union in terms of being a technical amendment needed to produce harmonization. Her dry and technocratic discussion of the copyright term extension is a marked contrast to her international counterparts. Ricketson, for instance, is trenchantly critical of the push for the extension of the copyright term in the very same journal issue.[132] The contrast is even greater between European commentators like von Lewinski and engaged American intellectuals such as Lawrence Lessig, Peter Jaszi and David Bollier.

Ginsburg J of the Supreme Court emphasized that the *Sonny Bono Act* was a rational exercise of the legislative authority conferred by the Copyright Clause in the United States Constitution:

> Consistent with the Berne Convention, the EU directed its members to deny this longer term to the works of any non-EU country whose laws did not secure the same extended term. By extending the baseline United States copyright term to life plus 70 years, Congress sought to ensure that American authors would receive the same copyright protection in Europe as their European counterparts. The [*Sonny Bono Act*] may also provide greater incentive for American and other authors to create and disseminate their work in the United States.[133]

Ginsburg J quotes with approval an article by Shirla Perlmutter[134] which argued that many benefits to knowledge and culture could be gained through active participation in the international copyright system.[135] Her Honour also relied upon a piece by Graeme Austin, which maintained that appeals in the Eldred briefs to history and theory were insular and provincial because of a failure to acknowledge the reality of copyright law's international context.[136] However, this vision of international copyright is hardly cosmopolitan. There was little concern about the impact of the copyright term extension on other countries – in particular, from an Antipodean point of view, there is no regard paid to Australia.

In his dissent, Breyer J questioned whether the *Sonny Bono Act* could be justified on the grounds that it would promote a healthy surplus balance of trade:

> I can find nothing in the Copyright Clause that would authorize Congress to enhance the copyright grant's monopoly power, likely leading to higher prices

> both at home and abroad, *solely* in order to produce higher foreign earnings. That objective is not a *copyright* objective. Nor, standing alone, is it related to any other objective more closely tied to the Clause itself. Neither can higher corporate profits alone justify the grant's enhancement. The Clause seeks public, not private, benefits.[137]

This complaint that the legislation is a form of corporate welfare is echoed elsewhere. David Bollier considers the dispute in the context of the information commons: 'The law is a clear case of corporate welfare for major corporations and amounts to a tax on the public and authors who want to use the public domain to create new works.'[138]

Breyer J comments that the United States Congress was not compelled to pass the *Sonny Bono Act* because of international treaty-making obligations. He observed that, notwithstanding important institutional and philosophical differences, the common law system of the United States and the civil tradition of European countries have been able to co-exist peacefully in the past: for instance, in relation to Europe's traditional respect for moral rights. Breyer J argued that the extension of the copyright term was not justified by the need for international uniformity of terms: 'Although it can be helpful to look to international norms and legal experience in understanding American law, in this case the justification based upon foreign rules is surprisingly weak.'[139] His Honour identifies a number of discrepancies between the United States model and the European standard. With respect to works 'made for hire', the *Sonny Bono Act* produces an extended term of 95 years while comparable European rights in 'for hire' works last for periods that vary from 50 years to 70 years to life plus 70 years. Neither does the statute create uniformity with respect to anonymous or pseudonymous works. The statute does produce uniformity with respect to copyrights in new, post-1977 works attributed to natural persons. However, these works constitute only a minority of works that retain commercial value after 75 years. Breyer J questions what, if any, benefit this partial future uniformity might achieve. He doubts whether the legislation would produce any incentive for American authors to create new work.

In the aftermath of the *Eldred* v. *Ashcroft* decision, the United States has relied upon bilateral free trade agreements with its major trading partners to extend the term of copyright protection in other jurisdictions. Peter Drahos and John Braithwaite have observed: 'US bilateralism on intellectual property rights remains relentless.'[140]

At the insistence of the United States, Australia has agreed to adopt a longer term of copyright protection for works and other subject matter. The *Australia–United States Free Trade Agreement* 2004 extended the copyright term for works of natural authors to the life of the author plus 70 years; and 70 years from publication for films and sound recordings. The

Australian Attorney General, Philip Ruddock, defended the copyright term extension at a conference:

> It is important that I say something about Australia's agreement to increase the term of protection for copyright works by an additional 20 years. Australia generally does not advocate higher standards of intellectual property protection than those determined internationally. However, it is sometimes in Australia's interest not to lag behind emerging standards of important trading countries. It is clear that an international standard is emerging amongst out major trading partners for a longer copyright term. In these circumstances, term extension is a necessary and positive thing. It will ensure that Australia remains a competitive destination for cultural investment. It will also ensure that Australians are better able to trade their interests in an increasingly global market.[141]

However, such harmonization has been partial and selective, at best. Australia has decided upon a prospective extension of the copyright term, as opposed to the retrospective extension of the copyright term in the European Union and the United States. Furthermore, Australia has not adopted features of United States law which favours copyright users, such as a higher threshold of originality, or a defence of fair use. As a result, there have been concerns that the *AUSFTA* will boost the position of copyright owners at the expense of the interests of libraries, archives, cultural institutions and other copyright users.

In Canada, Parliament provides for copyright protection for life of the author plus 50 years. There was a failed attempt to extend the copyright term for unpublished works. Lucy Maud Montgomery (1874–1942) was the author of the popular and lucrative *Anne of Green Gables* novels.[142] Her heirs wished to retain control over her unpublished writings. For posthumous unpublished works, the Canadian copyright legislation provides limited protection to the author's estate for 50 years after the death of the writer, plus a six-year 'window' for the estate either to publish or to communicate its intention to publish the material. Before 1997, perpetual copyright was granted to an estate for posthumous unpublished writings. Marian Hebb, a lawyer for the Montgomery estate, argued that, with respect to the Lucy Maud Montgomery diaries, material was left unpublished because it would cause offence to living people.[143] The Liberal Government pushed for amendments under Bill C-36, the so-called '*Lucy Maud Montgomery Copyright Term Extension Bill*', which would add anywhere from 14 years to 34 years of copyright to previously unpublished works of authors who died between 1 January 1930 and 1 January 1949.[144] A coalition of parties stopped the 'Lucy Maud Montgomery provision' from being passed through the Canadian Parliament.[145] The House of Commons rejected the bill to extend copyright protection for unpublished works in April 2004.[146]

Article 16.4.4 of the *United States–Singapore Free Trade Agreement* 2003[147] establishes that the term of copyright protection shall be at least the life of the author plus 70 years, or at least 70 years from first publication of the work. Article 17.5.4 of the *United States–Chile Free Trade Agreement* 2003[148] provides for similar terms. The United States has already persuaded the Dominican Republic and countries from Central America to extend the copyright term as part of the *United States–Dominican Republic–Central America Free Trade Agreement* 2005.[149] The United States has also been keen to encourage the rest of America to extend the copyright term as part of a proposed *Free Trade Area of the Americas*.[150] Some countries are even contemplating further extensions of the copyright term beyond the standards set by the United States. The Mexican Congress is considering a revision of the copyright law well beyond its obligations under the *North-American Free Trade Agreement* 1994 (NAFTA).[151] Among other changes the law will extend the term of copyright from life-plus-70 to life-plus-100 and, at the end of that term, the Mexican government has the right to charge royalties for works in the 'public domain'.[152] The United States of America will also push for the extension of the copyright term to be included in multilateral agreements. They will engage in forum-shopping across a range of forums, such as the *Berne Convention* 1886, the *TRIPs Agreement* 1994 under the World Trade Organization, and the World Intellectual Property Organization treaties.[153]

VI. 'IF I COULD TURN BACK TIME': PERPETUAL COPYRIGHT

In the 1995 Congressional Hearings, Peter Jaszi first raised the spectre of a constitutional challenge to legislation extending the copyright term:

> A cynical observer might be forgiven the suspicion that it represents a down payment on perpetual copyright on the installment plan, thus raising obvious and substantial constitutional issues. Nor does the legislation in its present form appear to satisfy the constitutional mandate to promote science and the useful arts. But even if these constitutional concerns are put to one side, the legislation, as it stands, cannot be justified within the framework of the sound approach to evaluating copyright reform proposals, which have served Congress so well for more than two centuries.[154]

The United States Supreme Court was concerned about the wider significance of the decision in *Eldred* v. *Ashcroft*. The majority feared that the invalidation of the *Sonny Bono Act* would in turn jeopardize the

Copyright Act 1976 (US). In other words, they were concerned about the retrospective impact of the decision on past legislation. By contrast, the minority were concerned that the validation of the *Sonny Bono Act* would create a 'perpetual copyright'. They suggested that a failure to act would mean that the government would be able to extend the copyright term on future occasions, without judicial restraint.

For the majority, Ginsburg J argued that, if the calculations of the amicus curiae brief of the economists were correct, then the *Copyright Act* 1976 (US) would be invalid as well as the *Sonny Bono Act*.[155] Her Honour concluded with the nightmarish vision that the time extensions which were enacted by the 1976 statute would also be vulnerable to constitutional challenge.[156] There was considerable argument in the Supreme Court of the United States as to whether the 1976 act would be affected by invalidating the *Sonny Bono Act*. In the oral proceedings, a number of judges expressed reservations about the impact of invalidating the 1998 Act.[157] It is curious that the majority of the Supreme Court were only willing to consider the practical impact of the legislation in this limited context, and not in relation to the economic consequences of the extension of the copyright term. Perhaps the judges are concerned that invalidating the statute will generate additional legal work, whereas the economic realities will not necessarily burden the court.

In his dissenting judgment, Breyer J rebutted such scaremongering by the majority of the court: 'I do not share the Court's concern that my view of the 1998 Act could automatically doom the 1976 Act.'[158] His Honour observed that, unlike the *Sonny Bono Act*, the *Copyright Act* 1976 (US) had thoroughly revised copyright law and enabled the United States to join the *Berne Convention* 1886. Consequently, the balance of copyright-related harms and benefits was far less one-sided.[159] Breyer J noted that the same was true of the 1909 and 1831 Acts. In any case, such legislation provided for maximum terms of 56 years or 42 years while requiring renewal after 28 years, with most copyrighted works falling into the public domain after that 28-year period, well before the putative maximum terms had elapsed. In any event, his Honour observes that the case focuses only on the *Sonny Bono Act* and it was therefore unnecessary to consider the constitutionality of other copyright statutes.[160]

In the footnotes, Ginsburg J stressed that there was no statement in the statutory text that installed a perpetual copyright.[161] She also observed that the House and Senate Reports accompanying the *Sonny Bono Act* reflected no purpose to create perpetual copyright. Responding to an inquiry whether copyrights could be extended 'forever', Register of Copyrights Marybeth Peters emphasized the dominant reason for the legislation:

> There certainly are proponents of perpetual copyright: we heard that in our proceeding on term extension. The Songwriters Guild suggested a perpetual term. However, our Constitution says limited times, but there really isn't a very good indication on what limited times is. The reason why you're going to life-plus-70 today is because Europe has gone that way.[162]

Notably, the Senate Report expressly acknowledged that the Constitution 'clearly precludes Congress from granting unlimited protection for copyrighted works',[163] and disclaimed any intent to contravene that prohibition. Members of Congress instrumental in the passage of the *Sonny Bono Act* spoke to similar effect. Representative Coble observed that 'copyright protection should be for a limited time only' and that '[p]erpetual protection does not benefit society'.[164] Furthermore, Congressional witnesses disavowed any intention of implementing a perpetual copyright term. However, Ginsburg J conveniently ignored the fact that the statute was named after a Member of Congress, who, the legislative history records, 'wanted the term of copyright protection to last forever'.[165]

Breyer J nevertheless insisted that the 'economic effect' of the *Copyright Term Extension Act* 1998 (US) was to make the copyright term 'virtually perpetual'.[166] He observed that the legislation created a copyright term worth 99.8 per cent of the value of a perpetual copyright:

> The economic effect of this 20-year extension – the longest blanket extension since the Nation's founding – is to make the copyright term not limited, but virtually perpetual. Its primary legal effect is to grant the extended term not to authors, but to their heirs, estates, or corporate successors. And most importantly, its practical effect is not to promote, but to inhibit, the progress of 'Science' by which word the Framers meant learning or knowledge.[167]

Stevens J also dissented on similar grounds:

> It is important to note, however, that a categorical rule prohibiting retroactive extensions would effectively preclude perpetual copyrights. More importantly, as the House of Lords recognized when it refused to amend the Statute of Anne in 1735, unless the Clause is construed to embody such a categorical rule, Congress may extend existing monopoly privileges *ad infinitum* under the majority's analysis.[168]

It is a strange regression that the law should lapse back into providing virtually perpetual protection of copyright works, when the *Statute of Anne* 1710 (UK) was supposed to guard against such a fate.

Despite such judicial prevarication, the *New York Times* spoke of the public domain in the past tense: 'In effect, the Supreme Court's decision makes it likely that we are seeing the beginning of the end of public domain and the birth of copyright perpetuity.'[169]

CONCLUSION

The failure of the case of *Eldred* v. *Ashcroft* highlights the need to address the problematic politics of Congress in the field of copyright law. In the United States, the *Sonny Bono Act* was passed with minimal debate. The legislation was undemocratic in spirit. Heavily lobbied by copyright owners, Congress was the captive of corporate interests, and acceded to demands for legislative reforms. The politicians largely ignored the voices of copyright users who protested against such changes. There was little debate about the long-term impact of the legislation upon economic, cultural and technological changes. The judgment in the case of *Eldred* v. *Ashcroft* will have an important impact in terms of educating the public about the role of the Congress in copyright law making. The spokesman for the Electronic Frontier Foundation, Cory Doctorow, said: 'I hope this case becomes a rallying point for people who care about the public domain, and this issue, which has been so obscure and hard to understand for most people, creates a more mainstream dialogue in which creators and audiences come to realize how important the public domain is.'[170] In the future, there must be a much more wide-ranging pragmatic debate about the benefits and costs, and the broader implications of copyright law reform. It would be wise to place greater reliance and trust upon independent expert committees to explore fully the policy issues. To ensure that governments do not become the captive of corporate interests, there needs to be greater political representation of the interests of copyright users in the law reform process.

The case of *Eldred* v. *Ashcroft* also highlights the role of the courts in gatekeeping the economic agenda, and reaffirming its ideological merits and silences. The majority of the Supreme Court of the United States subscribed to a philosophy of political quietism, and acted with abject deference towards the decisions of Congress. They were shy about making judgments on policy matters. The majority merely reiterated the main symbolic policy objectives of Congress. They were reluctant to consider the practical, instrumental effects of the legislation. The dominant discourse was one of economic investment and trade, and international harmonization and uniformity. Matters of history, culture and freedom of speech were marginalized. Jack Valenti of the Motion Picture Association of America was positive about the decision:

> We are pleased that the Court has reaffirmed the absolute authority of Congress to set copyright terms. We have always maintained and the law has long recognized that copyright, whose aim it is to provide incentive for the creation and preservation of creative works, is in the public interest. That is why this ruling is a victory not solely for rights holders but also for consumers everywhere.[171]

However, there are a number of possible antidotes to this pallid jurisprudence. Lessig and his fellow lawyers played an important role in litigating *Eldred* v. *Ashcroft*. The role of amicus curiae is certainly an important one, too, in highlighting the implications of disputes. Unfortunately, in the Eldred case, the judges only paid limited attention to the submissions made on the extension of the copyright term. The judiciary would be more socially and culturally authoritative if it was willing freely to engage in a robust debate about the policy consequences of copyright legislation. The judgment of Breyer J shows the way forward for such an engaged jurisprudence. Furthermore, there is a need for critical reading of judicial decisions in this field.

The supporters of the commons claimed the decision of the Supreme Court of the United States was a significant moral victory. This may in part be wishful thinking, a desire to believe that the long litigation was not in vain. In the aftermath of the verdict, Lessig commented wistfully: 'It has often been said that movements gain by losing in the Supreme Court.'[172] There remain a number of other constitutional challenges under way against the *Sonny Bono Act* in the United States courts.[173] In *Kahle* v. *Gonzales*,[174] the District Court dismissed a constitutional challenge by two archives, which sought a declaratory judgment that copyright restrictions on orphan works violated the United States Constitution. In *Golan* v. *Gonzales*,[175] the District Court ruled against a Colorado conductor who sought to have the *Sonny Bono Act* and the *Uruguay Round Agreements Act* 1994 (US) declared unconstitutional. In *Luck's Music Library* v. *Gonzales*,[176] the District Court and Court of Appeals rejected a constitutional challenge by the sellers of public-domain foreign music and motion pictures to the *Uruguay Round Agreements Act* 1994 (US) provision, which restored copyright protection to certain foreign works. Thus this series of constitutional challenges to the copyright term extension in the United States seem to be doomed to failure.

In the wake of the decision of the Supreme Court of the United States, Lessig has advocated the creation of a registration scheme in United States copyright law, in which copyright works would require the payment of renewal fees after 50 years.[177] He maintains that copyright law should be transformed into a registration system, such as patent law and trade mark law, with renewable protection.[178] Such a model has been developed by members of the Chicago school of law and economics, William Landes and Richard Posner.[179] Inspired by this academic commentary, the *Public Domain Enhancement Act* 2003 (US) was introduced into United States Congress in June 2003. The legislation sought to amend the *Copyright Act* 1976 (US) to allow abandoned copyrighted works to enter the public domain after 50 years.[180] It terminated the copyright unless payment of the applicable maintenance fee was received in the Copyright Office on or before its due date or within a grace period of six months thereafter. Representative Zoe Lofgren reintroduced a version of the bill to the 109th Congress in 2005.[181] The proposed legislation has yet to win the support of the United States Congress.

In response to the concerns of United States Congressmen about the impact of the copyright term extension, the United States Copyright Office has held an inquiry into the issues raised by orphan works: those copyright works in which the owner is unknown or untraceable.[182] In January 2006, Marybeth Peters, the Register of Copyrights at the United States Copyright Office, released the report on orphan works.[183] The Office recommended that a copyright owner should only be entitled to limited remedies where a copyright user had made reasonably diligent efforts to locate the owner of the copyright, and provided proper attribution to the author and the owner.[184] It is unclear whether the United States Copyright Office proposal would solve the orphan works problem. Indeed, it would be cold comfort for users of orphan works to learn that they could be liable for actions for copyright infringement, even though they had made diligent efforts to find the copyright owner. The group Public Knowledge has argued that there should instead be a new defence to copyright infringement for users who make a reasonable effort to locate the owner of a copyright work.[185] In any case, the proposal to limit remedies in respect of orphan works fails to provide a meaningful response to the magnitude of the problems created by the copyright term extension.

In December 2006, the *Gowers Review of Intellectual Property* made a number of recommendations on copyright law policy in the United Kingdom. After commissioning independent economic analysis[186], Andrew Gowers recommended that the European Commission should retain the length of protection on sound recordings and performers' rights at 50 years. Furthermore, he advised that policy makers should adopt the principle that the term and scope of protection for intellectual property rights should not be altered retrospectively. Gowers called upon the European Commission to fashion a legislative solution to deal with orphan works: 'Any such exception should permit the use of genuine orphan works, provided the user has performed a reasonable search and, where possible, gives attribution'.[187]

As imaginative as such initiatives are, it is arguable that more radical action is needed to defend the intellectual commons from incursions by private owners. In particular, there is a need to learn from the mistakes of the European Union, the United States and Australia. There is a need to prevent the *Sonny Bono Act* extensions from being accepted in other jurisdictions and becoming an international norm.

NOTES

1. Auden, W.H. (1976), 'In Memory of W.B. Yeats', *Selected Poems*, London: Faber & Faber, p. 81.
2. Associated Press (1998), 'Disney Lobbying for Copyright Extension No Mickey Mouse Effort. Congress OKs Bill Granting Creators 20 More Years', *The Chicago Tribune*, 17 October; and Sprigman, C. (2002), 'The Mouse That Ate The Public Domain: Disney, the Copyright Term Extension Act and Eldred v. Ashcroft', *Findlaw*, http://writ.news.findlaw.com/commentary/20020305_sprigman.html, 5 March.
3. Bono, M. (1998), 'Sonny Bono Copyright Term Extension Act', 144 Congressional Record H9946, 7 October, 9952.
4. Auden, W.H. (1976), 'In Memory of W.B. Yeats', *Selected Poems*, London: Faber & Faber, p. 81.
5. *Eldred* v. *Ashcroft* 123 S. Ct. 769 (2003).
6. The other nine plaintiffs were Eldritch Press, Higginson Book Company, Jill A. Crandall, Tri-Horn International, Luck's Music Library, Inc., Edwin F. Kalmus & Co., Inc., American Film Heritage Association, Moviecraft, Inc. and Dover Publications, Inc.
7. Fourteen amici supported Eldred in the Supreme Court, including College Art Association, Visual Resources Association, National Humanities Alliance, Consortium of College and University Media Centers and National Initiative for a Networked Cultural Heritage; five Constitutional Law Professors; Eagle Forum Education & Legal Defense Fund and Association of American Physicians and Surgeons; seventeen Economists; Free Software Foundation; Hal Roach Studios and Michael Agee; Intel Corporation; fifty-three Intellectual Property Law Professors; Internet Archive, Prelinger Archives, and Project Gutenberg Literary Archive Foundation; Fifteen Library Associations; National Writers Union et al., Tyler T. Ochoa, Mark Rose, Edward C. Walterscheid, Organization of American Historians, H-Net; Malla Pollack; and Progressive Intellectual Property Law Association and Union for the Public Domain.
8. Twenty amici supported the government in the Supreme Court, including American Intellectual Property Law Association; ASCAP, BMI, et al., Amsong, Inc; AOL Time Warner, Inc; Association of American Publishers et al., The Bureau of National Affairs, Inc; Symphonic and Concert Composers; Directors Guild of America et al., Dr. Seuss Enterprises, L.P. et al., Senator Orrin G. Hatch; Intellectual Property Owners Association; International Coalition for Copyright Protection; Motion Picture Association of America; The Nashville Songwriters Association International; New York Intellectual Property Law Association; Recording Artists Coalition; Recording Industry Association of America; New York Law School Professor Edward Samuels; House Judiciary Committee Members; and the Songwriters Guild of America.
9. *Eldred* v. *Reno* 74 F. Supp. 2d 1(1999).
10. *Eldred* v. *Reno* 239 Fd. 3d 372 (2001).
11. *Eldred* v. *Ashcroft* 123 S. Ct. 769 (2003).
12. Greenhouse, L. (2002), 'Supreme Court To Intervene In Internet Copyright Dispute', *The New York Times*, 19 February.
13. Ginsburg J delivered the opinion of the majority of the court. She was joined by Rehnquist CJ, and O'Connor, Scalia, Kennedy, Souter and Thomas JJ.
14. Such concerns have also been expressed notably in Jaszi, P. (1996), 'Goodbye To All That: A Reluctant (And Perhaps Premature) Adieu To A Constitutionally-Grounded Discourse Of Public Interest In Copyright Law', *Vanderbilt Journal Of Transnational Law*, **29**, 595–611.
15. Mark Rose is an expert on literary property in England; see Rose, Mark (1994), 'The Author As Proprietor: *Donaldson* v. *Becket* and the Genealogy Of Modern Authorship', in Sherman, Brad and Alain Strowel (eds), *Of Authors and Origins: Essays on Copyright Law*, Oxford: Clarendon Press, pp. 23–55; and Rose, Mark (1993), *Authors And Owners: The Invention Of Copyright*, Cambridge: Harvard University Press. Tyler Ochoa is interested in the history of intellectual property in the United States; see Ochoa, T.

(2001), 'Patent And Copyright Term Extension And The Constitution: A Historical Perspective', *Journal of the Copyright Society of the U.S.A*, **49**, 19–125. Edward Walterscheid has focused upon term limits and the intellectual property clause; see Walterscheid, E. (2000), 'Defining The Patent and Copyright Term: Term Limits and The Intellectual Property Clause', *Journal of Intellectual Property Law*, **7**, 315–94.

16. *Donaldson* v. *Beckett* (1774) 4 Burr 2408; 98 ER 257.
17. Anonymous (1735), 'A Letter to a Member of Parliament concerning the Bill now depending in the House of Commons, for making more effectual an Act in the 8th Year of the Reign of Queen Anne, entitled, An Act for the Encouragement of Learning, by Vesting the Copies of Printed Books in the Authors or Purchasers of such Copies, during the Times therein mentioned', document reproduced in Goldsmith's-Kress *Library of Economic Literature*, Segment 1: Printed Books Through 1800, Microfilm No. 7300 (Reel 430).
18. The historians expanded upon the amicus brief in an article published in a professional journal; Ochoa, T. and M. Rose (2002), 'The Anti-Monopoly Origins of the Patent and Copyright Clause', *Journal of the Copyright Society of the U.S.A*, **84**, 675–706.
19. *Eldred* v. *Ashcroft* 123 S. Ct. 769 at 779 (2003).
20. Nachbar, T. (2002), 'Constructing Copyright's Mythology', *Green Bag*, 6 2d (37), at 45.
21. *Mazer* v. *Stein* 347 U.S. 201 at 219 (1954).
22. *American Geophysical Union* v. *Texaco Inc.* 802 F. Supp. 1 (1992); 60 F.3d 913 (1994).
23. *American Geophysical Union* v. *Texaco Inc.* 802 F. Supp. 1 (1992); 60 F.3d 913 (1994).
24. *Eldred* v. *Ashcroft* 123 S. Ct. 769 at 785 (2003).
25. *Eldred* v. *Ashcroft* 123 S. Ct. 769 at 785 (2003).
26. *Eldred* v. *Ashcroft* 123 S. Ct. 769 at 785 (2003).
27. *Eldred* v. *Ashcroft* 123 S. Ct. 769 at 778 (2003)
28. *McClurg* v. *Kingsland* 1 How. 202 (1843).
29. *Eldred* v. *Ashcroft* 123 S. Ct. 769 at 781 (2003).
30. Madison, James (1817), 'Monopolies, Perpetuities, Corporations, and Ecclesiastical Endowments', in Rakove, Jack (ed.) (1999), *Writings*, New York: Library of America, 756; Jefferson, Thomas (1788), 'Letter to James Madison', 31 July, in Boyd, Julian Parkes (1956), *13 Papers of Thomas Jefferson*, Princeton: Princeton University Press, p. 443; and Solberg, Winton (1990), *The Constitutional Convention and the Formation of the Union*, Chicago: University of Illinois Press 2nd edn, pp. 334, 338.
31. Patterson, L.R. (2000), 'Understanding the Copyright Clause', *Journal of the Copyright Society of the USA*, **47**, 365–95; and Patterson, L. Ray (1968), *Copyright in Historical Perspective*, Nashville: Vanderbilt University Press, pp. 144–7.
32. Lessig L. et al. (2002), 'Brief For Petitioners in *Eldred* v. *Ashcroft*', 20 May, at 27.
33. Lord Macaulay (1841), 'A Speech Delivered On Serjeant Talfourd's Copyright Bill', 56 Parl. Deb. (3d Ser.) 341, 350; also reprinted in Lord Macaulay (1967), *Prose and Poetry*, Harvard: Harvard University Press, at 736.
34. *Eldred* v. *Ashcroft* 123 S. Ct. 769 (2003).
35. *Stewart* v. *Abend* 495 U.S. 207, 228 (1990).
36. *Mazer* v. *Stein* 347 U.S. 201, 219 (1954).
37. *Harper & Row* v. *Nation Enterprise* 471 US 539 at 545 (1985).
38. *Eldred* v. *Ashcroft* 123 S. Ct. 769 at 796 (2003).
39. *Eldred* v. *Ashcroft* 123 S. Ct. 769 at 799 (2003).
40. *Eldred* v. *Ashcroft* 123 S. Ct. 769 at 798 (2003).
41. *Eldred* v. *Ashcroft* 123 S. Ct. 769 at 790 (2003).
42. Bowrey, K. (1996), 'Who's Writing Copyright's History?', *European Intellectual Property Review*, **18**(6), 322–9 at 322.
43. *Eldred* v. *Ashcroft* 123 S. Ct. 769 (2003).
44. Geller, P.E. (2000), 'Copyright History And The Future: What's Culture Got To Do With It?', *Journal of the Copyright Society of the U.S.A.*, **47**, 209–64.
45. Jaszi, P. (1996), 'Goodbye To All That: A Reluctant (And Perhaps Premature) Adieu To A Constitutionally-Grounded Discourse Of Public Interest In Copyright Law', *Vanderbilt Journal Of Transnational Law*, **29**, 595–611.

46. Ibid.
47. *Eldred* v. *Ashcroft* 123 S. Ct. 769 at 781 (2003).
48. Arthur Miller observed: 'It is not for courts to substitute their judgment for Congress's judgment once Congress has passed that low threshold of rationality. It is not for courts to say, "Life plus seventy, no." A court cannot say, "I will buy life plus sixty-two and six months, but not life plus seventy." That is not what courts are in the business to do. Courts are not super-legislatures.' See Miller, A. (2000), 'Symposium: The Constitutionality of Copyright Term Extension', *Cardozo Arts & Entertainment Law Journal*, **18**, 651–737 at 689.
49. *Eldred* v. *Ashcroft* 123 S. Ct. 769 at 790 (2003).
50. *Eldred* v. *Ashcroft* 123 S. Ct. 769 at 778 (2003).
51. Sprigman, C. (2003), 'The Supreme Court's Copyright Extension Decision: A Mickey Mouse Ruling', *Findlaw*, http://writ.news.findlaw.com/commentary/20030120_sprigman.html, 20 January.
52. *Eldred* v. *Ashcroft* 123 S. Ct. 769 at 788 (2003).
53. *Eldred* v. *Ashcroft* 123 S. Ct. 769 at 788–789 (2003).
54. *Eldred* v. *Ashcroft* 123 S. Ct. 769 at 784 (2003).
55. Nimmer, M. (1970), 'Does Copyright Abridge The First Amendment Guarantees Of Free Speech and Press?', *The University of California Los Angeles Law Review*, **17**. 1180.
56. Drahos, Peter (1994), 'Decentring Communication: The Dark Side of Intellectual Property', in Campbell, Tom and Wojciech Sadurski (eds), *Freedom of Communication*, Aldershot: Dartmouth, p. 257.
57. Jaszi, P. (1991), 'Toward a Theory of Copyright: The Metamorphoses of "Authorship"', *Duke Law Journal*, 465–502.
58. *Harper & Row* v. *Nation Enterprises* 471 US 539 (1985).
59. *Eldred* v. *Ashcroft* 123 S. Ct. 769 at 789 (2003).
60. *Campbell* v. *Acuff-Rose Inc* 111 S. Ct. 1164 (1994).
61. It is surprising that Souter J should support the majority judgment of Ginsburg J, given that he was the author of the Supreme Court judgment in *Campbell* v. *Acuff-Rose Music, Inc.* 510 US 569 (1994), in which he developed a theory of transformative use to explain a broad reading of the fair use defence.
62. *Eldred* v. *Ashcroft* 123 S. Ct. 769 at 806 (2003).
63. *Rogers* v. *Koons* 960 F. 2nd 301 (1992).
64. *Eldred* v. *Ashcroft* 123 S. Ct. 769 (2003).
65. *Eldred* v. *Ashcroft* 123 S. Ct. 769 at 806 (2003).
66. *Eldred* v. *Ashcroft* 123 S. Ct. 769 at 812 (2003).
67. *Eldred* v. *Ashcroft* 123 S. Ct. 769 at 812 (2003).
68. *Eldred* v. *Ashcroft* 123 S. Ct. 769 at 801 (2003).
69. *Eldred* v. *Ashcroft* 123 S. Ct. 769 at 801 (2003).
70. Jaszi, P. (2002), 'Brief of Amici Curiae National Writers Union et al. in *Eldred* v. *Ashcroft*', 20 May.
71. Macmillan, F. (2002), 'The Cruel ©: Copyright Law and Film', *European Intellectual Property Review*, **24**(10), 483–92.
72. Bettig, Ronald (1996), *Copyrighting Culture. The Political Economy of Intellectual Property*, Boulder: Westview Press.
73. *Eldred* v. *Ashcroft* 123 S. Ct. 769 at 782 (2003).
74. *Eldred* v. *Ashcroft* 123 S. Ct. 769 at 813 (2003).
75. Macmillan, F. (2002), 'The Cruel ©: Copyright Law and Film', *European Intellectual Property Review*, **24**(10), 483–92.
76. *Eldred* v. *Ashcroft* 123 S. Ct. 769 at 805 (2003).
77. Rappaport, E. (1998), 'Copyright Term Extension: Estimating the Economic Values', Congressional Research Service, Library of Congress, 11 May.
78. *Eldred* v. *Ashcroft* 123 S. Ct. 769 at 806 (2003).
79. Lutzker, A. (2002), 'Brief for American Association of Law Libraries et al. as Amici Curiae Supporting Petitioners in *Eldred* v. *Ashcroft*', 20 May, at 20.

80. Cunard, J. (2002), 'Brief for College Art Association et al. as Amici Curiae Supporting Petitioners in *Eldred* v. *Ashcroft*', 20 May, 7–13.
81. Jaszi, P. (2002), 'Brief for the National Writers Union et al. as Amici Curiae Supporting Petitioners in *Eldred* v. *Ashcroft*', 20 May, pp. 25–7.
82. Lessig, L. and others (2002), 'Brief For Petitioners in *Eldred* v. *Ashcroft*', 20 May, pp. 3–5.
83. Arms, C. (1999), 'Getting the Picture: Observations from the Library of Congress on Providing Online Access to Pictorial Images', *Library Trends*, **48**, 379, 405.
84. Urbanski, L. (1997), 'Letter To Senator Strom Thurmand Opposing Copyright Extension', http://www.law.asu.edu/HomePages/Karjala/OpposingCopyrightExtension/letters/AFH.html, 31 March.
85. Powell, J. (2002), 'Brief of Hal Roach Studios and Michael Agee as Amici Curiae Supporting Petitioners in *Eldred* v. *Ashcroft*', 20 May.
86. Hamilton, Ian (1992), *Keepers of the Flame: Literary Estates and the Rise of Biography*, London: Hutchinson.
87. Shulman, S. (2002), 'Freeing Mickey Mouse', *Technology Review*, **105**(9), 81.
88. *Suntrust Bank* v. *Houghton Mifflin Company* 136 F. Supp. 2d 1357 (2001); *Suntrust Bank* v. *Houghton Mifflin Company*, 268 F 3d 1257 (11th Cir, 2001); and Lessig, L. (2001). 'Let the Stories Go', *The New York Times*, 30 April.
89. Weinberg, J. (2002), 'Brief Of Intellectual Property Law Professors As Amici Curiae Supporting Petitioners in *Eldred* v. *Ashcroft*', 20 May, pp. 2–3.
90. King, V. (2002), 'James Joyce's "Ulysses" – A Case Of Preparatory Manuscripts And Revived Copyright', *Entertainment Law Review*, **13**(4), 86–90.
91. Rimmer, M. (2004), 'Never Neverland: Peter Pan and Perpetual Copyright', *Incite*, **25** (12), 8–9.
92. Loughlan, P. (2002), 'Moral Rights (A View From The Town Square)', *Media And Arts Law Review*, **5**(1), 1–11.
93. Rimmer, M. (2001), 'Shine: Copyright Law And Film', *Australian Intellectual Property Journal*, **12**(3), 129–42.
94. Rimmer, M. (2005), 'Bloomsday: Copyright Estates and Cultural Festivals', *Scripted (University of Edinburgh)*, **2**(3), 383–428.
95. Carol Loeb Shloss, the biographer of Lucia Joyce, brought a law suit to obtain a declaration that her use of published and unpublished copyright works of Joyce on a scholarly website was protected by the defence of fair use: *Shloss* v. *Sweeney* C 06-3718 (US District Court for the Northern District of California, 2006). The action was supported by the Stanford Center for Internet and Society. In March 2007, the Joyce Estate agreed to enter into a settlement agreement, permitting Shloss to publish quotations relating to James and Lucia Joyce in her book and electronic supplement: http://cyberlaw.stanford.edu/system/files/Shloss+Settlement+Agreement.pdf.
96. Rimmer, M. (2006), 'Robbery Under Arms: Copyright Law and the Australia–United States Free Trade Agreement', *First Monday*, **11**(3), http://www.firstmonday.org/issues/issue11_3/rimmer/index.html.
97. Shiel, F. (2004), 'Libraries Caught In Copyright Changes', *The Age*, http://www.theage.com.au/articles/2004/02/10/1076388365432.html, 11 February.
98. Dodd, T. (2004), 'Trade Deal Bites Unis On Copyright Costs', *The Australian Financial Review*, 14 February, p. 16.
99. ABC (2003), 'Digitising Content in the ABC's Archive', Press Release, 8 July.
100. Ibid.
101. Posner, Richard (1998), *Economic Analysis Of Law*, New York: Aspen Law and Business, 5th edn; and Landes, William and Richard Posner (2004), *The Economic Structure of Intellectual Property Law*, Harvard: Harvard University Press.
102. Landes, W. and R. Posner (1989), 'An Economic Analysis of Copyright Law', *Journal of Legal Studies*, **18**, 325–64.
103. Rappaport, Edward (1998), *Copyright Term Extension: Estimating the Economic Values*, Congressional Research Service, Library of Congress, 11 May.
104. Englert, E. (2002), 'Brief of George Akerlof et al. as Amici Curiae in Support of Petitioners in *Eldred* v. *Ashcroft*', 20 May.

105. Lessig, L. (2002), 'Free Culture', Keynote Address at Oscon 2002, http://www.oreillynet.com/pub/a/policy/2002/08/15/lessig.html, 15 August.
106. *Eldred* v. *Ashcroft* 123 S. Ct. 769 at 784 (2003).
107. *Eldred* v. *Ashcroft* 123 S. Ct. 769 at 782 (2003).
108. *Eldred* v. *Ashcroft* 123 S. Ct. 769 at 807 (2003).
109. *Eldred* v. *Ashcroft* 123 S. Ct. 769 at 807 (2003).
110. Intellectual Property and Competition Review Committee (2000), 'Copyright Term' in *Review of Intellectual Property Legislation Under the Competition Principles Agreement*, at http://www.ipcr.gov.au/IPAustralia.pdf, September, pp. 80–84.
111. Ibid.
112. Ibid.
113. Senate Estimates Committee (2004), 'Foreign Affairs, Defence And Trade', Australian Parliament, 2 March.
114. Centre for International Economics (2004), *Economic Analysis of AUSFTA: Impact of the Bilateral Free Trade Agreement with the United States*, http://www.dfat.gov.au/trade/negotiations/us_fta/economic_analysis_report/austfta_report_040428.pdf.
115. Ibid., p. 39.
116. Dee, P. (2004), *The Australia–US Free Trade Agreement: An Assessment, A Report prepared for the Senate Select Committee on the Free Trade Agreement*, June, at http://www.aph.gov.au/Senate/committee/freetrade_ctte/rel_links/dee_fta_report.pdf.
117. Ibid., p. 13.
118. Ibid., p. 22.
119. Dee, P. (2004), *AUSFTA: A Response to Comments by the Department of Foreign Affairs and Trade*, the Senate Select Committee on the Free Trade Agreement, June, p. 4, at http://www.aph.gov.au/Senate/committee/freetrade_ctte/rel_links/response_dfat.pdf.
120. Ibid.
121. Ibid.
122. Ricketson, S. (1992), 'The Copyright Term', *IIC*, **23**(6), 753–84.
123. Jaszi, P. (1996), 'Goodbye To All That: A Reluctant (And Perhaps Premature) Adieu To A Constitutionally-Grounded Discourse Of Public Interest In Copyright Law', *Vanderbilt Journal Of Transnational Law*, **29**, 595–611.
124. Valenti, J. (1995), 'Testimony before the Subcommittee on Courts and Intellectual Property Committee on the Judiciary U.S. House of Representatives Hearing on Copyright Term Extension Act – H.R. 989', 1 June.
125. Ibid.
126. Council Directive 93/98/EEC of 29 October 1993 harmonizing the term of protection of copyright and certain related rights. *Official Journal* L 290, 24/11/1993 P. 0009 – 0013; Bard, Robert and Lewis Kurlantzick (1998), *Copyright Duration: Duration, Term Extension, The European Union, And The Making Of Copyright Policy*, Lanham, MD: Austin and Winfield.
127. Antill, J. and P. Coles (1996), 'Copyright Duration: The European Community Adopts "Three Score Years and Ten"', *European Intellectual Property Review*, **18** (7), 379–83.
128. Parrinder, Patrick (1997), 'Literary Copyright and the Public Domain', in Parrinder, Patrick and Warren Chernaik (eds), *Textual Monopolies Literary Copyright and the Public Domain*, London: Office for Humanities Communication, p. 1.
129. Sherman, Brad and Lionel Bently (1997), 'Balance and Harmony in the Duration of Copyright' in Parrinder, Patrick and Warren Chernaik (eds), *Textual Monopolies Literary Copyright and the Public Domain*, London: Office for Humanities Communication, p. 28.
130. Ibid., pp. 27–8.
131. von Lewinski, S. (1992), 'EC Proposal For A Council Directive Harmonizing The Term Of Protection Of Copyright And Certain Related Rights', *IIC*, **23**(6), 785–811.
132. Ricketson, S. (1992), 'The Copyright Term', *IIC*, **23**(6), 753–84.
133. *Eldred* v. *Ashcroft* 123 S. Ct. 769 at 781 (2003).
134. The author is a curious authority to cite given that she is currently the Vice President and Associate General Counsel, Intellectual Property Policy, AOL Time Warner Inc.

Perlmutter was also a former Consultant on Copyright and E-Commerce, World Intellectual Property Organization, a former Associate Register for Policy and International Affairs, U.S. Copyright Office, and a law professor at The Catholic University of America, teaching Copyright Law.
135. Perlmutter, S. (2002), 'Participation in the International Copyright System as a Means to Promote the Progress of Science and Useful Arts', *Loyola Los Angeles Law Review*, **36**, 323–35 at 330.
136. Austin, G. (2002), 'Does the Copyright Clause Mandate Isolationism?', *Columbia-VLA Journal of Law And The Arts*, **26**, 17–59.
137. *Eldred* v. *Ashcroft* 123 S. Ct. 769 at 811 (2003).
138. Bollier, D. (2001), 'Why We Must Talk About The Information Commons: New Technology, the Information Commons and the Future of Libraries', 2–4 November, p. 18.
139. *Eldred* v. *Ashcroft* 123 S. Ct. 769 at 808 (2003).
140. Drahos, Peter and John Braithwaite (2002), *Information Feudalism*, London: Earthscan Publications, p. 107.
141. Ruddock, P. (2004), 'Opening Address: Unlucky For Some', ACIPA Conference, 13 February.
142. Jack, I. (2003), 'Ottawa Champions Copyright – or Some of It: Amendment to Benefit Small Band of Authors with Unpublished Works,' *National Post*, 12 May, FP; Knopf, H. (2003), 'Mouse in the House: A New Bill in Ottawa Appears to Adopt U.S.-Style Copyright Term Extension', *National Post*, 7 June, FP 11; and Murray, L. (2003), 'Stop the Mickey Mouse', *National Post*, 16 June, FP 23.
143. Hebb, M. (2003), 'Modest Changes to Copyright Debated,' *National Post*, 17 June, FP 11.
144. Banks, S. (2003), 'Bill C-36: The Library and Archives of Canada Act', http://www.parl.gc.ca/common/Bills_ls.asp?lang=E&ls=C36&source=Bills_House_Government&Parl=37&Ses=2, 11 December.
145. Geist, M. (2006), 'Our Own Cultural Land: Cultural Monopoly and the Trouble with Copyright', The Hart House Lecture, http://individual.utoronto.ca/dtsang/hhlecture/Resources/Geist_2006.pdf, 28, 42.
146. Tuck, S. (2004), 'Lucy Maud Provision Fades Out', *Globe And Mail*, 1 April, R1.
147. *United States–Singapore Free Trade Agreement* 2003, URL: http://www.ustr.gov/new/fta/Singapore/consolidated_texts.htm.
148. *United States-Chile Free Trade Agreement* 2003, URL: http://www.ustr.gov/new/fta/Chile/text/index.htm.
149. *United States–Dominican Republican–Central America Free Trade Agreement* 2005, http://www.ustr.gov/Trade_Agreements/Bilateral/CAFTA/CAFTA-DR_Final_Texts/Section_Index.html.
150. *Free Trade Area of the Americas*, http://www.ftaa-alca.org/.
151. *North-American Free Trade Agreement* 1994 (NAFTA), http://www.nafta-sec-alena.org/DefaultSite/index.html.
152. Schmidt, L. (2003), 'Mexican Copyright Law', http://cyberlaw.stanford.edu/lessig/blog/archives/mexican.txt, 25 March.
153. Drahos, Peter and John Braithwaite (2002), *Information Feudalism: Who Owns The Knowledge Economy?*, London: Earthscan Productions.
154. Jaszi, P. (1995), 'The Copyright Term Extension Act of 1995: Testimony Before The Senate Committee on the Judiciary', 104th Cong., 1st Session, 20 September.
155. *Eldred* v. *Ashcroft* 123 S. Ct. 769 at 784 (2003).
156. *Eldred* v. *Ashcroft* 123 S. Ct. 769 at 790 (2003).
157. Rehnquist CJ, O'Connor and Kennedy JJ in *Eldred* v. *Ashcroft* US Trans Lexis 47 (2002).
158. *Eldred* v. *Ashcroft* 123 S. Ct. 769 at 812 (2003).
159. However, as an academic, Breyer J has previously expressed reservations about the copyright term extension under the *Copyright Act* 1976 (US): Breyer, S. (1970), 'An Uneasy Case for Copyright in Books, Photocopies and Computer Programs', *Harvard Law Review*, **84**, 281–351.

160. *Eldred* v. *Ashcroft* 123 S. Ct. 769 at 813 (2003).
161. *Eldred* v. *Ashcroft* 123 S. Ct. 769 at 784 (2003).
162. Peters, M. (1995), 'Copyright Term, Film Labeling, and Film Preservation Legislation: Hearings on H. R. 989 et al. before the Subcommittee on Courts and Intellectual Property of the House Committee on the Judiciary', 104th Cong., 1st Sess., 230.
163. Senate Committee on the Judiciary (1996), 'Copyright Term Extension Act of 1996', Senate Report No. 104-315, p. 11.
164. Coble, H. (1998), 'Sonny Bono Copyright Term Extension Act', *Congressional Record* 144, H1458 (25 March).
165. Bono, M. (1998), 'Sonny Bono Copyright Term Extension Act', 144 Congressional Record H9946, 7 October, 9952.
166. *Eldred* v. *Ashcroft* 123 S. Ct. 769 at 801 (2003).
167. *Eldred* v. *Ashcroft* 123 S. Ct. 769 at 801 (2003).
168. *Eldred* v. *Ashcroft* 123 S. Ct. 769 at 801 (2003).
169. Editorial (2003), 'The Coming Of Copyright Perpetuity', *The New York Times*, 16 January.
170. Koman, R. (2003), 'Eldred Opinion Met With Anger, Determination', The O'Reilly Network, http://www.oreillynet.com/pub/a/policy/2003/01/16/eldred.html, 16 January.
171. Valenti, J. (2003), 'Statement on the Supreme Court Ruling on Eldred v. Ashcroft', Motion Picture Association of America, http://www.mpaa.org/jack/2003/2003_01_15.htm, 15 January.
172. Lessig, L. (2003), 'Losing', Stanford Law School, http://cyberlaw.stanford.edu/lessig/blog/, 16 January.
173. Sprigman, C. (2004), 'Reform(aliz)ing Copyright', *Stanford Law Review*, **25**, 485–568.
174. *Kahle* v. *Ashcroft* 72 U.S.P.Q.2d 1888 (2004).
175. *Golan* v. *Ashcroft* 310 F.Supp.2d 1215 (2004); and *Golan* v. *Gonzales* 74 U.S.P.Q.2d 1808 (2005).
176. *Luck's Music Library* v. *Gonzales* 407 F.3d 1262 (2005).
177. Lessig, Lawrence (2001), *The Future of Ideas: The Fate Of The Commons In A Connected World*, New York: Random House, p. 250.
178. Lessig, L. (2003), 'Protecting Mickey Mouse at Art's Expense', *The New York Times*, 18 January.
179. 'The solution might be a system of indefinitely renewable copyrights. The initial grant might be for twenty-five years, renewable thereafter every five years. A stiff fee would assure that most works returned to the public domain. But those works requiring continuing investment or careful management to avoid consumer exhaustion would continue to be owned property': Landes, W. and R. Posner (2002), 'Indefinitely Renewable Copyright', Working Paper, Olin Center for Law and Economics, the University of Chicago, http://www.law.uchicago.edu/Lawecon/WkngPprs_151–175/154.wml-rap.copyright.new.pdf.
180. It required the Register of Copyrights to charge a fee of $1 for maintaining in force the copyright in any published U.S. work. It stipulated that the fee was due 50 years after the date of first publication or on 31 December 2004, whichever occurred later, and every ten years thereafter until the end of the copyright term.
181. *Public Domain Enhancement Act* 2005 (US) HR 2408 IH.
182. United States Copyright Office (2005), 'Orphaned Works', *Federal Register*, **70** (16), 3739–43.
183. United States Copyright Office (2006a), *Report on Orphan Works: A Report of the Register of Copyrights*, Library of Congress: United States Copyright Office.
184. Ibid.
185. Public Knowledge (2005), 'In the Matter of Orphaned Works', http://www.copyright.gov/orphan/comments/OW0629-PublicKnowledge.pdf, 25 March.
186. Gowers, Andrew (2006), *Gowers Review of Intellectual Property*, London: HM Treasury, December, http://www.hm-treasury.gov.uk/media/583/91/pbr06_gowers_report_755.pdf.
187. Ibid., 71.

2. Remote control: time-shifting and space-shifting

> The creation and near-universal adoption of the remote control arguably marks the beginning of the era of the personalization of technology. The remote control shifted power to the individual, and the technologies that have embraced this principle in its wake – the Walkman, the Video Cassette Recorder, Digital Video Recorders such as TiVo, and portable music devices like the iPod – have created a world where the individual's control over the content, style, and timing of what he consumes is nearly absolute. (Christine Rosen 'The Age of Egocasting'[1])

In 2005, there were commemorations of the 21st anniversary of the Supreme Court of the United States decision in *Sony* v. *Universal City Studios Inc* (the *Sony Betamax* case). In 1984, the Supreme Court ruled that, when consumers used the Sony Betamax VCR to make their own personal copies of copyrighted television programmes for single-use 'time-shifting' purposes, they were making a 'fair use' of the copyrighted work. Sony's distribution of the recorder was therefore legal because the Betamax was capable of substantial, non-infringing uses.[2] Notably, Gary Shapiro, the Chairman of the Home Recording Rights Coalition, paid an effusive tribute to the decision:

> The significance of the Supreme Court's decision, twenty years ago, cannot be overstated. For consumer electronics and consumer freedom, it is the Magna Carta and the Declaration of Independence rolled into one. But increasingly, major entertainment interests are arguing that the Betamax doctrine does not apply in the digital age. Without this doctrine's protection, the big motion picture studios and others would exercise a veto over every new function of every new product.[3]

Shapiro went on to emphasize the contemporary significance of the decision with particular reference to the litigation in *MGM Studios, Inc.* v. *Grokster, Ltd* (the *Grokster* case).[4] He observed: 'Almost all of the 60 briefs filed with the Supreme Court in the *Grokster* case, on all sides of the issues, recognized the validity of the Betamax framework, and its necessity if we are to avoid artificial constraints on technology, innovation and investment.'[5] Shapiro added: 'While there is scope for disagreement on its application, the core Betamax doctrine has become fundamental in U.S. law and society; it is time that it be recognized as such.'[6]

However, Jessica Litman has queried the rhetorical claim that the *Sony Betamax* case functions as the high technology industries' Magna Carta.[7,8] Litman responds to Shapiro with the retort:

> Historians remind us that the significance of the Magna Carta was more symbolic than practical: the English King neither respected nor complied with it. So, too, with what the Home Recording Rights Coalition calls the Magna Carta of the Technology Age. Briefs filed in the *Grokster* case argue that the Sony decision has protected innovators from overreaching, litigious copyright owners. If that's so, it's hard to argue that the case has done an especially effective job.[9]

Litman questions whether the *Sony* decision has protected innovators from copyright litigation: 'Sony has talismanic meaning in the community of high tech copyright lawyers, but it doesn't live up to its hype.'[10] She notes that, as new technologies have appeared, the *Sony Betamax* case has constantly been distinguished on factual grounds. She notes that copyright owners have argued that the decision did not apply to digital audio tape recorders, portable MP3 players and digital video recorders, because they are digital rather than analog. Litman concludes: 'Sony's doctrinal contributions have eroded over time.'[11]

Likewise, Lawrence Lessig has become disenchanted by subsequent litigation over the scope of the *Sony Betamax* case, lamenting that the rule has been interpreted in a narrow and restrictive fashion. He has expressed a sceptical view as to the value of the defence of fair use, emphasizing the social context in which it is used:

> Fair use in America simply means the right to hire a lawyer to defend your right to create. And as lawyers love to forget, our system for defending rights such as fair use is astonishingly bad – in practically every context, but especially here. It costs too much, it delivers too slowly, and what it delivers often has little connection to the justice underlying the claim. The legal system may be tolerable for the very rich. For everyone else, it is an embarrassment to a tradition that prides itself on the rule of law.[12]

Lessig doubts the high-minded claims of judges and lawyers that fair use provides adequate 'breathing room' between regulation by the law and the access the law should allow.[13] In his view, such a perspective bears little relationship to the social reality. Lessig observes: 'For in a world that threatens $150 000 for a single willful infringement of a copyright, and which demands tens of thousands of dollars to even defend against a copyright infringement claim, and which would never return to the wrongfully accused defendant anything of the costs she suffered to defend her right to speak – in that world, the astonishingly broad regulations that pass under the name "copyright" silence speech and creativity.'[14]

For his part, Randal Picker comments that the *Sony Betamax* decision very much reflects the closed nature of its technology design.[15] He observed that the Sony Betamax VCR was a stable product whose well-defined features would remain unchanged forever, once sold.[16] Picker argues that this closed design has been superseded by networked products, such as personal digital video recorders like TiVo, peer to peer networks, search engines such as Google and the Windows Media Player. He notes:

> Once we combine software with communication to create networked products we then have products that can evolve in real-time (and do). Smart products 'phone home' and update themselves. Phoning home – and the control that results from that – is a choice and one that designers of networked products make every day. Design ceases to be a one-time event and instead becomes a continuous process. And that is true not only for the next product sold, but also for the entire installed base. The dead hand of the past and the constraints of backwards compatibility are lifted.[17]

Picker has contended there is a need to revise the Sony rule to take into account networked products: 'We should modify the *Sony* test of substantial noninfringing use and replace it with a more textured test that reflects the control and evolution opportunities available with networked products.'[18]

This chapter considers the push to reform copyright law in order to protect and safeguard consumers' rights in the digital millennium. Section one examines the disputed legacy of the United States Supreme Court decision in the *Sony Betamax* case in respect of the defence of fair use and time-shifting. It revisits the philosophical divisions between the personalities of the court, notably, Stevens, O'Connor and Blackmun JJ. Section two explores the application of the *Sony Betamax* rule in respect of time-shifting by digital video recorders, pay television services and Internet broadcasting. It focuses upon new technologies, such as Replay TV, Clearplay, TiVo, Streamvision, and Slingbox. Section three considers whether the doctrine enunciated in the *Sony Betamax* case can be extended to the 'space-shifting' of copyright works. In particular, it examines the legal case involving the Rio MP3 Player, the failure of My.MP3.com, and the public debate over the iPod and podcasting. The Conclusion questions why the privileges accorded to United States consumers to engage in time-shifting and space-shifting have not been necessarily extended to citizens in other jurisdictions.

I. TIME-SHIFTING

In 1976, Universal and Disney filed a lawsuit in the District Court for the Central District of California, alleging that Sony Betamax recorders had been used to record copyrighted works, without authorization. The action was brought against the Sony Corporation, Sony's American subsidiary, five dealers in consumer electronics and a consumer named William Griffiths. The copyright owners claimed that the consumer manufacturers should be held liable for copyright infringement because of their marketing of Sony Betamax video recorders. They sought damages and an equitable accounting of profits from the companies, as well as an injunction against the manufacture and marketing of Betamax video recorders. At first instance, the District Court denied the copyright owners all the relief they sought and entered judgment for petitioners.[19] However, the United States Court of Appeals for the Ninth Circuit reversed the District Court's judgment, held Sony liable for contributory infringement and ordered the District Court to fashion appropriate relief.[20] The Supreme Court of the United States was deeply divided over the matter, finding for Sony by a majority of five to four.[21] Stevens J wrote the majority judgment, after winning late support from O'Connor J. Blackmun J wrote the dissenting judgment.

A. Stevens J

Professor Pamela Samuelson has observed: 'Of the nearly fifty IP decisions rendered by the Supreme Court during the thirty years that Justice Stevens has served on the Court, none has had a more significant economic or social impact than *Sony* v. *Universal*.'[22] She observed: 'Had Justice Stevens written no other opinion for the Court than this, he would be rightly remembered for the insightful and generative decision he wrote in *Sony*.'[23] With the benefit of hindsight, Samuelson comments that the decision of Stevens J was remarkably prescient: 'Not only did it pave the way for the untrammeled introduction into the market of iPods, MP3 players, digital video recorders, CD ripping software, CD burners, P2P technologies, and many others, but confirmed that use of such technologies for private and noncommercial purposes generally does not harm the interests of copyright owners.'[24]

In the lead judgment, Stevens J considers the dispute over the Sony Betamax video recorder in light of the broad sweep of the history of copyright law and new technologies. His Honour recalled:

> From its beginning, the law of copyright has developed in response to significant changes in technology. Indeed, it was the invention of a new form of copying equipment – the printing press – that gave rise to the original need for copyright protection. Repeatedly, as new developments have occurred in this country, it has been the Congress that has fashioned the new rules that new technology made necessary. Thus, long before the enactment of the Copyright Act of 1909, it was settled that the protection given to copyrights is wholly statutory. The remedies for infringement 'are only those prescribed by Congress'.

> The judiciary's reluctance to expand the protections afforded by the copyright without explicit legislative guidance is a recurring theme.[25]

In the course of the footnotes, Stevens J refers to a number of antecedents to the Sony Betamax recorder in the history of copyright law. His Honour comments that player pianos and perforated rolls of music challenged the assumptions of copyright owners, and led to the enactment of the *Copyright Act* 1909 (US).[26] The judge comments that the development of the photocopier gave rise to the statutory exemption for library copying embodied in section 108 of the 1976 revision of the copyright law. Furthermore, the development of the technology that made it possible to retransmit television programmes by cable or by microwave systems prompted the enactment of the complex statutory licence provisions after years of detailed congressional study.[27] Similarly, Congress enacted the *Sound Recording Amendment* 1971 (US) in response to the development of the audio tape recorder, and the practice of home recording.

In the course of the case, Stevens J seeks to formulate a test for contributory copyright infringement under copyright law. His Honour considered whether it was appropriate to draw upon the doctrinal principles of patent law to explain contributory infringement under copyright law:

> We recognize there are substantial differences between the patent and copyright laws. But in both areas the contributory infringement doctrine is grounded on the recognition that adequate protection of a monopoly may require the courts to look beyond actual duplication of a device or publication to the products or activities that make such duplication possible. The staple article of commerce doctrine must strike a balance between a copyright holder's legitimate demand for effective – not merely symbolic – protection of the statutory monopoly, and the rights of others freely to engage in substantially unrelated areas of commerce. Accordingly, the sale of copying equipment, like the sale of other articles of commerce, does not constitute contributory infringement if the product is widely used for legitimate, unobjectionable purposes. Indeed, it need merely be capable of substantial noninfringing uses.[28]

Stevens J held that a product cannot be banned simply because some, or even most, of its uses would result in copyright infringement. The judge ruled that manufacturers and retailers have a right to sell a product if it is capable of any commercially significant non-infringing uses. He concluded: 'The question is thus whether the Betamax is capable of commercially significant noninfringing uses.'[29]

Turning to the facts of the case, Stevens J observed that the primary use of the Sony Betamax video recorder for most owners was 'time-shifting', the practice of recording a programme to view it once at a later time.[30] The judge also acknowledged that some users of the Sony Betamax video recorder engaged in 'library-building', in which the user records a programme in order to keep it for repeated viewing over a longer term.[31] Stevens J established that private time-shifting in the home was essentially a non-commercial activity.[32] Moreover, time-shifting was likely to aid the Plaintiffs and increase the value of their copyrighted work rather than harm them.[33] His Honour observed that some broadcasters, relying on this assumption, did not object to home recording of their shows.[34] Time-shifting could thus be deemed a 'fair use' of copyrighted works and the video recorder seen as being used for an 'unobjectionable and legitimate purpose'.[35] The judge concluded: 'The Betamax is, therefore, capable of substantial noninfringing uses.'[36] Accordingly, 'Sony's sale of such equipment to the general public does not constitute contributory infringement of respondents' copyrights'.[37]

Finally, Stevens J considered the relationship between the judiciary and Congress in dealing with copyright law and new technologies. His Honour observed: 'Sound policy, as well as history, supports our consistent deference to Congress when major technological innovations alter the market for copyrighted materials.'[38] His Honour counselled judicial restraint: 'In a case like this, in which Congress has not plainly marked our course, we must be circumspect in construing the scope of rights created by a legislative enactment which never contemplated such a calculus of interests.'[39] Accordingly, the judge concluded:

> One may search the Copyright Act in vain for any sign that the elected representatives of the millions of people who watch television every day have made it unlawful to copy a program for later viewing at home, or have enacted a flat prohibition against the sale of machines that make such copying possible. It may well be that Congress will take a fresh look at this new technology, just as it so often has examined other innovations in the past. But it is not our job to apply laws that have not yet been written. Applying the copyright statute, as it now reads, to the facts as they have been developed in this case, the judgment of the Court of Appeals must be reversed.[40]

The judge says elsewhere: 'Congress has the constitutional authority and the institutional ability to accommodate fully the varied permutations of competing interests that are inevitably implicated by such new technology.'[41]

B. O'Connor J

The opinion of Stevens J was joined by Burger CJ, Brennan, White and O'Connor JJ. In his classic text, *Copyright's Highway: From Gutenberg to the Celestial Jukebox*, the scholar Paul Goldstein recounts the change of mind by the famous swing voter, O'Connor J, during the case.[42] Apparently her Honour was sympathetic to the view that Sony was liable for contributory copyright infringement. In the course of judicial deliberations, O'Connor J wrote to Blackmun J: 'I have considerable difficulty in rejecting the District Court's view that the respondents suffered no harm, actual or potential, as a result of Sony's use [of the Betamax].'[43] Blackmun J responded: 'In light of our different readings of the opinion, what would you think of remanding to the District Court for further consideration of the issue of harm?'[44] She declined his offer, observing: 'The burden of proof on harm and damages traditionally remains with the plaintiff, and I see no sufficient reason to shift it to the alleged infringer.'[45] In the end, Blackmun J refused to compromise his position any further: 'Five votes are not that important to me when I feel that proper legal principles are involved.'[46]

In the end, O'Connor J questioned Blackmun J's rejection of the 'staple article of commerce' doctrine:

> I had thought that the 'staple article' doctrine developed in order to limit the patent holder from depriving society of the good that comes from the existence of other enterprises that nevertheless frustrate the patent holder's monopoly to some degree. I see no reason why we should not be similarly concerned with what the copyright holder does with his monopoly.[47]

Her Honour noted: 'If the videorecorder has substantial noninfringing uses, we should be reluctant to find vicarious liability.'[48] Consequently, O'Connor J found herself inclined to support the position of Stevens J instead: 'I am closer to John's most recent draft than to any other now "on the table".'[49]

C. Blackmun J

In the opening to his dissenting judgment, Blackmun J provides a tart response to Stevens J's history of copyright law and technological change. His Honour observes:

> It is no answer, of course, to refer to and stress, as the Court does, this Court's 'consistent deference to Congress' whenever 'major technological innovations' appear. Perhaps a better and more accurate description is that the Court has tended to evade the hard issues when they arise in the area of copyright law. I see no reason for the Court to be particularly pleased with this tradition or to continue it. Indeed, it is fairly clear from the legislative history of the 1976 Act that Congress meant to change the old pattern and enact a statute that would cover new technologies, as well as old.[50]

In his judgment, Blackmun J objected to the new rules crafted by Stevens J on contributory infringement and the defence of fair use. His Honour noted: 'It may be tempting, as, in my view, the Court today is tempted, to stretch the doctrine of fair use so as to permit unfettered use of this new technology in order to increase access to television programming.'[51]

The judge warned that 'such an extension risks eroding the very basis of copyright law, by depriving authors of control over their works and consequently of their incentive to create'.[52] His Honour complained:

> The Court has adopted an approach very different from the one I have outlined. It is my view that the Court's approach alters dramatically the doctrines of fair use and contributory infringement as they have been developed by Congress and the courts. Should Congress choose to respond to the Court's decision, the old doctrines can be resurrected. As it stands, however, the decision today erodes much of the coherence that these doctrines have struggled to achieve.[53]

When discussing contributory infringement, Blackmun J objected to the technical judge-made doctrine of patent law, based in part on considerations irrelevant to the field of copyright, being imported wholesale into copyright law: 'Despite their common constitutional source, patent and copyright protections have not developed in a parallel fashion, and this Court in copyright cases in the past has borrowed patent concepts only sparingly.'[54] Nonetheless, his Honour conceded that 'if liability for contributory infringement were imposed on the manufacturer or seller of every product used to infringe – a typewriter, a camera, a photocopying machine – the "wheels of commerce" would be blocked'.[55]

On the facts of the case, Blackmun J submitted that time-shifting had a substantial adverse effect upon the 'potential market for' the Studios' copyrighted works:

> Although time-shifting may not replace theater or rerun viewing or the purchase of prerecorded tapes or discs, it may well replace rental usage; a VTR user who has recorded a first-run movie for later viewing will have no need to rent a copy when he wants to see it. Both library-builders and time-shifters may avoid commercials; the library-builder may use the pause control to record without them, and all users may fast-forward through commercials on playback.[56]

The judge concluded: 'A VTR owner who has taped a favorite movie for repeated viewing will be less likely to rent or buy a tape containing the same movie, watch a televised rerun, or pay to see the movie at a theater.'[57] His Honour suggested that library-building could also cause substantial harm.

Blackmun J emphasized that home-taping was an ordinary, rather than a productive use, or to use modern terminology, a transformative use, because the Betamax owners used the copy for the same purpose as the original and added nothing of their own. The judge argued that time-shifting cannot be deemed a fair use:

> It is true that the legislative history states repeatedly that the doctrine must be applied flexibly on a case-by-case basis, but those references were only in the

> context of productive uses. Such a limitation on fair use comports with its purpose, which is to facilitate the creation of new works. There is no indication that the fair use doctrine has any application for purely personal consumption on the scale involved in this case, and the Court's application of it here deprives fair use of the major cohesive force that has guided evolution of the doctrine in the past.[58]

The judge maintained, 'Time-shifting involves no such humanitarian impulse.'[59] His Honour argued that it was a mistake to characterize time-shifting as a non-commercial use: 'As one commentator has observed, time-shifting is noncommercial in the same sense that stealing jewelry and wearing it – instead of reselling it – is noncommercial.'[60] The judge concluded: 'Purely consumptive uses are certainly not what the fair use doctrine was designed to protect, and the awkwardness of applying the statutory language to time-shifting only makes clearer that fair use was designed to protect only uses that are productive.'[61]

Finally, Blackmun J objected to the judicial creativity of Stevens J:

> Like so many other problems created by the interaction of copyright law with a new technology, '[there] can be no really satisfactory solution to the problem presented here, until Congress acts'. But in the absence of a congressional solution, courts cannot avoid difficult problems by refusing to apply the law. We must 'take the Copyright Act . . . as we find it', and 'do as little damage as possible to traditional copyright principles . . . until the Congress legislates'.[62]

His Honour expressed the view: 'I would hope that these questions ultimately will be considered seriously and in depth by the Congress and be resolved there, despite the fact that the Court's decision today provides little incentive for congressional action.'[63] He preached a philosophy of jobbing, can-do jurisprudence: 'Our task in the meantime, however, is to resolve these issues as best we can in the light of ill-fitting existing copyright law.'[64]

Copyright owners were outraged by the outcome of the Supreme Court decision. Jack Valenti of the MPAA famously told a Congressional panel in 1982, 'I say to you that the VCR is to the American film producer and the American public as the Boston strangler is to the woman home alone.'[65] In the *Illustrated Story of Copyright Law*, Edward Samuels remembers his shock at the outcome of the Supreme Court of the United States decision:

> In any event, the copyright owners of movies and television programs got neither the license for home video recording nor the rental amendment that they said was necessary for their continued survival. Those of us who were sympathetic braced for the disaster that we predicted would occur.[66]

However, such a disastrous fate did not materialize for the movie industry. As Samuels observes, 'the VCR turned out to be one of the most lucrative inventions – for movie producers as well as hardware manufacturers – since movie projectors'.[67] The rental market proved to be a lucrative secondary market for film and television.

The divisions in the Supreme Court of the United States in the *Sony Betamax* case have been revisited in subsequent cases. Pamela Samuelson noted: 'The stark differences between the analytical frameworks of Justices Stevens and Blackmun in Sony have continued to play themselves out in the major copyright controversies of the day.'[68]

II. REPLAY TV

The precedent established by the *Sony Betamax* decision has been tested in the new context of personal video recorders (PVRs). William Fisher III discusses why copyright owners were uneasy about such recording technologies:

> Most PVRs have features that make them substantially more powerful and flexible than VCRs. Their digital storage systems facilitate the recording of large numbers of programs. Purchasers of PVRs typically subscribe to guide services that assist them in selecting programs they would like to watch. Some of the machines will even pick programs for you, predicting your tastes on the basis of what you have recorded in the past. All permit viewers to 'pause' or 'replay' programs that they are watching live.[69]

Significantly, a number of film studios and television networks brought legal action against the company Sonic Blue over its DVR (called 'ReplayTV 4000'). The technology developed was forced to file for bankruptcy before a court had the opportunity to consider a fair use defence. The Directors Guild of America brought legal action against the manufacturers of Clearplay, a form of software that enables viewers to skip offensive content on DVDs. However, timely legislative intervention by the Republican Congress protected the manufacturers from further litigation. The TiVo, Cablevision and Slingbox services have also raised issues about copyright law, digital video recorders and Internet distribution.

A. Sonic Blue

In *Paramount Pictures* v. *ReplayTV and Sonic Blue*, Paramount Pictures and 27 other major movie studios, television networks and cable companies brought a legal action in 2001 against the developers of an innovative new digital video recorder called 'ReplayTV 4000'.[70] First, it argued that the 'defendants enable, assist, and induce their ReplayTV 4000 customers to make unauthorized digital copies of plaintiffs' copyrighted television programming for the purpose of – at the touch of a button – viewing the programming with all commercial advertising automatically deleted'.[71] Second, it argued that the 'defendants provide their customers with a feature that makes it (in defendants' words) "a breeze" to make perfect digital copies of plaintiffs' copyrighted programmes, including entire theatrical motion pictures, and distribute them to other people – even many other people – through high-speed Internet connections'.[72] Paramount and the other major movie studios argued that ReplayTV and Sonic Blue were liable for contributory and vicarious copyright infringement. The studios also pleaded that the defendants were guilty of unfair competition and breaches of communications law. The studios asked the court to ban the sale of the ReplayTV DVR because it gave ReplayTV owners 'unprecedented new tools for violating [the Studios'] copyright interests'.[73]

Robert Schwartz, a Los Angeles attorney with the firm O'Melveny and Myers, acted for a number of the plaintiffs. He argued that the functions of ReplayTV could be distinguished from the time-shifting capacities protected as fair use under the *Sony Betamax* decision:

> The courts here in the United States have said that [recording free-to-air TV programs] is permissible, that's time-shifting, and if that's all that was going on here, we wouldn't be having this conversation because we wouldn't have filed this law suit. What's happening here is much more than just delaying the time in which I watch a show that I taped off the television. I'm delaying it, and watching it without the commercials, and that is something that our courts have never said is acceptable.[74]

Jamie Kellner, the head of Turner Broadcasting, was quoted as saying, 'People who watch TV without commercials are stealing from the entertainment producers.'[75] Robert Schwartz shared such sentiments: 'For 50 years here in the United States there's been something of a social contract, if you will, between people who watch TV and the people who put it on. If you're watching your TV set and a commercial comes on, you watch it.'[76]

Laurence Pulgram, partner with the San Francisco office of Fenwick and West, acted for Sonic Blue, the manufacturers of ReplayTV. He argued that such concerns were spurious, and the litigation would chill the development of new technologies that improved the lives of consumers. Pulgram argued that ReplayTV was certainly protected by the defence of fair use:

> I think the tension really comes down to defining fair use as we call it in the United States. And that is, what rights do consumers have to use the copyrighted materials that they have bought and paid for into their home. So this is not a situation where ReplayTV is distributing to the world, the product of the content

> companies, we're just making it easier for consumers to use that content that they've already paid their subscription fee for. And we're making it easier for a consumer to make a copy for a friend, which even the plaintiffs themselves, at least their CEOs, have recognised has gone on forever, and is going to continue to go on.[77]

Pulgram maintained that ReplayTV actually functioned to the advantage of copyright owners: 'In fact, what we're seeing is that people who buy the ReplayTV and people who buy personal video recorders, digital recorders like this generally, are subscribing to more broadcast and pay channels, more pay channels because they like TV so much more with all the conveniences that this kind of device affords you.'[78]

In the end, ReplayTV and Sonic Blue lacked the resources to defend the case. The chief executive officer for Sonic Blue, Greg Ballard, observed that his company spent $3 million per quarter on legal fees to defend itself and that the legal costs prevented the company from hiring new employees, which could engage in further research and development.[79] In March 2003, the ReplayTV creators filed for bankruptcy and sold off their assets. The purchaser of the ReplayTV technology, Digital Networks North America, announced in June 2003 that it was removing the contentious 'commercial advance' and 'send show' features in all future ReplayTV models, to 'address concerns of content copyright holders'. Shortly afterward, the copyright owners dismissed their lawsuit against ReplayTV and Sonic Blue.[80]

In *Newmark* v. *Turner Broadcasting System, Inc*, five people who owned ReplayTVs filed their own lawsuit represented by the Electronic Frontier Foundation (EFF) and attorneys Ira Rothken and Richard Wiebe.[81] They asked the court to rule that using their ReplayTVs to skip commercials, record shows for later viewing and send shows was fair use, was not copyright infringement. In 2004, Cooper J dismissed Newmark's case and request to convert the matter into a class action. The EFF lamented:

> The ReplayTV case is a cautionary tale for our times. The Hollywood studios used expensive litigation and an unproven threat of copyright liability to bankrupt two companies, and to force another to remove an innovative technology that threatened to disrupt their existing business models from the marketplace. As a result, there has been a noticeable chilling effect on technological innovation, and a corresponding reduction in consumer technology products.[82]

Lessig commented that the case had wider repercussions: '[Sonic Blue] spent years and millions of dollars litigating to defend its right to have the ReplayTV technology as it was. Essentially, it had to fold the company because the legal standard then was so uncertain that you had to get to trial before you could resolve the case.'[83]

B. Clearplay

In *Huntsman* v. *Soderbergh*, Steven Soderbergh, director of *Sex, Lies and Videotape*, together with other Hollywood Directors, the Directors Guild of America and the movie industry brought legal action against the manufacturers of Clearplay, a new form of software which allowed viewers to skip violent or sexual content while watching DVDs at home.[84] The President of the Guild, Martha Coolidge, observed:

> What these companies are doing is wrong, plain and simple. It is wrong to cut scenes from a film – just as it is to rip pages from a book – simply because we don't like the way something was portrayed or said, then resell it with the original title and creator's name still on it. It is wrong to circumvent the studios, who are the copyright holders, and the director, who is the film's creator – all in the name of turning a profit. It is unethical, it is shameful, and the DGA will aggressively pursue these claims.[85]

The movie industry argued that the companies were engaged in direct copyright infringement because they were renting, selling or distributing versions of movies without authorization. They also argued that the companies were in violation of the *Lanham Act* 1946 (US), a federal statute that prohibited false advertising, trademark infringement and unfair competition.

Robert Huntsman and Clean Flicks Inc. denied that it had engaged in direct copyright infringement or had committed any other offence. The EFF intervened as an amicus curiae, arguing that the motion picture studios sought to 'unlawfully usurp one of these rights, the right of private performance from the public via an unprecedented expansion of the exclusive right to create derivative works'.[86] Intel also intervened as an amicus curiae, protesting: 'Courts have been generally reluctant to expand copyright protection where such expansion would discourage legitimate technological innovation.'[87]

In response to such litigation, Republican Representative Lamar Smith introduced HR 357, the *Family Entertainment and Copyright Act* 2005 (US) to the House of Representatives. The legislation included the *Family Movie Act* 2005 (US), which provided an exemption for the editing of motion pictures by a member of a private household if no fixed copy of the altered version of the motion picture was created. Despite opposition from the Democrats, the legislation passed both the House of Representatives and the Senate. It was passed unanimously by voice vote. President Bush signed the *Family Entertainment and Copyright Act* in April 2005.[88]

Although legislation protected those selling technologies enabling private editing, the *Family Movie Act* 2005 (US) did not provide an exemption for actions resulting in fixed copies of altered works. In *Clean Flicks of*

Colorado, LLC v. *Soderbergh*, the Hollywood directors and other copyright owners sued Clean Flicks, Family Flix and Clean Films for selling and renting versions of movies that were edited to remove scenes containing sex, profanity and violence.[89] Matsch J of the United States District Court for the District of Colorado held that the alleged infringers had not made 'fair use' of the copyright works. The judge observed: 'There is nothing transformative about the edited copies.'[90] Matsch J added:

> The counterclaim defendants contend that there is no adverse effect from their use of the movies on the value of the copyrighted work to the Studios . . . The argument has superficial appeal but it ignores the intrinsic value of the right to control the content of the copyrighted work which is the essence of the law of copyright. Whether these films should be edited in a manner that would make them acceptable to more of the public playing them on DVD in a home environment is more than merely a matter of marketing; it is a question of what audience the copyright owner wants to reach.[91]

The judge held that the first sale doctrine did not protect alleged infringers; and granted an injunction barring sale and rental of infringing copies of the movies.

The outcome of the litigation is a mixed result. Huntsman, the manufacturer of Clearplay, was protected by the *Family Movie Act* 2005 (US). Nonetheless, Soderbergh and the copyright owners were successful in the legal action for copyright infringement against those remaining parties engaged in the alteration of fixed copies of motion pictures. The passage of the *Family Movie Act* 2005 (US) represents a rare setback for the motion picture industry in its battle to prevent the spread of digital recording technologies. It was a matter in which the Republican party's support for the interests of its 'moral majority' constituents overrode its usual sympathy for the copyright industries. However, it is worth remembering that the exemption provided for by the *Family Movie Act* 2005 (US) has only a limited scope of operation.

C. TiVo, Cablevision and Slingbox

The Californian company TiVo Inc has developed a digital video recorder, which is an impressive successor to the ReplayTV range. The TiVo enables the consumer to control live television, record a programme after it starts, skip advertisements and access an electronic programme guide. TiVo Inc has been understandably nervous about the threat of copyright infringement.[92] General counsel for TiVo, Matthew Zinn, observed: 'We're a little company caught between cable and satellite companies on one hand, and studios and other content providers on the other.'[93] Jonathan Zittrain has observed: 'TiVo has always been more circumspect than ReplayTV, but features like sharing content between TiVos or between a TiVo and a PC could cause problems.'[94] He noted: 'You can see TiVo running into a Napster problem', with the basic time-shifting capabilities allowed but the extra programme-sharing features prohibited.[95] Some conservative commentators have argued that the fair use doctrine should not extend to personal video recorders, such as TiVo.[96]

In May 2006, Twentieth Century Fox Film Corporation and a number of other copyright owners filed a legal action for copyright infringement against Cablevision Systems Corporation over its new remote digital access video recording service called 'RS-DVR'.[97] The plaintiffs argued that the television cable operator could not rely upon the narrow compulsory licence granted to cable services under s. 111 of the *Copyright Act* 1976 (US); nor was the service protected by fair use under s. 107 of the *Copyright Act* 1976 (US). In response, Cablevision argued that the service was protected under the defence of fair use because it enabled its customers to record and play back programming for their own viewing later – in other words, to engage in time-shifting. The company invoked the protection of the precedent of the *Sony Betamax* case: 'In sum, because the RS-DVR – like the Betamax, the VCR and the traditional set-top storage DVR before it – enables consumers to do nothing more than record television programming for later personal viewing, it does not infringe copyrights.'[98] Chin J ruled that the reliance on the *Sony Betamax* decision was misguided: 'Apart from their time-shifting functions, the RS-DVR and the VCR have little in common, and the relationship between Cablevision and potential RS-DVR customers is significantly different from the relationship between Sony and VCR users.'[99]

Slingbox is another new technology, which enables consumers to watch television programming remotely through any Internet-connected personal computer. CEO Blake Krikorian argues that, what TiVo and Replay TV did for time-shifting, Slingbox will do for place-shifting.[100] The company has boasted:

> The Slingbox™ [is] a groundbreaking piece of hardwired ingenuity that will literally transform the way you watch television. The Slingbox enables you to watch your TV programming from wherever you are by turning virtually any Internet-connected PC into your personal TV. Whether you're in another room or in another country, you'll always have access to your television.[101]

Motion picture studios and television networks are alarmed by place-shifting technologies such as Slingbox because they undermined proximity control, the restricted distribution of content to specific regions and times. CBS Executive Vice President Martin Franks observed: 'Slingbox is one manifestation of what we assume will be a cascade of similar products that are meant to manipulate our signals in ways that we think will be harmful to the network-affiliate business, if not the law.'[102] By contrast Fred von Lohmann of the EFF is enthusiastic about the product: 'They've done all the reasonable things to make this technology as palatable for the Hollywood studios as possible, but of course, that doesn't always stop a lawsuit.'[103]

III. SPACE-SHIFTING

There has been much legal and policy debate as to whether the defence of fair use, as enunciated in the *Sony Betamax* case, extends to the practice of 'space-shifting'. 'Space-shifting' refers to the practice whereby consumers transform their media collections into MP3 files. To such consumers, access to the media is no longer restricted to the physical space where their media player resides; they can access their collections through portable devices, like MP3 players, or via the Internet. There was some *obiter dicta* support in the case of *RIAA* v. *Diamond Multimedia Systems Inc* for the proposition that 'space-shifting' was a paradigmatic example of non-commercial personal use.[104] However, in *UMG Recordings, Inc.* v. *MP3.Com, Inc.*, the Federal Court distinguished this earlier precedent, and held that the website, MP3.com, could not avail itself of the defence of fair use on the grounds that it provided transformative space-shifting.[105] There has been much commentary as to whether the MP3 player, the iPod, has substantial non-infringing purposes.[106] In addition, the practice of podcasting has raised significant issues about the limits of the defence of fair use.

A. The Rio MP3 Player

After threats of legal action against digital recording devices and much industry debate, the United States Congress and President George Bush Senior passed the *Audio Home Recording Act* 1992 (US).[107] Paul Goldstein comments upon this initiative:

> Digital audiotape recording was a modest precursor to the problems that would inundate the record companies less than a decade later with the arrival of such digital tools for unauthorized copies as CD burning and Internet file sharing. The Internet in part illuminated the global scale of the problem. The levies introduced by the AHRA revealed an American willingness to borrow solutions from abroad – levies have been a feature of European copyright law since the Federal Republic of Germany's enactment in 1965 of a statute compensating copyright owners for the private copying of their works. But the United States was also prepared to export norms of its own, such as protection for encryption techniques like SCMS.[108]

This legislation required the incorporation of serial copy management system (SCMS) controls in digital equipment sold in the United States, and the payment of a statutory levy by the producers of blank digital audiotapes and equipment. The legislation also prohibited any copyright infringement action based on the manufacture, importation or distribution of an analog or a digital audio recording device, or the noncommercial use by a consumer of such a medium for making musical recordings.

There has been significant litigation in United States courts over the nature and the scope of the *Audio Home Recording Act* 1992 (US). In *RIAA* v. *Diamond Multimedia Systems Inc*, the Federal Court of Appeals for the Ninth Circuit considered whether the Rio portable music player was a digital audio recording device subject to the restrictions of the 1992 statute.[109]

The Consumer Electronics Manufacturers Association intervened in the dispute in an amicus brief, suggesting that the Rio MP3 player was perfectly entitled to protection under the *Audio Home Recording Act* 1992 (US).[110] The Association stressed that the legislation 'flatly rejects the notion that copyright owners should have the power to forbid consumer copying of musical recordings, either directly or by denying access to copying technology'.[111] The Association contended: 'Regrettably, the statute described in RIAA's brief bears little resemblance to the Act negotiated by the parties and enacted by Congress.'[112] The Association concludes that the 'RIAA's members simply are not injured by any possible technical non-compliance.'[113]

The Federal Court of Appeals for the Ninth Circuit ruled that the Rio portable music player was not a digital audio recording device subject to the restrictions of the *Audio Home Recording Act* 1992 (US). It found that the district court had properly denied the motion for a preliminary injunction against the Rio's manufacture and distribution. O'Scannlain J observed that the 'space-shifting' of sound recordings was acceptable under the 1992 statute:

> In fact, the Rio's operation is entirely consistent with the Act's main purpose – the facilitation of personal use. As the Senate Report explains, '[t]he purpose of [the Act] is to ensure the right of consumers to make analog or digital audio recordings of copyrighted music for their private, noncommercial use.' The Act does so through its home taping exemption, which 'protects all noncommercial copying by consumers of digital and analog musical recordings'. The Rio merely makes copies in order to render portable, or 'space-shift', those files that already reside on a user's hard drive. Such copying is paradigmatic noncommercial personal use entirely consistent with the purposes of the Act.[114]

However, there has been some debate over the value of this decision as a precedent. Some would suggest that the recognition of 'space-shifting' should also be recognized in the context of the defence of fair use. Others suggest that such remarks are at best *obiter dicta*, and do not necessarily have any force outside the immediate context of the *Audio Home Recording Act* 1992 (US). Such arguments have come to light in the context of litigation over digital music and peer to peer networks, such as Napster and Aimster.[115]

However, the *Audio Home Recording Act* 1992 (US) has been rendered otiose with further developments in technology. William Fisher III comments that the 'statute had three flaws, which have become increasingly glaring over time'.[116] First, he notes that the slow arrival of the legislation delayed the appearance of digital recorders. Second, the statute was highly technology-specific, focusing upon audio recording devices, rather than computers. Third, the statute was limited in its application to certain musical recordings. Fisher observes: 'The restrictions built into these definitions rapidly consigned the statute to a marginal role in the development of the music and consumer-electronics industries.'[117] He notes that the legislation has limited application nowadays to '[Digital Audiotape] recorders (of which very very few are sold), mini-disc recorders (still being produced in modest numbers by Sony) and the CD burners designed as components of stereo systems (not the much more popular burners housed in personal computers'.[118]

B. MP3.com and XM Satellite Radio

In January 2000, MP3.com launched its 'My.MP3.com' service, which would enable subscribers to store, customize and listen to the sound recordings contained on their CDs from any place where they have an Internet connection. The company made copies of 45 000 CDs to put onto its computer servers, and allowed subscribers to access such media files under certain conditions. To make use of this service, a subscriber to MP3.com would have to establish that they already owned a copy of the commercial CD (through the 'Beam-it Service') or purchase the CD from one of MP3.com's affiliated online retailers (the 'Instant Listening Service'). MP3.com believed that this service would act as a music locker for the storage of its subscribers' CDs.

Taking fright, the major record companies led by UMG recordings brought legal action against MP3.com, alleging that they had made unauthorized copies of 45 000 audio CDs, loaded those copies onto file servers and permitted users of its Internet service to download those copies. The music industry sought declaratory and injunctive relief, and statutory damages for wilful copyright infringement.[119]

In response, MP3.com pleaded that the service My.MP3.com should be protected by the defence of fair use in light of the *Sony Betamax* case, because it enabled consumers to engage in 'space-shifting' in an efficient manner:

> These services provide consumers with Internet access to MP3 files of the sound tracks from their personal CD collections, without requiring them first to convert the discs into MP3 files and then slowly upload the files to an Internet web site. The service thus allows CD owners to efficiently overcome the limitations of their Internet connections.[120]

The company stressed, though, that there were significant restrictions to the service, which protected the interests of copyright owners.

In *UMG Recordings, Inc.* v. *MP3.Com, Inc.*, Rakoff J of the District Court for the Southern District of New York observed: 'The complex marvels of cyberspatial communication may create difficult legal issues; but not in this case.'[121] The judge observed that the 'defendant's infringement of plaintiffs' copyrights is clear'.[122] Rakoff J denied that the website, MP3.com, could avail itself of the defence of fair use on the grounds that it provided transformative space-shifting:

> Here, although defendant recites that My.MP3.com provides a transformative 'space shift' by which subscribers can enjoy the sound recordings contained on their CDs without lugging around the physical discs themselves, this is simply another way of saying that the unauthorized copies are being retransmitted in another medium – an insufficient basis for any legitimate claim of transformation.[123]

The judge cited a number of cases to support the proposition that the repetition of copyrighted material that 'merely repackages or republishes the original' is unlikely to be deemed a fair use.[124]

After losing the litigation, the company MP3.com had to be sold off, in order to service the massive settlement costs of $US53.4 million.[125] In May 2001, Vivendi Universal, one of the leading plaintiffs in the copyright action, acquired MP3.com in return for $US372 million.[126] In the end, the remnants of MP3.com were sold off to CNET Networks. Fisher suggests that such legal action by the music industry was misguided: 'In their determination to maximize their short-term profits, they were attacking a service that benefited not only consumers but also the record companies themselves.'[127]

In January 2002, under new ownership, MP3.com filed a law suit in the Los Angeles County Superior Court against its former outside counsel, Cooley Godward LLP, alleging fraud, breach of fiduciary duty and malpractice.[128] The company alleged that Cooley Godward had failed to 'meaningfully advise about liability in an infringement suit' and misrepresented to MP3.com that it had secured expert opinion testimony that there was a strong and viable defence of fair use.[129] In the end, the parties settled the malpractice law suit. Sonia Katyal noted: 'It is important to remember that at the time Cooley advised MP3.com, the area of online music was a legal morass of unsettled questions.'[130]

Such issues about copyright law and subscription services for music have been revisited in recent litigation over satellite radio. In 2006, a number of record companies filed a legal action against XM Satellite Radio over its new subscription service called 'XM + MP3'.[131] Unlike the regular XM satellite radio service, the XM + MP3 service enables subscribers to receive permanent copies of individual songs and create permanent music libraries up to 50 hours long. The music industry argued that the new digital download subscription service infringed the copyright held in musical works and sound recordings. It also contended that the service would undermine lawful legitimate services, such as iTunes: 'XM explicitly advertises this substitution effect by touting its service's advantages over the iPod, one of many digital download systems: "It's not a Pod, it's the mothership".'[132]

In response, XM Satellite sought to reassure its subscribers that its efforts to provide consumers with greater choices would not be inhibited by such threats of copyright action:

> Consumers have enjoyed the right to tape off the air for their personal use for decades, from reel-to-reel and the cassette to the VCR and TiVo. Our new radios complement download services, they don't replace them. If you want a copy of a song to transfer to other players or burn onto CDs, we make it easy for you to buy them through XM + MP3. Satellite radio subscribers like you are law-abiding music consumers; a portion of your subscriber fee pays royalties directly to artists. Instead of going after pirates who don't pay a cent, the record labels are attacking the radios used for the enjoyment of music by consumers like you.[133]

The Home Recording Rights Coalition protested that, with such litigation, the music industry had betrayed its previous undertakings to consumers, the Congress and the courts.[134] An advocate for consumer electronics retailers, Robert Schwartz, comments: 'This is yet another attempt by the record industry to deny consumers access to new technologies and content, and to eliminate the right to private, noncommercial home recording that Americans have enjoyed for decades.'[135]

C. iPod, iTunes and Podcasting

On 21 October 2001, Apple Computer released the iPod, a brand of portable, digital MP3 player. The iPod has sold at an amazing rate, selling close to 20 million units over four years.[136] The iPod has dominated digital music player sales in the United States and elsewhere, with over 90 per cent of the market for hard drive-based players and over 70 per cent of the market for all types of players. Legal and cultural historian Dr Kathy Bowrey seeks to explain the appeal of this particular MP3 player:

> Part of the attraction of the iPod is that it is both a well integrated device that makes it easy to use and to share music, as well as fitting our expectations of a small, infinitely portable, wearable gadget. Whilst it is currently a very desirable commodity, given the fluidity of these identities we construct within a perpetual innovation cycle, there is an ongoing need for us to reinvest in new purchases, to refresh ours identities and aesthetic experiences, in response to the new trends. As experienced, affluent consumers we know the game element of this. We understand the functional obsolescence of the technologies and the disposability of the associated signs and devices.[137]

Apple designed the iPod to work with iTunes. This software allows users to manage the music libraries on their computers and on their iPods. iTunes can automatically synchronize a user's iPod with specific playlists or with the entire contents of a music library each time an iPod connects to a host computer. It is also an internet radio tuner that also allows users to share files across a network with other people using iTunes. Rather than charging a subscription fee to iTunes, Apple have developed an Internet store that allows for the purchase of digital downloads of individual songs and albums.

Steve Jobs, the Chief Executive Officer of Apple Computers, has explained that the company sought to capitalize upon the demand for digital download services while still respecting the interests of copyright owners:

> Napster and Kazaa certainly demonstrated that the Internet was built perfectly for delivering music. The problem is they're illegal. And the services that have sprung up that were legal are pretty anemic in terms of the rights they offer you, and they kind of treat you like a criminal. You can't burn a CD, or you can't put it on your MP3 player.
>
> And so our idea was to try to come up with a music service where you don't have to subscribe to it. You can just buy music at 99 cents a song, and . . . you have great rights to use it. You can burn as many CDs as you want for personal use, you can put it on your iPods, you can use it in your other applications, you can have it on multiple computers.
>
> And we were able to convince the big five music companies to go along with us on this. So it's a pretty landmark offering.[138]

In an effort to satisfy copyright owners, and no doubt conscious of the fate of My.MP3.com, Apple Computers placed limits upon what consumers could do with the music, which they downloaded. Consumers could engage in personal copying and transfers, but were unable to engage in mass file-sharing.[139] Nonetheless, there has been some apprehension that iPods can store both authorized and unauthorized digital downloads.

The Apple iPod has encouraged the phenomenon of podcasting. Recent developments in radio mean that radio broadcasts can be 'podcast' to MP3 players to be listened to at a later time. Podcasting is a method of publishing audio broadcasts via the Internet, allowing users to download and play MP3 files. It permits radio programmes to be accessed online, copied and stored on an MP3 player for use and reuse. Ben Hammersley explained the popular appeal of podcasting: 'It is a combination of the ease of creating content, and the way it can be consumed.'[140] He comments:

> Podcasting has arrived just as similar tools have appeared for audio, and new content is looking for distribution methods. The timing is impeccable. This timing, along with the popularity of iPods and the rest of the necessary ingredients, also comes as the idea of timeshifting hits the mainstream. TiVo units in America and Sky Plus in the UK, have shown that the idea that programming has to be consumed in the order and time that the broadcaster assigns it, is nonsense. An ordinary radio is an automated content delivery device, but you can't pause it, or rewind it, or adapt it to your own schedule.[141]

There are a number of complex and evolving copyright issues which arise in respect of podcasting.[142] Sheri Crofts and her collaborators observe: 'The problem is that, while current copyright law allows for streaming music online, or live Internet radio, it did not foresee that radio-like programming could be downloaded to MP3 players; thereby creating the potential for multiple copies to be made.'[143] Copyright collecting societies have expressed concerns that the podcasting of copyright work could infringe copyright owners' economic rights in respect of reproduction, public performance and communication to the public.[144]

There is some debate about what impact the *Grokster* decision will have upon the Apple iPod. In the *Grokster* case, the Supreme Court of the United States adopted a new inducement test in order to establish whether the producer of a device should be held secondarily liable for copyright infringement.[145] The Court held that one who distributes a device with the object of promoting its use to infringe copyright, as shown by clear expression or other affirmative steps taken to foster infringement, is liable for the resulting acts of infringement by third parties. This applies even where the device is capable of non-infringing uses.

Although the *Grokster* decision dealt with file sharing made possible by peer-to-peer networks, in the oral proceedings of the case, the Supreme Court of the United States was keen to discern what implications, if any, the decision would have for the iPod. Breyer J asked the attorney for the motion picture studios about the implications of the judgment for the inventors of new technologies, such as the Xerox Machine, the VCR and the iPod:

> On your test, are we sure, if you were the counsel to Mr. Carlson, that you recommend going ahead with the Xerox machine? Are you sure, if you were the counsel to the creator of the VCR, that you could recommend, given the use, copying movies, that we should ever have a VCR? Are you sure that you could recommend to the iPod inventor that he could go ahead and have an iPod, or, for that matter, Gutenberg, the press? I mean, you see the problem . . . Because in each case – for all I know, the monks had a fit when Gutenberg made his press – but the problem, of course, is that it could well be, in each of those instances, that there will be vast numbers of infringing uses that are foreseeable.[146]

Similarly, Souter J said he was very interested in iPods and during proceedings commented, 'I know perfectly well I could go out and buy a CD and put it on my iPod, but I also know perfectly well that if I can get the music on the iPod without buying the CD, that's what I'm going to do.'[147] He wondered out aloud: 'So why, in the iPod, do you not have this Damoclean sword?'[148] Furthermore, Kennedy J queried: 'How do we know in advance, on your test, anything that would give the inventor, or, more exactly, the developer, the confidence to go ahead?'[149]

Professor Lawrence Lessig was sceptical that the new inducement rule articulated in *Grokster* would provide certainty to innovators. He argued that Apple's position was uncertain because 'a court is supposed to decide whether a company like Apple "promot[ed]" or "fostered" copyright infringement through design, behavior, or words'.[150] He comments:

> Apple has sold about 15 million iPods, each capable of holding between 1000 and 15 000 songs. Its iTunes music store has sold about 500 million songs for 99 cents each. That works out to only 30 songs or so per device. Does this surprise Apple? Did it really expect that people would buy a 60-gig iPod for $400 and then put $14 850 of music in it? No. Apple expected precisely what it advertised – that people would 'Rip. Mix. Burn.' music from CDs to iTunes and, in turn, to their iPods. After all, as the ads say, 'It's your music.'[151]

Lessig rhetorically questions whether a start-up company would be able to afford such litigation: 'Would a small, young company ever build a business close to the insanely uncertain line of regulation that copyright law has become?'[152]

Steve Ballmer of Microsoft takes the controversial view that the iPod encourages copyright infringement:

> We've had DRM in Windows for years. The most common format of music on an iPod is 'stolen'. Part of the reason people steal music is money, but some of it is that the DRM stuff out there has not been that easy to use. We are going to

> continue to improve our DRM, to make it harder to crack, and easier, easier, easier, easier, to use. Most people still steal music. We can build the technology but there are still ways for people to steal music.[153]

Perhaps his real concern is that Apple hopes to obtain a monopoly in the marketplace, by using the iPod to interpose itself between consumers and computer hardware.

Record companies have placed increasing pressure upon Apple Computers to raise the price of digital downloads sold on iTunes. Warner Music CEO, Edgar Bronfam, argued that Apple should allow for greater flexibility in the pricing of iTunes digital downloads.[154] In response, Steve Jobs of Apple defended the low-pricing scheme:

> The problem is we are still competing with piracy. The labels make more money from selling tracks on iTunes than when they sell a CD. There are no marketing costs for them. We are competing with piracy, so it needs to be a fair price – if the price goes up people will go back to piracy. If they want to raise prices they are getting greedy.[155]

For their part, record companies are ambivalent about the iPod. As MacWorld puts it nicely, 'Labels love and loathe Apple: love for legitimizing and bringing to the mass market a digital distribution business that works; loathe for the dominant market share the company has achieved.'[156] In the end, the record companies have been forced to concede to the wishes of Apple Computers in respect of pricing of digital downloadings.[157]

Hollywood film companies have also expressed reservations about the uses of the iPod. In a lawsuit filed in the United States District Court, the Southern District of New York, *Paramount Pictures Corp.* v. *Load 'N Go Video*, motion picture studios have sued a small business, which loads videos onto personal media players, such as iPods.[158] The copyright owners argue that Load 'N Go Video Inc. has decrypted and copied DVDs, and thereby engaged in copyright infringement and circumvented technological protection measures. The motion pictures maintain that the small business does not have a licence to load DVDs into iPods. For its part, Load 'N Go Video Inc. has maintained that its customers have legitimately bought both the DVDs and the personal media players. The small business will undoubtedly argue that it is protected by the defence of fair use against both the claims of copyright infringement and circumvention of technological protection measures because it enables its customers to engage in 'space-shifting' of legitimately bought media.

Policy makers and regulators have expressed disquiet that the Apple iPod is only compatible with copyright content bought from iTunes.[159] A number of European countries have raised concerns that Apple's 'FairPlay' digital rights management system is anti-competitive, because it is not interoperable with other MP3 players and digital download services.[160] In March 2006, the French Parliament proposed amendments to its copyright legislation to ensure that copy-protection technologies did not 'result in the prevention of the effective application of interoperability'.[161] Apple protested, vigorously, that such a proposal was 'state-sponsored piracy'.[162] Jim Prendergast of Americans for Technology Leadership argued: 'Consumers will lose even more in the long term if France, and other nations, continue to strip away the intellectual property rights of companies like Apple.'[163] After complaints from Apple, the French parliament passed a diluted version of the law, which left online distributors with significant control over the code.

Scandinavian regulators have also worried about Apple's monopolistic tendencies.[164] In June 2006, the Consumer Ombudsmen of Norway, Sweden and Denmark notified Apple that its 'FairPlay' digital rights management system unfairly restricted consumer choice, that the terms and conditions for buying music from iTunes Music Store were too restrictive, and that its pricing was discriminatory.[165] In reply, Apple has defended its technological restrictions and refused to change its business model by opening iTunes purchases to rival devices. The Consumer Ombudsmen of the Scandinavian countries are considering whether to take Apple to court over the operations of the iTunes Music Store. The European Commission is also investigating certain competition matters relating to the operation of the iTunes Music Store.[166]

In addition to complaints over copyright law, consumer choice and competition, Apple has had to fend off claims of trademark and patent infringement.[167]

CONCLUSION

In testimony before the United States Senate Committee on the Judiciary, Gary Shapiro, the Chairman of the Home Recording Rights Coalition, reflected upon the significance of the *Sony Betamax* decision:

> The Betamax case, was, if not the vanguard, then the safeguard for a technological revolution that has empowered consumers and created new markets for content providers in ways that previous generations could only dream about. The Betamax decision gave technology companies the confidence to imagine, design and create today's digital revolution in audio, video, text, hypertext and interactive media.[168]

Nonetheless, Shapiro expressed concerns that 'the balance may have shifted from a pro-consumer revolution to maximum protection for proprietors'.[169]

He laments: 'Unfortunately, today, with changes in the law shifting the balance away from technology to copyright owner rights, some companies are engaging in "self-censorship" of innovative new and lawful products solely in hopes of avoiding the expense and risk of copyright litigation.'[170] It is certainly true that manufacturers of products such as TiVo and the iPod have been cautious, and taken measures to reduce their vulnerability to suits for copyright infringement. Other technology developers, like Sling Media, Cablevision and XM Satellite Radio, have been more bold and adventurous. However, such companies have attracted threats of legal action for copyright infringement.

Although it may lay claim to being the Magna Carta and the Declaration of Independence for consumers in the United States, the *Sony Betamax* decision has had little impact in other jurisdictions. The United States Trade Representative has been unwilling to export the privileges of fair use to other jurisdictions in the course of trade negotiations. Thus the legal ability of American consumers to engage in 'time-shifting' is not necessarily extended to the consumers of other marketplaces. Canadian scholar Rosemary Coombe laments: 'Discussion of the public domain in North American legal academic circles tends to concentrate upon issues of fair use and the First Amendment, with some attention to new forms of contractual licensing in digital environments and vague allusions to common property regimes.'[171] She warns that the 'proponents of the public domain should be aware that if we focus too exclusively upon concepts of fair use . . . and the First Amendment, we are concerning ourselves with local ordinances in a world of global interconnections'.[172] Coombe noted: 'Recent regional trade agreements clearly reflect this tendency to narrowly enumerate permissible usages and thereby usurp the policy balances enabled by fair use determinations.'[173] She observed that the United States was chary of allowing Canada to adopt a broad defence of fair use in the wake of the *North American Free Trade Agreement* 1994 (NAFTA). Coombe explains: 'We should also be cognizant of the fact that the major copyright industries have an interest in isolating the United States and its robust fair use jurisprudence and that these principles may be subject to challenge under international trade regimes.'[174] She concludes: 'We will forgo a necessary and valuable opportunity if we continue to address the public domain only through the lens of national and parochial legal categories rather than through a body of international law.'[175]

A similar dynamic was at work during the debate over the *Australia–United States Free Trade Agreement* 2004. The Australian Government was discouraged from adopting an open-ended defence of fair use. After much lobbying from pay television services[176] and consumer groups,[177] the Federal Australian Government provided new limited exceptions for private copying under the *Copyright Amendment Act* 2006 (Cth). The Attorney-General, Philip Ruddock, observed: 'These are commonsense amendments which will maintain Australia's copyright laws as the best in the world for the benefit of our creators and other copyright owners and for the many Australians who enjoy their creative works.'[178] The Attorney-General observed:

> Copyright is important and should be respected. That is why the Government is updating our laws to keep pace with technology. Everyday consumers shouldn't be treated like copyright pirates. Copyright pirates should be not treated like everyday consumers.[179]

The Federal Government provided for narrow technologically specific exceptions in respect of time-shifting, space-shifting, and format-shifting for private use. In addition, the Federal Government provided stronger backing for technological protection measures, and introduced new enforcement measures to combat copyright piracy and counterfeiting. However, the Australian Government has decided against the introduction of a general defence of fair use, along the lines of United States copyright law. As a result, Australian consumers do not enjoy the same privileges and liberties as their United States counterparts. The Federal Government also rejected the proposal of copyright collecting societies for there to be a levy in respect of home copying of copyright works.[180]

In the United Kingdom, there are moves afoot to introduce a private copying exception for consumers under the *European Community Information Society Directive*. In December 2006, the *Gowers Review of Intellectual Property* recommended the introduction of a private copying exception without a levy:

> If rightholders know in advance of a sale of a particular work that limited copying of that work can take place, the economic cost of the right to copy can be included in the sale price. The 'fair compensation' required by the Directive can be included in the normal sale price. This means, however, that any private right to copy cannot be extended retrospectively as copies of works already sold would not include this 'fair compensation'. Therefore, collecting societies may wish to consider making a single block licence available to allow consumers to format shift their back catalogues legitimately.[181]

Nonetheless, Andrew Gowers was of the firm belief that there should be strict limits on the scope of any private copying exception. The *Review* recommended that the private copying should be limited to 'format shifting' rather than simply allowing any copies to be made for private purposes. Again, such a position is much less expansive than the freedoms provided by the *Sony Betamax* decision in the United States.

NOTES

1. Rosen, C. (2004/2005), 'The Age of Egocasting', *The New Atlantis: A Journal of Technology and Society*, **7**, 51–72 at 51 http://www.thenewatlantis.com/archive/7/TNA07-Rosen.pdf.
2. *Sony Corporation of America* v. *Universal City Studios, Inc*, 464 US 417 (1984).
3. Home Recording Rights Coalition (2005), 'HRRC Urges Passage of Betamax Codification: Bill Would Promote User Freedom under DMCA', http://www.hrrc.org/news/PressRelease041405.html, 14 April.
4. *Metro-Goldwyn-Mayer Studios Inc*. v. *Grokster, Ltd*. 125 S.Ct. 2764 (2005).
5. Home Recording Rights Coalition (2005), 'HRRC Urges Passage of Betamax Codification: Bill Would Promote User Freedom under DMCA', http://www.hrrc.org/news/PressRelease041405.html, 14 April.
6. Ibid.
7. Litman, J. (2005), 'The Sony Paradox', *Case Western Reserve Law Review*, **55**, 917–61: see also Litman, J. (2005), 'The Story of Sony v. Universal Studios: Mary Poppins Meets the Boston Strangler', in Ginsburg, Jane and Rochelle Dreyfuss (eds), *Intellectual Property Stories*, New York: Foundation Press, pp. 358–94.
8. Ibid., at 919.
9. Ibid., at 951.
10. Ibid., at 960.
11. Ibid., at 960.
12. Lessig, Lawrence (2004), *Free Culture: How Big Media Uses Technology And Law To Lock Down Culture And Control Creativity*, New York: Penguin, p. 187.
13. Ibid.
14. Ibid.
15. Picker, R. (2005), 'Rewinding Sony: The Evolving Product, Phoning Home and the Duty of Ongoing Design', *University of Chicago Law and Economics Olin Working Paper*, **241**, 1–37.
16. Ibid.
17. Ibid., at 3.
18. Ibid., at 17.
19. *Universal City Studios, Inc* v. *Sony Corporation of America*, 480 F.Supp. 429 (1979).
20. *Universal City Studios, Inc* v. *Sony Corporation of America*, 659 F.2d 963 (1981).
21. *Sony Corporation of America* v. *Universal City Studios, Inc*, 464 US 417 (1984).
22. Samuelson, P. (2006), 'The Generativity of Sony v. Universal: The Intellectual Property Legacy of Justice Stevens', *Fordham Law Review*, **74**(4), 1831–76, 1875.
23. Ibid.
24. Ibid.
25. *Sony Corporation of America* v. *Universal City Studios, Inc*, 464 US 417 at 430 (1984).
26. *White-Smith Music Publishing Co*. v. *Apollo Co*., 209 U.S. 1 (1908).
27. *Fortnightly Corp*. v. *United Artists Television, Inc*., 392 U.S. 390 (1968), and *Teleprompter Corp*. v. *Columbia Broadcasting System, Inc*., 415 U.S. 394 (1974); and *Eastern Microwave, Inc*. v. *Doubleday Sports, Inc*., 691 F.2d 125, 129 (CA2 1982).
28. *Sony Corporation of America* v. *Universal City Studios, Inc*, 464 US 417 at 442 (1984).
29. *Sony Corporation of America* v. *Universal City Studios, Inc*, 464 US 417 at 442 (1984).
30. *Sony Corporation of America* v. *Universal City Studios, Inc*, 464 US 417 at 423 (1984).
31. *Sony Corporation of America* v. *Universal City Studios, Inc*, 464 US 417 at 424 (1984).
32. *Sony Corporation of America* v. *Universal City Studios, Inc*, 464 US 417 at 448–52 (1984).
33. *Sony Corporation of America* v. *Universal City Studios, Inc*, 464 US 417 at 452 (1984).
34. *Sony Corporation of America* v. *Universal City Studios, Inc*, 464 US 417 at 447 (1984).
35. *Sony Corporation of America* v. *Universal City Studios, Inc*, 464 US 417 at 442 (1984).
36. *Sony Corporation of America* v. *Universal City Studios, Inc*, 464 US 417 at 456 (1984).
37. *Sony Corporation of America* v. *Universal City Studios, Inc*, 464 US 417 at 456 (1984).
38. *Sony Corporation of America* v. *Universal City Studios, Inc*, 464 US 417 at 431 (1984).

39. *Sony Corporation of America* v. *Universal City Studios, Inc*, 464 US 417 at 431 (1984).
40. *Sony Corporation of America* v. *Universal City Studios, Inc*, 464 US 417 at 456 (1984).
41. *Sony Corporation of America* v. *Universal City Studios, Inc*, 464 US 417 at 431 (1984).
42. Goldstein, Paul (2003), *Copyright's Highway: From Gutenberg to the Celestial Jukebox*, Stanford: Stanford University Press. Jessica Litman also gives a good account of such oscillations in the court in her article, 'The Sony Paradox'; see Litman, J. (2005), 'The Sony Paradox', *Case Western Reserve Law Review*, **55**, 917–61.
43. Goldstein, Paul (2003), *Copyright's Highway: From Gutenberg to the Celestial Jukebox*, Stanford: Stanford University Press, p. 153.
44. Ibid.
45. Ibid.
46. Ibid., p. 154.
47. Litman, J. (2005), 'The Sony Paradox', *Case Western Reserve Law Review*, **55**, 917–61 at 933.
48. Ibid., 934.
49. Goldstein, Paul (2003), *Copyright's Highway: From Gutenberg to the Celestial Jukebox*, Stanford: Stanford University Press, p. 155.
50. *Sony Corporation of America* v. *Universal City Studios, Inc*, 464 US 417 at 457 (1984).
51. *Sony Corporation of America* v. *Universal City Studios, Inc*, 464 US 417 at 480–81 (1984).
52. *Sony Corporation of America* v. *Universal City Studios, Inc*, 464 US 417 at 481 (1984).
53. *Sony Corporation of America* v. *Universal City Studios, Inc*, 464 US 417 at 493 (1984).
54. *Sony Corporation of America* v. *Universal City Studios, Inc*, 464 US 417 at 491 (1984).
55. *Sony Corporation of America* v. *Universal City Studios, Inc*, 464 US 417 at 491 (1984).
56. *Sony Corporation of America* v. *Universal City Studios, Inc*, 464 US 417 at 483 (1984).
57. *Sony Corporation of America* v. *Universal City Studios, Inc*, 464 US 417 at 483 (1984).
58. *Sony Corporation of America* v. *Universal City Studios, Inc*, 464 US 417 at 495 (1984).
59. *Sony Corporation of America* v. *Universal City Studios, Inc*, 464 US 417 at 495 (1984).
60. *Sony Corporation of America* v. *Universal City Studios, Inc*, 464 US 417 at 496 (1984).
61. *Sony Corporation of America* v. *Universal City Studios, Inc*, 464 US 417 at 496 (1984).
62. *Sony Corporation of America* v. *Universal City Studios, Inc*, 464 US 417 at 500 (1984).
63. *Sony Corporation of America* v. *Universal City Studios, Inc*, 464 US 417 at 457 (1984).
64. *Sony Corporation of America* v. *Universal City Studios, Inc*, 464 US 417 at 457 (1984).
65. Valenti, J. (1982), 'Home Recording of Copyrighted Works', Subcommittee on Courts, Civil Liberties, and the Administration of Justice, the Committee on the Judiciary, House of Representatives, http://cryptome.org/hrcw-hear.htm, 12 April.
66. Samuels, Edward (2000), *The Illustrated Story of Copyright*, New York: Thomas Dunne Books, p. 70.
67. Ibid.
68. Samuelson, P. (2006), 'The Generativity of Sony v. Universal: The Intellectual Property Legacy of Justice Stevens', *Fordham Law Review*, **74**(4), 1831–76, 1876.
69. Fisher, William (2004), *Promises to Keep: Technology, Law, and the Future of Entertainment*, Stanford: Stanford University Press, p. 131.
70. *Paramount Pictures Corp*. v. *ReplayTV Inc.* 298 F.Supp.2d 921 (C.D.Cal, 2004).
71. *Paramount Pictures Corp*. v. *ReplayTV Inc* No. 2:01CV09358 (Docket) (C.D.Cal. Oct. 31, 2001).
72. Ibid.
73. Ibid.
74. Carrick, D. (2002), 'The Ruckus Over Replay TV', The Law Report, Radio National, http://www.abc.net.au/rn/talks/8.30/lawrpt/stories/s712304.htm, 29 October.
75. Ibid.
76. Ibid.
77. Ibid.
78. Ibid.
79. Evangelista, B. (2003), 'Piracy Suits Chill Valley, Moves Peril Profit, Techies Say', *San Francisco Chronicle*, 20 February.

80. EFF (2004), 'Digital Betamax: ReplayTV Owners Stand up to Hollywood to Defend Digital VCRs', http://www.eff.org/IP/Video/Newmark_v_Turner/.
81. *Newmark, et al.* v. *Turner Broadcasting System, Inc* (9 January 2004), http://www.eff.org/IP/Video/Newmark_v._Turner/20040109_Order.pdf.
82. Ibid.
83. Hof, R. (2005), 'Ten Years of Chilled Innovation: Interview with Lawrence Lessig', *Business Week*, http://www.businessweek.com/technology/content/jun2005/tc20050629_2928_tc057.htm, 29 June.
84. *Huntsman* v. *Soderbergh*, Not Reported in F.Supp.2d, 2005 WL 1993421 (D.Colo.,2005); and EFF 'Amicus Brief in *Huntsman* v. *Soderbergh*', http://www.eff.org/legal/cases/Huntsman_v._Soderbergh/20050822_eff_amicus.pdf, 22 August 2005.
85. DGA (2002), 'DGA responds and counterclaims against Robert Huntsman and CleanFlicks; adds motion picture studios to suit, DGA Press Releases', http://www.dga.org/index2.php 3?chg=, 20 September.
86. EFF (2003), 'Amicus Brief in *Huntsman* v. *Soderbergh*', http://www. eff.org/legal/cases/Huntsman_v._Soderbergh/20030618_eff_amicus.pdf, 1.
87. Intel (2003), 'Amicus Brief in *Huntsman* v. *Soderbergh*', http://www.eff.org/legal/cases/Huntsman_v._Soderbergh/intel_amicus.pdf, 4.
88. Boliek, B. (2005), 'President Bush Signs Family Entertainment and Copyright Act', *Hollywood Reporter*, http://www.hollywoodreporter.com/thr/article_display.jsp?vnu_content_id=1000900812, 28 April.
89. *Clean Flicks of Colorado, LLC* v. *Soderbergh* 433 F.Supp.2d 1236 (D.Colo., 2006.)
90. Ibid., 1241.
91. Ibid., 1241–2.
92. Cohen, A. (2004), 'The Trouble With TiVo: Content Owners are Crying Copyright Infringement, and Cable Companies are Talking Customers', *IP Law & Business*, http://www.ipww.com.
93. Ibid.
94. Ibid.
95. Ibid.
96. Rose Hilo, M. (2003), 'TiVo and the Incentive/Dissemination Conflict: The Economics of Extending Betamax to Personal Video Recorders', *Washington University Law Quarterly*, **81** (4), 1043–68.
97. *Twentieth Century Fox Film Corporation* v. *Cablevision Systems Corporation* 2007 WL 867093 (S.D.N.Y.), 82 U.S.P.Q.2d 1075 (2007).
98. *Twentieth Century Fox Film Corporation* v. *Cablevision Systems Corporation* 1:06-cv-03990-DC – Answer (2006).
99. *Twentieth Century Fox Film Corporation* v. *Cablevision Systems Corporation* 2007 WL 867093 (S.D.N.Y.), 82 U.S.P.Q.2d 1075 (2007).
100. Block, R. (2005), 'Interview with Blake Krikorian', *Engadget*, http://www.engadget.com/entry/1234000933050954/,18 July.
101. Slingbox, http://www.slingmedia.com/.
102. Slingbox, http://www.slingmedia.com/.
103. Wallenstein, A. (2005), 'Slingbox Could Spark New Lawsuits', *Hollywood Reporter*, http://www.hollywoodreporter.com/thr/article_display.jsp?vnu_content_id=1000973572, 6 July.
104. *RIAA* v. *Diamond Multimedia Systems Inc*. 180 F.3d 1072 (1999).
105. *UMG Recordings, Inc.* v. *MP3.Com, Inc*. 92 F.Supp.2d 349 S.D.N.Y (2000).
106. *Metro-Goldwyn-Mayer Studios Inc*. v. *Grokster, Ltd*. 125 S.Ct. 2764 (2005).
107. There is a sizeable amount of literature on the *Audio Home Recording Act* 1992 (US). See, for instance, Lutzker, G. (1992), 'DAT's All Folks: Cahn v. Sony and the Audio Home Recording Act of 1991 – Merrie Melodies or Looney Tunes', *Cardozo Arts and Entertainment Law Journal*, **11**, 145–90; McKuin, J. (1994), 'Home Audio Taping of Copyrighted Works and the Audio Home Recording Act of 1992: A Critical Analysis', *Hastings Communication and Entertainment Law Journal*, **16**, 317–48; Melville, A. (2001), 'The Future of the Audio Home Recording Act of 1992: Has It Survived the

Millennium Bug?', *Boston University Journal of Science and Technology Law*, **7**, 372–405; and Elkman, S. and A. Christie (2004), 'A Negotiated Solution to Audio Home Recording? Lessons from the US Audio Home Recording Act of 1992', *University of New South Wales Law Journal*, **27**(1), 123–46.

108. Goldstein, Paul (2003), *Copyright's Highway: From Gutenberg to the Celestial Jukebox*, Stanford: Stanford University Press, p. 133.
109. *RIAA* v. *Diamond Multimedia Systems Inc*. 180 F.3d 1072 (1999).
110. Consumer Electronics Manufacturers Association (1999), 'Amicus Brief in *RIAA* v. *Diamond Multimedia Systems Inc*'.
111. Ibid.
112. Ibid.
113. Ibid.
114. *RIAA* v. *Diamond Multimedia Systems Inc*. 180 F.3d 1072 (1999).
115. *A&M Records Inc* v. *Napster Inc* 114 F. Supp. 2d 896 (2000); 239 F.3d 1004 (2001); and *In re Aimster Copyright Litigation* 334 F.3d 643 (2003).
116. Fisher, William (2004), *Promises to Keep: Technology, Law, and the Future of Entertainment*, Stanford: Stanford University Press, p. 86.
117. Ibid.
118. Ibid., at 86–7.
119. *UMG Recordings, Inc.* v. *MP3.Com, Inc*. 92 F.Supp.2d 349 S.D.N.Y. (2000).
120. *UMG Recordings, Inc.* v. *MP3.Com, Inc*. 2000 WL 34474983, United States District Court, S.D. New York. Trial Pleading.
121. *UMG Recordings, Inc.* v. *MP3.Com, Inc*. 92 F.Supp.2d 349 S.D.N.Y. (2000).
122. Ibid.
123. *UMG Recordings, Inc.* v. *MP3.Com, Inc*. 92 F.Supp.2d 349 at 351 S.D.N.Y. (2000).
124. See, e.g., *Infinity Broadcast Corporation* v. *Kirkwood*, 150 F.3d 104, 108 (2d Cir.1998); *Los Angeles News Service* v. *Reuters Television Int'l Ltd.*, 149 F.3d 987 (9th Cir.1998), 525 U.S. 1141, 119 S.Ct. 1032, 143 L.Ed.2d 41 (1999); *American Geophysical Union* v. *Texaco Inc.*, 60 F.3d 913, 923 (2d Cir.), cert. dismissed, 516 U.S. 1005, 116 S.Ct. 592, 133 L.Ed.2d 486 (1995); and *Basic Books, Inc.* v. *Kinko's Graphics Corporation*, 758 F.Supp. 1522, 1530-31 S.D.N.Y. (1991).
125. Fisher, William (2004), *Promises to Keep: Technology, Law, and the Future of Entertainment*, Stanford: Stanford University Press, p. 102.
126. Vivendi Universal (2001), 'Vivendi Universal Acquires MP3.com in Move to Strengthen Digital Distribution Capacity and Web audience', Paris and San Diego, 21 May.
127. Fisher, William (2004), *Promises to Keep: Technology, Law, and the Future of Entertainment*, Stanford: Stanford University Press, p. 102.
128. *MP3.com, Inc*. v. *Cooley Godward LLP*, No. BC 266625 (Filed, L.A. Super. Ct., Jan. 2002).
129. Sandburg, B. (2002), 'Cooley Godward named in malpractice action', *The National Law Journal*, 28 January.
130. Katyal, S. (2002), 'A Legal Malpractice Claim By MP3.com: In The Changing Area Of Cyberlaw, Is A Crystal Ball Necessary To Avoid Liability?', Findlaw, 7 February.
131. *Atlantic Recording Corporation* et al. v. *XM Satellite Radio Inc*. NYSDCE 1:2006cv03733 (2006).
132. Ibid.
133. XM Satellite Radio (2006), 'Statement to XM Subscribers – The XM Nation', http://radio.about.com/od/xmsatelliteradio/a/aa051806a.htm.
134. Home Recording Rights Coalition (2006), 'Record Labels Break Compacts with Consumers, Congress, and Courts: Suit Against XM Trashes Labels' AHRA and Grokster Assurances', 17 May.
135. Schwartz, R. (2006), 'Recording Rights Under Attack Again', Public Knowledge, http://www.publicknowledge.org/node/306, 20 April.
136. Lee, J. (2004), 'Click at your Own Risk', *The Sydney Morning Herald*, 3 August.
137. Bowrey, Kathy (2005), *Law and Internet Cultures*, Cambridge: Cambridge University Press, p. 158.

138. O'Brien, M. (2003), 'CNN Talks to Steve Jobs About iTunes', http://www.cnn.com/2003/TECH/industry/04/29/jobs.interview/, 27 November.
139. Goldsmith, Jack and Tim Wu (2006), *Who Controls the Internet? Illusions of a Borderless World*, Oxford: Oxford University Press, pp. 118–20.
140. Hammersley, B. (2004), 'Personal Soundtracks', *The Guardian*, http://www.guardian.co.uk/online/howto/story/0,15824,1433785,00.html, 2 December.
141. Ibid.
142. Vogele, Colette and Mia Garlick (2006), 'Podcasting Legal Guide: Rules for the Revolution', The Berkman Center Clinical Program in Cyberlaw, Harvard Law School, http://mirrors.creativecommons.org/Podcasting_Legal_Guide.pdf, March; and Astle, M. (2006), 'Will Congress Kill the Podcasting Star?', *Harvard Journal of Law and Technology*, **19**(1), 162–210.
143. Crofts, S., Dilley, J., Fox, M., Retsema, A. and B. Williams (2005), 'Podcasting: A New Technology In Search of Viable Business Models', *First Monday*, **10**(9), http://firstmonday.org/issues/issue10_9/crofts/index.html.
144. APRA/AMCOS (2005), 'Fair Use and other Copyright Exceptions: An Examination of Fair Use, Fair Dealing and other Exceptions in the Digital Age', Submission to the Attorney General's Department.
145. *Metro-Goldwyn-Mayer Studios Inc.* v. *Grokster, Ltd.* 125 S.Ct. 2764 (2005).
146. Oral proceedings in *Metro-Goldwyn-Mayer Studios Inc.* v. *Grokster, Ltd.* 125 S.Ct. 2764 (2005).
147. Ibid.
148. Ibid.
149. Ibid.
150. Ibid.
151. Lessig, L. (2005), 'A Rotten Ruling', *Wired Magazine*, **13** (9), 94.
152. Ibid.
153. McCue, A. (2004), 'iPod Users are Music Thieves says Ballmer', Silicon.com, http://management.silicon.com/itpro/0,39024675,39124642,00.htm, 4 October.
154. MacWorld Staff (2005), 'Warner Chief Calls Apple iTunes Price "Unfair"', MacWorld UK, http://www.macworld.co.uk/news/index.cfm?home&NewsID=12716, 23 September.
155. Darlymple, S. (2005), 'Steve Job Discusses iPods, Music Labels and Intel Macs', *MacWorld*, http://www.macworld.com/news/2005/09/20/jobsparis/index.php, 20 September.
156. MacWorld Staff (2005), 'Warner Chief Calls Apple iTunes Price "Unfair"', MacWorld UK, http://www.macworld.co.uk/news/index.cfm?home& NewsID=12716, 23 September.
157. Veiga, A. (2006), 'Music Labels, Apple Divided Over Pricing, As Talks Approach', *Associated Press*, 2 April.
158. *Paramount Pictures* v. *Load 'N Go Video* 06 CV 12931, (United States District Court, Southern District of New York, 3 November 2006).
159. In *Slattery* v. *Apple Computer Inc.* Not Reported in F.Supp.2d, 2005 WL 2204981 (N.D.Cal.), the United States District Court for the Northern District of California is considering a class action against Apple Computer Inc., alleging the unlawful tying of music purchased on iTunes Music Store with the purchase of iPods, and the unlawful acquisition or maintenance of monopoly market power.
160. In *Union Fédérale des Consommateurs – Que Choisir* v. *Apple Computer France S.A.R.L. and iTunes S.A.R.L.* (9 February 2005), a French consumer association filed a complaint alleging that Apple violated consumer law by failing to mention that the iPod was incompatible with music from online music services other than the iTunes Music Store, and tying the sales of iPods to the iTunes Music Store.
161. Associated Press (2006), 'French Law Seeks Inter-Operability', *Wired News*, http://www.wired.com/news/politics/0,70436-0.html, 17 March.
162. BBC (2006), 'Apple Attacks Plan to Open iTunes', BBC News, http://news.bbc.co.uk/2/hi/technology/4833010.stm, 22 March.
163. Reuters (2006), 'French Law "Piracy"', *The Australian*, 23 March.

164. Consumer Council of Norway (2006), 'Complaint Against iTunes Music Store', http://forbrukerportalen.no/filearchive/Complaint%20against%20iTunes%20Music%20Store.pdf, 25 January.
165. Reuters (2006), 'Apple in Scandinavian iTunes Talks', *The Australian*, 17 August.
166. A United Kingdom consumer association, 'Which?', lodged a complaint with the United Kingdom Office of Fair Trading that Apple was violating European Union competition law by charging more for online music in the United Kingdom than in the Eurozone countries. The charges were referred to the European Commission, which is investigating the matter under Articles 81 and 82 of the European Commission treaty.
167. Apple Computers has been involved in a number of trade mark disputes with Apple Corps, which is owned by The Beatles. In *Apple Corps Ltd* v. *Apple Computers* [2006] EWHC 996 (Ch), Mann J in the English High Court of Justice, Chancellery Division, considered the argument of Apple Corps that the use of the Apple logo in respect of the iTunes Music Store would amount to a breach of past agreements in respect of trade marks. The judge denied that a consumer would be confused between Apple Computers and Apple Corps: 'In my view the presence of a logo which is the logo of the download service would not be likely to be taken by such a user, without more, as a sort of trade association with the content beyond that of being a retailer'. Apple Computers has also had to fend off claims that the iPod, the iTunes software, and the Quicktime streaming software infringe upon patents held by Burst.com: Krazit, T. (2006), 'Burst.com Sues For Patent Infringement', CNET News, http://news.com.com/2100-1047_3-6062067.html, 17 April.
168. Shapiro, G. (2005), 'Protecting Copyright and Innovation in a Post-Grokster World', Testimony, *United States Senate Committee on the Judiciary*, 28 September.
169. Ibid.
170. Ibid.
171. Coombe, R. (2003), 'Fear, Hope, and Longing for the Future of Authorship and a Revitalized Public Domain in Global Regimes of Intellectual Property', *De Paul Law Review*, **52**, 1171–91, 1177.
172. Ibid.
173. Ibid.
174. Ibid.
175. Ibid.
176. The Australian Subscription and Television Association (ASTRA) argued that Australia was out of step with international trends: 'Australia is the only major common law jurisdiction that does not provide a fair dealing or fair use right that permits copyright users at least the right to use video or hard drive recording devices to time-shift television programming'. ASTRA lamented: 'At present, the Act does not reflect the reality of the VCR, DVD recorder or PDR, let alone technologies that have yet to be developed'. Astra (2005), 'Fair Use and Other Copyright Exceptions', http://www.astra.org.au/content/ pdf/FairUseJuly05.pdf.
177. Black, M. (2005), 'Time for Fair Use to Free Up Technology', *The Sydney Morning Herald*, 28 January.
178. Ruddock, P. (2006), 'Major Copyright Reforms Strike Balance', Attorney-General's Department, Australian Government, 14 May.
179. Ibid.
180. Screenrights (2005), 'Screenrights' Response to the Attorney-General's *Fair Use and Other Copyright Exceptions* Issues Paper 2005', 13, http://ww.screen.org/submissions/ScreenrightsFairUseSu4BE09.pdf.
181. Gowers, Andrew (2006), *Gowers Review of Intellectual Property*, London: HM Treasury, December, http://www.hm-treasury.gov.uk/media/583/91/pbr 06gowersreport755.pdf, 63.

3. The privateers of the information age: copyright law and peer-to-peer networks

> We should think of peer-to-peer devotees not as buccaneers, but as privateers – the patriots of the information age. (Kathy Bowrey, *Law and Internet Cultures*[1])

In January 1999, as a teenager and freshman at Northeastern University, Shawn Fanning developed the original Napster application and service.[2] He combined the practicality of sharing personal music and finding MP3s online with the community features of Internet Relay Chat. The Napster technology allows users to exchange MP3 files stored on their own computer hard-drives directly, without payment. It also provides media fans with a forum to communicate their interests and tastes with one another via instant messaging, chat rooms, and Hot List user bookmarks. Napster originally had no technological means of checking the legitimacy of the files trading on the system.

The Recording Industry Association of America (RIAA) filed suit against Napster, Inc., operators of the website Napster.com, accusing them of violating federal and state laws through 'contributory and vicarious copyright infringement'.[3] The complaint describes the case as follows: 'Napster is similar to a giant online pirate bazaar: users log onto Napster servers and make their previously personal MP3 collections available for download by other Napster users who are logged on at the same time.'[4] The heavy metal band Metallica and the rap musician Dr Dre brought legal action against Napster, as well as Yale University, the University of Southern California and Indiana University, alleging that they were complicit in music piracy. They also named a number of anonymous Jane Does – individual consumers who had been using Napster.

Metallica staged and orchestrated a media event in order to publicize the litigation against Napster. The drummer of the band, Lars Ulrich, showed up at the Fourth Street headquarters of Napster Inc. to deliver the names of 334 435 Napster users who made 1.45 million Metallica songs available for free downloads. He told a news conference: 'If they want to steal Metallica's music, instead of hiding behind their computers in their bedrooms and dorm rooms then just go down to Tower Records and grab them off the shelves.'[5]

In the United States District Court for the Northern District of California, Patel J held that Napster was liable for contributory and vicarious copyright infringement.[6] Her Honour ruled that sampling, space-shifting and listening to authorized works were not substantial non-infringing uses of Napster. Patel J denied that Napster could shelter under the *Sony Betamax* decision:

> [The] Defendant fails to show that space-shifting constitutes a commercially significant use of Napster. Indeed, the most credible explanation for the exponential growth of traffic to the website is the vast array of free MP3 files offered by other users – *not* the ability of each individual to space-shift music she already owns. Thus, even if space-shifting is a fair use, it is not substantial enough to preclude liability under the staple article of commerce doctrine.[7]

Patel J also dismissed arguments about Napster users merely exercising home recording rights. She held that the *Audio Home Recording Act* 1992 (US) was irrelevant to the action: 'Neither the record company nor music publisher plaintiffs have brought claims under the [*Audio Home Recording Act* 1992 (US)]; moreover, the Ninth Circuit did not hold in Diamond Multimedia that the [*Audio Home Recording Act* 1992 (US)] covers the downloading of MP3 files.'[8] Patel J disagreed that Napster was a mere ISP entitled to 'safe harbour' protection under the *Digital Millennium Copyright Act* 1998 (US) (*DMCA*). In any case, she observed that the company was precluded from the benefit of such protection because its executives had actual knowledge of copyright infringement on the network.[9] Patel J was disinclined to take into account competition policy or First Amendment principles.[10] She granted a preliminary injunction to the record companies, preventing Napster 'from engaging in, or facilitating others in copying, downloading, uploading, transmitting, or distributing plaintiffs' copyrighted musical compositions and sound recordings'.[11]

The Federal Court of Appeals for the 9th Circuit considered the arguments of Napster that sampling, space-shifting and playing authorized sound recordings were substantial, non-infringing uses of the service.[12] The judges held that the practice of file-sharing was not analogous to time-shifting or space-shifting because it went beyond personal home copying and involved the distribution of copyrighted material to the general public. Beezer J doubted that Napster could avail itself of the protection provided under the *Sony Betamax* decision or the *Diamond Multimedia* case:

> We conclude that the district court did not err when it refused to apply the 'shifting' analyses of *Sony* and *Diamond.* Both *Diamond* and *Sony* are inapposite because the methods of shifting in these cases did not also simultaneously involve distribution of the copyrighted material to the general public; the time or spaceshifting of copyrighted material exposed the material only to the

original user. In *Diamond*, for example, the copyrighted music was transferred from the user's computer hard drive to the user's portable MP3 player. So too *Sony*, where 'the majority of VCR purchasers did not distribute taped television broadcasts, but merely enjoyed them at home'. Conversely, it is obvious that once a user lists a copy of music he already owns on the Napster system in order to access the music from another location, the song becomes 'available to millions of other individuals', not just the original CD owner.[13]

The Court affirmed the findings of Patel J in respect of the *Audio Home Recording Act* 1992 (US) and the safe harbour provisions of the *DMCA*.[14] Beezer J was similarly reluctant to indulge in wider policy discussion about competition law and freedom of speech. The Federal Court of Appeals for the 9th Circuit, though, did rule that the preliminary injunction granted by the District Court had been overly-broad. The judges emphasized that the record companies had the burden of providing notice to Napster of copyrighted works and files on the system: 'Napster, however, also bears the burden of policing the system within the limits of the system.'[15]

After losing cases in the District Court and the Federal Court of Appeals for the 9th Circuit, the company resisted being taken over by the German record company Bertelsmann,[16] and ended up in the bankruptcy court. Nonetheless, it seems that the Napster brand is not entirely moribund. A recent advertisement in the magazine *Wired* featured a long-haired millenarian waving around a sign promoting the second coming of Napster.[17] It seems that Napster, under new ownership, has been resurrected, in an act of necromancy, as an authorized distributor of on-line music, with the moniker 'It's Back (And It's Legal)'.[18]

In the wake of the litigation against Napster, the RIAA filed a lawsuit against a peer-to-peer network called Aimster, later renamed Madster.[19] In this case, Posner J for the Federal Court of Appeals for the 7th Circuit, held that Aimster was liable for contributory infringement because of its wilful blindness to the activities of its users.[20] His Honour ruled that the service was not entitled to the defence of fair use: 'Aimster has failed to produce any evidence that its service has ever been used for a noninfringing use, let alone evidence concerning the frequency of such uses.'[21] The judge also found that Aimster was not shielded by the safe harbour defence: 'Far from doing anything to discourage repeat infringers of the plaintiffs' copyrights, Aimster invited them to do so, showed them how they could do so with ease using its system, and by teaching its users how to encrypt their unlawful distribution of copyrighted materials disabled itself from doing anything to prevent infringement.'[22] Posner J was unsympathetic to arguments made about freedom of speech and constitutional law: 'Copyright law and the principles of equitable relief are quite complicated enough without the superimposition of First Amendment case law on them.'[23] Although a guru of the Chicago School of Law and Economics, Posner J was not the slightest bit concerned about the impact of copyright law upon competition in the marketplace. The judge also draws some bizarre analogies between peer-to-peer networks and criminal law, in the fields of drug trafficking and prostitution. The decision reveals a deep, abiding hostility to peer-to-peer networks.

This chapter considers recent litigation over peer-to-peer networks, such as Grokster, Kazaa, and BitTorrent.[24] It emphasizes the social life of copyright law, considering legal cases, political processes and media controversies. This inquiry focuses upon the practical application of copyright law, as well as its performative power. Cultural critic, Kate Crawford, comments:

> Just as the cases against centralized services such as Napster caused users to move towards more surreptitious and decentralized peer-to-peer networks, the crackdown on individuals' file-sharing has unwittingly generated a larger and more complex set of activities. This is driving the evolution of a new breed of camouflaged, encrypted networks.[25]

This discussion has three elements. Section one of this study examines the Supreme Court of the United States' ruling in the case of *Metro-Goldwyn-Mayer Studios Inc.* v. *Grokster, Ltd*[26] (*Grokster*) that Grokster and StreamCast had induced copyright infringement. Section two considers the Federal Court of Australia decision in *Universal Music Australia Pty Ltd* v. *Sharman License Holdings Ltd* (*Kazaa*)[27] that the operators of Kazaa had authorized copyright infringement. Section three considers the legal implications of the software, BitTorrent. It reflects upon legal action taken against BitTorrent websites such as TorrentSpy, eDonkey, Razorback2, Niteshadow.com and the Pirate Bay.

I. 'A 21ST-CENTURY PIRATICAL BAZAAR': GROKSTER AND STREAMCAST

The Motion Picture Association of America (MPAA) and the RIAA filed copyright infringement lawsuits against three file-trading services, Grokster, Streamcast and Kazaa BV. The pleadings of the entertainment companies declared: '[The] defendants have created a 21st-century piratical bazaar where the unlawful exchange of protected materials takes place across the vast expanses of the Internet, and where the materials being exchanged include first-run movies currently playing in theaters and hit songs from virtually every major recording artist'.[28]

In *Grokster*, Wilson J of the District Court for the Central District of California, held as a threshold matter that there was sufficient evidence of direct infringement by end users of the defendants' software: 'Just as in Napster, many of those who use Defendants' software do so to download copyrighted media files, including those owned by Plaintiffs, and thereby infringe Plaintiffs' rights of reproduction and distribution.'[29] Citing the decision of the United States Supreme Court in the *Sony Betamax* case, Wilson J affirmed: '[T]he sale of copying equipment, like the sale of other articles of commerce, does not constitute contributory infringement' if the product is 'capable of substantial noninfringing uses'.[30] His Honour observed that the Morpheus program was capable of substantial non-infringing uses:

> Here, it is undisputed that there are substantial noninfringing uses for Defendants' software, e.g., distributing movie trailers, free songs or other non-copyrighted works; using the software in countries where it is legal; or sharing the works of Shakespeare.[31]

Wilson J. held that the distributors were not liable for contributory infringement because there was no evidence that they had any material involvement in the users' conduct.[32] His Honour also held that the distributors were not liable for vicarious infringement because it had not been demonstrated that they had the right or ability to supervise users' conduct. Wilson J observed that 'neither StreamCast nor Grokster facilitates the exchange of files between users in the way Napster did'.[33] Wilson J acknowledged that the peer-to-peer networks had been structured in such a way as to evade the threat of contributory infringement: 'The Court is not blind to the possibility that Defendants may have intentionally structured their businesses to avoid secondary liability for copyright infringement, while benefiting financially from the illicit draw of their wares.'[34] Nonetheless, his Honour observed that it was the role of the United States Congress to reform copyright law: 'To justify a judicial remedy, however, Plaintiffs invite this Court to expand existing copyright law beyond its well-drawn boundaries.'[35] As a result, Wilson J granted summary judgment in favour of Grokster and Streamcast, albeit reluctantly.

The United States Court of Appeal for the 9th Circuit heard oral argument in the *Grokster* case in February 2004.[36] After deliberating on the matter, the court held that decentralized peer-to-peer networks such as Grokster could not be held liable for contributory or vicarious copyright infringement, because they could not police the conduct of their users, as Napster could.[37] Thomas J observed that the software was capable of substantial, non-infringing uses and mentioned the example of the popular band Wilco which was able to obtain a new recording contract after their work was circulated on peer-to-peer networks.[38] His Honour observed that the courts were an inappropriate forum to resolve such clashes over market forces and technological change:

> We live in a quicksilver technological environment with courts ill-suited to fix the flow of internet innovation. The introduction of new technology is always disruptive to old markets, and particularly to those copyright owners whose works are sold through well established distribution mechanisms. Yet history has shown that time and market forces often provide equilibrium in balancing interests, whether the new technology be a player piano, a copier, a tape recorder, a video recorder, a personal computer, a karaoke machine, or an MP3 player. Thus, it is prudent for courts to exercise caution before restructuring liability theories for the purpose of addressing specific market abuses, despite their apparent present magnitude.[39]

Thomas J was reluctant to accede to the demands of copyright owners to expand the reach of the doctrines of contributory and vicarious copyright infringement.[40] The Federal Circuit emphasized that it was the role of Congress to craft copyright laws in order to deal with new technologies.[41]

The Supreme Court of the United States agreed to consider whether Grokster and SteamCast Networks could be held responsible for their customers' online swapping of copyright songs and movies. A large number of amicus briefs were submitted in this matter.[42]

On appeal, the Supreme Court of the United States held that the Federal Court of Appeals for the 9th Circuit had erred in providing summary judgment in favour of Grokster and Streamcast, especially in view of the substantial evidence supporting MGM's case.[43] In the leading judgment, Souter J articulated a new theory of 'inducement' in order to explain the operation of contributory and vicarious copyright infringement. In a separate opinion, Ginsburg J expressed greater sympathy for the position of copyright owners. She was joined by Rehnquist CJ and Kennedy J. Breyer J wrote the third judgment, articulating and defending the benefits of the *Sony Betamax* rule. He was joined by Stevens J, the author of the original majority judgment in the *Sony Betamax* case, and O'Connor J, the late swing vote to the majority in the case.[44] It is worth exploring the three different visions as to the operation of copyright law in respect of peer-to-peer networks.

A. Souter J

In *Grokster*, the moderate Souter J crafts an 'inducement rule' in order to articulate secondary liability under the *Sony Betamax* judgment.[45] His Honour borrows liberally from patent law doctrine for inspiration:

> For the same reasons that *Sony* took the staple-article doctrine of patent law as a model for its copyright safe-harbor rule, the inducement rule, too, is a sensible

> one for copyright. We adopt it here, holding that one who distributes a device with the object of promoting its use to infringe copyright, as shown by clear expression or other affirmative steps taken to foster infringement, is liable for the resulting acts of infringement by third parties. We are, of course, mindful of the need to keep from trenching on regular commerce or discouraging the development of technologies with lawful and unlawful potential. Accordingly, just as *Sony* did not find intentional inducement despite the knowledge of the VCR manufacturer that its device could be used to infringe, mere knowledge of infringing potential or of actual infringing uses would not be enough here to subject a distributor to liability. Nor would ordinary acts incident to product distribution, such as offering customers technical support or product updates, support liability in themselves. The inducement rule, instead, premises liability on purposeful, culpable expression and conduct, and thus does nothing to compromise legitimate commerce or discourage innovation having a lawful promise.[46]

The judge held that 'the summary judgment record is replete with other evidence that Grokster and StreamCast, unlike the manufacturer and distributor in *Sony*, acted with a purpose to cause copyright violations by use of software suitable for illegal use'.[47]

Souter J held that there were three particularly notable features, which provided evidence of intent. First, Grokster and Streamcast sought to satisfy a known source of demand for copyright infringement, the market comprising former Napster users.[48] The judge believed such efforts indicated a principal, if not exclusive intent on the part of each to bring about infringement. Second, 'neither company attempted to develop filtering tools or other mechanisms to diminish the infringing activity using their software'.[49] This underscored the companies' intentional facilitation of their users' infringement. The judge added in a caveat that 'in the absence of other evidence of intent, a court would be unable to find contributory infringement liability merely based on a failure to take affirmative steps to prevent infringement, if the device otherwise was capable of substantial noninfringing uses'.[50] Finally, Souter J held that there was a further complement to the direct evidence of unlawful objective: 'It is useful to recall that StreamCast and Grokster make money by selling advertising space, by directing ads to the screens of computers employing their software.'[51]

Souter J concluded that the case of Grokster and StreamCast was significantly different from the classic *Sony Betamax* case. His Honour noted: '*Sony* dealt with a claim of liability based solely on distributing a product with alternative lawful and unlawful uses, with knowledge that some users would follow the unlawful course.'[52] By contrast, in this case, 'evidence of the distributors' words and deeds going beyond distribution as such shows a purpose to cause and profit from third-party acts of copyright infringement'.[53]

In a number of editorials, Lawrence Lessig argued that the elusive inducement test in *Grokster* would create great legal uncertainty.[54] He bemoaned 'Justice Souter's obtuseness to the costs of the complexity that he adds to the copyright system.'[55] Lessig observed that the decision would have a detrimental impact upon innovation by entrepreneurs and technologists. He complained that 'Justice Souter engages in common-law law-making, which is basically judges making up the law they want to apply to this particular case.'[56] Lessig argued that there is need to ensure that courts are not oblivious to the efficiency costs of legal rules.[57]

By contrast, Pamela Samuelson maintained that the Court's decision was welcome news for the technology community, because it did not revisit or disturb the safe harbour created by the *Sony Betamax* decision: 'This aspect of the Court's decision is, in itself, a considerable defeat for MGM and the entertainment industry which believed the "bad" facts of the Grokster case would be compelling enough to induce the Court to reinterpret Sony.'[58] Samuelson respectfully disagreed with the opinion of Lessig that the court's decision would have a chilling effect on innovation: 'Technology developers who induce copyright infringement should not expect to be treated any differently than those who induce patent infringement.'[59] She believed that 'there should be ample room for innovative technologies to continue to thrive', as long as 'the courts apply high standards for inducement liability'.[60] Samuelson observed: 'Although Justice Souter's opinion indicates that when there is other evidence of inducement, courts can consider technology design and business models in considering whether active inducement of infringement has occurred, it also makes clear that technology design and business models alone will not establish inducement liability.'[61]

Michael Geist took a similar tack, noting: 'While the highest court in the U.S. did indeed unanimously rule that two file sharing services – Grokster and Streamcast – can be sued for actively encouraging copyright infringement by their users, the decision is not the clear cut win its supporters suggest.'[62] He commented that the 'decision attempts to have it both ways, by holding out the prospect of liability for these particular services but preserving the principles that the technology community holds dear'.[63] Geist observed that 'the decision may actually provide helpful guidance to other file sharing services on how they can survive in the current legal climate'.[64]

Edward Felten, a computer scientist from Princeton University, was concerned that the Supreme Court 'engage[d] in exactly the kind of design second-guessing that technologists fear'.[65] He observed that 'the Court . . . criticizes Grokster and StreamCast for making a very reasonable engineering decision'.[66] Felten notes that 'there is every reason to believe that filtering technology would add to the cost and complexity of the companies' software, without substantially reducing infringement'.[67]

He worried about the risk of litigation: 'Legitimate technologists will still worry that a well-funded plaintiff can cook up a stew of product design second-guessing, business model second-guessing, and occasional failures of copyright compliance by low-level employees, into an active inducement case.'[68]

B. Ginsburg J

In *Grokster*, Ginsburg J reiterated her view that the primary purpose of copyright law is to promote the private interest of copyright owners – the profit motive. She believed that the lower courts, rather than granting summary judgment, should have considered whether Grokster and Streamcast could be held contributorily liable for user copyright infringements. Her Honour observed:

> In sum, when the record in this case was developed, there was evidence that Grokster's and StreamCast's products were, and had been for some time, overwhelmingly used to infringe, and that this infringement was the overwhelming source of revenue from the products. Fairly appraised, the evidence was insufficient to demonstrate, beyond genuine debate, a reasonable prospect that substantial or commercially significant noninfringing uses were likely to develop over time.[69]

Ginsburg J held that the case of Grokster and StreamCast differed markedly from the *Sony Betamax* case because there had been no finding of any fair use and little beyond 'anecdotal evidence' of non-infringing uses. She complained that the District Court and the Court of Appeals relied, uncritically, upon 'assertions (some of them hearsay) that a number of copyright owners authorise distribution of their works on the Internet and that some public domain material is available through peer-to-peer networks including those accessed through Grokster's and StreamCast's software'.[70] While she did not endorse the 'primary use' standard of contributory liability which MGM advocated, Ginsburg J seemed to place greater demands upon the developers of infringement-enabling technologies than other members of the Court.

Professor Timothy Wu, a former clerk of Posner J and Breyer J, was concerned about the emphasis placed in the decision upon the bad intent of Grokster.[71] He found this Jane Austen-like obsession with good manners, respectability and etiquette of the parties to be troubling:

> The theme is respectability and etiquette. The . . . view is that there are sometimes well-mannered and ill-mannered ways to do something – and that in hard cases, how you do things can make all the difference. It's almost like the

> Miss Manners' School of Jurisprudence – be polite and ask nicely, and you'd be surprised what can be done.[72]

Wu suggests that the peer-to-peer networks in *Grokster* lacked proper etiquette: 'The P2P companies were loud scofflaws, foreigners, and college students who blatantly encouraged illegal acts.'[73] He observed that, by contrast, Apple iTunes had avoided litigation because of its respectability: 'Steve Jobs is a rebel with manners.'[74]

C. Breyer J

In *Grokster*, Breyer J sought to provide a rearguard defence of the *Sony Betamax* decision, protecting its principles from revision or strict interpretation by copyright owners. His Honour emphasized that the *Sony Betamax* decision itself sought to 'strike a balance between a copyright holder's legitimate demand for effective – not merely symbolic – protection of the statutory monopoly, and the rights of others freely to engage in substantially unrelated areas of commerce'.[75] Breyer J articulated simply and cogently the benefits of the *Sony Betamax* rule. The judge denied the assertion of MGM that the decision incorrectly balanced copyright and new technology interests.

First of all, Breyer J argued that the *Sony Betamax* decision has worked to defend new technologies: '*Sony's* rule, as I interpret it, has provided entrepreneurs with needed assurance that they will be shielded from copyright liability as they bring valuable new technologies to market.'[76] The judge protested, '*Sony's* rule is clear.'[77] He noted that its 'clarity allows those who develop new products that are capable of substantial noninfringing uses to know, ex ante, that distribution of their product will not yield massive monetary liability'.[78] His Honour observed that the decision recognized that copyright laws should not discourage or control the emergence of new technologies that help disseminate ideas and information: '*Sony's* rule shelters VCRs, typewriters, tape recorders, photocopiers, computers, cassette players, compact disc burners, digital video recorders, MP3 players, Internet search engines, and peer-to-peer software.'[79] The judge emphasized that '*Sony's* rule is forward looking' because it focuses upon capability.[80] He observed: 'It does not confine its scope to a static snapshot of a product's current uses (thereby threatening technologies that have undeveloped future markets).'[81] Breyer J also stressed that '*Sony's* rule is mindful of the limitations facing judges where matters of technology are concerned.'[82] His Honour warned that judges should not be burdened with difficult determinations in relation to the feasibility, viability or marketability of new technologies.

Second, Breyer J questioned whether a modified *Sony Betamax* rule, or a strict interpretation, would significantly weaken the law's ability to protect new technology. His Honour commented that requiring technological developers to provide detailed evidence would provide additional risk and uncertainty:

> Inventors and entrepreneurs (in the garage, the dorm room, the corporate lab, or the boardroom) would have to fear (and in many cases endure) costly and extensive trials when they create, produce, or distribute the sort of information technology that can be used for copyright infringement. They would often be left guessing as to how a court, upon later review of the product and its uses, would decide when necessarily rough estimates amounted to sufficient evidence . . . The additional risk and uncertainty would mean a consequent additional chill of technological development.[83]

Breyer J was disinclined to adopt any of the numerous alternative tests for secondary infringement that MGM and those who supported its position had proffered for the Court's consideration, such as whether the principal use of a technology was for infringement. His Honour was also opposed to demanding a higher evidentiary burden: 'Justice Ginsburg's approach would require defendants to produce considerably more concrete evidence – more than was presented here – to earn Sony's shelter.'[84]

Third, Breyer J considered whether a positive impact for copyright holders, as a result of the reforms, would outweigh any technology-related loss. His Honour conceded: 'I do not doubt that a more intrusive *Sony* test would generally provide greater revenue security for copyright holders.'[85] Breyer J was unconvinced, though, that the gains for copyright owners would outweigh the losses caused to new technologies: 'For one thing, the law disfavors equating the two different kinds of gain and loss; rather, it leans in favor of protecting technology.'[86] He emphasized that courts must be circumspect in reading copyright law so as not to preclude the distribution of new technologies. It is worth recognizing how the judgment has been crafted to appeal more widely to Congress – by highlighting the need for fair use to protect innovation and entrepreneurial activities.

On the factual issues in the case, Breyer J shows a greater willingness than his counterpart, Ginsburg J, to accept evidence that there could be a significant future market for non-infringing uses of Grokster-type peer-to-peer software. His Honour observed that, as greater public domain information is stored in swappable form, it seems a likely inference that lawful peer-to-peer sharing will become increasingly prevalent:

> Such legitimate noninfringing uses are coming to include the swapping of research information (the initial purpose of many peer-to-peer networks); public domain films (e.g., those owned by the Prelinger Archive); historical

> recordings and digital educational materials (e.g., those stored on the Internet Archive); digital photos (OurPictures, for example, is starting a P2P photo-swapping service); 'shareware' and 'freeware' (e.g., Linux and certain Windows software); secure licensed music and movie files (Intent MediaWorks, for example, protects licensed content sent across P2P networks); news broadcasts past and present (the BBC Creative Archive lets users 'rip, mix and share the BBC'); user-created audio and video files (including 'podcasts' that may be distributed through P2P software); and all manner of free 'open content' works collected by Creative Commons (one can search for Creative Commons material on StreamCast).[87]

Such an expansive list will no doubt be useful in defining what legitimate non-infringing uses could fall within the defence of fair use. The special emphasis given to free software, open source software and Creative Commons licensed works suggests the potential for a positive interplay between the defence of fair use and contract law. The use of electronic publishing, podcasting and digital photograph exchanges are also defended. Breyer J observed: 'There may be other now-unforeseen noninfringing uses that develop for peer-to-peer software, just as the home-video rental industry (unmentioned in *Sony*) developed for the VCR.'[88] The judge argued that 'the foreseeable development of such uses, when taken together with an estimated 10% noninfringing material, is sufficient to meet Sony's standard'.[89]

As a result of the decision of the Supreme Court of the United States in *Grokster*, the operators of the peer-to-peer network, Grokster, agreed to a settlement with motion picture studios, record companies, and music publishers in November 2005.[90] Users logging onto the old website for Grokster receive the warning:

> The United States Supreme Court unanimously confirmed that using this service to trade copyrighted material is illegal. Copying copyrighted motion picture and music files using unauthorized peer-to-peer services is illegal and is prosecuted by copyright owners. There are legal services for downloading music and movies. This service is not one of them. YOUR IP ADDRESS . . . HAS BEEN LOGGED. Don't think you can't get caught. You are not anonymous.[91]

The site encourages visitors instead to log onto copyright industry websites, which promote respect for the exclusive rights of copyright owners.

Sharman Networks, the owners of Kazaa, reached a global settlement with the copyright owners in August 2006.

StreamCast continued to battle the copyright owners in court. The matter was remanded back to the United States District Court in the Central District of California.[92] Applying the Supreme Court of the United States' new doctrine of inducement, Wilson J ruled that evidence of StreamCast's unlawful intent was overwhelming. First, the judge noted that

StreamCast's software was used overwhelmingly for infringement. Second, Wilson J found that StreamCast actively courted Napster users through marketing, advertisements, and promotions. Third, the judge noted that StreamCast provided users with technical assistance for playback of copyrighted content. Fourth, Wilson J observed that StreamCast took steps to ensure that the technology it deployed would be capable of infringing use. Fifth, the judge commented that StreamCast's software was used overwhelmingly for infringement StreamCast's business model depended on massive infringing use. Sixth, Wilson J observed that StreamCast had taken no meaningful affirmative steps to prevent Infringement. Finally, the judge held that StreamCast could not reasonably claim ignorance of infringement. Accordingly, the court granted the motion for summary judgment as to StreamCast's liability for inducing copyright infringement through MusicCity/OpenNap and Morpheus.

II. HAIL TO THE THIEF: A TRIBUTE TO KAZAA

> The servers are in Denmark. The software is in Estonia. The domain is registered Down Under, the corporation on a tiny island in the South Pacific. The users – 60 million of them – are everywhere around the world. The next Napster? Think bigger. And pity the poor copyright cops trying to pull the plug.[93]

The peer-to-peer network Kazaa has been a formidable successor to Napster. This programme enables Internet users to search for and exchange digital media, including MP3 files, computer programs, films and e-books, with other users of file-sharing software powered by the FastTrack technology. Sharman Networks operates the Kazaa.com website, which serves as a central distribution and customer support hub for the software. The company is organized under the laws of the island-nation of Vanuatu and doing business principally in Australia. Nicola Hemming runs Sharman Networks through the Australian management company LEF Interactive, named after the French revolutionary slogan 'Liberty, Equality and Fraternity'. She waxes eloquent about the future of the venture:

> We are spearheading the delivery of possibly the biggest market-changing technologies ever available to human beings. It takes a visionary attitude to charter through difficult waters. What we are doing is an evolution, even, from the Internet.[94]

Sharman Networks entered into a joint enterprise partnership with Altnet, a subsidiary of Brilliant Digital Entertainment, a California-based multimedia company founded by Kevin Bermeister. Altnet provides digital rights management technology, a technology designed by Microsoft that 'wraps' licensed copyrighted content and enables users' access to that content on terms set by the copyright owner. When a Kazaa user searches for content, the Altnet files are displayed along with other content. An Altnet song or video game is downloaded like any other file. Unlike the case of illegally traded files, however, only those who pay a fee to Altnet can actually use the Altnet files. Sharman Networks optimistically claims that Kazaa is the world's largest distributor of licensed digital content over the internet.

Conversely, Kazaa has been denigrated by its detractors as a Robber Baron. It has been attacked as a purveyor of pornography, computer viruses and pirated copyright works. Jack Valenti of the MPAA had this to say about peer-to-peer networks:

> We know that the infestation of P2P not only threatens the well-being of the copyright industries but consumers and their families as well. As hearings in the House and Senate have conclusively established, downloading KaZaa, Gnutella, Morpheus, Grokster, etc., can lay bare your most private financial and personal information to identity thieves. It can bring into your home and expose your children to pornography of the most vile and depraved character imaginable. Most insidious of all, the pornography finds its way to your children disguised as wholesome material: your son or daughter may 'search' for 'Harry Potter' or 'Britney Spears', and be confronted with files that contain bestiality or child pornography . . . Therefore, the business model that current P2P networks celebrate as 'the digital democracy' is built on the fetid foundation of pornography and pilfered copyrighted works.[95]

Of course there is an element of truth in this statement. Peer-to-peer networks such as Kazaa have been used to circulate taboo and forbidden subject matter. However, Valenti overstates his case. He seems to be intent upon creating a moral panic about such networks amongst politicians and the wider public. His lurid claims deserve critical attention, as much as Kazaa's outlandish promises.

There has been litigation brought against Kazaa in three different jurisdictions: the Netherlands, the United States and Australia. In October 2001, the major American music labels and movie studios filed suit in the Netherlands against the company of Niklas Zennström, cofounder of Kazaa. Their goal was to shut down the service, and prevent the tens of millions of people sharing billions of copyrighted music, video and software files. In January 2002, while related legal action was pending against it in the Netherlands, Kazaa BV transferred ownership of key assets to the newly-formed Sharman Networks, Ltd.[96] Perhaps this flight was premature, given that Kazaa BV won its appeal in the Dutch Supreme Court.[97]

The record companies and motion picture studios filed law suits against the new owners of Kazaa in the United States. In *Grokster*, Wilson J of the

District Court of California held that Sharman Networks and LEF Interactive did enough business in the United States to be lawfully included as part of the *Grokster* lawsuit.[98] In response, Sharman Networks launched a law suit against the motion picture studios and record companies alleging that they were engaged in a conspiracy to monopolize and were refusing to deal with other parties, in violation of the *Sherman Act* 1890 (US).[99] Sharman Networks also sought declaratory relief for copyright misuse and unfair business practices.

Independent of the legal action in the Netherlands and the United States, the record industry initiated separate proceedings against Kazaa in Australia.[100] In *Kazaa*, Wilcox J held that the operators of Kazaa[101] authorized copyright infringement by the users of the system.[102] The judge declined, though, to find in favour of the record industry that Sharman Networks and its affiliates had breached the *Trade Practices Act* 1974 (Cth) and fair-trading laws by engaging in misleading and deceptive conduct.[103] His Honour also doubted whether Sharman Networks and its affiliates had entered into a conspiracy to use unlawful means to injure record companies. The judge noted that the case was best understood in terms of copyright law: 'It would have been preferable if the applicants had refrained from further burdening an already heavy case by including these claims.'[104]

A. Authorization

Early in the trial, Wilcox J directed the parties to concentrate upon the central question of whether Sharman Networks and Altnet had authorized copyright infringement through the peer-to-peer network, Kazaa. His Honour observed:

> It really comes down to whether or not you can be said to authorise the infringements and that in turn probably comes down to the question of what . . . steps, if any, you take that can be said to be [by] way of encouragement . . . That's what really the case is all about.[105]

Accordingly, the record industry sought to establish in the trial that Sharman and Altnet executives knew about copyright infringements on Kazaa, and that they failed to take reasonable steps to control it.

In the summary of his judgment, Wilcox J provides a pithy review of his findings in the case:

> The applicants overstated their case. It cannot be concluded, as the applicants claimed in their pleadings, that the respondents themselves engaged in communicating the applicants' copyright works. They did not do so. The more

> realistic claim is that the respondents authorised users to infringe the applicants' copyright in their sound recordings.[106]

Wilcox J found that a number of the respondents – Sharman Networks, management company LEF Interactive, Chief Executive Nicola Hemming, business partners Brilliant Digital Entertainment (BDE) and Altnet, and BDE Chief Executive Kevin Bermeister – were liable for authorizing copyright infringement.

Wilcox J emphasized that a number of factors supported this finding. First, his Honour held that respondents had long known that the Kazaa system was widely used for the sharing of copyright works:

> At all material times, it has been in Sharman's financial interest for there to be ever-increasing file-sharing, involving an ever-greater number of people. Sharman always knew users were likely to share files that were subject to copyright. At least since the Syzygy report in May 2003, Sharman, through Ms Hemming and Mr Morle, have been aware this was a major, even the predominant, use of the Kazaa system.[107]

His Honour concluded that 'despite the fact that the Kazaa website contains warnings against the sharing of copyright files, and an end user licence agreement under which users are made to agree not to infringe copyright, it has long been obvious that those measures are ineffective to prevent, or even substantially to curtail, copyright infringements by users'.[108] The judge surmised: 'It would have been obvious to [the operators of Kazaa] that, were those measures to prove effective, they would greatly reduce Kazaa's attractiveness to users and, therefore, its advertising revenue potential'.[109]

Second, the judge noted that the respondents had failed to take technological measures that would curtail the sharing of copyright files. Wilcox J believed that it was possible for Sharman Networks to take such measures:

> Sharman was in a position, through keyword filtering or gold file flood filtering, to prevent or restrict users' access to identified copyright works; in that sense, Sharman could control users' copyright infringing activities. Sharman did not do so; with the result that the relevant applicant's copyright in each of the Defined Recordings was infringed.[110]

The judge observed: 'It is in the respondents' financial interest to maximise, not to minimise, music file-sharing.'[111] His Honour concluded: 'Sharman had power (in the case of gold file flood filtering, in conjunction with Altnet) to prevent, or at least substantially to reduce, the incidence of copyright file-sharing'.[112]

Finally, Wilcox J was highly critical of the marketing campaign launched by Sharman Networks entitled 'Join the Revolution' designed to mobilize consumer support and garner industry acceptance. The campaign included print advertisements in a number of international and college newspapers, and online advertisements on *yahoo.com*, *billboard.com*, *wired.com* and *rollingstone.com*.[113] Wilcox J observed that 'far from taking steps that are likely effectively to curtail copyright file-sharing, Sharman Networks and Altnet have included on the Kazaa website exhortations to users to increase their file-sharing and a webpage headed "Join the Revolution" that criticises record companies for opposing peer-to-peer file-sharing'.[114] His Honour found that this web campaign would 'encourage visitors to think it "cool" to defy the record companies by ignoring copyright constraints'.[115]

Wilcox J agreed with the record companies that the Kazaa system was a joint venture between Sharman and Altnet under which Sharman provides the FastTrack peer-to-peer technology and Altnet supplies the TopSearch licensed file technology; the two systems were closely integrated and the two companies' interests were interdependent. His Honour observed: 'It is plain that Altnet had a lively, ongoing interest in the operation of the Kazaa system and its profitability'.[116] The judge held that Nicola Hemming could also be held liable for authorizing copyright infringement, because of her control over Sharman Networks: 'Whatever the ultimate ownership of the company, Ms Hemming has always been in charge of its day-to-day activities.'[117] In respect of the principal of Altnet, Wilcox J held that 'Mr Bermeister's degree of personal involvement in Altnet's and BDE's authorising conduct was such as to make it just that he be rendered liable for infringement of the applicants' copyright.'[118] His Honour doubted, though, that the chief technology officers of Sharman Networks and Altnet should be also held liable for authorizing copyright infringement.

B. Fair Dealing

Sharman Networks had hoped to raise the defence of fair use in the event of litigation over copyright infringement. The company's alliance with Altnet was designed to demonstrate that Kazaa had substantial non-infringing uses. Sharman Networks also made a number of press releases detailing further legitimate uses of the peer-to-peer network. For instance, it announced that it would distribute a Bollywood film–Hindi-language thriller *Supari*.[119] The company also distributed musical works by emerging artists, management organizations and independent record companies.[120]

In 2002, Sharman Networks argued that peer-to-peer networks such as Kazaa did not violate Australian copyright law. Nikki Hemming claimed rather tendentiously:

> P2P software is legal. The only superior court to have considered the copyright issues raised by P2P technology was the Dutch Appellate Court in 2001. That Court, relying on the precedent established in the *Sony Betamax* ruling of the United States Supreme Court, found the P2P software created and distributed by Kazaa BV and now distributed by Sharman was legal.[121]

However, Sharman Networks was concerned that the defence of fair dealing in Australia had been specifically confined to an exclusive set of purposes, such as research or study, criticism or review, reporting news and providing professional advice.[122] It was also worried that there was 'no "fair use" provision which would enable the owner of a legally purchased or legally downloaded music CD to make a back up copy or to copy onto hard disc including MP3s, iPods or similar'.[123]

The Communications Law Centre prepared an amicus curiae brief on behalf of the Australian Consumers' Association, Electronic Frontiers Australia, and New South Wales Civil Liberties Inc.[124] The Centre submitted that the Court should presume that authorization of the use of facilities is only for a lawful purpose, until rebutted. It argued that, where the product or technology was capable of substantial or commercially significant non-infringing uses, actual knowledge of infringing conduct should be required before authorization of infringement is found. The amici argued that it would be unfair and unrealistic to make software providers monitor content for infringement because Parliament intended to 'protect the messenger' through provisions such as sections 22(6) and 112E of the *Copyright Act* 1968 (Cth).

Wilcox J distinguished the Supreme Court of the United States decision in *Grokster* which had found that the peer-to-peer networks Grokster and Streamcast had induced copyright infringement.[125] His Honour noted: 'It had always been obvious that there were similarities between the Kazaa system and the Grokster and StreamCast systems.'[126] Nonetheless, Wilcox J emphasized that the Australian law on authorization of copyright infringement was distinct from United States law on contributory and vicarious infringement: 'Much of the Australian statutory law had no counterpart in United States law.'[127] His Honour concluded that, in the present case, 'the differences, both factual and legal, are such as to render *Grokster* of little assistance to me'.[128]

In any case, Wilcox J doubted that the peer-to-peer network was used for substantial non-infringing purposes:

> From time to time during the hearing of this case, counsel or a witness commented that Kazaa could be used in a non-infringing way. It was said that people might wish to share with others their own original literary or musical works, or they might desire to provide easy access to non-copyright works such as the plays of Shakespeare or poetry of Milton. In their Closing Submissions, counsel for the Sharman respondents referred to Project Gutenberg which, they said, 'contains 42,000 free public domain or licensed content files, including ebooks'. They said the ebooks include classic works such as *Don Quixote* and *Romeo and Juliet*, which may be shared using KMD. Counsel also mentioned Creative Commons, 'a method of licensing that allows users to distribute their own non-infringing material'.[129]

His Honour did not doubt that some people used Kazaa only in a non-infringing way, but he denied that was a substantial purpose of the peer-to-peer network: 'It seems unlikely that non-infringing uses would sustain the enormous Kazaa traffic claimed by the respondents.'[130]

C. Remedies

In the course of the trial, Wilcox J emphasized that any remedies granted to the copyright owners in the matter would be necessarily limited.[131] His Honour observed to the lawyers acting for the record industry: 'You're entitled to protect your copyright. You're not entitled to control the internet.'[132] Wilcox J also noted that any remedies he ordered would be limited to preventing the illegal distribution of copyrighted files on Kazaa and stressed that non-infringing uses of the peer-to-peer network would not be affected.[133] Furthermore, his Honour emphasized that the implied freedom to political communication recognized under the Australian Constitution would be important in deciding any remedies.[134]

Wilcox J commented in his judgment on the need to tailor the relief for the authorization of copyright infringement: 'There needs to be an opportunity for the relevant respondents to modify the Kazaa system in a targeted way, so as to protect the applicants' copyright interests (as far as possible) but without unnecessarily intruding on others' freedom of speech and communication.'[135] Wilcox J ordered that the respondents pay damages and 90 per cent of costs incurred by Universal Records. He also ordered that the Kazaa Internet file-sharing system could continue to operate but only if within two months it was modified to include technology to prevent copyright infringement.[136] As a result of the decision, there was a concern that the burden of enforcement may be shifted away from the rights holder and onto unrelated third parties, such as telecommunications carriers and ISPs.

The Full Federal Court of Australia heard an appeal against the decision of Wilcox J in *Kazaa*. Before the Court could hand down a judgment, the parties resolved their differences. In August 2006, Sharman Networks Ltd reached a global settlement of the *Kazaa* copyright cases in Australia and the United States.[137] As part of the agreement, the operators of Kazaa have agreed to pay US$115 million (AUD$152 million) compensation for past copyright infringements, and become a legal downloading business offering licensed music. The CEO of Sharman Networks, Nikki Hemming, observed optimistically of the agreement: 'This settlement marks the dawn of a new age of cooperation between P2P technology and content industries which will promise an exciting future for online distribution in general and Kazaa users in particular.'[138] The content industries were triumphant at the legal settlement obtained against Kazaa. Mitch Bainwol, the chairman and CEO of RIAA, observed: 'This is welcome news for the music community and the legal online music marketplace.'[139] It remains to be seen whether Sharman Networks Inc. and Altnet will have sufficient financial resources to bear the burden of such a heavy and onerous settlement.

Comparing the Supreme Court of the United States decision in *Grokster* and the Australian Federal Court decision in *Kazaa*, Jane Ginsburg and Sam Ricketson come to the conclusion that secondary liability for copyright infringement exists in Australia: 'While [it is] always difficult to predict future developments, it is possible that facilitators of online infringements may now be more vulnerable in Australia than in the US.'[140] Graeme Austin has also made comparisons between the two cases.[141]

Arguably, the *Kazaa* judgment is flawed in terms of its reasoning. The first problem with the judgment is that it is highly fact-specific. Although he makes heroic efforts, Wilcox J seems overwhelmed by the mass of detail in the trial. The second problem with the decision is that it fails to articulate clear principles as to what constitutes authorization. Wilcox J suggests that there are a number of factual indicia that might support a finding of authorization: knowledge of infringement, a failure to install proper filters, and a misguided public relations campaign, 'Join the Revolution'. However, he provides little guidance for technology developers and entrepreneurs in other factual scenarios: for instance, the developers of the iPod, TiVo, Foxtel iQ and Slingbox. The third problem with the case is its failure to address wider policy concerns. Wilcox J neglects to discuss the origins of P2P networks, and consider comparative law on the subject properly. He refuses to address wider policy concerns about competition and consumer rights. One can only hope future court cases seek to remedy the crude nature of Australian law on the authorization of copyright infringement.[142]

III. 'GIVE AND YE SHALL RECEIVE': BITTORRENT

In a note, Seth Miller observed that BitTorrent technology would come under scrutiny in the wake of the *Grokster* decision:

> The next frontier for the entertainment industry to tackle is BitTorrent technology. The torrent file is compact and provides close-to-original quality that is unmatched to date. Users of BitTorrent do not have to search a network for a file. Rather, users have to find a torrent by using websites that serve as databases; users only need to click on a torrent link to start downloading. BitTorrent is distinguishable from most P2Ps, though, because it 'is not advertising against its file transfers' and would pass if pressed under a financial benefit test.[143]

There has been much activity surrounding the BitTorrent technology, in terms of the agreement reached between BitTorrent Inc and Warner Bros about the distribution of authorized movie pictures and television programmes; as well as litigation against BitTorrent websites and trackers, such as Torrent Spy, isohunt.com, and The Pirate Bay.

A. BitTorrent

In 2002, software programmer Bram Cohen released BitTorrent as a free, open source project, a peer-to-peer file distribution tool. It has since been adopted by consumers of music, television and films. The name 'BitTorrent' refers to the distribution protocol, the original client application, and the .torrent file type. The website explains:

> BitTorrent is a free speech tool. BitTorrent gives you the same freedom to publish previously enjoyed by only a select few with special equipment and lots of money. ('Freedom of the press is limited to those who own one' – journalist A.J. Liebling.) The key to scaleable and robust distribution is cooperation. With BitTorrent, those who get your file tap into their upload capacity to give the file to others at the same time. Those that provide the most to others get the best treatment in return. ('Give and ye shall receive!').[144]

Cohen's approach is faster and more efficient than traditional P2P networking by sites like Kazaa and Morpheus. BitTorrent's architecture is based on a principle of reciprocity. The more files you are willing to share, the faster any individual torrent downloads to your computer. This prevents people from leeching, a classic peer-to-peer network problem in which too many people download files and refuse to upload, creating a drain on the system.

There has been both hope and fear that BitTorrent has the potential to have a wider application in television broadcasting. Journalist Clive

Thompson comments, 'BitTorrent transforms the Internet into the world's largest TiVo.'[145] In one case, a Stanford computer science graduate student put up on a web-site a 500-Mbyte torrent of *Outfoxed*, the documentary critical of Fox News. He had gained the permission of the film producer to distribute the work in this way. Within two months, 1500 people had downloaded the documentary. After that, the peers took over and hosted it themselves. The student observed, 'It's amazing – I'm a movie distributor. If I had my own content, I'd be a TV station.'[146] In the era of broadcasting, movie and television companies needed certain economies of scale in order to afford distribution. However, peer-casting could disrupt the established networks and channels of entertainment companies. Thompson suggests that 'the network of the future will resemble Yahoo! or Amazon.com – an aggregator that finds shows, distributes them in P2P video torrents, and sells ads or subscriptions to its portal'.[147]

Edward Felten argued that BitTorrent technology would be a litmus test for the Supreme Court standard for inducement.[148] He observed that the technology is widely used for both infringing and non-infringing purposes, with infringement probably predominating today. However, its creator originally created the software to support the sharing of concert recordings, only with the permission of the copyright owner. Felten notes: 'A court that followed the Grokster analysis closely would have to let BitTorrent off the hook.'[149] He observed, though, that the music and motion picture studios would be unwilling to tolerate the further existence of BitTorrent. Thus the scientist predicted a new round of strategic litigation by the copyright owners: 'We'll see a careful campaign of litigation against peer-to-peer services, trying to gradually stretch the noose of inducement liability until it fits around BitTorrent's neck.'[150] Failing that, he anticipated a push to get Congress to codify the industries' interpretation of the inducement rule.

In the wake of the *Grokster* decision, in November 2005, Bram Cohen, the creator of BitTorrent, entered into an agreement with Dan Glickman, the Chairman of the MPAA, to collaborate on inhibiting copyright piracy of films.[151] Bram Cohen commented that BitTorrent.com would remove links that direct users to copyright-protected content owned by MPAA companies from its search engine. He observed: 'BitTorrent, Inc. discourages the use of its technology for distributing films without a license to do so. As such, we are pleased to work with the film industry to remove unauthorized content from BitTorrent.com's search engine.'[152] As part of its corporate transformation, Bram Cohen and BitTorrent planned to enforce its trade marks in respect of BitTorrent against unauthorized users of the brand.[153]

In May 2006, the Warner Bros Home Entertainment Group entered into an agreement with BitTorrent Inc to use the technology to distribute television programmes and films.[154] Darcy Antonellis, Executive Vice

President, observed: 'The launch of a legal BitTorrent online video service allows us to extend our reach to places our content would not ordinarily be found legally and opens up new opportunities.'[155] BitTorrent will provide a platform to offer U.S. consumers legal content on both a video-on-demand and electronic sell-through basis, on the same date as the DVD release.[156]

B. TorrentSpy

At the same time, copyright owners have brought legal action against BitTorrent sites and web-sites, which facilitate the exchange of copyrighted materials.[157]

In February 2006, the MPAA announced a series of seven federal lawsuits against high BitTorrent sites such as TorrentSpy, isoHunt and eDonkey, Usenet hosts and peer-to-peer services.[158] This litigation was significant as it was the first time that the MPAA had targeted Web sites that index allegedly infringing content, as well as newsgroups that allowed users to attach infringing files to their messages containing movies, television shows, games and other protected works.

In February 2006, the MPAA brought legal action in the United States District Court – Central District for California against TorrentSpy, alleging that 'TorrentSpy.com is the world's most-visited site for obtaining infringing content using Torrent software.'[159] In its complaint, the MPAA asserted that the US District Court could claim personal jurisdiction, as the 'defendants enable users, including California residents, to access torrent files on their website'.[160] The movie studios argued:

> This is a case of willful and rampant infringement of copyright over the Internet. Defendants knowingly enable, encourage, induce and profit from massive online piracy – piracy Defendants could stop, but refuse to . . . As a direct result of Defendants' conduct, thousands of the most popular motion pictures and television shows – from new releases that are still in theaters to blockbuster DVD releases to today's most popular television shows – are infringed every day.[161]

Applying the formula for inducement developed in the *Grokster* case, the MPAA argued that the defendants should be held liable under the *Copyright Act* 1976 (US): 'Defendants' inducement of copyright infringement is apparent from, among other things, the overwhelming infringing content available on Defendants' torrent site and the indexing of torrent files according to the specific titles of copyrighted television programs'.[162] The MPAA argued that the defendants should be held liable as contributory copyright infringers for the infringing acts of users of their torrent site, especially as they had 'actual and constructive knowledge of the infringing activity that occurs on their torrent site'.[163] Moreover, the defendants should be held vicariously liable for the infringing acts of users because they could 'supervise and control the infringing activities that occur through the use of their torrent site'.[164]

In response, TorrentSpy argued that the case should be dismissed because the MPAA did not provide any evidence of primary infringement, or secondary responsibility. The attorneys for TorrentSpy warned: 'Plaintiffs' fears about copyright infringement over the Internet do not give them a license to launch a pre-emptive war against technical innovators whose products plaintiffs think are being used by infringers.'[165] The service sought shelter under the *Grokster* test, claiming that 'the complaint fails to allege any actual infringement whatsoever'.[166] TorrentSpy denied that it had the capacity to prevent copyright infringement through censoring torrent files on the basis of link and filename: 'Apparently, plaintiffs are demanding that defendants monitor the Internet as a whole for infringing materials at defendants' own expense and for the benefit of the entertainment industry.'[167] TorrentSpy also denied any actual or constructive knowledge of copyright infringement: 'At most there are claims that defendants have a duty to acquire knowledge by inspecting indices of uploads and comparing filenames found there with some speculative compendium of copyrighted titles.'[168] Finally, TorrentSpy denied that it had taken any affirmative steps to foster copyright infringement: 'Claims that defendants induced, caused or contributed to infringement are based on nothing more than categorical accusations and phantasms based on false impressions plaintiffs have intentionally constructed and that are analyzed in the factual presentation.'[169] Given such accusations, TorrentSpy argued that the same charges could be levelled against the search engine, Google: 'Everything alleged about defendants' website is true about Google, and even more so, because Google outperforms the allegations in the complaint.'[170]

EFF attorney Fred von Lohmann said that the courts had not yet ruled on whether search tools would be held liable for copyright infringement: 'We haven't had a case that really tests the case of whether providing an indexing service by itself is an infringement.'[171] The most relevant litigation – the record labels' suit against MP3.Board in 2000 – was settled before the issue came to trial.[172]

In *Columbia Pictures* v. *Fung*, the motion picture studios brought a legal action in the U.S. District Court for the Southern District of New York for copyright infringement against a Canadian, Gary Fung, and ten John Does in respect of the operations of isohunt.com, TorrentBox.com and Bthub.com.[173] The MPAA asserted jurisdiction, claiming that the defendants enabled users, including New York residents, to access torrent files. The complaint alleged:

> Defendants operate at least two torrent sites, Isohunt and Torrentbox, and related trackers. In doing so, the Defendants provide a material – indeed, an essential – contribution to the infringement of Plaintiffs' copyrighted movies and television programs. Furthermore, Defendants operate these websites and trackers with the object of enticing others to infringe Plaintiffs' copyrights . . . Defendants also have operated a service known as 'BTHub' in connection with the Isohunt website. This service increased the efficiency and reliability of successfully downloading Plaintiffs' copyrighted content when users selected torrents from the Isohunt website.[174]

The movie studios contended: 'The evidence of inducement is flagrant and voluminous and includes, but is not limited to, postings by the site operators discussing and encouraging the downloading of copyrighted content displays of images of infringing content on the site, an admission that Defendants' advertising revenue is tied to the draw of copyrighted content on the site, a refusal to filter infringing content and the intentional modification of torrent files obviously corresponding to infringing content to make it more likely that the torrents can be used to successfully download infringing works.'[175]

In *Columbia Pictures Industries Inc.* v. *Does 1–10*, the movie studios filed a John Doe lawsuit to learn the identity of the administrators of one of the most popular eDonkey sites, ED2K-It.com, located at Internet Protocol address 67.43.11.190.[176] The web-site was hosted by Liquid Web, an ISP headquartered in Lansing, Michigan, on a server located in or around Lansing, Michigan. The movie studios alleged that the defendants 'enable their users to locate and download infringing copies of Plaintiffs' valuable copyrighted motion pictures and television shows for free and without authorization'.[177] Moreover, the MPAA contended that the defendants 'profit unlawfully from the distribution of Plaintiffs' copyrighted movies and television programs.'[178] The complaint concludes that the administrators of ED2K-It.com were liable for inducement for copyright infringement, as well as contributory and vicarious copyright infringement. Rather than challenge the complaint, the administrators of the eDonkey site decided to shut it down.

The developer and distributor of eDonkey, and the President of MetaMachine Inc., Sam Yagan, gave testimony to the United States Senate Committee for the judiciary on the impact of the *Grokster* decision, and the legal tactics of the copyright industries:

> Many technology companies, including eDonkey, whose products can be used for infringement will simply find themselves unable to continue operations in a Post-Grokster world – not necessarily because they would lose under the new Grokster standard, but rather because they literally cannot afford the costs of mounting a legal defense. Companies like eDonkey must face the reality that confronting

> unimaginably larger opponents that can outspend small, under-funded technology companies to death makes the question of 'legal' or 'illegal' a moot point.[179]

Yagan explained that cease-and-desist notices from the RIAA had forced MetaMachine Inc. to dramatically change its business model and technological base: 'Because we cannot afford to fight a lawsuit – even one we think we would win – we have instead prepared to convert eDonkey's user base to an online content retailer operating in a 'closed'P2P environment.'[180] eDonkey has agreed to pay $US30 million to avoid potential copyright infringement lawsuits.[181]

In *Paramount Pictures Corp.* v. *Thompson*, the MPAA also brought a legal action against the administrators of NiteShadow.com, which had over 24 000 registered members and offered over 1000 science fiction television programmes and movie shows.[182] The complaint alleged that the 'defendants advertise their website and tracker as a place to find science fiction content, and they prominently display on the website home page the logos of various copyrighted science fiction movies and television programs'.[183] The MPAA also brought legal action against membership-based sites that enabled users of Newsgroups to find easily and download illegal content. Newsgroups are electronic bulletin boards which in recent years have become a major source of pirated content as users are able to attach movie, music and games files to their messages.[184] The MPAA argued that such newsgroups sought to induce copyright infringement of Plaintiffs' works, and operate their website with the object of promoting their use to infringe copyright.[185]

On 20 February 2006, Belgian and Swiss authorities shut down Razorback 2, the largest eDonkey server in the world, allowing 1.3 million users simultaneously to swap files. Dan Glickman, the chairman and CEO of the MPAA, exclaimed: 'By shaving the illegal traffic of copyrighted works facilitated by Razorback 2, we are depleting other illegal networks of their ability to supply Internet pirates with copyrighted works which is a positive step in our international effort to fight piracy.'[186] The Swiss authorities arrested the site's operator at his residence in Switzerland. At the same time, on the authority of a local magistrate, Belgian police seized the site's servers located at an Internet hosting centre in Zaventem, near Brussels. Executive Vice President and Worldwide Anti-Piracy Director of the MPAA, John Malcolm commented: 'I applaud the Swiss and Belgian authorities for their actions which are helping thwart Internet piracy around the world.'[187]

C. The Pirate Bay

A number of peer-to-peer networks raise larger issues about Internet jurisdiction and the operation of international law.[188] Neil Weinstock Netanel comments: 'Even if the industries win their battle in the United States, they face a serious risk of being unable to halt the operation of P2P file swapping sites from countries with laxer laws regarding copyright in general, or contributory infringement in particular.'[189] However, United States courts are increasingly taking an expansive view of jurisdiction. In *Grokster*, Wilson J of the District Court of California held that Sharman Networks and LEF Interactive did enough business in the United States to be lawfully included as part of the Morpheus–Grokster lawsuit.[190] In *Arista Records, Inc.* v. *Sakfield Holding Co.*, the District Court of Columbia asserted jurisdiction over puretunes.com, a Spanish based site that allowed users to download music.[191] In *Motown Record Co., L.P.* v. *iMesh.Com, Inc*, a number of record companies alleged that the 'peer-to-peer file sharing' system operated by the defendants facilitated the widespread theft of their valuable intellectual property.[192] Earth Station 5, apparently based in the Jenin refugee camp in the Palestinian Territories, boasted that it was beyond the range of legal threats from the RIAA and the MPAA.[193] Such controversies show that peer-to-peer networks will find it difficult to evade legal action for copyright infringement by secreting themselves in foreign jurisdictions outside the United States.

The BitTorrent website, The PirateBay.org, was founded by a Swedish anti-copyright group, Piratbyrån, or Pirate Bureau.[194] The site contains many torrents which point to copyright-protected material. The PirateBay.org has received a number of cease-and-desist notices and take down demands. For instance, attorneys from Dreamworks complained that the website reproduced, distributed and/or offered for sale the 'Shrek 2' motion picture. In response, the operators of The Pirate Bay responded, with some gratuitous insults:

> As you may or may not be aware, Sweden is not a state in the United States of America. Sweden is a country in northern Europe. Unless you figured it out by now, US law does not apply here. For your information, no Swedish law is being violated.[195]

A legal advisor for the service argues that The Pirate Bay is legal under Swedish statutory and case law, because the site's Stockholm-based servers provide only torrent files, without any copyright data: 'Until the law is changed so that it is clear that the trackers are illegal, or until the Swedish Supreme Court rules that current Swedish copyright law actually outlaws trackers, we'll continue our activities'.[196]

By contrast, the MPAA spokeswoman Kori Bernards insists The Pirate Bay violated copyright laws in a number of jurisdictions: 'Copyright laws are being enforced and upheld in countries all over the world and when you facilitate the illegal file swapping of millions of people around the world, you are subject to those laws.'[197] Sweden has since implemented the *European Community Information Society Directive*, which outlaws the copying, distribution, uploading and downloading of copyright material without the copyright holder's permission.[198]

In May 2006, Swedish police raided ten locations in central Sweden and shut down The Pirate Bay. Three people were detained for questioning on suspicion of violating copyright laws.[199] Dan Glickman applauded the action:

> The actions today taken in Sweden serve as a reminder to pirates all over the world that there are no safe harbors for Internet copyright thieves. Intellectual property theft is a problem for film industries all over the world and we are glad that the local government in Sweden has helped stop 'The Pirate Bay' from continuing to enable rampant copyright theft on the Internet.[200]

John Malcolm, an executive vice president of MPAA, accused the site of profiting from advertising associated with the site: 'The bottom line is that the operators of the Pirate Bay and others like them are criminals who profit handsomely by facilitating the distribution of millions of copyrighted creative works and files protected under the law.'[201]

Swedish copyright expert, Mathias Klang, provides an incisive analysis of the legal and ethical issues raised by the raid of The Pirate Bay:

> The Pirate Bay case is going to be exciting to watch because the people in control of The Pirate Bay are well aware of their legal position and of what they are doing. They will not have made the newbie mistake of having copyrighted material on their servers without permission. Is it illegal to do what The Pirate Bay does? . . . If The Pirate Bay are 'facilitating copyright infringement' then what about Google? or Flickr? Google helps me find images and texts of masses of copyrighted material. Flickr not only helps me find it but also helps me store it.[202]

He wonders whether the Swedish police exceeded their authority by removing property unconnected with The Pirate Bay: 'The Pirate Bay website today states that even servers containing material from organisations not connected with The Pirate Bay were taken – in this case this amounts to a serious violation of an organisation's ability to communicate.'[203] There has been much political controversy over the United States government and the MPAA pressuring the Swedish Minister for Justice, Thomas Bodström, to take action against The Pirate Bay.[204]

A few days after the police raid, the Pirate Bay was back online, as defiant as ever. As a result of the controversy, the Pirate Party ('Piratpartiet') – a Swedish political party committed to the abolishment of copyright law – boosted its membership.[205] Rasmus Fleischer, co-founder of the Piratbyrån, declared: 'We're actually delighted at the raids, as they have brought our issues to the front pages of newspapers, to the top of the TV news.'[206] The group espoused the credos of legalizing file sharing:

> The Pirate Party wants to restore the balance in the copyright legislation. All non-commercial copying and use should be completely free. File sharing and p2p networking should be encouraged rather than criminalized. Culture and knowledge are good things, that increase in value the more they are shared. The Internet could become the greatest public library ever created.[207]

There were physical demonstrations taken against the raid of The Pirate Bay in three of Sweden's largest cities, Stockholm, Malmö and Göteborg.[208] There has been denial of service attacks against the authorities and the Swedish Minister for Justice. The Pirate Party, though, failed to make an impact at the Swedish general election in 2006, recording about 33 000 votes, less than 1 per cent of the vote.[209]

CONCLUSION

In his concurring opinion in the *Grokster* case, Breyer J commented that 'the legislative option remains available'.[210] He noted that legislatures were better placed to deal with the myriad of policy issues arising in respect of copyright law and peer-to-peer networks: 'Courts are less well suited than Congress to the task of accommodat[ing] fully the varied permutations of competing interests that are inevitably implicated by such new technology.'[211]

The motion picture industries and recording industries were elated at the ruling of the Supreme Court of the United States in *Grokster*.[212] Mitch Bainwol, the chairman and chief executive officer of the RIAA, observed: 'With this unanimous decision, the Supreme Court has addressed a significant threat to the U.S. economy and moved to protect the livelihoods of the more than 11 million Americans employed by the copyright industries.'[213] Recalling the false epiphany after the *Napster* decision, his predecessor Hilary Rosen warned her colleagues not to be beguiled by the joys of the legal victory.[214] Rosen comments that 'what the consumer wants has been ignored far too often by both of these sides'.[215] She maintained: 'The euphoria of this decision does not and should not change the need for the entertainment industry to push foward and embrace these new distribution systems.'[216] The copyright industries will have to reassess whether there is any need to lobby Congress to pass further laws to clarify the meaning of inducement.[217]

The Congressional Internet Caucus Advisory Committee (ICAC) assembled a panel of the lead counsels associated with the *Grokster* case to discuss its significance.[218] Representative Robert Goodlatte applauded the unanimous decision, calling it 'pro-consumer' and noting its careful balance between encouraging innovation and protecting copyright. Don Verrilli of Jenner & Block argued that Congress should let the lower courts consider the issues and crystallize the decision: 'This is not the time for intervention by Congress.'[219] He said that the Supreme Court set a 'common sense standard' that gives the lower courts sufficient fodder to tackle illicit behaviour.[220] Andrew Greenberg of Carlton Fields suggested that 'Congress should monitor carefully' what the lower courts do.[221] He observed that the legislative route would be difficult: 'The technology industry and the music industry have both been absolutely incapable of working together to articulate credibly, clearly and understandably what the rules of the road are.'[222]

The staff attorney for the EFF, Fred von Lohmann, has called for law reform in the wake of the Supreme Court of the United States judgment in *Grokster*.[223] He said that the decision left too many unanswered questions, adding, 'I don't believe that uncertainty is balance.'[224] The attorney said: 'We need clear, bright-line rules so that technology companies can know in advance what they are and are not allowed to build.'[225] First, von Lohmann advocated a fair compensation system in respect of the downloading of copyright works on peer-to-peer networks. He believes that such technologies could be turned into a form of revenue. Second, von Lohmann supported a modernization and reformation of compulsory licensing. He maintained that such licences should not be merely limited to covers. Third, the attorney calls for a reform in copyright damages and remedies, because he considers them unbalanced. He argued that statutory damages should be removed in secondary liability cases and questioned whether copyright owners should be allowed to dictate the shape of technology markets. The attorney concluded: 'We shouldn't have a remedial system where, if Microsoft or Apple or Slingbox bet wrong, they go out of business.'[226]

There has also been feverish, hectic debate over the *DMCA*. Record companies and motion picture studios have engaged in a massive media and lobbying campaign. They have used the battle against peer-to-peer networks as a pretext to push for stronger protection of copyright law at a legislative level in the United States Congress. Public interest groups have struggled to counter such draconian measures in the legislative arena.[227] As Jessica Litman acerbically observes:

> There are not many Don Quixotes in Washington. The conflict over the scope of copyright in a digital age may have been fueled by differences in principles as much as narrow self-interest, but it is being fought in the usual way: representatives of private interests are simultaneously jockeying for advantage while offering to sit down at the bargaining table and negotiate a deal they find satisfactory.[228]

The future of digital copyright remains uncertain. As Antonio Gramsci once wrote in his prison notebooks, 'The old is dying and the new cannot be born; in this interregnum there arises a great diversity of morbid symptoms.'[229] The matrix of copyright protection proposed by record companies and movie studios will be countered by new technological innovations in peer-to-peer networks. Napster, Aimster, Grokster, Streamcast and Kazaa may have become defunct. However, they leave behind an important legacy. The strategies of resistance pioneered by the peer-to-peer networks will be refined by their rivals and successors. Peer-to-peer networks can deservedly be criticized for their slick marketing and overweening commercial ambitions, but they certainly deserve credit and respect for their ingenious legal and technical defences against copyright owners. Hail to the thief, indeed.

NOTES

1. Bowrey, Kathy (2005), *Law and Internet Cultures*, Cambridge: Cambridge University Press, p. 155.
2. There is a large literature on the Napster litigation. See, for instance, Rimmer, M. (2001), 'Napster: Infinite Digital Jukebox Or Pirate Bazaar', *Media International Australia incorporating Culture and Policy*, **98**, 27–38, Bowrey, K. and M. Rimmer (2002), 'Rip, Mix, Burn: The Politics of Peer to Peer and Copyright Law', *First Monday*, **7** (8), http://firstmonday.org/issues/issue7_8/bowrey/index.html; Fagin, M., Pasquale, F. and K. Weatherall (2002), 'Beyond Napster: Using Antitrust Law to Advance and Enhance Online Music Distribution', *Boston University Journal of Science and Technology Law*, **8**, 451–573; Ku, R. (2002), 'The Creative Destruction of Copyright: Napster and the New Economics of Digital Technology', *The University of Chicago Law Review*, **69**, 263–324; and Einhorn, M. (2002), 'Copyright, Prevention and Rational Governance: File-Sharing and Napster', *Columbia Journal for Law and the Arts*, **24**, 449–62.
3. *A&M Records Inc and others* v. *Napster Inc and Does 1–100*, Case No 99-5183-MHP, Complaint for Contributory and Vicarious Copyright Infringement, Violations of California Civil Code Section 980(a)(2), and Unfair Competition (N.D. Cal. 2000).
4. Ibid.
5. Higgins, D. (2000), 'Metallica Gets Heavy with its Fans', *The Sydney Morning Herald*, 5 May, p. 1.
6. *A&M Records Inc* v. *Napster Inc* 114 F. Supp. 2d 896 (N.D. Cal 2000).
7. *A&M Records Inc* v. *Napster Inc* 114 F. Supp. 2d 896 at 916 (N.D. Cal 2000).
8. *A&M Records Inc* v. *Napster Inc* 114 F. Supp. 2d 896 at 915 (N.D. Cal 2000).
9. *A&M Records Inc* v. *Napster Inc* 114 F. Supp. 2d 896 at 919 (N.D. Cal 2000).
10. *A&M Records Inc* v. *Napster Inc* 114 F. Supp. 2d 896 at 922 (N.D. Cal 2000).
11. *A&M Records Inc* v. *Napster Inc* 114 F. Supp. 2d 896 at 927 (N.D. Cal 2000).
12. *A&M Records Inc* v. *Napster Inc* 239 F.3d 1004 (9th 2001).
13. *A&M Records Inc* v. *Napster Inc* 239 F.3d 1004 at 1019 (9th 2001).
14. *A&M Records Inc* v. *Napster Inc* 239 F.3d 1004 at 1025 (9th 2001).
15. *A&M Records Inc* v. *Napster Inc* 239 F.3d 1004 at 1027 (9th 2001).
16. King, B. (2002), 'Napster's Assets Go For A Song', *Wired News*, http://www.wired.com/news/digiwood/0,1412,56633,00.html, 28 November.
17. Napster (2003), 'It's Coming Back', *Wired Magazine*, **11**(11), 213.
18. Napster, http://www.napster.com/.

19. *In re: Aimster Copyright Litigation* 334 F. 3d 643 (7th Cir. 2003).
20. *In re: Aimster Copyright Litigation* 334 F. 3d 643 at 650 (7th Cir. 2003).
21. *In re: Aimster Copyright Litigation* 334 F. 3d 643 at 653 (7th Cir. 2003).
22. *In re: Aimster Copyright Litigation* 334 F. 3d 643 at 655 (7th Cir. 2003).
23. *In re: Aimster Copyright Litigation* 334 F. 3d 643 at 656 (7th Cir. 2003).
24. Boyle, J. (1997), 'Foucault in Cyberspace: Surveillance, Sovereignty, and Hardwired Censors', *University of Cincinnati Law Review*, **66** (1), 177–205.
25. Crawford, K. (2005), 'Adaptation: Tracking the Ecologies of Music and Peer-to-Peer Networks', *Media International Australia incorporating Culture and Policy*, **114**, 30–39 at 34.
26. *Metro-Goldwyn-Mayer Studios Inc.* v. *Grokster, Ltd.* 125 S.Ct. 2764 (2005).
27. *Universal Music Australia Pty Ltd.* v. *Sharman License Holdings Ltd.* [2005] FCA 1242; (2005) 220 ALR 1.
28. MGM Studios and others, 'Complaint for Damages and Injunctive Relief for Copyright Infringement', 2 October 2001, 2.
29. *Metro-Goldwyn-Mayer Studios* v. *Grokster Ltd.* 259 F.Supp.2d 1029 at 1034–5 (2003).
30. *Sony Corporation of America* v. *Universal City Studios Inc.* 464 US 417 (1984).
31. *Metro-Goldwyn-Mayer Studios* v. *Grokster Ltd.* 259 F.Supp.2d 1029 at 1035 (2003).
32. *Metro-Goldwyn-Mayer Studios* v. *Grokster Ltd.* 259 F.Supp.2d 1029 at 1041–2 (2003).
33. *Metro-Goldwyn-Mayer Studios* v. *Grokster Ltd.* 259 F.Supp.2d 1029 at 1041 (2003).
34. *Metro-Goldwyn-Mayer Studios* v. *Grokster Ltd.* 259 F.Supp.2d 1029 at 1046 (2003).
35. *Metro-Goldwyn-Mayer Studios* v. *Grokster Ltd.* 259 F.Supp.2d 1029 at 1046 (2003).
36. *Metro-Goldwyn-Mayer Studios* v. *Grokster Ltd.* 380 F.3d 1154 (9th Cir. 2004).
37. *Metro-Goldwyn-Mayer Studios* v. *Grokster Ltd.* 380 F.3d 1154 (9th Cir. 2004).
38. *Metro-Goldwyn-Mayer Studios* v. *Grokster Ltd.* 380 F.3d 1154 at 1161 (9th Cir. 2004).
39. *Metro-Goldwyn-Mayer Studios* v. *Grokster Ltd.* 380 F.3d 1154 at 1167 (9th Cir. 2004).
40. *Metro-Goldwyn-Mayer Studios* v. *Grokster Ltd.* 380 F.3d 1154 at 1166 (9th Cir. 2004).
41. *Metro-Goldwyn-Mayer Studios* v. *Grokster Ltd.* 380 F.3d 1154 at 1167 (9th Cir. 2004).
42. A lawyer at Morrison & Foerster provides a good summary of the various positions taken in the Grokster amicus briefs: Band, J. (2005), 'The Grokster Scorecard', http://www.eff.org/IP/P2P/MGM_v._Grokster/summary.pdf.
43. *Metro-Goldwyn-Mayer Studios Inc.* v. *Grokster, Ltd.* 125 S.Ct. 2764 (2005).
44. Patry, W. (2005), 'The Court Punts', *Patry Blog*, http://williampatry.blogspot.com/2005/06/court-punts.html, 27 June. There is a growing commentary on the case. See, for instance, Vu, C. (2006), 'Tradition is the New Thing: The Supreme Court Holds That Creators of Peer-to-Peer Networks Could Be Liable Under Traditional Theories of Secondary Liability', *Whittier Law Review*, **27**, 1077–96; Hogberg, S. (2006), 'The Search for Intent-Based Doctrines of Secondary Liability in Copyright Law', *Columbia Law Review*, **106**, 909–57; Zittrain, J. (2006), 'The Generative Internet', *Harvard Law Review*, **119**, 1974–2040; and Ganley, P. (2006), 'Surviving Grokster: Innovation and the Future of Peer-to-Peer', *European Intellectual Property Review*, **28**(1), 15–25.
45. *Metro-Goldwyn-Mayer Studios Inc.* v. *Grokster, Ltd.* 125 S.Ct. 2764 (2005).
46. *Metro-Goldwyn-Mayer Studios Inc.* v. *Grokster, Ltd.* 125 S.Ct. 2764 at 2780 (2005).
47. *Metro-Goldwyn-Mayer Studios Inc.* v. *Grokster, Ltd.* 125 S.Ct. 2764 at 2781 (2005).
48. *Metro-Goldwyn-Mayer Studios Inc.* v. *Grokster, Ltd.* 125 S.Ct. 2764 at 2781 (2005).
49. *Metro-Goldwyn-Mayer Studios Inc.* v. *Grokster, Ltd.* 125 S.Ct. 2764 at 2781 (2005).
50. *Metro-Goldwyn-Mayer Studios Inc.* v. *Grokster, Ltd.* 125 S.Ct. 2764 at 2781 (2005).
51. *Metro-Goldwyn-Mayer Studios Inc.* v. *Grokster, Ltd.* 125 S.Ct. 2764 at 2781–2 (2005).
52. *Metro-Goldwyn-Mayer Studios Inc.* v. *Grokster, Ltd.* 125 S.Ct. 2764 at 2782 (2005).
53. *Metro-Goldwyn-Mayer Studios Inc.* v. *Grokster, Ltd.* 125 S.Ct. 2764 at 2782 (2005).
54. Hof, R. (2005), 'Ten Years of Chilled Innovation: That's the fallout from the Supreme Court ruling on file-sharing technologies, says Creative Commons Chair and Law Prof Larry Lessig', *Business Week*, 29 June.
55. Ibid.
56. Ibid.
57. Ibid.

58. Samuelson, P. (2005), 'Legally Speaking: Did MGM Really Win the Grokster Case?', *Communications of the ACM*, **48**, 19, http://www.sims.berkeley.edu/~pam/papers/CACM%20SCT%20decides%20MGM.pdf.
59. Ibid.
60. Ibid.
61. Ibid.
62. Geist, M. (2005), 'Grokster and the Future of File-Sharing', *Toronto Star*, http://www.michaelgeist.ca/resc/html_bkup/june292005.html, 29 June.
63. Ibid.
64. Ibid.
65. Felten, E. (2005), 'Legality of Design Decisions, and Footnote 12 in Grokster', *Freedom to Tinker*, http://www.freedom-to-tinker.com/?p=857, 27 June.
66. Ibid.
67. Ibid.
68. Ibid.
69. *Metro-Goldwyn-Mayer Studios Inc.* v. *Grokster, Ltd.* 125 S.Ct. 2764 at 2786 (2005).
70. *Metro-Goldwyn-Mayer Studios Inc.* v. *Grokster, Ltd.* 125 S.Ct. 2764 at 2785 (2005).
71. Wu, T. (2005), 'A Supreme Court Conversation', *Slate*, http://slate.msn.com/id/2121410/entry/2121673/, 28 June; for an expanded discussion, see Goldsmith, Jack and Tim Wu (2006), *Who Controls the Internet?: Illusions of a Borderless World*, Oxford: Oxford University Press, pp. 110–25.
72. Ibid.
73. Ibid.
74. Ibid.
75. *Metro-Goldwyn-Mayer Studios Inc.* v. *Grokster, Ltd.* 125 S.Ct. 2764 at 2787 (2005).
76. *Metro-Goldwyn-Mayer Studios Inc.* v. *Grokster, Ltd.* 125 S.Ct. 2764 at 2791 (2005).
77. *Metro-Goldwyn-Mayer Studios Inc.* v. *Grokster, Ltd.* 125 S.Ct. 2764 at 2791 (2005).
78. *Metro-Goldwyn-Mayer Studios Inc.* v. *Grokster, Ltd.* 125 S.Ct. 2764 at 2791 (2005).
79. *Metro-Goldwyn-Mayer Studios Inc.* v. *Grokster, Ltd.* 125 S.Ct. 2764 at 2791–2 (2005).
80. *Metro-Goldwyn-Mayer Studios Inc.* v. *Grokster, Ltd.* 125 S.Ct. 2764 at 2792 (2005).
81. *Metro-Goldwyn-Mayer Studios Inc.* v. *Grokster, Ltd.* 125 S.Ct. 2764 at 2792 (2005).
82. *Metro-Goldwyn-Mayer Studios Inc.* v. *Grokster, Ltd.* 125 S.Ct. 2764 at 2792 (2005).
83. *Metro-Goldwyn-Mayer Studios Inc.* v. *Grokster, Ltd.* 125 S.Ct. 2764 at 2793 (2005).
84. *Metro-Goldwyn-Mayer Studios Inc.* v *Grokster, Ltd.* 125 S.Ct. 2764 at 2792 (2005).
85. *Metro-Goldwyn-Mayer Studios Inc.* v. *Grokster, Ltd.* 125 S.Ct. 2764 at 2793 (2005).
86. *Metro-Goldwyn Mayer Studios Inc.* v. *Grokster, Ltd.* 125 S.Ct. 2764 at 2793 (2005).
87. *Metro-Goldwyn-Mayer Studios Inc.* v. *Grokster, Ltd.* 125 S.Ct. 2764 at 2790 (2005).
88. *Metro-Goldwyn-Mayer Studios Inc.* v. *Grokster, Ltd.* 125 S.Ct. 2764 at 2790 (2005).
89. *Metro-Goldwyn-Mayer Studios Inc.* v. *Grokster, Ltd.* 125 S.Ct. 2764 at 2790 (2005).
90. RIAA (2005), 'Music Industry Announces Grokster Settlement', http://www.riaa.com/news/newsletter/110705_2.asp, 11 November.
91. Grokster, http://www.grokster.com/.
92. *Metro-Goldwyn-Mayer Studios, Inc.* v. *Grokster, Ltd.*, 2006 WL 2806882 (United States District Court, Central District of California, 27 September, 2006).
93. Woody, T. (2003), 'The Race to Kill Kazaa', *Wired Magazine*, **11** (2), 104–7, 138, URL: http://www.wired.com/wired/archive/11.02/kazaa.html.
94. Johnston, C. (2003), 'Pirate Queen', *The Age*, http://www.theage.com.au/articles/2003/03/04/1046540185222.html, 5 March.
95. Valenti, J. (2003), 'Privacy and Piracy: The Paradox of Illegal File Sharing on Peer-to-Peer Networks and the Impact of Technology on the Entertainment Industry', Senate Committee on Governmental Affairs, 30 September.
96. Kazaa lost the initial case in *Buma and Stemra* v. *Kazaa* (unreported, 29 November 2001).
97. However, it won the appeal in *Kazaa* v. *Buma and Stemra* (unreported, 28 March 2002, Amsterdam Court of Appeal): http://www.eff.org/IP//P2P/BUMA_v._Kazaa/, as well as the final decision in *Buma and Stemra* v. *Kazaa* (unreported, 18 December 2003, the

Dutch Supreme Court). For a discussion of this litigation, see Van Bergh, G.-J. (2002), 'Case Comment: Copyright – File Sharing Service', *Entertainment Law Review*, **13** (6), 77–8; and Morrison, A. (2002), 'Case Comment: Kazaa v. Buma and Stemra', *European Intellectual Property Review*, **24**(8), 130–31.

98. *Metro-Goldwyn-Mayer Studios Inc.* v. *Grokster Ltd.* 243 F.Supp.2d 1073 (2003).
99. *Metro-Goldwyn-Mayer Studios Inc.* v. *Grokster Ltd.* 269 F.Supp.2d 1213 (2003).
100. Online Staff (2004), 'MIPI Serves Papers On Kazaa Offices In Vanuatu', *The Sydney Morning Herald*, http://www.smh.com.au/articles/2004/02/09/1076175068630.html?from=storyrhs, 9 February.
101. For a background account to the litigation over Kazaa, see Rimmer, M. (2005), 'Hail To The Thief: A Tribute To Kazaa', *The University of Ottawa Law and Technology Journal*, **2** (1), 173–218.
102. *Universal Music Australia Pty Ltd.* v. *Sharman License Holdings Ltd.* [2005] FCA 1242 (2005) 220 ALR 1.
103. Gray, P. (2004), 'Sharman Shuffles Legal Team', *Wired News*, http://www.wired.com/news/digiwood/0,1412,63062,00.html?tw=wn_tophead_4, 15 April.
104. *Universal Music Australia Pty Ltd.* v. *Sharman License Holdings Ltd.* [2005] FCA 1242; (2005) 220 ALR 1, 115.
105. Davidson, J. (2004), 'Billions at Stake in Kazaa Court Case', *Australian Financial Review*, 7 December, 30.
106. *Universal Music Australia Pty Ltd.* v. *Sharman License Holdings Ltd.* [2005] FCA 1242; (2005) 220 ALR, 15.
107. *Universal Music Australia Pty Ltd.* v. *Sharman License Holdings Ltd.* [2005] FCA 1242; (2005) 220 ALR, 198.
108. *Universal Music Australia Pty Ltd.* v. *Sharman License Holdings Ltd.* [2005] FCA 1242; (2005) 220 ALR 1, 5.
109. *Universal Music Australia Pty Ltd.* v. *Sharman License Holdings Ltd.* [2005] FCA 1242; (2005) 220 ALR 1, 99.
110. *Universal Music Australia Pty Ltd.* v. *Sharman License Holdings Ltd.* [2005] FCA 1242; (2005) 220 ALR 1, 100.
111. *Universal Music Australia Pty Ltd.* v. *Sharman License Holdings Ltd.* [2005] FCA 1242; (2005) 220 ALR 1, 5.
112. *Universal Music Australia Pty Ltd.* v. *Sharman License Holdings Ltd.* [2005] FCA 1242; (2005) 220 ALR 1, 99.
113. Sharman Networks (2003), 'Sharman Networks Launches "Join The Revolution"', Press Release, 19 November.
114. *Universal Music Australia Pty Ltd.* v. *Sharman License Holdings Ltd.* [2005] FCA 1242; (2005) 220 ALR 1, 5.
115. *Universal Music Australia Pty Ltd.* v. *Sharman License Holdings Ltd.* [2005] FCA 1242; (2005) 220 ALR 1, 6.
116. *Universal Music Australia Pty Ltd.* v. *Sharman License Holdings Ltd.* [2005] FCA 1242; (2005) 220 ALR 1, 108.
117. *Universal Music Australia Pty Ltd.* v. *Sharman License Holdings Ltd.* [2005] FCA 1242; (2005) 220 ALR 1, 104.
118. *Universal Music Australia Pty Ltd.* v. *Sharman License Holdings Ltd.* [2005] FCA 1242; (2005) 220 ALR 1, 109.
119. Sharman Networks (2003), 'Bollywood Comes To Kazaa: World's First Full-Length Feature Film Sold Online Using Peer-to-Peer Technology', Press Release, http://www.sharmannetworks.com/content/view/full/237, 12 November.
120. Goldman, J. (2003), 'KaZaA CEO Speaks Out', G4TV, http://www.g4tv.com/techtvvault/features/44860/KaZaA_CEO_Speaks_Out.html, 5 August.
121. Sharman Networks (2003), 'Review of Copyright Amendment (Digital Agenda) Act', http://www.phillipsfox.com/whats_on/Australia/DigitalAgenda/submissions/Sharman_submission.pdf, 30 September.
122. Copyright Law Review Committee (2002), *Simplification of the Copyright Act* 1968, Canberra: the Attorney General's Department [6.35].

123. Sharman Networks (2003), 'Review of Copyright Amendment (Digital Agenda) Act', http://www.phillipsfox.com/whats_on/Australia/DigitalAgenda/submissions/Sharman_submission.pdf, 30 September.
124. The Communications Law Centre (2005), 'Outline of Submissions on Behalf of Proposed Amici, the Australian Consumers' Association, Electronic Frontiers Australia Inc. and New South Wales Civil Liberties Inc in *Universal Music Australia Pty Ltd.* v. *Sharman License Holdings Ltd*, 16 March.
125. *Metro-Goldwyn-Mayer Studios Inc* v. *Grokster Ltd.* 125 S.Ct 2764 (2005).
126. *Universal Music Australia Pty Ltd.* v. *Sharman License Holdings Ltd.* [2005] FCA 1242; (2005) 220 ALR 1, 14.
127. *Universal Music Australia Pty Ltd.* v. *Sharman License Holdings Ltd.* [2005] FCA 1242; (2005) 220 ALR 1, 14.
128. *Universal Music Australia Pty Ltd.* v. *Sharman License Holdings Ltd.* [2005] FCA 1242; (2005) 220 ALR 1, 14.
129. *Universal Music Australia Pty Ltd.* v. *Sharman License Holdings Ltd.* [2005] FCA 1242; (2005) 220 ALR 1, 49.
130. *Universal Music Australia Pty Ltd.* v. *Sharman License Holdings Ltd.* [2005] FCA 1242; (2005) 220 ALR 1, 49.
131. Davidson, J. (2004), 'Win or Lose, Kazaa Won't Be Shut Down', *Australian Financial Review*, 3 December, 64.
132. Ibid.
133. Ibid.
134. Ibid.
135. *Universal Music Australia Pty Ltd.* v. *Sharman License Holdings Ltd.* [2005] FCA 1242; (2005) 220 ALR 1, 116.
136. *Universal Music Australia Pty Ltd.* v. *Sharman License Holdings Ltd.* [2005] FCA 1242; (2005) 220 ALR 1, 117.
137. Sharman Networks (2006), 'Content Industries and Sharman Networks Settle All Global Litigation', http://www.sharmannetworks.com/content/view/full/323, August.
138. Ibid.
139. IFPI (2006), 'Kazaa Settles with Record Industry and Goes Legitimate', http://www.ifpi.org/site-content/press/20060727.html, 27 July.
140. Ginsburg, J. and S. Ricketson (2006), 'Inducers and Authorisers: A Comparison of the US Supreme Court's Grokster decision and the Australian Federal Court's Kazaa ruling', *Media and Arts Law Review*, **11**(1), 1–25 at 23.
141. Austin, G. (2006), 'Importing Kazaa – Exporting Grokster', *Santa Clara Computer and High Technology Journal*, **22**, 577–619.
142. For a discussion of Australian case law on authorization, see Napthali, M. (2005), 'Unauthorised: Some Thoughts upon the Doctrine of Authorisation of Copyright Infringement in the Peer-to-Peer Age', *Australian Intellectual Property Journal*, **16**, 5–54.
143. Miller, S. (2006), 'Peer-to-Peer File Distribution: An Analysis of Design, Liability, Litigation, and Potential Solutions', *Review of Litigation*, **25**, 181–230 at 229–30.
144. BitTorrent, http://www.bittorrent.com/introduction.html.
145. Thompson, C. (2005), 'The BitTorrent Effect', *Wired Magazine*, **13** (1), 2, http://www.wired.com/wired/archive/13.01/bittorrent.html.
146. Ibid.
147. Ibid., 3.
148. Felten, E. (2005), 'BitTorrent: The Next Main Event', *Freedom to Tinker*, http://www.freedom-to-tinker.com/?p=859, 28 June.
149. Ibid.
150. Ibid.
151. MPAA (2005), 'BitTorrent and MPAA Join Forces: Companies Aim to Protect Film Copyrights', http://www.mpaa.org/press_releases/2005_11_22.pdf, 22 November.
152. Ibid.
153. Borland, J. (2006), 'BitTorrent to Crack Down on Use of Name', *ZDNet.com*, http://news.zdnet.com/2100-9588_22-6035800.html, 6 February.

154. Warner Bros (2006), 'Warner Bros. Home Entertainment Group Announces Revolutionary Deal to Publish Legal Film and TV Content Using the BitTorrent Platform', Press Release, 9 May.
155. Ibid.
156. Ibid.
157. In 2004, legal action was brought against the BitTorrent sites, Supranova, LokiTorrent and Finreactor. In 2005, the popular BitTorrent website EliteTorrents.org was shut down by the United States Federal Bureau of Investigation and Immigration and Customs Enforcement.
158. MPAA (2006), 'Studios Move to Thwart Illegal File Sharing on Major Pirate Networks', Press Release, http://www.mpaa.org/press_releases/2006_02_23.pdf, 23 February; *Columbia Pictures Industries Inc.* v. *Fung*, S.D.N.Y., No. 06-1471, complaint filed 2/23/06; *CBS Broadcasting Inc.* v. *Does 1–10*, N.D. Tex., No. 06-0338, complaint filed 2/23/06; *Disney Enterprises Inc.* v. *Does 1–10*, N.D. Fla., No. 06-0096, complaint filed 2/23/06; *Paramount Pictures Corp.* v. *Thompson*, D. Utah, No. 06-0156, complaint filed 2/23/06; *Columbia Pictures Industries Inc.* v. *Bunnell*, C.D. Cal., No. 06-1093, complaint filed 2/23/06; *Columbia Pictures Industries Inc.* v. *Does 1–10*, W.D. Pa., No. 06-0251, complaint filed 2/23/06; *Columbia Pictures Industries Inc.* v. *Does 1–10*, W.D. Mich., No. 06-0037, complaint filed 2/23/06.
159. *Columbia Pictures Industries Inc.* v. *Bunnell*, C.D. Cal., No. 06-1093, complaint filed 2/23/06.
160. *Columbia Pictures Industries Inc.* v. *Bunnell*, C.D. Cal., No. 06-1093, complaint filed 2/23/06.
161. *Columbia Pictures Industries Inc.* v. *Bunnell*, C.D. Cal., No. 06-1093, complaint filed 2/23/06.
162. *Columbia Pictures Industries Inc.* v. *Bunnell*, C.D. Cal., No. 06-1093, complaint filed 2/23/06.
163. *Columbia Pictures Industries Inc.* v. *Bunnell*, C.D. Cal., No. 06-1093, complaint filed 2/23/06.
164. *Columbia Pictures Industries Inc.* v. *Bunnell*, C.D. Cal., No. 06-1093, complaint filed 2/23/06.
165. *Columbia Pictures Industries Inc.* v. *Bunnell*, C.D. Cal., No. 06-1093, complaint filed 2/23/06, http://www.techfirm.com/mtdtorrentspy.pdf.
166. *Columbia Pictures Industries Inc.* v. *Bunnell*, C.D. Cal., No. 06-1093, complaint filed 2/23/06, http://www.techfirm.com/mtdtorrentspy.pdf.
167. *Columbia Pictures Industries Inc.* v. *Bunnell*, C.D. Cal., No. 06-1093, complaint filed 2/23/06, http://www.techfirm.com/mtdtorrentspy.pdf.
168. *Columbia Pictures Industries Inc.* v. *Bunnell*, C.D. Cal., No. 06-1093, complaint filed 2/23/06, http://www.techfirm.com/mtdtorrentspy.pdf.
169. *Columbia Pictures Industries Inc.* v. *Bunnell*, C.D. Cal., No. 06-1093, complaint filed 2/23/06, http://www.techfirm.com/mtdtorrentspy.pdf.
170. *Columbia Pictures Industries Inc.* v. *Bunnell*, C.D. Cal., No. 06-1093, complaint filed 2/23/06, http://www.techfirm.com/mtdtorrentspy.pdf.
171. Borland, J. (2006), 'MPAA Sues Newsgroup, P2P Search Sites', C/Net News.com, http://news.com.com/MPAA+sues+newsgroup%2C+P2P+search+sites/2100-1030_3-6042739.html, 23 February.
172. *Arista Records* v. *MP3.Board* (S.D.N.Y., no. 00 Civ. 4660 (SHS), 2000). For an archive of the litigation against MP3.Board, see http://www.riaa.com/News/filings/mp 3.asp.
173. *Columbia Pictures Industries Inc.* v. *Fung*, S.D.N.Y., No. 06-1471, complaint filed 2/23/06.
174. *Columbia Pictures Industries Inc.* v. *Fung*, S.D.N.Y., No. 06-1471, complaint filed 2/23/06.
175. *Columbia Pictures Industries Inc.* v. *Fung*, S.D.N.Y., No. 06-1471, complaint filed 2/23/06.
176. *Columbia Pictures Industries Inc.* v. *Does 1–10*, W.D. Mich., No. 06-0037, complaint filed 2/23/06.

177. *Columbia Pictures Industries Inc.* v. *Does 1–10*, W.D. Mich., No. 06-0037, complaint filed 2/23/06.
178. *Columbia Pictures Industries Inc.* v. *Does 1–10*, W.D. Mich., No. 06-0037, complaint filed 2/23/06.
179. Yagan, S. (2006), 'Testimony to the Senate Committee for the Judiciary', http://judiciary.senate.gov/testimony.cfm?id=1624&wit_id=4689, 28 September.
180. Ibid.
181. Associated Press (2006), 'Firm Behind eDonkey to Pay $30 Million to Avoid Piracy Claims', *Mercury News*, 12 September.
182. *Paramount Pictures Corporation* v. *Thompson*, D. Utah, No. 06-0156, complaint filed 2/23/06.
183. *Paramount Pictures Corporation* v. *Thompson*, D. Utah, No. 06-0156, complaint filed 2/23/06.
184. *Disney Enterprises Inc.* v. *Does 1–10*, N.D. Fla., No. 06-0096, complaint filed 2/23/06.
185. *Disney Enterprises Inc.* v. *Does 1–10*, N.D. Fla., No. 06-0096, complaint filed 2/23/06.
186. MPAA (2006), 'Belgian and Swiss Authorities Break Razorback 2', http://www.mpaa.org/press_releases/2006_02_21_razer.pdf, 21 February.
187. Ibid.
188. *Dow Jones & Co Inc* v. *Gutnick* (2002), 194 ALR 433; and Rolph, D. (2003), 'A Clearly Inappropriate Forum? Jurisdiction, Internet Defamation and The High Court of Australia', *Media And Arts Law Review*, **8** (1), 59–71.
189. Netanel, N.W. (2003), 'Impose A Noncommercial Use Levy To Allow Free Peer-to-Peer File Sharing', *Harvard Journal Of Law And Technology*, **17** (1), 1–84 at 18–19.
190. *Metro-Goldwyn-Mayer Studios Inc.* v. *Grokster Ltd.* (2003) 243 F.Supp.2d 1073.
191. *Arista Records* v. *Sakfield Holding Company* 314 F.Supp.2d 27 (2004).
192. *Motown Record Company* v. *IMesh.com Inc* WL 503720 (2004).
193. Honan, M. (2003), 'The Enigma of Earth Station 5', *Salon*, http://www.salon.com/tech/feature/2003/12/03/es 5/index.html, 3 December. In February 2004, the *Washington Post* investigated the bona fides of Earth Station 5. After travelling to Jenin in the West Bank to look for Earth Station 5's headquarters, the newspaper discovered that no voice or Internet services was ever provided to a company named Earth Station 5. See Anderson, J.W. (2004), 'Techno-Rebels in West Bank?; File Swapping Firm Claims Odd Hide-Out', *The Washington Post*, 22 February, A29.
194. Harrison, A. (2006), 'The Pirate Bay. Here to Stay', *Wired News*, 13 March.
195. Keats, McFarland and Wilson L.L.P. (2004), 'Unauthorised Use of Dreamworks SKG Property', http://thepiratebay.org/legal.php, 23 August; and The Pirate Bay response has been removed after recent raids.
196 Harrison, A. (2006), 'The Pirate Bay: Here to Stay', *Wired News*, 13 March.
197. Ibid.
198. *EC Information Society Directive*, Council Directive 2001/29/EC of 22 May 2001 on the harmonisation of certain aspects of copyright and related rights in the information society.
199. MPAA (2006), 'Swedish Authorities Sink "Pirate Bay"; Huge Worldwide Supplier of Illegal Movies Told No Safe Harbors for Facilitators of Piracy', 31 May.
200. Ibid.
201. Ibid.
202. Klang, M. (2006), 'Raiding Pirate Bay', Klang Blog: Sound and Fury, Signifying Nothing, http://www.ituniv.se/~klang/wrote/2006/05/31/raiding-pirate-bay/, 31 May.
203. Ibid.
204. Mennecke, T. (2006), 'United States Pressured Pirate Bay Closure', *Silicon Valley*, 1 June.
205. http://www2.piratpartiet.se/the_pirate_party.
206. South, G. (2006), 'Rip This: Piracy and Politics in Sweden', *Open Democracy*, http://www.opendemocracy.net/media-copyrightlaw/pirates_3626.jsp, 9 May.
207. The Pirate Party, http://www2.piratpartiet.se/the_pirate_party.
208. The Pirate Party, http://www2.piratpartiet.se/the_pirate_party.

209. Norton, Q. (2006), 'Voters Keelhaul Pirate Party', *Wired News*, http://www.wired.com/news/technology/0,71809-0.html, 18 September.
210. *Metro-Goldwyn-Mayer Studios Inc.* v. *Grokster, Ltd.* 125 S.Ct. 2764 (2005).
211. *Metro-Goldwyn-Mayer Studios Inc.* v. *Grokster, Ltd.* 125 S.Ct. 2764 (2005).
212. MPAA (2005), 'Statement from MPAA President and CEO Dan Glickman: Re: Supreme Court Ruling on MGM v. Grokster', http://www.mpaa.org/MPAAPress/2005/2005_06_27a.doc, 27 June.
213. RIAA (2005), 'Statement On MGM v. Grokster Supreme Court Ruling', http://www.riaa.com/news/newsletter/062705.asp, 27 June.
214. Rosen, H. (2005), 'The Wisdom of the Court: Part 2', *The Huffington Post*, http://www.huffingtonpost.com/theblog/archive/hilary-rosen/the-wisdom-of-the-court-_3259.html, 27 June.
215. Ibid.
216. Ibid.
217. Senator Orrin Hatch introduced the *Inducing Infringement of Copyrights Act* 2004 (US), or the so-called *Induce Act*, to provide for civil penalties against anyone who 'intentionally aids, abets, induces or procures' a copyright violation by a third person. Senator Hatch argued that there was a need to amend the *Copyright Act* 1976 (US) because lower courts had misapplied the standard in the *Sony Betamax* case.
218. Broache, A. (2005), 'Time for Lawmakers to Act on Grokster?', CNET News.com, http://news.com.com/2100-1028_3-5795314.html, 19 July.
219. Ibid.
220. Ibid.
221. Ibid.
222. Ibid.
223. Ibid; see also von Lohmann, F. (2004), 'Tech Dodges a Bullet', Law.com, 27 August.
224. Broache, A. (2005), 'Time for Lawmakers to Act on Grokster?', CNET News.com, http://news.com.com/2100-1028_3-5795314.html, 19 July.
225. Ibid.
226. Ibid.
227. Vaidhyanathan, S. (2004), 'The State Of Copyright Activism', *First Monday*, **9**(4), http://firstmonday.org/issues/issue9_4/siva/.
228. Litman, Jessica (2001), *Digital Copyright*, New York: Prometheus Books, p. 192.
229. Gramsci, Antonio (1971), *Selections from the Prison Notebooks of Antonio Gramsci*, London: Lawrence & Wishart, p. 276.

4. The grey album: copyright law, digital sampling and mash-ups

> By waging a war of litigation on file sharers and copyright infringers, the Recording Industry Association of America has unwittingly created a new kind of protest art. Mash-ups – digitally knitted-together compositions made up of two or more popular songs – are anti-authoritarian folk music for a generation whose 'establishment' is represented by corporate intellectual-property owners. (Annalee Newitz, 'Protest Music'[1])

Cultural critic and legal commentator, Siva Vaidhyanathan, comments: 'The most interesting and entertaining phenomenon of the MP3 libraries on peer-to-peer systems is the availability of "mashes" – new compositions created by combining the rhythm tracks of one song and the vocal track of another.'[2] He observed that mash-ups have a rich pedigree, dating back to literary pastiches, musical sampling and artistic appropriations: 'It is merely the latest incarnation of a widely shared, deeply embedded cultural habit of cultural recombination across time and space.'[3] Vaidhyanathan suggests that peer-to-peer networks do not just enable the distribution of popular mass-market musical works and sound recordings. He observes that peer-to-peer networks 'link diasporic communities and remake nations' as well as 'empower artists in new ways and connect communities of fans'.[4] The cultural critic lauded the riches of ephemera that can be found on such networks, ranging from Malcolm X's speeches to reggae remixes of Biggie Smalls' hits, club dance versions of Queen's 'Bohemian Rhapsody' and the comedy routines of Richard Pryor.

In 2001, the disc jockey called Roy Kerr, known by the pseudonym 'the Freelance Hellraiser', remixed the vocals of Christine Aguilera's 'Genie in a Bottle' with the guitars of The Strokes' 'Hard to Explain' in a mash-up entitled, 'A Stroke of Genie-us'.[5] This piece of bastard pop received both popular and critical acclaim. A critic from the *New Yorker*, Sasha Frere-Jones, wrote with admiration about the musical mash-up: 'Hellraiser brokers an amazing musical détente between the two styles.'[6] Although the work initially received a cease and desist order from the Radio Corporation of America Records, Roy Kerr's work was warmly received; indeed he was invited to create official remixes for Christine Aguilera.

In 2002, a Belgian group called Soulwax and also known as 2 Many DJs created a piece of bastard pop, combining the music of New Order's 'Blue

Monday 1988' with the Kylie Minogue vocal of 'Can't Get You Out Of My Head'. The track was known as 'Can't Get Blue Monday Out Of My Head' and was popular in discothèques and radio. Capitalizing on the vogue of the mash-up, the Australian pop princess, Kylie Minogue, performed a version of 'Can't Get Blue Monday Out of My Head' at the Brit Awards.[7] The live track was later released as an authorized B-side of one of her singles.

Sasha Frere-Jones observed: 'See mashups as piracy if you insist, but it is more useful, viewing them through the lens of the market, to see them as an expression of consumer dissatisfaction.'[8] He noted: 'Armed with free time and the right software, people are riffling through the lesser songs of pop music and, in frustration, choosing to make some of them as good as the great ones'.[9]

In addition to remixes of musical works and sound recordings, there have also been a number of notable audio-visual and Internet web mash-ups.[10] There are multiple prominent examples of this genre of mash-ups, including the parody 'Bush and Blair's Endless Love';[11] a mash-up of the Steven Spielberg's thriller *Jaws* and love songs, *Must Love Jaws*; a reinvention of the *Back to the Future* series as a story about gay cowboys; and various remixes of iTunes advertisments for the iPod.[12] Sometimes such audio-visual mash-ups attract legal attention. For instance, the music publisher Ludlow Music, Inc. threatened legal action against web animation studio JibJab Media Inc over the 'This Land' animated parody lampooning President Bush and Senator Kerry.[13] It was alleged that the video infringed copyright in the classic Woody Guthrie song, 'This Land is Your Land.' In response, JibJab argued that its work was a protected 'fair use' and did not infringe Ludlow's copyrights.[14] In any case, the group maintained that the Woody Guthrie song was part of the public domain and had been for many years. The case was settled, and JibJab was able to distribute the work, free from interference by the music publisher.

However, the most compelling mash-up is certainly the beguiling *The Grey Album*. In 2003, Brian Burton remixed the vocals from Jay-Z's *The Black Album* and The Beatles' *White Album* and called his creation *The Grey Album*.[15] He released 3000 promotional copies of the album under the pseudonym, DJ Danger Mouse, a nickname referring to the quaint British animation series.[16] Burton explained the complexities of the production of the work:

> A lot of people just assumed I took some Beatles and, you know, threw some Jay-Z on top of it or mixed it up or looped it around, but it's really a deconstruction. It's not an easy thing to do. I was obsessed with the whole project, that's all I was trying to do, see if I could do this. Once I got into it, I didn't think about anything but finishing it. I stuck to those two because I thought it would be more challenging and more fun and more of a statement to what you could do with

> sampling alone. It is an art form. It is music. You can do different things, it doesn't have to be just what some people call stealing. It can be a lot more than that.[17]

The musical creation of *The Grey Album* was accompanied by additional artistic creations. The artist Justin Hampton created a CD cover for the album, featuring Jay-Z, flanked by The Beatles, in shades of grey. Other artists experimented in mash-ups of the album covers of The Beatles and Jay-Z. In addition, a music video of the track 'Encore' from *The Grey Album* was made in the fall of 2004 by the directing team Ramon and Pedro. The video features clips from The Beatles' movie *A Hard Day's Night*, footage from a Jay-Z performance, as well as computer-generated imagery involving John Lennon and Ringo Starr. The video was distributed over the Internet, with the disclaimer that it was made for experimental purposes only.

The record company EMI, the owner of the rights to the sound recording of the *White Album*, sent cease and desist letters to DJ Danger Mouse and stores such as Fat Beats and hiphop.com, demanding they destroy copies of the album and remove them from their web-sites. DJ Danger Mouse agreed to cease distribution of *The Grey Album*.[18] He was quoted as saying, 'This wasn't supposed to happen . . . I just sent out a few tracks (and) now online stores are selling it and people are downloading it all over the place.'[19] He denies that he was being an agent provocateur: '[It] was not my intent to break copyright laws. It was my intent to make an art project.'[20]

On 24 February 2004, 170 web-sites posted copies of *The Grey Album* on the Internet in an act of protest and civil disobedience called 'Grey Tuesday'.[21] The organizers of the protest, Downhill Battle, declared on-line:

> This first-of-its-kind protest signals a refusal to let major label lawyers control what musicians can create and what the public can hear. *The Grey Album* is only one of the thousands of legitimate and valuable efforts that have been stifled by the record industry – not to mention the ones that were never even attempted because of the current legal climate. We cannot allow these corporations to continue censoring art; we need common-sense reforms to copyright law that can make sampling legal and practical for artists.[22]

A survey of the sites that hosted files during Grey Tuesday, and an analysis of file-sharing activity on that day, reported that *The Grey Album* was the number one album in the US on 24 February by a large margin.[23] The protestors boasted: 'Danger Mouse moved more "units" than Norah Jones and Kanye West, with well over 100 000 copies downloaded.'[24] The album was also actively distributed on peer-to-peer networks, such as Kazaa and Soulseek.

The controversy over the mash-up of *The Grey Album* is emblematic of the wider debate over copyright law and digital sampling of cultural works.[25] As one cultural critic, Sam Howard-Spink, observed: 'The tale of *The Grey Album* and Grey Tuesday offers a rich case study for the examination of a wide variety of contemporary cultural issues within the context of the "copyright wars" remix culture and the age of the digital network.'[26] This chapter focuses upon the legal dimensions of the debate over *The Grey Album*. Jonathan Zittrain has commented that the controversy illustrated a need for revisions in copyright law:

> As a matter of pure legal doctrine, the Grey Tuesday protest is breaking the law, end of story. But copyright law was written with a particular form of industry in mind. The flourishing of information technology gives amateurs and home-recording artists powerful tools to build and share interesting, transformative, and socially valuable art drawn from pieces of popular culture. There's no place to plug such an important cultural sea change into the current legal regime.[27]

The dispute poses a number of difficult legal issues. Section one considers whether a 'mash-up' goes beyond the *de minimis* use of a copyright work, and amounts to infringement of the economic rights of the owner. Section two examines whether *The Grey Album* is protected by the defence of fair use under copyright law because it provides a transformative use of copyright works. Section three speculates whether voluntary or compulsory licensing provide a means to legitimate the digital sampling and mash-ups of musical works. Section four considers whether digital sampling raises issues concerning the moral rights of attribution and integrity in certain jurisdictions.

I. 'THE LAW CARES NOT FOR TRIFLES': COPYRIGHT LAW AND *DE MINIMIS* USE

EMI and Sony/ATV Publishing instructed their lawyers to stop the distribution of *The Grey Album* on the Internet. J. Christopher Jensen from the New York law firm Cowan, Liebowitz and Latman, warned the host websites of the album: 'Any unauthorized distribution, reproduction, public performance and/or other exploitation of *The Grey Album* will constitute, among other things, common law copyright infringement/misappropriation, unfair competition and unjust enrichment rendering you and anyone engaged with you in such acts liable for all of the remedies provided by relevant laws.'[28] The lawyer emphasized that the samples used in *The Grey Album* constituted a substantial part of the sound recordings of The Beatles, and thus infringed the economic rights of the copyright owner. He observed: 'There is no dispute that *The Grey Album* incorporates Capitol Recordings, as Mr. Burton acknowledges on his website that "every kick, snare, and chord is taken from the Beatles *White Album* and is in their original recording somwhere [*sic*]".'[29] The lawyer demanded that host web-sites cease and desist from the reproduction, distribution and exploitation of *The Grey Album*. He threatened that the record company would seek legal remedies if there was a failure to remove the offending material from the Internet.

Interceding in the debate, the Electronic Frontier Foundation (EFF) issued a brief legal analysis of the issues raised by the controversy over *The Grey Album*.[30] It noted that there were at least four rights holders potentially involved in the matter: EMI, the owners of the rights to the recording for The Beatles' *White Album*; Sony Music/ATV Publishing, the owners of the rights to the musical works that appear on The Beatles' *White Album*; the owners of the rights to the sound recording for Jay-Z's *Black Album*; and the owners of the rights to the musical works that appear on Jay-Z's *Black Album*. The EFF observed that there was no federal copyright protection for sound recordings made before 1972: 'Because the *White Album* was released in 1968, it appears that EMI has no federal copyright rights in the sound recording.'[31] It noted, though, that State laws may protect sound recordings made before 1972.

In the United States, there has been much litigation over copyright infringement in respect of musical works and sound recordings. In *Bright Tunes Music Corp.* v. *Harrisongs Music, Ltd*, Owen J considered an action in which it was alleged that a former member of The Beatles, George Harrison, had plagiarized an earlier song, 'He's So Fine', in his number 'My Sweet Lord'.[32] The judge ruled that there had been an infringement of copyright, notwithstanding that the inspiration may have been an unconscious one:

> Did Harrison deliberately use the music of He's So Fine? I do not believe he did so deliberately. Nevertheless, it is clear that My Sweet Lord is the very same song as He's So Fine with different words, and Harrison had access to He's So Fine. This is, under the law, infringement of copyright, and is no less so even though subconsciously accomplished.[33]

Such a judgment was the result of a close comparison between the two musical works. The Court's decision was affirmed in subsequent litigation.[34]

In more recent copyright matters, the courts have stressed the legal maxim of 'de minimis non curat lex': 'the law cares not for trifles'.[35] In the case of *Newton* v. *Diamond*, the jazz flutist and composer, James W. Newton, claimed that the band, the Beastie Boys, had sampled a six-second, three-note performance of his composition, 'Choir'.[36] In 1992, Beastie Boys obtained a licence from ECM Records to use portions of the sound recording of 'Choir' in various renditions of their song 'Pass the Mic' in exchange for a one-time fee of $1000. The Beastie Boys did not obtain a licence from Newton to use the underlying composition.

At first instance, the District Court granted summary judgment that there was no copyright infringement in favour of the defendants.[37] For the majority, Schroeder CJ of the 9th Circuit Court of Appeals provides a definition and a history of the practice of 'digital sampling'. She affirmed that the Beastie Boys' use was *de minimis* and therefore not actionable:

> Because Newton conceded that 'Choir' and 'Pass the Mic' 'are substantially dissimilar in concept and feel, that is, in [their] overall thrust and meaning' and failed to offer any evidence to rebut Dr Ferrara's testimony that the sampled section is not a quantitatively or qualitatively significant portion of the 'Choir' composition, the Beastie Boys are entitled to prevail on summary judgment. On the undisputed facts of this case, we conclude that an average audience would not discern Newton's hand as a composer, apart from his talent as a performer, from Beastie Boys' use of the sample. The copying was not significant enough to constitute infringement. Beastie Boys' use of the 'Choir' composition was de minimis.[38]

The court observed that the sole basis of Newton's infringement action was his remaining copyright interest in the 'Choir' composition, because the Beastie Boys' use of the sound recording was authorized. It held that the Beastie Boys' use of a brief segment of that composition, consisting of three notes separated by a half-step over a background C note, was not sufficient to sustain a claim for copyright infringement. It affirmed the District Court's grant of summary judgment on the ground that the Beastie Boys' use of the composition was *de minimis* and therefore not actionable.

Dissenting, Graber J held that a jury reasonably could find that the Beastie Boys' use of the sampled material was not *de minimis*. She observed that the expert evidence actually showed that Newton's performance was indeed distinctive: 'The majority, then, reads the record selectively when it states that Newton failed to offer sufficient evidence that the sampled material is qualitatively significant.'[39] Accordingly, Graber J held that summary judgment was inappropriate in this case, because Newton had presented evidence establishing that reasonable ears differ over the qualitative significance of the composition of the sampled material. In her view, Newton should have been allowed to present his claims of infringement to a jury.

Newton petitioned for a writ of *certiorari*, complaining that the 'denial of copyright protection for "Choir" renders a substantial body of jazz, electronic and contemporary works by some of America's most distinguished composers virtually unprotected by copyright law'.[40] In support of Newton, an amicus brief by a group of musical composers claimed that the measurement of a musical sample was a matter of great public importance. Referring to the controversy over *The Grey Album*, the group observed:

> Low cost audio editing software such as Pro-Tools have enabled a new generation of amateur and professional musicians to craft new compositions out of pre-existing musical works on their home computer. The musical practice of digital sampling has also spawned numerous articles, books, and law review articles. This explosion of sampling technology and lack of uniform legal precedent brings to mind the pending high profile case of *MGM* v. *Grokster*, with one exception. Whereas the controversy surrounding file-sharing of musical works has existed for only a few years, the debate surrounding digital sampling in the music industry has continued unabated for over two decades.[41]

Nonetheless, the Supreme Court of the United States was unconvinced, and refused to grant special leave to Newton to appeal against the decision of the Federal Court.[42]

In *Bridgeport Music Inc.* v. *Dimension Films Inc*, the owner of a partial interest in copyright for the musical composition '100 Miles' brought an infringement action against the producer of the motion picture, *I Got the Hook Up*.[43] In the District Court, Higgins J held that there was *de minimis* use of the copyright work: 'The portion of the song at issue here is an arpeggiated chord – that is, three notes that, if struck together, comprise a chord but instead are played one at a time in very quick succession – that is repeated several times at the opening of "Get Off" '.[44] His Honour emphasized that 'a balance must be struck between protecting an artist's interests, and depriving other artists of the building blocks of future works'.[45] The judge concluded: 'Since the advent of Western music, musicians have freely borrowed themes and ideas from other musicians.'[46]

In the Court of Appeals for the 6th Circuit, Guy J reversed the District Court's decision to grant summary judgment in respect of the matter of copyright infringement.[47] His Honour observed that the requirement to seek permission from a copyright owner to sample a sound recording would not stifle artistic creativity:

> A sound recording owner has the exclusive right to 'sample' his own recording. We find much to recommend this interpretation. To begin with, there is ease of enforcement. Get a license or do not sample. We do not see this as stifling creativity in any significant way. It must be remembered that, if an artist wants to incorporate a 'riff' from another work in his or her recording, he is free to duplicate the sound of that 'riff' in the studio.[48]

The judge was disinclined to adopt an analysis of *de minimis* use: 'This case also illustrates the kind of mental, musicological and technological gymnastics that would have to be employed if one were to adopt a *de minimis* or substantial similarity analysis.'[49] The matter was remanded back to the District Court for a consideration of the availability of the defence of fair use. This hostility to digital sampling has attracted much unfavourable academic criticism.[50]

There is clearly a conflict between the approaches of the Court of Appeals for the 6th Circuit and the Court of Appeals for the 9th Circuit in respect of digital sampling and *de minimis* use. Perhaps the Supreme Court of the United States will eventually need to intervene to resolve this ongoing dispute. The issue is also prominent elsewhere. In other jurisdictions such as Australia[51] and the United Kingdom,[52] the courts have shown little fondness for the practices of digital sampling and remixing. Such Commonwealth judges have been willing to find that even the use of small portions of a musical work or a sound recording could amount to a 'substantial part' of a copyright work.

In light of such precedents in the United States and elsewhere, EMI and Sony/ATV will have to persuade a court that *The Grey Album* songs appropriated a substantial portion of each of the Lennon–McCartney compositions and the sound recordings that they claim have been infringed. The practice of 'mash-ups' pose a particular problem here. *The Grey Album* is not a minimalist piece of sampling; on the contrary, it is a maximalist appropriation of the work of The Beatles and Jay-Z. It is doubtful that a court would dismiss the amount of copying as merely trifling. Indeed, it would be likely that *The Grey Album* would be considered to use a substantial part of the musical works and the sound recordings.

II. THE GREY AREA OF FAIR USE

In the United States, there has been much debate about whether the digital sampling of musical works and sound recordings is protected under the defence of fair use.[53] The EFF commented that the hosts of *The Grey Album* could raise the defence of fair use against Sony: 'It is clear, however, that Grey Tuesday protesters have a credible fair use defense to any copyright claim by Sony/ATV.'[54]

The controversy over the *Grey Album* raised larger issues about the operation of the defence of fair use in respect of the creation and distribution of mash-ups. The holders of the copyright in the musical compositions in the *White Album*, Sony/ATV Publishing, sent a take down notice under the *Digital Millennium Copyright Act 1998* (US) to at least one Internet Service Provider. The website Stay Free! responded to the legal threats: 'Pursuant to our rights under the law, we posted *The Grey Album* and will continue to post it as part of our ongoing work on the Illegal Art Exhibit.'[55] The group observed that the web-site exhibit served to educate the public on the impact of copyright law upon the freedom of speech: 'Exercising our fair use rights, we have allowed the public to experience for themselves works such as *The Grey Album* that have been challenged on intellectual property grounds.'[56]

Traditionally, the courts have been protective of the musical works and sound recordings of The Beatles against derivative works. In *ATV Music Publishing* v. *Rogers Radio Broadcasting*, Van Camp J of the Ontario High Court ruled that a parody of the Canadian *Constitution Act* 1982 based on The Beatles' song 'You Say You Want a Revolution' was an infringement of copyright in the original work.[57] The judge lamented: 'It would be difficult ever again to listen to the original song without the words of the new song intruding.'[58] There was concern that such a decision would have a chilling effect upon freedom of artistic expression and political criticism.

Famously, in 1992, Island Records and music publisher Warner-Chappell Music instigated legal action against Negativland and SST Records Ltd in respect of the unauthorized and unattributed sampling of U2's song 'I Still Haven't Found what I'm Looking For'.[59] First, the plaintiffs claimed that the defendants were guilty of copyright infringement. Second, the plaintiffs argued that the defendants were engaged in misleading and deceptive conduct because the packaging and labelling of the CD gave the impression that it was a U2 album. Finally, the plaintiffs were concerned that the band's image would be tarnished by the expletives, curses and scatological language in the mash-up.

The matter was never resolved in court. Negativland was forced to settle over the U2 recording because it could not afford the tremendous costs involved in fighting for its rights in court. They agreed to pay $25 000 and half of the wholesale proceeds to Island Records and the music publisher Warner-Chappell Music. Negativland believed that there was an imbalance of power in the legal process, because musicians are unable to bear the financial and non-financial costs of litigation. It observed that 'when a corporation goes after a small business or low-income individuals, the conflict automatically rolls outside of the court system because of the defendant's inability to pay the costs of mounting a proper defense'.[60] Negativland commented that the dispute was resolved through bargaining power, without regard to the legality of the issue, let alone the morality. The danger is that the formal rules and principles of copyright law will be undercut and undermined by the practices of opportunistic parties.

After the litigation with U2, Negativland argued that the defence of fair use should be liberalized and expanded to allow any partial usage for any reason. They have supported the development of the public domain and the intellectual commons: 'In the isolated medium of the Internet, and in the suggestion of fair use for collage, we are being guided by new technologies to reacquaint ourselves with cultural urges toward a rejuvenated public domain, right here in the twenty-first century.'[61]

In *Campbell* v. *Acuff-Rose Music Inc.*, the Supreme Court of the United States provided a coherent theory and explanation for the fair use doctrine.[62] The case concerned whether a rap song, 'Pretty Woman', recorded by the group, 2 Live Crew, was a fair use of Roy Orbison's song, 'Oh Pretty Woman'. The Supreme Court of the United States emphasized that the fair use doctrine supported the transformative use of copyright material. Souter J stressed that the question is 'whether the new work merely "supersede[s] the objects" of the original creation, or instead adds something new, with a further purpose or different character, altering the first with new expression, meaning, or message'.[63] The Supreme Court held that parody, like other comment or criticism, deserves fair use protection. Souter J found that parody has an obvious claim to transformative value, because 'like less humorous forms of criticism, it can provide social benefit, by shedding light on an earlier work, and, in the process, creating a new one'.[64]

In *Abilene Music Inc.* v. *Sony Music Entertainment Inc.*, the plaintiffs alleged that Sony Music infringed their copyright in the famous song, 'What a Wonderful World', by issuing an album containing 'The Forest', a rap song that uses the first three lines of 'What a Wonderful World' as its introduction.[65] The District Court of New York held that the quotation of 'What a Wonderful World' in 'The Forest' was a parody and constituted fair use, and therefore did not infringe plaintiffs' copyright. Lynch J observed: 'The primary aim of *The Forest* is to portray the modern world as corrupted and venal, and it uses *Wonderful World* to underscore that message, by providing an ironic contrast to the body of the song.'[66] The judge also noted that the song itself was a target of parodic criticism, and that the creators of 'The Forest' were not merely using the original song as an ironic or satirical device to comment on what they viewed as a less than wonderful world – as was the case in the films *12 Monkeys* and *Good Morning, Vietnam*.

In considering the circumstances of *The Grey Album*, the United States courts could also take into account the rich vein of case law on appropriation art and the defence of fair use.[67]

In *Walt Disney Productions* v. *Air Pirates*, the Court of Appeals for the 9th Circuit considered an action brought by Walt Disney for copyright and trade mark infringement against two counter-culture magazines entitled 'Air Pirates Funnies'.[68] The cartoonists pleaded that their work was protected by the defence of fair use because it was a parody of the Walt Disney cartoon characters. Cummings J denied that the Air Pirates could be protected by the defence of fair use: 'By copying the images in their entirety, defendants took more than was necessary to place firmly in the reader's mind the parodied work and those specific attributes that are to be satirized.'[69]

In *Rogers* v. *Koons*, the Court of Appeals for the 2nd Circuit held that a sculpture by Jeff Koons was a copyright infringement of a photograph by Art Rogers called 'String of Puppies'.[70] Koons had argued that he was part of a tradition of post-modern art, which incorporates popular images and icons into art work to comment critically both on the incorporated art and on the political and economic system that created it.

Nonetheless, the Court of Appeals rejected Jeff Koons' defence that his work was a fair use of copyright material for the purposes of criticism or comment. It held that the copied work must be, at least in part, an object of the parody, and not just a critique of society.

In *Mattel Inc* v. *Walking Mountain Productions*, toy doll manufacturer Mattel sought to prohibit a Utah photographer called Thomas Forsythe from producing and selling photographs featuring its Barbie doll.[71] Pregerson J held that the artist Forsythe had created the sort of social criticism and parodic speech protected by the defence of fair use under copyright law, and the First Amendment. His Honour concluded that 'the benefits to the public in allowing such use – allowing artistic freedom and expression and criticism of a cultural icon – are great'.[72]

More recently, in *Blanch* v. *Koons*, Jeff Koons was successful in raising the defence of fair use in relation to his reproduction of Andrea Blanch's photograph, 'Silk Sandals by Gucci'.[73] Stanton J held that 'the painting's use does not "supersede" or duplicate the objective of the original, but uses it as raw material in a novel context to create new information, new aesthetics, and new insights'.[74] The judge added: 'Such use, whether successful or not artistically, is transformative.'[75]

Such precedents will be useful to make sense of the dispute over *The Grey Album*. In the present case, the EFF argued that there were a number of characteristics of the Grey Tuesday protest that would likely weigh in favour of those who posted *The Grey Album*:

1. the posting of *The Grey Album* is for a noncommercial purpose;
2. downloads of *The Grey Album* do not substitute for purchases of the White Album or other recordings of the Lennon–McCartney songs on the album;
3. a copyright owner is unlikely to license a work for use in a protest that is critical of the copyright owner itself;
4. *The Grey Album* is a transformative use of the White Album, not a wholesale copy; and
5. the posting of *The Grey Album* is intended as part of a commentary on the use of copyright law to stymie new kinds of musical creativity.[76]

The EFF, though, hedged its advice: 'Because fair use demands a case-by-case consideration of the particular facts surrounding any defendant, and because there is little case law addressing a situation like the one presented by Grey Tuesday, it is difficult to predict the outcome of any particular case.'[77] Nonetheless, the group believed that it was clear that Grey Tuesday protesters had a credible fair use defence to any copyright claim by the record companies.

It should be noted that the defence of fair dealing in Commonwealth countries is not as expansive as the defence of fair use in the United States. With the passage of the *Copyright Amendment Act* 2006 (Cth), the Australian Government has created a new defence of fair dealing specifically for parody and satire. The Australian defence is broader than the United States defence of fair use in that it protects satire; however, it is narrower than United States defence of fair use in that it does not embrace transformative uses. The Attorney-General, Philip Ruddock, commented on this change:

> Australians have always had an irreverent streak. Our cartoonists ensure sacred cows don't stay sacred for very long and comedians are merciless on those in public life. An integral part of their armoury is parody and satire – or, if you prefer, 'taking the mickey' out of someone. However, our copyright laws have until now done very little to protect the way people use others' works or images to parody and satirise others in the name of entertainment. I have a Bill currently before the Senate which will ensure Australia's fine tradition of satire is safe.[78]

In the United Kingdom, the Gowers Review of Intellectual Property has recommended that the British Parliament create a new copyright exception for the purpose of caricature, parody, or pastiche by 2008.[79] Andrew Gowers has also proposed that the *European Community Information Society Directive* be amended to allow for an exception for creative, transformative, or derivative works. It remains to be seen whether such policy recommendations will be adopted.

A number of scholars have argued that copyright law needs to be further reformed in order to accommodate mash-ups of copyright works. Damien O'Brien and Brian Fitzgerald have commented:

> We would suggest . . . that copyright law be reformed in such a manner as to allow certain reuses of copyright material without the permission of the copyright owner where those derivatives are highly transformative and do not impact upon the primary market of the copyright owner. There certainly appears to be a strong argument that non-commercial derivatives, which do not compete with the market for the original material, should be afforded some defence to copyright actions.[80]

Noah Balch has argued that mash-ups do not harm an artist when the new work created is entirely different from the original recording: 'In regard to

The Grey Album, it may be a matter of debate, but many music critics and fans are labeling this creation as one of the most impressive and innovative works of art in years.'[81] Nicholas Lewis maintains: 'Danger Mouse's mixture of 1960s pop legends The Beatles, with modern day rap artist Jay-Z, would present a plausible argument for fair use.'[82] Furthermore, Aaron Power observes that 'to quell this new form of cultural feedback would disserve the constitutional goal of copyright by restricting the public's access to free works that do not economically injure the original authors'.[83]

One wonders, though, whether mash-up artists, such as DJ Danger Mouse and Freelance Hellraiser, would enjoy the same cachet, if their outlaw work was accepted under mainstream copyright law.

III. COLLISION COURSE: LICENSING MASH-UPS

The Executive Director of the Creative Commons, Glenn Otis Brown, commented upon the controversy over Grey Tuesday:

> It's a great example of our two-tiered copyright system. Labels are saying, 'If you do (a remix) on the underground scene, it's OK. But if it's so compelling that people trade it all over the Internet, then we're going to sue you.'[84]

As the controversy over DJ Danger Mouse makes clear, there will be circumstances in which recording artists would be reluctant to grant permission for other artists to sample and remix their work. Jonathan Zittrain complains that copyright has become 'a means of control, rather than a means of profit'.[85] Once a musician has released a song commercially, other acts are free to perform and record their own versions of the song – as long as they pay a standard royalty. However, remixing and sampling are a different matter: 'There is no freedom to beat-match.'[86]

Lawrence Lessig of Stanford University contends that current copyright laws are biased against the production of derivative works and mash-ups because of the need for permission in respect of each use.[87] He has maintained that there was a need to reform copyright law to allow for greater latitude in respect of digital remixes and 'mash-ups'.[88] He argued that the right to control derivative works should be narrowed in scope and the defence of fair use should be expanded. Lessig called for the introduction of a system of compulsory licensing for digital sampling:

> Should the law give DJ Danger Mouse the right to remix without permission? I think so, though I understand how others find the matter a bit more grey. Should the law give DJ Danger Mouse a compulsory right to remix? That is, the right,

> conditioned upon his paying a small fee per sale? Again, I think so, and again, you might find this a bit less grey.[89]

In the absence of law reform, Lessig has proposed that remixers, mash-up artists and hackers should form trade associations – so-called 'mash-up' guilds – to make it possible to engage in creative acts, without fear of infringing copyright law.[90] In this context, Creative Commons licences designed for digital sampling and mash-ups could be of particular assistance.[91] Lessig also believed that there is a need for education – 'not about framing or law – but what you can do with the technology, and then the law will catch up'.[92]

However, it should not be assumed that recording artists and groups are necessarily as hostile to 'mash-ups' as The Beatles. Kembrew McLeod comments:

> Some forward-looking copyright owners are realizing that they ought to embrace these kinds of unauthorized acts, because it's free advertising. Instead of attacking these bastard pop confections – fruitlessly trying to track down the anonymous infringers – some record companies are appropriating the appropriations. They also realize that they can capitalize on these active audiences, expropriate this creative labor and make it theirs. Increasingly frequent in Europe is what Freelance Hellraiser calls a 'lawyer's mix', where an already existing mash-up is legally released by a record-company.[93]

The cultural critic observed that it was a paradox that digital artists should feel possessive about 'mash-ups' and object to copyright owners regaining control over derivative uses of their copyright works.

Sponsored by the car manufacturer, Audi, David Bowie staged a contest which involved the 'mash-ups' of his musical works. His web-site declared:

> The buzz in the music business is all about mash-ups. You've read about them, you've heard them, now it's time to create your own. A mash-up is a song created from parts of other songs, 'mashed-up'. Mix and match songs to create something new. That's what you'll do here with any track from David Bowie's 'Reality' CD and any other favorite Bowie track. Mix, match, mash-up and make something new.[94]

However, some underground DJs were suspicious of the commercial nature of the contest. Nicholas Reville, a co-founder of Downhill Music, observed that, although David Bowie allowed people to use and remix his copyright works, he nonetheless retained copyright over any adaptations of his works.[95] Indeed, the boilerplate contract for entrants to the contest prescribed that 'each entrant into the Contest hereby irrevocably grants . . . all copyrights, all music and music publishing rights, and all rights incidental, subsidiary, ancillary or allied thereto (including without limitation, all derivative rights) in and to the Mash-Up(s) for exploitation throughout the universe in perpetuity'.[96] There was some alarm that the practice of 'mash-ups' was being co-opted by the mainstream music industry.[97]

Seeking to emulate the success of *The Grey Album*, Jay-Z and Linkin Park collaborated on a series of mash-ups, which were recorded for posterity on compact disc and DVD entitled *Collision Course*.[98] The hybrid works included 'Dirt off Your Shoulder/Lying From You', 'Big Pimpin/Papercut', 'Numb/Encore', 'Jigga What/Faint', 'Izzo/In the End' and 'Points of Authority/99Problems/One Step Closer'. Mike Shinoda from Linkin Park and the producer of the studio recordings, observed:

> Mash-ups are best when they involve two songs that the listeners know. That's what was so promising about this project: we got to take songs that a lot of people are familiar with and totally reconstruct them. Tempo, key and style were all parts to a very elaborate balancing act.[99]

As opposed to the outlaw work of *The Grey Album*, the collaboration of *Collision Course* stayed within the bounds of legality. The work was licensed by the various owners of the musical works, the published lyrics and the sound recordings. Linkin Park's record label and Roc-a-Fella/Def Jam (Jay-Z) negotiated ownership of the 'new master', but licensed each master individually. Shinoda commented: 'With this many hands in the pot, a lot of us are not doing this for the money – people are behind this simply because they believe in the project.'[100]

Nicholas Firth, the chairman of BMG Music Publishing Worldwide, argued that the case of *Collision Course* rebutted and disproved the argument that copyright owners would refuse to license copyright works for mash-ups. He observed: 'There has been a lot of mythologizing and bad-mouthing about the inability to license these hybrid products.'[101] Firth hoped that such collaborations would provide a welcome creation of new consumer markets: 'With sales the way they are, we need innovative products.'[102] Similarly, Zomba's Melia concurs, adding, 'With this unprecedented Jay-Z/Linkin Park CD/DVD set, we are offering a solution: technology, coupled with necessity, will result in labels and publishers working more in tandem.'[103]

The artists, Jay Z and Linkin Park, also collaborated on a live performance of the mash-ups at the Roxy Theater in Los Angeles under the auspices of MTV. MTV's Calderone was enthusiastic about the performance:

> Kids today like many kinds of music. One kid will like rock, rap, hip-hop and electronic. So it's natural for them to take different-sounding records and merge them together. In this way, it shows the depth of their [musical] libraries.[104]

He observed that the live performance of the Jay-Z/Linkin Park collaboration helped make the mash-up become three-dimensional. 'Fans are watching the artists perform these songs live onstage.'[105]

Far from being admonished for his copyright misdemeanours, DJ Danger Mouse has been fêted by members of the musical industry. Much to the chagrin of EMI, Damon Albarn (formerly of Blur) hired DJ Danger Mouse to produce the second Gorillaz album, *Demon Days*, noting: 'I love the idea that you can take the past and present and make something futuristic.'[106] The project combines the eclectic music of Albarn, with animé illustrations of the fictional band by illustrator and animator, Jamie Hewlett. Notably, the musical works and sound recordings on *Demon Days* have been licensed by the copyright owners. Brian Burton earned a Grammy nomination for Producer of the Year for his work on this beguiling collaboration.

Following on from the triumph of the Gorillaz album, DJ Danger Mouse entered into collaboration with singer Cee-Lo Green, and formed the group, Gnarls Barkley. The group made history when their song 'Crazy' became the first to top the British charts through the sale of downloads alone. The album, *St Elsewhere*, has been a resounding success. In addition, DJ Danger Mouse has worked with rapper MF DOOM on the collaboration DANGERDOOM. Rather than posing a threat to the hegemony of the music industry, DJ Danger Mouse may indeed be a pioneer, leading a vanguard in terms of musical production and distribution. He has demonstrated that he can work within the confines of licensing copyright works, if need be.

IV. 'SHIZZLE MY NIZZLE': MORAL RIGHTS AND MASH-UPS

Article 6bis of the *Berne Convention* 1886 obliges nation states to provide recognition of two moral rights: in particular, the moral right of the author to be attributed as the author of a work; and the moral right of the author to object to derogatory treatment of a work which is prejudicial to their honour and reputation.

The United States Congress has resisted the introduction of moral rights into the framework of US copyright law. Famously, in *Gilliam* v. *ABC*, the creators of 'Monty Python's Flying Circus' took legal action against the American Broadcasting Corporation because they had drastically edited their programmes and edited out all profanities.[107] The Federal Court of Appeals for the 2nd Circuit observed:

> American copyright law, as presently written, does not recognize moral rights or provide a cause of action for their violation, since the law seeks to vindicate the

> economic, rather than the personal, rights of authors. Nevertheless, the economic incentive for artistic and intellectual creation that serves as the foundation for American copyright law cannot be reconciled with the inability of artists to obtain relief for mutilation or misrepresentation of their work to the public on which the artists are financially dependent. Thus courts have long granted relief for misrepresentation of an artist's work by relying on theories outside the statutory law of copyright, such as contract law, or the tort of unfair competition. Although such decisions are clothed in terms of proprietary right in one's creation, they also properly vindicate the author's personal right to prevent the presentation of his work to the public in a distorted form.[108]

In light of such precedents, the United States Congress maintains that the moral concerns of copyright creators are adequately recognized under such doctrines as the common law of misrepresentation and unfair competition: trade mark protection under the *Lanham Act* 1946 (US); and defamation law. At most, the Congress has only recognized limited moral rights protection for visual artists under the *Visual Artists Rights Act* 1990 (US).

In contrast to the United States Congress, the Australian Government introduced comprehensive moral rights legislation with the enactment of the *Copyright Amendment (Moral Rights) Act* 2000 (Cth). It recognized the right of attribution; the right against false attribution; and the right of integrity.[109]

The Federal Court of Australia considered the meaning of debasement in the intriguing matter of *Schott Musik International GmbH & Co* v. *Colossal Records Of Australia Pty Ltd And Others*.[110] The case concerned whether a techno dance adaptation made by the group Excalibur of the 'O Fortuna' chorus from Carl Orff's 'Carmina Burana' debased the original work. It involved section 55(2) of the *Copyright Act* 1968 (Cth), which provided that the entitlement to a compulsory licence for a record does not apply 'in relation to a record of an adaptation of a musical work if the adaptation debases the work'.

At first instance, Tamberlin J found that Excalibur preserved substantial and essential elements of the original intact, and communicated an exuberance and rhythmic character consistent with the spirit of the work.[111] His Honour counselled that, in assessing the notion of debasement, it was necessary to take a broad view of artistic tastes and values:

> As musical tastes are so divergent and varied (which is amply illustrated by the evidence in this case), it is necessary, in approaching the question, to pay due regard to that broad spectrum of taste and values. It would be wrong to take a strictly analytical or pedantic view of individual changes made in the adaptation and simply find the sum of those changes to reach a conclusion. Rather, it is necessary to consider the overall impression which it is likely to make on a community with a wide range of tastes and attitudes in relation to adaptations and musical forms.[112]

On appeal, the Full Federal Court upheld the finding of Tamberlin J. There was disagreement, though, over the proper test for debasement. Hill J favoured an objective test: 'I think that the test to be adopted is whether it is a consequence of the adaptation (taking into account that the adaptation differs from the original) that a reasonable person will be led to think less of the original work.'[113] However, Wilcox J rejected this method: 'I am not sure this approach would wholly relieve the Court from involvement in artistic censorship or matters of taste, as Hill J suggests.'[114] He agreed with Lindgren J that a subjective test of debasement had to be applied.

In the United Kingdom, there has also been judicial consideration of the debasement of musical works. In *Morrison Leahy Music Limited* v. *Lightbond Limited*, George Michael and Morrison Leahy Music Limited sought an injunction against Lightbond Limited from releasing samples of his work on the hits album *Bad Boys Megamix*.[115] The plaintiffs argued that Lightbond Limited should be denied a compulsory licence on the grounds that it subjected the work of George Michael to derogatory treatment. Morrit J examined whether the sampling of parts of the music altered the character of the work. He weighed evidence from the plaintiffs that the sampling had completely altered the character of the original compositions against evidence from the defendants in the form of letters of recommendation from disc jockeys who argued that the authenticity of the originals was faithfully preserved, even though only snatches had been taken from them. Morrit J also considered whether the lyrics had been modified by being taken from their context and put into a different context. There were three instances where the words 'bad boys' had been transposed onto the lyrics. Morrit J was quite willing to entertain the possibility that the remix of the work of George Michael amounted to derogatory treatment. He granted an injunction until there could be a trial.

In *Confetti Records* v. *Warner Music*, the Chancery Division of the High Court of Justice considered a claim based on the alleged derogatory treatment of 'Burnin' composed by Andrew Alcee in a remix by the United Kingdom garage band, The Heartless Crew.[116] The derogatory treatment was said to be the overlay of the song with a rap containing references to violence and drugs. Lewinson J commented that there was a need for expert evidence to decipher the meaning of the words used in the song.[117] He noted:

> Mr Howe submitted, correctly in my opinion, that the meaning of words in a foreign language could only be explained by experts. He also submitted, again correctly in my opinion, that the words of the rap, although in a form of English, were for practical purposes a foreign language. Thus he submitted that Mr Pascal's evidence, not being the evidence of an expert, was inadmissible. I think that he is right, although the occasions on which an expert drug dealer might be called to give evidence in the Chancery Division are likely to be rare.[118]

Lewinson J observed that the hearing involved 'the faintly surreal experience of three gentlemen in horsehair wigs examining the meaning of such phrases as 'mish mish man' and 'shizzle (or sizzle) my nizzle'.[119] He held: 'I hold that the mere fact that a work has been distorted or mutilated gives rise to no claim, unless the distortion or mutilation prejudices the author's honour or reputation.'[120] His Honour found that the fundamental weakness in the case was that there was no evidence about Mr Alcee's honour or reputation, or of any prejudice to either of them. As a result, the claim about derogatory treatment failed.

In light of such precedents, it is debatable whether *The Grey Album* would offend moral rights held by The Beatles and Jay-Z. DJ Danger Mouse expressed his view that *The Grey Album* was a labour of love, a tribute and a homage to the work of both The Beatles and Jay-Z.[121] He recalls being awestruck the first time he discovered the work of The Beatles:

> So when I heard that stuff for the first time, can you imagine? Beatles, Pink Floyd – it just hit me over the head. So I just stopped trying to fit in with what was around me and I just went with what I liked. I decided to be myself as much as I could be, before it was too late. And music was the thing that signified that change for me. It made it tangible. Music changed my life.[122]

DJ Danger Mouse has expressed concerns that The Beatles would dislike the mash-up: 'I'm just worried . . . whether Paul and Ringo will like it. If they say that they hate it, and that I messed up their music, I think I'll put my tail between my legs and go.'[123]

The organizers of the Grey Album protest, the music activism project Downhill Battle, denied that the album was a derogatory treatment of other musical works: 'Danger Mouse's album is one of the most "respectful" and undeniably positive examples of sampling; it honors both The Beatles and Jay-Z.'[124]

Faithful fans of The Beatles have found *The Grey Album* to be a perversion of all that is pure and good about the Fab Four. They have labelled the album as blasphemous, sacrilegious and disrespectful. One critic observed: 'The results are brilliant, frustrating, obnoxious, beautiful, and an insult to the legacy of The Beatles (though ironically, probably intended as a tribute)'.[125] He elaborates:

> Jay-Z's rap is not worthy of The Beatles backing music (even remixed). In fact, it creates the opposite effect: you get the feeling that one of the greatest records of all time by one of the greatest groups of all time has just had mud ladled all over it.[126]

The critic concluded: 'Listening, I go back and forth between digging this whole crazy messed-up adventure on one hand, and feeling like a great chapter in human creativity has been totally desecrated on the other.'[127] Such views would lend credence to the argument that *The Grey Album* debases the integrity of its musical sources. However, this evidence would have to be counter-balanced against the artist's intentions, and the full range of artistic tastes of musical audiences.

Not only do mash-ups raise concerns about the breach of economic and moral rights under copyright law, such musical works could also infringe performers' rights: so-called 'neighbouring rights'.[128] Mash-ups such as *The Grey Album* and *The Grey Video* could also violate publicity rights in the United States, which enable celebrities to control their name, voice and likeness.[129] For instance, in *Apple Corps Ltd.* v. *Leber*, The Beatles brought a legal action under the New York Civil Rights Law against a tribute band for breach of the right of publicity.[130] The group, Beatlemania, featured The Beatles look-alike, sound-alike, imitators performing popular Lennon–McCartney songs live on stage. Breckenridge J awarded substantial damages and an injunction to The Beatles.

There could be scope for actions against mash-up authors under other legal forms of regulation, such as trade mark law. However, there are limitations to legal actions for trade mark infringement and dilution. In *Dastar Corporation* v. *Twentieth Century Fox Film Corporation*, the Supreme Court of the United States held that section 43(a) of the *Lanham Act* 1946 (US) does not prevent the unaccredited copying of an uncopyrighted work.[131] Scalia J observed:

> The rights of a patentee or copyright holder are part of a carefully crafted bargain, under which, once the patent or copyright monopoly has expired, the public may use the invention or work at will and without attribution. Thus, in construing the Lanham Act, we have been careful to caution against misuse or over-extension of trademark and related protections into areas traditionally occupied by patent or copyright.[132]

His Honour concluded that 'allowing a cause of action under §43(a) for that representation would create a species of mutant copyright law that limits the public's federal right to copy and to use expired copyrights'.[133] Digital sampling and mash-ups sometimes even raise related questions of defamation.[134]

CONCLUSION

The controversy over the mash-up of *The Grey Album* is emblematic of the wider debate over consumer rights and copyright law. Music critic and cultural theorist, Sam Howard-Spink, comments:

> The remix today is part of how our culture operates and relates to itself. The blending of styles, the appropriation of signs and symbols, sounds and images – this is postmodernism at work. And yet it is more, because in its own way it is a form of progress in that it reveals the democratic and emancipatory potential of new technologies, and the capacity for cultural participation to actualize that potential . . . Mash-ups take familiar vocal and musical tracks and blend them together to create something new and unexpected. Grey Tuesday should be viewed as a case study of a similar blending of cultural activity and political activism, and as a model for future online political engagement in the space where culture and technology intersect with law and policy.[135]

Howard-Spink claims that Grey Tuesday was a significant protest by creators and consumers alike against the stifling copyright controls of a hegemonic music industry: 'The participation of amateur remixers and P2P users constitutes a newly emergent field of resistance to the dominating, centralized, bureaucratic control that is characteristic of the oligopolistic recorded music industry – and, by extension, all monopolizers of cultural and informational goods and the 'pay for play' copyright absolutism that is their goal.'[136] He hailed such online activism as a symbol of 'semiotic democracy'.[137]

The dispute over *The Grey Album* highlights the gulf that separates copyright law and social practices in the musical community. At present, copyright owners can exercise plenary control over use of their works, much to the detriment of creators and consumers. The author of the book *Digital Copyright*, Jessica Litman,[138] sagely observes that there is a need to simplify and reform copyright law:

> I suggest that if copyright law is going to apply to consumers as well as publishers and record labels, we need to replace the current long incomprehensible law with something short and intuitive. My suggestion is to junk the current structure entirely and recast copyright as an exclusive right of commercial exploitation. Copyright owners would have the sole right to exploit their works commercially or authorize others to do so, but would not be entitled to control noncommercial uses.[139]

Such a reformation of copyright law should be guided by the overriding goal of promoting the public interest in the encouragement and dissemination of works of the arts and intellect. It should be recognized that the *de minimis* use of copyright works is wholly acceptable. There ought to be an expansive application of the defence of fair use, especially in respect of transformative use of copyright works. There is a need for wider compulsory licensing of not only covers of sound recordings, but remixes and mash-ups as well. There could be scope for Creative Commons licences to allow for greater material to fall into the public domain. The moral rights of authors must be tempered to guard against the threat of artistic censorship.

A music journalist, Devon Powers, agreed that there was a need for a less reverential approach to The Beatles and other cultural icons:

> Maybe it's time to let go of the clout granted to [The] Beatles, and all these rock legends – that issue is one that's up for debate. But to me, it is beyond question that it is certainly time to free ourselves of the cultural nostalgia and legal stagnation that have allowed their music to fossilize. Music journalists must applaud Danger Mouse's astounding artistic accomplishment, and let their critical praise become part of the discussion about what's at stake as copyright goes awry. And for all of us who hold music dear, we owe it to ourselves to not only let our musical past footnote our musical present, but also allow that past to live and breathe, change and reform, disappear and reappear in unexpected ways.[140]

There is a need to ensure that copyright law does preserve cultural works in aspic, and prevent any modern reinterpretations of the material, or censor critical comment, however harsh and astringent it might sound.

NOTES

1. Newitz, A. (2004), 'Protest Music', AlterNet, http://www.alternet.org/columnists/story/19164/, 7 July.
2. Vaidhyanathan, Siva (2004), *The Anarchist In The Library: How the Clash Between Freedom and Control is Hacking the Real World and Crashing the System*, New York: Basic Books, p. 104.
3. Vaidhyanathan, S. (2005), 'Remote Control: The Rise of Electronic Cultural Policy', *The Annals of the American Academy of Political and Social Science*, **597** (1), 122–33 at 132.
4. Vaidhyanathan, Siva (2004), *The Anarchist In The Library: How the Clash Between Freedom and Control is Hacking the Real World and Crashing the System*, New York: Basic Books, p. 102.
5. The Freelance Hellraiser, http://www.freelancehellraiser.com.
6. Frere-Jones, S. (2005), 'The New Math of Mash-Ups', *The New Yorker*, http://www.newyorker.com/printables/critics/050110crmu_music, 3 January.
7. Phillips, D. (2002), 'Smells Like Teen Booty: What Do You Get If You Cross Destiny's Child With Nirvana?', *The Guardian*, 27 February, 22.
8. Frere-Jones, S. (2005), 'The New Math of Mash-Ups', *The New Yorker*, http://www.newyorker.com/printables/critics/050110crmu_music, 3 January.
9. Ibid.
10. Bradbury, D. (2006), 'Jockeying for Attention: Amateur Film Editors Can Subversively Recut Movies and Adverts', *The Guardian*, 20 April.
11. 'Endless Love', http://politicalhumor.about.com/cs/bushmultimedia/v/blendlesslove.htm.
12. O'Brien, D. and B. Fitzgerald (2006), 'Mashups, remixes and copyright law', *Internet Law Bulletin*, **9**(2), 17–19.
13. Hertz, K. (2004), 'Re: JibJab Media/Unauthorized Use of "This Land is Your Land",' in Sonnenschein, Nath and Rosenthal LLP, http://www.eff.org/legal/cases/JibJab_v._Ludlow/20040727_jibjabthreat.pdf.
14. *JibJab Media Inc.* v. *Ludlow Music Inc* (2004), http://www.eff.org/legal/cases/JibJab_v._Ludlow/20040729_JibJab_Complaint.pdf; and EFF (2004), 'Re JibJab Media Inc and Ludlow Music Inc', http://www.eff.org/legal/cases/JibJab_v._Ludlow/20040728_Ltr_to_LiCalsi.pdf.

15. Young, A. (2004), 'Music Generations Collide on the Grey Album', *Sidelines Online*, 4 March.
16. DJ Danger Mouse, www.djdangermouse.com.
17. Moss, C. (2004), 'Grey Album Producer Danger Mouse Explains How He Did It', *MTV News*, http://www.mtv.com/news/articles/1485693/20040311/jay_z.jhtml, 3 November.
18. Reuters (2004), 'DJ Mixes Beatles, Jay-Z Into Grey', CNN, http://edition.cnn.com/2004/SHOWBIZ/Music/02/19/leisure.grey.album.reut, 19 February.
19. Ibid.
20. Moody, N.M. (2004), 'Album Mixing Jay-Z's "Black Album" with Beatles "White Album" an Unauthorized Hit', *Associated Press*, 25 February.
21. Grey Tuesday, http://www.greytuesday.org.
22. Downhill Battle, http://www.downhillbattle.org.
23. Downhill Battle (2004), 'Incredible Success', Grey Tuesday, http://www.greytuesday.org.
24. Ibid.
25. For a history of copyright law and music, see Demers, Joanna (2006), *Steal This Music: How Intellectual Property Law Affects Musical Creativity*, Athens and London: The University of Georgia Press.
26. Howard-Spink, S. (2004), 'Grey Tuesday, Online Cultural Activism and the Mash-Up of Music and Politics', *First Monday*, **9**(10), http://www.firstmonday.org/issues/issue9_10/howard/index.html.
27. Werde, B. (2004), 'Defiant Downloads Rise From Underground', *The New York Times*, 25 February.
28. Jensen, J.C. (2004), 'Re: *The Grey Album* and Misappropriation of Capitol Records, Inc's Sound Recordings', Cowan, Liebowitz and Latman, P.C.
29. Ibid.
30. EFF (2004), 'Grey Tuesday: A Quick Overview of the Legal Terrain', http://www.eff.org/IP/grey_tuesday.php.
31. Ibid.
32. *Bright Tunes Music Corp*. v. *Harrisongs Music, Ltd*., 420 F. Supp. 177 (S.D.N.Y.1976).
33. *Bright Tunes Music Corp*. v. *Harrisongs Music, Ltd*., 420 F. Supp. 177 at 180 (S.D.N.Y. 1976).
34. *ABKCO Music, Inc*. v. *Harrisongs Music, Ltd*., 722 F.2d 988 (2d Cir. 1983).
35. Kaplicer, B. (2000), 'Rap Music and De Minimis Copying: Applying the Ringgold and Sandoval Approach to Digital Samples', *Cardozo Arts and Entertainment Law Journal*. **18**(1), 227–55; and Blessing, D. (2004), 'Who Speaks Latin Anymore?: Translating De Minimis Use For Application to Music Copyright Infringement and Sampling', *William and Mary Law Review*, **45**, 2399–2423.
36. *Newton* v. *Diamond* 204 F. Supp. 2d 1244 (2002); *Newton* v. *Diamond* 388 F.3d 1189 (9th Cir. 2004); and *Newton* v. *Diamond* 125 S.Ct. 2905 (2005).
37. *Newton* v. *Diamond* 204 F. Supp. 2d 1244 (2002).
38. *Newton* v. *Diamond* 388 F.3d 1189 at 1197 (9th Cir. 2004).
39. *Newton* v. *Diamond* 388 F.3d 1189 at 1198 (9th Cir. 2004).
40. Newton (2005), 'Appellate Petition, Motion and Filing in *Newton* v. *Diamond*', 2005 WL 585205, 27.
41. Meet the Composer (2005), 'Amicus Brief in *Newton* v. *Diamond*', 2005 WL 1170246, 10.
42. *Newton* v. *Diamond* 125 S.Ct. 2905 (2005).
43. *Bridgeport Music Inc*. v. *Dimension Films Inc*. 230 F. Supp. 2nd 830 (2002).
44. *Bridgeport Music Inc*. v. *Dimension Films Inc*. 230 F. Supp. 2nd 830 at 839 (2002).
45. *Bridgeport Music Inc*. v. *Dimension Films Inc*. 230 F. Supp. 2nd 830 at 842 (2002).
46. *Bridgeport Music Inc*. v. *Dimension Films Inc*. 230 F. Supp. 2nd 830 at 842 (2002).
47. *Bridgeport Music Inc*. v. *Dimension Films Inc*. 410 F.3d 792 (6th Cir. 2005).
48. *Bridgeport Music Inc*. v. *Dimension Films Inc*. 410 F.3d 792 at 801 (6th Cir. 2005).
49. *Bridgeport Music Inc*. v. *Dimension Films Inc*. 410 F.3d 792 at 802 (6th Cir. 2005).
50. Mueller, J. (2006), 'All Mixed Up: Bridgeport Music v. Dimension Films and de Minimis Digital Sampling', *Indiana Law Journal*, **81**, 435–63; Somoano, M.L. (2006), 'Bridgeport Music Inc. v. Dimension Films: Has Unlicensed Digital Sampling of

Copyrighted Sound Recordings Come to an End?', *Berkeley Technology Law Journal*, **21**, 289–309; and Kim, S. (2006), 'Taking De Minimis out of the Mix: The Sixth Circuit Threatens to Pull the Plug on Digital Sampling in Bridgeport Music Inc. v. Dimension Films', *Villanova Sports and Entertainment Law Journal*, **13**, 103–31.

51. In *Universal Music Australia Pty Ltd* v. *Miyamoto* [2003] FCA 812 (18 July 2003); [2004] FCA 982 (20 July 2004), Lindgren J held that five disk jockeys had infringed copyright because they had remixed tracks, and sold the resulting sound recordings, without the permission of the copyright holders, and Anthem Records who sold compact discs containing the remixed tracks, contained substantial parts of sound recordings. In *Commonwealth Director of Public Prosecutions* v. *Ng, Tran and Le* (unreported, Sydney Central Local Court, Henson DCM, 18 November 2003), Deputy Chief Magistrate Graeme Henson held that the operators of a website called MP3 WMA Land had infringed copyright by making CD albums and singles commercially available, and remixing such works.
52. In *Hyperion Records Ltd* v. *Warner Music (UK) Ltd* (unreported, Chancery Division of the High Court, 17 May 1991), Hugh Laddie, sitting as a deputy judge of the High Court, found that it was arguable on the facts as to whether seven or eight notes, lasting a mere four seconds, could be considered to be a substantial part of the plaintiff's sound recording. However, his Honour rejected the argument that copyright subsisted in the seven or eight notes in the introduction of the 'O Euchari' track as a separate work to the sound recording. In *Ludlow Music Inc.* v. *Williams* [2002] F.S.R. 57; and *Ludlow Music Inc.* v. *Williams* (No. 2) [2002] E.M.L.R. 29 [2002] EWHC 638 Ch D, The judge held that Robbie Williams' composition called 'Jesus in a Camper Van', infringed the copyright in the lyrics of the song, 'I Am The Way (New York Town)' by Loudon Wainwright, even though it only copied one out of four verses.
53. Bently, L. (1989), 'Sampling and Copyright: Is the Law on the Right Track?', *Journal of Business Law*, 113–25, 405–413; Bently, L. and B. Sherman (1992), 'Cultures of Copying: Digital Sampling and Copyright Law', *Entertainment Law Review*, **3** (5), 158–63; Arts Law Centre of Australia (2000), *Push the Button: Music Seminar*, Sydney: Harbourside Brasserie, 7 December; and Carnachan, R. (1999), 'Sampling and the Music Industry: A Discussion of the Implications of Copyright Law', *Te Mata Koi: Auckland University Law Review*, **8**(4), 1034–60.
54. EFF (2004), 'Grey Tuesday: A Quick Overview of the Legal Terrain', http://www.eff.org/IP/grey_tuesday.php.
55. Illegal Art, http://www.illegal-art.org.
56. Illegal Art, http://www.illegal-art.org.
57. *ATV Music Publishing* v. *Rogers Radio Broadcasting* (1982) 35 O.R. (2d) 417 (Ont. H.C.).
58. *ATV Music Publishing* v. *Rogers Radio Broadcasting* (1982) 35 O.R. (2d) 417 at 422 (Ont. H.C.).
59. Negativland (1995), *Fair Use: The Story of the Letter U and the Number 2*, Concord: Seeland.
60. Ibid.
61. Negativland (2003), 'Two Relationships to a Cultural Domain', *Law and Contemporary Problems*, **66**, 239–62.
62. *Campbell* v. *Acuff-Rose Music, Inc.* 510 U.S. 569 (1994).
63. *Campbell* v. *Acuff-Rose Music, Inc.* 510 U.S. 569 at 579 (1994).
64. *Campbell* v. *Acuff-Rose Music, Inc.* 510 U.S. 569 at 579 (1994).
65. *Abilene Music, Inc.* v. *Sony Music Entertainment, Inc.* 320 F.Supp.2d 84 (2003).
66. *Abilene Music, Inc.* v. *Sony Music Entertainment, Inc.* 320 F.Supp.2d 84 at 90 (2003).
67. See Greenberg, L. (1992), 'The Art Of Appropriation: Puppies, Piracy and Post-modernism', *Cardozo Arts And Entertainment Law Review*, **11**, 1–33; Bowrey, K. (1994), 'Copyright, The Paternity Of Artistic Works, And The Challenge Posed By Postmodern Artists', *Intellectual Property Journal*, **8**, 285–317; Wood, L.J. (1996), 'Copyright Law And Postmodern Artistic Practice: Paradox And Difference', *Media And Arts Law Review*, **1**, 72–85; Rimmer, M. (1998), 'Four Stories About Copyright Law And Appropriation Art', *Media And Arts Law Review*, **3** (4), 180–93; Rimmer, M.

(2002), 'Daubism: Copyright Law And Artistic Works', *Murdoch University Electronic Journal of Law*, **9**(4), http://www.murdoch.edu.au/elaw/issues/v9n4/rimmer94.html; McLean, Daniel, and Karsten Schubert (eds) (2002), *Dear Images: Art, Copyright and Culture*. London: Riding House; and Rimmer, M. (2004), 'The Valley Of The Dolls: Brand Protection And Artistic Parody', *Australian Intellectual Property Bulletin*, **16** (10), 160–63.

68. *Walt Disney Productions* v. *Air Pirates*, 581 F. 2d 751 (9th Cir, 1978); see also: Levin, Bob (2003), *The Pirates And The Mouse: Disney's War Against The Counterculture*, Seattle: Fantagraphics Books.
69. *Walt Disney Productions* v. *Air Pirates*, 581 F. 2d 751, 758 (9th Cir, 1978).
70. *Rogers* v. *Koons*, 960 F. 2d 301(2nd Cir, 1992).
71. *Mattel Inc* v. *Walking Mountain Productions* 353 F. 3d 792 (2004).
72. *Mattel Inc* v. *Walking Mountain Productions* 353 F. 3d 792, 806 (2004).
73. *Blanch* v. *Koons* U.S. Dist. LEXIS 26299 (2005).
74. *Blanch* v. *Koons* U.S. Dist. LEXIS 26299, 10 (2005).
75. *Blanch* v. *Koons* U.S. Dist. LEXIS 26299, 10 (2005).
76. EFF (2004), 'Grey Tuesday: A Quick Overview of the Legal Terrain', http://www.eff.rg/IP/grey_tuesday.php.
77. Ibid.
78. Ruddock, P. (2006), 'Parody Permit in the Spirit of Fair Play', *Daily Telegraph*, 30 November, p. 30.
79. Gowers, Andrew (2006), *Gowers Review of Intellectual Property*, London: HM Treasury, December, http://www.hmtreasury.gov.uk/media/583/91/pbr_06_gowersreport_755_pdf.
80. O'Brien, D. and B. Fitzgerald (2006), 'Mashups, Remixes and Copyright Law', *Internet Law Bulletin*, **9** (2), 17–19 at 18.
81. Balch, N. (2005), 'The Grey Note', *Review of Litigation*, **24**, 581–607 at 607.
82. Lewis, N. (2005), 'Shades of Grey: Can The Copyright Fair Use Defense Adapt to New Re-Contextualised Forms of Music and Art?', *American University Law Review*, **55**, 267–306 at 304.
83. Power, A. (2006), 'The Mouse that Roared: Addressing the Post-Modern Quandary of Mash-ups Through Traditional Fair Use Analysis', *Vanderbilt Journal of Entertainment and Technology Law*, **8**, 531–40 at 540.
84. Shachtman, N. (2004), 'Copyright Enters A Grey Area', *Wired News*, http://www.wired.com/news/digiwood/0,1412,62276,00.html, 14 February.
85. Ibid.
86. Ibid.
87. Farber, D. (2006), 'Mashups and the Law', ZDNet, http://blogs.zdnet.com/BTL/?p=2614, 20 February.
88. Lessig, Lawrence (2004), *Free Culture: How Big Media Uses Technology And The Law To Lock Down Culture And Control Creativity*. New York: Penguin Books.
89. Lessig, L. (2004), 'The Black and White Waged By Grey Tuesday', Lessig Blog, http://www.lessig.org/blog/archives/001754.shtml, 24 February.
90. Farber, D. (2006), 'Mashups and the Law', ZDNet, http://blogs.zdnet.com/BTL/?p=2614, 20 February.
91. The Creative Commons, http://creativecommons.org. The Creative Commons movement is discussed in detail in Chapter 8.
92. Farber, D. (2006), 'Mashups and the Law', ZDNet, http://blogs.zdnet.com/BTL/?p=2614, 20 February.
93. McLeod, Kembrew (2005), *Freedom of Expression$^{(R)}$: Overzealous Copyright Bozos and Other Enemies of Creativity*, New York: Doubleday, p. 163.
94. David Bowie, http://www.davidbowie.com/neverFollow.
95. Terdiman, D. (2004), Mashup Artists Face the Music, *Wired News*, http://www.wired.com/news/digiwood/0,1412,63314,00.html, 4 May.
96. David Bowie, http://www.davidbowie.com/neverFollow.
97. Terdiman, D (2004), Mashup Artists Face the Music, *Wired News*, http://www.wired.com/news/digiwood/0,1412,63314,00.html, 4 May.

98. Paoletta, M. (2004), 'Linkin Park, Jay-Z come together on "Collision Course"', *Billboard*, **116**(50), 3.
99. Ibid.
100. Ibid.
101. Ibid.
102. Ibid.
103. Ibid.
104. Ibid.
105. Ibid.
106. Bhattacharya, S. (2006), 'Genius in Disguise', Entertainment Guide, *The Age*, 12 May, 2.
107. *Gilliam and others* v. *American Broadcasting Corporation* 538 F.2d 14 (2d Circuit, 1976).
108. *Gilliam and others* v. *American Broadcasting Corporation* 538 F.2d 14 at 25-27 (2d Circuit, 1976).
109. Sainsbury, Maree (2003), *Moral Rights And Their Application In Australia*, Sydney: Federation Press.
110. *Schott Musik International GmbH & Co And Others* v. *Colossal Records Of Australia Pty Ltd And Others* (1996) 71 FCR 37, 36 IPR 267; aff'd (1997) 75 FCR 321, 38 IPR 1.
111. *Schott Musik International GmbH & Co And Others* v. *Colossal Records Of Australia Pty Ltd And Others* (1996) 71 FCR 37, 36 IPR 267.
112. *Schott Musik International GmbH & Co And Others* v. *Colossal Records Of Australia Pty Ltd And Others* (1996) 71 FCR 37, 36 IPR 267.
113. *Schott Musik International GmbH & Co And Others* v. *Colossal Records Of Australia Pty Ltd And Others* (1997) 75 FCR 321, 38 IPR 1.
114. *Schott Musik International GmbH & Co And Others* v. *Colossal Records Of Australia Pty Ltd And Others* (1997) 75 FCR 321, 38 IPR 1.
115. *Morrison Leahy Music Limited* v. *Lightbond Limited* [1993] EMLR 144.
116. *Confetti Records* v. *Warner Music* (2003) EWCH 1274 (CH).
117. Hamilton, A. (2003), 'Rap Is A Foreign Language, Rules Rueful Judge', *The Times*, http://www.timesonline.co.uk/article/0,2-704600,00.html, 6 June.
118. *Confetti Records* v. *Warner Music* (2003) EWCH 1274 (CH).
119. *Confetti Records* v. *Warner Music* (2003) EWCH 1274 (CH).
120. *Confetti Records* v. *Warner Music* (2003) EWCH 1274 (CH).
121. Reuters (2004), 'DJ Mixes Beatles, Jay-Z Into Grey', CNN, http://edition.cnn.com/2004/SHOWBIZ/Music/02/19/leisure.grey.album.reut, 19 February.
122. Bhattacharya, S. (2006), 'Genius in Disguise', Entertainment Guide, *The Age*, 12 May, 2.
123. Shachtman, N. (2004), 'Copyright Enters A Grey Area', *Wired News*, 14 February.
124. Ibid.
125. Hacker, S. (2004), 'Thoughts on the Grey Album', http://birdhouse.org/blog/archives/001233.php, 27 February.
126. Ibid.
127. Ibid.
128. Morgan, Owen (2002), *International Protection of Performers' Rights*, Oxford: Hart Publishing.
129. For a wider discussion of the right of publicity, see Beverley-Smith, Huw (2002), *The Commercial Appropriation of Personality*, Cambridge: Cambridge University Press.
130. *Apple Corps Ltd.* v. *Leber* 229 U.S.P.Q. 1015 (1986).
131. *Dastar Corporation* v. *Twentieth Century Fox Film Corporation* 539 U.S. 23 (2003).
132. *Dastar Corporation* v. *Twentieth Century Fox Film Corporation* 539 U.S. 23 at 33–4 (2003).
133. *Dastar Corporation* v. *Twentieth Century Fox Film Corporation* 539 U.S. 23 at 34 (2003).
134. For instance, the leader of One Nation, Pauline Hanson, successfully sued the ABC for defamation over a song called 'A Backdoor Man', which featured samples of her speeches arranged by a drag queen called Pauline Pantsdown: *Hanson* v. *ABC* (unreported, Supreme Court of Queensland, 1 September 1997); *ABC* v. *Hanson* (unreported, Supreme Court of Queensland Court of Appeal, 28 September 1998); and *ABC*

v. *Hanson* (unreported, High Court of Australia, special leave to appeal refused, 24 June 1999).
135. Howard-Spink, S. (2004), 'Grey Tuesday, Online Cultural Activism and the Mash-Up of Music and Politics', *First Monday*, **9** (10), http://www.firstmonday.org/issues/issue9_10/howard/index.html.
136. Ibid.
137. Ibid.
138. Litman, Jessica (2001), *Digital Copyright*, New York: Prometheus Books.
139. Pawlo, M. (2004), 'Jessica Litman on the Redesign of Copyright', *GrepLaw*. http://grep.law.harvard.edu/article.pl?sid=04/02/25/0344203&mode=flat, 23 February.
140. Powers, D. (2004), 'More Than Words: Musings on Music Journalism', *Pop Matters*, http://popmatters.com/music/columns/powers/040310.shtml, 10 March.

5. Grand turismo in the high court: copyright law and technological protection measures

> Sony Music wants to entertain you. Sony Electronics wants to equip you. The problem is that when it comes to digital media, their interests are diametrically opposed. (Frank Rose, 'The Civil War Inside Sony'[1])

In the 1990s, there was a push by copyright industries to obtain legal backing for technological protection measures (TPMs) designed to prevent copying. Article 11 of the *WIPO Copyright Treaty 1996* provided that 'contracting parties shall provide adequate legal protection and effective legal remedies against the circumvention of effective technological measures that are used by authors in connection with the exercise of their rights under this Treaty or the Berne Convention and that restrict acts, in respect of their works, which are not authorized by the authors concerned or permitted by law'.

The *Digital Millennium Copyright Act* 1998 (US) (*DMCA*) provided for new copyright offences related to circumventing TPMs[2] and disseminating decryption tools that could disable or avoid TPMs.[3] Pamela Samuelson has argued that the provisions of the *DMCA* were designed to buttress the interests of copyright industries:

> . . . by colorful use of high rhetoric and forceful lobbying, Hollywood and its allies were successful in persuading Congress to adopt the broad anti-circumvention legislation they favoured . . . Had the Administration sought to broker a fairer compromise between the interests of Hollywood and its allies and the interests of Silicon Valley and its allies, this process would almost certainly have produced better legislation than the anti-circumvention provisions of the DMCA.[4]

There has been concern expressed that the drafting of the anti-circumvention provisions was the result of lobbying by copyright industries, such as the Motion Picture Association of America (MPAA) and the Recording Industry Association of America (RIAA). Arguably, the long, convoluted, prescriptive provisions of the *DMCA* exceeded the minimalist requirements of the *WIPO Copyright Treaty* 1996.

Thus far, the *DMCA* has been interpreted in an expansive fashion by United States courts. In early case law, the United States courts were unwilling to countenance constitutional challenges to the TPMs regime in the *DMCA*.[5] Indeed, in the *2600: The Hacker Quarterly* case, Kaplan J denied that the *DMCA* should be read in the context of constitutional arguments about freedom of speech:

> Society must be able to regulate the use and dissemination of code in appropriate circumstances. The Constitution, after all, is a framework for building a just and democratic society. It is not a suicide pact.[6]

In addition, there have been concerns that TPMs have been deployed to undermine the defence of fair use, and the *Sony Betamax* decision. There have been a number of precedents, in which copyright owners have successfully sued technology developers for breach of TPMs, notwithstanding the substantial, non-infringing uses of their products.[7] Indeed, in his book, *Free Culture*, Lawrence Lessig complains that TPMs have disrupted the traditional balance in copyright law: 'Using code, copyright owners restrict fair use; using the *DMCA*, they punish those who would attempt to evade the restrictions on fair use that they impose through code.'[8] There have been concerns that TPMs have been used for anti-competitive purposes in attempts to control secondary markets for remote controls, printer cartridges, data storage and wireless telephone services.[9] There have also been a number of cases in which there have been difficulties engaging in security testing[10] and reverse engineering because of the use of TPMs.[11] Furthermore, there has been a push within Congress to review the operation of TPMs under the *DMCA*. There has also been a parallel debate about the use of a 'Broadcast Flag' to prevent the unauthorized copying and distribution of digital media.[12]

Fred von Lohmann of the Electronic Frontier Foundation (EFF) has argued that the regulation of TPMs has failed to achieve its stated goal of reducing copyright infringements:

> To put the matter simply, when enacting section 1201 of the DMCA, it appears that legislators may have chosen to regulate the wrong thing. The error is particularly grievous in light of the mounting evidence that the anti-circumvention provisions of the DMCA are inflicting serious collateral damage on other public values, including scientific research, free speech, innovation, fair use and competition. There have been more than a dozen reported incidents involving DMCA threats to researchers, journalists, and hobbyists. Bowing to DMCA liability fears, self-censorship is common: online service providers and bulletin board operators have censored discussions of copy-protection systems; programmers have removed computer security programs from their Web sites; and students, scientists, and security experts have stopped publishing the details of their research.[13]

The attorney concluded that policy makers in the US should give serious consideration to repealing the anti-circumvention provisions of the *DMCA* in favour of a new, workable approach to the digital crisis.[14] He advised that the trading partners of the US should refrain from adopting such a regime.

This chapter considers the debate over copyright law and TPMs, especially in the context of the Australian *Copyright Amendment (Digital Agenda) Act* 2000 (Cth) (*Digital Agenda Act*) and the *DMCA*. Rather than conduct a survey of the large and growing jurisprudence associated with TPMs, this chapter focuses upon the conduct of the multinational entertainment company, Sony.

Despite being the champion of home recording rights in the *Sony Betamax* decision, Sony has also relied upon TPMs to protect the content of its computer programs, compact discs and films. As Frank Rose observed in *Wired Magazine*, Sony is riven by divisions between its consumer electronics group and its recording companies and motion picture studios.[15] Section one focuses upon the Australian High Court decision in *Stevens* v. *Kabushiki Kaisha Sony Computer Entertainment*[16] *(Stevens* v. *Sony)*, the first time a superior court has had the opportunity to consider the operation of TPMs. The case is a synecdoche for the various theoretical and practical concerns expressed about digital rights management. The Australian High Court considers constitutional objections to TPMs, namely, that 'para-copyright' measures are beyond the scope of government power, and in any case violate protections of freedom of speech. The judges also examine whether TPMs will affect consumer rights to engage in fair dealing, and make use of library and archives exceptions. The Australian High Court canvassed larger policy issues about TPMs and competition policy as well. Section two examines the ramifications of the controversy over the Sony BMG Rootkit Software, particularly in relation to digital rights management information and privacy.[17] A commentator has observed that the scandal has 'reignited a dispute in the public sphere over the ways consumers should be allowed to use copyrighted digital information and, conversely, just how far copyright holders can go to secure their intellectual property against piracy'.[18] In the light of such controversies, the conclusion evaluates various US Congressional proposals designed to protect the interests of consumers, such as the *Digital Media Consumers' Rights Act* 2003 (US) and the *Benefit Authors without Limiting Advancement or Net Consumer Expectations (BALANCE) Act* 2003 (US).

I. SONY PLAYSTATION: COPYRIGHT LAW AND TECHNOLOGICAL PROTECTION MEASURES

> In 1493, Pope Alexander VI, perhaps the most corrupt of pontiffs, divided the New World of Americas between Spain and Portugal, in a supreme act of arrogance. These days global marketers don't require papal dispensation . . .

> Pope Alexander's 1493 wave of the papal staff found echoes in Australia's High Court recently, when it dealt with a case involving Sony's bid to divide the world into three separate markets for its Playstations and their accompanying CD-ROM games. (Allan Fels and Fred Brenchley, *The Australian Financial Review*[19])

In February 2005, there was an unusual spectacle in the High Court of Australia in the capital city of Canberra. Two junior lawyers were playing an arcade game called 'Grand Turismo' on a Sony PlayStation II (also known as 'Gran Turismo'). The motorcycle race was projected onto the walls of the highest court of the land. Six High Court judges watched this display, with a mixture of curiosity and intrigue. They were hitherto unfamiliar with the technology involved. The High Court had requested this demonstration in an effort to determine whether a Kensington man, Eddy Stevens, had circumvented any TPMs pertaining to the Sony PlayStation II. The matter concerned the amendments made to the *Copyright Act* 1968 (Cth) by the *Digital Agenda Act*. It also provided an opportunity for the High Court to contemplate the future impact of the *Australia–United States Free Trade Agreement* 2004 *(AUSFTA)* in respect of TPMs.

A. The *Digital Agenda Act*

In 2000, the *Digital Agenda Act* established a new regime providing remedies for copyright owners in respect of the circumvention of TPMs.

Section 116A of the *Copyright Act* 1968 (Cth) provides a right of action to the owner or exclusive licensee of the copyright in a work or other subject matter which is protected by a 'technological protection measure'. The right of action is against a person who makes, sells or does certain other acts in relation to, a 'circumvention device' capable of circumventing, or facilitating the circumvention of, the 'technological protection measure'.

Section 10(1) of the *Copyright Act* 1968 (Cth) provides a definition of TPMs:

> 'Technological protection measure' means a device or product, or a component incorporated into a process, that is designed, in the ordinary course of its operation, to prevent or inhibit the infringement of copyright in a work or other subject-matter by either or both of the following means:
>
> (a) by ensuring that access to the work or other subject matter is available solely by use of an access code or process (including decryption, unscrambling or other transformation of the work or other subject-matter) with the authority of the owner or exclusive licensee of the copyright;
> (b) through a copy control mechanism.

TPMs could include copy-control protection for compact discs, encryption for DVDs, software protected by passwords and registration codes.

Sony brought legal action against Eddy Stevens who had mod-chipped Sony Playstation consoles. The company claimed that Stevens had circumvented an access code protected as a TPM under the Australian *Copyright Act* 1968 (Cth). In the alternative, Sony argued that Eddy Stevens had infringed copyright in temporary reproductions and cinematographic films.

The competition regulator, the Australian Competition and Consumer Commission (ACCC), intervened early in this case as a friend of the court. The ACCC has expressed policy concerns about TPMs, suggesting that 'the provisions increase the likelihood of anti-competitive conduct with consequent detrimental outcomes for both consumers of the copyright works and society in general'.[20] The Australian Digital Alliance later appeared as a friend of the court in this case, because of fears that TPMs would undermine fair dealing and access to information.

At first instance in the Federal Court, Sackville J considered the meaning of TPMs under section 10(1) of the *Copyright Act* 1968 (Cth). His Honour ruled that the protective devices relied upon by the Sony companies could not be regarded as TPMs because they merely discouraged people from copying these games as a prelude to playing them on a PlayStation console:

> It is in this sense that the device or product must be designed, in the ordinary course of its operation, to prevent or inhibit the infringement of copyright in a work. I do not think the definition is concerned with devices or products that do not, by their operations, prevent or curtail specific acts infringing or facilitating the infringement of copyright in a work, but merely have a general deterrent or discouraging effect on those who might be contemplating infringing copyright in a class of works, for example by making unlawful copies of a CD-ROM.[21]

The judge doubted 'whether the temporary storage of part of a computer program in the RAM of a computer (in this case, the PlayStation console) can be said to constitute reproduction of a substantial part of the computer program "in a material form" and thus infringe copyright in the computer program'.[22] His Honour also questioned whether the PlayStation game embodied a 'cinematograph film'.

Following the lead of United Kingdom authorities on TPMs,[23] the Full Federal Court allowed the appeal by Sony. The Bench held that the definition of TPMs embraces inhibition in the sense of deterrence or discouragement of infringement, which results from a denial of access to a program copied in infringement of copyright.[24] Having regard to extraneous materials, Lindgren J believed that a broader approach to the interpretation of TPMs was intended by the legislature:

> If, as in the present case, the owner of copyright in a computer program devises a technological measure which has the purpose of inhibiting infringement of that copyright, the legislature intended that measure to be protected (subject to any express exception), even though the inhibition is indirect and operates prior to the hypothetical attempt at access and the hypothetical operation of the circumvention device.[25]

For his part, French J expressed his frustration at the complicated legislative regime, noting: 'The law develops its own access codes requiring special readers.'[26] Although aware of policy concerns about the expansion of copyright protection and related issues of competition policy, he adopted a broad definition of TPMs, observing: 'It is not for the Court to cage the ordinary meaning of the words which have been adopted by reference to policy considerations of its own divining.'[27] Finkelstein J concurred.

However, the majority of the Full Federal Court agreed with Sackville J's resolution of the two other issues against Sony. French and Lindgren JJ held that there was not a reproduction of the computer programs in the Random Access Memory of the PlayStation console when a game was played.[28] The judges also ruled that there was also no copy of the game, regarded as a 'cinematographic film', made in RAM when a game was played.[29] Finkelstein J dissented on these points. Citing US precedents,[30] his Honour supported an American approach in respect of the protection of temporary copies. Finkelstein J also believed that the arcade game should be protected as a cinematographic film.[31]

B. High Court Decision

The High Court of Australia heard debate on *Stevens* v. *Sony* in February 2005, and handed down its judgment in October 2005. All six sitting judges held that the Sony protection device was not a TPM because it did not prevent copyright infringement. It found that the device merely inhibited copyright infringement. The High Court also rejected the alternative arguments of Sony. It denied that there had been any infringement of copyright through a temporary reproduction. The judges also doubted that the work of Sony could be protected as 'cinematographic films'.

The High Court was frustrated that the task of statutory interpretation was complicated by the ambiguities in the *Digital Agenda Act*, and the lack of clear legislative guidance. The joint judgment observed:

> Copyright legislation, both in Australia and elsewhere, gives rise to difficult questions of construction. Given the complexity of the characteristics of this form of intangible property, that, perhaps, is inevitable. It may be going too far to say of the definition of 'technological protection measure' and of s. 116A, as

> Benjamin Kaplan wrote of the American law even as it stood in 1967, that the provisions have a 'maddeningly casual prolixity and imprecision'. However, in this Court no party advanced the proposition that its task on this appeal was satisfied merely by a consideration of the ordinary meaning of the words in the definition of 'technological protection measure'.[32]

Similarly, McHugh J noted that 'the Federal Parliament resolved an important conflict between copyright owners and copyright users by an autochthonous solution'.[33] His Honour reflected: 'Much modern legislation regulating an industry reflects a compromise reached between, or forced upon, powerful and competing groups in the industry whose interests are likely to be enhanced or impaired by the legislation.'[34] McHugh J commented: 'There is a good deal of evidence that supports the view that the legislative provisions with which this litigation is concerned are the product of a compromise agreed to, or forced upon, interest groups in the industry affected by the legislation.'[35] His Honour despaired that it was difficult to divine the purpose of legislation created during such free-wheeling political debate.

Kirby J emphasized the need to engage in statutory interpretation with an appreciation of the larger matters of domestic politics and international law: 'A court, not fully aware of the compromises that have been struck nationally and internationally and of the large debates that have addressed so-called super or "übercopyright", is well advised, in the end, to confine itself to offering its best solution to the contested task of statutory interpretation.'[36]

The High Court favoured a narrow construction of TPMs because there were penal provisions involved. The joint judgment noted 'that, in choosing between a relatively broad and a relatively narrow construction of legislation, it is desirable to take into account its penal character'.[37] Furthermore, the joint decision noted that 'an appreciation of the heavy hand that may be brought down by the criminal law suggests the need for caution in accepting any loose, albeit "practical", construction of Div 2A itself'.[38] Similarly, Kirby J noted that the presence of penal provisions was a final, albeit less important, consideration. His Honour observed: 'The fact that the phrase TPM appears in the new criminal offences, as well as in the provision for civil remedies under s.116A, pursuant to which the appellant was sued for copyright infringement, lends some weight to a stricter meaning of the contested definition of TPM, in preference to the broader meaning adopted by the Full Court.'[39]

In the course of oral argument, two opposing views were presented to the High Court as to the nature of the relationship between the defence of fair dealing under the *Copyright Act* 1968 (Cth) and the TPM provisions in the

Digital Agenda Act. On behalf of Sony, David Catterns argued that there were no explicit exemptions for the defence of fair dealing under the TPM regime: 'If we allowed every single person, under the rubric of fair dealing, to be an exception to the circumvention device provisions, then it would be practically useless.'[40] By contrast, Basten QC for the Australian Digital Alliance maintained that the TPM regime should not undermine the defence of fair dealing: 'It is in the case where the customer already has acquired, legitimately, let us assume, a copyright work and seeks apprehension of that work, that too broad a construction to the terms of this provision will ultimately provide the copyright owner with a right to control all forms of apprehension going well beyond the control of reproduction of copyright material.'[41]

The High Court was concerned that the expansive definition of TPMs would have a detrimental impact upon the defence of fair dealing, and special exceptions for libraries and archives.[42] The joint judgment emphasized:

> The true construction of the definition of 'technological protection measure' must be one which catches devices which prevent infringement. The Sony device does not prevent infringement. Nor do many of the devices falling within the definition advanced by Sony. The Sony device and devices like it prevent access only after any infringement has taken place.[43]

McHugh J observed that 'the s. 10(1) definition of "technological protection measure" ought to be read according to its ordinary meaning and not artificially stretched to include within its scope acts of copyright infringement that are not comprised in the copyright'.[44] Kirby J noted concerns of libraries that 'Sony's interpretation of s. 116A would enable rights holders effectively to opt out of the fair dealing scheme of the Act'.[45] He maintained: 'This is not an interpretation that should be readily accepted'.[46]

Kirby J was alert to the irony that Sony had in the past advocated broad fair use rights for consumers in superior courts. Famously, in the *Sony Betamax* case, the Supreme Court of the United States held that Sony, as the distributor and seller of the Betamax video cassette recorder, was not liable if users of that recorder infringed the copyright of others in television broadcasts.[47] The superior court found that it was a fair use for consumers to be engaged in 'time-shifting' – namely, the taping of television programmes for viewing at more convenient times. The Supreme Court of the United States recently reaffirmed the *Sony Betamax* rule in the case of *MGM* v. *Grokster*.[48] In particular, Breyer J observed that the *Sony Betamax* decision was strongly protective of new technology and avoided the introduction of a 'chill of technological development' in the name of responding to alleged copyright infringement. Kirby J noted: 'Many of these considerations apply in the present case to suggest a preference for a stricter, rather than a broader, meaning of the expression TPM in s. 10(1) of the Copyright Act.'[49]

In *Stevens* v. *Sony*, the High Court was concerned that an expansive interpretation of 'TPMs' would provide unwarranted protection to regional coding devices, which would allow copyright owners to engage in price discrimination between markets. This concern about the anti-competitive effects of TPMs was no doubt a result in part of the earlier intervention of the ACCC. Kirby J observed:

> By their line the Popes of old divided the world into two spheres of influence. Sony, it appears, has divided the world (for the moment) into at least three spheres or markets. By the combined operation of the CD ROM access code and the Boot ROM in the PlayStation consoles, Sony sought to impose restrictions on the ordinary rights of owners, respectively of the CD ROMS and consoles, beyond those relevant to any copyright infringement as such. In effect, and apparently intentionally, those restrictions reduce global market competition. They inhibit rights ordinarily acquired by Australian owners of chattels to use and adapt the same, once acquired, to their advantage and for their use as they see fit.[50]

His Honour concluded that 'where a choice of interpretation has to be made, the existence of the additional non-copyright purpose of enforcing global market price differentiation does constitute a reason to prefer an outcome that is consistent with the balances ordinarily inherent in copyright legislation over a result that is not'.[51]

Similarly, the joint judgment considered that 'in construing a definition which focuses on a device designed to prevent or inhibit the infringement of copyright, it is important to avoid an overbroad construction which would extend the copyright monopoly rather than match it'.[52] The decision noted that the broad construction would 'extend the copyright monopoly by including within the definition not only technological protection measures which stop the infringement of copyright, but also devices which prevent the carrying out of conduct which does not infringe copyright and is not otherwise unlawful'.[53] The High Court was no doubt sensitive to a number of United States cases, in which companies had relied upon TPMs to control secondary markets and stifle competition.[54]

There has been great debate over the constitutionality of so-called 'para-copyright', in terms both of its relationship to a government's intellectual property power, and of constitutional guarantees of the freedom of communication.

In *Stevens* v. *Sony*, Kirby J favoured a narrow construction of 'TPMs' because it would uphold fundamental rights under the Australian

Constitution.[55] His Honour noted: 'Ordinary principles of statutory construction, observed by this Court since its earliest days, have construed legislation, where there is doubt, to protect the fundamental rights of the individual.'[56] The judge observed: 'The right of the individual to enjoy lawfully acquired private property (a CD ROM game or a PlayStation console purchased in another region of the world or possibly to make a backup copy of the CD ROM) would ordinarily be a right inherent in Australian law upon the acquisition of such a chattel.'[57] The judge stressed that copyright law operates against the backdrop of Australian constitutional law: 'The provisions of the Australian Constitution affording the power to make laws with respect to copyright operate in a constitutional and legal setting that normally upholds the rights of the individual to deal with his or her property as that individual thinks fit.'[58] He warned that over-reaching copyright legislation could encounter constitutional problems: 'To the extent that attempts are made to push the provisions of Australian copyright law beyond the legitimate purposes traditional to copyright protection at law, the Parliament loses its nexus to the constitutional source of power.'[59]

The High Court was quite careful to ensure that its decision would be relevant for future legislative changes. Kirby J, in particular, comments upon the need to address very particular concerns in any future iterations of the law with respect to TPMs:

> Such considerations included the proper protection of fair dealing in works or other subject matters entitled to protection against infringement of copyright; proper protection of the rights of owners of chattels in the use and reasonable enjoyment of such chattels; the preservation of fair copying by purchasers for personal purposes; and the need to protect and uphold technological innovation which an over-rigid definition of TPMs might discourage. These considerations are essential attributes of copyright law as it applies in Australia. They are integrated in the protection which that law offers to the copyright owner's interest in its intellectual property.[60]

The Federal Government will have to comply with the High Court's demands that any future laws on TPMs be drafted with precision and clarity. The government will also need to take into account wider policy concerns, so that there are not inadvertent, detrimental impacts for competition, access to information and fundamental freedoms.[61] If the Federal Government fails to take heed of the decision, the High Court has made it quite clear that they will exercise judicial restraint, and read down the law. There is even the possibility that a constitutional challenge could be successfully launched against over-reaching copyright regulation.

There have been similar concerns expressed about the constitutionality of 'para-copyright' in the United States and Canada.[62] United States scholar,

Neil Weinstock Netanel, has argued: 'Even if copyright's traditional safety valves did continue to afford some semblance of First Amendment protection, those limitations on copyright-holder prerogatives are poised to give way before a technology and contract-based "paracopyright".'[63] He observed that such 'paracopyright' expanded content provider control over content significantly beyond that which was traditionally obtained under the *Copyright Act* 1976 (US). First of all, Netanel noted: 'the DMCA enables content providers effectively to control access to content, not merely control uses that fall within the parameters of copyright holders' exclusive rights'.[64] Second, he observed that 'nothing in the Act requires content providers to use that technology only for copyrighted works or only for portions of content that are protected by copyright'.[65] Finally, Netanel objected: 'The DMCA prohibits circumvention of access controls and trafficking in circumvention devices even when necessary to enable users to use copyrighted works in ways, such as fair use, that are permitted under copyright law.'[66] He concluded that such provisions should not survive First Amendment scrutiny, because of their internal contradictions, undue burdens on freedom of speech, and expansive scope.

Alarmed by developments in the United States, a number of Canadian academics have questioned whether the Canadian Parliament has the constitutional power to pass laws with respect to TPMs and electronic rights management systems. Jeremy deBeer has observed: 'Although paracopyright provisions are in a way connected to copyrights, they simultaneously implicate issues typically reserved for provincial legislators, such as contractual obligations, consumer protection, e-commerce and the regulation of classic property.'[67] He observed that legislation dealing with TPMs could only be tangentially related to the Federal Government's copyright power or even treaty implementation; the matter might more appropriately be placed within provincial authority over Property and Civil Rights. Jane Bailey expressed concerns that legislative protection of TPMs would conflict with the *Canadian Charter of Rights and Freedoms*. She emphasized: 'Any legislative prohibition on circumvention of TPMs must take into account not only copyright holders' rights, but users' rights and the public interest in access to and use of information and knowledge.'[68]

C. International Law

In *Stevens* v. *Sony*, the High Court noted that the *Copyright Amendment (Digital Agenda) Act* 2000 (Cth) was intended to ensure that Australia provided adequate legal protection and effective legal remedies to comply with 'the technological measures obligations' in two treaties negotiated in 1996 in the WIPO.[69] Article 11 of the *WIPO Copyright Treaty* stated:

'Contracting Parties shall provide adequate legal protection and effective legal remedies against the circumvention of effective technological measures that are used by authors in connection with the exercise of their rights under this Treaty or the Berne Convention and that restrict acts, in respect of their works, which are not authorized by the authors concerned or permitted by law.' The joint judgment noted: 'It will be apparent that the provision is expressed in broad terms, leaving considerable scope to individual States in deciding on the manner of implementation.'[70]

There has been much debate about the best means of implementation of such measures. The Phillips Fox Digital Agenda Review made a number of recommendations in respect of TPMs.[71] The Review advised that the reasoning of Sackville J should be followed and the definition of a TPM should be limited to measures to protect or control only rights that fall within copyright.[72] Furthermore, the Review recommended an extension of the 'permitted purposes' or exceptions to the prohibition on circumvention devices under the Act. This would include exceptions for fair dealing and for access to a legitimately acquired non-pirated product. The Digital Agenda Review believed that, if these recommendations were accepted, the objectives of the *Digital Agenda Act* would be better met, and a more appropriate balance, reflecting the Government's previous policy decisions, would be created.

However, the recent *AUSFTA* required Australia to adopt a TPM regime very similar to that established in the *DMCA*. Article 17.4.7 (b) expands the definition of a TPM: 'Effective technological measure means any technology, device, or component that, in the normal course of its operation, controls access to a protected work, performance, phonogram, or other protected subject matter, or protects any copyright.' There has been concern that such a broad definition could also cover regional coding devices. As Jacob Varghese comments:

> A ban on devices that circumvent TPMs significantly strengthens the copyright holder's ability to prevent parallel importing, by making it illegal to circumvent the region-coding, and thus play a DVD or computer game purchased in another country on an Australian-bought machine. It does seem incongruous that a 'free trade' agreement, purportedly intended to liberalise trade, should assist copyright holders to establish their own trade barriers.[73]

As well, Article 17.4.7(a) of *AUSFTA* requires Australia to provide civil and criminal liability for the circumvention of any TPM (this would include circumvention by an end-user). The Article also provides remedies against the 'trafficking' in devices that are designed or promoted as enabling or facilitating the circumvention of TPMs or for 'trafficking' in devices which have only limited commercial purpose other than circumvention of TPMs.

Article 17.4.7(d) stipulates: 'Each Party shall provide that a violation of a measure implementing this paragraph is a separate civil or criminal offence and independent of any infringement that might occur under the Party's copyright law.' Moreover, Article 17.4.7(e) narrows the range of certain exemptions or defences to these actions and offences.

In addition, Article 17.4.9 of the *AUSFTA* required Australia to provide stronger protection for electronic rights management information. Article 17.7 obliged Australia to provide protection against the decoding of encrypted broadcast television signals.

Furthermore, Article 17.4.1 of the *AUSFTA* compels Australia to extend the definition of reproduction to cover all reproductions in any manner or form, permanent or temporary (including temporary storage in material form). However, Australia has retained its ability to include specific exceptions to allow reproductions in certain circumstances. There were concerns that the protection of temporary copying under the *AUSFTA* could disadvantage Australia's ISPs, the cultural and educational sectors and consumers.[74]

The Federal Government professed itself to be indifferent to the outcome of the decision of the High Court. Asked about the pending decision in *Stevens* v. *Sony*, Senator Robert Hill observed during the parliamentary debates over *AUSFTA*:

> The parliament is the master of its own destiny. The parliament sets the law. The High Court interprets the situation as it existed at the time the case was brought. So be it. The idea that the parliament should not determine the appropriate future legislative structure because previous matters are being litigated does not seem to me to be particularly persuasive.[75]

Nonetheless, the extent of legislative change to the existing regime depended in large part upon the outcome in *Stevens* v. *Sony*.

Furthermore, the Attorney-General, Philip Ruddock, asked the House of Representatives Standing Committee on Legal and Constitutional Affairs to inquire into TPM exceptions.[76] The Committee recommended that the balance between copyright owners and copyright users achieved by the *Copyright Act* 1968 (Cth) should be maintained upon implementation of Article 17.4.7 of the *AUSFTA*. The Committee advised that, in the legislation, the definition of a TPM should clearly require a direct link between access control and copyright protection. In its view, the Government should ensure that access control measures are related to the protection of copyright, rather than to the restriction of competition in markets for non-copyright goods and services. The Committee warned that regional coding devices should be specifically excluded from the definition of a TPM in the legislation. The Committee recommended that the Government allow for as broad as possible exceptions for TPMs in relation to a range of activities – including fair dealing, library and archive exceptions, the use of copyright material by educational institutions, security testing and reverse engineering. The Committee recommended that future administrative reviews required under Article 17.4.7(e)(viii) be conducted by the Attorney-General's Department. There has been some debate, though, as to whether such recommendations are consistent with the *AUSFTA*.

In December 2006, the Federal Government passed the *Copyright Amendment Act* 2006 (Cth) to ensure compliance with Article 17.4.7 of the *AUSFTA*.[77] Such amendments introduce civil and criminal remedies in relation to circumvention of TPMs that prevent access to copyrighted material, and 'dealings with' devices and services that may be used to circumvent a TPM that either controls access to copyright material, or otherwise protects the copyrighted material. The Federal Government will introduce exceptions, recommended by the House of Representatives Standing Committee on Legal and Constitutional Affairs, through the means of regulations.

Bilateral trade agreements, such as the *AUSFTA*, serve the dual purpose of entrenching the regime of TPMs into United States domestic law, while at the same time exporting those standards of protection to other jurisdictions.

II. SPIES LIKE US: *IN RE SONY BMG CD TECHNOLOGIES LITIGATION*

A number of activists and academics have provided a critique of TPMs and digital rights management systems on the grounds of privacy. The project leaders of the privacy project, *On the Identity Trail*, Ian Kerr and Jane Bailey, have expressed concerns about the broader social consequences of enabling digital rights management (DRM).[78] The authors have concluded that the current use of digital rights management has the potential to seriously undermine fundamental public commitments to personal privacy and freedom of expression:

> To express our concern in the language of Andrew Carnegie, many of today's digital rights management systems are designed to help only those who pay. They pauperize. They impede the aspiring and lock away from these chief treasures of the world – renting to them instead only brief glimpses, tracking their every move all the while. A taste for such systems drives out higher tastes.[79]

Kerr and Bailey contend that lawyers and policy makers must be vigilant and uncover the structure of particular DRM architectures that violate fair information practices. They submit that there is a need for technology developers to work with ethicists, lawyers and policy makers in developing more robust privacy standards within the design of DRM software.

Such concerns about privacy and security being compromised by TPMs were crystallized in the public controversy over Sony BMG rootkit software in late 2005. The major entertainment company sold CDs containing digital rights management systems, which compromised the privacy and security of consumers' personal computers. Wade Roush comments upon the larger significance of the controversy:

> The story of the Sony BMG rootkit fiasco is about more than bad corporate judgment or the ongoing struggle over the rights of consumers to do what they want with the things they own. It is also about fear and the excesses it can arouse. When media companies apply such powerful, secret tools to content protection, it suggests that their nervousness over piracy has turned to panic. Although Sony BMG insists that the rootkit was deployed unintentionally, the episode persuaded many observers that the music industry had come to see deception as an indispensable component of digital rights management. It should be no surprise when customers who feel they are being treated like thieves stop buying things. If there is one message in Sony BMG's experience for other companies entering the digital world, it is that distrust engenders distrust.[80]

The litigation over the Sony BMG rootkit software demonstrated that consumer concerns over TPMs can be addressed both within the confines of copyright law and through adjoining systems of legal regulation, such as consumer protection law and anti-spyware law.

A. The Sony BMG Rootkit Software

In 2005, Sony BMG Music Entertainment released CDs, which were subject to two distinct digital rights management systems: XCP software and Mediamax software.[81] These TPMs sought to prevent disc-to-disc copying and inhibit the circulation of musical works and sound recordings on peer-to-peer networks. The digital rights management systems were designed to limit how consumers could use music contained on Sony BMG CDs, for instance, by restricting the number of back-up copies that could be made of musical works. J. Alex Halderman and Edward Felten observed that 'major record companies such as Sony-BMG are parts of larger, diversified companies, and can be expected to bolster the competitive position of their corporate siblings'.[82] The pair noted that 'parts of Sony sell portable music players in competition with Apple, so Sony-BMG has an incentive to take steps to undermine Apple's market power'.[83]

First, Sony BMG hired a United Kingdom company called First 4 Internet to provide a Windows copy protection program called XCP (eXtended Copy Protection) software. The EFF summed up the nature of this technology:

> Security researchers have shown that the XCP technology was designed to have many of the qualities of a 'rootkit'. It was written with the intent of concealing its presence and operation from the owner of the computer, and once installed, it degrades the performance of the machine, opens new security vulnerabilities, and installs updates through an Internet connection to Sony BMG's servers. The nature of a rootkit makes it extremely difficult to remove, often leaving reformatting the computer's hard drive as the only solution.[84]

The XCP software was intended to deter the copying of music, both by Sony BMG's own employees and customers, and by consumers.

Second, Sony BMG licensed a dual Macintosh/Windows program called MediaMax from Phoenix-based company, SunnComm. The EFF commented:

> The MediaMax software, which is included on over 20 million Sony BMG CDs, has different, but similarly troubling problems. It installs on the users' computers even if they click 'no' on the EULA, and does not include a way to uninstall the program. The security issue involves a file folder installed on users' computers by the MediaMax software that could allow malicious third parties who have localized, lower-privilege access to gain control over a consumer's computer running the Windows operating system. The software also transmits data about users to SunnComm through an Internet connection whenever purchasers listen to CDs, allowing the company to track listening habits.[85]

Such spyware was especially problematic given that Sony's End User License Agreement stated that the software would not be used to collect personal information and SunnComm's website stressed that 'no information was collected about consumers or personal computers'.[86]

In September 2005, John Guarino, the owner of TecAngels, a two-man computer consultancy in Manhattan, discovered that a number of his customers' computers had been infected by mysterious rootkit software.[87] He was forced to reinstall the operating systems in order to remove the software. Guarino then discovered that his own personal computer had been afflicted by a similar problem. He observed:

> That's what really pissed me off. I was like, 'I can't believe it. I have the latest firewall, the latest antivirus software, three or four antispyware programs. How did this get here?'[88]

Guarino deduced that the culprit was a Sony BMG album called *Touch*, by the rhythm and blues singer, Amerie. The compact disc had carried a form of digital rights management, which had installed the rootkit software.

In response, Guarino e-mailed his logs to a Finland-based computer security firm, F-Secure, whose software had detected the files. The security company was concerned that the rootkit could compromise the security of personal computers by making them vulnerable to viruses, Trojan horses and malware (malicious software).[89] F-Secure notified Sony BMG of the problem on 4 October 2005. Mikko Hypponen, F-Secure's director of anti-virus research, observed: 'If [Sony] had woken up and smelled the coffee when we told them there was a problem, they could have avoided this trouble.'[90] Nonetheless, Sony BMG failed to respond to such concerns in an expeditious fashion. As Wade Roush observed, the matter 'escalated into a full-blown scandal, complete with backroom negotiations, public exposés, heated denials, angry boycotts, vengeful lawsuits, and rueful apologies'.[91]

On Halloween, 31 October 2005, an independent computer researcher, Mark Russinovich, reported on his blog that he was shocked to discover that a rootkit had been installed on his computer by a Sony BMG compact disc. He observed:

> The entire experience was frustrating and irritating. Not only had Sony put software on my system that uses techniques commonly used by malware to mask its presence, the software is poorly written and provides no means for uninstall. Worse, most users that stumble across the cloaked files with a RKR scan will cripple their computer if they attempt the obvious step of deleting the cloaked files. While I believe in the media industry's right to use copy protection mechanisms to prevent illegal copying, I don't think that we've found the right balance of fair use and copy protection, yet. This is a clear case of Sony taking DRM too far.[92]

The posting generated a wide public outcry, which reached the mainstream media and the story was taken up by such mainstream outlets as USA Today and the BBC.[93]

Worldwide, Sony BMG used copy-protection on 52 of its CDs., which installed a software program known as a rootkit on users' computers.[94] The affected CDs included popular titles such as The Backstreet Boys' *Never Gone*, Foo Fighters' *In Your Honour*, Neil Diamond's *12 Songs*, Sarah McLachlan's *Afterglow Live* and Velvet Revolver's *Contraband*.[95] Researchers suggested that the program had affected 500 000 computers in 165 countries.[96] The Anti-Spyware Coalition and computer security firm, Computer Associates, labelled the Sony BMG software as 'spyware' because the rootkit was placed on computers without the user's consent or authorization.[97] The software compromised the privacy of consumers, and the security of their computers. Furthermore, the rootkit could not be uninstalled without the assistance of Sony BMG.

B. Lawsuits

In November 2005, the EFF wrote an open letter to Sony BMG, expressing concerns regarding the XCP and SunnComm MediaMax software:

> You must be aware that the discovery of this software has shocked and angered your customers. Software that deceives the owner of the computer it runs upon and opens that computer up to attacks by third parties may be expected to come from malicious cyber-attacks; it is certainly not expected nor acceptable to be distributed and sold to paying customers by a major music company.[98]

The EFF urged Sony BMG to recall all CDs that contained the XCP and SunnComm MediaMax technology, offer to refund the purchase price of infected CDs, and compensate consumers for any damage to their computers caused by the infected products, including the time, effort and expenditure required to remedy the damage or verify that their computer systems or networks were not altered or damaged by XCP or SunnComm MediaMax products.[99]

The EFF launched a class action complaint on behalf of consumers against Sony BMG in the Superior Court of the State of California.[100] The EFF argued that the software was a computer contaminant. The class action alleged that Sony BMG had engaged in deceptive practices, unlawful methods of competition and unfair acts in violation of the *Consumer Legal Remedies Act* and the *California Business and Professions Code*. The law suit also alleged that Sony BMG had breached an implied covenant of good faith and fair dealing. The EFF sought compensatory damages, punitive damages, a restitution and disgorgement of profits, and equitable relief for consumers.

As well, a series of law suits were filed against Sony BMG in the US District Court for the Southern District of New York.[101] There were a host of lawsuits filed against Sony BMG in a variety of other jurisdictions.[102] Such matters were collected in the complaint *In re Sony BMG CD Technologies Litigation* in the US District Court for the Southern District of New York.[103] The complaint summarized the various actions as follows:

> [The] actions claim that SONY BMG and F4I, by disseminating the XCP Software on XCP CDs, and that SONY BMG and SunnComm, by disseminating the MediaMax Software on MediaMax CDs, violated, among other things, the *Computer Fraud and Abuse Act*, 18 U.S.C. §§1030, et seq.; the consumer

> fraud, false advertising, and/or deceptive trade practices laws of the several states, and state and federal common law.[104]

The complaint sought injunctive relief, equitable relief, restitution and damages on behalf of a nationwide class of consumers who used any of the MediaMax CDs and the XCP CDs. The plaintiffs in other actions sought essentially the same relief on behalf of a nationwide class or the residents of individual states.

The Texan Attorney-General Greg Abbott filed suit against Sony BMG for violations of that state's anti-spyware legislation.[105] It alleges that the New York-based company violated the *Consumer Protection Against Computer Spyware Act* 2005 (Texas) protecting consumers from hidden spyware. The company accomplished this by using new technology on certain music CDs to install files onto consumers' computers that hide other files installed by SONY. This secret 'cloaking' component is installed without the knowledge of consumers and can cause their computers to become vulnerable to computer viruses and other forms of attack. Abbott commented:

> SONY has engaged in a technological version of cloak and dagger deceit against consumers by hiding secret files on their computers. Consumers who purchased a SONY CD thought they were buying music. Instead, they received spyware that can damage a computer, subject it to viruses and expose the consumer to possible identity crime.[106]

The Attorney-General's investigation found that the XCP technology remains hidden and active at all times after installation, even when SONY's media player is inactive, prompting concerns about its true purpose. The Attorney-General sought civil penalties of $100 000 for each violation of the law, attorneys' fees and investigative costs.

In addition, there was an inquiry by the Federal Trade Commission, and numerous investigations by state attorneys-general and other governmental authorities in various jurisdictions, such as the Attorney-General of Florida and the New York State Attorney-General.[107]

Similarly, a lawsuit in Canada claimed that Sony-BMG had breached the manufacturer's warranty, the terms under the End User License Agreement, and the consumer protection legislation.[108] The lawsuit noted that, in Canada, 'Sony BMG distributed at least 34 titles with XCP' and '120 thousand CDs were sold'.[109] The lawsuit stated, 'Sony's artists include Canadians, whose titles were sold with the artist [unaware] of XCP including the artist Celine Dion.'[110]

In response to this public outcry and array of legal actions, Sony BMG has decided to suspend the use of the rootkit software and recall affected CDs. The record company observed in a statement:

> We are aware that a computer virus is circulating that may affect computers with XCP content protection software. We stand by content protection technology as an important tool to protect our intellectual property rights and those of our artists. Nonetheless, as a precautionary measure, Sony BMG is temporarily suspending the manufacture of CDs containing XCP technology.[111]

The United States Government has expressed concern about the case. Stewart Baker, the Department of Homeland Security's assistant secretary for policy said: 'In the pursuit of protection of intellectual property, it's important not to defeat or undermine the security measures that people need to adopt in these days.'[112]

A number of performing artists and bands were upset that Sony BMG had included the digital rights management systems into compact discs featuring their work. Tim Foreman, the guitarist for Switchfoot, was shocked to discover that their album *Nothing is Sound* was subject to the rootkit. He posted on a fan site instructions for disabling Sony content protections. He observed:

> We were horrified when we first heard about the new copy-protection policy. It is heartbreaking to see our blood, sweat, and tears over the past two years blurred by the confusion and frustration surrounding new technology.[113]

Damian Kulash, the lead singer for the band OK Go, speculated: 'As for musicians, we are left to wonder how many more people could be listening to our music if it weren't such a hassle, and how many more iPods might have our albums on them if our labels hadn't sabotaged our releases with cumbersome software.'[114]

C. Settlement

After a consolidation of a number of similar law suits, Sony BMG agreed to a settlement of the matter in December 2005.[115] In May 2006, a Federal judge granted final approval of the settlement between Sony BMG and consumers who had filed the class action law suit.[116]

As part of the settlement with consumers, Sony BMG compensated purchasers with a replacement CD, which was free of copyright protection. In addition, the entertainment company also provided purchasers with the choice of $US7.50 plus one free album download, or three free album downloads. Strikingly, Sony BMG provided the undertaking that the purchasers could download such work from one of three services, including its competitor, the Apple iTunes service: 'SONY BMG will use commercially reasonable efforts to ensure that one of the three download services offered as an option to Settlement Class Members is the "iTunes" service'.[117] Sony BMG offered a choice of 200 titles for download.

As a part of the legal settlement, Sony BMG made a number of undertakings in respect of the future development of TPMs. The company agreed not to manufacture or distribute audio CDs with XCP Software, or MediaMax 3.0 or MediaMax 5.0. Sony BMG promised that it would address any suspected security vulnerability in copy-control software in an expeditious and public fashion in future.

Sony BMG also agreed to comply with ten conditions regarding the manufacture of CDs with any Content Protection Software during the period of the injunction. It is worth highlighting the broad themes of such undertakings. Sony BMG emphasized that the future introduction of Content Protection Software should be transparent, vowing that 'no software will be installed on the hard disk drive of a user's computer unless and until the user has agreed to such installation by accepting an End-User Licence Agreement or by otherwise affirmatively consenting to such installation'.[118] The company also accepted that Content Protection Software should be able to be readily uninstalled by users. Sony BMG promised to show Content Protection Software and End-User Licence Agreements to independent third parties to ensure that the technology respected the privacy and security of consumers. The company agreed to 'obtain an opinion from that third party that the installation and use of the software would create no Security Vulnerabilities that would be considered Confirmed Security Vulnerabilities'.[119] Sony BMG promised to provide a written disclosure to consumers that 'the CD contains such Content Protection Software and a brief description of such Content Protection Software, and, unless such connection is only made upon the user's prior informed, affirmative consent, that the CD seeks to connect to a SONY BMG (or a contractor's) server'.[120]

Cindy Cohn of the EFF commented: 'The proposed settlement will provide significant benefits for consumers who bought the flawed CDs.'[121] She noted, though: 'EFF is continuing discussions with Sony BMG, however, and believes that there is more they can do to protect music lovers in the future'.[122] Kurt Opsahl, a staff attorney of the EFF, added: 'We hope that other record labels will learn from Sony's hard experience and focus more on the carrot of quality music and less on the stick of copy protection.'[123]

The Canadian class action was eventually settled on similar terms to its United States counterpart.[124]

Michael Geist observes that there remain a number of critics of the Sony/BMG settlement:

> Opponents of the settlement will argue that a few music downloads is a small price to pay given the damage that Sony has created to personal computers

around the world. Moreover, consumers living outside of the United States are excluded from the settlement, leaving thousands without compensation and protection against ongoing TPM misuse. The Sony CDs found their way onto computers in more than 100 countries, with thousands of consumers throughout the UK and Europe among the victims. While it remains possible that Sony will provide similar compensation to consumers worldwide, that appears unlikely.[125]

The Canadian professor comments: 'The European Union Copyright Directive and the US *DMCA* have set up legal protections for TPMs by establishing anti-circumvention measures; however, the rootkit incident illustrates that there is the need for parallel consumer legal protections from TPMs.'[126] Nevertheless, he observes: 'Notwithstanding its shortcomings, the Sony settlement does provide a potential starting point for a much-needed model statute to protect consumers from TPMs.'[127] The disclosure requirements of the Sony settlement provide a model for treating TPMs much like cigarettes and alcohol, with appropriate warnings on their potential negative consequences. Geist believes that these security measures may be the first step toward a comprehensive TPM approval and licensing system that places the security needs of the general public ahead of private commercial interests. He also suggests that the privacy provision of the settlement acknowledges that mere disclosure of the privacy impact of TPMs does not provide the public with adequate privacy protection. Given that national privacy legislation does not provide sufficient privacy safeguards, new statutory limits on the collection and use of such information that cannot be overridden through licence agreements are needed.

Michael Geist observed that the controversy affected the brand reputation of Sony BMG: 'Sony BMG, the world's second largest record label, has for the past three weeks been the subject of a corporate embarrassment that rivals earlier public relations nightmares involving tampered Tylenol and contaminated Perrier.'[128] He noted that the dispute had wider consequences: 'While in the short-term one of the world's best-known brands has suffered enormous damage, the longer term implications are even more significant – a fundamental re-thinking of policies toward digital locks known as TPMs.'[129] Overall, the dispute suggested that TPMs not only put users' property at risk, but they also limit the use of lawfully acquired personal property.

In December 2005, the Samuelson Law, Technology, and Public Policy Clinic submitted a comment to the United States Copyright Office on behalf of Edward Felten and his Princeton colleague, J. Alex Halderman.[130] The computer scientists observed:

We respectfully request an exemption to §1201(A)(1)(a) for sound recordings and audiovisual works distributed in compact disc format and protected by

> technological measures that impede access to lawfully purchased works by creating or exploiting security vulnerabilities that compromise the security of personal computers. The creation of security vulnerabilities includes running or installing rootkits or other software code that jeopardize the security of a computer or the data it contains. The exploitation of security vulnerabilities includes running or installing software protection measures without conspicuous notice and explicit consent and failing to provide a permanent and complete method of uninstalling or disabling the technological measure.[131]

The pair sought an exemption to the *DMCA* that would permit circumvention of TPMs protecting sound recordings and audiovisual works on compact discs that impede access to lawfully purchased works by creating or exploiting security vulnerabilities that compromise the security of personal computers.

The submission observed that digital rights management systems, such as the Sony BMG Rootkit, adversely affected at least four varieties of non-infringing uses, including listening, engaging in security research, device and format-shifting, and creating back-ups. Felten and Halderman commented:

> Even for those consumers satisfied with the Windows Media file format, the presence of protection measures that satisfy the definition set out above interfere unreasonably with consumers' fair use rights to transfer CDs to other devices and convert them to other formats. Because the protection measures jeopardize security, many users will be unwilling to copy their CDs with the supplied software out of a justified fear of compromising the security of their computers.[132]

The submission observes: 'The proposed exemption, in keeping with the Congressional intent underlying the DMCA, would allow consumers to undertake the sort of self-help measures necessary to access and lawfully use the CDs they purchase without accepting unnecessary risks created by carelessly designed protection measures.'[133] The Comment was submitted as part of the Copyright Office's periodic rulemaking proceeding in which the Office considers whether to exempt certain classes of works from the prohibition against circumvention of TPMs that control access to copyrighted works.

In November 2006, the Librarian of Congress, on the recommendation of the Register of Copyrights, announced classes of works exempt from the prohibition against circumvention of TPMs that control access to copyrighted works for the next three years.[134] There was a new exemption designed to deal with security flaws and vulnerabilities, such as those which arose with the Sony BMG Rootkit: Sound recordings, and audiovisual works associated with those sound recordings, distributed in compact disc format and protected by technological protection measures that control access to lawfully purchased works and create or exploit security flaws or vulnerabilities that compromise the security of personal computers, when circumvention is accomplished solely for the purpose of good faith testing, investigating, or correcting such security flaws or vulnerabilities.[135] Such an exception, though, seems to be a weak means of dealing with TPMs, which compromise consumer privacy and computer privacy. Surely, a much more effective solution would be to prohibit TPMs, which had such detrimental impacts.

Unfortunately, the process for reviewing exceptions under the *DMCA* has been a cumbersome means of addressing consumer concerns such as those in relation to the Sony BMG Rootkit controversy. The EFF has protested that 'the DMCA triennial rulemaking is fundamentally unable to protect the interests of today's digital media consumers'.[136] The EFF observes that the exemptions can only be used by a few people, because circumvention tools are not provided: 'The DMCA provides that the Librarian of Congress can only grant exemptions from the DMCA's prohibition on *acts* of circumvention; exemptions from the DMCA's prohibition on distributing *tools* of circumvention are not within the scope of the rulemaking.'[137] As a consequence, the group concludes that 'this restriction effectively shuts the door on digital consumers.'[138] The EFF observes that the legislation suffers from an impenetrable complexity: 'Any digital consumer interested in participating meaningfully in the DMCA rulemaking process must first decipher a bewildering array of legal arcana and independently gather considerable evidence.'[139] Furthermore, the EFF complains that the Copyright Office has undermined fair use principles in the *DMCA* rulemaking process: 'Rather than treating fair use as a forward-looking, evolving regime, the Copyright Office has made it backward-looking, effectively barring courts from addressing the fair use implications of new digital consumer technologies in the 21st century.'[140]

The Sony BMG Rootkit controversy illustrates that there is a need for governments to put in place positive measures to protect and safeguard the privacy interests of consumers against the abuse of TPMs. Jeremy deBeer has argued that the matter involves not only copyright law, but a network of regulatory regimes:

> A number of laws might apply here, including competition, consumer protection and privacy statutes as well as common law tort and contract doctrines. Protection is piecemeal, and gaps do exist, but it seems that the main problem is not finding a viable cause of action. Successfully litigating a claim is another matter.[141]

The academic suggests that the controversy might prompt the development of legislation to guard against the abuse of TPMs: 'Specific legislation could be enacted to deal with abuses of DRM systems, general anti-spyware statutes could be developed or consumer protection law as a whole could be bolstered.'[142] Of course, there would be a need to weigh the merits of technology neutral legislation against specifically tailored solutions.

CONCLUSION

2005 was an *annus horribilis* for the Sony Group. Not only did the entertainment company lose its action against Eddy Stevens for breach of TPMs in the High Court of Australia, Sony BMG was embarrassed by the revelations that its Copyright Protection Software compromised the privacy and security of its consumers. The twin pieces of litigation have provided impetus to reform copyright provisions relating to TPMs in order to better protect and safeguard the interests of consumers.

Congressman Rick Boucher introduced the *Digital Media Consumers' Rights Act* 2003 (US) into Congress in order to restore the historic balance to US Copyright law.[143] He has discussed his credos that copyright law should promote the interests of consumers:

> When consumers who purchase digital media can enjoy a broad range of uses of the media for their own convenience in ways which do not infringe copyrights, everyone wins . . . This principle has been borne out in history time and time again as new technologies have been developed which make the media products ultimately more valuable to consumers. The challenge for content creators is to embrace these new technologies and to create business models around them, rather than shun them by seeking more and more control over the downstream uses of media.[144]

The Congressman argued that the exemptions to the TPMs should be expanded to include the defence of fair use; musical sampling and space-shifting; the first sale doctrine; and making a back-up copy of any copyrighted data. The legislation also provided for proper labelling of 'copy-protected compact discs'. Boucher observed: 'The bill seeks to restore the balance in our nation's copyright laws in ways that will promote technological innovation and consumer freedom, while at the same time ensuring that record companies, movie studios, and book producers can stop pirates from stealing.'[145]

This legislative bill received the strong endorsement of leading technology companies and industry associations, including Intel, Sun Microsystems, Verizon, BellSouth, Philips Electronics North America, Gateway, the Consumer Electronics Association, and the Computer & Communications Industry Association.[146] It also has the equally strong support of public interests organizations, including libraries, universities and consumer groups.[147] However, it did not win support from the Congress as a whole.

Similarly, Representative Zoe Lofgren introduced the *Benefit Authors without Limiting Advancement or Net Consumer Expectations (BALANCE) Act* 2003 (US) into Congress. She explains the intent of this legislation:

> Today's challenge is to maintain the balance in the digital age by finding ways to prevent digital piracy without treating every consumer as a pirate. Digital technology allows for perfect copies of copyrighted works. At the same time, digital technology lets copyright holders control how consumers enjoy the books, music and movies they lawfully purchase. Contrary to the intent of Congress, the DMCA has been used to legitimize this control over consumer uses. It's been used to prohibit lawful users from circumventing technical restrictions, even to pursue rights they have.[148]

Section 3 of the Bill would serve to clarify that America's historic principles of fair use – protected under Section 107 of the *Copyright Act* 1976 (US) – would apply to analog and digital transmissions. Section 4 extends the first sale doctrine, codified in section 109 of Title 17, to digital transmissions. Under section 5, a copyright owner is free to employ technical measures to protect his or her work. However, the copyright owner must ensure that those measures allow purchasers to make non-infringing uses of the work. The Bill would also permit purchasers to bypass technical measures that impede their consumer rights and expectations.

Promoting the Bill, Lofgren maintained: 'Consumers are poised to work with the technology and entertainment industries to ensure that in the future, copyrights are protected, innovation is encouraged, and legitimate rights and expectations are respected.'[149] Much like its counterpart in the Senate, the BALANCE Act failed to garner the favour of the Congress as a whole. Lofgren lamented: 'We didn't have any counterforce against the Hollywood people, the RIAA people, and the publishers.'[150] Lofgren emphasized that the battles over the DMCA and fair use were not limited or localized to the United States. She noted with concern that the United States Trade Representative, Richard Zoellick, had entered into a bilateral free trade agreement with Australia, contingent on their adoption of the United States' version of the DMCA.[151] Lofgren and Boucher wrote a letter to the United States Trade Representative, protesting against its trade policy with respect to intellectual property.[152]

In reaction, the supporters of copyright industries have introduced the *Intellectual Property Protection Act* 2006 (US). Instead of merely targeting distribution, Representative Lamar Smith is keen to prohibit parties from making, importing, exporting, obtaining control of, or possessing such anti-circumvention tools if they may be redistributed to someone else. Such legislation seeks to broaden the operation of the trafficking provisions. Professor Peter Jaszi has lamented: 'It's one degree more likely that mere communication about the means of accomplishing a hack would be subject to penalties.'[153]

NOTES

1. Rose, F. (2003), 'The Civil War Inside Sony', *Wired Magazine*, **11**(2), http://www.wired.com/wired/archive/11.02/sony_pr.html.
2. S1201(a)(1) of the *Digital Millennium Copyright Act* 1998 (US).
3. S1201(a)(2) and (b)(1) of the *Digital Millennium Copyright Act* 1998 (US).
4. Samuelson, P. (1999), 'Intellectual Property and the Digital Economy: Why the Anti-Circumvention Regulations Need to be Revised', *Berkeley Technology Law Journal*, **14**, 519–66 at 523.
5. *Universal City Studios* v. *Reimerdes* 82 F.Supp.2d 211 (S.D.N.Y.2000); *Universal City Studios* v. *Corley*, 273 F.3d 429 (Fed. Cir. 2nd, 2001); and *United States of America* v. *Elcom Ltd* 203 F.Supp.2d 1111 (N.D.Cal.2002). For a more extensive discussion, see Bowrey, K. and M. Rimmer (2002), 'Rip, Mix, Burn: The Politics of Peer to Peer and Copyright Law', *First Monday*, **7**(8), http://firstmonday.org/issues/issue7_8/bowrey/index.html.
6. *Universal City Studios* v. *Reimerdes* 111 F.Supp.2d 294 at 304-305 (S.D.N.Y.2000).
7. *RealNetworks, Inc.* v. *Streambox, Inc.*, No. 2:99CV02070, 2000 WL 127311 (W.D.Wash., Jan 18, 2000); *Macrovision Corp.* v. *321 Studios*, Not Reported in F.Supp.2d, 2004 WL 1066323 (S.D.N.Y.) and 2005 WL 678851 (S.D.N.Y.); and *Macrovision* v. *Sima Products Corporation* WL 1063284 (S.D.N.Y. 20 April 2006); and WL 1472152 (S.D.N.Y. 26 May, 2006).
8. Lessig, Lawrence (2004), *Free Culture: How Big Media Uses Technology And Law To Lockdown Culture And Control Creativity*, New York: Penguin, p. 160.
9. *Chamberlain Group, Inc.* v. *Skylink Techologies, Inc.* 292 F.Supp.2d 1040 (N.D.Ill. 2003) and on appeal 381 F.3d 1178 (Fed. Cir. 2004); *Lexmark International, Inc.* v. *Static Control Components, Inc* 253 F.Supp.2d 943 (E.D.Ky. 2003) and 387 F.3d 522 (Fed Cir 6th, 2004); *Storage Technology Corporation* v. *Custom Hardware Engineering & Consulting, Inc.* 421 F.3d 1307 (Fed. Cir. 2005); and *Tracfone Wireless Inc.* v. *Sol Wireless Group Inc* 05-23279 (US District Court for the Southern District of Florida, 21 December 2005), http://www.copyright.gov/1201/2006/reply/14granick_WA.pdf.
10. *Felten and others* v. *RIAA* (unreported, United States District Court of New Jersey, 28 November 2001), http://www.eff.org/IP/DMCA/Felten_v._RIAA/20011128_hearing_transcript.html.
11. *Davidson & Associates, Inc.* v. *Internet Gateway* 334 F.Supp.2d 1164 (E.D. Mo. 2004) and, on appeal, *Davidson & Associates* v. *Jung* 422 F.3d 630 (Fed Cir 8th 2005).
12. The Court of Appeals for the District Circuit of Columbia ruled that the Federal Communications Commission had exceeded its statutory authority by promulgating regulations on the 'Broadcast Flag', *American Library Association* v. *Federal Communications Commission* 406 F.3d 689 (C.A.D.C., 2005). For a review of the 'Broadcast Flag', see Crawford, S. (2003), 'The Biology of the Broadcast Flag', *Hastings Communications and Entertainment Law Journal*, **25**, 603–52.
13. von Lohmann, F. (2004), 'Measuring the Digital Millennium Copyright Act against the Darknet: Implications for the Regulation of Technological Protection Measures', *Loyola of Los Angeles Entertainment Law Review*, **24**, 635–48 at 647.
14. Ibid., 648.
15. Rose, F. (2003), 'The Civil War Inside Sony', *Wired Magazine*, **11**(2), http://www.wired.com/wired/archive/11.02/sony_pr.html.

16. *Stevens* v. *Kabushiki Kaisha Sony Computer Entertainment* (2005) 221 ALR 448.
17. *In re Sony BMG CD Technologies Litigation* No 1:05-cv-09575 (NRB) (US District Court for the Southern District of New York, 2005).
18. Roush, W. (2006), 'Inside the Spyware Scandal', *Technology Review*, **109**(2), 48–57 at 50.
19. Fels, A. and F. Brenchley (2005), 'Copyright: Divide and Rule', *The Australian Financial Review*, 18 October, p. 62.
20. ACCC (2003), 'Submission to the Digital Agenda Review: Circumvention Devices and Services, Technological Protection Measures and Rights Management Information', http://www.aph.gov.au/Senate/committee/freetrade_ctte/submissions/sub294aatt1.pdf, October.
21. *Kabushiki Kaisha Sony Computer* v. *Stevens* (2002) 55 IPR 497 at 523–4.
22. *Kabushiki Kaisha Sony Computer* v. *Stevens* (2002) 55 IPR 497 at 524.
23. In *Sony Computer Entertainment Inc* v. *Owen* [2002] EWHC 45, Jacob J of the High Court of Justice, Chancery Division, held that the authorization codes for a Sony Playstation were a device or means intended to prevent or restrict copying of copyright works. The judge held that the Messiah chip was a device or means specifically designed or adapted to circumvent the form of copy protection employed. This decision was later followed by Laddie J in the High Court of Justice, Chancery Division, in *Sony Computer Entertainment Inc* v. *Ball* [2004] EWHC 1738 (Ch). His Honour held that the use of the Messiah2 mod-chip on a Playstation 2 was a circumvention of a TPM.
24. *Kabushiki Kaisha Sony Computer* v. *Stevens* (2003) 57 IPR 161.
25. *Kabushiki Kaisha Sony Computer* v. *Stevens* (2003) 57 IPR 161 at 201.
26. *Kabushiki Kaisha Sony Computer* v. *Stevens* (2003) 57 IPR 161 at 173.
27. *Kabushiki Kaisha Sony Computer* v. *Stevens* (2003) 57 IPR 161 at 174.
28. *Kabushiki Kaisha Sony Computer* v. *Stevens* (2003) 57 IPR 161.
29. *Kabushiki Kaisha Sony Computer* v. *Stevens* (2003) 57 IPR 161.
30. *MAI Systems Corp* v. *Peak Computer Inc* 991 F2d 511 (9th Cir 1993); cert. denied 114 S Ct 671 (1994); and *Advanced Computer Services of Michigan Inc* v. *MAI Systems Corporation* 845 F.Supp 356 (E.D. Va 1994).
31. *Kabushiki Kaisha Sony Computer* v. *Stevens* (2003) 57 IPR 161 at 212.
32. *Stevens* v. *Kabushiki Kaisha Sony Computer Entertainment* (2005) 221 ALR 448 at 461.
33. *Stevens* v. *Kabushiki Kaisha Sony Computer Entertainment* (2005) 221 ALR 448 at 476.
34. *Stevens* v. *Kabushiki Kaisha Sony Computer Entertainment* (2005) 221 ALR 448 at 476.
35. *Stevens* v. *Kabushiki Kaisha Sony Computer Entertainment* (2005) 221 ALR 448 at 476.
36. *Stevens* v. *Kabushiki Kaisha Sony Computer Entertainment* (2005) 221 ALR 448 at 493.
37. *Stevens* v. *Kabushiki Kaisha Sony Computer Entertainment* (2005) 221 ALR 448 at 459.
38. *Stevens* v. *Kabushiki Kaisha Sony Computer Entertainment* (2005) 221 ALR 448 at 459.
39. *Stevens* v. *Kabushiki Kaisha Sony Computer Entertainment* (2005) 221 ALR 448 at 501.
40. *Stevens* v. *Kabushiki Kaisha Sony Computer Entertainment & Ors* [2005] HCATrans 30 (8 February 2005).
41. *Stevens* v. *Kabushiki Kaisha Sony Computer Entertainment & Ors* [2005] HCATrans 30 (8 February 2005).
42. *Stevens* v. *Kabushiki Kaisha Sony Computer Entertainment* (2005) 221 ALR 448 at 496.
43. *Stevens* v. *Kabushiki Kaisha Sony Computer Entertainment* (2005) 221 ALR 448 at 459.
44. *Stevens* v. *Kabushiki Kaisha Sony Computer Entertainment* (2005) 221 ALR 448 at 480.
45. *Stevens* v. *Kabushiki Kaisha Sony Computer Entertainment* (2005) 221 ALR 448 at 496.
46. *Stevens* v. *Kabushiki Kaisha Sony Computer Entertainment* (2005) 221 ALR 448 at 496.
47. *Sony Corporation of America* v. *Universal City Studios, Inc*, 464 US 417 (1984).
48. *Metro-Goldwyn-Mayer Studios Inc* v. *Grokster Ltd* 125 S.Ct 2764 (2006).
49. *Stevens* v. *Kabushiki Kaisha Sony Computer Entertainment* (2005) 221 ALR 448 at 493.
50. *Stevens* v. *Kabushiki Kaisha Sony Computer Entertainment* (2005) 221 ALR 448 at 486.
51. *Stevens* v. *Kabushiki Kaisha Sony Computer Entertainment* (2005) 221 ALR 448 at 497.
52. *Stevens* v. *Kabushiki Kaisha Sony Computer Entertainment* (2005) 221 ALR 448 at 459.
53. *Stevens* v. *Kabushiki Kaisha Sony Computer Entertainment* (2005) 221 ALR 448 at 459.
54. For a review of the debate over technological protection measures and competition policy in North America, see Geist, Michael (2005), 'Anti-Circumvention Legislation

and Competition Policy: Defining a Canadian Way' in Michael Geist (ed.), *In The Public Interest: The Future of Canadian Copyright Law*, Toronto: Irwin Law, pp. 221–50; *Chamberlain Group, Inc.* v. *Skylink Techologies, Inc.* 292 F.Supp.2d 1040 (N.D.Ill. 2003) and, on appeal, 381 F.3d 1178 (Fed. Cir. 2004); *Lexmark International, Inc.* v. *Static Control Components, Inc* 253 F.Supp.2d 943 (E.D.Ky. 2003) and 387 F.3d 522 (Fed Cir 6th, 2004); *Storage Technology Corporation* v. *Custom Hardware Engineering & Consulting, Inc.* 421 F.3d 1307 (Fed. Cir. 2005); and *Tracfone Wireless Inc.* v. *Sol Wireless Group Inc* 05-23279 (US District Court for the Southern District of Florida, 21 December 2005), http://www.copyright.gov/1201/2006/reply/14granick_WA.pdf.

55. *Stevens* v. *Kabushiki Kaisha Sony Computer Entertainment* (2005) 221 ALR 448 at 497.
56. *Stevens* v. *Kabushiki Kaisha Sony Computer Entertainment* (2005) 221 ALR 448 at 497.
57. *Stevens* v. *Kabushiki Kaisha Sony Computer Entertainment* (2005) 221 ALR 448 at 497–8.
58. *Stevens* v. *Kabushiki Kaisha Sony Computer Entertainment* (2005) 221 ALR 448 at 498.
59. *Stevens* v. *Kabushiki Kaisha Sony Computer Entertainment* (2005) 221 ALR 448 at 498.
60. *Stevens* v. *Kabushiki Kaisha Sony Computer Entertainment* (2005) 221 ALR 448 at 500.
61. For a consideration of the linkage between digital rights management and privacy, see Kerr, Ian (2005), 'If Left to their Own Devices . . . How DRM and Anti-Circumvention Laws Can Be Used to Hack Privacy', in Michael Geist (ed.), *In The Public Interest: The Future of Canadian Copyright Law*, Toronto: Irwin Law, pp. 167–210.
62. Netanel, N.W. (2005), 'Copyright and the First Amendment: What Eldred Misses and Portends', in Jonathan Griffiths and Uma Suthersanen (eds), *Copyright and Free Speech: Comparative and International Analyses*, Oxford: Oxford University Press, pp. 127–52.
63. Netanel, N.W. (2001), 'Locating Copyright Within the First Amendment Skein', *Stanford Law Review*, **54**, 1–83 at 22.
64. Ibid., 75.
65. Ibid., 75.
66. Ibid., 75.
67. deBeer, Jeremy (2005), 'Constitutional Jurisdiction over Paracopyright Laws', in Michael Geist (ed.), *In The Public Interest: The Future of Canadian Copyright Law*, Toronto: Irwin Law, pp. 89–124.
68. Bailey, Jane (2005), 'Deflating the Michelin Man: Protecting Users' Rights in the Canadian Copyright Reform Process', in Michael Geist (ed.), *In The Public Interest: The Future of Canadian Copyright Law*, Toronto: Irwin Law, pp. 125–66.
69. For an overview of these treaties, see Kerr, I., A. Maurushat and C. Tacit (2003), 'Technical Protection Measures: Tilting at the Copyright Windmill', *Ottawa Law Review*, **34**, 9–82.
70. *Stevens* v. *Kabushiki Kaisha Sony Computer Entertainment* (2005) 221 ALR 448.
71. Phillips Fox (2004), *Digital Agenda Review*, Canberra: Attorney General's Department, http://www.ag.gov.au/DigitalAgendaReview/reportrecommendations.
72. Ibid.
73. Varghese, J. (2004/ 2005), 'Guide to Copyright and Patent Law Changes in the US Free Trade Agreement Implementation Bill 2004', *Parliamentary Library Current Issues Brief*, **3** (17), http://www.aph.gov.au/library/pubs/CIB/2004-05/05cib03.pdf.
74. Ibid.
75. Hill, R. (2004), 'US Free Trade Agreement Implementation Bill 2004 (Cth)', Senate Hansard, 12 August, 26428, http://www.aph.gov.au/hansard/senate/dailys/ ds 120804.pdf.
76. House of Representatives Standing Committee on Legal and Constitutional Affairs (2006), *Review of Technological Protection Measures Exceptions*, http://www.aph.gov.au/house/committee/laca/protection/report/fullreport.pdf.
77. The Federal Government implemented the new regime for technological protection measures in December 2006 with the *Copyright Amendment Act* 2006 (Cth).
78. Kerr, I. and J. Bailey (2004), 'The Implications of Digital Rights Management for Privacy and Freedom of Expression', *Journal of Information, Communication & Ethics in Society*, **2**, 87–97.
79. Ibid., 94.

80. Roush, W. (2006), 'Inside the Spyware Scandal', *Technology Review*, **109**(2), 48–57 at 50.
81. For a comprehensive analysis of the design, implementation and deployment of such technologies, see Halderman, J.A. and E. Felten (2006), 'Lessons from the Sony CD DRM Episode', http://itpolicy.princeton.edu/pub/sonydrm-ext.pdf, 14 February; and deBeer, J. (2006), 'How Restrictive Terms and Technologies Backfired on Sony BMG Music: Part 1', *Internet and E-Commerce Law in Canada*, **6**(12), 93–9.
82. Halderman, J.A. and E. Felten (2006), 'Lessons from the Sony CD DRM Episode', http://itpolicy.princeton.edu/pub/sonydrm-ext.pdf, 14 February, 4.
83. Ibid.
84. EFF (2005), 'Sony BMG Info', http://www.eff.org/IP/DRM/Sony-BMG/.
85. Ibid.
86. Roush, W. (2006), 'Inside the Spyware Scandal', *Technology Review*, **109**(2), 48–57.
87. Ibid.
88. Ibid., 49.
89. Ibid.
90. Hamm, S. (2005), 'Sony BMG's Costly Silence', *Business Week*, 29 November.
91. Roush, W. (2006), 'Inside the Spyware Scandal', *Technology Review*, **109**(2), 48–57 at 50.
92. Russinovich, M. (2005), 'Sony, Rootkits, and Digital Rights Management Gone Too Far', Mark's Sysinternals Blog, http://www.sysinternals.com/blog/2005/10/sonyrootkits-and-digital-rights.html, 31 October.
93. Geist, M. (2005), 'Sony's Long-term Rootkit CD Woes', BBC News, 21 November; and Kantor, A. (2005), 'Sony: The Rootkit of All Evil?', *USA Today*, http://www.usatoday.com/tech/columnist/andrewkantor/2005-11-17-sony-rootkit_x.htm, 17 November.
94. Sony BMG (2006), 'CDs Included in the Settlement', http://www.sonybmgcdtechsettlement.com/CDList.htm.
95. Ibid.
96. Geist, M. (2005), 'Sony's Long-term Rootkit CD Woes', BBC News, 21 November.
97. Discussed in *Hull* v. *Sony BMG Music Entertainment*, No. BC343385 (Cal. Super. Ct. Nov. 21, 2005), http://www.eff.org/IP/DRM/Sony-BMG/sony_complaint.pdf.
98. EFF (2005), 'An Open Letter to Sony BMG', http://www.eff.org/IP/DRM/Sony-BMG/?f=open-letter-2005-11-14.html, 14 November.
99. Ibid.
100. *Hull* v. *Sony BMG Music Entertainment*, No. BC343385 (Cal. Super. Ct. Nov. 21, 2005), http://www.eff.org/IP/DRM/Sony-BMG/sony_complaint.pdf.
101. *Maletta* v. *Sony BMG Music Entertainment, No. 05 CV 10637 (UA) (S.D.N.Y. Dec. 19, 2005); Ricciuti* v. *Sony BMG Music Entertainment, No. 05 CV 10190 (BSJ) (S.D.N.Y. Dec. 5, 2005); Klewan* v. *Arista Holdings Inc. d/b/a Sony BMG Music Entertainment, No. 05 CV 9609, consolidated as No. 05 CV 9575 (NRB) (S.D.N.Y. Nov. 14, 2005); Michaelson* v. *Sony BMG Music, Inc., No. 05 CV 9575 (NRB) (S.D.N.Y. Nov. 14, 2005); Potter* v. *Sony BMG Music Entertainment, No. 05 CV 9607, consolidated as No. 05 CV 9575 (NRB) (S.D.N.Y. Nov. 14, 2005); Rivas* v *Sony BMG Music Entertainment, No. 05 CV 9598, consolidated as No. 05 CV 9575 (NRB) (S.D.N.Y. Nov. 14, 2005).*
102. *Black* v. *Sony BMG Music Entertainment*, No. CIV-05-1315 WDS/RLP (D. N.M. Dec. 19, 2005); *Klemm* v. *Sony BMG Music Entertainment*, No. C 05 5111 BZ (N.D. Cal. Dec. 9, 2005); *Melcon* v. *Sony BMG Music Entertainment*, No. C 05 5084 MHP (N.D. Cal. Dec. 8, 2005); *Ponting* v. *SONYBMG Music Entertainment, LLC*, No. CV-05-08472-JFW(AJWx) (C.D. Cal. Dec. 2, 2005); *Jacoby* v. *Sony BMG Music Entertainment*, No. 05/116679 (N.Y. Sup. Ct. Nov. 30, 2005); *Bahnmaier* v. *Sony BMG Music Entertainment*, No. CJ 2005 06968 (Okla. Dist. Ct. Nov. 28, 2005); *Xanthakos* v. *Sony BMG Music Entertainment, LLC*, No. 05-0009203 (D.C. Super. Ct. Nov. 28, 2005); *Maletta* v. *Sony BMG Music Entertainment Corp.*, No. BC343615 (Cal. Super. Ct. Nov. 28, 2005); *Burke* v. *Sony BMG Music Entertainment*, No. 857213 (Cal. Super. Ct. Nov. 22, 2005); *Hull* v. *Sony BMG Music Entertainment*, No. BC343385 (Cal. Super. Ct. Nov. 21, 2005); *Cooke*

v. *Sony BMG Music Entertainment*, No. 05-0009093 (D.C. Super. Ct. Nov. 18, 2005); *DeMarco* v. *Sony BMG Music*, No. 2:05-cv-05485-WHW-SDW (D.N.J. Nov. 17, 2005); *Stynchula* v. *Sony Corporation of America*, No. BC343100 (Cal. Super. Ct. Nov. 15, 2005); *Gruber* v. *Sony Corporation of America*, No. BC342805 (Cal. Super. Ct. Nov. 9, 2005); *Guevara* v. *Sony BMG Music Entertainment*, No. BC342359 (Cal. Super. Ct. Nov. 1, 2005).

103. *In re Sony BMG CD Technologies Litigation* No 1:05-cv-09575 (NRB) (US District Court for the Southern District of New York, 2005).
104. *In re Sony BMG CD Technologies Litigation* No 1:05-cv-09575 (NRB) (US District Court for the Southern District of New York, 2005).
105. *Texas* v. *Sony BMG Music Entertainment* (Dist. Ct., Travis Co, Tex, 2005).
106. Abbott, G. (2005), 'Attorney General Abbott Brings First Enforcement Action In Nation Against Sony BMG For Spyware Violations', http://www.oag.state.tx.us/oagnews/release.php?id=1266, 21 November.
107. Various government policy investigations discussed in *In re Sony BMG CD Technologies Litigation* No 1:05-cv-09575 (NRB) (US District Court for the Southern District of New York, 2005).
108. *Palmer and Cook* v. *First 4 Internet, Sony BMG Music (Canada) Inc and Sony BMG Music Entertainment* (Ontario Superior Court of Justice, 16 January 2006).
109. *Palmer and Cook* v. *First 4 Internet, Sony BMG Music (Canada) Inc and Sony BMG Music Entertainment* (Ontario Superior Court of Justice, 16 January 2006).
110. *Palmer and Cook* v. *First 4 Internet, Sony BMG Music (Canada) Inc and Sony BMG Music Entertainment* (Ontario Superior Court of Justice, 16 January 2006).
111. Evers, J. (2005), 'Sony Halts Production of "Rootkit" CDs', CNet.News, 11 November.
112. Geist, M. (2005), 'Sony's Long-term Rootkit CD Woes', BBC News, 21 November.
113. Woellert, L. (2005), 'Sony's Escalating "Spyware" Fiasco', *Businessweek*, 22 November.
114. Kulash, D. (2005), 'Buy, Play, Trade, Repeat', *The New York Times*, 6 December, p. 27.
115. *In re Sony BMG CD Technologies Litigation* No 1:05-cv-09575 (NRB) (US District Court for the Southern District of New York, 2005).
116. EFF (2006), 'Judge Grants Final Approval for Sony BMG CD Settlement', http://www.eff.org/news/archives/2006_05.php, May 22.
117. *In re Sony BMG CD Technologies Litigation* No 1:05-cv-09575 (NRB) (US District Court for the Southern District of New York, 2005).
118. *In re Sony BMG CD Technologies Litigation* No 1:05-cv-09575 (NRB) (US District Court for the Southern District of New York, 2005).
119. *In re Sony BMG CD Technologies Litigation* No 1:05-cv-09575 (NRB) (US District Court for the Southern District of New York, 2005).
120. *In re Sony BMG CD Technologies Litigation* No 1:05-cv-09575 (NRB) (US District Court for the Southern District of New York, 2005).
121. EFF (2005), 'EFF and Sony BMG Reached Settlement over Flawed DRM', http://www.eff.org/news/archives/2005_12.php#004287, 29 December.
122. Ibid.
123. Ibid.
124. deBeer, J. (2006), 'Sony Settles Canadian Class Actions', http://www.jeremydebeer.ca/content/view/87/2/, 31 August.
125. Geist, M. (2006), 'Legal Fallout from Sony's CD Woes', BBC News, 3 January.
126. Ibid.
127. Ibid.
128. Geist, M. (2005), 'Sony's Long-Term Rootkit CD Woes', BBC, 21 November.
129. Ibid.
130. Samuelson Clinic (2005), 'Re: RM 2005-11 – Exemption to Prohibition on Circumvention of Copyright Protection Systems for Access Control Technologies', http://www.law.berkeley.edu/clinics/samuelson/papers/other/Halderman_Felten_Comment_Final.pdf.
131. Ibid., 1.
132. Ibid., 8.
133. Ibid., 13.

134. United States Copyright Office (2006), 'Exemption to Prohibition on Circumvention of Copyright Protection Systems for Access Control Technologies', *Federal Register*, **71**(227), http://www.copyright.gov/fedreg/2006/71fr68472.pdf, 68472-68479.
135. United States Copyright Office (2006), *Rulemaking on Exemptions from Prohibition on Circumvention of Technological Measures that Control Access to Copyrighted Works*, http://www.copyright.gov/1201/, November.
136. EFF (2005), 'DMCA Triennial Rulemaking: Failing the Digital Consumer' 2005, http://www.eff.org/IP/DMCA/copyrightoffice/DMCA_rulemaking_broken.pdf, 1 December.
137. Ibid.
138. Ibid.
139. Ibid.
140. Ibid.
141. deBeer, J. (2006), 'How Restrictive Terms and Technologies Backfired on Sony BMG Music: Part 2', *Internet and E-Commerce Law in Canada*, **7**(1), 1–8 at 6.
142. Ibid.
143. *Digital Media Consumers' Rights Act* 2003 (US) HR 107.
144. Boucher, R. (2003), 'Copyright and Fair Use: The Present and Future Perspective', *Harvard Journal of Law and Technology Symposium*, http://www.house.gov/boucher/docs/harvard.htm, 15 March.
145. Ibid.
146. Mark, R. (2003), 'Boucher Introduces Fair Use Rights Bill', Internetnews.com, http://dc.internet.com/news/article.php/1565901, 8 January.
147. Boucher, R. (2003) 'Supporters of Digital Media Consumers Act', http://www.boucher.house.gov/index.php?option=com_content&task=view&id=25&Itemid=.
148. Lofgren, Z. (2003), 'Digital Rights', http://www.house.gov/lofgren/iss_digital-rights.shtml.
149. Ibid.
150. Lofgren, Z. (2003), 'Symposium: Law and Technology of Digital Rights Management', *Berkeley Technology Law Journal*, **18**, 495–500.
151. Ibid.
152. Carney, D. (2003), 'Reps. Lofgren and Boucher Address FTAs and DMCA', *Tech Law Journal*, http://www.techlawjournal.com/topstories/2003/20030618.asp, 18 June.
153. McCullagh, D. (2006), 'Congress Readies New Broad Digital Copyright Bill', CNet.News, http://news.com.com/2100-1028_3-6064016.html, 23 April.

6. Agent Smith and the matrix: copyright law and intermediary liability

> It seems that you've been living two lives. One life, you're Thomas A. Anderson, program writer for a respectable software company. You have a social security number, pay your taxes, and you . . . help your landlady carry out her garbage. The other life is lived in computers, where you go by the hacker alias 'Neo' and are guilty of virtually every computer crime we have a law for. One of these lives has a future, and one of them does not. (Agent Smith, *The Matrix*)

The dystopian thriller, *The Matrix*, featured a cat-and-mouse chase between Agent Smith, and Thomas A. Anderson, a fugitive hacker known by the alias, Neo. The film played upon fears that the Internet had become a panopticon, a surveillance society, without civil liberties or privacy. The motion picture gained contemporary resonance in public debates about copyright enforcement, as copyright owners went to great lengths to unmask and prosecute individual copyright infringers, and peer-to-peer networks hid behind a complex web of intermediaries.

In the 1990s, there was much legal debate as to the extent of legal liability of Internet service providers (ISPs) and other intermediaries in respect of copyright infringement in a digital environment.[1]

In response to such concerns, the United States Congress passed Part II of the *Digital Millennium Copyright Act* 1998 (US) (*DMCA*), which was named the *Online Copyright Infringement Liability Limitation Act*. Jessica Litman has observed that this legislation represented a compromise between the competing interest groups: 'Copyright owners agreed that Internet service providers should not be liable for their subscribers' infringing transmissions so long as the provider had no reason to suspect infringement was taking place, on the condition that the service provider agreed to shut down copyright violators and remove infringing material as soon as a content owner notified it of a violation.'[2] The legislation limited the liability of ISPs in respect of on-line copyright material. The *DMCA* created a number of safe harbours for ISPs engaged in a number of activities: transitory communications,[3] system caching,[4] the hosting of information on systems and networks at the directions of users,[5] and the provision of information location tools,[6] such as search engines. The legislation sought to define a 'service provider' for such various purposes.[7]

In order to benefit from the safe harbour provisions, a service provider had to satisfy two conditions. First, the service provider must have adopted and reasonably implemented a copyright policy, and provided for termination of the subscription accounts of repeat offenders. Second, the service provider had to accommodate and not interfere with standard technical measures.

If such threshold conditions were satisfied, the service provider had to demonstrate that they did not have actual knowledge that the material or an activity using the material on the system or network is infringing; they did not receive a financial benefit directly attributable to the infringing activity, in a case in which the service provider has the right and ability to control such activity; and upon notification of claimed infringement responded expeditiously to remove copyright infringing material.[8]

There has been much debate about the efficacy of the intermediary liability scheme under the *DMCA*.[9] A recent, probing study by Jennifer Urban and Laura Quilter of the Samuelson Law, Technology and Public Policy Clinic suggests that the regime has 'chilling effects':

> Policy concerns related to questionable takedowns seem likely to increase in importance – however successful or problematic the process is, our data show that its use appears to be rising. Some notices are certainly sent in order to accomplish the paradigmatic goal of 512 – the inexpensive takedown of clearly infringing hosted content or links to infringing web sites. But our data also show the process is commonly used for other purposes: to create leverage in a competitive marketplace, to protect rights not given by copyright (or perhaps any other law), and to stifle criticism, commentary and fair use. These unanticipated or unintended uses of the process are having a continuous and perhaps unquantifiable effect on public discourse.[10]

There has been concern that the notice and take down scheme has targeted material, which has a strong or at least reasonable likelihood of raising the defence of fair use.[11] As Marjorie Heins and Tricia Beckles comment: 'A major force contributing to the erosion of fair use is the culture of gatekeeper-intermediaries – publishers, broadcasters, distributors, and many ISPs – who care less about legal niceties or the rights of users than about avoiding expensive lawsuits.'[12]

This chapter considers the litigation brought by the Recording Industry Association of America (RIAA) and the Motion Picture Association of America (MPAA) against a range of intermediaries under the *Digital Millennium Copyright Act* (DMCA). Section one examines litigation by copyright owners against ISPs. In particular, it considers the litigation taken against Verizon, and Charter Communications over the subpoena provisions of the *DMCA*.[13] There has also been concern about strategic legal action taken against universities and educational institutions. For instance, there was much disquiet about a case in which Diebold Inc. sent out cease-and-desist letters to the various ISPs over students from Swarthmore College publishing documents revealing security flaws and software problems in electronic voting machines.[14] The Electronic Frontier Foundation (EFF) intervened in the dispute, filing a lawsuit declaring that the postings were protected under the defence of fair use and the First Amendment.[15] Section two considers the litigation by copyright owners against individual file-sharers in the United States. There has been much debate over the right of distribution in *Elektra Entertainment Group* v. *Barker*;[16] there has also been a consideration of the available defences to end-users in the case of *BMG* v. *Gonzales*.[17] It examines the mooted amnesty by the RIAA. The conclusion to the chapter questions whether there is a need for a personal copying or private levy scheme to be introduced.

I. DISCIPLINE AND PUNISH: COPYRIGHT PIRACY AND DIGITAL PRIVACY

In 'The New Surveillance', Sonia Katyal comments that copyright owners have been exercising an increasingly intrusive control over consumer choices and behaviour:

> A few years ago, it was fanciful to imagine a world where intellectual property owners – such as record companies, software owners, and publishers – were capable of invading the most sacred areas of the home in order to track, deter, and control uses of their products. Yet, today, precisely that is taking place. Emboldened by courts and legislators, copyright owners now undertake a widening degree of control over cultural products through the guise of piracy detection.[18]

In the effort to shut down off-shore peer-to-peer networks, copyright owners have placed increasing pressure on ISPs and telecommunications networks to reveal the identities of subscribers involved in the exchange of copyright-protected media. As Seagrumn Smith comments: 'Without U.S. assets to seize, the recording and movie industries are left with few options, namely government cooperation, DMCA Section 512 requests to ISPs and pressuring universities – all of which have garnered formidable concern and resistance.'[19] There has been much debate as to whether the intermediary liability regime established by the *DMCA* has compromised the privacy and civil liberties of consumers.

A. *RIAA* v. *Verizon*

Since July 2003, the RIAA used a controversial subpoena provision introduced by the *DMCA* and issued over 1600 subpoenas to ISPs, requesting the names and contact information of particular subscribers. In most cases, the return period listed on the subpoena for the information sought was seven days. Some ISPs acceded to such demands by the RIAA out of commercial prudence. However, a few exceptional companies sought to protect the privacy and anonymity of their consumers.

RIAA brought a legal action against Verizon Internet Services because it refused to reveal the identity of a Verizon subscriber who allegedly used Kazaa peer-to-peer software to share music online. The President of the RIAA, Cary Sherman, challenged the claims of Verizon that they were protecting the privacy of their subscribers:

> Verizon disingenuously implies that they are protecting the 'privacy' of their subscribers. But they are not. Recognizing there is no right to commit an illegal act anonymously, Verizon readily concedes that they will turn over the name of the subscriber once a lawsuit has been filed against 'John Doe'. So their subscribers' 'privacy' is not going to be protected regardless. The only thing Verizon is protecting is Verizon's own business interests. They are trying to avoid the cost of identifying infringers as provided for in the DMCA by imposing unrealistic and burdensome obligations on copyright owners instead.[20]

Sherman was scathing about the lack of the co-operation of the ISP, Verizon: 'Verizon seems to be playing a legal shell game that ignores the balances and compromises embodied in the DMCA.'[21]

In response, Verizon declared that Congress should not allow copyright owners to trample upon users' privacy rights under the *DMCA*: 'We must preserve the balance among all stakeholders and discourage attempts by copyright owners to shift liabilities and burdens for protecting their copyrights onto third parties.'[22] Verizon argued that the relevant provision of the *DMCA* did not cover copyright-infringing material that resided on individuals' own computers – only material that resided on the system of the ISP.

Verizon argued that the subpoena sought by the record companies violated a number of constitutional guarantees. First of all, Verizon contended that section 512(h) violated Article III of the Constitution because it authorized federal courts to issue subpoenas in the absence of a pending case or controversy. Second of all, Verizon also contends that the subpoena authority in 512(h) violated the First Amendment rights of Internet users – piercing their anonymity – both because it did not provide sufficient procedural protection for expressive and associational rights and because it was overbroad and sweeping in the breadth of protected expression. Third, Verizon maintained that the *DMCA* did not provide adequate safeguards to protect Internet users' rights of expression and association. Finally, Verizon claimed that the section 5121(h) subpoena authority was substantially overbroad and would chill protected anonymous speech and association.

In January 2003, Bates J of the Washington D.C. District Court rejected Verizon's interpretation of the *DMCA* subpoena provision, ordering Verizon to reveal the subscriber's identity.[23] Bates J refused to quash the subpoena sought by the RIAA: 'The Court finds that §512 of the DMCA, as construed by this Court in its *First Subpoena Decision*, does not violate the "case or controversy" requirement of Article III of the Constitution, and does not abridge the First Amendment rights of Internet users.'[24] The judge concluded: 'In the end, Verizon's customers should have little expectation of privacy (or anonymity) in infringing copyrights.'[25]

Verizon appealed the judgment of the District Court. An amicus curiae submission was made by the American Civil Liberties Union, the EFF and other public interest groups to the United States Court of Appeals for the District Court of Columbia Circuit. The submission observed: 'This Court should be mindful of the need to protect the constitutional rights of Internet users against abuse by private individuals.'[26] The submission complained that section 512(h) had been misused and mistakenly applied to Internet users who are not infringing copyrights. They observe that there have been a number of incidents, in which copyright owners have lodged subpoenas over uncopyrightable facts, public domain materials and copyright works that were the subject of fair use.

In the appeal against the decision of Bates J, the Court of Appeals was surprisingly sympathetic to the arguments of Verizon about the statutory interpretation of section 512(h) of the *DMCA*.[27] First, Ginsburg J held: '[T]he text of §512(h) and the overall structure of §512 clearly establish, as we have seen, that §512(h) does not authorize the issuance of a subpoena to an ISP acting as a mere conduit for the transmission of information sent by others.'[28] His Honour commented that ISPs such as Verizon had no capacity to police copyright material on its subscribers' computers:

> Infringing material obtained or distributed via P2P file sharing is located in the computer (or in an off-line storage device, such as a compact disc) of an individual user. No matter what information the copyright owner may provide, the ISP can neither 'remove' nor 'disable access' to 'the infringing material because that material is not stored on the ISP's servers. Verizon cannot remove or disable one user's access to infringing material resident on another user's

> computer because Verizon does not control the content on its subscribers' computers.[29]

His Honour held that 'a subpoena may be issued only to an ISP engaged in storing on its servers material that is infringing or the subject of infringing activity'.[30]

Second, Ginsburg J comments that this interpretation of section 512(h) was consistent with the legislative history behind the *DMCA*:

> The Congress had no reason to foresee the application of §512(h) to P2P file sharing, nor did they draft the DMCA broadly enough to reach the new technology when it came along. Had the Congress been aware of P2P technology, or anticipated its development, §512(h) might have been drafted more generally. Be that as it may, contrary to the RIAA's claim, nothing in the legislative history supports the issuance of a §512(h)subpoena to an ISP acting as a conduit for P2P file sharing.[31]

In any case, Ginsburg J noted that recourse to legislative history was only possible where there was ambiguity in the text: 'Legislative history can serve to inform the court's reading of an otherwise ambiguous text; it cannot lead the court to contradict the legislation itself.'[32]

Third, Ginsburg J commented that the decision was in keeping with the purpose of the *DMCA*. His Honour observed:

> We are not unsympathetic either to the RIAA's concern regarding the widespread infringement of its members' copyrights, or to the need for legal tools to protect those rights. It is not the province of the courts, however, to rewrite the DMCA in order to make it fit a new and unforeseen internet architecture, no matter how damaging that development has been to the music industry or threatens being to the motion picture and software industries. The plight of copyright holders must be addressed in the first instance by the Congress; only the 'Congress has the constitutional authority and the institutional ability to accommodate fully the varied permutations of competing interests that are inevitably implicated by such new technology.'[33]

This statement is reminiscent of the comments of Wilson J in the *Grokster* case. It displays a fidelity to legal formalism in remaining faithful to the meaning of the statutory intention. It shows a similar reluctance to engage in judicial creativity to enhance the rights of copyright owners beyond what was provided for by Congress.

Finally, Ginsburg J declined to address the constitutional arguments of Verizon: 'Because we agree with Verizon's interpretation of the statute, we reverse the orders of the district court enforcing the subpoenas and do not reach either of Verizon's constitutional arguments.'[34] In 2004, the copyright owners sought special leave to appeal against the decision in the Supreme Court of the United States.[35] The president of RIAA, Cary Sherman, commented:

> This is a disappointing procedural decision, but it only changes the process by which we will file lawsuits against online infringers. This decision in no way changes our right to sue, or the fact that those who upload or download copyrighted music without authorization are engaging in illegal activity. We can and will continue to file copyright infringement lawsuits against illegal file sharers.[36]

The RIAA argued that the decision of the Federal Court circuit undermined the text, structure and the purpose of the *DMCA*: 'The decision below gutted a federal statute essential to protecting intellectual property rights from piracy on the Internet.'[37] The RIAA despaired: 'The decision below has effectively stopped the issuance of DMCA subpoenas in the context of peer-to-peer copyright infringement.'[38] This submission was supported by an amicus brief from a broad coalition of copyright industries.[39] As both the owner of copyright content and the provider of Internet services, Time Warner put forward an amicus brief in support of the petitioner: 'Time Warner's interest lies in a balanced result that will protect the interests of copyright holders in the battle against online piracy, while ensuring that ISPs do not face unreasonable burdens and costs.'[40]

In response to such submissions, Verizon defended the decision of the Federal Circuit: 'The court of appeals also quite properly observed that the application of copyright laws to new technologies requires a careful balancing of interests that this Court repeatedly has held is for Congress, not the federal courts, to perform.'[41]

After considering such submissions, the Supreme Court of the United States rejected the submission for leave. Perhaps the Bench felt that it could more directly address concerns about internet piracy in the context of the *Grokster* case. Verizon were triumphant at the verdict, observing that it was a 'victory for consumer safety and privacy'.[42] Sarah Deutsch of Verizon submitted that this action was a significant victory for consumers and the Internet: 'The Supreme Court has shut the door on a dangerous and illegal subpoena campaign that threatened the constitutional rights of all Americans.'[43] She commented on the ruling:

> Today's ruling is an important victory for Internet users and all consumers. The court has knocked down a dangerous procedure that threatens Americans' traditional legal guarantees and violates their constitutional rights. This decision removes the threat of a radical, new subpoena process that empowers copyright holders or anyone merely claiming to be a copyright holder to obtain personal

> information about Internet users by simply filing a one-page form with a court clerk. This harmful procedure exposes anyone who uses the Internet to potential predators, scam artists and crooks – including identity thieves and stalkers.[44]

Similarly, the EFF sought to champion the decision as a victory for consumers' privacy and freedom of speech. Wendy Seltzer heralded the decision, observing: 'The ruling stops the record labels from taking our free speech rights as collateral damage in the campaign against the American music fan.'[45] However, such a misreading of the case is wishful thinking on the part of Seltzer. Far from being a ringing endorsement of civil liberties, the decision of the Court of Appeals and the refusal of the Supreme Court of the United States showed a great reluctance to read copyright law in light of wider constitutional concerns about freedom of speech and privacy. This remains a consistent judicial trend in the United States.

B. *In re Charter Communications*

In Re Charter Communications, a trade association representing owners of copyrights in musical recordings sought to require an ISP to disclose identities of its subscribers who were using 'peer-to-peer' file sharing programs to transmit copyrighted songs.[46]

At first instance, the United States District Court for the Eastern District of Missouri issued a subpoena.

Consumer and privacy groups intervened on behalf of Charter Communications. Cindy Cohn of the EFF argued that Section 512(h) violated the Due Process Clause because it does not contain adequate procedural protections against the curtailment of constitutionally protected expression. She maintained that Internet users have a substantial and constitutionally protected liberty interest in privacy and anonymous expression:

> This long-standing right to anonymity is especially critical to a modern medium of expression: the Internet. The rise of the Internet has created an opportunity for dialogue and expression on a scale and in a manner previously unimaginable. Now, alongside the traditional print and broadcasting media, individuals can utilize the Internet to convey their opinions, thoughts or ideas whenever they want, and to anyone who cares to read them. As the Supreme Court has recognized, the Internet is a new and powerful democratic forum in which anyone can become a 'pamphleteer' or 'a town crier with a voice that resonates farther than it could from any soapbox'. The Court noted that there is 'no basis for qualifying the level of First Amendment scrutiny that should be applied to this medium'.[47]

Cohn alleged that the minimal procedural protections of Section 512(h) create a substantial risk of erroneous deprivation of constitutional rights that could be diminished by the use of adequate procedural safeguards. She observed that the legitimate interests of the Government and copyright holders will not be substantially affected by requiring the use of adequate and normal procedural protections. Cohn concluded that Section 512(h) violates the First Amendment when it strips speakers of their anonymity without procedural protections: 'Whether viewed through the lens of the Due Process Clause or the First Amendment, Section 512 without additional procedural protections fails to pass constitutional muster.'[48]

The Eighth Circuit of the United States Court of Appeals held by a majority that the subpoena provisions of the *DMCA* did not authorize copyright owners to obtain and serve subpoenas on ISPs to obtain personal information about subscribers using peer-to-peer networks. In the leading judgment, Bye J followed the precedent of the *Verizon* case:

> We agree with and adopt the reasoning of the United States Court of Appeals for the District of Columbia Circuit in *Verizon* as it pertains to this statutory issue. Thus, because the parties do not dispute that Charter's function was limited to acting as a conduit for the allegedly copyright protected material, we agree §512(h) does not authorize the subpoenas issued here. As a court we are bound to interpret the terms of the statute and not to contort the statute so as to cover the situation presented by this case.[49]

In a footnote, the majority judge recognized: 'This case has wide-reaching ramifications, because as a practical matter, copyright owners cannot deter unlawful peer-to-peer file transfers unless they can learn the identities of persons engaged in that activity.'[50] However, the judge noted that organizations such as the RIAA could also employ alternative avenues to seek this information, such as 'John Doe' lawsuits, which would allow for third-party discovery of the identity of the otherwise anonymous 'John Doe' defendant.[51]

Bye J declined to rule decisively upon the larger constitutional questions raised by Charter and the amicus curiae. However, the judge did express some concern about the subpoena provision of s.512(h) in obiter:

> We comment without deciding that this provision *may* unconstitutionally invade the power of the judiciary by creating a statutory framework pursuant to which Congress, via statute, compels a clerk of a court to issue a subpoena, thereby invoking the court's power. Further, we believe Charter has at least a colorable argument that a judicial subpoena is a court order that must be supported by a case or controversy at the time of its issuance.[52]

The judge emphasized, though, that, for purposes of this appeal, the court did not reach these issues and decided the merits of this case on the grounds of statutory interpretation. Again, this position is very similar to that arrived at in the *Verizon* litigation.

In dissent, Murphy J argued that the majority had erred in its narrow reading of the *DMCA*, overlooking the plain language used by Congress, and failing to give effect to the statute as a whole. She maintained that the interpretation of the majority undermined the intent of the *DMCA* to address the 'massive piracy' of copyright works over digital networks without hampering the development of the Internet:

> The majority's interpretation of the statute undermines this structure [of the *DMCA*]. It denies copyright holders the ability to obtain identification of those subscribers who purloin protected materials through §512(a) conduit ISPs. This interpretation also shields conduit ISPs from liability without requiring their assistance in protecting copyrights. The suggestion that copyright holders should be left to file John Doe lawsuits to protect themselves from infringement by subscribers of conduit ISPs like Charter, instead of availing themselves of the mechanism Congress provided in the DMCA, is impractical and contrary to legislative intent. John Doe actions are costly and time consuming. Nowhere in the DMCA did Congress indicate that copyright holders should be relegated to such cumbersome and expensive measures against conduit ISPs.[53]

The judge emphasized that the legislative history showed that the purpose of the subpoena power under the DMCA was to facilitate the co-operation of ISPs in the expeditious removal of infringing copyright content.

Murphy J denied that the subpoena provisions of the *DMCA* could be considered to be unconstitutional. She denied that the argument of Charter that 'internet speakers' had a 'presumptively protected anonymity' and that section 512(h) permitted the disclosure of subscriber identity based only on suspicion of infringing conduct. The judge observed:

> There is no suppression of material based on its expressive content and the First Amendment is not implicated. Moreover, the DMCA has considerable procedural safeguards in its requirements for a subpoena request. These include identification of the work claimed to have been infringed and of the infringing material, statement of a 'good faith belief' that unlawful use has occurred, verification of the accuracy of the statements, and a sworn declaration that the information disclosed is sought for and will be used only to enforce ownership rights. Charter has not shown that the DMCA restrains or censors speech or that it violates the First Amendment.[54]

The judge concludes: 'Because the subpoena to Charter was properly issued and was authorized under the terms of the DMCA, and there being no constitutional or statutory impediments to its enforcement, the order of the district court should be affirmed.'[55]

Charter welcomed the decision. David Anderson, the senior vice president for communications, observed:

> Charter takes its responsibility to protect the private information of our customers very seriously. Our customers place their trust in Charter, so we took all appropriate legal measures in this matter to fulfill this responsibility. This said, our actions in this case should assure them that this trust is justified.[56]

Verizon General Counsel, Sara Deutsch, was pleased that the tactic of the RIAA to obtain split decisions in the Federal Circuit had failed: 'This ruling closes the door on the Supreme Court's taking the case.'[57] Legal Director of the EFF, Cindy Cohn, praised the decision for protecting the interests of consumers: 'Charter should be congratulated for following in the footsteps of Verizon in standing up for the privacy of its users.'[58]

C. *Online Policy Group* v. *Diebold Inc.*

There has also been significant legal action against universities and educational institutions as intermediaries in respect of copyright-infringing material.[59] Furthermore, there has been much concern about strategic legal action taken against public participation: so-called 'SLAPP' law suits.

In 2003, two students from Swarthmore College, Nelson Pavlosky and Luke Smith, founded the Swarthmore Coalition for the Digital Commons. The group was inspired by the EFF, the Free Software Foundation and the Creative Commons. The Swarthmore Coalition for the Digital Commons is dedicated, in the words of Pavlosky, 'to promoting a bottom-up, participatory structure for society and culture characterized by the free and open exchange of information'.[60]

The two students used Internet access provided by Swarthmore to post an email archive on various websites.[61] The pair published thousands of internal documents from a company called Diebold Inc., detailing security flaws and software problems in its electronic voting machines. The archive contained internal criticism by employees of Diebold Inc. of the reliability and verification procedures of the machines. The archive also showed Diebold's inability to account for reporting results such as in the 2000 United States election for President, in the contested state of Florida.

An on-line newspaper, IndyMedia, published an article criticizing Diebold's electronic voting machines and containing a hyperlink to the email archive. The Online Policy Group acted as their ISP; in turn, that Group received services from an upstream ISP, Hurricane Electric. In response, Diebold Inc. sent out cease-and-desist letters to the various ISPs, including Swarthmore College, the Online Policy Group and Hurricane

Electric, citing copyright violations under the *DMCA*. The ISPs were advised that pursuant to these provisions they would be shielded from a copyright infringement suit by Diebold if they disabled access to or removed the allegedly infringing material.

Swarthmore College required Pavlosky and Smith to remove the email archive from their website. Swarthmore's counsel advised the College that 'a federal district court ruling in a 1999 case, *Intellectual Reserve* v. *Utah Lighthouse Ministry*,[62] suggests that providing direct hyperlinks may be construed as contributory copyright infringement'.[63] Swarthmore's President observed that 'civic responsibility encourages students to act on their commitment to a better society by first seeking approaches within the law to reach socially significant goals, before considering civil disobedience'.[64] Hurricane notified the Online Policy Group that it might be required to terminate its Internet access if IndyMedia's hyperlink to the email archive was not removed.

In his testimony, Pavlosky expressed concerns that the use of the *DMCA* had a chilling effect on political debate and learning. He commented that the intervention of Diebold Inc. had negatively affected his education, and had undermined his faith in Swarthmore College: 'My group, the SCDC, cannot fully dedicate itself to elevating our knowledge and the public's knowledge about issues that affect our ability to participate in our government and in our society in general. I fear that the resulting lack of transparency in the voting process will mean flawed election results and will decrease voter confidence and participation.'[65] In his testimony, Smith observed: 'Our goal was to show the public the serious and deep-seated problems with the Diebold machines, and we posted the emails on SCDC's website as part of our mission to educate the public about the need for a transparent voting system.'[66] He worried: 'Diebold's letter to Swarthmore prevents me from using the SCDC and its website as a tool for learning and debate about our core mission interest of informing the public about issues that affect citizens' ability to participate in our government and in our society in general.'[67]

The EFF intervened in the dispute, filing a lawsuit to protect the e-voting activists' First Amendment rights. Wendy Seltzer argued that Diebold's cease-and-desist notices were a blatant abuse of copyright law: 'Publication of the Diebold documents is clear fair use because of their direct relevance to the debate over the accuracy of electronic voting machines.'[68] First, she noted that the Online Policy Group was merely providing co-location to IndyMedia, which in turn is only providing hyperlinks to material that was alleged to have infringed Diebold copyrights. In other words, Online Policy Group did not host the Diebold materials and neither did IndyMedia. Consequently, the entities could not be held liable for copyright infringement.

Second, Seltzer argued that the postings themselves were plainly fair use for the purposes of research, criticism, comment, and news reporting, not copyright infringement. She added that 'the First Amendment plainly protects speech about this very essence of our democracy – the right to a free and fair election'.[69] Finally, Seltzer warned Diebold Inc. that it was harassing numerous ISPs with these frivolous demand letters, misusing claimed copyright to interfere with numerous subscribers' contracts for Internet service. She noted that the company risked counter-suits.

In response, Diebold Inc. argued that the Online Policy Group could be held liable for copyright infringement if it knowingly hosted web-sites containing hyperlinks to infringing material. The electronic voting company argued that the Swarthmore Coalition for Digital Commons could not be protected by the defence of fair use, because it had not made creative or transformative use of 'stolen' materials:

> Plaintiffs are subject to a heightened standard of proof, because unpublished materials are given special protection under fair use analysis. As the Supreme Court explained in *Harper & Row*, unpublished material is not normally subject to fair use in light of the fact that 'the author's right to control the first public appearance of his undisseminated expression will outweigh a claim of fair use'.[70]

Diebold Inc. insisted that the company was not misusing copyright law or abusing the take-down procedures of the *DMCA*. The company noted that 'the student plaintiffs sought to avoid the DMCA's "take-down" provisions by switching the material to other websites'.[71] Diebold Inc. emphasized that the safe harbour provisions of the *DMCA* carefully balanced the First Amendment rights of users with the rights of an injured copyright owner: 'Taken together, the procedures provide a streamlined, practical approach to copyright enforcement on the Internet.'[72] However, in the end, Diebold Inc. decided to withdraw the law suit against the Swarthmore Coalition for the Digital Commons.

The litigation has attracted much attention. Yale Professor Yochai Benkler praised 'the efficacy of the students' continued persistent publication in the teeth of the cease-and-desist letters and the willingness of the universities to comply'.[73] Kembrew McLeod sought to make sense of the controversy over the electronic voting machines:

> In so many instances of overzealous copyright bozoism, the law is not on the side of those who try to apply it improperly. Many times, all it takes is an individual to call a company's bluff or an organization such as the Electronic Frontier Foundation to counter attacks on free speech. In fact, many of these censorious uses of copyright law have had a boomerang effect. In making frivolous claims on its copyrights, Diebold succeeded only in setting a precedent that opened up *more* possibilities for Freedom of Expression(R) online. This event

> demonstrated to activists and ordinary people that they need not be afraid of threats that are based on unfounded assertions of intellectual-property rights. Or, at least, they should be less fearful.[74]

McLeod was concerned about the ramifications of private electronic voting, with third parties being unable to check the reliability of proprietary software because of a combination of patent, copyright and trade secrets protection. He concluded that society and democracy is better served by open source voting systems, in which anyone can examine the software code and check its security.

D. Other Jurisdictions

Similar legal and policy debates have taken place in other jurisdictions in respect of limited liability for online intermediaries in respect of copyright infringement.[75] Charlotte Waelde and Lillian Edwards observe that there is a great diversity in the regulatory models for intermediaries, ranging from a 'total liability' approach to the 'safe harbors' regime and even 'self-regulation' and 'total immunity schemes'.[76] The academics observe that there has been great fluctuation in the responsibilities and duties imposed upon intermediaries.

> The competing interests of the stakeholders in the Internet content industry – intermediaries, content providers, rights-holders, and the public interest or 'users' – led at the turn of the millennium to creation of a 'limited liability/notice and take-down' approach to online intermediary immunity. However, if it is accepted that the level and extent of ISP duties is a matter of balancing policy needs, and not simply a matter of historical accident, or natural justice, then it becomes plausible that, as the Internet industry matures and policy interests change, so the imposition of ISP liability – or immunity from such – may also fluctuate.[77]

The emergence of file-sharing using peer-to-peer networks has led to a reconsideration of intermediary liability in a number of jurisdictions. There have been a number of significant legal actions brought by copyright owners against Internet intermediaries in Australia, Canada and Ireland. Although an extensive discussion of such cases is beyond the scope of this study, it is well worth providing a brief thumbnail sketch of such actions.

In Australia, intermediaries have been placed in a vulnerable position, because of the controversially broad approach taken by the courts to the authorization of copyright infringement. In *University of New South Wales* v. *Moorhouse*, the High Court of Australia held that the failure by a university to exercise control or supervision in relation to a photocopying machine installed in a library amounted to an authorization of infringement of copyright.[78] In *Telstra Corp Ltd* v. *APRA*, the telecommunications carrier was held directly liable for the playing of music-on-hold by its subscribers to their clients, even though Telstra exercised no control in determining the content of the music played.[79] In *Universal Music Australia Pty Ltd* v. *Cooper*, Tamberlin J held that the proprietor of a web-site and an ISP had infringed copyright to sound recordings made available on a web-site, mp3s4free.net, which provided links to music files on other web-sites.[80] In *Warner Music Australia Pty Ltd* v. *Swiftel Communications Pty Ltd*, a number of record companies launched legal action against a Perth-based ISP, for authorizing copyright infringement by allegedly hosting and maintaining two Internet computer servers and a web-site called Archie's Hub which deployed the BitTorrent application.[81] In the end, the matter was settled out of court.

By contrast, Canadian courts have taken a much more narrow approach to the authorization of copyright infringement. In *CCH Canadian Ltd* v. *Law Society of Upper Canada*, the Supreme Court of Canada emphasized that authorization of copyright infringement should be interpreted in a stringent fashion.[82] In *BMG Canada* v. *John Doe*, the Canadian Federal Court and the Full Federal Court considered an action taken by record companies against ISPs to reveal the identities of subscribers who, it was alleged, had infringed copyright laws by illegally trading in music downloaded from the Internet.[83] The judges were highly protective of consumers' privacy. In *Society of Composers, Authors and Music Publishers of Canada* v. *Canadian Association of Internet Providers*, the Supreme Court of Canada considered whether Internet intermediaries, such as ISPs, could be held liable for the transmission of copyrighted content on their networks.[84] Binnie J observed:

> This appeal raises the difficult issue of who should compensate musical composers and artists for their Canadian copyright in music downloaded in Canada from a foreign country via the Internet. In an era when it is as easy to access a website hosted by a server in Bangalore as it is to access a website with a server in Mississauga, where is the protection for the financial rights of the people who created the music in the first place? Who, if anyone, is to pay the piper?[85]

The Supreme Court of Canada ruled that the Canadian ISPs could not be held liable to copyright owners, because they acted as merely conduits of content.

In contrast to the *DMCA*'s particular focus on liability of ISPs for copyright infringement, the European Union provides for general regulation of content liability for intermediaries under the *European Community Electronic Commerce Directive* 2000 (ECD).[86]

In *EMI Records (Ireland) Ltd et al.* v. *Eirecom Ltd, BT Telecommunications Ireland Ltd*, members of the Irish recorded music association sought the disclosure of the identities and addresses of 17 alleged copyright infringers who were known to the plaintiffs only by the unique numbers that constituted their respective Internet Protocol addresses.[87] The defendants withheld the information on the basis that they were bound by law to respect the confidentiality of their subscribers' identities. Kelly J of the Irish High Court held that the plaintiffs were entitled to the order sought. The judge observed: 'I am satisfied that whether the right to confidentiality arises by statute or by contract or at common law, it cannot be relied on by a wrongdoer or a person against whom there is evidence of wrongdoing to protect his or her identity.'[88] Kelly J noted: 'The right to privacy or confidentiality of identity must give way where there is prima facie evidence of wrongdoing.'[89]

In contrast, a Dutch appeals court has rejected attempts by the Dutch anti-piracy organization BREIN to get the identities of file-sharers from five ISPs, including Wanadoo and Tiscali.[90] The court found that the manner in which IP addresses were collected and processed by a US company, MediaSentry, had no lawful basis under European privacy laws.

In spite of the criticisms of the *DMCA* safe harbour scheme for intermediaries, the United States Trade Representative has sought to encourage other nations to adopt similar limited liability schemes for online intermediaries. Notably, the *Australia–United States Free Trade Agreement* 2004 requires Australia to establish a system for dealing with allegedly infringing material on ISP systems and networks. An ISP will receive 'safe harbour' immunity when dealing with alleged copyright infringements on their system or networks if they comply with certain conditions. Article 17.11.29 (b)(i) defines four functions for which a limitation of liability is available: transmission of material without modification of content (a category A activity); caching carried out as part of an automatic process (a category B activity); storage at the direction of a user of material 'residing on a system operated by or for the service provider' (a category C activity) and referring users to an online location using information location tools or technology, such as hyperlinking (a category D activity). If an infringement occurs in the course of carrying on one of these activities, but an ISP complies with the relevant conditions, a court cannot grant relief against the ISP which consists of damages or other monetary relief. Article 17.11.29 (xi) and (x) of the *AUSFTA* provides for a notification and counter-notification procedure, the form of which is outlined in an accompanying side letter. The procedures exempt an ISP from liability where they expeditiously remove the allegedly infringing material in good faith based on receiving a notice from copyright owners. It was surprising that the Federal Government would impose such a stringent regime upon telecommunications carriers and ISPs, especially given its desire to sell its remaining stake in the public telecommunications carrier, Telstra.[91]

Rather than the current diversity of regimes governing Internet intermediaries, the United States Trade Representative would no doubt prefer a uniform international approach to the liability of ISPs and telecommunications carriers, mirroring the regime established by the *DMCA*.

II. THE RECORD INDUSTRY V. THE PEOPLE: THE NEW INTERMEDIARIES

In addition to such litigation against ISPs, copyright owners have also brought legal action against a number of alternative pressure points, including search engines, financial institutions and users of peer-to-peer networks. Michael Geist comments upon this important trend:

> With Internet users joining ISPs, e-commerce companies, financial institutions and search engines as intermediaries, we must begin to reconsider what it means to be an intermediary on the Internet. While the initial reaction was to provide broad legal protection for intermediaries, it may be time to re-evaluate that approach. The issue has ceased to become whether an intermediary bears responsibility when harmful activity occurs online. The question is now which intermediary bears responsibility.[92]

There has been legal action taken against members of the legal profession. MP3.com has brought a legal malpractice suit for $175 million damages against their former counsel, Cooley Godward LLP, in the Los Angeles Superior Court.[93] The music industry has sought to take legal action against venture capitalists to deprive peer-to-peer networks of capital. EMI and Universal Records have sued Hummer Winblad, the venture capital firm that raised the initial funds for the Napster program and its distribution, as well as Bertelsmann, a supporter of Napster.[94] There has been much controversy about such legal action against venture capitalists and financiers.[95] This matrix of legal action is designed to isolate and sequester peer-to-peer networks – such as Kazaa. It is intended to deprive such networks of financial support and investment, legal advice and expertise, media content and, of course, users.

In an extraordinary development, the record industry has launched thousands of legal actions against individuals who participated in file-sharing peer-to-peer networks. Since September 2003, the RIAA has brought civil copyright infringement law suits against 18 602 individuals engaged in file-sharing. There have been 4263 settlements to date, with the parties paying costs of between $US4000 and $US5000. President of the RIAA, Cary Sherman, commented in 2005:

> Enforcing our rights against both businesses and individuals engaged in online music theft is a key component of our overall effort to discourage illegal downloading and encourage fans to turn to legal services. These lawsuits have helped to contain illegal peer-to-peer use during a period of phenomenal broadband growth. They have helped to establish clear moral and legal rules of the road, weed out the bad actors and give lift to a robust legitimate marketplace. While this remains a marketplace with much room to grow, there is no question that these lawsuits have already altered the digital landscape for the better.[96]

The record industry contends that file-sharing has resulted in a fall in the sales of music. The RIAA maintained that such legal action served as an effective deterrence against individual file-sharers. The record industry also believed that the litigation would help educate consumers about the nature of copyright law. The RIAA hoped that such legal action would encourage consumers to employ legitimate authorized download services, such as iTunes, SonyConnect, Rhapsody, and Napster 2.0. Some pundits have argued that such litigation against end-users is an effective strategy. Justin Hughes, for instance, contends: 'Instead of being a bad idea, "suing your own customer" could become a financially self-sustaining activity for the record industry.'[97]

Such litigation has not been confined to the jurisdiction of the United States. The International Federation of the Phonographic Industry (IFPI) has co-ordinated a number of combinations of criminal and civil suits aimed at individuals who have uploaded hundreds or thousands of copyrighted songs onto Internet file-sharing networks without permission from the copyright owners. John Kennedy, the chairman and chair executive of IFPI, explained the nature of the worldwide campaign against file-sharing: 'People who file-share illegally often claim to be music fans but in fact they are hurting investment in music, breaking the law and risking financial penalties by their actions.'[98] The record industry denied that it was suing its own consumers: 'These are not our true customers – these are people who are distributing large amounts of copyrighted music illegally.'[99] The law suits have covered 5522 file-sharers of peer-to-peer networks, including FastTrack (Kazaa), Gnutella (BearShare), eDonkey, DirectConnect, BitTorrent, Limewire, WinMX and SoulSeek. Legal actions were brought in 18 different countries, including European nations such as France,[100] Germany, Italy and the United Kingdom;[101] Asian–Pacific countries, such as China,[102] Japan and Singapore; and a South American country, Argentina. IFPI noted that the targets of the legal action included 'a

Finnish carpenter, a British postman, a Czech IT manager, a German judge, a French chef, a British local councillor and a retired German couple'.[103] It should be noted that there are jurisdictions, such as Australia and New Zealand, where record companies have thus far refrained from taking legal action against individual end-users.

There has been some alarm and disquiet expressed about the willingness of copyright owners to sue individual end-users of file-sharing networks. The EFF has objected to the lawsuits launched by the RIAA against the users of file-sharing networks: 'There is no question that the RIAA's lawsuit campaign is unfairly singling out a few people for a disproportionate amount of punishment.'[104] The EFF has been concerned that many of the targeted individuals have lacked the resources to defend themselves, and have not been able to afford to settle the litigation. The EFF contend that the litigation against individuals engaged in file-sharing has not dampened demand: 'While some surveys suggest a modest reduction in file sharing since the recording industry lawsuits against individuals began, empirical monitoring of the P2P networks has shown P2P usage increasing.'[105] The group suggests that the litigation is a poor educational tool: 'If the goal of the RIAA was to increase awareness of the copyright laws, that mission has been accomplished, albeit at the expense of financial hardship to over 15 000 arbitrarily chosen individuals.'[106] The EFF maintains that the record industry would be better off developing more appealing authorized download services. The group comments that the litigation will have the effect of incubating new 'Darknet' technologies: 'The RIAA lawsuit campaign may also be encouraging music fans to migrate to file sharing technologies that will be both more efficient for users and harder for the RIAA to infiltrate.'[107] Indeed, the EFF comments: 'To the extent file sharers are worried about the RIAA lawsuits, many are simply opting to continue downloading while refraining from uploading (this is known as "leeching" in the lexicon of the P2P world).'[108]

There have been a number of doctrinal issues that have arisen in the context of such litigation against individual file-sharers.[109] First, there has been much debate in the case of *Elektra* v. *Barker* as to whether the right of distribution extends to uploading and downloading copyright works. Second, there has been legal argument in *BMG* v. *Gonzales* as to whether the users of peer-to-peer networks can claim to be fair users of copyright work, or at the very least, innocent infringers. Third, there have been concerns raised about copyright owners suing individuals because of mistaken identities. As illustrated by the litigation in *Parke* v. *RIAA*, there have been doubts raised about 'amnesties' granted by the RIAA.

A. *Elektra Entertainment Group* v. *Barker*

In *Elektra Entertainment Group* v. *Barker*, a number of record companies have brought an action for copyright infringement against Tenise Barker, a nursing student from the Bronx, in a Manhattan Federal Court before Karas J.[110] The companies alleged that she had used the Kazaa file sharing program to engage in copyright infringement under the screen name, 'Phoenyxx@KaZaZ': 'This individual had 611 music files on her computer and offered them freely for distribution to the millions of people who use similar peer-to-peer networks.'[111] The record companies maintained that 'making actual files available for distribution is a violation of the copyright owner's exclusive right to distribution'.[112] The record companies maintained that the plain language of the WIPO Internet treaties provided strong support for the conclusion that the right to make available is part of the distribution right. Elektra and others argued that the defendant was liable for copyright infringement regardless of who downloaded the files that were contained in their share folder.

In a motion to dismiss the complaint, Tenise Barker argued that the complaint should be dismissed because it did not disclose any specific acts or times of copyright infringement. Her lawyer noted: 'It is incomprehensible for the federal courts to be burdened with tens of thousands of identical lawsuits based on boilerplate complaints which allege, in essence, nothing – and for each defendant to be required to spend tens of thousands of dollars on litigation to do battle over the merits of "claims" that have not even been made.'[113]

The EFF intervened in the case of *Elektra Entertainment Group* v. *Barker*, complaining about the broad interpretation given to the distribution right. Fred von Lohmann comments:

> Defendant Tenise Barker, like more than 19000 others, is accused by several major record companies of using peer-to-peer (P2P) file sharing software to download and upload music. When individuals use P2P file sharing software to make unauthorized copies of sound recordings, record companies are within their rights to sue them for making unauthorized reproductions. In the thousands of suits filed thus far, however, the record companies have also alleged infringement of their distribution rights under 17 U.S.C. §106(3), apparently in hopes that an expansive judicial interpretation of the distribution right may support quick summary judgments based on the bare fact that a defendant has 'offered' files for download.[114]

The EFF argued that not all 'distributions', however, infringed section 106(3) of the *Copyright Act* 1976 (US).[115] The group maintained: 'The plain language of the Act – as well as legislative history, historical practice, and binding Second Circuit precedent – requires that a physical, tangible, material object change hands before the distribution right can be infringed.'[116] The EFF alleged: 'Plaintiffs' complaint ignores this plain statutory language and instead attempts to expand §106(3) to encompass intangible transmissions between computers over the Internet.'[117] Furthermore, the group argued that the WIPO Treaties provided no support for the plaintiffs' conception of the right of distribution.

Similarly, the Computer and Communications Industry Association and US Internet Industry Association filed an *amici curiae* brief, complaining that the expansion of the distribution right would ignore the plain language and structure of the *Copyright Act* 1976 (US) and distort copyright law in a way that would threaten varied interests across the American economy and society.[118] The Associations advised: 'While the establishment of intellectual property rights provides important incentives for creativity and innovation, the undue extension and overenforcement of those rights may have the opposite effect, of choking creativity and innovation.'[119] The groups advised: 'Efforts by Plaintiffs to rewrite copyright law should not be countenanced by a court.'[120]

Intervening as an amicus curiae, the MPAA argued that the plain language of the statute, the case law, and the legislative history supported the contention that the right of distribution was indeed a right of making available: 'If the Defendant, without authorization, loaded copies of Plaintiffs' sound recordings on her computer (whether legal or illegal copies), and made them available for other users of the peer-to-peer network to download, she infringed Plaintiffs' §106(3) distribution rights, regardless of whether any other user of the peer-to-peer service can be shown to have downloaded a copy from the Defendant's computer.'[121] The MPAA alleged: 'It is no different than if Defendant had put a table on a street corner with copies of Plaintiffs' works and a sign that said "Free – Take One" – except that in the present case Plaintiffs' works were being made available for the taking simultaneously to millions of Internet users.'[122] The MPAA observed that the ratification of the WIPO Internet Treaties by the United States Congress confirmed that the 'right of making available' was subsumed under the distribution right. The MPAA feared that, 'unless the Copyright Law is interpreted to provide copyright owners with the protections that Congress and the President intended it to provide, the ever-expanding forms of unauthorized dissemination that the Internet makes possible will eviscerate the value of the Plaintiffs' copyrights along with those of millions of other copyright owners'.[123]

The United States Department of Justice intervened in the case, because it feared that a ruling in favour of the defendant in respect of the distribution right and the electronic transfer of digital files would adversely affect its ability to engage in the federal prosecution of criminal copyright infringement.[124] The United States Government argued that the defendant's and the EFF's interpretation of the statute and the legislative history "distorts the clear language of the Act and has the nonsensical result of excluding from its reach distribution of copyrighted works through the most powerful and efficient method of distribution available" '.[125]

Oral argument in *Elektra Entertainment Group* v. *Barker* was held in January 2007; the parties are awaiting judgement.

B. *BMG* v. *Gonzales*

The EFF singled out the case of Cecilia Gonzalez as a *cause célèbre* in the ongoing litigation between the copyright industries and individual end-users of peer-to-peer networks:

> Take the case of Cecilia Gonzalez, a recently laid-off mother of five, who owes five major record companies a total of $22 500 for illegally downloading off the Internet. That's more than three-fourths of what she made the previous year as a secretary. Ironically, Gonzalez primarily downloaded songs she *already owned* on CD – the downloads were meant to help her avoid the labor of manually loading the 250 CDs she owns onto her computer. In fact, the record companies are going after a steady customer – Gonzalez and her husband spent about $30 per month on CDs. Nevertheless, the RIAA insisted that it would not consider a settlement for less than $3000, an amount that would bankrupt the Gonzalez family.[126]

In this matter, a number of record companies brought a legal action, seeking a summary judgment against Cecilia Gonzalez for copyright infringement of music recordings, in violation of s.101 of the *Copyright Act* 1976 (US), by downloading 30 songs onto her home computer.

At first instance, Manning J of the District Court observed: 'Gonzalez admits that she infringed upon the Recording Companies' copyrights by downloading 30 songs from the internet which she did not own.'[127] She noted: 'Numerous courts have held that downloading music from the internet, which the user does not own, constitutes "direct infringement".'[128] Citing the decision of the Ninth Circuit in *A & M Records Inc* v. *Napster*, the judge found that sampling by direct infringers was not fair use, and that the cumulative effect of direct infringers, like Gonzalez, harms the recording industry by reducing sales and 'raising barriers' to the recording industry's 'entry into the market for digital downloading of music'.[129] The District Court also rejected the argument of Gonzales that she was an innocent infringer. The judge observed: 'To allow Gonzalez to assert this defense based on her ignorance would eviscerate copyright protection and the old adage that "ignorance is no defense to the law".'[130] Blanche Manning also rejected the contention of Gonzales that injunctive relief was inappropriate because 'she no longer has online access, and therefore, she does not present a risk of future infringement'.[131] She observed: 'There is nothing, however, to stop her from reconnecting to the internet and resuming her infringement.'[132] The court enjoined Gonzalez from further infringement and awarded $22 500 in damages to the record companies.

In December 2005, the Federal Court of Appeals for the Seventh Circuit handed down judgment in *BMG* v. *Gonzalez*.[133] The lead judgment was by Easterbook J, an expert in antitrust law and criminal law, a specialist in law and economics, and a former Chicago Law School Professor. The judgment considered primary copyright infringement, the defence of fair use, the position of the innocent infringer, and the statutory award of damages.

First, Easterbrook J considered past precedents of the United States Federal Court in the *Aimster* litigation,[134] and the Supreme Court of the United States in the *Grokster* case,[135] and concluded that consumers who posted or downloaded music files were irrefutably primary infringers of copyright.[136] His Honour observed that Cecilia Gonzales denied the premise of *Aimster* and *Grokster*, because she believed that downloading copyrighted music through the Kazaa filesharing network was a fair use rather than infringement. Easterbrook J compared Gonzales to a 'shoplifter': 'Nor can she defend by observing that other persons were greater offenders; Gonzalez's theme that she obtained "only 30" (or "only 1,300") copyrighted songs is no more relevant than a thief's contention that he shoplifted "only 30" compact discs, planning to listen to them at home and pay later for any he liked'.[137] The judge emphasized that authors retained ultimate control over the distribution of their copyright works: 'Copyright law lets authors make their own decisions about how best to promote their works; copiers such as Gonzalez cannot ask courts (and juries) to second-guess the market and call wholesale copying "fair use" if they think that authors err in understanding their own economic interests or that Congress erred in granting authors the rights in the copyright statute.'[138]

Second, Easterbook J denied that Cecilia Gonzales was engaged in the fair use of copyright works. His Honour invoked the distinction drawn in the *Sony Betamax* decision between the legitimate practice of time-shifting, and the illegitimate practice of library-building. Easterbrook J observed that Gonzales had downloaded and retained MP3 files of musical works and sound recordings, rather than making merely ephemeral copies:

> Instead of erasing songs that she decided not to buy, [Gonzales] retained them. It is these 30 songs about which there is no dispute concerning ownership that

> formed the basis of the damages award. This is not a form of time-shifting, along the lines of [the *Sony Betamax* decision]. A copy downloaded, played, and retained on one's hard drive for future use is a direct substitute for a purchased copy – and without the benefit of the license fee paid to the broadcaster.[139]

Citing the judgments in the *Napster*, *Aimster* and *Grokster* litigation, Easterbrook J rejected the argument of Gonzales that sampling musical works was a fair use: 'Music downloaded free from the Internet is a close substitute for purchased music; many people are bound to keep the downloaded files without buying originals.'[140] The judge held that 'downloads from peer-to-peer networks such as Kazaa compete with licensed broadcasts and hence undermine the income available to authors'.[141]

Easterbrook J held that Gonzales could have listened to streaming music on Internet radio stations or sampled musical works and sound recordings on authorized MP3 services, such as the iTunes Music Store, Yahoo Music Unlimited, Real Rhapsody and Napster 2.0.[142]

Third, Easterbrook J refused to mitigate the damages awarded against Gonzales because he did not believe that she was an 'innocent infringer'. His Honour considered the provision that, if an 'infringer sustains the burden of proving, and the court finds, that such infringer was not aware and had no reason to believe that his or her acts constituted an infringement of copyright, the court in its discretion may reduce the award of statutory damages to a sum of not less than $200'. Easterbook J commented: 'Gonzalez readily could have learned, had she inquired, that the music was under copyright.'[143] This finding is troubling, especially as the judge refused to have a jury trial to test this evidence.

Fourth, Easterbook J refused the request of Gonzales for a jury trial, because BMG had asked for the minimum statutory damages of $US750 per song.[144] His Honour observed: 'The Justices did not purport to give defendants in copyright cases the right to ask jurors to return verdicts in the teeth of the law.'[145] The judge also rejected the request of Gonzales that the injunction should be vacated because 'she has learned her lesson, has dropped her broadband access to the Internet, and is unlikely to download copyrighted material again'.[146] His Honour observed: 'A private party's discontinuation of unlawful conduct does not make the dispute moot, however.'[147]

A number of commentators expressed reservations about the reasoning of Easterbrook J in *BMG* v. *Gonzales*. Cathy Kirkman observed: 'While the outcome here is unsurprising as a matter of fair use analysis, the Court's characterization of the holding in *Sony*, while it may be technically correct, does seem like a rather narrow reading of the landmark *Sony Betamax* case.'[148] Ann Bartow commented that the decision of Easterbrook J undermined Supreme Court precedents on the defence of fair use: 'Even though the Supreme Court's opinion in *Campbell* v. *Acuff Rose* explicitly disavowed the purported principle that unauthorized commercial uses are presumptively unfair, it seems to be alive and well in Easterbrook's jurisprudence.'[149] The commentator William Patry suggested that Easterbook J misapplied the judgment in *UMG Recordings, Inc.* v. *MP3.com, Inc.*,[150] because 'MP3.com didn't involve downloading at all: MP3.com bought lawfully-made CDs, copied them on to its servers and through a verification process permitted consumers who had also purchased lawfully-made copies to space-shift stream the CD.'[151] Joe Gratz comments: 'The innocent infringer defense should act as an incentive for copyright owners to place proper copyright notice on copies they distribute, while lessening the punishments for infringers who had no reason to think they were infringing.'[152] He suggested that it was possible that a jury could well find that Gonzales had good reason to believe her acts were non-infringing.[153]

C. *Parke* v. *RIAA*

The EFF have also documented that the record industry have filed lawsuits against individuals who were not engaged in file-sharing. First of all, the music industry was criticized for taking legal action against a 12-year-old girl, Brianna LaHara, who lived in a public housing apartment in the Upper West Side of New York.[154] The EFF observed: 'Rather than working to create a rational, legal means by which its customers can take advantage of file-sharing technology and pay a fair price for the music they love, [the music industry] has chosen to sue people like Brianna LaHara, a 12-year-old girl living in New York City public housing.'[155] The group stressed: 'Copyright law shouldn't make criminals out of 60 million Americans.'[156] The girl was frightened to learn that she had been sued: 'I got really scared. My stomach is all turning. I thought it was OK to download music because my mom paid a service fee for it. Out of all people, why did they pick me?'[157] Her mother Sylvia Torres paid $2000 to settle her daughter's law suit.

Second, the record companies were criticized for bringing an action against the wrong person.[158] The IP address listed in the subpoena was traced to an account held by a Romanian graduate student studying at the Massachusetts Institute of Technology. After initially opposing the subpoena on educational privacy and jurisdictional grounds, MIT revealed the student's name in response to a motion to enforce brought by the RIAA. However, the student identified had been out of the United States in Romania at the time of the alleged file-trading on the MIT campus, did not own a computer, and therefore could not have uploaded the songs from that IP address as alleged.

Third, the music industry was criticized for bringing an action for copyright infringement against a 66-year-old artist, educator and grandmother, Sarah Seabury Ward.[159] She was accused of illegally downloading and sharing more than 2000 songs online, including *I'm a Thug* by Trick Daddy. With the help of the EFF, Ward defended herself, replying that she and her husband only used the Internet to e-mail their family and did not have the software to download music. Indeed her Macintosh computer would be unable to run the Kazaa file-sharing software. In any case, she explained that she listened to classical and folk music, not the rock and hip hop music referred to in the complaint. The seven record labels sued Ward solely on the basis of 'screen shots' from the Kazaa network and information obtained from a subpoena issued to Comcast, Ward's ISP. There was no attempt made to contact Ward by either Comcast or the record companies before the legal action was taken. RIAA admitted it may have been a case of mistaken identity. It withdrew the law suit as 'a gesture of good faith'.[160] Although the RIAA ultimately withdrew the law suit against her, a RIAA spokesperson commented, 'When you go fishing with a driftnet, sometimes you catch a dolphin.'[161]

Fourth, the EFF raises the case of Patricia Santangelo, a 43-year-old single mother of five from Wappingers Falls, sued for allegedly pirating music through file-sharing networks. In the matter of *Elektra Entertainment Group, Inc.* v. *Santangelo*, a number of record companies, including the Elekra Entertainment Group, alleged that Santangelo had downloaded a number of copyright works, without permission of the copyright owners. The record companies demanded that she pay $US7500 to settle the matter.[162] Denying the allegation of copyright infringement, Santangelo responded that she had never downloaded a single song on her computer. McMullan J in the United States District Court for the Southern District of New York made some preliminary comments upon the nature of the matter. She noted that the question raised by the litigation was whether 'an Internet-illiterate parent, who does not know Kazaa from a kazoo, and who can barely retrieve her e-mail, is liable for copyright infringement committed by that parent's minor child, who downloads music over the Web without the parent's knowledge or permission – but using the parent's Internet account.'[163] It would appear unlikely that she would have downloaded songs such as Incubus's *Nowhere Fast*, Godsmack's *Whatever* and Third Eye Blind's *Semi-Charmed Life*. The case has been dismissed.

The RIAA announced that the industry was prepared to grant what amounts to 'amnesty' to P2P users who voluntarily identify themselves and pledge to stop illegally sharing music on the Internet.[164] The choice of language is interesting: 'amnesty' derives from the term 'amnestia', which means 'to forget'. The RIAA guaranteed not to sue file sharers who have not yet been identified in any RIAA investigations and who provide a signed and notarized affidavit in which they promise to respect recording-company copyrights. The website www.musicunited.org provided detailed information on this amnesty. However, the EFF warned P2P users against the plan to offer 'amnesty' to file-sharers who sign admissions of guilt.[165]

The EFF elaborated that the offer of an amnesty was largely illusory, because the RIAA did not own any copyrights, and its member labels were not bound by this arrangement: 'In reality, the RIAA cannot actually protect anyone from all civil suits, and individuals who sign these affidavits may open themselves up to criminal prosecution.'[166] Peter Yu commented upon the deficiencies of the amnesty scheme proposed by the RIAA:

> On its surface, the RIAA's amnesty program was quite attractive and creative. In reality, it represented another ineffective, costly, and disturbing attempt by the recording industry to fight the copyright wars. The most egregious copyright infringers were unlikely to participate in the program, as they typically did not believe, or did not care, that what they were doing was illegal. The RIAA was likely to end up enlisting mostly minor offenders in whom the recording industry had limited interest.[167]

The EFF filed a lawsuit in *Parke* v. *RIAA* against the Amnesty programme for being false and misleading.[168] The law suit sought a remedy to stop 'the RIAA from engaging in unlawful, misleading, and fraudulent business practices including advertising an "Amnesty Program" that does not provide real amnesty from lawsuit and a "Clean Slate Program" that does not provide a real "clean slate".'[169]

CONCLUSION

In this climate of litigation against individual end-users of peer-to-peer networks, the EFF has advocated the establishment of a voluntary collective licensing regime as a mechanism to fairly compensate artists and rights-holders for peer-to-peer network file sharing.[170] The EFF hoped that such arrangements would absolve consumers from liability for copyright infringement: 'In exchange, file-sharing music fans who pay (or have their ISP or software provider or other intermediary pay on their behalf) will be free to download whatever they like, using whatever software works best for them.'[171]

There have been a plethora of academic proposals and suggestions to develop a statutory licensing scheme or a private copying levy to deal with Internet transmissions. The advocates of such models hope that such schemes might broker reconciliation between copyright owners and private copiers. In 2002, Raymond Ku proposed that a digital recording act should fund artists through a statutory levy scheme with the distribution of funding tied to aggregate Internet downloading or use.[172] Neil Weinstock Netanel has suggested that there should be a non-commercial use levy to allow file sharing on peer-to-peer networks.[173] In his book *Promises to Keep*, William Fisher III has proposed an administrative scheme to compensate copyright owners through a tax on the devices and services that consumers use to gain access to digital entertainment.[174] In his text, *Free Culture*, Lawrence Lessig advocates law reform as a solution to such an addictive technology: 'Rather than seeking to destroy the Internet or the P2P technologies that are currently harming content providers on the Internet, we should find a relatively simple way to compensate those who are harmed.'[175] Jessica Litman contends that a blanket fee or a private licence should not just allow the downloading of media, but also facilitate the dissemination of material between consumers.[176] Peter Eckersley has suggested that there should be virtual market reward systems for musicians and writers.[177] For his part, Daniel Gervais has argued that the copyright owners should embrace and license file sharing, 'either because the industry will not be able ultimately to stop P2P file sharing, or simply because it is good business'.[178] He envisaged that such licensing could be done by ISPs, copyright collectives, and technology companies.[179]

However, not all commentators are partial to such schemes for statutory licensing and private levies. Jeremy deBeer is one who has philosophical objections to such regimes:

> There is no principled reason to impose the burden of levies on third parties in the technology and communication industries. Such shotgun approaches, which splatter liability around with the hope that some of the intended targets will be hit, may cause unacceptable collateral damage in the war on putative piracy.[180]

Historically, statutory levies have been vulnerable to challenges to their constitutional validity.[181] The precedent of the blank tape and audio home recording levies are revealing in this respect.[182] Private levying schemes have been quickly outmoded and rendered obsolescent by the appearance of new technologies.[183] There has been conflict between statutory levies and technological protection measures.[184] Furthermore, the establishment of statutory levies may augment and reinforce the increasing power of the copyright collecting societies, and lead to greater litigation. There would be immense practical difficulties involved in establishing and imposing upon various industries such a bureaucratic scheme of copyright management.

In any case, such a regimented scheme of a personal copying levy in respect of Internet downloading remains premature, given the relative youth of the technology and the culture that has sprung up around it. As J.D. Lasica has observed: 'Let a thousand business models bloom.'[185]

NOTES

1. For a historical overview, see Zittrain, J. (2006), 'A History of Online Gatekeeping', *Harvard Journal of Law and Technology*, **19**(2), 253–98. For case law, see for instance, the various conflicting decisions on the liability of online service providers in *Playboy Enterprises Inc* v. *Frena* 839 F. Supp 1552 (MD Fl 1993); *Religious Technology Center* v. *Netcom* 907 F. Supp 1361 (ND Cal 1995); *Marobie-FL Inc* v. *National Association of Fire Equipment Distribs* 983 F. Supp 1167 (ND Ill 1997); and *Sega Enterprises Ltd* v. *MAPHIA* 1997 WL337558 (ND Cal, 8 June 1997).
2. Litman, Jessica (2001), *Digital Copyright*, New York: Prometheus Books, p. 135.
3. S.512 (a) of the *Digital Millennium Copyright Act* 1998 (US).
4. S.512 (b) of the *Digital Millennium Copyright Act* 1998 (US).
5. S.512 (c) of the *Digital Millennium Copyright Act* 1998 (US).
6. S.512 (d) of the *Digital Millennium Copyright Act* 1998 (US).
7. S.512 (k) (1)(a) of the *Digital Millennium Copyright Act* 1998 (US); and S.512 (k) (1)(b) of the *Digital Millennium Copyright Act* 1998 (US).
8. S.512 (c) (1) of the *Digital Millennium Copyright Act* 1998 (US).
9. Scott, M. (2005–06), 'Safe Harbors Under the Digital Millennium Copyright Act', *New York University Journal of Legislation and Public Policy*, **9**, 99–166; and Skillrud, S.E. (2005), 'An Umbrella or a Canopy? Why the 17 U.S.C. Section 512 (a) Safe Harbor Should be Read Broadly', *Marquette Intellectual Property Law Review*, **9**, 91–109.
10. Urban, J. and L. Quilten (2005), 'Efficient Process or "Chilling Effects"? Takedown Notices Under Section 512 of the Digital Millennium Copyright Act', *Santa Clara Computer and High Technology Law Journal*, **22**, 621–93 at 687.
11. Pollock, M. (2006), 'Rebalancing Section 512 to Protect Fair Users from Herds of Mice-Trampling Elephants, or a Little Due Process is not Such a Dangerous Thing', *Santa Clara Computer and High Technology Law Journal*, **22**, 547–76.
12. Heins, Marjorie and Tricia Beckles (2005), *Will Fair Use Survive?: Free Expression in the Age of Copyright Control*, Brennan Center for Justice, New York University School of Law, http://www.fepproject.org/policyreports/WillFairUseSurvive.pdf, p. 55.
13. *Verizon Internet Services* v. *RIAA* 351 F. 3d 1229 (DC Cir 2003); and *In re Charter Communications*, 393 F.3d 771 (8th Cir. 2005).
14. *Online Policy Group et al.* v. *Diebold Inc.* 337 F. Supp. 2d 1195 (2004).
15. EFF (2004), *Online Policy Group et al.* v. *Diebold Inc.* at http://www.eff.org/legal/ISP_liability/OPG_v._Diebold/.
16. *Elektra Entertainment Group* v. *Barker* No. 05 CV 7340 (SDNY, filed Feb. 24, 2006).
17. *BMG et al.* v. *Cecilia Gonzalez* WL 106592 (N.D.Ill.) (2005).
18. Katyal, S. (2004), 'The New Surveillance', *Case Western Law Review*, **54**, 297–385 at 297.
19. Smith, S. (2003), 'From Napster to Kazaa: The Battle Over Peer to Peer File-Sharing Goes International', *Duke Law and Technology Review*, http://www.law.duke.edu/journals/dltr/articles/2003dltr0008.html, 28 March.
20. RIAA (2002), 'Cary Sherman On Dispute With Verizon', Press Release, 11 September.
21. Ibid.
22. Ibid.
23. *RIAA* v. *Verizon Internet Services* 257 F Supp 2d 244 (2003).
24. *RIAA* v. *Verizon Internet Services* 257 F Supp 2d 244 (2003).
25. *RIAA* v. *Verizon Internet Services* 257 F Supp 2d 244 at 275 (2003).
26. Alliance for Public Technology (2003), 'Amicus curiae brief in *RIAA* v. *Verizon*', http://www.eff.org/legal/cases/RIAA_v._Verizon/20030516_eff_amicus.pdf, 22.
27. *Verizon Internet Services* v. *RIAA* 351 F. 3d 1229 (DC Cir 2003).

28. *Verizon Internet Services* v. *RIAA* 351 F. 3d 1229 at 1237 (DC Cir 2003).
29. *Verizon Internet Services* v. *RIAA* 351 F. 3d 1229 at 1235 (DC Cir 2003).
30. *Verizon Internet Services* v. *RIAA* 351 F. 3d 1229 at 1233 (DC Cir 2003).
31. *Verizon Internet Services* v. *RIAA* 351 F. 3d 1229 at 1238 (DC Cir 2003).
32. *Verizon Internet Services* v. *RIAA* 351 F. 3d 1229 at 1237 (DC Cir 2003).
33. *Verizon Internet Services* v. *RIAA* 351 F. 3d 1229 at 1238 (DC Cir 2003).
34. *Verizon Internet Services* v. *RIAA* 351 F. 3d 1229 at 1231 (DC Cir 2003).
35. *RIAA* v. *Verizon Internet Services*, 543 U.S. 924, 125 S.Ct. 309 U.S (2004).
36. Sherman. C. (2003), 'RIAA on Verizon Appeals Court Decision', Press Release, http://www.riaa.com/news/newsletter/121903.asp, 19 December.
37. RIAA (2004), 'Petition for a Writ of Certiorari in *RIAA* v. *Verizon Internet Services*', appellate petition, motion, and filing, 2004 WL 1175134, 24 May.
38. Ibid.
39. MPAA *et al.* (2004), 'Amicus Brief in support of the petitioner in *RIAA* v. *Verizon Internet Services*', 2004 WL 1466644 (U.S.).
40. Time Warner (2004), 'Amicus Brief in support of the petitioner in *RIAA* v. *Verizon Internet Services*', 2004 WL 1453026.
41. Verizon (2004), 'Brief in Opposition in *RIAA* v. *Verizon Internet Services*', 2004 WL 1466645.
42. Verizon (2003), 'Verizon Wins Fight to Protect Internet Safety and Privacy: Anti-Consumer Subpoena Process Struck Down by Appeals Court', 19 December.
43. Deutsch, S. and D. McGuire (2004), 'Supreme Court Internet Privacy Decision', *Washington Post*, 14 October.
44. Ibid.
45. EFF (2003), 'Court Rules Verizon Can Refuse to ID Customers to Music Industry', 19 December.
46. *In re Charter Communications*, 393 F.3d 771 (8th Cir. 2005).
47. EFF (2004), 'Amicus Curiae Brief of Consumer and Privacy Groups in Support of Appellant Charter Communications, Inc.', 23 January.
48. EFF (2004), 'Amicus Curiae Brief of Consumer and Privacy Groups in Support of Appellant Charter Communications, Inc.', 23 January.
49. *In re Charter Communications*, 393 F.3d 771 at 777 (8th Cir. 2005).
50. *In re Charter Communications*, 393 F.3d 771 at 775 (8th Cir. 2005).
51. *In re Charter Communications*, 393 F.3d 771 at 775 (8th Cir. 2005).
52. *In re Charter Communications*, 393 F.3d 771at 777 (8th Cir. 2005).
53. *In re Charter Communications*, 393 F.3d 771at 782 (8th Cir. 2005).
54. *In re Charter Communications*, 393 F.3d 771 at 785 (8th Cir. 2005).
55. *In re Charter Communications*, 393 F.3d 771 at 786 (8th Cir. 2005).
56. Bloomberg (2005), 'U.S. Appeals Court Quashes Subpoenas for Charter Subscribers', http://www.bloomberg.com/apps/news?pid=10000103&sid=a0sCSInA_RrA, 4 January.
57. Barrett, R. (2005), 'Court Says RIAA Can't Subpoena ISPs Under DMCA', *Communications Daily*, **25**(3).
58. EFF (2005), 'Music Industry Must Respect Privacy of Filesharers: Ruling in Charter Case Smashes DMCA Subpoena Powers', 4 January.
59. Putter, J. (2006), 'Copyright Infringement v. Academic Freedom on the Internet: Dealing with Infringing Use of Peer-to-Peer Technology on Campus Networks', *Journal of Law and Policy*, **14**, 419–69.
60. Pavlosky, N.C. (2003), 'Declaration of Nelson Chu Pavlosky in Support of Plaintiff's Action for a Temporary Restraining Order and for Preliminary Injunction in *Online Policy Group et al.* v. *Diebold Inc.*', http://www.eff.org/legal/ISP_liability/ OPG_v._Diebold/Pavlosky.pdf.
61. *Online Policy Group et al.* v. *Diebold Inc.* 337 F. Supp. 2d 1195 (2004).
62. *Intellectual Reserve* v. *Utah Lighthouse Ministry* 75 F. Supp. 2d 1290 (1999).
63. Diebold Inc. (2003), 'Opposition to motion for Preliminary Injunction in *Online Policy Group et al.* v. *Diebold Inc.*', http://www.eff.org/legal/ISP_liability/OPG_v._Diebold/diebold_opp_prelim_injunct.pdf.

64. Ibid.
65. Pavlosky, N.C. (2003), 'Declaration of Nelson Chu Pavlosky in Support of Plaintiff's Action for a Temporary Restraining Order and for Preliminary Injunction in *Online Policy Group et al.* v. *Diebold Inc.*', http://www.eff.org/legal/ISP_liability/OPG_v._Diebold/Pavlosky.pdf.
66. Smith, L.T. (2003), 'Declaration of Luke Thomas Smith in Support of Plaintiff's Action for a Temporary Restraining Order and for Preliminary Injunction in *Online Policy Group et al.* v. *Diebold Inc.*', http://www.eff.org/legal/ISP_liability/OPG_v._Diebold/Smith.pdf.
67. Ibid.
68. EFF (2004), *Online Policy Group et al.* v. *Diebold Inc.* at http://www.eff.org/legal/ISP_liability/OPG_v._Diebold/.
69. Seltzer, W. (2003), 'Declaration of Wendy Seltzer in Support of Plaintiff's Action for a Temporary Restraining Order and for Preliminary Injunction in *Online Policy Group et al.* v. *Diebold Inc.*', http://www.eff.org/legal/ISP_liability/OPG_v._Diebold/Seltzer.pdf.
70. Diebold Inc. (2003), 'Opposition to motion for Preliminary Injunction in *Online Policy Group et al.* v. *Diebold Inc.*', http://www.eff.org/legal/ISP_liability/OPG_v._Diebold/diebold_opp_prelim_injunct.pdf.
71. Ibid.
72. Ibid.
73. Benkler, Yochai (2006), *The Wealth of Networks: How Social Production Transforms Markets and Freedom*, New Haven and London: Yale University Press, p. 231.
74. McLeod, Kembrew (2005), *Freedom of Expression(R): Overzealous Copyright Bozos and other Enemies of Creativity*, New York: Doubleday, p. 244.
75. For a comparative analysis of intermediary liability schemes in respect of copyright law, see Hamilton, Sheryl (2005), 'Made in Canada: A Unique Approach to Internet Service Provider Liability and Copyright Infringement' in Michael Geist (ed.), *In The Public Interest: The Future of Canadian Copyright Law*, Toronto: Irwin Press, pp. 285–308.
76. Waelde, C. and E. Lillian (2005), 'Online Intermediaries and Liability for Copyright Infringement', World Intellectual Property Organization, Geneva, 18 April.
77. Ibid., 59–60.
78. *University of New South Wales* v. *Moorhouse* (1975) 133 CLR 1.
79. *Telstra Corp Ltd* v. *APRA* (1997) 191 CLR 140.
80. *Universal Music Australia Pty Ltd* v. *Cooper* [2005] FCA 972.
81. *Warner Music Australia Pty Ltd* v. *Swiftel Communications Pty Ltd* [2005] FMCA 627; and *(No. 2)* [2005] FMCA 706.
82. *CCH Canadian Ltd.* v. *Law Society of Upper Canada*, [2004] 1 S.C.R. 339.
83. *BMG Canada* v. *John Doe* [2004] 3 F.C. 241; and [2005] FCA 193 (on appeal).
84. *Society of Composers, Authors and Music Publishers of Canada* v. *Canadian Association of Internet Providers*, [2004] 2 S.C.R. 427.
85. *Society of Composers, Authors and Music Publishers of Canada* v. *Canadian Association of Internet Providers*, [2004] 2 S.C.R. 427.
86. *EC Electronic Commerce Directive* 2000/31/EC, passed 8 June 2000.
87. *EMI Records (Ireland) Ltd et al.* v. *Eirecom Ltd, BT Telecommunications Ireland Ltd* [2005] IEHC 233.
88. *EMI Records (Ireland) Ltd et al.* v. *Eirecom Ltd, BT Telecommunications Ireland Ltd* [2005] IEHC 233.
89. *EMI Records (Ireland) Ltd et al.* v. *Eirecom Ltd, BT Telecommunications Ireland Ltd* [2005] IEHC 233.
90. *Foundation* v. *UPC Nederland* (2005); and on appeal (2006); Libbenga, J. (2006), 'File-Swappers' Identities Protected by a Dutch Court', *The Register*, http://www.theregister.com/2006/07/14/fileswappers_protected/, 14 July.
91. Rimmer, M. (2006), 'Robbery Under Arms: Copyright Law and the Australia–United States Free Trade Agreement', *First Monday*, **11**(3), http://www.firstmonday.org/issues/issue11_3/rimmer/index.html.

92. Geist, M. (2003), 'Web Quandary For Regulators', *Toronto Star*, 25 August; and Lessig, Lawrence (2004), *Free Culture: How Big Media Uses Technology And The Law To Lock Down Culture And Control Creativity*, New York: Penguin Books, pp. 189–90.
93. *MP3.com, Inc.* v. *Cooley Godward LLP*, No. BC 266625 (Filed, L.A. Super. Ct., Jan. 2002); Francis Cahill, S. (2002), 'Dot-Com Sues Law Firm Over Advice: MP3.com Says Cooley Godward Should Have Warned of Copyright Issues', udcyberspacelaw.org, 7 February; Beck, S. (2002), 'Out of Tune', *American Lawyer*, 28 March; Sandburg, B. (2002), 'Cooley Godward named in malpractice action', *The National Law Journal*, 28 January; Katyal, S. (2002), 'A Legal Malpractice Claim By MP3.com: In The Changing Area Of Cyberlaw, Is A Crystal Ball Necessary To Avoid Liability?', Findlaw, 7 February; Orlowski, A. (2003), 'Hungover CNET Wakes Up Next To MP3.com', The Register, http://www.theregister.co.uk/2003/11/15/hungover_cnet_wakes_up_next/, 15 November; and Lessig, Lawrence (2004), *Free Culture: How Big Media Uses Technology and the Law to Lock Down Culture and Control Creativity*, New York: The Penguin Press, pp. 190–91.
94. After extensive procedural litigation, Hummer Winblad and Bertelsmann have reached settlements with EMI and Universal: *UMG Recordings, Inc.* v. *Bertelsmann* AG 222 F.R.D. 408 (N.D.Cal.,2004); *In re Napster, Inc. Copyright Litigation*, Not Reported in F.Supp.2d, 2005 WL 289977, N.D.Cal., Feb 03, 2005; *In re Napster, Inc. Copyright Litigation*, 354 F.Supp.2d 1113, 2005-1 Trade Cases P 74 743, N.D.Cal., Feb 03, 2005; *In re Napster, Inc. Copyright Litigation*, 377 F.Supp.2d 796, 77 U.S.P.Q.2d 1833, N.D.Cal., May 31, 2005; *In re Napster, Inc. Copyright Litigation*, 235 F.R.D. 463, 2006-1 Trade Cases P 75 205, N.D.Cal., Apr 20, 2006; and *In re Napster, Inc. Copyright Litigation*, Slip Copy, 2006 WL 1348555, N.D.Cal., May 17, 2006.
95. Reuters (2003), 'EMI, Universal Sue Napster Backers', *USA Today*, 23 April; and Lessig, Lawrence (2004), *Free Culture: How Big Media Uses Technology And The Law To Lock Down Culture And Control Creativity*, New York: Penguin Books, p. 191; Glatstein, B. (2004), 'Tertiary Copyright Liability', *The University of Chicago Law Review*, **71**, 1605–35; Coats, W., M. Weinstein and E. Zimmerman (2005), 'Pre- and Post-Grokster Copyright Infringement Liability for Secondary and Tertiary Parties', 11th Annual Institute on Intellectual Property Law, Practising Law Institute Patents, Copyrights, Trademarks, and Literary Property Course Handbook Series, PLI Order No. 6036, 221.
96. RIAA (2005), 'Music Industry Files New Lawsuits in Ongoing Enforcement Against Online Theft', Press Release, http://www.riaa.com/news/newsletter/113005.asp, 20 November.
97. Hughes, J. (2005), 'On the Logic of Suing One's Customers and the Dilemma of Infringement Based Business Models', *Cardozo Arts and Entertainment Law Journal*, **22**, 725.
98. IFPI (2006), 'Illegal music file-sharers targeted by fresh wave of legal action', http://www.ifpi.org/content/section_news/20060404.html, 4 April.
99. Ibid.
100. In *Société Civile des Producteurs Phonographiques* v. *Antoine G and the Association of Audionautes* (December 2005), a French record producer association known as the SCPP sued Antoine G for downloading and uploading 1212 music tracks. The Association of Audionautes intervened in this matter on behalf of Antoine G. The District Court of Paris released Antoine G free of charges, finding that the acts of downloading and uploading qualified as 'private copying'.
101. In *Polydor Limited and Others* v. *Brown and Others* [2005] EWHC 3191 (Ch), Collins J of the High Court of Justice Chancery Division held that Brown had directly infringed copyright by 'connecting a computer to the Internet, where the computer is running P2P software, and in which music files containing copies of the claimant's copyright works are placed in a shared directory'. The judge emphasized that 'it does not matter whether the person knows, or has reason to believe, that what they are doing is an infringement, because innocence or ignorance is no defence'.
102. There has been much discussion of the prosecution of Chan Nai-Ming for using BitTorrent software to engage in Internet film piracy: *Hong Kong Special*

Administrative Region v. *Chan Nai-Ming* (TMCC 1268/2005, 24 October 2005); and on appeal (HCMA 1221/2005, 12 December 2006); Tofalides, M. and G. Fearn (2006), 'Bittorrent Copyright Infringement', *Entertainment Law Review*, **17**(2), 81–3; and Low, W.T. (2006), 'Tackling Online Copyright Infringers in Hong Kong', *Entertainment Law Review*, **17**(4), 122–4.
103. IFPI (2006), 'Illegal music file-sharers targeted by fresh wave of legal action', http://www.ifpi.org/content/section_news/20060404.html, 4 April.
104. EFF (2005), 'RIAA v. the People: Two Years Later', http://www.eff.org/IP/P2P/RIAAatTWO_FINAL.pdf, 3 November.
105. Ibid.
106. Ibid.
107. Ibid.
108. Ibid.
109. There is a large amount of litigation against end-users of peer-to-peer networks. Lawyers representing such defendants maintain a web site, with extensive details of such litigation: http://recordingindustryvspeople.blogspot.com/.
110. *Elektra Entertainment Group* v. *Barker* No. 05 CV 7340 (SDNY, filed 24 Feb. 2006).
111. Elektra Entertainment Group (2006), 'Plaintiff's Opposition to Defendant's Motion to Dismiss the Complaint in *Elektra Entertainment Group* v. *Barker*', http://www. ilrweb.com/viewILRPDF.asp?filename=elektra_barker_oppositiontomotion.
112. Ibid.
113. Barker, T. (2006), 'Memorandum of Tenise Barker in Support of her Motion to Dismiss the Complaint', http://www.ilrweb.com/viewILRPDF.asp?filename=elektra_barker_memooflaw.
114. EFF (2006), 'Amicus Brief in support of Defendant's Motion to Dismiss the Complaint in *Elektra Entertainment Group* v. *Barker*', http://www.eff.org/IP/P2P/RIAA_v._ThePeople/elektra_v._barker/elektra-amicus-efiled.pdf.
115. Ibid.
116. Ibid.
117. Ibid.
118. The Computer and Communications Industry Association and US Internet Industry Association (2006), 'Brief of Amici Curiae in Support of the Defendant's Motion to Dismiss the Complaint in *Elektra Entertainment Group* v. *Barker*', http://www.ilrweb.com/viewILRPDF.asp?filename=elektra_barker_amicusbriefcomputercomm.
119. Ibid.
120. Ibid.
121. MPAA (2006), 'Brief of Amicus Curiae in Relation to the Defendant's Motion to Dismiss the Complaint in *Elektra Entertainment Group* v. *Barker*', http://www.ilrweb.com/viewILRPDF.asp?filename=elektra_barker_mpaabrief.
122. Ibid.
123. Ibid.
124. United States Government (2006), 'Statement of Interest in Opposition to Defendant's Motion to Dismiss the Complaint in *Elektra Entertainment Group* v. *Barker*', http://www.ilrweb.com/viewILRPDF.asp?filename=elektra_barker_usstatement.
125. Ibid.
126. EFF (2005), 'RIAA v. the People: Two Years Later' (3 November), http://www.eff.org/IP/P2P/RIAAatTWO_FINAL.pdf.
127. *BMG et al.* v. *Cecilia Gonzalez* WL 106592 (N.D.Ill.) (2005).
128. *BMG et al.* v. *Cecilia Gonzalez* WL 106592 (N.D.Ill.) (2005).
129. *BMG et al.* v. *Cecilia Gonzalez* WL 106592 (N.D.Ill.) (2005).
130. *BMG et al.* v. *Cecilia Gonzalez* WL 106592 (N.D.Ill.) (2005).
131. *BMG et al.* v. *Cecilia Gonzalez* WL 106592 (N.D.Ill.) (2005).
132. *BMG et al.* v. *Cecilia Gonzalez* WL 106592 (N.D.Ill.) (2005).
133. *BMG et al.* v. *Cecilia Gonzalez* 430 F.3d 888 (2005).
134. *In re Aimster Copyright Litigation*, 334 F.3d 643, 645 (7th Cir. 2003).
135. *MGM Studios, Inc.* v. *Grokster, Ltd.*, 125 S. Ct. 2764 (2005).

136. *BMG et al.* v. *Cecilia Gonzalez* 430 F.3d 888 (2005).
137. *BMG et al.* v. *Cecilia Gonzalez* 430 F.3d 888 at 891(2005).
138. *BMG et al.* v. *Cecilia Gonzalez* 430 F.3d 888 at 891 (2005).
139. *BMG et al.* v. *Cecilia Gonzalez* 430 F.3d 888 at 890 (2005).
140. *BMG et al.* v. *Cecilia Gonzalez* 430 F.3d 888 at 890 (2005).
141. *BMG et al.* v. *Cecilia Gonzalez* 430 F.3d 888 at 891 (2005).
142. *BMG et al.* v. *Cecilia Gonzalez* 430 F.3d 888 at 891 (2005).
143. *BMG et al.* v. *Cecilia Gonzalez* 430 F.3d 888 at 892 (2005).
144. *BMG et al.* v. *Cecilia Gonzalez* 430 F.3d 888 at 892 (2005).
145. *BMG et al.* v. *Cecilia Gonzalez* 430 F.3d 888 at 892 (2005).
146. *BMG et al.* v. *Cecilia Gonzalez* 430 F.3d 888 at 893 (2005).
147. *BMG et al.* v. *Cecilia Gonzalez* 430 F.3d 888 at 893 (2005).
148. Kirkman, C. (2005), '7th Circuit Rules in P2P Infringement User Case', Silicon Valley Media Law Blog, http://www.joegratz.net/archives/2005/12/10/7th-cir-p2p-downloading-is-not-fair-use/, 10 December.
149. Bartow, A. (2005), 'BMG v. Gonzalez', Sivacracy.net, http://www.nyu.edu/classes/siva/archives/002533.html, 12 December.
150. *UMG Recordings, Inc.* v. *MP3.com, Inc.*, 92 F. Supp. 2d 349 (S.D.N.Y. 2000).
151. Patry, W. (2005), 'BMG v. Cecilia Gonzalez', The Patry Copyright Blog, http://williampatry.blogspot.com/2005/12/bmg-v-cecilia-gonzalez.html, 11 December.
152. Gratz, J. (2005), '7th Circuit: Downloading is not Fair Use', joegratz.net, http://www.joegratz.net/archives/2005/12/10/7th-cir-p 2p-downloading-is-not-fair-use/, 10 December.
153. Ibid.
154. Mongelli, L. (2003), 'Music Pirate', *New York Post*, http://www.nypost.com/cgi-bin/printfriendly.pl, 9 September.
155. BBC News (2003), 'Grandmother Piracy Lawsuit Dropped', BBC News, http://news.bbc.co.uk/go/pr/fr/-/1/hi/entertainment/music/3140160.stm, 25 September.
156. Ibid.
157. Ibid.
158. Hinze, G. (2003), 'The Electronic Frontier Foundation Comments Regarding Phillips Fox, Issues Papers On The Australian Digital Agenda Review', http://www.eff.org/IP/DRM/DMCA/20031003_australian_comments.php, 30 September.
159. EFF (2003), 'Recording Industry Withdraws Music Sharing Lawsuit: Lack Of Due Process Leads To Mistaken Identity', 24 September.
160. Associated Press (2003), 'Downloading Claim Against Granny Dropped', *The Sydney Morning Herald*, 25 September.
161. Roddy, D. (2003), 'The Song Remains the Same', *Pittsburgh Post-Gazette.com*, 16 September.
162. *Elektra Entertainment Group, Inc.* v. *Santangelo* Slip Copy, 2005 WL 3199841 (S.D.N.Y., 2005).
163. *Elektra Entertainment Group, Inc.* v. *Santangelo* Slip Copy, 2005 WL 3199841 (S.D.N.Y., 2005).
164. RIAA (2003), 'Recording Industry Begins Suing P2P File Sharers Who Illegally Offer Copyrighted Music Online', Press Release, Washington, 8 September.
165. EFF (2003), 'Recording Industry Plans "Amnesty" for Music Sharers: Electronic Frontier Foundation Says Share, Get Artists Paid', 5 September.
166. EFF (2003), 'Why RIAA's "Amnesty" Offer Is A Sham', 9 September.
167. Yu, P. (2005), 'P2P and the Future of Private Copying', *University of Colorado Law Review*, **76**, 653–765 at 664.
168. *Parke* v. *RIAA* ('No Clean Slate lawsuit') 9 September 2003, http://www.eff.org/IP/P2P/Parke_v._RIAA/Parke_RIAA_Complaint.pdf.
169. Ibid.
170. EFF (2005), 'RIAA v. the People: Two Years Later', http://www.eff.org/IP/P2P/RIAAatTWO_FINAL.pdf, 3 November.
171. Ibid.

172. Ku, R. (2002), 'The Creative Destruction of Copyright: Napster and the New Economics of Digital Technology', *University of Chicago Law Review*, **69**, 263–324.
173. Netanel, N.W. (2003), 'Impose A Noncommercial Use Levy To Allow Free Peer-to-Peer File Sharing', *Harvard Journal Of Law And Technology*, **17**(1), 1–84.
174. Fisher, William (2004), *Promises to Keep: Technology, Law, and the Future of Entertainment*, Stanford: Stanford University Press.
175. Lessig, Lawrence (2004), *Free Culture: How Big Media Uses Technology And The Law To Lock Down Culture And Control Creativity*, New York: Penguin Books, p. 201.
176. Litman, J. (2004), 'Sharing and Stealing', *Hastings Law Communications and Entertainment Law Journal*, **27**, 1.
177. Eckersley, P. (2004), 'Virtual Markets for Virtual Goods: The Mirror Image of Digital Copyright?', *Harvard Journal of Law and Technology*, **18**(1), 85–166.
178. Gervais, D. (2004), 'The Price of Social Norms: Towards a Liability Regime for File-Sharing', *Journal of Intellectual Property Law*, **12**(1), 39–73.
179. Ibid.
180. de Beer, J. (2005), 'The Role of Levies in Canada's Digital Music Market', *Canadian Journal of Law & Technology*, **4**(3), 153 at 164.
181. In *Australian Tape Manufacturers Association Ltd* v. *Commonwealth* (1993) 176 CLR 480 the High Court of Australia held that the *Copyright Amendment Act* 1989 (Cth), which levied a royalty on the vendors of blank tapes, was invalid as a tax under s.55 of the Constitution.
182. *Audio Home Recording Act* 1992 (US).
183. In *Canadian Private Copying Collective* v. *Canadian Storage Media Alliance* (2004) FCA 424, the Federal Court ruled that the Canadian private copying levy scheme did not apply to digital audio recorders such as iPods because such technologies were not contemplated by the statute.
184. In *Stéphane P and Association UFC* v. *Universal Pictures Video France* (22 April 2005), the Court d'Appel de Paris in France considered the interaction between personal levy schemes and technological protection measures. The matter concerned Mr P. who had purchased a DVD of 'Mulholland Drive', and wanted to play it at his mother's house, which only had a VHS player. Mr P. was unable to transfer the DVD onto a VHS cassette because of digital rights management protection. He brought his case to the French consumer union (UFC) who agreed to bring an action against Universal Pictures and Studio Canal. The appellate court recognized that the French Intellectual Property Code guaranteed the rights of consumers 'to make a private copy' (Article L.122–5) and obligated vendors to inform consumers of essential characteristics of goods (Article L.111–1). It found that the digital rights management system was a breach of the exception for private copy and that Universal had failed to provide sufficient information about the mechanism, which is an essential characteristic of the product. As a remedy, the Parisian court ordered that the companies cease from using TPMs which were incompatible, with an exception for private copy and to pay damages. In *Perquin and UFC Que Choisir* v. *SA Films, Alain Sarde Ste, Universal Pictures Video France* (28 February 2006), the Supreme Court (Court de Cassation) set aside the decision, ruling that the appeal court had misconstrued the law. The Supreme Court held that the exception for private copying could not prohibit the use of TPMs where such copying would conflict with the normal exploitation of the work.
185. Lasica, J.D. (2005), *Darknet: Hollywood's War against the Digital Generation*, Hoboken, NJ: Wiley & Sons, p. 209.

7. Google: search or destroy?

> When it was proclaimed that the Library contained all books, the first impression was one of extravagant happiness. All men felt themselves to be the masters of an intact and secret treasure. There was no personal or world problem whose eloquent solution did not exist in some hexagon . . . As was natural, this inordinate hope was followed by an excessive depression. The certitude that some shelf in some hexagon held precious books and that these precious books were inaccessible, seemed almost intolerable. (Jorge Luis Borges, 'The Library of Babel'[1])

The popular search engine Google is named after the mathematical term 'googol' which refers to the number 1 followed by one hundred zeroes.[2] The service enables users to search the Web, Usenet and images. Google's features include PageRank, caching and translation of results and an option to find similar pages. Its search engine depends on a 'crawler', that accesses and indexes a substantial proportion of the content accessible on the Web, and on a 'precedence algorithm' which sorts the pages that match any given search-string into a sequence. The company's breakthrough technology and continued innovation serve its mission of 'organizing the world's information and making it universally accessible and useful'.[3]

Google was established in 1995 by Sergey Brin and Larry Page, two Stanford University students in Palo Alto, California.[4] In 1998, Sergey and Larry established a private company with $1 million in funding from family, friends and angel investors. In August 2004, Google offered 25.7 million shares in a Dutch auction, and became a public company. The search engine has used its advertising revenue and investment monies to expand into a wide range of additional lines of business, some through takeover and some through internal development. It has sought both greater vertical and horizontal integration. Google Desktop enables users to search their own computer.[5] Google Scholar allows specialized searches of materials relevant in the academic world.[6] Google Book Search provides an index to a vast array of books from leading libraries around the world.[7] Google Images provides a comprehensive search engine of images.[8] Google News enables users to search and browse 4500 sources of news.[9] Google Earth provides satellite imagery of the earth's surface at high levels of resolution.[10] Froogle – a rival to eBay – is a product search engine and shopping directory, which assists consumers with locating products for sale online by presenting photos of relevant products.[11] A beta version of

Google Video enables users to search television programmes and videos.[12] Google has also been investing in on-line communication: it has developed GMail,[13] an email service which freely provides 1 gigabyte per account; Picasa, a management system for digital photographs; Blogger,[14] which enables personal expression through blogging; and Orkut,[15] an online web community, which provides a social networking service.

In a piece entitled 'Who's Afraid of Google? Everyone', Kevin Kelleher comments that the company poses a threat to a number of competitors:

> It seems no one is safe: Google is doing Wi-Fi; Google is searching inside books; Google has a plan for ecommerce. Of course, Google has always wanted to be more than a search engine. Even in the early days, its ultimate goal was extravagant: to organize the world's information. High-minded as that sounds, Google's ever-expanding agenda has put it on a collision course with nearly every company in the information technology industry: Amazon.com, Comcast, eBay, Yahoo!, even Microsoft.[16]

Nonetheless, the commentator notes that Google is sensitive to the fears that it will be a rival. The Google sales manager, Omid Kordestani, observed at a recent conference, 'We're trying to find ways so we are not viewed as a gorilla.'[17] Kevin Kelleher notes: 'Given its outsize ambitions, that's one search Google might not be able to handle.'[18]

Since the search engine became a public company, there has been much debate about Google and the implications of its activities for copyright law, privacy and competition. In its 2005 annual report, the search engine is candid about its reliance upon intellectual property, noting: 'We rely on a combination of patent, trademark, copyright and trade secret laws in the U.S. and other jurisdictions . . . to protect our proprietary technology and our brand.'[19] Furthermore the company notes that Google, AdSense, I'm Feeling Lucky, PageRank and Keyhole are registered trademarks in the United States, as well as Blogger, Orkut.com, Froogle, Gmail and Picasa. Google also relies upon an exclusive licence to PageRank technology. In the same report, Google also admits that it is vulnerable to legal action for breach of copyright law:

> Certain entities have also filed copyright claims against us, alleging that features of certain of our products, including Google Web Search, Google News, Google Image Search, and Google Book Search, infringe their rights. Adverse results in these lawsuits may include awards of damages and may also result in, or even compel, a change in our business practices, which could result in a loss of revenue for us or otherwise harm our business. In addition, generally speaking, any time that we have a product or serve that links to or hosts material in which others allege to own copyrights, we face the risk of being sued for copyright infringement or related claims. Because these products and services comprise the

> majority of our products and services, the risk of potential harm from such lawsuits is substantial.[20]

The company is particularly conscious that digital copyright law impinges upon its business: 'For example, the *Digital Millennium Copyright Act* 1998 (US) [*DMCA*] has provisions that limit, but do not eliminate, our liability for listing or linking to third-party web sites that include materials that infringe copyrights or other rights.'[21]

In addition, there has been increasing competition between Google Inc and Microsoft Corporation, leading to litigation over intellectual property rights.[22] Google has endured patent litigation brought by its rival, Yahoo.[23] Google Inc. has also been facing a number of trademark infringement lawsuits from various parties, including the American Chemical Society,[24] the insurance company Geico,[25] the American Blind and Wall Paper Factory,[26] and Louis Vuitton.[27] The search engine has also battled Digital Envoy over trade secrets, technology licensing and unfair competition.[28] Furthermore, there have also been concerns about the privacy implications of Google services, such as GMail, and Google Earth.[29] The share price for Google plummeted after it resisted subpoenas from the US Government seeking evidence to support its child pornography laws. The government asked for a list of relevant requests entered into the search engine during an unspecified single week: 'a breakdown that could conceivably span tens of millions of queries'.[30]

This chapter contends that the *DMCA* is ill-equipped to deal with the technical and legal issues raised by search engines, especially as it was drafted in 1998 when the providers of information tools were still in their infancy. It focused, in particular, upon the controversy over Google Book Search. Section one considers the collaboration between Google and a number of university libraries and the New York Public Library to 'digitally scan books from their collections so that users worldwide can search them in Google'.[31] The search engine claimed that this would be an 'expansion of the Google Print program, which assists publishers in making books and other offline information searchable online'.[32] Section two considers the class action filed by the Authors' Guild in September 2005 against Google alleging that the Google Library program had infringed copyright in literary works.[33] This section also considers a similar lawsuit brought by the Association of American Publishers against the search engine in October 2005.[34] Section three explores whether Google could raise a defence of fair use against such allegations. It is worthwhile considering, in this context, past precedents on photocopying, indexing and Internet search engines.

This chapter counterpoints such litigation over Google Book Search with parallel litigation over Google News, Google Images, and Google

Cache. Section four considers litigation over Google News. In *Agence France Presse* v. *Google Inc*, the Agence France Presse sued Google in the District Court of the District of Columbia, claiming that the use of the Agency's headlines, lead sentences and photographs on the Google News website constitutes copyright infringement.[35] Section five examines copyright litigation over Google Images. The Californian adult company, Perfect 10, has also filed a lawsuit against Google, claiming that the reproduction of its images infringes the company's copyright, trade marks and publicity rights.[36] Section six focuses upon copyright lawsuits over web archiving and caching by Google. In *Field* v. *Google Inc*., the District Court of Nevada dismissed the claim of a Nevada lawyer and writer, that Google had infringed his copyright in 51 literary works from his personal website, blakeswritings.com, which the search engine had stored in an online repository.[37] In *Parker* v. *Google Inc*, the United States District Court for the Eastern District of Pennsylvania dismissed the claims of Gordon Ray Parker that Google had infringed his copyright in works published on the Internet, such as his e-book, '29 Reasons Not to Be A Nice Guy', under the name Snodgrass Publishing Group.[38] The conclusion to the chapter notes the emergence of new copyright litigation in respect of Internet videos featured on Google Video and YouTube.

I. 'IMAGINE ALL THE WORLD'S BOOKS AT YOUR FINGERTIPS': THE LIBRARY OF BABEL

In the beguiling parable 'The Library of Babel', the Argentinian author, Jorge Luis Borges, explores the joy and fear inspired by an infinite library.[39] The Google Book Search project has inspired opinions as polarized as those found in this parable. On the one side, there are grand hopes Google Book Search will bring about a new Enlightenment, spreading knowledge far and wide. On the other, there are fears that the service will pose a threat to the traditional roles of libraries and publishers alike.

A. Google Book Search

In his breathless new book *The Google Story*, David A. Vise proclaims that the search engine promises a new Gutenberg revolution: 'Not since Gutenberg invented the modern printing press . . . has any new invention empowered individuals, and transformed access to information, as profoundly as Google.'[40]

It should be acknowledged that Google is certainly not the first attempt at digitizing the world's literature. In 1971, Michael Hart founded Project

Gutenberg, a project devoted to digitizing and distributing html books.[41] This venture relied upon the contributions of volunteers. The Prelinger Archive was founded in 1983 by Rick Prelinger.[42] Over the next twenty years, it grew into a collection of over 48 000 'ephemeral' films. In 1996, Brewster Kahle established the Internet Archive.[43] This project sought to build an 'Internet library', with the purpose of offering permanent access for researchers, historians and scholars to historical collections that exist in digital format. The Carnegie Mellon University has embarked upon the Million Books Project, with the goal of scanning and indexing one million books.[44] The University has sought to digitize public domain and out-of-print, in-copyright material with the permission of the publishers. The Google Book Search project is significant, because it outstrips such precedents in terms of the scale of the undertaking, and the power of the search engine.

Google envisions: 'Our ultimate goal is to work with publishers and libraries to create a comprehensive, searchable, virtual card catalog of all books in all languages that helps users discover new books and publishers find new readers.'[45] The company explains the nature of the project:

> Google Book Search is a book-finding tool, not a book-reading tool. We only show the full pages of books if the copyright holders have given us permission or if the book is out of copyright. Otherwise we show bibliographic information about the book plus at most a few sentences of your search term in context.[46]

Using secret proprietary copying technologies, Google plans to scan into its database materials from the libraries of Harvard, Stanford and Oxford Universities, the University of Michigan, the University of California the University of Wisconsin-Madison, the New York Public Library, and the Complutense University of Madrid in Spain. In response to search queries, users will be able to read the full text of public domain materials. However, Google will only allow readers to read a few sentences of text around the search term in books still covered by copyright. The Internet search engine will display sample pages of books, with the permission of the publisher or the copyright holder. The company sums up the ambitions of Google Book Search with the catchphrase, 'Imagine all the world's books at your fingertips.'[47]

B. The Library Partners

The libraries participating in Google Book Search have been optimistic about the digitization project. The University of Michigan has entered into a partnership with Google to scan its entire collection: 7.8 million public domain and copyright works.[48] Provost Paul N. Courant commented: 'By placing the great works of the past on the Internet, this endeavor helps ensure that the texts that have informed the development of thought and human understanding throughout recorded history will continue to do so.'[49] University librarian, William Gosling, observed that the project would benefit its users in direct and transformative ways: 'This partnership with Google affords us the opportunity to chart new methods of bringing these resources and the expertise of the Library to the academic community and as a public good to a broader user population.'[50]

In an address to the Professional/Scholarly Publishing Division of the Association of American Publishers, Mary Sue Coleman, the Michigan University President, argued that the venture was 'a legal, ethical, and noble endeavor that will transform our society:'[51]

> Legal because we believe copyright law allows us the fair use of millions of books that are being digitized. Ethical because the preservation and protection of knowledge is critically important to the betterment of humankind. And noble because this enterprise is right for the time, right for the future, right for the world of publishing, right for all of us.[52]

Coleman observes: 'The University of Michigan's partnership with Google offers three overarching qualities that help fulfill our mission: the preservation of books; worldwide access to information; and, most importantly, the public good of the diffusion of knowledge.'[53] She comments, in particular, on the need to protect cultural heritage from potential catastrophes: talking about how the Japanese army destroyed the Filipino library in World War II; how the Khmer Rouge ransacked the National Library of Cambodia; and how Hurricane Katrina wrecked the libraries of New Orleans.

Stanford University has also engaged in industrial-scale digitization with the help of Google. Michael Keller, university librarian and publisher of the Stanford University Press and the HighWire Press, Stanford's online co-publishing service for scholarly journals, remarked that the venture helped overcome the technical and financial limitations which had hampered the university's own digitization efforts: 'The Google arrangement catapults our effective digital output from the boutique scale to the truly industrial.'[54]

Harvard University has also agreed to Google undertaking a pilot project of scanning and digitizing 40 000 books that are both in and out of copyright. The Director of the University Library, Sidney Verba, explained:

> The new century presents important new opportunities for libraries, including Harvard's, and for those individuals who use them. The collaboration between major research libraries and Google will create an important public

> good of benefit to students, teachers, scholars, and readers everywhere. The project harnesses the power of the Internet to allow users to identify books of interest with a precision and at a speed previously unimaginable. The user will then be guided to find books in local libraries or to purchase them from publishers and book vendors. And, for books in the public domain, there will be even broader access.[55]

Verba emphasized that the large-scale digitization of Harvard's library books did not in any way diminish the University's commitment to the collection and preservation of books as physical objects: 'The digital copy will not be a substitute for the books themselves.'[56] The University was confident that Google's treatment of in-copyright works would be consistent with copyright law.

Similarly, the New York Public Library agreed to allow Google to scan, digitize and distribute public domain works in a pilot project. Dr Paul LeClerc, President of the New York Public Library, said:

> This is an historic moment for libraries everywhere, and for this library in particular. NYPL has over 50 million items in its vast collections, 20 million of which are books. The public has been able to search the bibliographic online catalog of the NYPL for over a decade, but never before has one been able to search the full content of any of our holdings electronically. The books that will be digitized in this pilot project were chosen based on three important criteria: they are all in the public domain, they are not too fragile to scan, and we know that they are of great interest to the public.[57]

For the duration of this pilot project, Google's innovative scanning operation will come onsite to NYPL. LeClerc added, 'The New York Public Library is participating in the project because it is central to our mission – making our collections democratically accessible to a global audience, free of charge.'[58] He added: 'Without Google's assistance, the cost of digitizing our books – in both time and dollars – would be prohibitive.'[59]

Oxford University has also allowed Google to digitize public domain works. Reg. Carr, Director of Oxford University Library Services, said, 'The Bodleian's 19th century collections, which include many out-of-print titles which otherwise would be incredibly hard to find, will be scanned as part of the Google Print programme.'[60] Ronald Milne, the acting director of Oxford University Library and Bodley's Librarian, further commented: 'The initiative will carry forward Sir Thomas Bodley's vision and the ethos of the Bodleian Library into the digital age, allowing readers from around the world to access the Library's collections over the World Wide Web.'[61] However, the English library did not permit the search engine to scan copyright books, because of concerns about the limitations of the defence of fair dealing under United Kingdom copyright law.

In August 2006, the University of California joined the Google Book Search Project.[62] John Oakley, Chair of UC's Academic Senate and professor of law at UC Davis, observed:

> The academic enterprise is fundamentally about discovery. We contribute to it immeasurably by unlocking the wealth of information maintained within our libraries and exposing it to the latest that search technologies have to offer.[63]

Google will scan books from the hundreds of academic libraries associated with the ten campuses of the University of California, and make the items searchable on the web.[64] In return, the University of California will receive a digital copy of the works.

Google has also entered into partnership agreements with the University of Wisconsin-Madison in the United States and the Complutense University of Madrid in Spain. No doubt the search engine will enter into further library partnerships in the future.

It should, however, be stressed that not all libraries were enamoured of Google Book Search. The President of the American Library Association, Michael Gorman, has accused what he calls the 'boogie-woogie Google boys' of suffering from an overwhelming hubris: 'If you are taken in by all the fanfare and hoopla that have attended their project to digitize all the books in a number of major libraries . . . you would think they are well on their way to godliness.'[65] The President maintains that Google Book Search is no 'Mind of God'. Indeed, he believes there is no substitute for traditional libraries: 'It is beyond premature to prepare to mourn the death of libraries and the death of the book.'[66] He acerbically predicted: 'This latest version of Google hype will no doubt join taking personal commuter helicopters to work and carrying the Library of Congress in a briefcase on microfilm as "back to the future" failures, for the simple reason that they were solutions in search of a problem.'[67]

C. Rival Digitization Projects

A number of the rivals to Google have launched competing digitization projects. Most notably, the search engine Yahoo! established the Open Content Alliance, which aims to digitize historical works of fiction and specialized technical papers over the next few years.[68] The project members include the Internet Archive, the University of California, the University of Toronto and the National Archives of the United Kingdom. Internet Archive founder, Brewster Kahle, has been critical of libraries participating in the Google Book Search project:

> They're effectively giving their library to a single corporation. Having a public institution decide to go with Google's restrictions doesn't help the idea of libraries being open in the future.[69]

The Alliance will encourage the greatest possible degree of access to and reuse of collections in the archive, while respecting the rights of content owners and contributors. Contributors must secure the permission of concerned copyright holders prior to submitting materials for digitization or inclusion in the archive.[70] They will also determine the terms and conditions under which their collections are distributed and how attribution should be made. The Alliance need not be obligated to accept all content that is offered to it and may give preference to that which can be made widely accessible. It will offer collection and item-level metadata of its hosted collections in a variety of formats and welcomes efforts to create and offer tools that will enhance the usability of the materials in the archive. Copies of the collections will reside in multiple archives internationally to ensure their long-term preservation and accessibility to all.

As well, in November 2005, Microsoft and the British Library announced a strategic partnership to digitize 25 million pages of content from the library's collections in 2006, with a long-term commitment to digitize still more in the future.[71] Bill Gates, Chairman and Chief Software Architect of Microsoft, stressed: 'Our partnership with the British Library is not only about digitisation and preservation, but also about delivering a great experience for people accessing this amazing collection through British Library and MSN Web sites.'[72] Microsoft and the British Library will work together to digitize around 100 000 out-of-copyright books. MSN Search will launch an initial public beta offering in 2006.

In November 2005, the on-line bookseller, Amazon.com, announced plans to expand its 'Search Inside the Book', which provides searchable content from thousands of books.[73] The first program, Amazon Pages, will enable customers to simply and inexpensively purchase and read online just the pages they need. The second program, Amazon Upgrade, will allow customers to 'upgrade' their purchase of a physical book on Amazon.com to include complete online access.

The French President, Jacques Chirac, and the European Commission expressed concern about the Anglo-centric nature of Google Book Search. As Agence-France Press reported: 'Google's plans have rattled the cultural establishment in Paris, raising fears that the French language and ideas could be just sidelined on the worldwide web, which is already dominated by English.'[74] The European Commission announced in October 2005 that it would turn Europe's 'historical and cultural heritage into digital content' and make it available online to all European citizens.[75]

II. 'WAGE JUSTICE FOR POETS': THE AUTHORS' GUILD AND GOOGLE BOOK SEARCH

In 'Opening In England', Australian poet Les Murray declares: 'Wage justice for poets, a living/like that of all who live off our words.'[76] Such heartfelt sentiments have recently been expressed in the context of litigation by the Authors' Guild against Google Book Search.

In response to the concerns of authors and publishers, Google announced in August 2005 that, if publishers provided it with a list of its titles that it did not want Google to scan at libraries, Google would respect that request. The search engine stated that it would not scan any more copyrighted works until November 2005. Such concessions did not placate the holders of copyright in literary works.

A. The Authors' Guild

In September 2005, the Authors' Guild filed a class action against Google alleging that the Google Book Search project had infringed copyright in literary works through its unauthorized scanning and copying of books.[77] The representatives named in the action included Herbert Mitgang, the author of *The Fiery Trial: A Life of Lincoln*, children's author Betty Miles and literary critic Daniel Hoffman. The Authors' Guild claimed:

> Google knew or should have known that the Copyright Act, 17 U.S.C. §101 et seq. required it to obtain authorization from the holders of the copyrights in these literary works before creating and reproducing digital copies of the Works for its own commercial use and for the use of others. Despite this knowledge, Google has unlawfully reproduced the Works and has announced plans to reproduce and display the Works without the copyright holders' authorization. Google intends to derive revenue from this program by attracting more viewers and advertisers to its site.[78]

The Authors' Guild has sought injunctive and declaratory relief with respect to Google's present infringement, and declaratory and injunctive relief with respect to Google's planned unauthorized commercial use of the works.

The President of the Authors' Guild, Nick Taylor, argued that the Google Book Search Project presented a Faustian bargain for authors: 'By digitizing mountains of copyrighted books without permission, Google is exercising a renegade notion of eminent domain: Google decides what's good for us and seizes private property to get it done.'[79] Taylor asserted: 'The alphabet ought to be free, most certainly, but the people who painstakingly arrange it into books deserve to be paid for their work.'[80] He further contends that exposure of authors alone would be insufficient compensation for the appropriation of their books: 'Is that the only form of compensation Google can come up with when it makes huge profits on the ads it sells along the channels its users are compelled to navigate?'[81] He demanded respect for the intellectual property rights of authors: 'When did we decide that socialism was the way to run the Internet?'[82]

The legal action by the Authors' Guild against Google is by no means guaranteed to be a success. It will be difficult to establish that the Abe Lincoln biographer Herbert Mitgang, children's storyteller Betty Miles and poet Daniel Hoffman form a representative class, and would be harmed by the Google Book Search venture. Even if it wins its action, the Authors' Guild is not necessarily guaranteed to receive a windfall from the advertising revenue of Google.

B. The Association of American Publishers

In October 2005, the Association of American Publishers filed a separate action for copyright infringement. In the suit in *McGraw Hill Companies* v. *Google Inc.*, the publishers alleged:

> Because Google's entirely commercial endeavor requires, among things, massive, wholesale and systematic copying of entire books still protected by copyright for public distribution and public display, it infringes one or more of each Publisher's exclusive rights under the Copyright Act, 17 USC S.106. Neither (a) the fair use provisions of 17 USC S.107 nor (b) the narrow provisions of 17 USC S.108, which in very different circumstances would allow a library but, in no event, Google, to make digital copies of these works in a library's collection, excuse Google's wholesale unauthorized copying.[83]

The publishers have sought a declaration of copyright infringement against Google as well as an order enjoining Google from reproducing, publicly distributing or displaying any of the publishers' works. They have also asked for an order from the court to require Google to delete or otherwise destroy all unauthorized copies made by the search engine. Finally, they have requested any other further relief deemed equitable and proper by the court.

Pat Schroeder, the President of the Association of American Publishers, was livid about the Google Book Search Project: 'Google's position essentially amounts to a license to steal, so long as it returns the loot upon a formal request by their victims.'[84] She was unsatisfied by the offer of Google to allow authors of copyrighted works to 'opt-out' of the free online library by notifying Google that they do not want their works online.

However, Timothy Wu comments that the battle over the Google Book Search project features two different visions of what might best promote authorship: 'One side trumpets the culture of authorial *exposure*, the other urges the culture of authorial *control*.'[85] He observed: 'Authors and their advocates have long favored maximal control – but we are undergoing a sea-change in our understanding of the author's interests in both exposure and control.'[86] Wu noted:

> I believe that everyone who considers themselves an author or an author's advocate should take a deep breath and, at least this time, praise Google Print. In the end, it is just a search, not a replacement product. We readers need help finding what exists, and we authors also need help being found. There is here, as anywhere, such a thing as too much control. It may be time for the offline media to learn something from online media – namely, the virtues of letting go.[87]

Wu argues the claims of authors and publishers are based upon a misunderstanding of the Google Book Search project which he explains 'is a way to *search* books, not a way to get books for free'.[88] In other words, 'It is not, in short, Napster for books.'[89]

The computer publisher, Tim O'Reilly, has been rhapsodic about the opportunities the project will present for authors and publishers alike:

> A search engine for books will be revolutionary in its benefits. Obscurity is a far greater threat to authors than copyright infringement, or even outright piracy . . . I'm sorry to see authors buy into the old-school protectionism of the Authors Guild, not realizing they're acting against their own self-interest. Their resistance can come only from a failure to understand the nature of the program. Google Library is intended to help readers discover copyrighted works, not to give copies away. It's a tremendous service to authors that will help them beat the dismal odds of publishing as usual.[90]

O'Reilly adds that Google Book Search solves a huge problem for the publishing industry in respect of copyright management, especially in respect of forgotten rights and ignored texts: 'As the public discovers the value of these works, publishers and authors are incentivized to track down and assert their ownership in order to opt-in to the revenue sharing offered by the Google Print service.'[91]

Author and advocate Cory Doctorow takes this criticism further, claiming that 'the writer/publisher objections to Google amount to nothing more than rent-seeking: an attempt to use legal threats to milk Google for some of the money it will make by providing this vital service'.[92] He argued that Google Book Search may provide an opportunity for authors and publishers to compete on an equal footing with other media: 'The Internet makes it possible for the social factors that sell books – the sense of community engendered by shared cultural referents, the conversation that books enable – to flourish.'[93]

Stephen Arnold contends that Google's Book Search project does not pose a real threat to the publishing industry.[94] Rather, he introduces an alternative concern suggesting that the press should be more wary about Google's potential to become a publisher itself and deal directly with authors by publishing their new works online: 'U.S. publishers chase windmills while ignoring Google's real challenge to the traditional approach to scholarly and professional publishing.'[95]

C. The Status of the Artist

The law suits launched against Google Book Search raise larger questions about the relationship between authors and publishers. Undeniably, artists have been poorly compensated for their creative endeavours. As Australian musician and politician Peter Garrett notes: 'The best that the majority of working contemporary artists can hope for is a paltry, uneven return for their creative effort.'[96] However, copyright law has proved to be an inadequate mechanism to provide an 'even return'. The economic rights of authors have traditionally been assigned or licensed to publishers in exchange for the dissemination of literary work. Authors have often been insufficiently compensated by publishers for the reproduction and distribution of their work. Furthermore, in the United States, there is no adequate protection of the moral rights of authors in relation to attribution and the integrity of their work, although other jurisdictions, such as Australia, Canada and the European Union, provide better legal protection of the honour and reputation of creators.

If it is really concerned about providing a living wage for artists, the Authors' Guild would be better off exploring alternative policy mechanisms, such as industrial relations and taxation law, to protect the livelihoods of authors. In Canada, for example, the Government passed the *Status of the Artist Act* 1992 (Canada) to recognize the contribution made by artists to various aspects of Canadian life. The legislation allows creative artists to engage in collective bargaining for industrial relations under the auspices of Canadian Artists and Producers Professional Relations Tribunal.[97] In the European Union, Luxembourg has implemented similar legislation.[98] Notably, the Republic of Ireland has sought to implement policies to help secure a living wage for authors. Most significantly, since 1969, the work of authors, creative artists and musicians living and working in Ireland is exempt from income tax on income derived from work of cultural merit.[99] Such policy options seem better tailored to achieve the wistful hopes of authors like Les Murray who yearn for 'Wage justice for poets'.[100]

III. THE PROGRESS OF SCIENCE AND THE USEFUL ARTS: COPYRIGHT LAW AND FAIR USE

In response to these claims of copyright infringement, Google has reserved a number of defences. The search engine argues that the plaintiffs' lack standing and fail to state a claim upon which relief may be granted. The company contends that the plaintiffs' claims and remedies are barred by the First Amendment of the United States Constitution. The company has thus signalled a willingness to make constitutional defences in this case. Google also claims that its use of and activities with respect to books that are subject to copyright fall within the exceptions in sections 107 to 122 of the *Copyright Act* 1976 (US). This covers the defence of fair use, exemptions for libraries and archives, and other miscellaneous exceptions. The search engine further argues that some or all of the plaintiffs' works are not copyrightable because they lack originality and material expression, and fall in the public domain. Google maintains the plaintiffs' claims should be barred because they failed to comply with the formalities of renewal, notice and registration. Finally, Google asserts that the plaintiffs' claims should be barred because of copyright misuse and unclean hands. In any case, the search engine invokes the equitable doctrines of waiver, estoppel, laches and acquiescence.

Above all else in this log of claims, there has been much debate as to whether Google Book Search is protected under s.107 of the *Copyright Act* 1976 (US) by the defence of fair use under United States copyright law. The Google legal action takes place against the background of a long history of litigation over the meaning of fair use between publishers, libraries and educational institutions. Of particular relevance are past precedents dealing with library photocopying, freelance authors and Internet search engines. There has been much debate about the proper interpretation of the nature and scope of the defence of fair use. Some commentators have argued that Google's activities fall under an expansive reading of the defence of fair use.[101] Other critics have contended that Google's activities fall outside a strict, narrow interpretation of fair use.[102] In truth, the case law provides a mixed set of rules, understandings and outcomes, which both sides will be able to draw upon in their arguments.

A. Photocopiers

In the United States, there are a number of important precedents dealing with the use of photocopiers in respect of educational materials, which would be of relevance to the Google case.

In *Williams & Wilkins Co* v. *The United States*, a scientific publisher sued the National Library of Medicine and the National Institutes of Health for copyright infringement of its journals by engaging in massive photocopying of its works.[103] The Supreme Court of the United States was evenly divided four to four as to whether such conduct was protected under the defence of fair use. As a result, the decision in the Court of Appeals was allowed to stand.

In *Basic Books Inc* v. *Kinko's Graphics Corp*, the Federal Court held that Kinko's Graphics Corporation was liable for copyright infringement because it printed course packs for use in universities.[104] By contrast, in *Princeton University Press* v. *Michigan Document Services*, the United States Court of Appeals for the Sixth Circuit ruled that Michigan Document Services was protected by the defence of fair use when it copied materials for course-packs for university students without seeking permission from the publishers or paying royalties.[105]

In *American Geophysical Union* v. *Texaco, Inc.*, the majority of the 2nd Circuit Court held that corporate copying of a small number of scientific and medical journals was not fair use under United States copyright law, because the systematic and archival copying of the journal articles had an adverse impact on the publisher's market.[106] However, there was a strong dissent from Jacobs J. Drawing upon the history of science, the sociology of scientific communication and anthropology, his Honour argued that the photocopying of journal articles was integral to the transformative and productive ends of scientific research. Jacobs J concludes that there is a need to reinterpret copyright law and the defence of fair use in light of its impact upon scientific practice: 'Since the copyright laws seek to stimulate *creativity* we should consider the incentives chiefly from the perspective of the authors and scientists.'[107]

Google will emphasize that the copying of literary texts serves a larger educational purpose. By contrast, the authors and publishers will stress that the Internet search engine is scanning whole copyright works, reproducing this collection on its internal database and then distributing such work to the public.

B. Indexes and Electronic Databases

There are also significant decisions dealing with indexes and electronic databases, which will be relevant to the litigation between Google, the Authors' Guild and the Association of American Publishers.

In *New York Times Co. Inc.* v. *Roxbury Interface, Inc.*, Meanor J of the United States District Court for the District of New Jersey considered whether 'a copyrighted work may be indexed by an outsider without the permission of the holders of the copyrights to the original work'.[108] The publishers of the New York Times index brought an action against the publishers of the 'Personal Name Index to "The New York Times Index"', claiming copyright infringement. Meanor J held that the defendants' publication was protected by the doctrine of the defence of fair use, especially considering 'that the personal name index would serve the public interest in the dissemination of information'.[109]

In *New York Times Co., Inc.* v. *Tasini*, a majority of the Supreme Court of the United States held that the copyright of freelance authors was infringed when print and electronic publishers placed their articles in electronic databases, such as NEXIS, NYTO and GPO.[110] In the wake of the decision, the Authors Guild, the American Society of Journalists and the National Writers Union obtained approval of an $US 18 million settlement in the class action suit filed on behalf of freelance writers whose work appeared in electronic databases without their consent.

Seeking to raise the defence of fair use, Google has sought to characterize its book search project as being 'like a card catalog', which will 'show users information about the book, and in some cases, a few snippets – a few sentences of their search term in context'.[111] By contrast, the authors and publishers will stress that this is just another case of copyright work being placed in electronic databases, without the prior permission of the copyright owners.

C. Internet Search Engines

In *Kelly* v. *Arriba Soft*, the Federal Court of Appeals for the Ninth Circuit considered 'the application of copyright law to the vast world of the internet and internet search engines'.[112]

A professional photographer, Leslie Kelly, brought a legal action against a search engine, Arriba (later renamed Ditto), which reproduced his images of the American West as thumbnails, and in-line links. A number of search engines, including Google, Altavista and Yahoo, intervened as amicus curiae in support of Arriba Soft. The brief observed: 'As providers of some of the leading information tools on the World Wide Web, we believe that it is vital that courts apply the copyright laws in a manner that fosters the continued healthy growth of the Web and the search tools that are necessary to navigate its ever-growing expanses.'[113]

In 2002, the Court of Appeals considered the application of the defence of fair use in respect of the use of thumbnail images on Internet search engines. Circuit judge T.G. Nelson observed:

> Arriba's use of Kelly's images promotes the goals of the Copyright Act and the fair use exception. The thumbnails do not stifle artistic creativity because they are not used for illustrative or artistic purposes and therefore do not supplant

> the need for the originals. In addition, they benefit the public by enhancing information-gathering techniques on the internet.[114]

The Court of Appeals considered the argument of Kelly that Arriba was not protected by the defence of the fair use because the images were reproduced exactly and hence the use of the photographs was not transformative. Kelly cited a number of cases in which courts were reluctant to find fair use where an original work was merely retransmitted in a different medium. The Court of Appeals was unconvinced by such claims, making the observation: 'This case involves more than merely a retransmission of Kelly's images in a different medium. Arriba's use of the images serves a different function than Kelly's use – improving access to information on the internet versus artistic expression.'[115] The Court of Appeals preferred the decision in *Un Nezez* v. *Caribbean International News Corporation*, in which the First Circuit found that copying a photograph that was intended to be used in a modelling portfolio and using it instead in a news article was a transformative use.[116] The judge observed: 'The use of Kelly's images in Arriba's search engine is more analogous to the situation in *Un Nezez* because Arriba has created a new purpose for the images and is not simply superseding Kelly's purpose.'[117]

Their Honours also concluded that Arriba's use of Kelly's images in its thumbnails did not harm the market for Kelly's images or the value of those images. Even if users were more interested in the image itself rather than the information on the web page, they would still have to go to Kelly's site to see the full-sized image. The thumbnails would not be a substitute for the full-sized images because the thumbnails lose their clarity when enlarged. This would hold true whether the thumbnails are solely in Arriba's database or are more widespread and found in other search engine databases. However, the Court held that the in-line links that displayed the full pictures were not fair use and so were infringing the exclusive rights of Kelly.

D. Other Jurisdictions

The debate over the Google Book Search Project has international dimensions. Jonathan Band notes that other jurisdictions may have more limited scope for the use of copyright works:

> Fair use under the US Copyright Act is generally broader and more flexible than the copyright exceptions in other countries . . . While the copyright laws of most countries might not be so generous as to allow the reproduction of an entire book, almost all copyright laws do permit short quotations. These exceptions for quotations should be sufficient to protect Google's transmission of Library Project search results to users.[118]

It would be true that the defence of fair dealing would be read in a more rigid fashion in other jurisdictions. In Australia, for example, the courts would be likely to take a restrictive interpretation of the defence of fair dealing in this context, especially in light of the High Court decision in *University of New South Wales* v. *Moorhouse*, in which a university library was held to have authorized copyright infringement through the provision of photocopiers.[119] Michael Fraser, the chief executive of the Australian copyright collecting society, the Copyright Agency Ltd, has expressed the view that Google Book Search would infringe the exclusive rights of authors and publishers:

> Google Library takes away the creative content and puts it into their business without permission. . . . That's in violation of international copyright principles of copyright law, in our view, that they should be copying and making available content on line without the licence, the permission of the rights owners, the authors and publishers.[120]

Fraser maintains that the online service will only benefit authors, publishers and consumers, if it obtains the permission of copyright owners.

In respect of United Kingdom law, Paul Ganley comments that U.K. copyright law would struggle to accommodate uses such as Google's within its existing scheme of exceptions:

> Under existing U.K. law principles, Google has two problems. Firstly, the intermediary copying of the entire work is only relevant at the 'fair dealing' stage of the analysis. Secondly, none of the fair dealing categories fit: using a searchable electronic index of works for 'informational' purposes is simply not an exempted category of use.[121]

Ganley suggests that there is a need to reconceptualize United Kingdom copyright law exceptions in order to accommodate generative technologies. He also recommends the introduction of a new defence of 'fair dealing for informational purposes'.[122]

In Europe, there has been a parallel debate over whether Google Book Search infringes the copyright of publishers. A scientific publisher Wissenschaftliche Buchgesellschaft (WBG), backed by the German publishers association, asked a Hamburg court for an injunction preventing Google from scanning its books as part of its library project.[123] Google argued before the Hamburg court that the display of short snippets from in-copyright books did not infringe German copyright law. The copyright chamber of the regional court of Hamburg indicated that WGB's petition for an injunction was unlikely to succeed. The court rejected WBG's argument that the scanning of its books in the US infringed German copyright law. As a result, WGB has decided to drop its petition for a preliminary injunction.

The French publishing group La Martinere and a French publisher's association has filed a lawsuit in a Paris court against Google Inc. and Google France, seeking an injunction to stop the search engine from scanning books for Google Book Search, and damages. This matter is still at a preliminary stage.

Of course, there are some exceptional jurisdictions, which may be more sympathetic to the Google Book Search Project. Canada, for instance, seems a particularly safe haven. The Supreme Court of Canada has taken an expansive view of the defence of fair dealing in the case of *CCH Canadian Limited* v. *The Law Society of Upper Canada*.[124] Furthermore, the Canadian copyright law only provides copyright protection for life of the author plus 50 years – instead of life plus 70 years, as required in the United States and the European Union. Indeed, Michael Geist from the University of Ottawa contends that the Google Book Search Project is eminently protectable: 'For books that remain subject to copyright, Google will still scan a copy of the book, but will only grant the general public more modest access to its content, providing users with smaller excerpts of the work – a policy that is consistent with principles of fair use under copyright law.'[125] He contends that the Canadian Government should take advantage of its position and establish a national digital library in order to 'provide an exceptional resource for Canadians at home as well as advantageously promote the export of Canadian culture abroad'.[126]

IV. THE FRENCH PAPARAZZI: GOOGLE NEWS

In the wake of the terrorist attack on the World Trade Center and the Pentagon on 11 September 2001, engineers at Google realized the importance of a search engine to collect and rank news. Google News, launched on 23 September 2002, provides a news aggregation service – a collection of current stories and photographs from over 4500 news sources for a period of a month. These news stories are divided into sections for the world, business, sci/tech, sports, entertainment and health. They are then ranked according to significance and date.

Agence France Presse is the world's oldest news agency. It was founded in 1835 by the journalist Charles-Louis Havas. Agence France Presse provides a worldwide subscription service for stories and photographs. The company emphasizes:

> AFP invests a great deal of time and money to acquire its news data to guarantee its top quality international service, which is tailored to the specific needs of clients in each region around the world. AFP's photographs and news stories are

> original and creative works. AFP does not give away its content for free . . . AFP provides services to its customers either as a subscription, whereby AFP's wire(s) are available, or on an à la carte basis, whereby customers may purchase single graphics or photographs.[127]

The press agency made a number of allegations against Google. First, Agence France Presse claimed that Google had infringed copyright in its photographs. Second, the company pleaded that Google had infringed copyright in its headlines, which it claims are original and creative text. Third, the company argued that the search engine has infringed copyright in its story leads. Fourth, Agence France Presse complained that Google has removed or altered electronic rights management information. Finally, the press agency argued that there has been state law misappropriation of 'hot news'.

In response, Google sought a declaration stating that 'AFP's headlines and parts of "story leads" or other text that it alleges are infringed consist, in whole or in substantial part, of mere facts and ideas that are not subject to copyright protection.'[128] Indeed Google stressed that 'AFP has added no creative expression, or *de minimis* expression, to those facts and ideas.'[129]

Furthermore, the search engine claimed Google News was engaged in the lawful use of any copyright works held by Agence France Presse. The company emphasized that it was protected by the defence of fair use because it had transformed the news stories and photographs:

> Google News provides links to news stories and news photographs and may have previously provided links to alleged copyrighted works created or owned by AFP. At no time has Google News provided users with any AFP story or photograph in its entirety. Rather, Google News provides, at most, links containing the headline, lead fragment, and a thumbnail link . . . Google News further transforms the headlines, lead fragments and thumbnails by categorizing them by subject matter and creating an index of news stories and thumbnail images that users may use to find and select web sites containing information relevant to them. Google News transforms the headlines, lead fragments and thumbnails from underlying news stories by indexing them by subject matter.[130]

The search engine maintains that Google News serves the wider public interest in educating citizens as to current events and other items of news. It cited the observation of the Supreme Court of the United States that the Worldwide Web is 'comparable, from the readers' viewpoint, to . . . a vast library including millions of readily available and indexed publications'.[131]

The search engine also argued that Google News could be defended by the existence of an implied licence: 'Accordingly, to the extent Google News utilizes any works or other material owned by AFP, Google's utilization thereof is licensed or authorized by AFP, implicitly if not explicitly, based *inter alia* upon AFP's conduct, knowledge, and contracts with third parties.'[132] Google asked the court to dismiss the law suit against them.

In January 2006, there was oral argument between the two parties before Kessler J. Both parties filed summary judgment motions on the issue of whether news headlines are copyrightable subject matter. The Counsel for both parties acknowledged that there was no clear United States precedent on this issue. The press agency's counsel, Joshua Kaufman, observed: 'I do think this is a case of first impression.'[133] He sought to distinguish news headlines from 'titles' and 'short phrases', which are not copyrightable. In response, Google counsel, Thomas Kirby, argued: 'Headlines are not protectible. Period.'[134] He argued that a news headline is essentially the title of the story and should be subject to the same prohibition against copyright protection; a ruling in favour of copyrightability would impose a 'substantial, needless obstacle' on the dissemination of news.

The Australian commentator Michael Handler reflects upon the decision of Google to withdraw content of the French press agency from the Google News website:

> Google responded to AFP's lawsuit by removing AFP content from the Google News site. It has made similar decisions in response to other legal threats. This illustrates that Google's choices as to the sites to which it links are not only mathematical, but also legal and political. It is thus incumbent on us to remind ourselves that, while highly useful, Google is not, and never will be, a global repository of information.[135]

Indeed, Google is forced to respond to the claims of copyright owners on a regular basis under the notice and take-down system of the *DMCA*.

In August 2006, Google entered into a licensing arrangement with Associated Press to use its content.[136] Chief Executive, Eric Schmidt, observed:

> The people who own the content did a lot of work to generate the content. We want them to get the majority of the revenue from advertising.[137]

Associated Press Chief Executive Tom Curley commented: 'The AP and others in the industry early on did not appreciate the value of the content and understand the economics of the marketplace as we do today.'[138] The licensing arrangement perhaps signals a détente between search engines and press agencies.

In September 2006, Google was ordered by a Belgian court to remove articles by the Belgian publisher, Copiepresse, from its service, Google News.[139] The Court of First Instance of Brussels observed that 'the activities of Google Inc. jeopardize the electronic sale of press articles as well as the daily press and, in the short term, the quality of the articles as the publishers run the risk of not being able to avail [themselves] of sufficient resources to pay their journalists properly'.[140] Indeed, the judges held that 'the nature of the defendant's activity makes the publishers lose a considerable part of their income which stems from sales of advertisements'.[141] Accordingly, the court held that Google had infringed copyright and the database rights of Copiepresse, and ordered the Internet search engine to remove the material owned by the Belgian publisher. This decision was re-affirmed in February 2007.

In addition, Google News has also attracted threats of litigation from the Israeli portal, Walla Communications Ltd, which has threatened to prevent Google from publishing news items and material originating from Walla.[142]

V. PERFECT 10: GOOGLE IMAGES

The Californian adult company, Perfect 10, has also filed a lawsuit in the United States District Court for the Central District of California in Los Angeles against Google, claiming that reproduction of its adult images infringes the company's copyright, trade marks and publicity rights.

Perfect 10 alleged that the 'search engine giant provided Internet users with at least 800,000 unauthorized links to images of Perfect 10's nude models, stealing membership fees and advertising revenue from the Los Angeles publisher'.[143] The law suit complains:

> Perfect 10 is informed and, on that basis avers, that Defendants have received millions of dollars in revenue from their Adwords and Adsense agreements with Stolen Content Websites and other websites, and from advertising revenues generated as a result of the massive amounts of high quality infringing copies of Perfect 10 Copyrighted Works both on Defendants' own servers and on linked Stolen Content Websites.[144]

The company requested Google to remove the offending Web sites from its index and stop displaying thumbnail versions of the photographs in its image search results.

A similar law suit has been filed against Amazon.inc. and the United States District Court for the Central District of California has therefore consolidated the pair of copyright infringement lawsuits brought by Perfect 10.[145]

In its opposition to the action, Amazon has argued that the safe harbour provisions of the *DMCA* shelter the company from Perfect 10's Copyright Claims. Furthermore, the electronic publisher has argued that the *Grokster* and *Sony* Supreme Court decisions preclude holding Amazon liable for direct or contributory infringement. Amazon has argued that any use of copyrighted images is protected under the defence of fair use, especially in light of the decision in *Kelly* v. *Arriba Soft*:

> In sum, Amazon is providing a pure research tool, a visual and textual map of the Internet. The thumbnails are necessary to visually describe the locations that the users have asked for information about. Amazon does not make any copies of the copyrighted works. Amazon merely makes available to its users URLs pointing to the source of images.[146]

In the alternative, Amazon argued that the equitable balancing factors weigh strongly against the requested injunction.

John Palfrey, executive director of the Berkman Center for Internet and Society at Harvard Law School, comments that Google may be able to defend itself from the claims of copyright infringement: 'Courts have generally seen search engines as serving a public interest and have tended to afford them certain leeway as a result, at least whenever a balancing test is involved, as it is in the fair use analysis on most of the relevant copyright claims.'[147] Palfrey observes that Google is an obvious target for such claims of infringement of intellectual property rights, as it is a well-endowed and well-resourced intermediary: 'I suspect that Perfect 10 will not be the last to go after Google's riches with such a series of claims.'[148]

Furthermore, the Electronic Frontier Foundation (EFF) has filed a brief in support of Google Image Search, arguing that the federal district court should reject a request for an injunction to shut the service down. The amicus brief concludes: 'Shutting down Google's image search will have a serious and immediate detrimental effect on the public's access to knowledge and the benefits they receive every day from Google's innovation.'[149]

In the United States District Court for the Central District of California, Matz J considered the extent of Google's direct liability for linking to material infringing copyright law. His Honour preferred a 'server test' to determine what constituted a 'display' of copyright works: 'The Court concludes that in determining whether Google's lower frames are a "display" of infringing material, the most appropriate test is also the most straightforward: the website on which content is stored and by which it is served directly to a user, not the website that in-line links to it, is the website that "displays" the content.'[150] The judged adopted the server test, for several reasons. First, the test reflected, in his view, 'the reality of how content actually travels over the internet before it is shown on users' computers'.[151] Second, the judge observed that the 'adoption of the server test neither invites copyright infringing activity by a search engine such as Google nor flatly precludes liability for such activity'.[152] Third, the judge noted that 'website operators can readily understand the server test and courts can apply it relatively easily'.[153] His Honour concluded that the server test maintained, however uneasily, a balance between encouraging the creation of creative works and encouraging the dissemination of information: 'Merely to index the web so that users can more readily find the information they seek should not constitute direct infringement, but to *host* and *serve* infringing content may directly violate the rights of copyright holders.'[154]

Applying the server test, the Court concluded that, for the purpose of direct copyright infringement, Google's use of frames and in-line links did not constitute a 'display' of the full-size images stored on and served by infringing third-party websites. Thus Perfect 10's claim of direct infringement with respect to these actions would likely fail. However, his Honour found that Perfect 10 had established a likelihood of proving that Google's creation and public display images directly infringed Perfect 10's copyrights: 'Google acknowledges that it creates and stores those thumbnails on its own servers – and that, upon receiving search queries, it responds by displaying a grid of those thumbnails.'[155]

Matz J held that Google's creation and display of thumbnail images could not be protected under the defence of fair use. His Honour noted: 'Although the Court is reluctant to issue a ruling that might impede the advance of internet technology, and although it is appropriate for courts to consider the immense value to the public of such technologies, existing judicial precedents do not allow such considerations to trump a reasoned analysis of the four fair use factors.'[156]

On the first factor for fair use, the judge held that Google's uses of the photographs were both transformative and consumptive:

> Google's use of thumbnails to simplify and expedite access to information is transformative of P10's use of reduced-size images to entertain. But that does not end the analysis, because Google's use is simultaneously consumptive as well.[157]

The judge makes much of the fact that Perfect 10 entered into a licensing agreement with Fonestarz Media Limited for the sale and distribution of reduced-size images for download to and use on cell phones. His Honour ruled: 'Google's use of thumbnails does supersede this use of P10's images, because mobile users can download and save the thumbnails displayed by Google Image Search onto their phones.'[158] The judge appears to rather speciously distinguish the case of *Kelly* v. *Arriba Soft* on the basis of such facts.

On the second factor, the judge emphasized the creative nature of the photographic works, observing:

> The P10 photographs consistently reflect professional, skillful, and sometimes tasteful artistry. That they are of scantily-clothed or nude women is of no

consequence; such images have been popular subjects for artists since before the time of 'Venus de Milo'.[159]

Arguably, the judge overrates the artistic quality and merits of the pornographic works: perhaps they are not deserving of comparison to the 'Venus de Milo'.

His Honour then ruled that the third factor – the amount and substantiality of the portion used – was neutral and that 'Google's use of the infringing copies of P10's images . . . is no greater than necessary to achieve the objective of providing effective image search capabilities.'[160]

Finally, concerning the fourth factor – the effect of the use upon the potential market for and value of the copyrighted work – the judge held in favour of Perfect 10. His Honour observed: 'Google's use of thumbnails likely *does* harm the potential market for the downloading of P10's reduced-size images onto cell phones.'[161]

Matz J doubted whether Google should be held secondarily liable for the infringements of others, however. His Honour held that the *Sony Betamax*, *Napster* and *Grokster* precedents were of little use to Perfect 10 in the facts of this case. Similarly, the judge rejected arguments that Google could be held to be vicariously liable.

Google is appealing against the decision of Matz J to the United States Court of Appeals for the 9th Circuit. Counsel for the search engine, Michael Kwun, commented: 'While we're disappointed with portions of the ruling, we are pleased with Judge Matz's favourable ruling on linking and other aspects of Google Image Search.'[162] There is a high likelihood that the 9th Circuit Court of Appeals will strike down the somewhat bizarre decision of the District Court. As Siva Vaidhyanathan observed: 'This case seems to contradict the important and sweeping precedent in *Kelly* v. *Arriba Soft*, in which the 9th Circuit Court of Appeals ruled that thumbnails were fair uses of copyrighted images for the purpose of generating search engines.'[163] The District Court judge is unpersuasive in his efforts to distinguish the precedent on the basis that Google has the ability to share advertising revenues from infringing sites, because of AdSense, and Perfect 10's deal with Fonestarz to provide low-resolution images for cellphones.

VI. GOOGLE CACHE

In *Field* v. *Google Inc*., the District Court of Nevada considered the claim of a Nevada lawyer and writer, Blake A. Field, that Google had infringed his copyright in 51 literary works from his personal website, blakeswritings.com, which the search engine had stored in an online repository.[164]

Google provided 'cached' links to the website, providing a snapshot of the last time the Googlebot visited the site. The search engine enabled users to access its copy of Web pages through 'Cached' links, for several reasons. Google's 'Cached' links allow users to view archival pages that the user cannot, for whatever reason, access directly. Google Cache also enables Web Page Comparisons: it allows users to determine how a particular Web page has been altered over time. The 'Cached' links further enable users to determine immediately why a particular page was deemed responsive to their search by highlighting the terms from the user's query as they appear on the page.

Jones J of the United States District Court of Nevada granted Google's motion for summary judgment on a number of grounds. First, the judge held that the search engine had not directly infringed the work of Blake. His Honour stressed that a plaintiff must also show volitional conduct on the part of the defendant in order to support a finding of direct copyright infringement. The judge observed that Google was passive, providing automated responses to the users' requests.

Second, Jones J ruled that Google had an implied licence to reproduce and distribute the works. His Honour observed:

> A Web site publisher can instruct a search engine not to cache the publisher's Web site by using a 'no-archive' meta-tag . . . Field concedes he was aware of these industry standard mechanisms, and knew that the presence of a 'no archive' meta-tag on the pages of his Web site would have informed Google not to display 'Cached' links to his pages. Despite this knowledge, Field chose not to include the no-archive meta-tag on the pages of his site . . . His conduct is reasonably interpreted as the grant of a license to Google for that use.[165]

Accordingly, the Court granted Google's motion that it is entitled to the defence of implied licence, and denied Field's cross-motion that the defence was inapplicable.

Third, the judge noted that a plaintiff is estopped from asserting a copyright claim if he has aided the defendant in infringing or otherwise induced it to infringe or has committed covert acts such as holding out by silence or inaction. His Honour ruled that Google could raise the defence of estoppel because Field knew of Google's allegedly infringing conduct; Field intended that Google rely upon his conduct or acted so that Google had a right to believe it was so intended; Google was ignorant of the true facts; and Google detrimentally relied on Field's conduct.

Fourth, Jones J applied *Kelly* v. *Arriba Soft* in interpreting the defence of fair use. His Honour held that Google's use was a fair use:

> Assuming that Field intended his copyrighted works to serve an artistic function and entertain others as he claims, Google's presentation of 'cached' links to the

> copyrighted works at issue here does not serve the same functions. For a variety of reasons, the 'Cached' links 'add something new' and do not merely supersede the work.[166]

Given that Google served different and socially important purposes in offering access to copyrighted works through 'Cached' links and did not merely supersede the 'artistic' objectives of the original creations, the Court concluded that Google's alleged copying and distribution of Field's Web pages containing copyrighted works was transformative.

Finally, the judge held Google was entitled to protection under a series of safe harbour provisions for online service providers contained in the *DMCA*. Section 512(b) is directed to system caches and states that '[a] service provider shall not be liable for monetary relief . . . for infringement of copyright by reason of the intermediate and temporary storage of material on a system or network controlled or operated by or for the service provider' provided certain requirements are met. Jones J concluded that Google made 'intermediate and temporary storage' of the material stored in its cache, within the meaning of the *DMCA*.[167]

The decision has been hailed by supporters of the search engine. Fred von Lohmann, the EFF attorney, observed:

> This ruling makes it clear that the Google Cache is legal and clears away copyright questions that have troubled the entire search engine industry. The ruling should also help Google in defending against the lawsuit brought by book publishers over its Google Library Project, as well as assisting organizations like the Internet Archive that rely on caching.[168]

Others have played down the significance of the decision, suggesting that it is an inconsequential ruling of a minor court.

In *Parker* v. *Google Inc*, the United States District Court for the Eastern District of Pennsylvania considered the claims of Gordon Ray Parker that Google had infringed his copyright in works published on the Internet, such as his e-book, '29 Reasons Not to Be A Nice Guy', under the name Snodgrass Publishing Group.[169]

Parker asserted that Google's automatic archiving of this USENET posting constituted a direct infringement of his copyright. He also claimed that, when Google produced a list of hyperlinks in response to a user's search query and provided excerpts from his website in that list, Google was again directly infringing his copyrighted work. Parker also claimed that, by archiving USENET postings and providing a feature that allows users to search for all postings by a specific author, Google engaged in contributory and vicarious copyright infringement.

Surrick J ruled: 'It is clear that Google's automatic archiving of USENET postings and excerpting of websites in its results to users' search queries do not include the necessary volitional element to constitute direct copyright infringement.'[170] The judge added: 'In addition, while it is not entirely clear from Plaintiff's rambling Complaint, should Parker be claiming direct copyright infringement based on Google's automatic caching of web pages as a means of indexing websites and producing results to search queries, this activity does not constitute direct infringement either.'[171] The judge noted that Google Inc enjoyed a safe harbour for system caching under the *DMCA*. In respect of contributory and vicarious infringement, Surrick J held that Parker had not provided any evidence of copyright infringement, or established that Google had authorized any copyright infringement. The judge concluded that the plaintiff had failed to state a claim on which relief could be granted.

Parker has appealed against the decision to the United States Court of Appeals for the Third Circuit.

CONCLUSION

In terms of its philosophy, Google has sought to position itself as a decent corporate citizen. One of the company's mottos is 'You can make money without doing evil.' The search engine has been particularly keen to stress that its integrity will not be corrupted by the sale of advertising.[172] The Google Book Search project has provided an incredible fillip for the digitization of books and the cultural heritage of libraries around the world. The initiative has also attracted much consternation, particularly amongst copyright owners. Litigation between Google and the Authors' Guild and the Association of American Publishers promises to be groundbreaking, particularly in the application of copyright law and defence of fair use to Internet search engines. Google has been enmeshed in additional litigation over the hyperlinking to news headlines and thumbnails. Such matters will also provide important guidance as to copyright law, and the scope of the defence of fair use in respect of reporting the news, and indexing images. There remain larger questions about the future of Google, and whether it will retain its counter-culture identity and ethos, or become a monopolist in the field of information technology.

The counter-culture Google has been lauded for challenging the dominance and hegemony of Bill Gates' Microsoft. There has been concern, however, about the expansive and, some would say, imperialistic ambitions of the search engine. Some predict that Google will overcome its rivals and competitors and become a dominant, hegemonic force in the marketplace.

The cultural critic, Siva Vaidhyanathan, cautions that the search engine has the potential to be a monopolist, given the right market conditions. While he admits that Google currently enjoys a good reputation as a corporate citizen, Vaidhyanathan is wary of the company's pretence to speak for the public interest, believing it to be a 'contingent pledge based on convenience and temporary market conditions'.[173] He finds this process of privatization particularly troubling and worried about the potential for Google to fail in the marketplace: 'For that reason alone, it's imperative that stable public institutions take the lead in such an ambitious project.'[174] The critic is concerned that the libraries in Google Book Search are outsourcing the risk and responsibility for digitizing texts and making them searchable online: 'If a New York court rules clumsily, indelicately, or too broadly in an attempt to express umbrage at Google's audacity, then the principles of *Kelly* are in danger.'[175] He is worried that an adverse verdict against Google will have a chilling effect on the activities of libraries and universities:

> I can't help but envision this fight as one between Godzilla and Megalon. Whoever the bad guy turns out to be, a whole lot of good things are going to get crushed in the melee.[176]

One can only pray that the grand hopes of the Google Book Search project will not be smashed in a B-grade monster-mash, copyright battle.

However, not everyone is convinced that Google has the potential to become an unscrupulous monopolist. Sarah Waladan from the Australian Digital Alliance contends that such fears are unfounded:

> So far, Google has indicated its willingness to be seen as a 'good corporate citizen'. In any event, if Google's activities develop in such a way that it effectively uses its market power to harm either consumers or its competitors, competition laws should provide an appropriate remedy to curb those activities. Google Book Search offers many public benefits, and US law is flexible enough to embrace this technology. Let's move forward.[177]

There is hope amongst libraries and cultural institutions that Google will become a champion of the public domain, in terms of both litigation and policy debates.[178]

In the future, Google faces increasing copyright litigation over Internet videos – both in respect of Google Video and YouTube.[179] In November 2006, Google acquired YouTube for the princely sum of $US1.65 billion.[180] The search engine, though, has maintained a reserve of $US200 million in escrow to ward off potential copyright litigation. Recording companies, film studios, and television networks have expressed concerns that the site YouTube and other Internet video sites have facilitated the exchange of copyright-infringing media. Universal Music Group, has demanded compensation from YouTube for copyright infringement of music videos and other content involving Universal artists. The Recording Industry Association of America has sent cease-and-desist notices to YouTube users who have uploaded copyright-protected musical works and sound recordings. There has also been much concern about bootlegged material from live concerts – such as mobile phone recordings of the U2 performance in Sydney – being put up on YouTube. Furthermore, Hollywood studios have expressed concern that clips from popular movies, such as the Harry Potter films, were available on YouTube, without authorization. United States television network, NBC Universal, demanded YouTube remove two skits from its Saturday Night Live show. Copyright owner Robert Tur has filed an action against YouTube in a Californian court, alleging copyright infringement of famous videos, including the LA riots, and the OJ Simpson police chase.[181] YouTube has also removed nearly 30000 copyrighted files after receiving complaints of copyright infringement from the Japanese Society for Rights of Authors, Composers and Publishers. Google will be hard pressed to make YouTube profitable, and defend the website from copyright actions. In 2007, Viacom International Inc., the owner of MTV, has brought legal action against YouTube Inc., alleging massive copyright infringement of its music videos and other copyright material.[182] The litigation will provide an important test case for copyright law and internet videos.

NOTES

1. Borges, Jorge Luis (1964), 'The Library of Babel', in Labyrinths: *Selected Stories and Other Writings*, New York: New Directions. For a wider discussion of the history of libraries, see Battles, Matthew (2004), *Library: An Unquiet History*, London: Random House.
2. Google, www.google.com.
3. Google Corporate Information, http://www.google.com/corporate/facts.html.
4. For a popular history of Google, see Vise, David (2005), *The Google Story: Inside the Hottest Business, Media and Technology Success of our Time*, New York: Macmillan.
5. Google Desktop, http://desktop.google.com/.
6. Google Scholar, http://scholar.google.com/.
7. Google Book Search, http://books.google.com/.
8. Google Images, http://images.google.com/.
9. Google News, http://www.google.com/news.
10. Google Earth, http://earth.google.com/.
11. Froogle, http://froogle.google.com/.
12. Gmail, gmail.google.com/.
13. Picasa, http://picasa.google.com/.
14. Blogger, http://www.blogger.com/start.
15. Orkut, http://www.orkut.com.
16. Kelleher, K. (2005), 'Who's Afraid of Google? Everyone', *Wired Magazine*, **13**(12), 233, http://www.wired.com/wired/archive/13.12/google.html.

17. Ibid.
18. Ibid.
19. Google (2005), *Annual Report*, Mountain View, California, p. 16.
20. Google (2005), *Annual Report*, Mountain View, California, p. 27.
21. Google (2005), *Annual Report*, Mountain View, California, p. 29.
22. Microsoft filed a complaint against Google and Kai-Fu Lee, a former Microsoft employee, alleging a breach of the covenant not to compete, a breach of non-disclosure promises and misappropriation of trade secrets, and a tortious interference with contractual relations: *Google, Inc.* v. *Microsoft Corporation* 415 F.Supp.2d 1018 (N.D.Cal., 2005).
23. In late 2004, Google Inc. reached a settlement with Yahoo! Inc. Under the terms of the settlement agreement, Google obtained a licence to U.S. Patent No. 6,269,361, a 'System and method for influencing a position on a search result list generated by a computer network search engine', and several related patents, held by Yahoo!'s wholly-owned subsidiary, Overture. In connection with the settlement of the dispute, Google issued shares of its Class A common stock to Yahoo! Google (2004), 'Yahoo and Google Resolve Disputes', http://www.google.com/press/pressrel/yahoo.html 9 August.
24. American Chemical Society (2004), 'ACS Takes Legal Action against Google', http://pubs.acs.org/cen/news/8250/8250acs.html, 10 December; and McCullagh, D. (2006), 'Google Scholar Trademark Case Ends', CNet News.com, http://news.com.com/2100-1025_3-6096240.html, 9 July.
25. *GEICO* v. *Google Inc.* Not Reported in F.Supp.2d, 2005 WL 1903128 (E.D.Va., 2005).
26. *Google Inc.* v. *American Blind & Wallpaper Factory, Inc.* Not Reported in F.Supp.2d, 2005 WL 832398 (N.D.Cal., 2005).
27. *Louis Vuitton* v. *Google Inc.* (Paris District Court, February 2005), and on appeal (Paris Court of Appeals, June 2006).
28. *Digital Envoy, Inc.* v. *Google, Inc.* 370 F.Supp.2d 1025 (N.D.Cal., 2005).
29. BBC News (2004), 'Google's GMail Sparks Privacy Row', http://news.bbc.co.uk/2/hi/business/3602745.stm, 5 April.
30. In the wake of the Supreme Court of the United States ruling in *Ashcroft* v. *American Civil Liberties Union* 542 U.S. 656 (2004), the United States Government has sought to defend the *Child Online Protection Act* 1998 (US): *Gonzales* v. *Google* Case No. 5:06-mc-80006-JW (US District for the Northern District of California, 2006); Mohammed, A. (2006), 'Google Refuses Demand for Search Information: Government Asked 4 Firms for Data in Effort to Revive Anti-Porn Law', *Washington Post*, 20 January 2006.
31. Google (2004), 'Google Checks Out Library Books', http://www.google.com/press/pressrel/print_library.html, 14 December.
32. Ibid.
33. *The Authors' Guild* v. *Google Inc.* Case No. 05 CV 8136-JES (2005), http://www.boingboing.net/images/AuthorsGuildGoogleComplaint1.pdf.
34. *McGraw-Hill Companies et al.* v. *Google Inc.* Case No. 05 CV 8881-JES (2005), http://www.publishers.org/press/pdf/40%20McGraw-Hill%20v.%20Google.pdf.
35. *Agence France Presse* v. *Google Inc.*, D. D.C., No. 05-00546 (2005), http://blog.searchenginewatch.com/blog/050321-175410.
36. *Perfect 10 Inc.* v. *Google Inc.*, 16 F.Supp.2d 828 (2006).
37. *Field* v. *Google Inc.* 412 F.Supp.2d 1106 D.Nev. (2006), http://www.eff.org/IP/blake_v._google/google_nevada_order.pdf.
38. *Parker* v. *Google, Inc.* 422 F.Supp.2d 492 (2006).
39. Borges, Jorge Luis (1964), 'The Library of Babel', in *Labyrinths: Selected Stories and Other Writings*, New York: New Directions. For a wider discussion of the history of libraries, see Battles, Matthew (2004), *Library: An Unquiet History*, London: Random House.
40. Vise, David (2005), *The Google Story: Inside the Hottest Business, Media and Technology Success of our Time*, New York: Macmillan, p. 1.
41. Project Gutenberg, http://www.gutenberg.org/.
42. Prelinger Archive, http://www.archive.org/details/prelinger.

43. Internet Archive, http://www.archive.org/index.php.
44. The Million Books Project, http://www.archive.org/details/millionbooks.
45. Google Book Search, http://books.google.com/googleprint/library.html.
46. Google Book Search, http://books.google.com/googlebooks/vision.html.
47. Google Book Search, http://books.google.com/googlebooks/vision.html.
48. The University of Michigan is the only one of the libraries to publish its co-operative agreement with Google: http://www.lib.umich.edu/mdp/umgooglecooperativeagreement.html.
49. The University of Michigan (2004), 'Google/ U-M Project Opens the Way to Universal Access to Information', http://www.umich.edu/news/?Releases/2004/Dec04/library/index, 14 December.
50. Ibid.
51. Coleman, M.S. (2006), 'Google, the Khmer Rouge, and the Public Good', Address to the Professional/Scholarly Publishing Division of the Association of American Publishers, http://www.umich.edu/pres/speeches/060206google.html, 6 February.
52. Ibid.
53. Ibid.
54. Keller, M. (2004), 'Stanford and Google to Make Library Books Available Online'. http://www.stanford.edu/dept/news/pr/2004/pr-google-011205.html, 14 December. See also Stanford University (2005), 'Stanford and Google Book Search Statement of Support and Participation, 'http://library.stanford.edu/about_sulair/news_and_events/stanford_google_project.html.
55. Verba, S. (2004), 'Google Library Partners', Google, http://books.google.com/googlebooks/partners.html; see also Verba, S. (2005), 'Libraries, Books, Equality – Google', Harvard University Library, http://hul.harvard.edu/hgproject/verba.html.
56. Verba, S. (2004), 'Google to Digitize Some Harvard Library Holdings', *Harvard Gazette*, http://www.news.harvard.edu/gazette/2004/12.16/01-google.html, 16 December.
57. LeClerc, P. (2004), 'NYPL Partners with Google: Full Text of Thousands of Books to be Made Searchable', New York Public Library, http://www.nypl.org/press/2004/google.cfm, 14 December.
58. Ibid.
59. Ibid.
60. Carr, R. (2005), 'Oxford–Google Digitisation Agreement', http://www.bodley.ox.ac.uk/google/.
61. Milne, R. (2005), 'Google Book Search Library Partners', http://books.google.com/googlebooks/partners.html.
62. Google (2006), 'Google Book Search and US Library Partnership', Press Release, http://www.google.com/press/annc/books_uclibrary.html, August.
63. Ibid.
64. The Google Books Library Project and the University of California, http://www.cdlib.org/news/google.html.
65. Gorman, M. (2004), 'Google and God's Mind', *Los Angeles Times*, 17 November.
66. Ibid.
67. Ibid.
68. Open Content Alliance, http://www.opencontentalliance.org/.
69. Mills, E. (2006), 'Google and U.C. Sign Contract to Digitize Books', CNet News.com, http://news.zdnet.com/2100-9588_22-6103540.html, 8 August.
70. Open Content Alliance, http://www.opencontentalliance.org/faq.html#link4.
71. British Library (2005), 'Microsoft and British Library Work Together to Make 25 Million Pages of Content Available To All', http://www.bl.uk/news/2005/pressrelease20051104.html , 4 November.
72. Ibid.
73. Amazon.com (2005), 'Amazon.com Announces Plans for Innovative Digital Books That Will Enable Customers to Purchase Online Access to Any Page, Section or Chapter of a Book, as well as a Book in its Entirety', http://phx.corporate-ir.net/phoenix.zhtml?c=176060&p=irol-newsArticle&ID=778248, 3 November.

74. Macmillan, R. (2005), 'Google Unites Europe', *The Washington Post*, 29 April; and AAP (2005), 'European Libraries Join Forces Against Google', *The Sydney Morning Herald*, 28 April.
75. European Commission (2005), 'European Digital Library Proposed', http://europa.eu.int/idabc/en/document/4239/330, 4 May; and European Commission (2006), 'i2010 Digital Libraries Initiative', http://europa.eu.int/information_society/activities/digital_libraries/index_en.htm.
76. Murray, L. (1996), 'Opening in England', in *Subhuman Redneck Poems*, Sydney: Duffy & Snellgrove.
77. *The Authors' Guild* v. *Google Inc.* (2005), http://www.boingboing.net/images/AuthorsGuildGoogleComplaint1.pdf.
78. *The Authors' Guild* v. *Google Inc.* (2005), http://www.boingboing.net/images/AuthorsGuildGoogleComplaint1.pdf.
79. Taylor, N. (2005), 'Response to Tim O'Reilly of the Google Advisory Board', *The New York Times*, http://www.authorsguild.org/news/10_02_05.htm, 29 September.
80. Taylor, N. (2005), 'Not at the Writer's Expense', *The Washington Post*, 22 October, A21.
81. Ibid.
82. Ibid.
83. *McGraw-Hill Companies et al.* v. *Google Inc.* (2005), http://www.publishers.org/press/pdf/40%20McGraw-Hill%20v.%20Google.pdf.
84. Schroeder, P. and B. Barr (2005), 'Reining in Google', *The Washington Times*, http://www.washtimes.com/commentary/20051102-093349-7482r.htm, 3 November.
85. Wu, T. (2005), 'Google Print and the Other Culture War', *Slate*, http://www.slate.com/id/2128094/, 17 October.
86. Ibid.
87. Ibid.
88. Ibid.
89. Ibid.
90. O'Reilly, T. (2005), 'Search and Rescue', *The New York Times*, http://radar.oreilly.com/archives/2005/09/ny_times_op_ed_on_authors_guil.html, 28 September.
91. Ibid.
92. Doctorow, C. (2006), 'Why Publishing Houses Should Send Fruit-Baskets to Google', Boing Boing, http://www.boingboing.net/2006/02/14/why_publishing_shoul.html, 14 February.
93. Ibid.
94. Arnold, S. (2005), 'Disintermediation, Not Copyright Infringement: Is Google's Real Threat to Publishers?', Bogart Communications, http://www.arnoldit.com/press/News_Release-Google_Disintermediation.doc, 24 October.
95. Ibid.
96. Garrett, P. (2005), 'Currency House: Arts and Public Life', http://www.petergarrett.com.au/c.asp?id=95, 20 October. For a discussion of the professional status of artists, see Myer, Rupert (2002), *Report of the Contemporary Visual Arts and Craft Inquiry*, Canberra: Department of Communications, Information Technology and the Arts.
97. Canadian Artists and Producers Professional Relations Tribunal, http://www.capprt-tcrpap.gc.ca/epic/internet/incapprt-tcrpap.nsf/en/home.
98. Sanavia, P. (2000), 'The Status of the Independent Professional Artist: Aid Granted by the Virtue of the Status', Tallinan.
99. Section 195 of the *Taxes Consolidation Act* 1997 (Ireland) allows the Revenue Commissioners to make a determination that certain artistic works are original and creative works, and that earnings from such works are exempt from income tax from the year in which the claim is made. There have been moves afoot to review such exemptions: Chrisafis, A. (2005), 'Secret Talks Threaten Cultural Incentive', *The Guardian*, http://books.guardian.co.uk/news/articles/0,6109,1509280,00.html, 18 June.
100. Murray, Les (1996), 'Opening in England', in *Subhuman Redneck Poems*, Sydney: Duffy & Snellgrove.

101. Band, J. (2006), 'Copyright Owners v. The Google Print Library Project', *Entertainment Law Review*, **17**(1), 21–24; Lee, T. (2005), 'Don't Stop Google', *Cato Institute*, http://www.cato.org/pub_display.php?pub_id=4000, 23 July; and Lessig, L. (2005), 'The "Discussion": The Morning After', Lessig Blog, http://www.lessig.org/blog/archives/003224.shtml, 18 November.
102. Hanratty, E. (2005), 'Google Library: Beyond Fair Use?', *Duke Law and Technology Review*, **10**, http://www.law.duke.edu/journals/dltr/articles/2005dltr0010.html, 15 April; and Nimmer, R. (2005), 'Google Lawsuit Begins: Fair Use', Contemporary Intellectual Property, Licensing and Information Law, http://www.ipinfoblog.com/archives/intellectual-property-33-google-lawsuit-begins-fair-use.html, 3 October.
103. *Williams & Wilkins Co*. v. *The United States* 420 US 376 (1975).
104. *Basic Books Inc* v. *Kinko's Graphics Corp* 758 F. Supp. 1522 (1991).
105. *Princeton University Press* v. *Michigan Document Services* 99 F.3d 1381 (1996).
106. *American Geophysical Union* v. *Texaco, Inc*., 60 F.3d 913 (1994).
107. *American Geophysical Union* v. *Texaco, Inc*., 60 F.3d 913 at 940 (1994).
108. *New York Times Co. Inc*. v. *Roxbury Interface, Inc*., 434 F.Supp. 217 at 218 (D.N.J.1977).
109. *New York Times Co. Inc*. v. *Roxbury Interface, Inc*., 434 F.Supp. 217 at 226 (D.N.J.1977).
110. *New York Times Co., Inc*. v. *Tasini* 533 U.S. 483 (2001).
111. Google Book Search Library Project, http://books.google.com/googlebooks/library.html
112. *Kelly* v. *Arriba Soft* 336 F.3d 811 at 815 (2003).
113. Altavista *et al*. (2000), 'Appellate Brief of Internet Search Engines Altavista Company, Google, Incorporated, and Yahoo! Incorporated as Amici Curiae in Support of Defendant–Appellee Arriba Soft Corporation', 2000 WL 33994358, 11 September.
114. *Kelly* v. *Arriba Soft* 336 F.3d 811 at 820 (2003).
115. *Kelly* v. *Arriba Soft* 336 F.3d 811 at 819 (2003).
116. *Un Nezez* v. *Caribbean International News Corporation* 235 F.3d 18 (1st Cir.2000).
117. *Kelly* v. *Arriba Soft* 336 F.3d 811 at 819 (2003).
118. Band, J. (2006), 'Copyright Owners v. The Google Print Library Project', *Entertainment Law Review*, **17**(1), 21–4.
119. *University of New South Wales* v. *Moorhouse* (1975) 133 CLR 1; and Wiseman, L. (2002), 'Beyond The Photocopier: Copyright and Publishing in Australia', *Media And Arts Law Review*, **7**(4), 299–314.
120. Crisp, L. (2006), 'Gearing up for a Title Fight', *Australian Financial Review*, 25 January, p. 52.
121. Ganley, P. (2006), 'Google Book Search: Fair Use, Fair Dealing and the Case for Intermediary Copying', Baker and McKenzie, http://papers.ssrn.com/sol3/papers.cfm?abstract_id=875384.
122. Ibid.
123. Wray, R. (2006), 'Legal Victory for Google in Library Project', *The Guardian*, 29 June.
124. *CCH Canadian Limited* v. *The Law Society of Upper Canada* (2004) SCC 13. For commentary on the decision, see Rimmer, M. (2004), 'Canadian Rhapsody: Copyright Law and Research Libraries', *Australian Academic and Research Libraries*, **25**(3), 193–213: Gervais, D. (2004), 'Canadian Copyright Law Post-CCH', *Intellectual Property Journal*, **18**(2), 131–67; Murray, L. (2005), 'Bill C-60 and Copyright in Canada: Opportunities Lost and Found', *Canadian Journal of Communication*, **30**, 649–54; Wilkinson, Margaret Ann (2005), 'Filtering the Flow from the Fountains of Knowledge: Access and Copyright in Education and Libraries', in Michael Geist (ed.), *In The Public Interest: The Future of Canadian Copyright Law*, Toronto: Irwin Law, pp. 331–74; and Drassinower, Abraham (2005), 'Taking User Rights Seriously' in Michael Geist (ed.), *In The Public Interest: The Future of Canadian Copyright Law*, Toronto: Irwin Law, pp. 462–79.
125. Geist, M. (2005), 'National Web Library – Doable, Affordable, Visionary', *The Toronto Star*, 10 January.
126. Ibid.
127. *Agence France Presse* v. *Google Inc*., D. D.C., No. 05-00546 (2005), http://blog.searchenginewatch.com/blog/050321-175410.

128. *Agence France Presse* v. *Google Inc.*, D. D.C., No. 05-00546 (2005), http://blog.searchenginewatch.com/blog/050321-175410.
129. *Agence France Presse* v. *Google Inc.*, D. D.C., No. 05-00546 (2005), http://blog.searchenginewatch.com/blog/050321-175410.
130. *Agence France Presse* v. *Google Inc.*, D. D.C., No. 05-00546 (2005), http://blog.searchenginewatch.com/blog/050321-175410.
131. *Agence France Presse* v. *Google Inc.*, D. D.C., No. 05-00546 (2005), http://blog.searchenginewatch.com/blog/050321-175410.
132. *Agence France Presse* v. *Google Inc.*, D. D.C., No. 05-00546 (2005), http://blog.searchenginewatch.com/blog/050321-175410.
133. *Agence France Presse* v. *Google Inc.*, D. D.C., No. 05-00546, *oral argument* 1/11/06); Warnecke, M. (2006), 'In Battle Over Use of News Headlines, Court Focuses on Policy Implications for Web', e-Commerce Law Daily, **11**(3), http://ipcenter.bna.com/pic2/ip.nsf/id/BNAP-6KYKF9, 12 January.
134. Ibid.
135. Handler, M. (2005), 'Lessons from the Google News Controversy', *Open Democracy*, http://www.opendemocracy.net/media-copyrightlaw/google_3130.jsp, 16 December.
136. Akerman, E. (2006), 'New Media Making Deals with 'Old News Providers', *San Jose Mercury News*, http://www.mercurynews.com/mld/mercurynews/news/15157800.htm, 30 July.
137. Ibid.
138. Ibid.
139. *Copiepresse* v. *Google Inc.* (Court of First Instance of Brussels, 5 September 2006), http://www.chillingeffects.org/international/notice.cgi?action=image_7796; order reproduced by Chilling Effects (2006) 'Google Ordered by Belgian Court to Remove All Belgian News and Photographs' http://www.chillingeffects.org/international/notice.cgi?NoticeID=5133, 5 September.
140. *Copiepresse* v. *Google Inc.* (Court of First Instance of Brussels, 5 September 2006), http://www.chillingeffects.org/international/notice.cgi?action=image_7796.
141. *Copiepresse* v. *Google Inc.* (Court of First Instance of Brussels, 5 September 2006), http://www.chillingeffects.org/international/notice.cgi?action=image_7796.
142. Globes (2006), 'Walla! Threatens to Sue Google over News Site', TMCNet.com, http://www.tmcnet.com/usubmit/2006/03/07/1438447.htm, 7 March.
143. Perfect 10 (2004), 'Complaint and Demand for a Jury Trial in *Perfect 10 Inc.* v. *Google Inc*', 19 November.
144. Perfect 10 (2004), 'Complaint and Demand for a Jury Trial in *Perfect 10 Inc.* v. *Google Inc*', 19 November.
145. *Perfect 10 Inc.* v. *Amazon.com Inc.* CV05-4753 AHM (SHx) (US District Court for the Central District of California, 2005).
146. Amazon.com, 'Defendant's Memorandum of Points and Authorities in Opposition to Plaintiff's Motion for Preliminary Injunction in *Perfect 10 Inc.* v. *Amazon.com Inc.*', 7 November 2005.
147. Palfrey, J. (2004), 'Pornographer Sues Google on 12 Grounds', Berkman Center for Internet and Society, Harvard Law School, http://blogs.law.harvard.edu/palfrey/2004/11/20, 20 November.
148. Ibid.
149. EFF (2005), 'Amicus Brief in *Perfect 10 Inc.* v. *Google Inc.*', 12 October.
150. *Perfect 10 Inc.* v. *Google Inc.*, 16 F.Supp.2d 828 at 843 (2006).
151. *Perfect 10 Inc.* v. *Google Inc.*, 16 F.Supp.2d 828 at 843 (2006).
152. *Perfect 10 Inc.* v. *Google Inc.*, 16 F.Supp.2d 828 at 843–844 (2006).
153. *Perfect 10 Inc.* v. *Google Inc.*, 16 F.Supp.2d 828 at 844 (2006).
154. *Perfect 10 Inc.* v. *Google Inc.*, 16 F.Supp.2d 828 at 844 (2006).
155. *Perfect 10 Inc.* v. *Google Inc.*, 16 F.Supp.2d 828 at 844 (2006).
156. *Perfect 10 Inc.* v. *Google Inc.*, 16 F.Supp.2d 828 at 851 (2006).
157. *Perfect 10 Inc.* v. *Google Inc.*, 16 F.Supp.2d 828 at 849 (2006).
158. *Perfect 10 Inc.* v. *Google Inc.*, 16 F.Supp.2d 828 at 849 (2006).

159. *Perfect 10 Inc.* v. *Google Inc.*, 16 F.Supp.2d 828 at 849 (2006).
160. *Perfect 10 Inc.* v. *Google Inc.*, 16 F.Supp.2d 828 at 850 (2006).
161. *Perfect 10 Inc.* v. *Google Inc.*, 16 F.Supp.2d 828 at 851 (2006).
162. McCullagh, D. (2006), 'Nude-photo Site Wins Injunction against Google', CNet News.com, http://news.com.com/Nude-photo+site+wins+injunction+against+Google/2100-1030_3-6041724.html, 22 February.
163. Vaidhyanathan, S. (2006), 'Thumbnails (and Google) in Danger', Sivacracy.net, http://www.nyu.edu/classes/siva/archives/002827.html, 22 February.
164. *Field* v. *Google Inc.* 412 F.Supp.2d 1106 (D.Nev., 2006).
165. *Field* v. *Google Inc.* 412 F.Supp.2d 1106 at 1116 (D.Nev., 2006).
166. *Field* v. *Google Inc.* 412 F.Supp.2d 1106 at 1118 (D.Nev., 2006).
167. *Field* v. *Google Inc.* 412 F.Supp.2d 1106 at 1124 (D.Nev., 2006).
168. von Lohmann, F. (2006) 'Nevada Court Rules Google Cache Fair Use', Electronic Frontier Foundation, http://www.eff.org/news/archives/2006_01.php, 25 January.
169. *Parker* v. *Google, Inc.* 422 F.Supp.2d 492 (2006).
170. *Parker* v. *Google, Inc.* 422 F.Supp.2d 492 at 496 (2006).
171. *Parker* v. *Google, Inc.* 422 F.Supp.2d 492 at 496 (2006).
172. Google Corporate Information: Our Philosophy, http://www.google.com/corporate/tenthings.html.
173. Vaidhyanathan, S. (2005), 'A Risky Gamble with Google', *A Chronicle of Higher Education*, http://www.nyu.edu/classes/siva/archives/002445.html, 2 December.
174. Ibid.
175. Ibid.
176. Ibid.
177. Waladan, S. (2005), 'Google: Search or Destroy?', *Open Democracy*, http://www.opendemocracy.net/media-copyrightlaw/google_3130.jsp, 16 December.
178. Google is supporting the Stanford Center for Law and Society's Fair Use Project, which includes litigation such as *Shloss* v. *Sweeney* (US District Court Northern District of California, 2006).
179. Liedtke, M. (2006), 'Google Video Suit Could Signal YouTube Trouble Ahead', *The Associated Press*, 8 November.
180. Google and YouTube (2006), 'Google Closes Acquisition of YouTube', http:// www.youtube.com/press_room_entry?entry=AwPf9c9qJDc, 13 November.
181. *Tur* v. *YouTube* case number CV 06-4436-GAF (FMO_x) (United States District Court, Central District of California, 14 July 2006).
182. *Viacom International Inc. et al.* v. *YouTube Inc., YouTube LLC. and Google Inc.* (United States District Court for the Southern District of New York, 13 March 2007).

8. Remix culture: the creative commons and its discontents

> Remix culture . . . upholds the remix as an open challenge to a culture predicated on exclusive ownership, authorship, and controlled distribution. Against these cultural forces, the subterranean remix opposes an ongoing questioning of economic and cultural givens. Against ownership it upholds an ethic of creative borrowing and sharing. Against the original it holds out an open process of recombination and creative transformation. It equally calls into question the categories, rifts and borders between high and low cultures, pop and elitist art practices, as well as blurring lines between artistic disciplines. (Bernard Schutze, 'Samples from the Heap'[1])

Headquartered in San Francisco, the Creative Commons was officially launched in 2001. The group is a non-profit organization, which has relied upon contract law to expand the range of creative work available for others to build upon and share legally. This project relies upon a variety of standard contract and licensing schemes to enable copyright holders to grant some of their rights to the public while retaining others.

The Creative Commons movement had its origins in the failed efforts to challenge the *Sonny Bono Act*. Founder Lawrence Lessig recounts that the electronic publisher Eric Eldred encouraged him to develop a constructive alternative to the current copyright laws.[2] The academic envisaged a volunteer, collaborative project, which would seek to promote 'free culture':

> Creative Commons is just one example of voluntary efforts by individuals and creators to change the mix of rights that now govern the creative field. The project does not compete with copyright; it complements it. Its aim is not to defeat the rights of authors, but to make it easier for authors and creators to exercise their rights more flexibly and cheaply. That difference, we believe, will enable creativity to spread more easily.[3]

The Creative Commons movement positions itself as a voice of reason and moderation in an otherwise polarized political debate. It invokes the slogan 'some rights reserved' as a mission statement and preaches a message of bringing balance and harmony to the legal system.[4] The movement has sought to counter the effects of the dominant and restrictive permission culture pervading modern society: 'A single goal unites Creative Commons' current and future projects: to build a layer of reasonable, flexible copyright in the face of increasingly restrictive default rules.'[5] Nonetheless, the group disclaims any broader advocacy role in the copyright debate.

The Creative Commons draws inspiration from a number of theoretical traditions and intellectual heritages. The group invokes the key legal concepts of 'the public domain', 'the commons', 'open content' and 'intellectual property conservancies'. First, it emphasizes the importance of the public domain: 'We stand on the shoulders of giants by revisiting, reusing, and transforming the ideas and works of our peers and predecessors.'[6] The group hoped to replenish a public domain which has been depleted by successive copyright term extensions and the dramatic expansion of digital copyright protection.[7] Second, the movement endeavours to invoke the notion of the 'Commons', property held in common: 'Creative Commons aspires to cultivate a commons in which people can feel free to reuse not only ideas, but also words, images, and music without asking permission – because permission has already been granted to everyone.'[8] Third, the Creative Commons draws upon the idea of 'Open Content' as developed by the free software movement, open source software developers and projects like the on-line encyclopaedia, *Wikipedia*.[9] The group notes: 'Creative Commons hopes to build on the work of these pioneers by creating a menu of license provisions that people can combine to make their work available for copying and creative reuses.'[10] Fourth, it serves as a conservation group, hoping to provide a public sanctuary for works of special value.[11] The Creative Commons movement enunciates its ambition: 'Our ultimate goal is to develop a rich repository of high-quality works in a variety of media, and to promote an ethos of sharing, public education, and creative interactivity.'[12]

There are several types of Creative Commons licences, including attribution, non-commercial, no derivative and share alike licences. An *attribution* licence means that the creator requires attribution as a condition of using his or her creative work.[13] A *non-commercial* licence means that the creator allows only non-commercial uses of his or her work.[14] A *no derivative works* licence means the creator asks that the work be used as is and not as the basis for something else.[15] A *share alike* licence means that any derivative you make using the licensed work must also be released under the same terms.[16] Creative Commons licences bear a clause preserving fair use rights: 'Nothing in this license is intended to reduce, limit, or restrict any rights arising from fair use, first sale or other limitations on the exclusive rights of the copyright owner under copyright law or other applicable laws.'[17] The agreements are also a means of counteracting technological protection measures and digital rights management. Indeed, the organization observes: 'We are in the business of digital rights expression, not management.'[18]

Ultimately, the Creative Commons licences recognize that, subject to the conditions of the contracts, users have the freedom to copy and distribute, display and perform the work.

The Creative Commons movement has also developed and customized a number of other licences with specialist applications. The group has sought to ameliorate the harshness of the *Sonny Bono Act* through the use of Public Domain Dedications and 'Founders' Copyright' contracts.[19] Public Domain Dedications free works from copyright protection altogether. The group explains: 'We will encourage people to donate their works to Creative Commons to be held in public trust; in some cases, we may purchase important works to help guarantee both their integrity and widespread availability.'[20] Under a 'Founders' Copyright' contract, the Creative Commons and a contributor guarantee that the relevant creative work will enter the public domain after 14 years, unless the author chooses to extend for another 14. In addition, sampling licences have been developed to enable snippets to be remixed into new works, even commercially.[21] The movement also offers GNU General Public Licences and GNU LGPL licences for software developers. Finally, Creative Commons has been working on a Developing Nations Licence, which would allow less restrictive terms to those countries with a low income as defined by the World Bank.[22]

The Creative Commons cause has been championed by a combination of lawyers and public intellectuals, creators and samplers, publishers and broadcasters. Most notably, Professor Lawrence Lessig has acted as a charismatic leader and promoter for the movement. He has extolled the virtues of free culture and the Creative Commons in his trilogy of books, *Code and Other Laws of Cyberspace*, *The Future of Ideas* and *Free Culture*.[23] Similarly, Professor Michael Geist has provided support for Creative Commons Canada, releasing his edited book *In The Public Interest: The Future of Canadian Copyright Law* under such a licence.[24] Professor Brian Fitzgerald has promoted the cause in Australia.[25] The lively on-line journals *Open Democracy*, *First Monday* and *The Public Library of Science* have encouraged their authors to give permission to release their literary works under Creative Commons licences.[26] Also, the BBC has begun a pilot project called BBC Creative Archive in partnership with other public sector organizations to create a public and legal domain of audio visual material for the benefit of consumers in the United Kingdom.[27] Moreover, a number of Promethean creative artists, musicians and film-makers have also employed Creative Commons licences. Most notably, the science-fiction writer and journalist, Cory Doctorow, has allowed his books, including *Down and Out in the Magic Kingdom*, and his short stories to be downloaded and distributed freely under Creative Commons licences.[28]

In response to such enthusiasm, a number of copyright owners and collecting societies have argued the Creative Commons movement undermines the value and integrity of licensing regimes. Michael Fraser, the Chief Executive Officer of the Copyright Agency Limited, the Australian copyright collecting society, is antipathetic to the 'copyleft' movement: 'Copyleft adherents promote a weakening of copyright in policy and in law, especially by making the claim that copyright restricts the flow of ideas.'[29]

A number of academics have also expressed reservations about whether the Creative Commons movement can realize its theoretical values and practical ambitions.[30] Although sympathetic to the concern of Creative Commons with copyright fundamentalism, Niven Elkin-Koren is sceptical of the strategies deployed by the movement.[31] She argues that a reliance on property rights, in the absence of a shared sense of free access, may serve to strengthen the proprietary regime. Furthermore, Elkin-Koren observes that the movement is a diffuse coalition that spans libertarians and anarchists, anti-market advocates and free-market advocates. She claims that the movement lacks ideological clarity: 'Creative Commons lacks a comprehensive vision of the information society and a clear definition of prerequisites for open access to creative works.'[32] Finally, the group has been attacked by members of the Free Software Foundation (FSF) and the libre society for lapsing into political and economic liberalism, and lacking a radical agenda for law reform.

This chapter charts some of the key projects and initiatives within the Creative Commons movement. It charts the wide spectrum of opinion: from the Creative Commons evangelists to the advocates of libre commons and the pragmatic critics to the pro-copyright loyalists. Section one considers the relationship between free software and open software, and the Creative Commons movement. It seeks to analyse the repercussions of the litigation between the SCO Group and Linux. Section two focuses upon Flickr, a web-site which enables the exchange of photographs. There is a discussion of the legal action taken by Adam Curry against a Netherlands tabloid magazine publishing photographs from Flickr, in breach of the terms of the Creative Commons licences. Section three examines the use of Creative Commons licences to facilitate digital sampling and mash-ups. It looks at the conflict between the Creative Commons movement and collecting societies. Section four focuses upon the remixable film, *Sanctuary*. Section five considers the contradictions of the BBC Creative Archive project. It examines the opposition to the project by the Media Entertainment and Arts Alliance. Section six considers the Public Library of Science and the development of the Scientific Commons. The conclusion charts the growing pains involved in the establishment of a global Creative Commons movement – iCommons.

I. COMMONERS, 'COMMONISTS', AND 'MARXIST-LESSIGISTS': FREE AND OPEN SOFTWARE

In the software field, copyright owners have been suspicious of 'copyleft' licences, which seek to keep code free from proprietary protection. In an interview, Bill Gates, the chairman and chief software architect of Microsoft, suggested that the critics of copyright law were fundamentally 'communists':

> There are some new modern-day sort of communists who want to get rid of the incentive for musicians and moviemakers and software makers under various guises. They don't think that those incentives should exist.[33]

Glenn Otis Brown denied the Creative Commons could be criticized in such terms: 'Bill Gates is too smart to confuse a voluntary, market-based approach to copyright like Creative Commons with a statist, centrally planned economy.'[34] In response, Lawrence Lessig contended that copyright reform advocates were 'commonists', not 'communists'. He observed: 'Indeed, our message from the start has been that for at least some creative work, and some artists, the exposure that a Creative Commons license offers could help the artist profit from his or her work.'[35] For his part, Dan Hunter wittily suggested that the adherents of the movement should be labelled 'Marxist–Lessigists'.[36]

In an effort to counter the proprietary ownership of computer software and hardware, Richard Stallman set up the Free Software Foundation (FSF). The organization believes that people should be free to study, share and improve all the software they use, and that this right is an essential aspect of the system of free expression in a technological society. The FSF has been working to achieve this goal since 1985 by directly developing and distributing, and by helping others to develop and distribute, software that is licensed on terms that permit all users to copy, modify and redistribute the works, so long as they give others the same freedoms to use, modify and redistribute in turn. The FSF is the largest single contributor to the GNU operating system, an alternative to the Unix system. Its GNU General Public Licence is the most widely used 'free software' licence, covering major components of the GNU operating system and tens of thousands of other computer programs used on tens of millions of computers around the world. The FSF is strongly interested in the use and development of copyright law to encourage sharing, and to protect the rights of users and the public domain.

Evolving out of the FSF, the Open Source Movement was established in 1997.[37] The movement was committed to 'the ability to distribute software freely, the availability of the source code, and the right to create derived works through modification'.[38] The Open Source Movement did not adhere to an absolute version of freedom, as espoused by the FSF. It was willing to operate within the commercial marketplace. There are a collection of companies whose business is based around the distribution of open source software – most famously, Red Hat and Cygnus Solutions. Furthermore a number of mainstream companies such as IBM, Netscape and Hewlett Packard have been interested in the potential of open source software.

The Creative Commons was inspired by the innovative contractual strategies of the FSF and the Open Source movement. In the acknowledgments to his book *Free Culture*, Lawrence Lessig pays tribute to the work of Richard Stallman and the FSF: 'As I reread Stallman's own work, especially the essays in *Free Software, Free Society*, I realize that all of the theoretical insights I develop here are insights Stallman described decades ago.'[39] The Stanford Professor comments that the Creative Commons is similar to the FSF in that it seeks to 'open a space for creativity freed of much of the burden of copyright'.[40] However, he noted that the Creative Commons does not seek to eliminate proprietary culture like the FSF: 'Instead, we believed that by building a buttress of free culture (meaning culture that can be used freely at least for some important purposes), we could resist the trends that push the other way.'[41] Moreover, the Creative Commons has a broader scope and ambition than its progenitors. Rather than merely being confined to software developers, the movement seeks to appeal to a wide range of cultural creators, including writers, musicians, film-makers and photographers.

There has been an increasing number of skirmishes about the validity and legitimacy of free and open source software licences. No doubt the outcomes of such contract battles will have a bearing upon the legal validity of Creative Commons licences. Thus the preliminary litigation and battles over the GPL and open source licences is of some interest to the Creative Commons movement. Such contests, though, have been somewhat inconclusive.

In 2002, MySQL AB sued Progress NuSphere for copyright and trademark infringement in the United States District Court for the District of Massachusetts.[42] NuSphere had allegedly violated MySQL's copyright by linking code for the Gemini table type into the MySQL server. After a preliminary hearing before Saris J, the parties eventually settled. At the hearing, Saris J expressed the view that she saw no reason why the GPL would not be enforceable.

In March 2003, the SCO Group (formerly known as Caldera Systems) filed a lawsuit in the United States against IBM for allegedly 'devaluing' its version of the UNIX operating system.[43] The group claimed IBM had, without authorization, contributed SCO's intellectual property to the codebase of the open source, Unix-like Linux operating system. In May 2003, the SCO Group sent letters to members of the Fortune 1000 and Global 500 companies warning them of the possibility of liability if they used Linux. In response, IBM and Linux distributor Red Hat brought legal proceedings against SCO.[44] SCO has brought additional lawsuits against Novell, AutoZone and DaimlerChrysler.[45]

Jonathan Zittrain comments: 'The ongoing case of *SCO Group* v. *International Business Machines Inc.* represents a major legal battle between the spheres of free and proprietary software, at a moment when dominance over operating systems for Internet server-related purposes is truly up for grabs.'[46] Reviewing the history of the litigation, Ishtiaque Omar commented that 'intellectual property lies at the heart of the action'.[47] Yet he observes:

> Despite the centrality of this conflict, it may be preempted by the contractual rights created by agreements betweeen IBM and SCO. Further, each party argues the other's behaviour constitutes unfair competition. The interconnecting influences of the myriad legal doctrines will be the determining factor in the outcome of the dispute.[48]

Elkin-Koren notes that 'the *SCO* v. *IBM* dispute demonstrates the increased concern related to conflicting claims, and the difficulty of verifying rights'.[49] She claims that 'these concerns call into question the sustainability of a contractual regime for coordinating rights over time, among different generations of owners and users, where rights may be divided and held by different holders and consequently raise conflicting claims'.[50]

In 2004, the 'Netfilter/iptables' project was granted a preliminary injunction against SiteCom Germany by Munich District Court because the company refused to desist from distributing Netfilter's GPLed software in violation of the terms of the GPL. The Munich District Court confirmed this injunction as a final ruling against SiteCom, finding the company was bound to adhere to the licence conditions of the GPL.[51] This ruling was important because it was the first time in the world that a court had confirmed that the GPL is a legally enforceable licence.

In *Wallace* v. *Free Software Foundation, Inc.*, Daniel Wallace sought injunctive relief against the FSF under the *Sherman Act* 1946 (US) to remedy 'the restraint of trade by way of a licensing scheme to fix the prices of computer software products'.[52] He contended that the FSF conspired with commercial distributors IBM, Red Hat Inc., Novell Inc. and others to fix the price of intellectual property in computer programs that are collectively known as the Linux (or GNU/Linux) operating system. The suit was dismissed in March 2006, on the grounds that Wallace had failed to state a valid anti-trust claim. The court noted, 'the GPL encourages, rather than discourages, free competition and the distribution of computer operating systems, the benefits of which directly pass to consumers'.[53]

Such litigation will no doubt be relevant to the status of Creative Commons licences. It should be noted that the fond affection of the Creative Commons movement for the FSF remains unrequited.

In a critique, Benjamin Mako Hill observed: 'CC's goal to escape a world of "all rights reserved" is laudable but they fail to describe what it will be replaced with except to say it will be better.'[54] He suggests that 'conservatism risks reducing CC's concept of balance toward little more than 'slightly better than the status quo'.[55] According to Hill, Creative Commons licences are compromised by the conservativism of creators:

> When asked at the World Summit on the Information Society about non-commercial use clauses, Lessig said that he thought they were overused and frequently a bad idea. For whatever reasons, 3/4 of CC-licensed works prohibit commercial use. Lessig provided licenses and he hoped most creators' conservatism and fears would not get the better of them. Apparently, they did; artistic works under these licenses are less accessible to a large number of creators.[56]

In accord with such disappointment, Richard Stallman commented: 'I used to support Creative Commons, but then it adopted some additional licenses which do not give everyone that minimum freedom, and now I can no longer endorse it as an activity.'[57]

Furthermore, some have questioned whether Creative Commons licences are sympathetic to the needs and interests of consumers. Alex Boswell comments: 'The problem is that Creative Commons licenses have been custom tailored to appeal to the random whims of publishers with no regard for consumers of the commons content.'[58] He contends that 'the principle problem with Creative Commons is that most of the creative commons content is not actually reuseable at all'.[59] He concludes: 'When the licenses are a compromise between the publisher and consumer and a simple standard, we'll see a true creative commons.'[60]

In a political critique, David Berry and Giles Moss of Libre Society claim that the Creative Commons is compromised by its inherent political and economic liberalism and lack of a radical agenda for reform. The commentators are disappointed that the movement lacks a radical agenda:

> We argue that the Creative Commons project on the whole fails to confront and look beyond the logic and power asymmetries of the present. It tends to conflate how the world is with what it could be, with what we might want it to be. It's too of this time – *it is too timely*. We find an organisation with an ideology and worldview that agrees too readily with that of the global 'creative' and media industries.[61]

The authors claim the Creative Commons network provides only a simulacrum of a commons: 'Under the name of the commons, we actually have a privatised, individuated and dispersed collection of objects and resources that subsist in a technical–legal space of confusing and differential legal restrictions, ownership rights and permissions.'[62] They complain that the Creative Commons movement is perverse because it has increased the complexity and combination of licences.[63]

No doubt such FSF purists would be further incensed by the recent collaboration between the Creative Commons and Microsoft. The two organizations have released a copyright licensing tool, which enables the addition of Creative Commons licensing information for works in popular Microsoft Office applications.[64] Lawrence Lessig enthused: 'We're incredibly excited to work with Microsoft to make that ability easily available to the hundreds of millions of users of Microsoft Office.'[65] Alan Yates of Microsoft observed: 'The collaboration of Microsoft and Creative Commons to bring Creative Commons licenses to Microsoft Office applications underscores how for-profit companies and nonprofit organizations can work together to bring innovative ideas and tools to the public.'[66] The wider open source movement was less than delighted by this collaboration. The editor of *Open Democracy*, Becky Hogge, observed: 'Like a cuckoo in the nest, Microsoft's arrival in the Creative Commons movement threatens trouble in the free culture family.'[67]

II. FLICKR FESTIVAL: CREATIVE COMMONS AND ARTISTIC WORKS

In a climate of antagonistic conflict and mistrust, the Cultural Commons movement seeks to defuse the strained relations between copyright owners and creative artists, and reduce the transaction costs associated with seeking permissions for use of copyright works. Derek Slater comments that the movement enables legitimate appropriations of artistic works, with the blessing of the authors:

> Creative Commons licensing is in one sense a pragmatic solution to copyright's ills. Artists who want to license their works can easily express their preferences in a way that others can identify and trust. In this way, Creative Commons licensing has enabled collaborations that might otherwise require a lawyer and a dozen inquiries.[68]

Slater comments that the Creative Commons licensing regime also serves other symbolic purposes, namely, presenting alternatives to the current legal regime. He observes: 'Artists can create a world where the law meets their expectations about legitimate appropriations – where museums and sterile McMash-Up contests aren't the only places to see new kinds of art.'[69]

In this context, the Creative Commons movement has sought to encourage the sharing of photographs on the Internet, especially amongst amateurs. Flickr is an on-line photograph management and sharing application, which was bought by the search engine Yahoo in 2005.[70] Founder Stewart Butterfield explained how Flickr relies upon Creative Commons licences to facilitate the exchange of photographs between creators and visitors:

> We allow members to select a default Creative Commons license for all photos they upload and the ability to control licensing on a photo-by-photo basis. This gives people the most flexibility. And I think it does solve a real problem for some people: they want to be able to post their photos on the web and still express their preference as to how their work gets used. This was an important step for us; as individuals and as a company we believe in and want to support free culture. Creative Commons licensing is great because it just sort of 'snaps in' – the hard thinking has already been done, and even some of the technical work. In the longer term we'll be adding a lot of features which will help viewers find Creative Commons-licensed photos: by license type, by subject, by photographer, and so on. With a powerful search interface we hope that this will become a valuable resource.[71]

The web-site has two main goals. First, in the words of the company, 'We want to help people make their photos available to the people who matter to them.'[72] Second, the company stresses: 'We want to enable new ways of organizing photos.'[73]

The use of Creative Commons licences on Flickr was tested in the District Court of Amsterdam.[74] The plaintiff was Adam Curry, a broadcasting and Internet personality. Curry brought a lawsuit against *Weekend*, a Dutch gossip magazine, for breach of copyright and violation of privacy for publishing four photographs of his family retrieved from www.flickr.com without permission. Curry alleged the magazine had engaged in the 'reproduction of pictures I own and publish on flickr under the creative commons 'attribution-non commercial-share alike' license'.[75] He also alleged the magazine was responsible for 'endangering our 15-year-old daughter by publishing the name and location of her school and her means of transport to and from school'.[76]

As to the copyright claim, *Weekend* argued that it was misled by the notice 'this photo is public' and that the link to the CC licence was not obvious. Audax, the publisher of *Weekend*, argued that it was informed of the existence of the licence only much later by its legal counsel. In sum, *Weekend* had assumed in good faith that no authorization from Curry was needed. In regard to the privacy infringement, the magazine maintained that Curry had not incurred any damages by the publication of the photos, since the photos were freely available to the public on Flickr.

On 9 March 2006, in a summary judgment, the District Court of Amsterdam rejected *Weekend*'s defence on the copyright claim, and upheld the validity of the Creative Commons licence:

> In principle, Curry owns the copyright in the four photos, and the photos, by posting them on that website, are subject to the [Creative Commons] License. Therefore Audax should observe the conditions that control the use by third parties of the photos as stated in the License. The Court understands that Audax was misled by the notice 'This photo is public' (and therefore did not take note of the conditions of the License). However, it may be expected from a professional party like Audax that it conduct a thorough and precise examination before publishing in *Weekend* photos originating from the internet.[77]

The court added: 'In case of doubt as to the applicability and the contents of the License [Audax] should have requested authorization for publication from the copyright holder of the photos (Curry).'[78] Ruling that Audax had failed to observe the conditions of the licence, the court enjoined the defendants from publishing the photographs that Curry had published on www.flickr.com, unless this occurs in accordance with the conditions of the License.[79] The judge observed that, if the magazine used the copyrighted photographs in the future, it would be fined 1000 € for each photograph used without permission. The court did not find that a case could be made in respect of the breach of privacy.

Bernt Hugenholtz from the University of Amsterdam observed: 'The Dutch Court's decision is especially noteworthy because it confirms that the conditions of a Creative Commons license automatically apply to the content licensed under it and bind users of such content even without expressly agreeing to, or having knowledge of, the conditions of the license.'[80] Paul Keller, Public Project Lead for Creative Commons in the Netherlands, observed: 'We are very happy with this decision as it demonstrates that the millions of creators who use creative commons licenses are effectively protected against abuses of their willingness to contribute to the commons.'[81] Lawrence Lessig noted: 'This decision confirms that the Creative Commons licensing system is an effective way for content creators to manage their copyrights online.'[82]

The outcome of the Curry dispute lends support to the idea that Creative Commons licensing enables artists to share their works with the public without compromising copyright and without the need for legal expertise. However, some remain unconvinced that creative artists will benefit from Creative Commons licences. Australian academic Kathy Bowrey observes that such a licensing regimen may be attractive to libraries, universities and the sciences because these institutions are familiar with bureaucratic practices.[83] Yet, for all its rhetoric, the Creative Commons project remains difficult to access for non-legal actors:

> There is more to this concern about the prominence of intellectual property issues than simply tiredness, apathy or ignorance. There is an intuitive resistance to juridification, because previously it was possible to express a creative practice without rights awareness assuming such a priority. No doubt how comfortable one is with a rights based consciousness (commonly associated with US civics) [it] is culturally variable. In any case, the spread of intellectual property rights globally is not intrinsically a good thing, even where the license purports to be on the side of the angels.[84]

Bowrey contends that artists will intuitively resist the intrusion of law into everyday practices: 'The "civility" of the commons is that of the respectable property holder, graciously consenting to specified free or less restrictive uses, so long as the prescribed notice stays attached.'[85] In her view, it might not be a bad thing that creative artists scorn legal relations.

III. TROPICALISMO: DIGITAL SAMPLING IN THE DISCOTHEQUE

In 2003, the Creative Commons developed new Sampling Licences in collaboration with the experimental music collective, Negativland. Don Joyce of Negativland called for the legal acknowledgment of the 'state of modern audio/visual creativity in which quoting, sampling, direct referencing, copying, and collaging have become a major part of modern inspiration'.[86] The sampling group observed:

> There's a crucial difference between bootlegging another's work and the creative transformation of it. Collage is a technique that has an undisputed currency in virtually all art forms today. Originally, copyright was designed to prohibit the piracy or bootlegging of complete works; that was and remains a worthy goal. But copyright is now also routinely used to prohibit collage, as if it were no different from outright piracy. With Creative Commons, we're trying to build a license that will allow copyright holders to invite transformation of their works – even for money – while preventing this sort of verbatim bootlegging.[87]

The Creative Commons offered two models of Sampling Licences. Under the first version, 'The Sampling license will let authors invite others to tranform their work, even for commercial purposes, while prohibiting distribution of verbatim copies, or any use in advertising.'[88] Under the second version, 'the Sampling-Plus license will offer the same freedoms as the Sampling license, but will also allow noncommercial sharing of the verbatim work'.[89] The Creative Commons explained: 'So, an artist could release her song under a Sampling-Plus license to encourage her fans to trade it on file-sharing networks, then remix or build upon it however they like.'[90] The Creative Commons deed provides that a user is free to 'sample, mash-up, or otherwise creatively transform this work for commercial or noncommercial purposes.'[91]

The Creative Commons movement also enlisted Gilberto Gil, the Minister for Culture of the Brazilian Government, to help develop the Sampling Licences. The Minister for Culture, and *tropicalismo* musician Gilberto Gil observed:

> A world opened up by communications cannot remain closed up in a feudal vision of property. No country, not the US, not Europe, can stand in the way of it. It's a global trend. It's part of the very process of civilization. It's the semantic abundance of the modern world, of the postmodern world – and there's no use resisting it.[92]

Gilberto Gil has sought to 'tropicalize' Brazil's approach to intellectual property in the networked age. His hope is 'to make the digital world join in the samba'.[93] Gil has given his imprimatur to the digital sampling licences of the Creative Commons. Rather than call them 'Sampling licences', Creative Commons Brazil has renamed them 'Recombo licences', a name inspired by a Brazilian art collective, called Re: Combo.[94]

The technology bible, *Wired Magazine*, released a collection of 16 songs produced under the Creative Commons licences, encouraging its consumers, 'Rip, Mix, Burn. Swap till you drop. The music cops can't do a thing – it's 100 percent legal, licensed by the bands.'[95] The journalist, Thomas Goetz commented: 'At root, Creative Commons is simply codifying what modern culture has already decided it wants to be: a hybrid nation of explicit influences, generous borrowings, and inside references.'[96] The concept album even featured a piece by DJ Danger Mouse and Jemini entitled, 'What U Sittin' On?'

The mainstream rock band, Pearl Jam, released a music video for the song, 'Life Wasted' under a Creative Commons licence, which required attribution, no commercial use and no derivative use.[97] The clip was offered as a free download for a limited time under Google Video, after which time, the music video was made available for sale. The musician, Jeff Tweedy, of the alternative country band Wilco is also positive about the venture.[98] He argued that creating an adversarial relationship with music consumers was a mistake: 'The industry is hiding behind a smokescreen of artists' rights – it is terrified of people being able to listen to music and deciding whether they like it before the industry can tell them what to like.'[99]

There has been much tension between the Creative Commons movement and copyright collecting societies in charge of the management of the economic rights of composers, music publishers and record companies. The Creative Commons movement has been concerned that recording artists are unable to avail themselves of Creative Commons licences in some circumstances, because they have assigned ownership of their economic rights to copyright collecting societies. For their part, copyright collecting societies are concerned that Creative Commons licences undermine the economic value of copyright subsisting in musical works, public performances and sound recordings.

Emma Pike, the Director General of British Music Rights, is sceptical of the Creative Commons movement. She approved of the assessment in *Forbes* magazine that Lessig was not a friend of copyright creators: 'His assault on copyright largely helps a ragtag bunch of gleaners who claim that copying is "creativity" because they can't create anything without directly reusing copyright material.'[100] She warned: 'In effect, by entering into a Creative Commons licence, creators are signing away their rights irrevocably, in perpetuity, for the whole world, for free.'[101] She was hostile to Creative Commons licences: 'For the huge tranche of writers falling between the extremes of hobbyist versus big time, Creative Commons fails to deliver any real benefits, yet some may be lured into it by its seductive rhetoric.'[102]

Such tensions have resulted in litigation in the European Union. In the Fall of 2005, the main Spanish collecting society – Sociedad General de Autores y Editores ('SGAE') – sued Ricardo Andrés Utrera Fernández, the owner of Metropol, a disco bar located in Badajoz.[103] SGAE alleged that the bar owner had failed to pay SGAE's licence fee of 4816.74 € for the period from November 2002 to August 2005 for the public performance of music managed by the collecting society.

On 17 February 2006, the Lower Court number six of Badajoz rejected the collecting society's claims because the owner of the bar proved that the music he was using was not managed by the society. The music performed in the bar was licensed under CC licences that allow public performance since the authors had already granted those rights. Specifically, the judge said:

> The author possesses some moral and economic rights on his creation. And the owner of these rights, he can manage them as he considers appropriate, being able to yield the free use, or hand it over partially. 'Creative Commons' licenses are different classes of authorizations that the holder of his work gives for a more or less free or no cost use of it. They exist as . . . different classes of licenses of

> this type . . . they allow third parties to be able to use music freely and without cost with greater or minor extension; and in some of these licenses, specific uses require the payment of royalties. The defendant proves that he makes use of music that is handled by their authors through these Creative Commons licenses.[104]

The leader of the Creative Commons Spain project, Ignasi Labastida, observed: 'This decision demonstrates that authors can choose how to manage their rights for their own benefit and anyone can benefit from that choice, too.'[105]

There have been similar conflicts in other jurisdictions. The Australasian Performing Rights Association (APRA) is a collecting society administering the rights of composers, songwriters and publishers in Australia and New Zealand. The association has been implacably hostile to the use of Creative Commons licences. APRA claims that Creative Commons licenses are an inappropriate vehicle for music because they were based on a model for free software and open software. They have also expressed concerns about 'the irrevocability of licences, the possible conflict with recording or publishing agreements, the need to attend to formalities associated with either opt out or licence back from APRA, and the uncertainty and difficulty of defining exactly what 'non-commercial use' means'.[106] APRA stressed that it is 'imperative for any member to ensure that he or she obtains competent legal advice before signing up'.[107]

The Creative Commons movement was concerned that APRA required its members to assign economic rights to the collecting society. Chief counsel Mia Garlick was concerned that APRA members would be precluded from the opportunity of using Creative Commons licences:

> We believe that Australian musicians are at a significant disadvantage with regard to other musicians around the world. Due to APRA's current licensing and contract arrangements, Australian musicians do not have the flexibility to distribute their music on terms of their choosing. We are not suggesting that all Australian musicians will choose to license their works under a Creative Commons licence. We do believe, however, that they should have a choice. There are successful models in other jurisdictions of collective rights management that are co-existent with open content licensing systems.[108]

The Creative Commons movement appealed to the competition regulator, the Australian Competition and Consumer Commission (ACCC), to intervene to require APRA to build flexibility into its input and output arrangements.

In its determination, the ACCC noted: 'To the extent that APRA's licence back provisions, or the uncertainty as to their applicability, inhibits the non-commercial sharing of musical works for private use, such as through creative commons licenses, this would generate a public detriment.'[109] However, the ACCC observed: 'However, more generally, the creative commons licensing model is not, nor is it intended to be, an alternative means of monitoring public performance of musical works and/or collecting royalties in respect of public performance.'[110]

IV. SANCTUARY: PERFORMERS' RIGHTS AND THE CREATIVE COMMONS

In *Free Culture*, Lawrence Lessig discusses how film-makers' creative work has been unnecessarily interrupted by the transaction costs and royalties associated with copyright clearances and permissions.[111] He hoped that Creative Commons licences would overcome the complexity of copyright clearances and licensing in the film industry: 'If you can begin to wrap content in licenses where the original creator signals there are subsequent uses available for this content, you could begin to develop a different norm – a norm around people being free to remix and build upon, to sample out of, to supplement, to criticize content.'[112] The Stanford Professor believed that Creative Commons licences would be of particular appeal to amateur film-makers and documentary makers.

Recently, the director Michela Ledwidge has been developing a short film called *Sanctuary* to explore the potential for interactive contributions by the audience. She yearned for film sampling to become as common as music sampling:

> Film is going to change dramatically in the next 10 years. Not just in production values, as in the last decade, but in production methods and how the films are packaged for audiences. Digital asset management is going to be the key to commercial and creative re-use, increasing the likelihood of any film investment returns. I want to build an artistic bridge between film and interactive entertainment, designing the film story as a musical instrument. No cinema-quality film has ever been given to its audience in pieces, in the form of a library of re-mixable art. No director has encouraged the audience to tamper with the work to this degree. An architect builds something for it to be inhabited.[113]

Ledwidge hoped to employ the Australian-specific Creative Commons Licences released in February 2005. Such licences allowed the audience to exercise greater control over purchased film content, and take advantage of the opportunity for mash-ups and re-mixes. She sees her project as a 'new type of film that comes assembled like a Rubik's cube' and which treats film as an online stage with the ability to incorporate live performance.[114]

In a dispute over *Sanctuary*, the Media Entertainment and Arts Alliance complained about the lack of comprehensive copyright protection for screen performers. The union has blocked the remixable film project out of fear that footage of actors could be misused. Rather dogmatically, the national director Simon Whipp complained:

> We don't see any safe way a performer can appear in this. Footage could be taken and included in a pro-abortion advertisement or a pro-choice advertisement. Any non-commercial usage the performer may or may not agree with. Then for commercial work, performers are asked to sign a statement about what other commercials they have appeared in and this can be used to determine whether or not to include that performer. Without full knowledge of future usage of the film, it could unwittingly place that performer in breach of future commercial agreements.[115]

The union leader suggested that there was no adequate protection for the interests of performers: 'This means that a film that starts out with a performer in a specific role could end up spliced and diced into a pornographic scenario a million miles away from what the performer agreed to or would feel comfortable with.'[116]

Simon Whipp was particularly incensed that the Australian Film Commission was willing to found the film, *Sanctuary*. He contended hyperbolically: 'A performer with the head of a goat, spruiking for the Trotskyist party on a pro-abortion platform, it's all just part of the future of film encouraged by the Australian Film Commission (AFC).'[117] The union leader alleged that Creative Commons licences would do little to redress the poor financial performance of Australian film makers: 'With Australian box office at historic lows of 1.3% of total film box office, it seems that the AFC has some pretty strange ideas on how to build box office.'[118] He concluded: 'The local film industry is precious to all Australians, and the federal Government should have a long hard think about whether it wants to fund our home grown performers digitally manipulated to sound like aliens with heads of farmyard geese, talking about sex with donkeys as they perform terrorist acts on the Sydney CBD.'[119] Whipp emphasized that his stance was supported by the United States Screen Actors' Guild: 'The US Screen Actors Guild (SAG) have endorsed our stance on *Sanctuary* and stated that their members will not sign to any productions, either on film, tape or digital, made under a creative commons licence.'[120]

However, the cast of *Sanctuary* did not necessarily agree with the position of the union. One performer, Mark Owen-Taylor, was a member of the union but nonetheless supported Ledwidge's concept: 'For me, it's like doing any other film. I don't mind if people put my face on a donkey at home.'[121] He dismissed Whipp's concerns as far-fetched: 'Why would a political party even care? They could get their mum to do it in the backyard.'[122]

For her part, the director Michela Ledwidge expressed her dismay at the decision of the union:

> Having worked for years to fund this project and bring it back home to Australia to showcase local talent, I'm both dismayed and rather embarrassed by the MEAA position. It is no small irony that the actors and talent agents, who supported our little pilot and our submission to the MEAA, have the most to lose from this decision. We will still make the film but plans for an Australian shoot will have to be revised.[123]

Ledwidge suggested that re-mixable films would be adopted in the marketplace in the future: 'Commercial film sampling will eventually happen because film sampling is already taking place.'[124]

The leaders of the Creative Commons Australia project, Brian Fitzgerald and Ian Oi, sought to reassure the Alliance that their fears were baseless.[125] They observed that a Creative Commons licence could contain clauses which provided safeguards in respect of attribution and integrity of a work. Brian Fitzgerald noted:

> [I]t is important to point out that the base Australian creative commons license that has been drafted does actually protect the moral rights as defined in the Australian copyright legislation. So we need to also keep in mind that creative commons is not totally against moral rights protection.[126]

Fitzgerald observed: 'we certainly do understand the real concerns that MEAA has put forward about actors.'[127] He sought, however, to obtain a rapprochement with the union: 'One of the things that we would like to encourage though is, to some extent, a sentiment of experimentation, controlled as it may be, in various projects so that we can see what happens in terms of this new dimension of remixable film.'[128]

The underlying grievance of the union related to the lack of comprehensive performers' rights for audio-visual performers. The Media Entertainment and Arts Alliance has lobbied, so far in vain, for the introduction of comprehensive economic and moral rights for performers in respect of audio-visual work. The actor Steve Bisley provided evidence to the Senate Legal and Constitutional Committee about the need for the protection of the economic and moral rights of performers. He referred to two defining experiences in his career: the first, in which his character, 'Goose' in the film *Mad Max* had his Australian accent dubbed over with the voice of a Montana cowboy; and the second, in which his character in *The Big Steal* was billboarded in a television advertisement without his consent or permission.[129] However, such arguments did not sway the Government of the day.

Historically, there has been much debate in Australia over performers' rights, but little substantive legislative reform.[130] As part of the *Australia–United States Free Trade Agreement* 2004 (*AUSFTA*), the Federal Government was obliged to accede to the *WIPO Performances and Phonograms Treaty* (1996). The *US Free Trade Agreement Implementation Act* 2004 (Cth) provides economic rights to performers in sound recordings, albeit in a limited and circumscribed fashion. The legislation also provides moral rights to performers in sound recordings under Part IX of the *Copyright Act* 1968 (Cth). However, the *AUSFTA* failed to provide comprehensive protection of the economic and moral rights of performers in respect of audio-visual performances.

Some have suggested Australian copyright users should rely upon Creative Commons licences as an adaptive strategy in order to counter the pernicious impacts of the *AUSFTA*. Christoper Moore maintains that the Creative Commons licence system offers an effective method of co-operative activity, which lowers the barriers to access and distribution of cultural works. However, he comments:

> There is some debate as to the appropriateness of resorting to a licence system, a response generated by US cultural and legal traditions, in addressing the problems of our national copyright system when there are key differences between the two countries' models of cultural production and values. The reality is that Australia has just inherited a reconfigured model of copyright and intellectual property law from the United States.[131]

He maintains that the Creative Commons licence system offers an effective method of co-operative activity, which lowers the barriers to access and distribution of cultural works.

V. THE BBC CREATIVE ARCHIVE: BROADCASTING AND THE BRITISH COMMONS

There is an urgent need to archive television and radio broadcasts of the twentieth century.[132] Accordingly, at the Edinburgh Television Festival of 2003, the Director-General, Greg Dyke, announced the establishment of the BBC Creative Archive:

> We intend to allow parts of our programmes, where we own the rights, to be available to anyone in the UK to download so long as they don't use them for commercial purposes. Under a simple licensing system, we will allow users to adapt BBC content for their own use.[133]

He revealed that the BBC is planning to digitize and offer for download, free, as much of its back catalogue of programmes that it can legally do, from the earliest radio reels to nature documentaries to educational programmes. The project had been in part inspired by visits from Lawrence Lessig and Brewster Kahle.

In its 2004 document, *Building Public Value: Renewing the BBC for a Digital World*, the broadcaster outlined its broader vision for BBC Creative Archive:

> The BBC Creative Archive will establish a pool of high-quality content which can be legally drawn on by collectors, enthusiasts, artists, musicians, students, teachers and many others, who can search and use this material non-commercially. And where exciting new works and products are made using this material, we will showcase them on BBC services.[134]

The broadcaster concluded: 'Our ambition is to help establish a common resource which will extend the public's access while protecting the commercial rights of intellectual property owners.'[135]

The broadcaster intended to release factual material, starting with extracts from natural history programmes. Paula Le Dieu, Joint Director of the BBC Creative Archive, observed: 'Should we be successful with our approach, we may be able to release, over time, more programme genres – sport, music, drama – and possibly longer formats to the public.'[136] The BBC hoped to engage its audience in a creative collaboration. Le Dieu commented: 'The Creative Archive is, if you like, our first step into the BBC, changing slightly its relationship with audiences from one of being a pure broadcaster, to one that's taking a step into the realm of becoming part of a sort of creative domain, being part of a world in which its audiences join the BBC in the creative process.'[137] In order to increase the amount of content available in the public domain, the broadcaster had engaged in consultations with major public and commercial holders of audio visual collections in the United Kingdom, including broadcasters, archives, libraries and museums

The BBC promoted the Creative Archive under the slogan, 'Find it, Rip it, Share it, Come and Get it.'[138] Thus far, however, only a small proportion of its archives have been made available for downloading. The BBC Natural History Unit in Bristol has made 230 clips available in the Open Earth Archive, including clips from programmes featuring Sir David Attenborough and Bill Oddie as well as unbroadcast rushes from the anticipated new series 'Planet Earth'. The broadcaster has also released 80 reports from the News Archives, including Michael Buerk's report on the Ethiopian famine of 1984 that launched Band Aid, footage of the England team preparing for their 1966 World Cup victory and the aftermath of Nelson Mandela's release. It has also made available 100 programme extracts and clips on Radio 1's Superstar VJ's site, including skylines, sunsets, seascapes, wildlife, time-lapse photography and retro gadgets.

Lawrence Lessig was supportive of the project: 'The BBC Creative Archive would enable the British to cultivate this national resource – for which they have already paid – for educational, critical or comedic purposes.'[139] He believed that the venture would embody 'the BBC's founding mission – as Lord Reith put it – to "inform, educate and entertain"'.[140] Lessig was conscious, though, of the commercial imperatives facing public broadcasters such as the BBC. He anticipated there would be a natural resistance to the prospect of relinquishing control over copyright content: 'For the natural intuition of content owners is control.'[141] Lessig argued, however, that greater public access to broadcasting material 'would increase the BBC's chances of selling content commercially and make it more likely that the technology to cultivate this content (computers) will be more eagerly bought'.[142] He suggests that the Creative Archive project will have broader benefits for the economy of the United Kingdom: 'If the vision proves a reality, Britain will become a centre for digital creativity, and will drive many markets – in broadband deployment and technology – that digital creativity will support.'[143]

David Tannenbaum, the Coordinator of the Union for the Public Domain, expressed concerns about the modest output of the BBC Creative Archive:

> We want to make sure that the archive is more than just shagging marmots. There's been no public discussion of how they are going to get beyond these nature clips.[144]

The Friends of the Creative Domain – including the Union for the Public Domain, the Electronic Frontier Foundation and the Creative Commons – sent out a letter to the Department of Culture, Ministry and Sport, Members of Parliament, the Office of the e-Envoy and the BBC.[145] The letter was signed by artists, filmmakers, educators, students, researchers and archivists. The Friends of the Creative Domain argued that the archive must have breadth, and draw from 'all areas of the BBC's broadcasting, from factual to light entertainment, from drama to sport, and everything in between'.[146] Furthermore, the group maintained that the archive must be accessible, 'files must be made available in open, standards-defined formats without "digital rights management" or other technology locks that will keep Britons from creatively re-using the BBC's offerings'.[147] They stated that the content should be free and whole: 'Material should be licensed under conditions that do not restrict any licence payer from accessing, storing, modifying or sharing archive material for non-commercial use.'[148] The Friends of the Creative Domain expressed their concern about the commercialization of the archive: 'Some commercial broadcasters have already expressed opposition to an accessible archive of free material for non-commercial use, even while asking the BBC to "seed" the market for digital content.'[149]

In testimony to a select committee, Cory Doctorow of the Electronic Frontier Foundation expressed his support for the venture.[150] He argued that the project would enable consumers to remake and transform popular culture: 'The Creative Archive project will take the very essence of British popular culture – the material that the United Kingdom spent billions of pounds on in order to entertain, educate and inform itself – and give it to Britons to extend, to make their own, to interweave with the stories they tell and hear.'[151] Doctorow enumerates the many benefits arising from the Creative Archive: 'It has the power to lend cultural identity to the coming generation of Britons, to benefit UK cultural institutions, artists and commercial broadcasters, and to push the whole world towards a new height of freedom and cooperation.'[152]

The BBC has decided to limit access to Creative Archive Licence Campaign content to UK residents to 'ensure best value for the UK licence fee'.[153] Users outside of the UK are not able to access clips and programmes that form part of this campaign. The BBC explains on the web-site:

> The archive content . . . is restricted in this pilot to the UK because the member organisations who supply the content are funded with public money to serve the UK population. They are therefore unable to bear the cost of distribution to overseas audiences. In addition, there may be broadcast rights restrictions which means that content intended for a UK audience should not be made available overseas.[154]

Paula Le Dieu provided some small hope that this policy diktat would change in the future: 'I think it would be in everybody's interest, including the BBC, if it was available internationally.'[155] She noted, though, that there was no scope for the revision of this policy in the short term.[156]

Arguably, the value of the BBC Creative Archive project has been compromised by its refusal to allow non-British residents to access archival material. The broadcaster has created a provincial 'British' commons, rather than a global creative commons. The restriction of content to British users compromises the ideals of the Creative Commons. There is a disjuncture between the rhetoric and public relations of the BBC Creative Archive and its operation. 'Find it, Rip it, Share it, Come and Get it' – but only if you are a resident of the British Isles. The unmistakable impression is that the BBC is rather half-hearted about making its archives available to all. There still seems to be an overriding desire to license content for fees and royalties to other territories. It is certainly disappointing that the BBC is being so insular and is not taking its function as a global broadcaster very seriously.

There is a tension here between a global view of the commons, and a national construction of the commons. The intellectual commons has often been constructed as a global entity constructed by the collective labours of all humanity over all time. However, there are other possibilities. In *A Philosophy of Intellectual Property*, Peter Drahos comments: 'The idea that there are objects that belong in a global cultural commons is an idea which has been discussed, but has in no way replaced the belief that the cultural commons is predominantly national or regional.'[157] There remains ongoing debate about whether the BBC is acting in bad faith, and failing to realize the opportunities presented by the BBC Creative Archive, because of a lack of institutional support, and conflicting priorities.

For all its flaws, the BBC Creative Archive initiative is no doubt preferable to the increasing commercialization of United States archives and collections.[158]

VI. THE PUBLIC LIBRARY OF SCIENCE: THE CREATIVE COMMONS AND SCIENTIFIC PUBLISHING

In a famous article, Rebecca Eisenberg and Michael Heller expressed concerns about the tragedy of the anti-commons in biomedical research:

> The 'tragedy of the commons' metaphor helps explain why people overuse shared resources. However, the recent proliferation of intellectual property rights in biomedical research suggests a different tragedy, an 'anticommons' in which people underuse scarce resources because too many owners can block each other. Privatization of biomedical research must be more carefully deployed to sustain both upstream research and downstream product development. Otherwise, more intellectual property rights may lead paradoxically to fewer useful products for improving human health.[159]

The pair argued that 'a proliferation of intellectual property rights upstream may be stifling life-saving innovations further downstream in the course of research and product development'.[160] The focus of the pair's comments was very much upon patents, research tools and material transfer agreements. However, such arguments have wider resonance in the context of scientific publishing and data sharing.

In September 2001, the Public Library of Science (the Library) provided a clarion call for the reform of scientific publishing:

> Since the time of the great library of Alexandria, scholars have recognized the value of central repositories of knowledge. As scientists, we are particularly dependent on ready and unimpeded access to our published literature, the only permanent record of our ideas, discoveries, and research results, upon which future scientific activity and progress are based. The growth of the Internet is changing the way we access this literature, as more scientific journals produce online editions to supplement or replace printed versions. We urge journal publishers, their editors, and all working scientists to join together to create public, electronic archives of the scientific literature, containing complete copies of all published scientific papers.[161]

The group circulated a letter proposing a boycott of journals which did not provide 'unrestricted free distribution rights to any and all original research reports . . . within six months of their initial publication date'.[162] They believed the record of scientific research and ideas should neither be owned nor controlled by publishers, but should belong to the public and should be freely available through an international online public library. The open letter was signed by over 30 000 scientists from 180 countries.

This initiative prompted some significant efforts amongst a few scientific publishers towards providing free and open access to published research. Notably, *Science* and the *Journal of Cell Biology* announced that they would make their articles freely available on their respective websites 12 months after publication. *Nature* opened an online forum for discussion on the impact of the web on scientific publishing. However, in the main, commercial scientific publishers were hostile to the proposal. The editors of the prestigious journal, *Science*, commented:

> The proposition of Roberts et al. raises problems for *Science*, and for other journals. First, it will reroute an economically important source of online traffic for journals . . . Second, unlimited redistribution of content could lead to misuse of content and loss of quality control. Third, it may expose users to risks historically associated with monopoly suppliers. For example, recently PubMed – on which PMC will depend – unexpectedly failed to process new content for over a month, inconveniencing authors and publishers.[163]

The Library eventually conceded that the boycott was not effective. Scientists and researchers were still keen to publish in commercial journals for status and kudos, notwithstanding that they might have less control of their published work.

Undaunted by this response, the Library has since obtained funding from the Gordon and Betty Moore Foundation to publish its own journals.

It has hired a number of distinguished editors and established two new journals: *Public Library of Science Biology* and *Public Library of Science Medicine*. Controversially, the authors contributing to the journals have to contribute an up-front fee for publication to help cover expenses incurred by editorial oversight, managing peer review and maintaining production standards. Harold Varmus seeks to defend this business plan:

> People criticise the business plan of open-access publishers because it involves authors – and that means usually the funding agencies the authors use – paying a fee upfront of $1000 or $1500. They say that is a new expense. But it's not. The organisations – the funding agencies and research organisations – paying those costs will not change. It's the way the payment is done that's changing and the total costs will certainly go down. The research environment has been sustaining the publishing industry for years. That's not a bad thing. Publishing is crucial to research. In fact, one of the things we are trying to get across loud and clear is that publishing has to be considered part of the cost of doing research.[164]

The Library emphasized that there was scope for fee waivers. It noted: 'We understand that there are many scientists who might wish to publish in our journals but do not have access to grant funds or institutional support to allow them to pay publication fees, and we will substantially reduce or waive the publication fees for any authors for whom such fees would be a burden.' It sought further funding from outside research organizations.

Of critical importance to this publishing venture is the design and scope of copyright law. In the inaugural issue of *The Public Library of Science Biology*, Glenn Otis Brown of the Creative Commons laments the intrusion of copyright law into the daily lives of scientists.[165] He comments that policy makers have created a draconian system of copyright law under the influence of lobbyists: 'The result is a legal regime tailored to a powerful minority but ill-suited to a number of other constituencies – scientists and scholars chief among them – that thrive on openness.'[166] He observes that there is a need to reform copyright law to remedy this problem.

The Library seeks to provide authors with high-quality journals, which will allow them to make their papers freely accessible and useable, while still receiving proper credit for their work. This provides a solution to what Michael Eisner calls 'the central problem in scientific publishing' caused by 'authors of scientific papers assigning copyright to journals, thereby giving publishers ownership of scientific literature'.[167] He stressed: 'The monopoly control enjoyed by publishers over specific publications allows them to charge exorbitant access fees to individuals and institutions that need access to this material – which they cannot get anywhere else.'[168]

The Library allows authors and publishers to retain copyright on the work, but licenses the work to any third party to redistribute and use the work, subject to the condition that proper attribution be given whenever the work is reproduced or redistributed. Michael Eisner commented: 'Creative Commons and [the Public Library of Science] share the common goal of strengthening the science commons, and we want to take advantage of all the work Creative Commons and the growing number of Creative Commons licence users are doing to create, defend, and internationalize licences that define the commons.'[169]

In 2005, Science Commons was launched as a subsidiary of Creative Commons. John Wilbanks explains that this venture is designed to address a number of disparate problems, including 'inaccessible journal articles, tools locked up behind complex contracts, socially irresponsible patent licensing, and data obscured by technology or end-user licensing agreements'.[170] He comments that the Scientific Commons necessarily has a broader remit:

> We translate this into projects, with work in three distinctly different project spaces: publishing (covered by copyright), licensing (covered by patent and contract) and data (in the US, covered only by contract). We work on agreements between funders and grant recipients, between universities and researchers and between funders and universities – all in the service of opening up scientific knowledge, tools and data for reuse. We also promote the use of CC licensing in scientific publishing, on the belief that scientific papers need to be available to everyone in the world, not simply available to those with enough resources to afford subscription fees.[171]

As part of its publishing project, Science Commons seeks to support science publishers experimenting with Creative Commons licences, such as the Public Library of Science, BioMed Central and Springer OpenChoice. In its licensing project, Science Commons is seeking to address problems associated with the 'anti-commons', through means such as patent pooling, licensing research tools and conserving intellectual property rights. Finally, in its data project, the Science Commons seeks to resist the expansion of copyright protection over databases.[172]

Of course, there are even more radical open content ventures in the field of science. In 2001, James Wales founded *Wikipedia*, a multilingual Web-based free-content encyclopedia.[173] He called it 'an effort to create and distribute a multilingual free encyclopaedia of the highest possible quality to every single person on the planet in their own language.'[174] The encyclopaedia exists as a wiki, allowing volunteer Internet users to add, edit and delete entries. There has been some controversy over the reliability and accuracy of the encyclopaedia, with allegations of vandalism and errors.[175] The science journal, *Nature*, undertook a comparison of the accuracy of *Wikipedia* with the online version of *Encyclopaedia Britannica*.[176] Jim Giles concluded from the study: 'The exercise revealed numerous errors in both encyclopaedias, but among 42 entries tested, the difference in accuracy was not particularly great: the average science entry in *Wikipedia* contained around four inaccuracies; Britannica, about three.'[177] For its part, *Encyclopaedia Britannica* was indignant at the report, offering a refutation of the *Nature* study, which claimed 'almost everything about the journal's investigation, from the criteria for identifying inaccuracies to the discrepancy between the article text and its headline, was wrong and misleading'.[178] *Wikipedia* poses a particular threat to the norms and hierarchies of learned societies, scientific journals and encyclopaedia.[179]

CONCLUSION

The Creative Commons is an alternative to the polar extremes of the proprietary culture of the copyright industries and the 'free for all' of the users of peer-to-peer networks. The movement is an ambitious project, which seeks to address the needs of a wide range of creators across a variety of art-forms in multiple jurisdictions. The venture has won the backing of a diverse range of interest groups, including academics, and creative artists, archives and libraries, broadcasters and film producers. However, the Creative Commons has also attracted a number of detractors and critics, ranging from copyright owners and collecting societies, to industrial unions and professional associations, to theoreticians and radical proponents of free software. There has been an increasing number of skirmishes about the validity and legitimacy of free software, open source and Creative Commons licences. Elkin-Koren has observed: 'The first major challenge for Creative Commons is to ensure that license provisions, and particularly Share Alike provisions, would be enforceable against third parties.'[180] She notes: 'If subsequent users of the original work are not subject to the terms of the original license, the licensing scheme would become meaningless.'[181] Yet, in the face of such suspicion and hostility from established industries, the Creative Commons movement has proved to be surprisingly resilient.

There have been reservations expressed, though, about the reluctance of the group to engage in broader advocacy for copyright law reform. Berry and Moss of the Libre Society suggest that the Creative Commons movement is too conciliatory and accommodating of copyright owners: 'We find an organisation with an ideology and worldview that agrees too readily with that of the global "creative" and media industries.'[182] Indeed, Niva Elkin-Koren contends, 'In the long run, creating an alternative to copyright will require a copyright reform.'[183] The 'Founder's' Copyright licences have made little headway in redressing the ill-effects of the copyright term extension. There is a need to wind back the successive lengthenings of copyright duration. There is a need to expand the defence of fair use to allow for greater transformative and derivative uses of copyright works. In order to be effective, the Creative Commons movement will have to challenge the *DMCA*. In particular, there is a need to ensure that technological protection measures do not stymie the efforts to dedicate works to the public domain. The attribution and integrity of authors' works would be better protected in the United States, if Creative Commons licences had the backing of a comprehensive moral rights scheme.

The Creative Commons movement has sought to expand its base from the United States to a range of jurisdictions.[184] Lawrence Lessig has discussed the growth and development of this initiative: 'Our aim was to build an infrastructure of free licenses internationally so that creative work could move from jurisdiction to jurisdiction while preserving the freedoms that the creator chose.'[185] There are over 70 volunteer projects working to develop Creative Commons licences and 25 jurisdictions that have already launched their local licences. A federation of the movement, called iCommons, has been established as a separate nonprofit organization based in the United Kingdom, with a board comprising a wide range of activists from around the world. iCommons held a summit in Rio de Janeiro in Brazil in June 2006 in an effort to bridge the various interests within the international movement.[186] Undoubtedly, there will be tensions between the original model for the Creative Commons licences, which was founded on the template of United States copyright law, and the translations and adaptations of those licences in other jurisdictions. Lessig has responded: 'These ideals of a "Commons" are not American. They are human.'[187] The Creative Commons movement will have to see whether it can overcome various internal and external pressures to achieve its ambition of creating a 'global digital commons'.[188]

NOTES

1. Schutze, B. (2003), 'Samples from the Heap: Notes on Recycling the Detritus of a Remixed Culture', *Horizon Zero: Digital Art and Culture in Canada*, **8**, http://www.horizonzero.ca/textsite/remix.php?is=8&art=0&file=5&tlang=0, April/ May.
2. Lessig, L. (2005), 'CC in Review', The Creative Commons, http://creativecommons.org/weblog/entry/5661, 5 October.
3. Lessig, Lawrence (2004), *Free Culture: How Big Media Uses Technology and the Law to Lock Down Culture and Control Creativity*, New York: The Penguin Press, p. 286.
4. The Creative Commons, 'Some Rights Reserved: Building a Layer of Reasonable Copyright', http://creativecommons.org/about/history.
5. The Creative Commons, 'Some Rights Reserved: Building a Layer of Reasonable Copyright', http://creativecommons.org/about/history.
6. The Creative Commons Legal Concepts, http://creativecommons.org/about/legal.

7. For a discussion of the various meanings ascribed to the 'public domain', see Samuelson, P. (2003), 'Mapping the Digital Public Domain: Threats and Opportunities', *Law and Contemporary Problems*, **66**, 147–71; and Samuelson, P. (2006), 'Enriching Discourse on Public Domain', *Duke Law Journal*, **55**, 783–4.
8. The Creative Commons Legal Concepts, http://creativecommons.org/about/legal.
9. Pfaffenberger, B. (2001), 'Why Open Content Matters?', *Linux Journal*, http://www.linuxjournal.com/article/4709, 11 April.
10. The Creative Commons Legal Concepts, http://creativecommons.org/about/legal.
11. Boyle, J. (1997), 'A Politics of Intellectual Property: Environmentalism for the Net?', *Duke Law Journal*, **47**, 87–116; Kahle, B., R. Prelinger and M. Jackson (2001), 'Public Access to Digital Material,' *D-Lib Magazine*, **7**(10), http://www.dlib.org/dlib/october01/kahle/10kahle.html, October; and Bearman, D. (2000), 'Intellectual Property Conservancies', *D-Lib Magazine*, **6**(12) http://www.dlib.org/dlib/december00/bearman/12bearman.html, December.
12. The Creative Commons Legal Concepts, http://creativecommons.org/about/legal.
13. The Creative Commons Attribution Licence 2.5, http://creativecommons.org/licenses/by/2.5/legalcode. Of course, the Creative Commons licences are not unique in this respect. There have been many attempts in the past to use private contracts to bolster the moral interests of artists, in the absence of comprehensive moral rights legislation. See, for instance, the agreements developed by the playwright David Williamson and the Indigenous performing arts company, Bangarra Dance Theatre: Rimmer, M. (2002), 'Heretic: Copyright Law And Dramatic Works', *Queensland University of Technology Law And Justice Journal*, **2**(1), 131–49; and Rimmer, M. (2000), 'Bangarra Dance Theatre: Copyright Law And Indigenous Culture', *Griffith Law Review*, **9**(2), 274–302. The Creative Commons movement is an important progression in that it seeks to provide such licences on an industry-wide level, rather than on a merely local level.
14. The Creative Commons Attribution-Non Commercial Licence 2.5, http://creativecommons.org/licenses/by-nc/2.5/legalcode.
15. The Creative Commons Attribution No Derivatives Licence 2.5, http://creativecommons.org/licenses/by-nd/2.5/legalcode.
16. The Creative Commons Attribution Share Alike Licence, http://creativecommons.org/licenses/by-sa/2.5/legalcode.
17. The Creative Commons legal code, http://creativecommons.org/licenses/by-nc-nd/2.0/legalcode.
18. The Creative Commons Frequently Asked Questions, http://wiki.creativecommons.org/FAQ.
19. The Creative Commons, Founder's Copyright, http://creativecommons.org/projects/founderscopyright/.
20. The Creative Commons Legal Concepts, http://creativecommons.org/about/legal.
21. The Creative Commons, Sampling Licences, http://creativecommons.org/about/sampling.
22. The Creative Commons Developing Nations Licence, http://creativecommons.org/licenses/devnations/2.0/.
23. Lessig, Lawrence (1999), *Code And Other Laws Of Cyberspace*, New York: Basic Books; Lessig, Lawrence (2001), *The Future Of Ideas: The Fate Of The Commons In A Connected World*, New York: Random House; and Lessig, Lawrence (2004), *Free Culture: How Big Media Uses Technology And Law To Lock Down Culture And Control Creativity*, New York: Penguin.
24. Geist, Michael (ed.) (2005), *In The Public Interest: The Future of Canadian Copyright Law*, Toronto: Irwin Law.
25. Fitzgerald, B. (2005), 'Creative Choices: Changes to the Creative Commons', *Media International Australia*, **114**, 83–6; and Fitzgerald, B. and N. Suzor (2005), 'Legal Issues For the Use of Free and Open Source Software in Government', *Melbourne University Law Review*, **29**, 412–47.
26. Vaidhyanathan, S. (2005), 'Creative Commons: Making Copyright Work for Democracy', *Open Democracy*, http://www.opendemocracy.net/media-copyrightlaw/creativecommons_2596.jsp, 13 June.

27. The Creative Archive Licence Group, http://creativearchive.bbc.co.uk/.
28. Oberg, T. (2006), 'Sharing a Novel Future', *The Courier-Mail*, 25 March, p. 1, M23.
29. Fraser, M. (2005), 'Information Wants to be Free?', Presentation to the Copyright Symposium, http://www.copyright.com.au/reports%20&%20papers/Copyright_symposium_2005.pdf, 17 November.
30. For a summary of such theoretical complaints made against the Creative Commons, see Weatherall, K. (2006), 'Would You Ever Recommend a Creative Commons License?', *Australian Intellectual Property Resources*, **4**, http://www.austlii.edu.au/au/other/AIPLRes/2006/4.html.
31. Elkin-Koren, N. (2005), 'What Contracts Can't Do: The Limits of Private Ordering in Facilitating a Creative Commons', *Fordham Law Review*, **74**, 375–422.
32. Ibid., 377.
33. Kanellos, M. (2005), 'Gates Taking a Seat in Your Den', C/Net News.com, http://news.com.com/2102-1041_3-5514121.html, 11 January.
34. Dean, K. (2005), 'We're Creative Commonists, Bill', *Wired News*, http://www.wired.com/news/culture/0,1284,66209,00.html, 8 January; and Brown, G.O. (2005), 'Response to Bill Gates', The Creative Commons, http://creativecommons.org/weblog/entry/5223, 9 January.
35. Lessig, L. (2005), 'CC in Review', The Creative Commons, 23 November.
36. Hunter, D. (2005), 'Culture War', *Texas Law Review*, **83**(4), 1105–36 at 1105.
37. Raymond, Eric (1999), *The Cathedral and the Bazaar: Musings on Linux and Open Source by an Accidental Revolutionary*, Cambridge, Mass.: O'Reilly and Associates; Moody, Glyn (2001), *Rebel Code: Linus Torvalds, Open Source, and the War for the Soul of Software*, London: Penguin Books; Ghosh, Rishab Aiyer (ed.) (2005), *Code: Collaborative Ownership and the Digital Economy*, Cambridge, Mass. and London: The MIT Press.
38. Open Source, http://www.opensource.org/docs/definition.php.
39. Lessig, Lawrence (2004), *Free Culture: How Big Media Uses Technology and the Law to Lock Down Culture and Control Creativity*, New York: The Penguin Press, p. xv.
40. Lessig, L. (2005), 'CC in Review', The Creative Commons, http://creativecommons.org/weblog/entry/5668, 12 October.
41. Ibid.
42. *Progress Software Corp*. v. *MySQL AB* 195 F.Supp.2d 328 (D.Mass., 2002); see Moglen, E. (2002), 'Declaration in Support of Defendant's Motion for Preliminary Injunction on its Counterclaims in *Progress Software Corp* v. *MySQL AB*', http://www.gnu.org/press/mysql-affidavit.pdf.
43. *SCO Group, Inc*. v. *IBM Corp*., Not Reported in F.Supp.2d, 2005 WL 318784, 2005 Copr.L.Dec. P 28,957, (D.Utah, Feb, 09, 2005); *SCO Group, Inc*. v. *IBM Corp*., Not Reported in F.Supp.2d, 2005 WL 3776323, 2005 Copr.L.Dec. P 29,027, (D.Utah, Jul 01, 2005); and *SCO Group, Inc*. v. *IBM Corp*., Slip Copy, 2006 WL 2434229, (D.Utah, 21 Aug. 2006).
44. *Red Hat, Inc*. v. *The SCO Group, Inc*., Not Reported in F.Supp.2d, 2004 WL 883400, (D.Del., 06 Apr. 2004).
45. *SCO Group, Inc*. v. *Novell, Inc*. Slip Copy, 2006 WL 2403578 (D.Utah, 2006).
46. Zittrain, J. (2004), 'Normative Principles for Evaluating Free and Proprietary Software', *University of Chicago Law Review*, **71**(1), 1–21.
47. Omar, I. (2005), 'The Penguin in Peril: SCO's Legal Threats to Linux', *First Monday*, **10**(1), http://www.firstmonday.org/issues/issue10_1/omar/index.html.
48. Ibid.
49. Elkin-Koren, N. (2005), 'What Contracts Can't Do: The Limits of Private Ordering in Facilitating a Creative Commons', *Fordham Law Review*, **74**, 375–422 at 419.
50. Ibid., 420.
51. *In re Harald Welte* v. *SiteCom Germany* No. 21 0 6123/04 District Court of Munich I (19 May 2004), http://www.jbb.de/judgment_dc_munich_gpl.pdf#search=%22netfilter%20sitecom%22.
52. *Wallace* v. *Free Software Foundation, Inc*. Slip Copy, 2005 WL 3239208 (S.D.Ind., 2005).

53. Ibid.
54. Hill, B.M. (2005), 'Towards a Standard of Freedom: Creative Commons and the Free Software Movement', http://mako.cc/writing/toward_a_standard_of_freedom.html, 29 July.
55. Ibid.
56. Ibid.
57. Stallman, R. (2005), 'Fireworks in Montreal', Free Software Foundation http://www.fsf.org/blogs/rms/entry-20050920.html, 5 July.
58. Boswell, A. (2006), 'Creative Commons is Broken', Source Labs, http://www.sourcelabs.com/blogs/ajb/2006/02/creative_commons_is_broken.html, 21 February.
59. Ibid.
60. Ibid.
61. Berry, D.M. and G. Moss, (2005), 'On the "Creative Commons": A Critique of the Commons Without Commonalty', *Free Software Magazine*, http://www.freesoftwaremagazine.com/articles/commons_without_commonality/, 15 July.
62. Ibid.
63. Ibid.
64. Microsoft and the Creative Commons (2006), 'Microsoft and Creative Commons release Tool for Copyright Licensing', 20 June.
65. Ibid.
66. Ibid.
67. Hogge, B. (2006), 'What Moves a Movement?', *Open Democracy*, http://www.opendemocracy.net/media-commons/movement_3686.jsp, 27 June.
68. Slater, D. (2003), 'Take Another Little Piece of My Art', The Creative Commons, http://creativecommons.org/image/illegalart, July.
69. Ibid.
70. Flickr, http://www.flickr.com/about.gne.
71. Haughey, M. (2004), 'Interview with Stewart Butterfield, Flickr', The Creative Commons, http://creativecommons.org/image/flickr, July.
72. Flickr, http://www.flickr.com/about.gne.
73. Flickr, http://www.flickr.com/about.gne.
74. *Curry* v. *Audax* Case no. 334492 / KG 06-176 SR (District Court of Amsterdam, 9 March 2006), http://mirrors.creativecommons.org/judgements/Curry-Audax-English.pdf.
75. Curry, A. (2006), 'Judgement Day', Curry.com, http://curry.podshow.com/?p=49, 9 March 2006.
76. Ibid.
77. *Curry* v. *Audax* Case no. 334492/KG 06-176 SR (District Court of Amsterdam, 9 March 2006), http://mirrors.creativecommons.org/judgements/Curry-Audax-English.pdf.
78. *Curry* v. *Audax* Case no. 334492 / KG 06-176 SR (District Court of Amsterdam, 9 March 2006), http://mirrors.creativecommons.org/judgements/Curry-Audax-English.pdf.
79. *Curry* v. *Audax* Case no. 334492 / KG 06-176 SR (District Court of Amsterdam, 9 March 2006), http://mirrors.creativecommons.org/judgements/Curry-Audax-English.pdf.
80. Hugenholtz, P.B. (2006), 'Dutch Court Upholds Creative Commons Licence', Creative Commons Canada, http://creativecommons.ca/blog/?p=165, 14 March.
81. Garlick, M. (2006), 'Creative Commons Licenses Upheld in Dutch Court', The Creative Commons, http://creativecommons.org/press-releases/entry/5822, 15 March.
82. Ibid.
83. Bowrey, Kathy (2006), 'The New, the Bad, the Hot, the Fad – Popular Music, Technology and the Culture of Freedom', in Fiona Macmillan, *New Directions in Copyright Law: Volume 2*, Cheltenham, UK and Northampton, MA, USA: Edward Elgar, pp. 262–72.
84. Ibid., 270.
85. Ibid., 269.
86. Brown, G.O. (2003), 'Mmm . . . Free Samples (Innovation 1A)', The Creative Commons, http://creativecommons.org/weblog/archive/2003/03, 11 March.

87. The Creative Commons (2003), 'Creative Commons and Negativland Begin Work on Free Sampling and Collage', http://creativecommons.org/press-releases/entry/3707, 29 May.
88. The Creative Commons (2003), 'The Sampling Licences', http://mail.sarai.net/pipermail/commons-law/2003-October/000448.html, October.
89. Ibid.
90. Ibid.
91. Ibid.
92. Dibbell, J. (2004), 'We Pledge Allegiance to the Penguin', *Wired Magazine*, **12**(11), http://www.wired.com/wired/archive/12.11/linux.html.
93. Ibid.
94. Brown, G. O. (2004), 'Recombo Brazil', The Creative Commons, http://creativecommons.org/weblog/entry/4234, 4 June; and http://www.recombo.art.br/.
95. Goetz, T. (2004), 'Sample the Future', *Wired Magazine*, **12**(11), http://www.wired.com/wired/archive/12.11/sample.html.
96. Ibid.
97. Steuer, E. (2006), 'Pearl Jam's "Life Wasted" Video Released Under a CC Licence', The Creative Commons, http://creativecommons.org/weblog/entry/5913, 19 May.
98. Mackintosh, H. (2005), 'Talk Time: Jeff Tweedy', *The Guardian*, http://technology.guardian.co.uk/online/story/0,3605,1476170,00.html, 5 May.
99. Ibid.
100. Pike, E. (2005), 'What You Need to Know about Creative Commons', *Members' Music Magazine*, http://www.bmr.org/html/news/news53.htm, 15 March.
101. Ibid.
102. Ibid.
103. Garlick, M. (2006), 'Spanish Court Recognizes CC-Music', The Creative Commons, http://creativecommons.org/weblog/entry/5830, 23 March.
104. Ibid.
105. Ibid.
106. APRA/AMOCS (2006), 'Creative Commons', http://www.apra.com.au/writers/forms_and_guidelines/creative_commons.asp.
107. Ibid.
108. Fitzgerald, B., T. Cochrane, M. Garlick and N. Suzor (2005), 'Re Re-Authorisation of Collective Administration of Music Performing Rights by APRA', The Creative Commons, http://www.law.qut.edu.au/files/ACCCFinal31.pdf, 7 October.
109. *Australasian Performing Right Association Limited Application for Authorisation* A90918 to A90925 ACCC Final Determination (8 March 2006).
110. *Australasian Performing Right Association Limited Application for Authorisation* A90918 to A90925 ACCC Final Determination (8 March 2006).
111. Lessig, Lawrence (2004), *Free Culture: How Big Media Uses Technology and the Law to Lock Down Culture and Control Creativity*, New York: The Penguin Press, pp. 95–107.
112. Koman, R. (2005), 'Remixing Culture: An Interview with Lawrence Lessig', O'Reilly Network, http://www.oreillynet.com/pub/a/policy/2005/02/24/lessig.html, 24 February.
113. NESTA (2004), 'Profile: Michela Ledwidge: Mod Films', (June), at http://www.nesta.org.uk/ourawardees/profiles/4397/.
114. Ibid.
115. Byrne, S. (2005), 'Actors' Union Shouts "Cut" on Digital Film', *The Age*, 12 April.
116. Media, Entertainment and Arts Alliance (2005), 'Media Release: AFC Provides No *Sanctuary* for Australian Performers', 30 March.
117. Ibid.
118. Ibid.
119. Ibid.
120. Ibid.
121. Moses, A. (2005), 'Mixing Movies at Home', *The Sydney Morning Herald*, 7 June.
122. Ibid.

123. MOD Films (2005), 'MEAA Halts World-first Film Project in Australia', http://rights.apc.org.au/culture/2005/03/meaa_halts_worldfirst_film_project_in_australia.php, 10 May.
124. Moses, A. (2005), 'Mixing Movies at Home', *The Sydney Morning Herald*, 7 June.
125. Carrick, D. (2005). 'Remixable Films', Law Report, Radio National ABC, http://www.abc.net.au/rn/talks/8.30/lawrpt/stories/s1379751.htm, 31 May.
126. Ibid.
127. Ibid.
128. Ibid.
129. Senate Legal And Constitutional Legislation Committee (1997), 'Public Hearings: Copyright Amendment Bill 1997 (Cth)', 19 August, pp. 123–5.
130. *Performers' Copyright Bill* 1975 (Cth); *Sony Music Productions Pty Ltd* v. *Tansing (t/a Apple House Music)* (1993) 27 IPR 640; Attorney General's Department (1997), *Performers' Intellectual Property Rights: Scope of Extended Rights for Performers under the Copyright Act 1968*, Canberra: Attorney General's Department.
131. Moore, C. (2005), 'Creative Choices: Changes to Australian Copyright Law and the Future of the Public Domain', *Media International Australia*, **114**, 71–82 at 79.
132. Lessig, Lawrence (2004), *Free Culture: How Big Media Uses Technology and the Law to Lock Down Culture and Control Creativity*, New York: The Penguin Press, p. 111.
133. Dyke, G. (2003), 'Richard Dunn Memorial Lecture', BBC, http:// www.bbc.co.uk/pressoffice/speeches/stories/dyke_richard_dunn.shtml, 24 August.
134. BBC (2004), *Building Public Value: Renewing the BBC for a Digital World*, http://www.bbc.co.uk/thefuture/pdfs/bbc_bpv.pdf, June.
135. Ibid.
136. Aedy, R. (2005), 'Creative Archives', The Media Report, ABC, http://www.abc.net.au/rn/talks/8.30/mediarpt/stories/s1314858.htm, 3 March.
137. Ibid.
138. BBC Creative Archive, http://creativearchive.bbc.co.uk/archives/for_download/.
139. Lessig, L. (2003), 'The BBC's Lessons for America', *The Financial Times*, 8 September.
140. Ibid.
141. Ibid.
142. Ibid.
143. BBC (2004), *Building Public Value: Renewing the BBC for a Digital World*, http://www.bbc.co.uk/thefuture/pdfs/bbc_bpv.pdf, June.
144. Dean, K. (2004), 'BBC to Open Floodgates', *Wired News*, 16 June.
145. Friends of the Creative Domain (2004), 'Friends of the Creative Domain Call for a True Creative Archive', the Union for the Public Domain, http://www.public-domain.org/?q=node/36&PHPSESSID=1f6fbf319a31fe9a6cb2fbc3ec12dadb, 10 June.
146. Ibid.
147. Ibid.
148. Ibid.
149. Ibid.
150. Doctorow, C. (2004), 'Written Testimony to Select Committee on Culture, Media and Sport', Electronic Frontier Foundation, http://www.eff.org/IP/BBC_CMSC testimony.php, 11 September.
151. Ibid.
152. Ibid.
153. BBC Creative Archive, http://creativearchive.bbc.co.uk/archives/what_is_the_licence/licence_faqs/.
154. Ibid.
155. Aedy, R. (2005), 'Creative Archives', The Media Report, ABC, http://www.abc.net.au/rn/talks/8.30/mediarpt/stories/s1314858.htm, 3 March.
156. Ibid.
157. Drahos, Peter (1996), *A Philosophy of Intellectual Property*, Aldershot: Dartmouth, p. 58.

158. For instance, the Smithsonian institution and Showtime announced the creation of Smithsonian Networks, a joint venture to develop television programming. Under the agreement, the joint venture has the right of first refusal to commercial documentaries that rely upon Smithsonian collections or staff. Ken Burns, the documentary filmmaker of 'The Civil War', 'Baseball', and 'Jazz', was critical of this exclusive arrangement with the public archive: 'It feels like the Smithsonian has essentially optioned America's attic to one company, and to have access to that attic, we would have to be signed off with, and perhaps co-opted by, that entity.' The case illustrates the increasing commercial pressures placed upon the collections of public institutions: Wyatt, E. (2006), 'Smithsonian Agreement Angers Filmmakers', *The New York Times*, 1 April.
159. Heller, M. and R. Eisenberg (1998), 'Can Patents Deter Innovation? The Anticommons in Biomedical Research', *Science*, 1 May, **280**(5364), 698–701 at 698.
160. Ibid.
161. Roberts, R., H. Varmus, M. Ashburner, P. Brown, M. Eisen, C. Khosla, M. Kirschner, R. Nusse, M. Scott and B. Wold (2001), 'Information Access: Building a "GenBank" of the Published Literature', *Science*, 23 March, **291**(5512), 2318–19.
162. The Public Library of Science, http://www.publiclibraryofscience.org.
163. Editorial (2001), 'Is a Government Archive the Best Option?', *Science*, 23 March, **291**(5512), 2318–19.
164. Kleiner, K. (2003), 'Freedom Fighter: Interview With Harold Varmus', *New Scientist*, 1 November, **2419**, 46–9.
165. Brown, G.O. (2003), 'Out Of The Way: How The Next Copyright Revolution Can Help The Next Scientific Revolution', *Public Library Of Science Biology*, **1**(1), 30–31.
166. Ibid.
167. Lynch, L. (2003), 'Michael Eisner. Featured Commoner: Public Library of Science', The Creative Commons, http://creativecommons.org/text/plos, October.
168. Ibid.
169. Ibid.
170. Wilbanks, J. (2005), 'What is Science Commons?', The Creative Commons, http://creativecommons.org/weblog/entry/5695, 9 November.
171. Ibid.
172. Rimmer, M. (2005), 'Japonica Rice: Intellectual Property, Scientific Publishing, and Data-Sharing', *Prometheus*, **23**(3), 325–47.
173. Wikipedia, http://en.wikipedia.org/wiki/Main_Page; Goetz, T. (2003), 'Open Source Everywhere', *Wired Magazine*, **11**(11), http://www.wired.com/wired/archive/11.11/opensource_pr.html; Ciffolilli, A. (2003), 'Phantom Authority, Self-Selective Recruitment and Retention of Members in Virtual Communities: The Case of Wikipedia', *First Monday*, **8**(12), http://www.firstmonday.org/issues/issue8_12/ciffolilli/index.html; Benkler, Yochai (2006), *The Wealth of Networks: How Social Production Transforms Markets and Freedom*, New Haven and London: Yale University Press, pp. 70–74; and Younge, G. (2006), 'The Addictive Encyclopaedia', *The Guardian Weekly*, 1–7 September 2006.
174. Wales, J. (2005), 'Wikipedia is an Encyclopedia', wikipedia-l@wikimedia.org, 8 March.
175. Seigenthaler, J. (2005), 'A False Wikipedia "Biography"', USA Today, 29 November.
176. Giles, J. (2005), 'Internet Encyclopaedias Go Head to Head', Nature, http://www.nature.com/news/2005/051212/full/438900a.html, 15 December, 900–901.
177. Ibid.
178. Encyclopaedia Britannica (2005), 'Fatally Flawed: Refuting the Recent Study on Encyclopedic Accuracy by the Journal *Nature*', http://corporate.britannica.com/britannica_nature_response.pdf, March.
179. There is a long history of debate about copyright protection of encyclopaedias. See Yeo, Richard (2001), *Encyclopaedic Visions: Scientific Dictionaries And Enlightenment Culture*, Cambridge: Cambridge University Press, pp. 195–221.
180. Elkin-Koren, N. (2005), 'What Contracts Can't Do: The Limits of Private Ordering in Facilitating a Creative Commons', *Fordham Law Review*, **74**, 375–422 at 402.
181. Ibid., 402.

182. Berry, D.M. and G. Moss, (2005), 'On the "Creative Commons": A Critique of the Commons Without Commonalty', *Free Software Magazine*, http://www.freesoftwaremagazine.com/articles/commons_without_commonality/, 15 July.
183. Elkin-Koren, N. (2005), 'What Contracts Can't Do: The Limits of Private Ordering in Facilitating a Creative Commons', *Fordham Law Review*, **74**, 375–422 at 422.
184. iCommons, http://creativecommons.org/worldwide/overview.
185. Lessig, L. (2005), 'CC in Review', The Creative Commons, http://lists.ibiblio.org/pipermail/cc-lessigletter/2005/000005.html, 16 November.
186. iCommons Summit 2006, http://www.icommons.org/isummit/.
187. Lessig, L. (2005), 'CC in Review', The Creative Commons, http://lists.ibiblio.org/pipermail/cc-lessigletter/2005/000005.html, 16 November.
188. The electronic journal *Open Democracy* provided a forum of commentary on the Rio iSummit: Curzon Price, T. (2006), 'iCommons for Beginners', *Open Democracy*, http://www.opendemocracy.net/arts-commons/lowdown_3659.jsp, 20 June; Stark, E. (2006), 'Free Culture and the Internet: A New Semiotic Democracy, *Open Democracy*, http://www.opendemocracy.net/arts-commons/semiotic_3662.jsp, 20 June; Halbert, D., C. Darch, A. Story and C. South (2006), 'Education and Development on the High Seas of Copyright Infringement', *Open Democracy*, http://www.opendemocracy.net/arts-commons/icommons_3664.jsp, 21 June; Bechler, R. (2006), 'Should Artists Know Better? The British Copyright Experience', *Open Democracy*, http://www.opendemocracy.net/arts-commons/genius_3667.jsp, 21 June; Berry, D. (2006), 'The Global Digital Commons and Other Unlikely Tales', *Open Democracy*, http://www. opendemocracy.net/arts-commons/tales_3668.jsp, 22 June; Howard-Spink, S. (2006), 'Tropicalia and The Quest for a Cultural Commons', *Open Democracy*, http://www.opendemocracy.net/arts-commons/tropicalia_3675.jsp, 23 June; and Hogge, B. (2006), 'What Moves a Movement?', *Open Democracy*, http://www. opendemocracy.net/media-commons/movement_3686.jsp, 27 June.

Conclusion: a consumer's manifesto, the declaration of innovation independence

> Consumers hold the key to the balance of power for tomorrow's Internet. They are powerful because they drive markets and because many vote. If they remain satisfied with the Internet's generative characteristics – continuing to buy the hardware and software that make it possible and to subscribe to ISPs that offer unfiltered access to the Internet at large – then the regulatory and industry forces that might otherwise wish to constrain the Internet will remain in check, maintaining a generative equilibrium. If, in contrast, consumers change their view – not simply tolerating a locked-down Internet but embracing it outright – then the balance among competing interests that has favored generative innovation will tilt away from it. (Jonathan Zittrain, 'The Generative Internet'[1])

This book has depicted a consumer revolution against digital copyright laws, particularly as they are represented by the *Sonny Bono Copyright Term Extension Act* 1998 (US) (the *Sonny Bono Act*) and the *Digital Millennium Copyright Act* 1998 (US) (*DMCA*). As David Bollier notes, this movement has a broad membership:

> Despite the troubling trajectory that intellectual property law has taken over the past generation, a new movement to assert the public interest is starting to take shape and gain momentum. Key constituencies such as consumers, artists, librarians, computer professionals, academics, and scientists have become active players in the debates, and partners in advocacy. The general public, too, has become far more attentive. Ever since the Napster controversy dramatized the everyday implications of copyright law, ordinary people are more aware that technological and legal battles can directly affect them. Now that tens of millions of people use the Internet, networking software, CD burners, iPods, WiFi, and dozens of other innovations, few will knowingly accept a great cultural lockdown without a fight.[2]

Such constituencies have demanded that digital copyright laws should be recast in light of a better theoretical and practical understanding of role of the consumer. As Julie Cohen has emphasized: 'Scholars and policymakers should ask how much latitude the situated user needs to perform her functions most effectively, and how the entitlement structure of copyright law might change to accommodate that need.'[3]

There have been efforts by consumers and their allies to put forward constructive proposals for the reform of copyright law, policy and jurisprudence.

In 2005, the Consumer Electronics Association issued a Declaration of Innovation Independence.[4] President, and Chief Executive Officer, Gary Shapiro acknowledged that digital technology threatened the content industry: 'History is replete with technology disrupting existing businesses.'[5] However he was not pleased that copyright owners were seeking to inhibit scientific and technological progress: 'I am unsympathetic if they insist on handcuffing new technologies with efforts to poison and undermine the critical Betamax holdings.'[6] Shapiro observed:

> For too long, the content community has been allowed to define the terms of the IP debate. Today we reassert our independence. We reassert our independence from the content community's stranglehold on determining the language of the debate. We reassert our independence to counter their efforts to inhibit the democratization of creativity enabled by digital technology. And we reassert our independence to ensure that legal activities conducted by consumers remain legal and are not inaccurately labeled as 'piracy'. The principles we present today are designed to protect the critical American values of innovation and creativity while preserving basic consumer rights.[7]

In the Declaration of Innovation Independence, the Association enumerated a series of principles to ensure that fair use, home recording rights and innovation are protected in legislative, judicial and regulatory debates regarding the protection of intellectual property. It called on allied groups and policymakers to sign on and work toward the goal outlined within the document. The Association hopes to liberate democratic policy-making processes from capture: 'The influential content lobby has in many respects shaped the current state of copyright law.'[8]

Chapter 1 considered the failed constitutional challenge to the validity of the *Sonny Bono Act*. There remains great disquiet about the impact of the copyright term extension in the European Union, the United States and Australia. The Consumer Electronics Association has called on policy makers to recognize that 'our founders instituted copyright law to promote creation, innovation and culture rather than to maximize copyright holders' profits, and that it can do this only if new technologies are not stifled and fair use rights are upheld'.[9] The Association has emphasized the need to 're-examine the length of the copyright term and explore avenues for content to be reliably available for creative endeavors, scholarship, education, history, documentaries and innovation benefiting society at large'.[10] Even the Register of Copyright, Marybeth Peters, has confessed that the *Sonny Bono Act* was an error of legislative judgment:

> We've certainly lengthened the term [of copyright] perhaps – I won't even say perhaps – too long a term. I think it is too long. I think that was probably a big mistake, but one that Congress can make.[11]

Ideally, the *Sonny Bono Act* and its counterparts should be repealed, and the copyright term should return to the minimum standard laid down by the *Berne Convention* 1886. There is no compelling political, economic or cultural justification for the copyright term to last longer than life and 50 years. Failing such a reversal of the copyright term extension, it is worthwhile exploring amendments, which could ameliorate the impact of such laws. As mooted in *The Public Domain Enhancement Act* 2005 (US) there ought to be scope for copyright works to fall into the public domain, if they are not being exploited. There should be a solution for orphan works: preferably, a proposal that is more robust than that put forward by the United States Copyright Office.

Some commentators have gone further, and argued that the length of the copyright term should be drastically reduced. David Lametti of McGill University, for instance, provocatively suggests: 'In my view, we need to not only shorten the term of copyright generally, but also to vary the terms of copyright as between different kinds of works according to the context of the right and the resource protected by copyright.'[12] Even the usually staid *The Economist* has flirted with the reduction of the copyright term to a mere fourteen years.[13]

Chapter 2 considered the contested legacy of the *Sony Betamax* decision of the Supreme Court of the United States. The Consumer Electronics Association has sought to reaffirm the significance of the *Sony Betamax* decision:

> The Supreme Court in 1984 held that it is legal under the copyright law to sell a product if the product has substantial non-infringing uses. This Betamax holding paved the way for the introduction of revolutionary technologies enabling recording, storage and shifting of content in time and space without the prior permission of the copyright holders. Technologies such as MP3 encoding, the PC, the Internet and digital and audio recorders have supported a creative renaissance that has enriched the content community, empowered consumers and helped establish the United States as the world's economic leader.[14]

The Association has emphasized that there is a need to 'reaffirm the Betamax holding that a product is legal if it has significant legal uses' and 're-establish the fundamental rights of consumers to time-shift, place-shift and make backup copies of lawfully acquired content, and use that content on a platform of their choice'.[15] There is a need for the *Sony Betamax* decision to be codified and entrenched in copyright legislation, so that its application is not circumscribed or limited to obsolescent technology. In other words, the judgment should aspire to be, as Gary Shapiro has suggested, 'the Magna Carta and the Declaration of Independence rolled into one'.[16]

The privileges accorded to United States consumers by the *Sony Betamax* decision should also be extended to other jurisdictions.

Chapter 3 examined the regulation of peer-to-peer networks, the 'privateers of the information age'. In particular, it looked at litigation over Grokster, Kazaa and BitTorrent. The rules on secondary liability for copyright infringement remain unclear. Gary Shapiro of the Consumer Electronics Association has worried about the application of the *Grokster* decision to new consumer technologies:

> The Grokster case itself was about defendants that the Court viewed as bad actors engaging in egregious conduct, on a massive scale, sending content among millions of people who had no relationship with either the sender or the proprietor of the content. But will the courts now apply the same doctrine to technologies and companies that serve consumers who pay for their content in their cable bills or satellite bills, buy it on a CD or DVD, and listen to advertising on the radio? If a single court were now to declare one of their recordings to be an 'infringement', what is the status of all the product design, research, development, production, marketing, and distribution activity that went into serving these consumers? They may all be targets for potential plaintiffs, and their contingent fee lawyers.[17]

The Association warns: 'The recording and motion picture industries have often resisted, opposed or sought to stifle new technologies and products, despite the fact that these technologies transform markets and create new avenues for profitable content creation and distribution.'[18] It fears that litigation will have a deleterious impact upon technology innovation: 'Makers of pioneering technologies are now routinely subject to expensive and time-consuming lawsuits that discourage innovation and impede U.S. companies from competing globally.'[19] There are an array of legislative proposals to reform copyright law and peer-to-peer networks.[20]

Chapter 4 considered the remarkable creative phenomenon of 'mash-ups', looking at such classic examples as 'A Stroke of Genie-us', 'Can't Get Blue Monday out of my Head', and DJ Danger Mouse's symphony, *The Grey Album*. There is at best grudging tolerance towards digital sampling under copyright doctrine at present, and little sympathy for mash-ups, which involve the maximum use of copyright works. One commentator, Aaron Power, hopes that the defence of fair use can be flexible enough to accommodate mash-ups within the notion of 'transformative uses':

> As evidenced by the popularity of *The Grey Album*, society is willing to accept this new genre as a type of legitimate, creative work, and courts will be forced to deal with the copyright issues raised by mash-ups as long as record labels attempt to silence them. Fair use may provide a defense for mash-ups if courts are willing to acknowledge that the genre shares the core elements of parody and

> apply that line of cases. Mash-ups are transformative uses that do not supplant the market for the original, nor do they harm the market for traditional sample licenses. Like parodies, they must be allowed to use parts of preexisting works to 'conjure up' the originals in the listener in order to be created.[21]

There could also be scope for greater voluntary licensing in respect of 'mash-ups'. There also ought to be an expansion of compulsory licensing provisions to allow for mash-ups and remixes of musical works and sound recordings. There would also be a need to take into account the operation of the moral rights of authors and creative artists in jurisdictions such as Australia, England, Canada and the European Union.

Chapter 5 expressed dismay at the development of technological protection measures (TPMs) under the *DMCA*. Paul Goldstein has commented that the regime for TPMs in the *DMCA* has failed to pass the triple bottom-line of 'brevity, simplicity, and fairness'.[22] There have been complaints that TPMs have failed to achieve the objective of quelling copyright infringement in the digital environment. Fred von Lohmann of the EFF has observed:

> Despite the use of TPMs by copyright owners, it is evident that online copyright infringement has become a global and epidemic problem in part *because* of such uses. Since the entertainment industries have been slow to make their wares available online, this has further fueled consumer demand for copyrighted works which are ultimately obtained from unauthorized sources.[23]

Moreover, such digital rights management technologies have had an adverse impact upon such values as access to information, competition and consumer privacy.

As the Australian High Court decision in *Stevens* v. *Sony* made clear, there is a need to ensure that TPMs do not serve as a form of super or 'über-copyright'.[24] There is a need for TPMs to be civilized and tamed, so that they act as an adjunct to the traditional rights of copyright owners, and not a superior, more lethal form of protection. Fred von Lohmann comments:

> It is time to reconsider the wisdom of relying on legal protections for TPMs to address the challenges posed by digital technologies for the copyright industries. Countries that have not yet embarked down this path should refrain from doing so. Policy-makers in the United States, meanwhile, should give serious consideration to repealing the anticircumvention provisions of the DMCA in favor of allowing a new solution to the digital crisis – preferably, one that works.[25]

There have been a number of Congressional proposals to reform the regime of TPMs in the *DMCA*, including the *Digital Media Consumers' Rights Act* 2003 (US) and the *Benefit Authors without Limiting Advancement or Net Consumer Expectations (BALANCE) Act* 2003 (US).[26] Such measures would help provide safeguards for consumers' rights to engage in fair use and other legitimate actions – as laid down by the *Sony Betamax* decision – without fear of circumventing TPMs on copyright works. In the wake of the controversy over the Sony BMG rootkit, there is a need for stronger measures to dissuade technology developers from abusing TPMs. The *DMCA* and its foreign counterparts should not only include penalties for those who circumvent TPMs, but there should be countervailing penalties for technology developers who use TPMs for illegitimate purposes.

Chapter 6 explored the regulation of intermediaries under copyright law, ranging from Internet Service Providers to financial institutions and lawyers, and even individual end-users of peer-to-peer networks. There has been concern expressed in cases involving Verizon, Charter Communications and Swarthmore College, that intrusive copyright laws compromised the privacy, anonymity and freedom of speech of consumers. Jonathan Zittrain comments that there is a need for policy-makers to exercise forbearance in the regulation of intermediaries and gatekeepers:

> The history of online gatekeeping is partly one of the exercise of raw political power by intermediaries to limit their responsibilities. But it is also one of policy judgment in the judicial as well as legislative spheres that generative technologies ought to be given wide latitude to find a variety of uses – including ones that encroach upon other interests. These encroachments may be undesirable individually, but particularly in the realm of malum prohibitum wrongs such as those associated with the American intellectual property system – a system primarily conceived to maximize creative output rather than to vindicate moral rights of authors and publishers – they may also point to opportunities to reconceptualize the rights underlying the markets and the business models based upon them. An information technology environment capable of recursive innovation in the realms of business, art, and culture will best thrive with continued regulatory forbearance.[27]

There has been much attention paid to the lawsuits which have been launched against thousands of end-users of peer-to-peer networks. Lessig advocates a form of personal copying levy as a solution to such an addictive technology: 'Rather than seeking to destroy the Internet or the P2P technologies that are currently harming content providers on the Internet, we should find a relatively simple way to compensate those who are harmed.'[28] William Fisher III has put forward a comprehensive proposal for artists to be compensated for the distribution of content by an appropriate tax.[29] Similarly, Neil Weinstock Netanel has suggested that there should be a non-commercial use levy to allow file-sharing on peer to peer networks.[30] However, such proposals have not necessarily commanded respect and deference. It has been argued, in this book, that consumers and their allies would resist the imposition of a personal copying levy.

As shown in Chapter 7, the morass of litigation involving Google suggests that digital copyright laws are ill-equipped to deal with Internet search engines. Passed in 1998, the *DMCA* failed to apprehend the future prominent role and significance of Internet search engines. The limited exception for the providers of information location tools in the safe harbour provisions is demonstrably inadequate. Jessica Litman has observed:

> The Google lawsuits remind us that networked digital technology constrained by a copyright law that is both spare and sensible can expand our access to knowledge enormously. If, instead, our copyright law takes the form that the entertainment and information industries seem determined to purchase from the United States Congress, access to knowledge and the ability to make use of it may become subject to ever-more draconian controls.[31]

There is a need to provide better protection for technological innovators, such as Google. That would involve reforming the safe harbours provisions dealing with Internet search engines, and building upon the defence of fair use, so that it could better encompass the activities of Internet search engines. In addition, there should be further amendments to enable libraries, archives and educational institutions to undertake digitization projects, without being hobbled by copyright restrictions.[32]

Chapter 8 looked at the use of Creative Commons licences to facilitate a range of creative endeavours. It considered the use of such innovative contractual strategies in computer programming, digital photography, music mixing and sharing, television and radio broadcasting, film-making and scientific publishing. Speaking about the BBC Creative Archive, Cory Doctorow argued that such open content projects would be a boon for education, scholarship and innovation:

> Television today is being supplanted by interactivity. Today, children increasingly use PVRs to time-shift their favorite programming, and spend the rest of their TV-time playing games, including multiplayer games. They engage in file-sharing, and as they get a little older, they begin to play with their media, remixing and recutting it. It's the dawn of a 'creative nation' – a Britain which, like many other countries around the globe, makes use of the new tools to actively participate in media, a nation of recasters and reworkers, folk artists and appreciators of folk art.[33]

There is a need for national governments to nurture and foster such open content ventures. The Brazilian Government has taken the lead in supporting open source projects and adopting Creative Commons licences. Sam Howard-Spink comments: 'The country has recently emerged as one of the leading provocateurs in a global fraternity of developing nations that is challenging US and western assumptions about copyright, patents, trademarks – and cultural ownership.'[34]

Such developments suggest that the consumer revolution against digital copyright is not just a parochial concern of elite United States consumers of culture and technology. It is a fully-fledged international movement, with close collaboration between United States groups, and international academics, civil society and nation states. Kathy Bowrey comments:

> Support that strengths the profile and role of select US civil society groups globally can contribute to the moderation of some of the more objectionable current policies advocated by the US government, such as the global advocacy of proprietary models of software protection and strong patent rights. Arguably it is only changes to US domestic policy that will moderate further global IP rights advancement.[35]

Notably, there has been much concern about how the United States Trade Representative has sought to export key features of the *DMCA* and the *Sonny Bono Act* through international trade agreements.

In reaction, civil society actors have supported a development agenda to promote access to knowledge. Ralph Nader's Consumer Project on Technology (CP Tech) has taken the lead in the drafting of a *Treaty on Access to Knowledge* (the *A2K Treaty*).[36] Such an instrument would seek to protect, enhance and expand access to knowledge, and to facilitate the transfer of technology to developing countries.[37] There has been much theoretical and academic debate over the form and substance of the *A2K Treaty*. Yale Law School convened a conference to 'help build an intellectual framework that will protect access to knowledge both as the basis for sustainable human development and to safeguard human rights'.[38] Madhavi Sunder has argued that the A2K movement needs to be grounded on firmer theoretical foundations, commenting:

> But A2K is both revolutionary and conservative at the same time. A2K addresses the promise of new technologies, for example, not by exploiting the potential of the law to enhance semiotic democracy, but to return to the balance that earlier existed between producers and consumers. And while it would redistribute knowledge products, in its current state A2K does little to address the need for enhancing poor people's capacity to produce knowledge themselves, which is considered increasingly important for realizing the development goals of the new millennium.[39]

Jane Anderson and Kathy Bowrey have also expressed reservations about the failure of the A2K movement adequately to address questions of power and governance, particularly in the contexts of traditional knowledge, intellectual property and a digital networked society.[40]

There has been much debate over the future of the *A2K Treaty* proposal. Peter Drahos comments that much will depend upon the leadership of countries such as South Africa, Brazil and China, as well as diplomatic go-betweens:

> The fate of the treaty will depend heavily on the leadership of a few. The moral strength and determination of Nelson Mandela strides across the landscape of the twentieth century, a brilliant reminder of what a real leadership of values can accomplish against injustice. If developing countries are to take a stand on the governance of knowledge and make laws that address the structural injustices of the present regime, much will depend on the creative energies of Brazil and President Lula and thoughtful multilateral diplomacy of the kind practiced by Norway. Even more important will be China's beliefs about the rights and duties of owners of knowledge.[41]

Drahos also suggested that such a treaty would require backing from key corporations: 'It should be said that the success of a treaty on access to knowledge depends profoundly on the involvement of business, especially that segment of business entrepreneurship that sees in open source innovation the possibility of business models that will drive the knowledge markets of the 21st century.'[42]

The developer of the iPod, Apple, will be at the vanguard of such legal, commercial social, and technological change. In February 2007, Steve Jobs envisaged a future, in which copyright works would be distributed, free of the encumbrance of TPMs:

> Imagine a world where every online store sells DRM-free music encoded in open licensable formats. In such a world, any player can play music purchased from any store, and any store can sell music which is playable on all players. This is clearly the best alternative for consumers, and Apple would embrace it in a heartbeat. If the big four music companies would license Apple their music without the requirement that it be protected with a DRM, we would switch to selling only DRM-free music on our iTunes store. Every iPod ever made will play this DRM-free music.[43]

In April 2007, Apple announced that the entire digital catalogue of music held by EMI would be available for purchase at a premium on iTunes, without any DRM restrictions.[44] This important development is a harbinger of a wider consumer revolution against the restrictions of digital copyright law.

NOTES

1. Zittrain, J. (2006), 'The Generative Internet', *Harvard Law Review*, **119**, 1974–2040 at 2003.
2. Bollier, David (2005), *Brand Name Bullies: The Quest to Own and Control Culture*, Hoboken, NJ: John Wiley & Sons Inc. pp. 245–6.

3. Cohen, J. (2005), 'The Place of the User in Copyright Law', *Fordham Law Review*, **74**, 347–74 at 374.
4. Consumer Electronics Association (2005), 'CEA Announces Declaration of Innovation Independence: Presents Six Principles to Guide Intellectual Property Debate', Arlington, Virginia, 16 March.
5. Ibid.
6. Ibid.
7. Ibid.
8. Ibid.
9. Ibid.
10. Ibid.
11. Doctorow, C. (2006), 'Copyright Office Head Denounces "Big Mistake" of Extending Copyright', Boing Boing, http://www.boingboing.net/2006/02/21/copyright_office_hea.html, 21 February.
12. Lametti, David (2005), 'Coming to Terms with Copyright' in Michael Geist (ed.), *In The Public Interest: The Future of Canadian Copyright Law*, Toronto: Irwin Inc., pp. 480–516 at 482.
13. Editorial (2003), 'A Radical Rethink', *The Economist*, http://www.economist.com/opinion/displayStory.cfm?story_id=1547223, 23 January.
14. Consumer Electronics Association (2005), 'CEA Announces Declaration of Innovation Independence: Presents Six Principles to Guide Intellectual Property Debate', Arlington, Virginia, 16 March.
15. Ibid.
16. Home Recording Rights Coalition (2005), 'HRRC Urges Passage of Betamax Codification: Bill Would Promote User Freedom Under DMCA', http://www.hrrc.org/news/PressRelease041405.html, 14 April.
17. Shapiro, G. (2005), 'Protecting Copyright and Innovation in a Post-Grokster World', United States Senate Committee on the Judiciary, 28 September.
18. Ibid.
19. Ibid.
20. Fagin, M., F. Pasquale and K. Weatherall (2002), 'Beyond Napster: Using Antitrust Law to Advance and Enhance Online Music Distribution', *Boston University Journal of Science and Technology Law*, **8**, 451–573.
21. Power, A. (2006), 'The Mouse that Roared: Addressing the Post-Modern Quandary of Mash-ups Through Traditional Fair Use Analysis', *Vanderbilt Journal of Entertainment and Technology Law*, **8**, 531 at 539–40.
22. Goldstein, Paul (2003), *Copyright's Highway: From Gutenberg to the Celestial Jukebox*, Stanford: Stanford University Press, p. 216.
23. Von Lohmann, F. (2004), 'Measuring the Digital Millennium Copyright Act Against the Darknet: Implications for the Regulation of Technological Protection Measures', *Loyola of Los Angeles Entertainment Law Review*, **24**, 635–48 at 639.
24. *Stevens* v. *Kabushiki Kaisha Sony Computer Entertainment* (2005) 221 ALR 448 at 493.
25. Ibid.
26. *Digital Media Consumers' Rights Act* 2003 (US), and *Benefit Authors Without Limiting Advancement or Net Consumer Expectations (BALANCE) Act* 2003 (US).
27. Zittrain, J. (2006), 'A History of Online Gatekeeping', *Harvard Journal of Law and Technology*, **19** (2), 253–98 at 298.
28. Lessig, Lawrence (2004), *Free Culture: How Big Media Uses Technology And Law To Lock Down Culture And Control Creativity*, New York: Penguin, p. 201.
29. Fisher, William (2004), *Promises to Keep: Technology, Law, and the Future of Entertainment*, Stanford: Stanford University Press.
30. Netanel, N.W. (2003), 'Impose A Noncommercial Use Levy To Allow Free Peer-to-Peer File Sharing', *Harvard Journal Of Law And Technology*, **17**(1), 1–84.
31. Litman, Jessica (2001), *Digital Copyright*, 2nd edn, New York: Prometheus, Humanity Books, reprinted 2006, p. 202.

32. Tushnet, R. (2006), 'My Library: Copyright and the Role of Institutions in a Peer-to-Peer World', *The University of California Los Angeles Law Review*, **53**, 978–1029.
33. Doctorow, C. (2004), 'Written Testimony to Select Committee on Culture, Media and Sport', Electronic Frontier Foundation, http://www.eff.org/IP/BBC_CMSC_testimony.php, 11 September.
34. Howard-Spink, S. (2006), 'Tropicalia and The Quest for a Cultural Commons', *Open Democracy*, http://www.opendemocracy.net/arts-commons/tropicalia_3675.jsp, 23 June.
35. Bowrey, Kathy (2005), *Law and Internet Cultures*, Cambridge: Cambridge University Press, pp. 188–9.
36. Consumer Project on Technology, http://www.cptech.org/a2k/.
37. *Draft Treaty on Access to Knowledge* (the *A2K Treaty*), http://www.cptech.org/a2k/consolidatedtext-may9.pdf.
38. Yale Law School, Access to Knowledge Conference, http://research.yale.edu/isp/eventsa2k.html.
39. Sunder, M. (2006), 'IP^3', *Stanford Law Review*, **59**, 257–332 at 311–12.
40. Anderson, J. and K. Bowrey (2006), 'The Imaginary Politics of Access to Knowledge: Whose Cultural Agendas are Being Advanced?', *Australian Intellectual Property Law Resources*, **13**, 'http://www.austlii.edu.au/au/other/AIPLRes/2006/13.html.
41. Drahos, P. (2005), 'Access to Knowledge: Time for a Treaty', *Bridges*, **4**, 15–17 at 17.
42. Ibid., 17.
43. Jobs, S. (2007), 'Thoughts on Music', Apple, http://www.apple.com/hotnews/thoughtsonmusic/, 6 February.
44. Apple and EMI (2007), 'Apple Unveils Higher Quality DRM-Free Music on the iTunes Store: DRM-Free Songs from EMI Available on iTunes for $1.29 in May', http://www.apple.com/pr/library/2007/04/02itunes.html, 2 April.

Bibliography

REFERENCES

AAP (2005), 'European Libraries Join Forces Against Google', *The Sydney Morning Herald*, 28 April.

Abbott, G. (2005), 'Attorney General Abbott Brings First Enforcement Action In Nation Against Sony BMG For Spyware Violations', http://www.oag.state.tx.us/oagnews/release.php?id=1266, 21 November.

ABC (2003), 'Digitising Content in the ABC's Archive', Press Release, 8 July.

ACCC (2003), 'Submission to the Digital Agenda Review: Circumvention Devices and Services, Technological Protection Measures and Rights Management Information', http://www.aph.gov.au/Senate/committee/freetrade_ctte/submissions/sub294aatt1.pdf, October.

Aedy, R. (2005), 'Creative Archives', The Media Report, ABC, http://www.abc.net.au/rn/talks/8.30/mediarpt/stories/s1314858.htm, 3 March.

Akerman, E. (2006), 'New Media Making Deals with "Old News Providers"', *San Jose Mercury News*, http://www.mercurynews.com/mld/mercurynews/news/15157800.htm, 30 July.

Alliance for Public Technology (2003), 'Amicus curiae brief in *RIAA* v. *Verizon*', http://www.eff.org/legal/cases/RIAA_v._Verizon/20030516_eff_amicus.pdf.

Altavista (2000), 'Appellate Brief of Internet Search Engines Altavista Company, Google, Incorporated, and Yahoo! Incorporated as Amici Curiae in Support of Defendant-Appellee Arriba Soft Corporation' 2000 WL 33994358, 11 September.

Amazon.com (2005), 'Amazon.com Announces Plans for Innovative Digital Books That Will Enable Customers to Purchase Online Access to Any Page, Section or Chapter of a Book, as well as a Book in its Entirety', http://phx.corporate-ir.net/phoenix.zhtml?c=176060&p=irol-newsArticle&ID=778248, 3 November.

Amazon.com (2005), 'Defendant's Memorandum of Points and Authorities in Opposition to Plaintiff's Motion for Preliminary Injunction in *Perfect 10 Inc.* v. *Amazon.com Inc.*', 7 November.

American Chemical Society (2004), 'ACS Takes Legal Action Against Google', http://pubs.acs.org/cen/news/8250/8250acs.html, 10 December.

American Open Technology Consortium (2003), 'Going Deep', http://www.aotc.info/archives/2003_01.html, 20 January.

Anderson, J. and K. Bowrey (2006), 'The Imaginary Politics of Access to Knowledge: Whose Cultural Agendas are Being Advanced?', *Australian Intellectual Property Law Resources*, **13**, 'http://www.austlii.edu.au/au/other/AIPLRes/2006/13.html.

Anderson, J.W. (2004), 'Techno-Rebels in West Bank?; File Swapping Firm Claims Odd Hide-Out', *The Washington Post*, 22 February, A29.

Anonymous (1735), 'A Letter to a Member of Parliament concerning the Bill now depending in the House of Commons, for making more effectual an Act in the 8th Year of the Reign of Queen Anne, entitled, An Act for the Encouragement of Learning, by Vesting the Copies of Printed Books in the Authors or Purchasers of such Copies, during the Times therein mentioned', document reproduced in Goldsmith's-Kress *Library of Economic Literature*, Segment 1: Printed Books Through 1800, Microfilm No. 7300 (Reel 430).

Antill, J. and P. Coles (1996), 'Copyright Duration: The European Community Adopts "Three Score Years and Ten" ', *European Intellectual Property Review*, **18**(7), 379–83.

Apple and EMI (2007), 'Apple Unveils Higher Quality DRM-Free Music on the iTunes Store: DRM-Free Songs from EMI Available on iTunes for $1.29 in May', http://www.apple.com/pr/library/2007/04/02itunes.html, 2 April.

APRA/AMCOS (2005), 'Fair Use and Other Copyright Exceptions: An Examination of Fair Use, Fair Dealing and Other Exceptions in the Digital Age', Submission to the Attorney General's Department.

APRA/AMOCS (2006), 'Creative Commons', http://www.apra.com.au/writers/forms_and_guidelines/creative_commons.asp.

Arms, C. (1999), 'Getting the Picture: Observations from the Library of Congress on Providing Online Access to Pictorial Images', *Library Trends*, **48**, 379, 405.

Arnold, S. (2005), 'Disintermediation, Not Copyright Infringement: Is Google's Real Threat to Publishers?', Bogart Communications, http://www.arnoldit.com/press/News_Release-Google_Disintermediation.doc, 24 October.

Arts Law Centre of Australia (2000), *Push the Button: Music Seminar*, Sydney: Harbourside Brasserie, 7 December.

Associated Press (1998), 'Disney Lobbying for Copyright Extension No Mickey Mouse Effort: Congress OKs Bill Granting Creators 20 More Years', *The Chicago Tribune*, 17 October.

Associated Press (2003), 'Downloading Claim Against Granny Dropped', *The Sydney Morning Herald*, 25 September.

Associated Press (2006), 'Firm Behind eDonkey to Pay $30 Million to Avoid Piracy Claims', *Mercury News*, 12 September.

Associated Press (2006), 'French Law Seeks Inter-Operability', *Wired News*, http://www.wired.com/news/politics/0,70436-0.html, 17 March.

Astle, M. (2006), 'Will Congress Kill the Podcasting Star?', *Harvard Journal of Law and Technology*, **19**(1), 162–210.

Astra (2005), 'Fair Use and Other Copyright Exceptions', http://www.astra.org.au/content/pdf/FairUseJuly05.pdf.

Attorney General's Department (1997), *Performers' Intellectual Property Rights: Scope of Extended Rights for Performers Under the Copyright Act 1968*, Canberra: Attorney General's Department.

Auden, W.H. (1976), 'In Memory of W.B. Yeats', *Selected Poems*, London: Faber & Faber.

Austin, G. (2002), 'Does the Copyright Clause Mandate Isolationism?', *Columbia-VLA Journal of Law And The Arts*, **26**, 17–59.

Austin, G. (2006), 'Importing Kazaa – Exporting Grokster', *Santa Clara Computer and High Technology Journal*, **22**, 577–619.

Bailey, Jane (2005), 'Deflating the Michelin Man: Protecting Users' Rights in the Canadian Copyright Reform Process', in Michael Geist (ed.), *In The Public Interest: The Future of Canadian Copyright Law*, Toronto: Irwin Law, pp. 125–66.

Balch, N. (2005), 'The Grey Note', *Review of Litigation*, **24**, 581–607.

Band, J. (2005), 'The Grokster Scorecard', http://www.eff.org/IP/P2P/MGM_v._Grokster/summary.pdf.

Band, J. (2006), 'Copyright Owners v. The Google Print Library Project', *Entertainment Law Review*, **17**(1), 21–4.

Banks, S. (2003), 'Bill C-36: The Library and Archives of Canada Act', http://www.parl.gc.ca/common/Bills_ls.asp?lang=E&ls=C36&source=Bills_House_Government&Parl=37&Ses=2, 11 December.

Bard, Robert and Lewis Kurlantzick (1998), *Copyright Duration: Duration, Term Extension, The European Union, And The Making Of Copyright Policy*, Lanham, MD: Austin and Winfield.

Barker, T. (2006), 'Memorandum of Tenise Barker in Support of her Motion to Dismiss the Complaint', http://www.ilrweb.com/viewILRPDF.asp?filename=elektra_barker_memooflaw.

Barrett, R. (2005), 'Court Says RIAA Can't Subpoena ISPs Under DMCA', *Communications Daily*, **25**(3).

Bartow, A. (2005), 'BMG v. Gonzalez', Sivacracy.net, http://www.nyu.edu/classes/siva/archives/002533.html, 12 December.

Battles, Matthew (2004), *Library: An Unquiet History*, London: Random House.

BBC (2003), 'Grandmother Piracy Lawsuit Dropped', BBC News, http://news.bbc.co.uk/go/pr/fr/-/1/hi/entertainment/music/3140160.stm, 25 September.

BBC (2004), *Building Public Value: Renewing the BBC for a Digital World*, http://www.bbc.co.uk/thefuture/pdfs/bbc_bpv.pdf, June.

BBC (2004), 'Google's GMail Sparks Privacy Row', BBC News, http://news.bbc.co.uk/2/hi/business/3602745.stm, 5 April.

BBC (2006), 'Apple Attacks Plan to Open iTunes', BBC News, http://news.bbc.co.uk/2/hi/technology/4833010.stm, 22 March.

Bearman, D. (2000), 'Intellectual Property Conservancies', *D-Lib Magazine*, **6**(12), http://www.dlib.org/dlib/december 00/bearman/12bearman.html, December.

Bechler, R. (2006), 'Should Artists Know Better? The British Copyright Experience', *Open Democracy*, http://www.opendemocracy.net/arts-commons/genius_3667.jsp, 21 June.

Beck, S. (2002), 'Out of Tune', *American Lawyer*, 28 March.

Benkler, Y. (2000), 'From Consumers to Users: Shifting the Deeper Structures of Regulation Toward Sustainable Commons and User Access', *Federal Communications Law Journal*, **52**, 561–79.

Benkler, Yochai (2006), *The Wealth of Networks: How Social Production Transforms Markets and Freedom*, New Haven and London: Yale University Press.

Bently, L. (1989), 'Sampling and Copyright: Is the Law on the Right Track?', *Journal of Business Law*, 113–25, 405–13.

Bently, L. and B. Sherman (1992), 'Cultures of Copying: Digital Sampling and Copyright Law', *Entertainment Law Review*, **3**(5), 158–63.

Bently, Lionel and Brad Sherman (2004), *Intellectual Property*, 2nd edn, Oxford: Oxford University Press.

Berry, D. (2006), 'The Global Digital Commons and Other Unlikely Tales', *Open Democracy*, http://www.opendemocracy.net/arts-commons/tales_3668.jsp, 22 June

Berry, D.M. and G. Moss (2005), 'On the "Creative Commons": A Critique of the Commons Without Commonalty', *Free Software Magazine*, http://www.freesoftwaremagazine.com/articles/commons_without_commonality/, 15 July.

Bettig, Ronald (1996), *Copyrighting Culture: The Political Economy of Intellectual Property*, Boulder: Westview Press.

Beverley-Smith, Huw (2002), *The Commercial Appropriation of Personality*, Cambridge: Cambridge University Press.

Bhattacharya, S. (2006), 'Genius in Disguise', Entertainment Guide, *The Age*, 12 May, p. 2.

Black, M. (2005), 'Time for Fair Use to Free Up Technology', *The Sydney Morning Herald*, 28 January.

Blessing, D. (2004), 'Who Speaks Latin Anymore? Translating De Minimis Use For Application to Music Copyright Infringement and Sampling', *William and Mary Law Review*, **45**, 2399–423.

Block, R. (2005), 'Interview with Blake Krikorian', *Engadget*, http://www.engadget.com/entry/1234000933050954/,18 July.

Bloomberg (2005), 'U.S. Appeals Court Quashes Subpoenas for Charter Subscribers', http://www.bloomberg.com/apps/news?pid=10000103&sid=a0sCSInA_RrA, 4 January.

Boliek, B. (2005), 'President Bush Signs Family Entertainment and Copyright Act', *Hollywood Reporter*, http://www.hollywoodreporter.com/thr/article_display.jsp?vnu_content_id=1000900812, 28 April.

Bollier, D. (2001), 'Why We Must Talk About The Information Commons', New Technology, the Information Commons and the Future of Libraries, 2–4 November.

Bollier, David (2002), *Silent Theft: The Private Plunder of Our Common Wealth*, New York: Routledge.

Bollier, David (2005), *Brand Name Bullies: The Quest to Own and Control Culture*, Hoboken, NJ: John Wiley & Sons Inc.

Bono, M. (1998), 'Sonny Bono Copyright Term Extension Act', 144 Congressional Record H9946, 7 October, 9952.

Borges, Jorge Luis (1964), 'The Library of Babel', *Labyrinths: Selected Stories and Other Writings*, New York: New Directions.

Borland, J. (2006), 'BitTorrent to Crack Down on Use of Name', *ZDNet.com*, http://news.zdnet.com/2100-9588_22-6035800.html, 6 February.

Borland, J. (2006), 'MPAA Sues Newsgroup, P2P Search Sites', C/Net News.com, http://news.com.com/MPAA+sues+newsgroup%2C+P2P+search+sites/2100-1030_3-6042739.html, 23 February.

Boswell, A. (2006), 'Creative Commons is Broken', Source Labs, http://www.sourcelabs.com/blogs/ajb/2006/02/creative_commons_is_broken.html, 21 February.

Boucher, R. (2003), 'Copyright and Fair Use: The Present and Future Perspective', Harvard Journal of Law and Technology Symposium, http://www.house.gov/boucher/docs/harvard.htm, 15 March.

Boucher, R. (2003), 'Supporters of Digital Media Consumers Act', http://www.boucher.house.gov/index.php?option=com_content&task=view&id=25&Itemid=.

Bowrey, K. (1994), 'Copyright, The Paternity Of Artistic Works, And The Challenge Posed By Postmodern Artists', *Intellectual Property Journal*, **8**, 285–317.

Bowrey, K. (1996), 'Who's Writing Copyright's History?', *European Intellectual Property Review*, **18**(6), 322–9.

Bowrey, Kathy (2005), *Law and Internet Cultures*, Cambridge: Cambridge University Press.

Bowrey, Kathy (2006), 'The New, the Bad, the Hot, the Fad – Popular Music, Technology and the Culture of Freedom', in Fiona Macmillan (ed.), *New Directions in Copyright Law: Volume 2*, Cheltenham, UK and Northampton, MA, USA: Edward Elgar, pp. 262–72.

Bowrey, K. and M. Rimmer (2002), 'Rip, Mix, Burn: The Politics of Peer to Peer and Copyright Law', *First Monday*, **7**(8), http://firstmonday.org/issues/issue7_8/bowrey/index.html.

Boyle, James (1996), *Shamans, Software, and Spleens: Law and the Construction of the Information Society*, Cambridge: Harvard University Press.

Boyle, J. (1997), 'A Politics of Intellectual Property: Environmentalism for the Net', *Duke Law Journal*, **47**, 87–116.

Boyle, J. (1997), 'Foucault in Cyberspace: Surveillance, Sovereignty, and Hardwired Censors', *University of Cincinnati Law Review*, **66**(1), 177–205.

Boyle, J. (2003), 'The Second Enclosure Movement and the Construction of the Public Domain', *Law and Contemporary Problems*, **66**, 33–74.

Bradbury, D. (2006), 'Jockeying for Attention: Amateur Film Editors Can Subversively Recut Movies and Adverts', *The Guardian*, 20 April.

Braithwaite, John and Peter Drahos (2000), *Global Business Regulation*, Cambridge: Cambridge University Press.

Breyer, S. (1970), 'An Uneasy Case for Copyright in Books, Photocopies and Computer Programs', *Harvard Law Review*, **84**, 281–351.

British Library (2005), 'Microsoft and British Library Work Together to Make 25 Million Pages of Content Available To All', http://www.bl.uk/news/2005/pressrelease20051104.html, 4 November.

Broache, A. (2005), 'Time for Lawmakers to Act on Grokster?', CNet.News, http://news.com.com/2100-1028_3-5795314.html, 19 July.

Brown, G.O. (2003), 'Mmm . . . Free Samples (Innovation 1A)', The Creative Commons, http://creativecommons.org/weblog/archive/2003/03, 11 March.

Brown, G.O. (2003), 'Out Of The Way: How The Next Copyright Revolution Can Help The Next Scientific Revolution', *Public Library Of Science Biology*, **1**(1), 30–31.

Brown, G.O. (2004), 'Recombo Brazil', The Creative Commons, http://creativecommons.org/weblog/entry/4234, 4 June; and http://www.recombo.art.br/.

Brown, G.O. (2005), 'Response to Bill Gates', The Creative Commons, http://creativecommons.org/weblog/entry/5223, 9 January.

Burrell, Robert and Allison Coleman (2005), *Copyright Exceptions: The Digital Impact*, Cambridge: Cambridge University Press.

Byrne, S. (2005), 'Actors' Union Shouts "Cut" on Digital Film', *The Age*, 12 April.

Carnachan, R. (1999), 'Sampling and the Music Industry: A Discussion of the Implications of Copyright Law', *Te Mata Koi: Auckland University Law Review*, **8**(4), 1034–60.

Carney, D. (2003), 'Reps. Lofgren and Boucher Address FTAs and DMCA', *Tech Law Journal*, http://www.techlawjournal.com/topstories/2003/20030618.asp, 18 June.

Carr, R. (2005), 'Oxford–Google Digitisation Agreement', http://www.bodley.ox.ac.uk/google/.

Carrick, D. (2002), 'The Ruckus Over Replay TV', The Law Report, Radio National, http://www.abc.net.au/rn/talks/8.30/lawrpt/stories/s712304.htm, 29 October.

Carrick, D. (2005), 'Remixable Films', Law Report, Radio National ABC, http://www.abc.net.au/rn/talks/8.30/lawrpt/stories/s1379751.htm. 31 May.

Centre for International Economics (2004), *Economic Analysis of AUSFTA: Impact of the Bilateral Free Trade Agreement with the United States*, http://www.dfat.gov.au/trade/negotiations/us_fta/economic_analysis_report/austfta_report_040428.pdf.

Chilling Effects (2006), 'Google Ordered by Belgian Court to Remove all Belgian News and Photographs', http://www.chillingeffects.org/international/notice.cgi?NoticeID=5133, 5 September.

Chrisafis, A. (2005), 'Secret Talks Threaten Cultural Incentive', *The Guardian*, http://books.guardian.co.uk/news/articles/0,6109,1509280,00.html, 18 June.

Ciffolilli, A. (2003), 'Phantom Authority, Self-Selective Recruitment and Retention of Members in Virtual Communities: The Case of Wikipedia', *First Monday*, **8**(12), http://www.firstmonday.org/issues/issue8_12/ciffolilli/index.html.

Coats, W., M. Weinstein and E. Zimmerman (2005), 'Pre- and Post-Grokster Copyright Infringement Liability for Secondary and Tertiary Parties', 11th Annual Institute on Intellectual Property Law, Practising Law Institute Patents, Copyrights, Trademarks, and Literary Property Course Handbook Series, PLI Order No. 6036, 221.

Coble, H. (1998), 'Sonny Bono Copyright Term Extension Act', 144 Congressional Record H1458, 25 March.

Cohen, A. (2004), 'The Trouble With TiVo: Content Owners are Crying Copyright Infringement, and Cable Companies are Talking Customers', *IP Law & Business*, http://www.ipww.com.

Cohen, J. (2005), 'The Place of the User in Copyright Law', *Fordham Law Review*, **74**, 347–74.

Coleman, M.S. (2006), 'Google, the Khmer Rouge, and the Public Good', Address to the Professional/Scholarly Publishing Division of

the Association of American Publishers, http://www.umich.edu/pres/speeches/060206google.html, 6 February.
The Communications Law Centre (2005), 'Outline of Submissions on Behalf of Proposed Amici, the Australian Consumers' Association, Electronic Frontiers Australia Inc. and New South Wales Civil Liberties Inc. in *Universal Music Australia Pty Ltd.* v. *Sharman License Holdings Ltd*', 16 March.
The Computer and Communications Industry Association and US Internet Industry Association (2006), 'Brief of Amici Curiae in Support of the Defendant's Motion to Dismiss the Complaint in *Elektra Entertainment Group* v. *Barker*', http://www.ilrweb.com/viewILRPDF.asp?filename=elektra_barker_amicusbriefcomputercomm.
Consumer Electronics Association (2005), 'CEA Announces Declaration of Innovation Independence: Presents Six Principles to Guide Intellectual Property Debate', Arlington, Virginia, 16 March.
Consumer Electronics Manufacturers Association (1999), 'Amicus Brief in *RIAA* v. *Diamond Multimedia Systems Inc.*'
Coombe, Rosemary (1998), *The Cultural Life Of Intellectual Properties*, Durham, NC: Duke University Press.
Coombe, R. (2003), 'Fear, Hope, and Longing for the Future of Authorship and a Revitalized Public Domain in Global Regimes of Intellectual Property', *De Paul Law Review*, **52**, 1171–91.
Copyright Law Review Committee (2002), *Simplification of the Copyright Act* 1968, Canberra: Attorney-General's Department.
Cornish, William and David Llewelyn (2003), *Intellectual Property: Patents, Copyright, Trade Marks and Allied Rights*, 5th edn, London: Sweet & Maxwell.
Crawford, K. (2005), 'Adaptation: Tracking the Ecologies of Music and Peer-to-Peer Networks', *Media International Australia incorporating Culture and Policy*, **114**, 30–39.
Crawford, S. (2003), 'The Biology of the Broadcast Flag', *Hastings Communications and Entertainment Law Journal*, **25**, 603–52.
Crisp, L. (2006), 'Gearing Up for a Title Fight', *Australian Financial Review*, 25 January, p. 52.
Crofts, S., J. Dilley, M. Fox, A. Retsema and B. Williams (2005), 'Podcasting: A New Technology In Search of Viable Business Models', *First Monday*, **10**(9), http://firstmonday.org/issues/issue10_9/crofts/index.html.
Cunard, J. (2002), 'Brief for College Art Association et al. as Amici Curiae Supporting Petitioners in *Eldred* v. *Ashcroft*', 20 May.
Curry, A. (2006), 'Judgement Day', Curry.com, http://curry.podshow.com/?p=49, 9 March 2006.

Curzon Price, T. (2006), 'iCommons for Beginners', *Open Democracy*, http://www.opendemocracy.net/arts-commons/lowdown_3659.jsp, 20 June.
Darlymple, S. (2005), 'Steve Job Discusses iPods, Music Labels and Intel Macs', *MacWorld*, http://www.macworld.com/news/2005/09/20/jobsparis/index.php, 20 September.
Darnton, Robert (1982), *The Literary Underground of the Old Regime*, Cambridge, Mass: Harvard University Press.
Darnton, Robert (1990), *The Kiss of Lamourette: Reflections in Cultural History*, New York and London: W.W. Norton and Company.
Darnton, Robert (1995), *The Forbidden Best-Sellers of Pre-Revolutionary France*, New York and London: W.W. Norton and Company.
Davidson, J. (2004), 'Billions at Stake in Kazaa Court Case', *Australian Financial Review*, 7 December, p. 30.
Davidson, J. (2004), 'Win or Lose, Kazaa Won't Be Shut Down', *Australian Financial Review*, 3 December, p. 64.
Dean, K. (2004), 'BBC to Open Floodgates', *Wired News*, 16 June.
Dean, K. (2005), 'We're Creative Commonists, Bill', *Wired News*, http://www.wired.com/news/culture/0,1284,66209,00.html, 8 January.
Deazley, Ronan (2004), *On the Origin of the Right to Copy: Charting the Movement of Copyright in Eighteenth Century Britain*, Oxford: Hart Publishing.
deBeer, Jeremy (2005), 'Constitutional Jurisdiction over Para-copyright Laws', in Michael Geist (ed.), *In The Public Interest: The Future of Canadian Copyright Law*, Toronto: Irwin Law, pp. 89–124.
deBeer, J. (2005), 'The Role of Levies in Canada's Digital Music Market', *Canadian Journal of Law & Technology*, **4**(3), 153–68.
deBeer, J. (2006), 'How Restrictive Terms and Technologies Backfired on Sony BMG Music: Part 1', *Internet and E-Commerce Law in Canada*, **6**(12), 93–9.
deBeer, J. (2006), 'How Restrictive Terms and Technologies Backfired on Sony BMG Music: Part 2', *Internet and E-Commerce Law in Canada*, **7**(1), 1–8.
deBeer, J. (2006), 'Sony Settles Canadian Class Actions', http://www.jeremydebeer.ca/content/view/87/2/, 31 August.
Dee, P. (2004), *AUSFTA: A Response to Comments by the Department of Foreign Affairs and Trade*, the Senate Select Committee on the Free Trade Agreement, June, http://www.aph.gov.au/Senate/committee/freetrade_ctte/rel_links/response_dfat.pdf.
Dee, P. (2004), *The Australia–US Free Trade Agreement: An Assessment, A Report Prepared for the Senate Select Committee on the Free Trade*

Agreement, June, http://www.aph.gov.au/Senate/committee/freetrade_ctte/rel_links/dee_fta_report.pdf.

Demers, Joanna (2006), *Steal This Music: How Intellectual Property Law Affects Musical Creativity*, Athens and London: The University of Georgia Press.

Deutsch, S. and D. McGuire (2004), 'Supreme Court Internet Privacy Decision', *Washington Post*, 14 October.

DGA (2002), 'DGA responds and counterclaims against Robert Huntsman and CleanFlicks; adds motion picture studios to suit, DGA Press Releases, http://www.dga.org/index2.php 3?chg=', 20 September.

Dibbell, J. (2004), 'We Pledge Allegiance to the Penguin', *Wired Magazine*, **12**(11), http://www.wired.com/wired/archive/12.11/linux.html.

Diebold Inc. (2003), 'Opposition to motion for Preliminary Injunction in *Online Policy Group* et al. v. *Diebold Inc*.' http://www.eff.org/legal/ISP_liability/OPG_v._Diebold/diebold_opp_prelim_injunct.pdf.

Doctorow, C. (2004), 'Written Testimony to Select Committee on Culture, Media and Sport', Electronic Frontier Foundation, http://www.eff.org/IP/BBC_CMSC_testimony.php, 11 September.

Doctorow, C. (2006), 'Copyright Office Head Denounces "Big Mistake" of Extending Copyright', Boing Boing, http://www.boingboing.net/2006/02/21/copyright_office_hea.html, 21 February.

Doctorow, C. (2006), 'Why Publishing Houses Should Send Fruit-Baskets to Google', Boing Boing, http://www.boingboing.net/2006/02/14/why_publishing_shoul.html, 14 February.

Dodd, T. (2004), 'Trade Deal Bites Unis On Copyright Costs', *The Australian Financial Review*, 14 February, p. 16.

Downhill Battle (2004), 'Incredible Success', Grey Tuesday, http://www.greytuesday.org/.

Drahos, Peter (1994), 'Decentring Communication: The Dark Side of Intellectual Property', in Tom Campbell and Wojciech Sadurski (eds), *Freedom of Communication*, Aldershot: Dartmouth, p. 257.

Drahos, Peter (1996), *A Philosophy of Intellectual Property*, Aldershot: Dartmouth.

Drahos, P. (2005), 'Access to Knowledge: Time for a Treaty', *Bridges*, **4**, 15–17.

Drahos, Peter and John Braithwaite (2002), *Information Feudalism*, London: Earthscan Publications.

Drassinower, Abraham (2005), 'Taking User Rights Seriously', in Michael Geist (ed.), *In The Public Interest: The Future of Canadian Copyright Law*, Toronto: Irwin Law, pp. 462–79.

Dyke, G. (2003), 'Richard Dunn Memorial Lecture', BBC, http://www.bbc.co.uk/pressoffice/speeches/stories/dyke_richard_dunn.shtml, 24 August.

Eckersley, P (2004), 'Virtual Markets for Virtual Goods: The Mirror Image of Digital Copyright?', *Harvard Journal of Law and Technology*, **18**(1), 85–166.
Edelman, Bernard (1979), *Ownership of the Image: Elements for a Marxist Theory of Law*, London: Routledge.
Editorial (2001), 'Is a Government Archive the Best Option?', *Science*, 23 March, **291**(5512), 2318–19.
Editorial (2003), 'A Radical Rethink', *The Economist*, http://www.economist.com/opinion/displayStory.cfm?story_id=1547223, 23 January.
Editorial (2003), 'The Coming Of Copyright Perpetuity', *The New York Times*, 16 January.
EFF (2003), 'Amicus Brief in *Huntsman* v. *Soderbergh*', http://www.eff.org/legal/cases/Huntsman_v._Soderbergh/20030618_eff_amicus.pdf.
EFF (2003), 'Court Rules Verizon Can Refuse to ID Customers to Music Industry', 19 December.
EFF (2003), 'Recording Industry Plans "Amnesty" for Music Sharers: Electronic Frontier Foundation Says Share, Get Artists Paid', 5 September.
EFF (2003), 'Recording Industry Withdraws Music Sharing Lawsuit: Lack Of Due Process Leads To Mistaken Identity', 24 September.
EFF (2003), 'Why RIAA's "Amnesty" Offer Is A Sham', 9 September.
EFF (2004), 'Amicus Curiae Brief of Consumer and Privacy Groups in Support of Appellant Charter Communications, Inc.', 23 January.
EFF (2004), 'Digital Betamax: ReplayTV Owners Stand up to Hollywood to Defend Digital VCRs', http://www.eff.org/IP/Video/Newmark_v._Turner/.
EFF (2004), 'Grey Tuesday: A Quick Overview of the Legal Terrain', http://www.eff.org/IP/grey tuesday.php.
EFF (2004), *Online Policy Group* et al. v. *Diebold Inc*. at http://www.eff.org/legal/ISP_liability/OPG_v._Diebold/.
EFF (2004), 'Re JibJab Media Inc and Ludlow Music Inc', http://www.eff.org/legal/cases/JibJab_v._Ludlow/20040728_Ltr_to_LiCalsi.pdf.
EFF (2005), 'Amicus Brief in *Perfect 10 Inc.* v. *Google Inc.*', 12 October.
EFF (2005), 'An Open Letter to Sony BMG', http://www.eff.org/IP/DRM/Sony-BMG/?f=open-letter-2005-11-14.html, 14 November.
EFF (2005), 'DMCA Triennial Rulemaking: Failing the Digital Consumer', http://www.eff.org/IP/DMCA/copyrightoffice/DMCA_rulemaking_broken.pdf, 1 December.
EFF (2005), 'EFF and Sony BMG Reached Settlement over Flawed DRM', http://www.eff.org/news/archives/2005_12.php#004287, 29 December.
EFF (2005), 'Music Industry Must Respect Privacy of Filesharers: Ruling in Charter Case Smashes DMCA Subpoena Powers', 4 January.

EFF (2005), 'RIAA v. the People: Two Years Later', http://www.eff.org/IP/P2P/RIAAatTWO_FINAL.pdf, 3 November.

EFF (2005), 'Sony BMG Info', http://www.eff.org/IP/DRM/Sony-BMG/.

EFF (2006), 'Amicus Brief in Support of Defendant's Motion to Dismiss the Complaint in *Elektra Entertainment Group* v. *Barker*', http://www.eff.org/IP/P2P/RIAA_v._ThePeople/elektra_v._barker/elektra-amicus-efiled.pdf.

EFF (2006), 'Judge Grants Final Approval for Sony BMG CD Settlement', http://www.eff.org/news/archives/2006_05.php, May 22.

Einhorn, M. (2002), 'Copyright, Prevention, and Rational Governance: File-Sharing and Napster', *Columbia Journal for Law and the Arts*, **24**, 449–62.

Elektra Entertainment Group et al. (2006), 'Plaintiff's Opposition to Defendant's Motion to Dismiss the Complaint in *Elektra Entertainment Group* v. *Barker*', http://www.ilrweb.com/viewILRPDF.asp?filename=elektra_barker_oppositiontomoti.

Elkin-Koren, N. (2005), 'What Contracts Can't Do: The Limits of Private Ordering in Facilitating a Creative Commons', *Fordham Law Review*, **74**, 375–422.

Elkman, S. and A. Christie (2004), 'A Negotiated Solution to Audio Home Recording? Lessons from the US Audio Home Recording Act of 1992', *University of New South Wales Law Journal*, **27**(1), 123–46.

Encyclopaedia Britannica (2005), 'Fatally Flawed: Refuting the Recent Study on Encyclopedic Accuracy by the Journal *Nature*', http://corporate.britannica.com/britannica_nature_response.pdf, March.

Englert, E. (2002), 'Brief of George Akerlof et al. as Amici Curiae in Support of Petitioners in *Eldred* v. *Ashcroft*', 20 May.

European Commission (2005), 'European Digital Library Proposed', http://europa.eu.int/idabc/en/document/4239/330, 4 May.

European Commission (2006), 'i2010 Digital Libraries Initiative', http://europa.eu.int/information_society/activities/digital_libraries/index_en.htm.

European Consumer Law Group (2005), *Copyright Law and Consumer Protection*, Institute of Information Law, the University of Amsterdam, http://www.ivir.nl/publications/other/copyrightlawconsumerprotection.pdf

Evangelista, B. (2003), 'Piracy Suits Chill Valley, Moves Peril Profit, Techies Say', *San Francisco Chronicle*, 20 February.

Evers, J. (2005), 'Sony Halts Production of "Rootkit" CDs', CNet.News, 11 November.

Fagin, M., F. Pasquale and K. Weatherall (2002), 'Beyond Napster: Using Antitrust Law to Advance and Enhance Online Music Distribution', *Boston University Journal of Science and Technology Law*, **8**, 451–73.

Farber, D. (2006), 'Mashups and the Law', ZDNet, http://blogs.zdnet.com/BTL/?p=2614, 20 February.

Fels, A. and F. Brenchley (2005), 'Copyright: Divide and Rule', *The Australian Financial Review*, 18 October, p. 62.

Felten, E. (2005), 'BitTorrent: The Next Main Event', *Freedom to Tinker*, http://www.freedom-to-tinker.com/?p=859, 28 June.

Felten, E. (2005), 'Legality of Design Decisions, and Footnote 12 in Grokster', *Freedom to Tinker*, http://www.freedom-to-tinker.com/?p=857, 27 June.

Fisher, William (2004), *Promises to Keep: Technology, Law, and the Future of Entertainment*, Stanford: Stanford University Press.

Fitzgerald, B. (2005), 'Creative Choices: Changes to the Creative Commons', *Media International Australia*, **114**, 83–6.

Fitzgerald, B. and N. Suzor (2005), 'Legal Issues For the Use of Free and Open Source Software in Government', *Melbourne University Law Review*, **29**, 412–47.

Fitzgerald, B., T. Cochrane, M. Garlick and N. Suzor (2005), 'Re Re-Authorisation of Collective Administration of Music Performing Rights by APRA', The Creative Commons, http://www.law.qut.edu.au/files/ACCCFinal31.pdf, 7 October.

Francis Cahill, S. (2002), 'Dot-Com Sues Law Firm Over Advice: MP3.com Says Cooley Godward Should Have Warned of Copyright Issues', udcyberspacelaw.org, 7 February.

Fraser, M. (2005), 'Information Wants to be Free?', Presentation to the Copyright Symposium, http://www.copyright.com.au/reports%20&%20papers/Copyright_symposium_2005.pdf, 17 November.

Frere-Jones, S. (2005), 'The New Math of Mash-Ups', *The New Yorker*, http://www.newyorker.com/printables/critics/050110crmu_music, 3 January.

Friends of the Creative Domain (2004), 'Friends of the Creative Domain Call for a True Creative Archive', the Union for the Public Domain, http://www.public-domain.org/?q=node/36&PHPSESSID=1f6fbf319a31fe9a6eb2fbc3ec12dadb, 10 June.

Frow, John (1997), *Time and Commodity Culture: Essays in Cultural Theory and Postmodernity*, Oxford: Oxford University Press.

Gaines, Jane (1992), *Contested Culture: The Image, the Voice and the Law*, London: British Film Industry Publishing.

Ganley, P. (2006), 'Google Book Search: Fair Use, Fair Dealing and the Case for Intermediary Copying', Baker and McKenzie, http://papers.ssrn.com/sol3/papers.cfm?abstract_id=875384.

Ganley, P. (2006), 'Surviving Grokster: Innovation and the Future of Peer-to-Peer', *European Intellectual Property Review*, **28**(1), 15–25.

Gantz, John and Jack Rochester (2005), *Pirates of the Digital Millennium: How the Intellectual Property Wars Damage Our Personal Freedoms, Our Jobs, and the World Economy*, Upper Saddle River, NJ: Prentice-Hall/Financial Times.

Garlick, M. (2006), 'Creative Commons Licenses Upheld in Dutch Court', The Creative Commons, http://creativecommons.org/press-releases/entry/5822, 15 March.

Garlick, M. (2006), 'Spanish Court Recognizes CC-Music', The Creative Commons, http://creativecommons.org/weblog/entry/5830, 23 March.

Garrett, P. (2005), 'Currency House: Arts and Public Life', http://www.petergarrett.com.au/c.asp?id=95, 20 October.

Geist, Michael (ed.) (2005), *In The Public Interest: The Future of Canadian Copyright Law*, Toronto: Irwin Law.

Geist, M. (2003), 'Web Quandary For Regulators', *Toronto Star*, 25 August.

Geist, Michael (2005), 'Anti-Circumvention Legislation and Competition Policy: Defining a Canadian Way', in Michael Geist (ed.), *In The Public Interest: The Future of Canadian Copyright Law*, Toronto: Irwin Law, pp. 221–50.

Geist, M. (2005), 'Grokster and the Future of File-Sharing', *Toronto Star*, http://www.michaelgeist.ca/resc/html_bkup/june292005.html, 29 June.

Geist, M. (2005), 'National Web Library – Doable, Affordable, Visionary', *The Toronto Star*, 10 January.

Geist, M. (2005), 'Sony's Long-term Rootkit CD Woes', BBC News, 21 November.

Geist, M. (2006), 'Legal Fallout from Sony's CD Woes', BBC News, 3 January.

Geist, M. (2006), 'Our Own Cultural Land: Cultural Monopoly and the Trouble with Copyright', The Hart House Lecture, http://individual.utoronto.ca/dtsang/hhlecture/Resources/Geist_2006.pdf.

Geller, P.E. (2000), 'Copyright History And The Future: What's Culture Got To Do With It?', *Journal of the Copyright Society of the U.S.A.*, **47**, 209–64.

Gervais, D. (2004), 'Canadian Copyright Law Post-CCH', *Intellectual Property Journal*, **18**(2), 131–67.

Gervais, D. (2004), 'The Price of Social Norms: Towards a Liability Regime for File-Sharing', *Journal of Intellectual Property Law*, **12**(1), 39–73.

Gervais, Daniel and Elizabeth Judge (2005), *Intellectual Property: The Law in Canada*, Toronto: Thomson Carswell.

Ghosh, Rishab Aiyer (ed.) (2005), *Code: Collaborative Ownership and the Digital Economy*, Cambridge, Mass. and London: The MIT Press.

Giles, J. (2005), 'Internet Encyclopaedias Go Head to Head', *Nature*, http://www.nature.com/news/2005/051212/full/438900a.html, 15 December, 900–901.

Ginsburg, J. (2002), 'How Copyright Got A Bad Name For Itself', *Columbia Journal of Law and the Arts,* **26**(1), 61–73.

Ginsburg, Jane and Rochelle Dreyfuss (eds) (2005), *Intellectual Property Stories*, New York: Foundation Press.

Ginsburg, J. and S. Ricketson (2006), 'Inducers and Authorisers: A Comparison of the US Supreme Court's Grokster Decision and the Australian Federal Court's Kazaa Ruling', *Media and Arts Law Review*, **11**(1), 1–25.

Glatstein, B. (2004), 'Tertiary Copyright Liability', *The University of Chicago Law Review*, **71**, 1605–35.

Globes (2006), 'Walla! Threatens to Sue Google over News Site', TMCNet.com, http://www.tmcnet.com/usubmit/2006/03/07/1438447.htm, 7 March.

Goetz, T. (2003), 'Open Source Everywhere', *Wired Magazine*, **11**(11), http://www.wired.com/wired/archive/11.11/opensource_pr.html.

Goetz, T. (2004), 'Sample the Future', *Wired Magazine*, **12**(11), http://www.wired.com/wired/archive/12.11/sample.html.

Goldman, J. (2003), 'KaZaA CEO Speaks Out', G4TV, http://www.g4tv.com/techtvvault/features/44860/KaZaA_CEO_Speaks_Out.html, 5 August.

Goldsmith, Jack and Tim Wu (2006), *Who Controls the Internet? Illusions of a Borderless World*, Oxford: Oxford University Press.

Goldstein, Paul (2003), *Copyright's Highway: From Gutenberg to the Celestial Jukebox*, Stanford: Stanford University Press.

Google (2004), 'Google Checks Out Library Books', http://www.google.com/press/pressrel/print_library.html, 14 December.

Google (2004), 'Yahoo and Google Resolve Disputes', http://www.google.com/press/pressrel/yahoo.html, 9 August.

Google (2005), *Annual Report*, Mountain View, California.

Google (2006), 'Google Book Search and US Library Partnership', Press Release, http://www.google.com/press/annc/books_uclibrary.html, August.

Google (2006), 'The Google Books Library Project and the University of California', http://www.cdlib.org/news/google.html.

Google and YouTube (2006), 'Google Closes Acquisition of YouTube', http:www.youtube.com/press_room_entry?entry=Awpf9c9qJDC, 13 November.

Gorman, M. (2004), 'Google and God's Mind', *Los Angeles Times*, 17 November.

Gowers, Andrew (2006), *Gowers Review of Intellectual Property*, London: HM Treasury, December, http://www.hm-treasury.gov.uk/media/583/91/pbr06_gowers_report_755.pdf.

Gramsci, Antonio (1971), *Selections from the Prison Notebooks of Antonio Gramsci*, London: Lawrence & Wishart.

Gratz, J. (2005), '7th Circuit: Downloading is not Fair Use', joegratz.net, http://www.joegratz.net/archives/2005/12/10/7th-cir-p2p-downloading-is-not-fair-use/, 10 December.

Gray, P. (2004), 'Sharman Shuffles Legal Team' *Wired News*, http://www.wired.com/news/digiwood/0,1412,63062,00.html?tw=wn_tophead_4, 15 April.

Greenberg, L. (1992), 'The Art of Appropriation: Puppies, Piracy and Post-modernism', *Cardozo Arts And Entertainment Law Review*, **11**, 1–33.

Greenhouse, L. (2002), 'Supreme Court To Intervene In Internet Copyright Dispute', *The New York Times*, 19 February.

Griffiths, Jonathan and Uma Suthersanen (eds) (2005), *Copyright and Free Speech: Comparative and International Analyses*, Oxford: Oxford University Press.

Groom, Nick (2002), *The Forger's Shadow: How Forgery Changed The Course Of Literature*, London: Picador.

Hacker, S. (2004), 'Thoughts on the Grey Album', http://birdhouse.org/blog/archives/001233.php, 27 February.

Halbert, D., C. Darch, A. Story and C. South (2006), 'Education and Development on the High Seas of Copyright Infringement', *Open Democracy*, http://www.opendemocracy.net/arts-commons/icommons_3664.jsp, 21 June.

Halderman, J.A. and E. Felten (2006), 'Lessons from the Sony CD DRM Episode', http://itpolicy.princeton.edu/pub/sonydrm-ext.pdf, 14 February.

Hamilton, A. (2003), 'Rap Is A Foreign Language, Rules Rueful Judge', *The Times*, http://www.timesonline.co.uk/article/0,2-704600,00.html, 6 June.

Hamilton, Ian (1992), *Keepers of the Flame: Literary Estates and the Rise of Biography*, London: Hutchinson.

Hamilton, Sheryl (2005), 'Made in Canada: A Unique Approach to Internet Service Provider Liability and Copyright Infringement', in Michael Geist (ed.), *In The Public Interest: The Future of Canadian Copyright Law*, Toronto: Irwin Press, pp. 285–308.

Hamm, S. (2005), 'Sony BMG's Costly Silence', *Business Week*, 29 November.

Hammersley, B. (2004), 'Personal Soundtracks', *The Guardian*, http://www.guardian.co.uk/online/howto/story/0,15824,1433785,00.html, 2 December.

Handler, M. (2005), 'Lessons from the Google News Controversy', *Open Democracy*, http://www.opendemocracy.net/media-copyrightlaw/google_3130.jsp, 16 December.

Hanratty, E. (2005), 'Google Library: Beyond Fair Use?', *Duke Law and Technology Review*, **10**, http://www.law.duke.edu/journals/dltr/articles/2005dltr0010.html, 15 April.

Harrison, A. (2006), 'The Pirate Bay: Here to Stay', *Wired News*, 13 March.

Haughey, M. (2004), 'Interview with Stewart Butterfield, Flickr', The Creative Commons, http://creativecommons.org/image/flickr, July.

Hebb, M. (2003), 'Modest Changes to Copyright Debated', *National Post*, 17 June, FP 11.

Heins, Marjorie and Tricia Beckles (2005), *Will Fair Use Survive? Free Expression in the Age of Copyright Control*, Brennan Center for Justice, New York University School of Law, http://www.fepproject.org/policyreports/WillFairUseSurvive.pdf.

Heller, M. and R. Eisenberg (1998), 'Can Patents Deter Innovation? The Anticommons in Biomedical Research', *Science*, **280**(5364), 698–701, 1 May.

Hertz, K. (2004), 'Re: JibJab Media/Unauthorized Use of "This Land is Your Land"', Sonnenschein, Nath and Rosenthal LLP, http://www.eff.org/legal/cases/JibJab_v._Ludlow/20040727_jibjabthreat.pdf.

Higgins, D. (2000), 'Metallica Gets Heavy with its Fans', *The Sydney Morning Herald*, 5 May, p. 1.

Hill, B.M. (2005), 'Towards a Standard of Freedom: Creative Commons and the Free Software Movement', http://mako.cc/writing/toward_a_standard_of_freedom.html, 29 July.

Hill, R. (2004), 'US Free Trade Agreement Implementation Bill 2004 (Cth)', *Senate Hansard*, 12 August, 26428, http://www.aph.gov.au/hansard/senate/dailys/ds120804.pdf.

Hinze, G. (2003), 'The Electronic Frontier Foundation Comments Regarding Phillips Fox' Issues Papers On The Australian Digital Agenda Review', http://www.eff.org/IP/DRM/DMCA/20031003_australian_comments.php, 30 September.

Hof, R. (2005), 'Ten Years of Chilled Innovation: That's the fallout from the Supreme Court ruling on file-sharing technologies, says Creative Commons Chair and Law Prof Larry Lessig', *Business Week*, 29 June.

Hogberg, S. (2006), 'The Search for Intent-Based Doctrines of Secondary Liability in Copyright Law', *Columbia Law Review*, **106**, 909–57.

Hogge, B. (2006), 'What Moves a Movement?', *Open Democracy*, http://www.opendemocracy.net/media-commons/movement_3686.jsp, 27 June.

Home Recording Rights Coalition (2005), 'HRRC Urges Passage of Betamax Codification: Bill Would Promote User Freedom under DMCA', http://www.hrrc.org/news/PressRelease041405.html, 14 April.
Home Recording Rights Coalition (2006), 'Record Labels Break Compacts with Consumers, Congress, and Courts: Suit Against XM Trashes Labels' AHRA and Grokster Assurances', 17 May.
Honan, M. (2003), 'The Enigma of Earth Station 5', *Salon*, http://www.salon.com/tech/feature/2003/12/03/es 5/index.html, 3 December.
House of Representatives Standing Committee on Legal and Constitutional Affairs (2006), *Review of Technological Protection Measures Exceptions*, Canberra: Australian Parliament, http://www.aph.gov.au/house/committee/laca/protection/report/fullreport.pdf.
Howard-Spink, S. (2004), 'Grey Tuesday, Online Cultural Activism and the Mash-Up of Music and Politics', *First Monday*, **9**(10), http://www.firstmonday.org/issues/issue9_10/howard/index.html.
Howard-Spink, S. (2006), 'Tropicalia and The Quest for a Cultural Commons', *Open Democracy*, http://www.opendemocracy.net/arts-commons/tropicalia_3675.jsp, 23 June.
Hugenholtz, Bernt (ed.) (1996), *The Future of Copyright in a Digital Environment*, The Hague: Kluwer Law International.
Hugenholtz, B. (2006), 'Dutch Court Upholds Creative Commons Licence', Creative Commons Canada, http://creativecommons.ca/blog/?p=165, 14 March.
Hugenholtz, Bernt and Lucie Guilbault (eds) (2006), *The Future of the Public Domain – Identifying the Commons in Information Law*, The Hague: Kluwer Law International.
Hughes, J. (2005), 'On the Logic of Suing One's Customers and the Dilemma of Infringement-Based Business Models', *Cardozo Arts and Entertainment Law Journal*, **22**, 725–66.
Hunter, D. (2005), 'Culture War', *Texas Law Review*, **83**(4), 1105–36.
Hunter, D. and G. Lastowka (2004), 'Amateur-to-Amateur', *William and Mary Law Review,* **46**, 951–1030.
IFPI (2006), 'Illegal Music File-sharers Targeted by Fresh Wave of Legal Action', http://www.ifpi.org/content/section_news/20060404. html, 4 April.
IFPI (2006), 'Kazaa Settles with Record Industry and Goes Legitimate', http://www.ifpi.org/site-content/press/20060727.html, 27 July.
Intel (2003), 'Amicus Brief in *Huntsman* v. *Soderbergh*', http://www.eff.org/legal/cases/Huntsman_v._Soderbergh/intel_amicus.pdf.
Intellectual Property and Competition Review Committee (2000), *Review of Intellectual Property Legislation Under the Competition Principles Agreement*, http://www.ipcr.gov.au/IPAustralia.pdf, September.

Jack, I. (2003), 'Ottawa Champions Copyright – or Some of It: Amendment to Benefit Small Band of Authors with Unpublished Works', *National Post*, 12 May, FP.

Jaszi, P. (1991), 'Toward a Theory of Copyright: The Metamorphoses of "Authorship"', *Duke Law Journal*, 465–502.

Jaszi, P. (1995), 'The Copyright Term Extension Act of 1995: Testimony Before The Senate Committee on the Judiciary', 104th Cong., 1st Session, 20 September.

Jaszi, P. (1996), 'Goodbye To All That: A Reluctant (And Perhaps Premature) Adieu To A Constitutionally-Grounded Discourse Of Public Interest In Copyright Law', *Vanderbilt Journal Of Transnational Law*, **29**, 595–611.

Jaszi, P. (2002), 'Brief of Amici Curiae National Writers Union et al. in *Eldred* v. *Ashcroft*', 20 May.

Jefferson, Thomas (1788), 'Letter to James Madison', 31 July, in Julian Parkes Boyd (1956), *13 Papers of Thomas Jefferson*, Princeton: Princeton University Press.

Jensen, J.C. (2004), 'Re: *The Grey Album* and Misappropriation of Capitol Records, Inc.'s Sound Recordings', Cowan, Liebowitz and Latman, P.C.

Job, S. (2007), 'Thoughts on Music', Apple, http://www.apple.com/hotnews/thoughtsonmusic/, 6 February.

Johnston, C. (2003), 'Pirate Queen', *The Age*, http://www.theage.com.au/articles/2003/03/04/1046540185222.html, 5 March.

Jones, Dylan (2005), *iPod, Therefore I Am: Thinking Inside the White Box*, London and New York: Bloomsbury.

Kahle, B., R. Prelinger and M. Jackson (2001), 'Public Access to Digital Material', *D-Lib Magazine*, **7**(10) http://www.dlib.org/dlib/october01/kahle/10kahle.html, October.

Kanellos, M. (2005), 'Gates Taking a Seat in Your Den', C/Net News.com, http://news.com.com/2102-1041_3-5514121.html, 11 January.

Kantor, A. (2005), 'Sony: The Rootkit of All Evil?', *USA Today*, http://www.usatoday.com/tech/columnist/andrewkantor/2005-11-17-sony-rootkit_x.htm, 17 November.

Kaplicer, B. (2000), 'Rap Music and De Minimis Copying: Applying the Ringgold and Sandoval Approach to Digital Samples', *Cardozo Arts and Entertainment Law Journal*, **18**(1), 227–55.

Katyal, S. (2002), 'A Legal Malpractice Claim By MP3.com: In The Changing Area Of Cyberlaw, Is A Crystal Ball Necessary To Avoid Liability?', Findlaw, 7 February.

Katyal, S. (2004), 'The New Surveillance', *Case Western Law Review*, **54**, 297–385.

Katyal, S. (2006), 'Performance, Property and the Slashing of Gender in Fan Fiction', *American University of Gender, Social Policy and the Law*, **14**, 461–518.

Kelleher, K. (2005), 'Who's Afraid of Google? Everyone', *Wired Magazine*, **13**(12), 233, http://www.wired.com/wired/archive/13.12/google.html.

Keller, M. (2004), 'Stanford and Google to Make Library Books Available Online', http://www.stanford.edu/dept/news/pr/2004/pr-google-011205.html, 14 December.

Kerr, Ian (2005), 'If Left to their Own Devices . . . How DRM and Anti-Circumvention Laws Can Be Used to Hack Privacy', in Michael Geist (ed.), *In The Public Interest: The Future of Canadian Copyright Law*, Toronto: Irwin Law, pp. 167–210.

Kerr, I. and J. Bailey (2004), 'The Implications of Digital Rights Management for Privacy and Freedom of Expression', *Journal of Information, Communication & Ethics in Society*, **2**, 87–97.

Kerr, I., A. Maurushat and C. Tacit (2003), 'Technical Protection Measures: Tilting at the Copyright Windmill', *Ottawa Law Review*, **34**, 9–82.

Kim, S. (2006), 'Taking De Minimis out of the Mix: The Sixth Circuit Threatens to Pull the Plug on Digital Sampling in Bridgeport Music Inc. v. Dimension Films', *Villanova Sports and Entertainment Law Journal*, **13**, 103–31.

King, B. (2002), 'Napster's Assets Go For A Song', *Wired News*, http://www.wired.com/news/digiwood/0,1412,56633,00.html, 28 November.

King, V. (2002), 'James Joyce's "Ulysses" – A Case Of Preparatory Manuscripts And Revived Copyright', *Entertainment Law Review*, **13**(4), 86–90.

Kirkman, C. (2005), '7th Circuit Rules in P2P Infringement User Case', Silicon Valley Media Law Blog, http://www.joegratz.net/archives/2005/12/10/7th-cir-p2p-downloading-is-not-fair-use/, 10 December.

Klang, M. (2006), 'Raiding Pirate Bay', Klang Blog: Sound and Fury, Signifying Nothing, http://www.ituniv.se/~klang/wrote/2006/05/31/raiding-pirate-bay/, 31 May.

Klang, Mathias (2006), *Disruptive Technologies: Effects of Technology Regulation on Democracy*, doctoral dissertation, Göteborg University.

Klein, Naomi (2000), *No Logo: Taking Aim At The Brand Bullies*, London: Harper Collins.

Kleiner, K. (2003), 'Freedom Fighter: Interview With Harold Varmus', *New Scientist*, 1 November, **2419**, 46–9.

Knopf, H. (2003), 'Mouse in the House: A New Bill in Ottawa Appears to Adopt U.S.-Style Copyright Term Extension', *National Post*, 7 June, FP 11.

Koman, R. (2003), 'Eldred Opinion Met With Anger, Determination', The O'Reilly Network, http://www.oreillynet.com/pub/a/policy/2003/01/16/eldred.html, 16 January.

Koman, R. (2005), 'Remixing Culture: An Interview with Lawrence Lessig', O'Reilly Network, http://www.oreillynet.com/pub/a/policy/2005/02/24/lessig.html, 24 February.

Krazit, T. (2006), 'Burst.com Sues For Patent Infringement', CNET News, http://news.com.com/2100-1047_3-6062067.html, 17 April.

Ku, R. (2002), 'The Creative Destruction of Copyright: Napster and the New Economics of Digital Technology', *The University of Chicago Law Review*, **69**, 263–324.

Kulash, D. (2005), 'Buy, Play, Trade, Repeat', *The New York Times*, 6 December, p. 27.

Lametti, David (2005), 'Coming to Terms with Copyright', in Michael Geist (ed.), *In The Public Interest: The Future of Canadian Copyright Law*, Toronto: Irwin Inc., pp. 480–516.

Landes, W. and R. Posner (1989), 'An Economic Analysis of Copyright Law', *Journal of Legal Studies*, **18**, 325–64.

Landes, W. and R. Posner (2002), 'Indefinitely Renewable Copyright', Working Paper, Olin Center for Law and Economics, the University of Chicago, http://www.law.uchicago.edu/Lawecon/WkngPprs_151–175/154.wml-rap.copyright.new.pdf.

Landes, William and Richard Posner (2004), *The Economic Structure of Intellectual Property Law*, Harvard: Harvard University Press.

Lasica, J.D. (2005), *Darknet: Hollywood's War Against the Digital Generation*, Hoboken, NJ: Wiley & Sons.

LeClerc, P. (2004), 'NYPL Partners with Google: Full Text of Thousands of Books to be Made Searchable', New York Public Library, http://www.nypl.org/press/2004/google.cfm, 14 December.

Lee, J. (2004), 'Click at Your Own Risk', *The Sydney Morning Herald*, 3 August.

Lee, T. (2005), 'Don't Stop Google', *Cato Institute*, http://www.cato.org/pub_display.php?pub_id=4000, 23 July.

Lessig, L. (2001), 'Let the Stories Go', *The New York Times*, 30 April.

Lessig, L. (2002), 'Free Culture', Keynote Address at Oscon, http://www.oreillynet.com/pub/a/policy/2002/08/15/lessig.html, 15 August.

Lessig, L. (2003), 'Losing', Stanford Law School, http://cyberlaw.stanford.edu/lessig/blog/, 16 January.

Lessig, L. (2003), 'Protecting Mickey Mouse at Art's Expense', *The New York Times*, 18 January.

Lessig, L. (2003), 'The BBC's Lessons for America', *The Financial Times*, 8 September.

Lessig, L. (2004), 'The Black and White Waged By Grey Tuesday', Lessig Blog, http://www.lessig.org/blog/archives/001754.shtml, 24 February.
Lessig, L. (2005), 'A Rotten Ruling', *Wired Magazine*, **13**(9), 94.
Lessig, L. (2005), 'CC in Review', The Creative Commons, http://creativecommons.org/weblog/entry/5661, 5 October.
Lessig, L. (2005), 'CC in Review', The Creative Commons, http://creativecommons.org/weblog/entry/5668, 12 October.
Lessig, L. (2005), 'CC in Review', The Creative Commons, http://lists.ibiblio.org/pipermail/cc-lessigletter/2005/000005.html, 16 November.
Lessig, L. (2005), 'CC in Review', The Creative Commons, 23 November.
Lessig, L. (2005), 'The "Discussion": The Morning After', Lessig Blog, http://www.lessig.org/blog/archives/003224.shtml, 18 November.
Lessig, Lawrence (1999), *Code And Other Laws Of Cyberspace*, New York: Basic Books.
Lessig, Lawrence (2001), *The Future Of Ideas: The Fate Of The Commons In A Connected World*, New York: Random House.
Lessig, Lawrence (2004), *Free Culture: How Big Media Uses Technology And Law To Lock Down Culture And Control Creativity*, New York: Penguin.
Levin, Bob (2003), *The Pirates And The Mouse: Disney's War Against The Counterculture*, Seattle: Fantagraphics Books.
Lewis, N. (2005), 'Shades of Grey: Can The Copyright Fair Use Defense Adapt to New Re-Contextualised Forms of Music and Art?', *American University Law Review*, **55**, 267–306.
Libbenga, J. (2006), 'File-Swappers' Identities Protected by a Dutch Court', *The Register*, http://www.theregister.com/2006/07/14/fileswappers_protected/, 14 July.
Liedtke, M. (2006), 'Google Video Suit Could Signal YouTube Trouble Ahead', *The Associated Press*, 8 November.
Litman, Jessica (2001), *Digital Copyright*, New York: Prometheus Books.
Litman, Jessica (2001), *Digital Copyright*, 2nd edn, New York: Prometheus, Humanity Books; reprinted 2006.
Litman, J. (2004), 'Sharing and Stealing', *Hastings Law Communications and Entertainment Law Journal*, **27**, 1–50.
Litman, J. (2005), 'The Sony Paradox', *Case Western Reserve Law Review*, **55**, 917–61.
Litman, J. (2005), 'The Story of Sony v. Universal Studios: Mary Poppins Meets the Boston Strangler', in Jane Ginsburg and Rochelle Dreyfuss (eds), *Intellectual Property Stories*, New York: Foundation Press, pp. 358–94.
Liu, J. (2003), 'Copyright Law's Theory of the Consumer', *Boston College Law Review*, **44**(2), 397–438.
Lofgren, Z. (2003), 'Digital Rights', http://www.house.gov/lofgren/iss_

digital-rights.shtml.
Lofgren, Z. (2003), 'Symposium: Law and Technology of Digital Rights Management', *Berkeley Technology Law Journal*, **18**, 495–500.
Loughlan, P. (2002), 'Moral Rights (A View From The Town Square)', *Media And Arts Law Review*, **5**(1), 1–11.
Low, W.T. (2006), 'Tackling Online Copyright Infringers in Hong Kong', *Entertainment Law Review*, **17**(4), 122–4.
Lutzker, A. (2002), 'Brief for American Association of Law Libraries et al. as Amici Curiae Supporting Petitioners in *Eldred* v. *Ashcroft*', 20 May.
Lutzker, G. (1992), 'DAT's All Folks: Cahn v. Sony and the Audio Home Recording Act of 1991 – Merrie Melodies or Looney Tunes', *Cardozo Arts and Entertainment Law Journal*, **11**, 145–90.
Lord Macaulay (1841), 'A Speech Delivered On Serjeant Talfourd's Copyright Bill', 56 Parl. Deb. (3d Ser.) 341, 350; also reprinted in Lord Macaulay (1967), *Prose and Poetry*, Harvard: Harvard University Press, p. 736.
Lynch, L. (2003), 'Michael Eisner. Featured Commoner: Public Library of Science', The Creative Commons, http://creativecommons.org/text/plos, October.
Mackintosh, H. (2005), 'Talk Time: Jeff Tweedy', *The Guardian*, http://technology.guardian.co.uk/online/story/0,3605,1476170,00.html, 5 May.
Macmillan, F. (2002), 'The Cruel ©: Copyright Law and Film', *European Intellectual Property Review*, **24**(10), 483–92.
Macmillan, Fiona (ed.) (2005), *New Directions in Copyright Law, Volume 1*, Cheltenham, UK and Northampton, MA, USA: Edward Elgar.
Macmillan, Fiona (ed.) (2006), *New Directions in Copyright Law, Volume 2*, Cheltenham, UK and Northampton, MA, USA: Edward Elgar.
Macmillan, Fiona and Kathy Bowrey (eds) (2006), *New Directions in Copyright Law, Volume 3*, Cheltenham, UK and Northampton, MA, USA: Edward Elgar.
Macmillan, R. (2005), 'Google Unites Europe', *The Washington Post*, 29 April.
MacWorld Staff (2005), 'Warner Chief Calls Apple iTunes Price "Unfair"', MacWorld UK, http://www.macworld.co.uk/news/index.cfm?home&NewsID=12716, 23 September.
Madison, James (1817), 'Monopolies, Perpetuities, Corporations, and Ecclesiastical Endowments', in Jack Rakove (ed.) (1999), *Writings*, New York: Library of America.
Mark, R. (2003), 'Boucher Introduces Fair Use Rights Bill', Internetnews.com, http://dc.internet.com/news/article.php/1565901, 8 January.
Manes, S. (2004), 'Let's Have Less of Lessig', *Forbes Magazine*, 4 February.

Martin, S. (2002), 'The Mythology of the Public Domain: Exploring the Myths Behind Attacks on the Duration of Copyright Protection', *Loyola of Los Angeles Law Review*, **36**, 253–321.

McCue, A. (2004), 'iPod Users are Music Thieves says Ballmer', Silicon.com, http://management.silicon.com/itpro/0,39024675,39124642,00.htm, 4 October.

McCullagh, Declan (2005), 'Don't Touch my TiVo Sign Outside Supreme Court During Grokster Peer-to-Peer Case', http://www.mccullagh.org/photo/1ds2-5/dont-touch-my-tivo, March.

McCullagh, Declan (2005), 'Protestors Outside Grokster Supreme Court Arguments: "Feed a Musician – Download Legally"', http://www.mccullagh.org/photo/1ds2-5/feed-a-musician-music-piracy, March.

McCullagh, Declan (2005), 'Protestors Outside Grokster Supreme Court Arguments: "Hands Off my iPod" Fileswapping Photo', http://www.mccullagh.org/photo/1ds2-5/hands-off-my-ipod-flie-swapping, March.

McCullagh, D. (2006), 'Congress Readies New Broad Digital Copyright Bill', CNet.News, http://news.com.com/2100-1028_3-6064016.html, 23 April.

McCullagh, D. (2006), 'Google Scholar Trademark Case Ends', CNet News.com, http://news.com.com/2100-1025_3-6096240.html, 9 July.

McCullagh, D. (2006), 'Nude-photo Site Wins Injunction against Google', CNet News.com, http://news.com.com/Nude-photo+site+wins+injunction+against+Google/2100-1030_3-6041724.html, 22 February.

McKeough, Jill, Kathy Bowrey and Philip Griffith (2007), *Intellectual Property: Commentary and Materials*, 4th edn, Sydney: Law Book Co.

McKeough, Jill, Andrew Stewart and Philip Griffith (2004), *Intellectual Property in Australia*, 3rd edn, Sydney: LexisNexis Butterworths.

McKuin, J. (1994), 'Home Audio Taping of Copyrighted Works and the Audio Home Recording Act of 1992: A Critical Analysis', *Hastings Communication and Entertainment Law Journal*, **16**, 317–48.

McLean, Daniel and Karsten Schubert (eds) (2002), *Dear Images: Art, Copyright and Culture*, London: Riding House.

McLeod, Kembrew (2005), *Freedom of Expression*$^{(R)}$*: Overzealous Copyright Bozos and Other Enemies of Creativity*, New York: Doubleday.

Media, Entertainment and Arts Alliance (2005), 'Media Release: AFC Provides No *Sanctuary* for Australian Performers', 30 March.

Meet the Composer (2005), 'Amicus Brief in *Newton* v. *Diamond*', 2005 WL 1170246.

Melville, A. (2001), 'The Future of the Audio Home Recording Act of 1992: Has It Survived the Millennium Bug?', *Boston University Journal of Science and Technology Law*, **7**(2), 372–405.

Mennecke, T. (2006), 'United States Pressured Pirate Bay Closure', *Silicon*

Valley, 1 June.
Microsoft and the Creative Commons (2006), 'Microsoft and Creative Commons release Tool for Copyright Licensing', 20 June.
Miller, A. (2000), 'Symposium: The Constitutionality of Copyright Term Extension', *Cardozo Arts & Entertainment Law Journal*, **18**, 651–737.
Miller, S. (2006), 'Peer-to-Peer File Distribution: An Analysis of Design, Liability, Litigation, and Potential Solutions', *Review of Litigation*, **25**, 181–230.
Mills. E. (2006), 'Google and U.C. Sign Contract to Digitize Books', CNet News.com, http://news.zdnet.com/2100-9588_22-6103540.html, 8 August.
Milne, R. (2005), 'Google Book Search Library Partners', http://books.google.com/googlebooks/partners.html.
MOD Films (2005), 'MEAA Halts World-first Film Project in Australia', http://rights.apc.org.au/culture/2005/03/meaa_halts_world first_film_project_in_australia.php, 10 May.
Moglen, E. (2002), 'Declaration in Support of Defendant's Motion for Preliminary Injunction on its Counterclaims in *Progress Software Corp v. MySQL AB*', http://www.gnu.org/press/mysql-affidavit.pdf.
Mohammed, A. (2006), 'Google Refuses Demand for Search Information: Government Asked 4 Firms for Data in Effort to Revive Anti-Porn Law', *Washington Post*, 20 January 2006.
Mongelli, L. (2003), 'Music Pirate', *New York Post*, http://www.nypost.com/cgi-bin/printfriendly.pl, 9 September.
Moody, Glyn (2001), *Rebel Code: Linus Torvalds, Open Source, and the War for the Soul of Software*, London: Penguin Books.
Moody, N.M. (2004), 'Album Mixing Jay-Z's "Black Album" with Beatles "White Album" an Unauthorized Hit', *Associated Press*, 25 February.
Moore, C. (2005), 'Creative Choices: Changes to Australian Copyright Law and the Future of the Public Domain', *Media International Australia*, **114**, 71–82.
Morgan, Owen (2002), *International Protection of Performers' Rights*, Oxford: Hart Publishing.
Morrison, A. (2002), 'Case Comment: Kazaa v. Buma and Stemra', *European Intellectual Property Review*, **24**(8), 130 31.
Moses, A. (2005), 'Mixing Movies at Home', *The Sydney Morning Herald*, 7 June.
Moss, C. (2004), 'Grey Album Producer Danger Mouse Explains How He Did It', *MTV News*, http://www.mtv.com/news/articles/1485693/20040311/jay_z.jhtml, 3 November.
MPAA et al. (2004), 'Amicus Brief in support of the petitioner in *RIAA* v. *Verizon Internet Services*', 2004 WL 1466644 (U.S.).

MPAA (2005), 'BitTorrent and MPAA Join Forces: Companies Aim to Protect Film Copyrights', http://www.mpaa.org/press_releases/2005_11_22.pdf, 22 November.

MPAA (2005), 'Statement from MPAA President and CEO Dan Glickman: Re: Supreme Court Ruling on MGM v. Grokster', http://www.mpaa.org/MPAAPress/2005/2005_06_27a.doc, 27 June.

MPAA (2006), 'Belgian and Swiss Authorities Break Razorback 2', http://www.mpaa.org/press_releases/2006_02_21_razer.pdf, 21 February.

MPAA (2006), 'Brief of Amicus Curiae in Relation to the Defendant's Motion to Dismiss the Complaint in *Elektra Entertainment Group* v. *Barker*', http://www.ilrweb.com/viewILRPDF.asp?filename=elektra_barker_mpaabrief.

MPAA (2006), 'Studios Move to Thwart Illegal File Sharing on Major Pirate Networks', Press Release, http://www.mpaa.org/press_releases/2006_02_23.pdf, 23 February.

MPAA (2006), 'Swedish Authorities Sink "Pirate Bay"; Huge Worldwide Supplier of Illegal Movies Told No Safe Harbors for Facilitators of Piracy', 31 May.

Mueller, J. (2006), 'All Mixed Up: Bridgeport Music v. Dimension Films and de Minimis Digital Sampling', *Indiana Law Journal*, **81**, 435–63.

Murota, T. (2004), 'History and Current State of the Commons in England and Wales: John S. Mill at a Turning Point', Research Center for Social Common Capital, Doshisha University.

Murray, L. (2003), 'Stop the Mickey Mouse', *National Post*, 16 June, FP 23.

Murray, L. (2005), 'Bill C-60 and Copyright in Canada: Opportunities Lost and Found', *Canadian Journal of Communication*, **30**, 649–54.

Murray, Les (1996), *Subhuman Redneck Poems*, Sydney: Duffy & Snellgrove.

Myer, Rupert (2002), *Report of the Contemporary Visual Arts and Craft Inquiry*, Canberra: Department of Communications, Information Technology, and the Arts.

Nachbar, T. (2002), 'Constructing Copyright's Mythology', *Green Bag*. 6 2d (37).

Napster (2003), 'It's Coming Back', *Wired Magazine*, **11**(11), 213.

Napthali, M. (2005), 'Unauthorised: Some Thoughts upon the Doctrine of Authorisation of Copyright Infringement in the Peer-to-Peer Age', *Australian Intellectual Property Journal*, **16**, 5–54.

Negativland (1995), *Fair Use: The Story of the Letter U and the Number 2*, Concord: Seeland.

Negativland (2003), 'Two Relationships to a Cultural Domain', *Law and Contemporary Problems*, **66**, 239–62.

NESTA (2004), 'Profile: Michela Ledwidge: Mod Films' (June), at

http://www.nesta.org.uk/ourawardees/profiles/4397/.
Netanel, N.W. (2001), 'Locating Copyright Within the First Amendment Skein', *Stanford Law Review*, **54**, 1–83.
Netanel, N.W. (2003), 'Impose A Noncommercial Use Levy To Allow Free Peer-to-Peer File Sharing', *Harvard Journal Of Law And Technology*, **17**(1), 1–84.
Netanel, N.W. (2005), 'Copyright and the First Amendment: What Eldred Misses and Portends', in Jonathan Griffiths and Uma Suthersanen (eds), *Copyright and Free Speech: Comparative and International Analyses*, Oxford: Oxford University Press, pp. 127–52.
Newitz, A. (2004), 'Protest Music', AlterNet, http://www.alternet.org/columnists/story/19164/, 7 July.
Nimmer, M. (1970), 'Does Copyright Abridge The First Amendment Guarantees Of Free Speech and Press?', *The University of California Los Angeles Law Review*, **17**, 1180–204.
Nimmer, R. (2005), 'Google Lawsuit Begins: Fair Use', Contemporary Intellectual Property, Licensing and Information Law, http://www.ipinfoblog.com/archives/intellectual-property-33-google-lawsuit-begins-fair-use.html, 3 October.
Oberg, T. (2006), 'Sharing a Novel Future', *The Courier-Mail*, 25 March, p. 23.
O'Brien, D. and B. Fitzgerald (2006), 'Mashups, Remixes and Copyright Law', *Internet Law Bulletin*, **9**(2), 17–19.
O'Brien, M. (2003), 'CNN Talks to Steve Jobs About iTunes', http://www.cnn.com/2003/TECH/industry/04/29/jobs.interview/, 27 November.
Ochoa, T. (2001), 'Patent And Copyright Term Extension And The Constitution: A Historical Perspective', *Journal of the Copyright Society of the U.S.A*, **49**, 19–125.
Ochoa, T. and M. Rose (2002), 'The Anti-Monopoly Origins of the Patent and Copyright Clause', *Journal of the Copyright Society of the U.S.A*, **84**, 675–706.
Omar, I. (2005), 'The Penguin in Peril: SCO's Legal Threats to Linux', *First Monday*, **10**(1), http://www.firstmonday.org/issues/issue10_1/omar/index.html.
Online Staff (2004), 'MIPI Serves Papers On Kazaa Offices In Vanuatu', *The Sydney Morning Herald*, http://www.smh.com.au/articles/2004/02/09/1076175068630.html?from=storyrhs, 9 February.
O'Reilly, T. (2005), 'Search and Rescue', *The New York Times*, http://radar.oreilly.com/archives/2005/09/ny_times_op_ed_on_authors_guil.html, 28 September.
Orlowski, A. (2003), 'Hungover CNET Wakes Up Next To MP3.com', *The Register*, http://www.theregister.co.uk/2003/11/15/hungover_cnet_wakes_up_next/, 15 November.

Palfrey, J. (2004), 'Pornographer Sues Google on 12 Grounds', Berkman Center for Internet and Society, Harvard Law School, http://blogs.law.harvard.edu/palfrey/2004/11/20, 20 November.

Paoletta, M. (2004), 'Linkin Park, Jay-Z Come Together on "Collision Course" ', *Billboard*, **116**(50), 3.

Parrinder, Patrick (1997), 'Literary Copyright and the Public Domain', in Patrick Parrinder and Warren Chernaik (eds), *Textual Monopolies Literary Copyright and the Public Domain*, London: Office for Humanities Communication, p. 1.

Patry, W. (2005), 'BMG v. Cecilia Gonzalez', The Patry Copyright Blog, http://williampatry.blogspot.com/2005/12/bmg-v-cecilia-gonzalez.html, 11 December.

Patry, W. (2005), 'The Court Punts', *Patry Blog*, http://williampatry.blogspot.com/2005/06/court-punts.html, 27 June.

Patterson, L. Ray (1968), *Copyright in Historical Perspective*, Nashville: Vanderbilt University Press.

Patterson, L.R. (2000), 'Understanding the Copyright Clause', *Journal of the Copyright Society of the USA*, **47**, 365–95.

Pavlosky, N.C. (2003), 'Declaration of Nelson Chu Pavlosky in Support of Plaintiff's Action for a Temporary Restraining Order and for Preliminary Injunction in *Online Policy Group* et al. v. *Diebold Inc.*', http://www.eff.org/legal/ISP_liability/OPG_v._Diebold/Pavlosky.pdf.

Pawlo, M. (2004), 'Jessica Litman on the Redesign of Copyright', *GrepLaw*, http://grep.law.harvard.edu/article.pl?sid=04/02/25/0344203&mode=flat, 23 February.

Perfect 10 (2004), 'Complaint and Demand for a Jury Trial in *Perfect 10 Inc.* v. *Google Inc*', 19 November.

Perlmutter, S. (2002), 'Participation in the International Copyright System as a Means to Promote the Progress of Science and Useful Arts', *Loyola Los Angeles Law Review*, **36**, 323–35.

Peters, M. (1995), 'Copyright Term, Film Labeling, and Film Preservation Legislation: Hearings on H.R. 989 et al. before the Subcommittee on Courts and Intellectual Property of the House Committee on the Judiciary', 104th Cong., 1st Sess., 230.

Pfaffenberger, B. (2001), 'Why Open Content Matters', *Linux Journal*, http://www.linuxjournal.com/article/4709, April 11.

Phillips, D. (2002), 'Smells Like Teen Booty: What Do You Get If You Cross Destiny's Child With Nirvana?', *The Guardian*, 27 February, p. 22.

Phillips Fox (2004), *Digital Agenda Review*, Canberra: Attorney General's Department, http://www.ag.gov.au/DigitalAgendaReview/reportrecommendations.

Picker, R. (2005), 'Rewinding Sony: The Evolving Product, Phoning Home and the Duty of Ongoing Design', *University of Chicago Law and Economics Olin Working Paper*, **241**, 1–37.

Pike, E. (2005), 'What You Need to Know about Creative Commons', *Members' Music Magazine*, http://www.bmr.org/html/news/news53.htm, 15 March.

Pollock, M. (2006), 'Rebalancing Section 512 to Protect Fair Users from Herds of Mice-Trampling Elephants, or a Little Due Process is not Such a Dangerous Thing', *Santa Clara Computer and High Technology Law Journal*, **22**, 547–76.

Posner, Richard (1998), *Economic Analysis Of Law*, 5th edn, New York: Aspen Law and Business.

Powell, J. (2002), 'Brief of Hal Roach Studios and Michael Agee as Amici Curiae Supporting Petitioners in *Eldred* v. *Ashcroft*', 20 May.

Power, A. (2006), 'The Mouse that Roared: Addressing the Post-Modern Quandary of Mash-ups Through Traditional Fair Use Analysis', *Vanderbilt Journal of Entertainment and Technology Law*, **8**, 531–40.

Powers, D. (2004), 'More Than Words: Musings on Music Journalism', *Pop Matters*, http://popmatters.com/music/columns/powers/040310.shtml, 10 March.

Public Knowledge (2005), 'In the Matter of Orphaned Works', http://www.copyright.gov/orphan/comments/OW0629-PublicKnowledge.pdf, 25 March.

Putter, J. (2006), 'Copyright Infringement v. Academic Freedom on the Internet: Dealing with Infringing Use of Peer-to-Peer Technology on Campus Networks', *Journal of Law and Policy*, **14**, 419–69.

Rappaport, Edward (1998), *Copyright Term Extension: Estimating the Economic Values*, Congressional Research Service, Library of Congress, 11 May.

Raymond, Eric (1999), *The Cathedral and the Bazaar: Musings on Linux and Open Source by an Accidental Revolutionary*, Cambridge, Mass.: O'Reilly and Associates.

Reuters (2003), 'EMI, Universal Sue Napster Backers', *USA Today*, 23 April.

Reuters (2004), 'DJ Mixes Beatles, Jay-Z Into Grey', CNN, http://edition.cnn.com/2004/SHOWBIZ/Music/02/19/leisure.grey.album.reut, 19 February.

Reuters (2006), 'Apple in Scandinavian iTunes Talks', *The Australian*, 17 August.

Reuters (2006), 'French Law "Piracy" ', *The Australian*, 23 March.

RIAA (2002), 'Cary Sherman On Dispute With Verizon', Press Release, 11 September.

RIAA (2003), 'Recording Industry Begins Suing P2P File Sharers Who Illegally Offer Copyrighted Music Online', Press Release, Washington, 8 September.

RIAA (2004), 'Petition for a Writ of Certiorari in *RIAA* v. *Verizon Internet Services*', appellate petition, motion, and filing, 2004 WL 1175134, 24 May.

RIAA (2005), 'Music Industry Announces Grokster Settlement', http://www.riaa.com/news/newsletter/110705_2.asp, 11 November.

RIAA (2005), 'Music Industry Files New Lawsuits in Ongoing Enforcement Against Online Theft', Press Release, http://www.riaa.com/news/newsletter/113005.asp, 20 November.

RIAA (2005), 'Statement On MGM v. Grokster Supreme Court Ruling', http://www.riaa.com/news/newsletter/062705.asp, 27 June.

Ricketson, S. (1992), 'The Copyright Term', *IIC*, **23**(6), 753–84.

Ricketson, Sam and Megan Richardson (2005), *Intellectual Property: Cases and Materials*, 3rd edn, Sydney: LexisNexis Butterworths.

Rimmer, M. (1998), 'Four Stories About Copyright Law And Appropriation Art', *Media And Arts Law Review*, **3**(4), 180–93.

Rimmer, M. (2000), 'Bangarra Dance Theatre: Copyright Law And Indigenous Culture', *Griffith Law Review*, **9**(2), 274–302.

Rimmer, M. (2001), 'Napster: Infinite Digital Jukebox Or Pirate Bazaar', *Media International Australia incorporating Culture and Policy*, **98**, 27–38.

Rimmer, M. (2001), 'Shine: Copyright Law And Film', *Australian Intellectual Property Journal*, **12**(3), 129–42.

Rimmer, M. (2002), 'Daubism: Copyright Law And Artistic Works', *Murdoch University Electronic Journal of Law*, **9**(4), http://www.murdoch.edu.au/elaw/issues/v9n4/rimmer 94.html

Rimmer, M. (2002), 'Heretic: Copyright Law And Dramatic Works', *Queensland University of Technology Law And Justice Journal*, **2**(1), 131–49.

Rimmer, M. (2004), 'Canadian Rhapsody: Copyright Law and Research Libraries', *Australian Academic and Research Libraries*, **25**(3), 193–213.

Rimmer, M. (2004), 'Never Neverland: Peter Pan and Perpetual Copyright', *Incite*, **25**(12), 8–9.

Rimmer, M, (2004), 'The Valley Of The Dolls: Brand Protection And Artistic Parody', *Australian Intellectual Property Bulletin*, **16**(10), 160–63.

Rimmer, M. (2005), 'Bloomsday: Copyright Estates and Cultural Festivals', *Scripted (University of Edinburgh)*, **2**(3), 383–428.

Rimmer, M. (2005), 'Hail To The Thief: A Tribute To Kazaa', *The University of Ottawa Law and Technology Journal*, **2**(1), 173–218.

Rimmer, M. (2006), 'Robbery Under Arms: Copyright Law and the Australia–United States Free Trade Agreement', *First Monday*, **11**(3), http://www.firstmonday.org/issues/issue11_3/rimmer/index.html.

Roberts, R., H. Varmus, M. Ashburner, P. Brown, M. Eisen, C. Khosla, M. Kirschner, R. Nusse, M. Scott and B. Wold (2001), 'Information Access: Building a "GenBank" of the Published Literature', *Science*, 23 March, **291**(5512), 2318–19.

Roddy, D. (2003), 'The Song Remains the Same', *Pittsburgh Post-Gazette.com*, 16 September.

Rolph, D. (2003), 'A Clearly Inappropriate Forum? Jurisdiction, Internet Defamation and The High Court of Australia', *Media And Arts Law Review*, **8**(1), 59–71.

Rose, F. (2003), 'The Civil War Inside Sony', *Wired Magazine*, **11**(2), http://www.wired.com/wired/archive/11.02/sony_pr.html.

Rose, Mark (1993), *Authors And Owners: The Invention Of Copyright*, Cambridge: Harvard University Press.

Rose, Mark (1994), 'The Author As Proprietor: *Donaldson* v. *Becket* and the Genealogy Of Modern Authorship', in Brad Sherman and Alain Strowel (eds), *Of Authors and Origins: Essays on Copyright Law*, Oxford: Clarendon Press, pp. 23–55.

Rose Hilo, M. (2003), 'Tivo and the Incentive/ Dissemination Conflict: The Economics of Extending Betamax to Personal Video Recorders', *Washington University Law Quarterly*, **81**(4), 1043–68.

Rosen, C. (2004/2005), 'The Age of Egocasting', *The New Atlantis: A Journal of Technology and Society*, **7**, 51–72, http://www. thenewatlantis. com/archive/7/TNA07-Rosen.pdf.

Rosen, H. (2005), 'The Wisdom of the Court: Part 2', *The Huffington Post*, http://www.huffingtonpost.com/theblog/archive/hilary-rosen/the-wisdom-of-the-court-_3259.html, 27 June.

Roush, W. (2006), 'Inside the Spyware Scandal', *Technology Review*, **109**(2), 48–57.

Ruddock, P. (2004), 'Opening Address: Unlucky For Some', ACIPA Conference, 13 February.

Ruddock, P. (2006), 'Major Copyright Reforms Strike Balance', Attorney-General's Department, Australian Government, 14 May.

Ruddock, P. (2006), 'Parody Permit in the Spirit of Fair Play', *Daily Telegraph*, 30 November, p. 30.

Russinovich, M. (2005), 'Sony, Rootkits, and Digital Rights Management Gone Too Far', Mark's Sysinternals Blog, http://www.sysinternals.com/blog/2005/10/sony-rootkits-and-digital-rights.html, 31 October.

Said, Edward (1994), *Representations of the Intellectual: the 1993 Reith Lectures*, New York: Pantheon Books.

Sainsbury, Maree (2003), *Moral Rights And Their Application In Australia*, Sydney: Federation Press.

Samuels, Edward (2000), *The Illustrated Story of Copyright*, New York: Thomas Dunne Books.

Samuelson, P. (1999), 'Intellectual Property and the Digital Economy: Why the Anti Circumvention Regulations Need to be Revised', *Berkeley Technology Law Journal*, **14**, 519–66.

Samuelson, P. (2003), 'Mapping the Digital Public Domain: Threats and Opportunities', *Law and Contemporary Problems*, **66**, 147–71.

Samuelson, P. (2005), 'Legally Speaking: Did MGM Really Win the Grokster Case?', *Communications of the ACM*, **48**, 19, http://www.sims.berkeley.edu/~pam/papers/CACM%20SCT%20decides%20MGM. pdf.

Samuelson, P. (2006), 'Enriching Discourse on Public Domain', *Duke Law Journal*, **55**, 783–834.

Samuelson, P. (2006), 'The Generativity of Sony v. Universal: The Intellectual Property Legacy of Justice Stevens', *Fordham Law Review*, **74**(4), 1831–76.

Samuelson Clinic (2005), 'Re: RM 2005–11 – Exemption to Prohibition on Circumvention of Copyright Protection Systems for Access Control Technologies', http://www.law.berkeley.edu/clinics/samuelson/papers/other/Halderman_Felten_Comment_Final.pdf.

Sanavia, P. (2000), 'The Status of the Independent Professional Artist: Aid Granted by the Virtue of the Status', Tallinan.

Sandburg, B. (2002), 'Cooley Godward Named in Malpractice Action', *The National Law Journal*, 28 January.

Schmidt, L. (2003), 'Mexican Copyright Law', http://cyberlaw.stanford.edu/lessig/blog/archives/mexican.txt, 25 March.

Schroeder, P. and B. Barr (2005), 'Reining in Google', *The Washington Times*, http://www.washtimes.com/commentary/20051102-093349-7482r.htm, 3 November.

Schutze, B. (2003), 'Samples from the Heap: Notes on Recycling the Detritus of a Remixed Culture', *Horizon Zero: Digital Art and Culture in Canada*, **8**, http://www.horizonzero.ca/textsite/remix.php?is=8&art=0&file=5&tlang=0, April/ May.

Schwartz, R. (2006), 'Recording Rights Under Attack Again', Public Knowledge, http://www.publicknowledge.org/node/306, 20 April.

Scott, M. (2005–2006), 'Safe Harbors Under the Digital Millennium Copyright Act', *New York University Journal of Legislation and Public Policy*, **9**, 99–166.

Screenrights (2005), 'Screenrights' Response to the Attorney-General's *Fair Use and Other Copyright Exceptions* Issues Paper 2005', http://www.screen.org/submissions/ScreenrightsFairUseSu4BE09.pdf.

Seigenthaler, J. (2005), 'A False Wikipedia "Biography"', *USA Today*, 29 November.

Seltzer, W. (2003), 'Declaration of Wendy Seltzer in Support of Plaintiff's Action for a Temporary Restraining Order and for Preliminary Injunction in *Online Policy Group* et al. v. *Diebold Inc.*', http://www.eff.org/legal/ISP_liability/OPG_v._Diebold/Seltzer.pdf.

Senate Committee on the Judiciary (1996), 'Copyright Term Extension Act of 1996', Senate Report No. 104-315, p. 11.

Senate Estimates Committee (2004), 'Foreign Affairs, Defence And Trade', Australian Parliament, 2 March.

Senate Legal And Constitutional Legislation Committee (1997), 'Public Hearings: Copyright Amendment Bill 1997 (Cth)', 19 August, pp. 123–5.

Seville, Catherine (1999), *Literary Copyright Reform in Early Victorian England: The Framing of the 1842 Copyright Act*, Cambridge: Cambridge University Press.

Shachtman, N. (2004), 'Copyright Enters A Grey Area', *Wired News*, http://www.wired.com/news/digiwood/0,1412,62276,00.html, 14 February.

Shapiro, G. (2005), 'Protecting Copyright and Innovation in a Post-Grokster World', Testimony, United States Senate Committee on the Judiciary, 28 September.

Sharman Networks (2003), 'Review of Copyright Amendment (Digital Agenda) Act', http://www.phillipsfox.com/whats_on/Australia/Digital Agenda/submissions/Sharman_submission.pdf, 30 September.

Sharman Networks (2003), 'Bollywood Comes To Kazaa: World's First Full-Length Feature Film Sold Online Using Peer-to-Peer Technology', Press Release, http://www.sharmannetworks.com/content/view/full/237, 12 November.

Sharman Networks (2003), 'Sharman Networks Launches "Join The Revolution"', Press Release, 19 November.

Sharman Networks (2006), 'Content Industries and Sharman Networks Settle All Global Litigation', http://www.sharmannetworks.com/content/view/full/323, August.

Sherman, Brad and Lionel Bently (1997), 'Balance and Harmony in the Duration of Copyright', in Patrick Parrinder and Warren Chernaik (eds), *Textual Monopolies Literary Copyright and the Public Domain*, London, London: Office for Humanities Communication, p. 28.

Sherman, Brad and Lionel Bently (1999), *The Making Of Modern Intellectual Property Law: The British Experience 1760–1911*, Cambridge: Cambridge University Press.

Sherman, Brad and Alain Strowel (eds) (1994), *Of Authors And Origins: Essays On Copyright Law*, Oxford: Clarendon Press.

Sherman. C. (2003), 'RIAA on Verizon Appeals Court Decision', Press Release, http://www.riaa.com/news/newsletter/121903.asp, 19 December.

Shiel, F. (2004), 'Libraries Caught In Copyright Changes', *The Age*, http://www.theage.com.au/articles/2004/02/10/1076388365432.html, 11 February.

Shulman, Seth (1999), *Owning the Future*, Boston and New York: Houghton Mifflin Company.

Shulman, S. (2002), 'Freeing Mickey Mouse', *Technology Review*, **105**(9), 81.

Skillrud, S.E. (2005), 'An Umbrella or a Canopy? Why the 17 U.S.C. Section 512 (a) Safe Harbor Should be Read Broadly', *Marquette Intellectual Property Law Review*, **9**, 91–109.

Slater, D. (2003), 'Take Another Little Piece of My Art', The Creative Commons, http://creativecommons.org/image/illegalart, July.

Smith, L.T. (2003), 'Declaration of Luke Thomas Smith in Support of Plaintiff's Action for a Temporary Restraining Order and for Preliminary Injunction in *Online Policy Group* et al. v. *Diebold Inc.*', http://www.eff.org/legal/ISP_liability/OPG_v._Diebold/Smith.pdf.

Smith, S. (2003), 'From Napster to Kazaa: The Battle Over Peer to Peer File-Sharing Goes International', *Duke Law and Technology Review*, http://www.law.duke.edu/journals/dltr/articles/2003dltr0008.html, 28 March.

Solberg, Winton (1990), *The Constitutional Convention and the Formation of the Union*, 2nd edn, Chicago: University of Illinois Press.

Somoano, M.L. (2006), 'Bridgeport Music Inc. v. Dimension Films: Has Unlicensed Digital Sampling of Copyrighted Sound Recordings Come to an End?', *Berkeley Technology Law Journal*, **21**, 289–309.

Sony BMG (2006), 'CDs Included in the Settlement', http://www.sonybmgcdtechsettlement.com/CDList.htm.

South, G. (2006), 'Rip This: Piracy and Politics in Sweden', *Open Democracy*, http://www.opendemocracy.net/media-copyrightlaw/pirates_3626.jsp, 9 May.

Sprigman, C. (2002), 'The Mouse That Ate The Public Domain: Disney, the Copyright Term Extension Act and Eldred v. Ashcroft', *Findlaw*, http://writ.news.findlaw.com/commentary/20020305_sprigman.html, 5 March.

Sprigman, C. (2003), 'The Supreme Court's Copyright Extension Decision: A Mickey Mouse Ruling', *Findlaw*, http://writ.news.findlaw.com/commentary/20030120_sprigman.html, 20 January.

Sprigman, C. (2004), 'Reform(aliz)ing Copyright', *Stanford Law Review*, **25**, 485–568.

Stallman, R. (2005), 'Fireworks in Montreal', Free Software Foundation, http://www.fsf.org/blogs/rms/entry-20050920.html, 5 July.

Stanford University (2005), 'Stanford and Google Book Search Statement of Support and Participation', http://library.stanford.edu/about_sulair/news_and_events/stanford_google_project.html.

Stark, E. (2006), 'Free Culture and the Internet: A New Semiotic Democracy, *Open Democracy*, http://www.opendemocracy.net/arts-commons/semiotic_3662.jsp, 20 June.

Steuer, E. (2006), 'Pearl Jam's "Life Wasted" Video Released Under a CC Licence', The Creative Commons, http://creativecommons.org/weblog/entry/5913, 19 May.

Sunder, M. (2006), 'IP^3', *Stanford Law Review*, **59**, 257–332.

Taylor, N. (2005), 'Not at the Writer's Expense', *The Washington Post*, 22 October, A21.

Taylor, N. (2005), 'Response to Tim O'Reilly of the Google Advisory Board', *The New York Times*, http://www.authorsguild.org/news/10_02_05.htm, 29 September.

Terdiman, D (2004), 'Mashup Artists Face the Music', *Wired News*, http://www.wired.com/news/digiwood/0,1412,63314,00.html, 4 May.

Thompson, C. (2005), 'The BitTorrent Effect', *Wired Magazine*, **13**(1), 2, http://www.wired.com/wired/archive/13.01/bittorrent.html.

Time Warner (2004), 'Amicus Brief in support of the Petitioner in Petitioner in *RIAA* v. *Verizon Internet Services*', 2004 WL 1453026.

Tofalides, M. and G. Fearn (2006), 'Bittorrent Copyright Infringement', *Entertainment Law Review*, **17**(2), 81–3.

Tuck, S. (2004), 'Lucy Maud Provision Fades Out', *Globe And Mail*, 1 April, R1.

Tushnet, R. (2006), 'My Library: Copyright and the Role of Institutions in a Peer-to-Peer World', *The University of California Los Angeles Law Review*, **53**, 978–1029.

United States Copyright Office (2005), 'Orphaned Works', *Federal Register*, **70**(16), 3739–43.

United States Copyright Office (2006), *Report on Orphan Works: A Report of the Register of Copyrights*, Library of Congress: United States Copyright Office.

United States Copyright Office (2006), 'Exemption to Prohibition on Circumvention of Copyright Protection Systems for Access Control Technologies', *Federal Register*, **71**(227), http://www.copyright.gov/fedreg/2006/71fr 68472.pdf, 68472–9.

United States Copyright Office (2006), *Rulemaking on Exemptions from Prohibition on Circumvention of Technological Measures that Control Access to Copyrighted Works*, http://www.copyright.gov/1201/, November.

United States Government (2006), 'Statement of Interest in Opposition to Defendant's Motion to Dismiss the Complaint in *Elektra Entertainment*

Group v. *Barker*', http://www.ilrweb.com/viewILRPDF.asp?filename=elektra_barker_usstatement.

University of Michigan (2004), 'Google/ U-M Project Opens the Way to Universal Access to Information', http://www.umich.edu/news/?Releases/2004/Dec04/library/index, 14 December.

Urban, J. and L. Quilten (2005), 'Efficient Process or "Chilling Effects"? Takedown Notices Under Section 512 of the Digital Millennium Copyright Act', *Santa Clara Computer and High Technology Law Journal*, **22**, 621–93.

Urbanski, L. (1997), 'Letter To Senator Strom Thurmand Opposing Copyright Extension', http://www.law.asu.edu/HomePages/Karjala/OpposingCopyrightExtension/letters/AFH.html, 31 March.

Vaidhyanathan, Siva (2001), *Copyrights And Copywrongs: The Rise Of Intellectual Property And How It Threatens Creativity*, New York: New York University Press.

Vaidhyanathan, Siva (2004), *The Anarchist In The Library: How the Clash Between Freedom and Control is Hacking the Real World and Crashing the System*, New York: Basic Books.

Vaidhyanathan, S. (2004), 'The State Of Copyright Activism', *First Monday*, **9**(4), http://firstmonday.org/issues/issue9_4/siva/.

Vaidhyanathan, S. (2005), 'Remote Control: The Rise of Electronic Cultural Policy', *The Annals of the American Academy of Political and Social Science*, **597**(1), 122–33.

Vaidhyanathan, S. (2005), 'A Risky Gamble with Google', *A Chronicle of Higher Education*, http://www.nyu.edu/classes/siva/archives/002445.html, 2 December.

Vaidhyanathan, S. (2005), 'Creative Commons: Making Copyright Work for Democracy', *Open Democracy*, http://www.opendemocracy.net/media-copyrightlaw/creativecommons_2596.jsp, 13 June.

Vaidhyanathan, S. (2006), 'Thumbnails (and Google) in Danger', Sivacracy. net, http://www.nyu.edu/classes/siva/archives/002827.html, 22 February.

Valenti, J. (1982), 'Home Recording of Copyrighted Works', Subcommittee on Courts, Civil Liberties, and the Administration of Justice, the Committee on the Judiciary, House of Representatives, http://cryptome.org/hrcw-hear.htm, 12 April.

Valenti, J. (1995), 'Testimony before the Subcommittee on Courts and Intellectual Property Committee on the Judiciary U.S. House of Representatives Hearing on Copyright Term Extension Act – H.R. 989', 1 June.

Valenti, J. (2003), 'Privacy and Piracy: The Paradox of Illegal File Sharing on Peer-to-Peer Networks and the Impact of Technology on the

Entertainment Industry', Senate Committee on Governmental Affairs, 30 September.

Valenti, J. (2003), 'Statement on the Supreme Court Ruling on Eldred v. Ashcroft', Motion Picture Association of America, http://www.mpaa.org/jack/2003/2003_01_15.htm, 15 January.

Van Bergh, G.-J. (2002), 'Case Comment: Copyright – File Sharing Service', *Entertainment Law Review*, **13**(6), 77–8.

Varghese, J. (2004/05), 'Guide to Copyright and Patent Law Changes in the US Free Trade Agreement Implementation Bill 2004', *Parliamentary Library Current Issues Brief*, **3**(17), http://www.aph.gov.au/ library/pubs/CIB/2004-05/05cib03.pdf.

Vaver, David (2000), *Copyright Law*, Toronto: Irwin Law Inc.

Veiga, A. (2006), 'Music Labels, Apple Divided Over Pricing, As Talks Approach', *Associated Press*, 2 April.

Verba, S. (2004), 'Google to Digitize Some Harvard Library Holdings', *Harvard Gazette*, http://www.news.harvard.edu/gazette/2004/12.16/01-google.html, 16 December.

Verba, S. (2004), 'Google Library Partners', Google, http://books.google.com/googlebooks/partners.html.

Verba, S. (2005), 'Libraries, Books, Equality – Google', Harvard University Library, http://hul.harvard.edu/hgproject/verba.html.

Verizon (2003), 'Verizon Wins Fight to Protect Internet Safety and Privacy: Anti-Consumer Subpoena Process Struck Down by Appeals Court', 19 December.

Verizon (2004), 'Brief in Opposition in *RIAA* v. *Verizon Internet Services*', 2004 WL 1466645.

Vise, David (2005), *The Google Story: Inside the Hottest Business, Media and Technology Success of our Time*, New York: Macmillan.

Vivendi Universal (2001), 'Vivendi Universal acquires MP3.com in move to strengthen digital distribution capacity and web audience', Paris and San Diego, 21 May.

Vogele, Colette and Mia Garlick (2006), *Podcasting Legal Guide: Rules for the Revolution*, The Berkman Center Clinical Program in Cyberlaw, Harvard Law School, http://mirrors.creativecommons.org/Podcasting_Legal_Guide.pdf, March.

von Lewinski, S. (1992), 'EC Proposal For A Council Directive Harmonizing The Term Of Protection Of Copyright And Certain Related Rights', *IIC*, **23**(6), 785–811.

von Lohmann, F. (2004), 'Measuring the Digital Millennium Copyright Act Against the Darknet: Implications for the Regulation of Technological Protection Measures', *Loyola of Los Angeles Entertainment Law Review*, **24**, 635–48.

von Lohmann, F. (2004), 'Tech Dodges a Bullet', Law.com, 27 August.

von Lohmann, F. (2006), 'Nevada Court Rules Google Cache Fair Use', Electronic Frontier Foundation, http://www.eff.org/news/archives/2006_01.php, 25 January.

Vu, C. (2006), 'Tradition is the New Thing: The Supreme Court Holds That Creators of Peer-to-Peer Networks Could Be Liable Under Traditional Theories of Secondary Liability', *Whittier Law Review*, **27**, 1077–96.

Waelde, C. and E. Lillian (2005), 'Online Intermediaries and Liability for Copyright Infringement', World Intellectual Property Organization, Geneva, 18 April.

Waladan, S. (2005), 'Google: Search or Destroy?', *Open Democracy*, http://www.opendemocracy.net/media-copyrightlaw/google_3130.jsp, 16 December.

Wales, J. (2005), 'Wikipedia is an Encyclopedia', wikipedia-l@wikimedia.org, 8 March.

Wallenstein, A. (2005), 'Slingbox Could Spark New Lawsuits', *Hollywood Reporter*, http://www.hollywoodreporter.com/thr/article_display.jsp?vnu_content_id=1000973572, 6 July.

Walterscheid, E. (2000), 'Defining The Patent and Copyright Term: Term Limits and The Intellectual Property Clause', *Journal of Intellectual Property Law*, **7**, 315–94.

Warnecke, M. (2006), 'In Battle Over Use of News Headlines, Court Focuses on Policy Implications for Web', *e-Commerce Law Daily*, **11**(3), http://ipcenter.bna.com/pic2/ip.nsf/id/BNAP-6KYKF9, 12 January.

Warner Bros (2006), 'Warner Bros. Home Entertainment Group Announces Revolutionary Deal to Publish Legal Film and TV Content using the BitTorrent Platform', Press Release, 9 May.

Weatherall, K. (2006), 'Would You Ever Recommend a Creative Commons License?', *Australian Intellectual Property Resources*, **4**, http://www.austlii.edu.au/au/other/AIPLRes/2006/4.html.

Weinberg, J. (2002), 'Brief Of Intellectual Property Law Professors As Amici Curiae Supporting Petitioners in *Eldred* v. *Ashcroft*', 20 May.

Werde, B. (2004), 'Defiant Downloads Rise From Underground', *The New York Times*, 25 February.

Wilbanks, J. (2005), 'What is Science Commons?', The Creative Commons, http://creativecommons.org/weblog/entry/5695, 9 November.

Wilkinson, Margaret Ann (2005), 'Filtering the Flow from the Fountains of Knowledge: Access and Copyright in Education and Libraries', in Michael Geist (ed.), *In The Public Interest: The Future of Canadian Copyright Law*, Toronto: Irwin Law, pp. 331–74.

Wirten, Eva Hemmungs (2003), *No Trespassing: Authorship, Intellectual Property Rights, And The Boundaries Of Globalization*, Toronto: University of Toronto Press.

Wirten, E.H. (2006), 'Out of Sight and Out of Mind: On the Cultural Hegemony of Intellectual Property (Critique)', *Cultural Studies*, **20**(2–3), 282–91.

Wirten, Eva Hemmungs (2008), *Terms of Use: Negotiating the Jungle of the Intellectual Commons*, Toronto: University of Toronto Press.

Wiseman, L. (2002), 'Beyond The Photocopier: Copyright and Publishing in Australia', *Media And Arts Law Review*, **7**(4), 299–314.

Woellert, L. (2005), 'Sony's Escalating "Spyware" Fiasco', *Businessweek*, 22 November.

Wood, L.J. (1996), 'Copyright Law And Postmodern Artistic Practice: Paradox And Difference', *Media And Arts Law Review*, **1**, 72–85.

Woodmansee, Martha (1994), *The Author, Art, And The Market: Rereading The History Of Aesthetics*, New York: Columbia University Press.

Woodmansee, Martha and Peter Jaszi (eds) (1994), *The Construction Of Authorship: Textual Appropriation In Law And Literature*, Durham, London: Duke University Press.

Woody, T. (2003), 'The Race to Kill Kazaa', *Wired Magazine*, **11**(2), 104–7, 138, http://www.wired.com/wired/archive/11.02/kazaa.html.

Wray, R. (2006), 'Legal Victory for Google in Library project', *The Guardian*, 29 June.

Wu, T. (2005), 'A Supreme Court Conversation', *Slate*, http://slate.msn.com/id/2121410/entry/2121673/, 28 June.

Wu, T. (2005), 'Google Print and the Other Culture War', *Slate*, http://www.slate.com/id/2128094/, 17 October.

Wyatt, E. (2006), 'Smithsonian Agreement Angers Filmmakers', *The New York Times*, 1 April.

XM Satellite Radio (2006), 'Statement to XM Subscribers - The XM Nation', http://radio.about.com/od/xmsatelliteradio/a/aa051806a.htm.

Yagan, S. (2006), 'Testimony to the Senate Committee for the Judiciary', http://judiciary.senate.gov/testimony.cfm?id=1624&wit_id=4689, 28 September.

Yeo, Richard (2001), *Encyclopaedic Visions: Scientific Dictionaries And Enlightenment Culture*, Cambridge: Cambridge University Press.

Young, A. (2004), 'Music Generations Collide on the Grey Album', *Sidelines Online*, 4 March.

Younge, G. (2006), 'The Addictive Encyclopaedia', *The Guardian Weekly*, 1–7 September.

Yu, P. (2005), 'P2P and the Future of Private Copying', *University of Colorado Law Review*, **76**, 653–765.

Zittrain, J. (2006), 'A History of Online Gatekeeping', *Harvard Journal of Law and Technology*, **19**(2), 253–98.

Zittrain, J, (2004), 'Normative Principles for Evaluating Free and Proprietary Software', *University of Chicago Law Review*, **71**(1), 1–21.

Zittrain, J. (2006), 'The Generative Internet', *Harvard Law Review*, **119**, 1974–2040.

CASE LAW

A&M Records Inc v. *Napster Inc* 114 F. Supp. 2d 896 (N.D. Cal 2000).

A&M Records Inc v. *Napster Inc* 239 F.3d 1004 (9th 2001).

ABC v. *Hanson* (unreported, Supreme Court of Queensland Court of Appeal, 28 September 1998).

ABC v. *Hanson* (unreported, High Court of Australia, special leave to appeal refused, 24 June 1999).

Abilene Music, Inc. v. *Sony Music Entertainment, Inc.* 320 F.Supp.2d 84 (2003).

ABKCO Music, Inc. v. *Harrisongs Music, Ltd.*, 722 F.2d 988 (2d Cir. 1983).

Advanced Computer Services of Michigan Inc v. *MAI Systems Corporation* 845 F.Supp 356 (E.D. Va 1994).

Agence France Presse v. *Google Inc.*, D. D.C., No. 05-00546 (2005), http://blog.searchenginewatch.com/blog/050321-175410.

American Geophysical Union v. *Texaco Inc.*, 60 F.3d 913, 923 (2d Cir.), cert. dismissed, 516 U.S. 1005, 116 S.Ct. 592, 133 L.Ed.2d 486 (1995).

American Library Association v. *Federal Communications Commission* 406 F.3d 689 (C.A.D.C., 2005).

Apple Corps Ltd v. *Apple Computers* [2006] EWHC 996 (Ch).

Apple Corps Ltd. v. *Leber* 229 U.S.P.Q. 1015 (1986).

Arista Records v. *MP3.Board* (S.D.N.Y., no. 00 Civ. 4660 (SHS), 2000).

Arista Records v. *Sakfield Holding Company* 314 F.Supp.2d 27 (2004).

Ashcroft v. *American Civil Liberties Union* 542 U.S. 656 (2004).

Atlantic Recording Corporation et al. v. *XM Satellite Radio Inc.* NYSDCE 1:2006cv03733 (2006).

ATV Music Publishing v. *Rogers Radio Broadcasting* (1982) 35 O.R. (2d) 417 (Ont. H.C.).

Australian Tape Manufacturers Association Ltd v. *Commonwealth* (1993) 176 CLR 480.

Australasian Performing Right Association Limited Application for Authorisation A90918 to A90925 ACCC Final Determination (8 March 2006).

The Authors' Guild v. *Google Inc.* Case No. 05 CV 8136-JES (2005), http://

www.boingboing.net/images/AuthorsGuildGoogleComplaint1.pdf.
Bahnmaier v. *Sony BMG Music Entertainment*, No. CJ 2005 06968 (Okla. Dist. Ct. Nov. 28, 2005).
Basic Books, Inc. v. *Kinko's Graphics Corporation*, 758 F.Supp. 1522 (S.D.N.Y. 1991).
Black v. *Sony BMG Music Entertainment*, No. CIV-05-1315 WDS/RLP (D.N.M. Dec. 19, 2005).
Blanch v. *Koons* U.S. Dist. LEXIS 26299 (2005).
BMG et al. v. *Cecilia Gonzalez* WL 106592 (N.D.Ill.) (2005).
BMG et al. v. *Cecilia Gonzalez* 430 F.3d 888 (2005).
BMG Canada v. *John Doe* [2004] 3 F.C. 241; and [2005] FCA 193 (on appeal).
Bridgeport Music Inc. v. *Dimension Films Inc.* 230 F Supp 2nd 830 (2002).
Bridgeport Music Inc. v. *Dimension Films Inc.* 410 F.3d 792 (6th Cir. 2005).
Bright Tunes Music Corp. v. *Harrisongs Music, Ltd.*, 420 F. Supp. 177 (S.D.N.Y. 1976).
Buma and Stemra v. *Kazaa* (unreported, 29th November 2001).
Buma and Stemra v. *Kazaa* (unreported, 18 December 2003, the Dutch Supreme Court).
Burke v. *Sony BMG Music Entertainment*, No. 857213 (Cal. Super. Ct. Nov. 22, 2005).
Campbell v. *Acuff-Rose Music, Inc.* 510 U.S. 569 (1994).
Canadian Private Copying Collective v. *Canadian Storage Media Alliance* (2004) FCA 424.
CBS Broadcasting Inc. v. *Does 1–10*, N.D. Tex., No. 06–0338, complaint filed 2/23/06.
CCH Canadian Limited v. *The Law Society of Upper Canada* (2004) SCC 13.
Chamberlain Group, Inc. v. *Skylink Techologies, Inc.* 292 F.Supp.2d 1040 (N.D.Ill. 2003) and on appeal 381 F.3d 1178 (Fed. Cir. 2004).
Clean Flicks of Colorado, LLC v. *Soderbergh* 433 F.Supp.2d 1236 (D.Colo., 2006).
Columbia Pictures Industries Inc. v. *Bunnell*, C.D. Cal., No. 06-1093, complaint filed 2/23/06.
Columbia Pictures Industries Inc. v. *Does 1–10*, W.D. Pa., No. 06-0251, complaint filed 2/23/06.
Columbia Pictures Industries Inc. v. *Does 1–10*, W.D. Mich., No. 06-0037, complaint filed 2/23/06.
Columbia Pictures Industries Inc. v. *Fung*, S.D.N.Y., No. 06-1471, complaint filed 2/23/06.
Commonwealth Director of Public Prosecutions v. *Ng, Tran and Le* (unreported, Sydney Central Local Court, Henson DCM, 18 November 2003).

Confetti Records v. *Warner Music* (2003) EWCH 1274 (CH).
Consumer Council of Norway (2006), 'Complaint Against iTunes Music Store', http://forbrukerportalen.no/filearchive/Complaint%20against%20iTunes%20Music%20Store.pdf, 25 January.
Cooke v. *Sony BMG Music Entertainment*, No. 05-0009093 (D.C. Super. Ct. Nov. 18, 2005).
Copiepresse v. *Google Inc.* (Court of First Instance of Brussels, 5 September 2006), http://www.chillingeffects.org/international/notice.cgi?action=image_7796.
Curry v. *Audax* Case no. 334492 / KG 06-176 SR (District Court of Amsterdam, 9 March 2006), http://mirrors.creativecommons.org/judgements/Curry-Audax-English.pdf.
Dastar Corporation v. *Twentieth Century Fox Film Corporation* 539 U.S. 23 (2003).
Davidson & Associates, Inc. v. *Internet Gateway* 334 F.Supp.2d 1164 (E.D. Mo. 2004).
Davidson & Associates v. *Jung* 422 F.3d 630 (Fed Cir 8th 2005).
DeMarco v. *Sony BMG Music*, No. 2:05-cv-05485-WHW-SDW (D.N.J. Nov. 17, 2005).
Digital Envoy, Inc. v. *Google, Inc.* 370 F.Supp.2d 1025 (N.D.Cal., 2005).
Disney Enterprises Inc. v. *Does* 1–10, N.D. Fla., No. 06-0096, complaint filed 2/23/06.
Donaldson v. *Beckett* (1774) 4 Burr 2408; 98 ER 257.
Dow Jones & Co Inc v. *Gutnick* (2002) 194 ALR 433.
Eastern Microwave, Inc. v. *Doubleday Sports, Inc.*, 691 F.2d 125, 129 (CA2 1982).
Eldred v. *Ashcroft* 123 S. Ct. 769 (2003).
Eldred v. *Reno* 74 F. Supp. 2d 1(1999).
Eldred v. *Reno* 239 Fd. 3d 372 (2001).
Elektra Entertainment Group v. *Barker* No. 05 CV 7340 (S.D.N.Y., filed Feb. 24, 2006).
Elektra Entertainment Group, Inc. v. *Santangelo* Slip Copy, 2005 WL 3199841 (S.D.N.Y., 2005).
EMI Records (Ireland) Ltd et al. v. *Eirecom Ltd, BT Telecommunications Ireland Ltd* [2005] IEHC 233.
Felten and others v. *RIAA* (unreported, United States District Court of New Jersey, 28 November 2001), http://www.eff.org/IP/DMCA/Felten_v._RIAA/20011128_ hearing_transcript.html.
Field v. *Google Inc.* 412 F.Supp.2d 1106 (D.Nev., 2006).
Fortnightly Corp. v. *United Artists Television, Inc.*, 392 U.S. 390 (1968).
Foundation v. *UPC Nederland* (2005); and on appeal (2006).
GEICO v. *Google Inc.* Not Reported in F.Supp.2d, 2005 WL 1903128 (E.D.Va., 2005).

Gilliam and others v. *American Broadcasting Corporation* 538 F.2d 14 (2d Circuit, 1976).

Golan v. *Ashcroft* 310 F.Supp.2d 1215 (2004).

Golan v. *Gonzales* 74 U.S.P.Q.2d 1808 (2005).

Gonzales v. *Google Inc.* 5:06-mc-80006-JW (US District for the Northern District of California, 2006).

Google Inc. v. *American Blind & Wallpaper Factory, Inc.* Not Reported in F.Supp.2d, 2005 WL 832398 (N.D.Cal., 2005).

Google, Inc. v. *Microsoft Corporation* 415 F.Supp.2d 1018 (N.D.Cal., 2005).

Gruber v. *Sony Corporation of America*, No. BC342805 (Cal. Super. Ct. Nov. 9, 2005).

Guevara v. *Sony BMG Music Entertainment*, No. BC342359 (Cal. Super. Ct. Nov. 1, 2005).

Hanson v. *ABC* (unreported, Supreme Court of Queensland, 1 September 1997).

Harper & Row v. *Nation Enterprises* 471 US 539 (1985).

Hong Kong Special Administrative Region v. *Chan Nai-Ming* (TMCC 1268/2005, 24 October 2005); and, on appeal (HCMA 1221/2005, 12 December 2006).

Hull v. *Sony BMG Music Entertainment*, No. BC343385 (Cal. Super. Ct. Nov. 21, 2005), http://www.eff.org/IP/DRM/Sony-BMG/sony_complaint.pdf.

Huntsman v. *Soderbergh*, Not Reported in F.Supp.2d, 2005 WL 1993421 (D.Colo., 2005).

Hyperion Records Ltd v. *Warner Music (UK) Ltd* (unreported, Chancery Division of the High Court, 17 May 1991).

In re: Aimster Copyright Litigation 334 F. 3d 643 (7th Cir. 2003).

In re Charter Communications, 393 F.3d 771 (8th Cir. 2005).

In re Harald Welte v. *SiteCom Germany* No. 21 0 6123/04 District Court of Munich I (19 May 2004), http://www.jbb.de/judgment_dc_munich_gpl.pdf#search=% 22netfilter%20sitecom%22.

In re Napster, Inc. Copyright Litigation, Not Reported in F.Supp.2d, 2005 WL 289977, N.D.Cal., Feb. 03, 2005.

In re Napster, Inc. Copyright Litigation, 354 F.Supp.2d 1113, 2005-1 Trade Cases P 74, 743, N.D.Cal., Feb. 03, 2005.

In re Napster, Inc. Copyright Litigation, 377 F.Supp.2d 796, 77 U.S.P.Q.2d 1833, N.D.Cal., 31 May 2005.

In re Napster, Inc. Copyright Litigation, 235 F.R.D. 463, 2006-1 Trade Cases P 75, 205, N.D.Cal., Apr. 20, 2006.

In re Napster, Inc. Copyright Litigation, Slip Copy, 2006 WL 1348555, N.D.Cal., May 17, 2006.

In re Sony BMG CD Technologies Litigation No 1:05-cv-09575 (NRB) (US District Court for the Southern District of New York, 2005).

Infinity Broadcast Corporation v. *Kirkwood*, 150 F.3d 104, 108 (2d Cir. 1998).

Intellectual Reserve v. *Utah Lighthouse Ministry* 75 F. Supp. 2d 1290 (1999).

Jacoby v. *Sony BMG Music Entertainment*, No. 05/116679 (N.Y. Sup. Ct. Nov. 30, 2005).

JibJab Media Inc. v. *Ludlow Music Inc* (2004), http://www.eff.org/legal/cases/JibJab_v._ Ludlow/20040729_JibJab_Complaint.pdf.

Kabushiki Kaisha Sony Computer v. *Stevens* (2002) 55 IPR 497.

Kabushiki Kaisha Sony Computer v. *Stevens* (2003) 57 IPR 161.

Kahle v. *Ashcroft* 72 U.S.P.Q.2d 1888 (2004).

Kazaa v. *Buma and Stemra* (unreported, 28 March 2002, Amsterdam Court of Appeal): http://www.eff.org/IP//P2P/BUMA_v._Kazaa/.

Kelly v. *Arriba Soft* 336 F.3d 811 (2003).

Klemm v. *Sony BMG Music Entertainment*, No. C 05 5111 BZ (N.D. Cal. Dec. 9, 2005).

Klewan v. *Arista Holdings Inc. d/b/a Sony BMG Music Entertainment,* No. 05 CV 9609, consolidated as No. 05 CV 9575 (NRB) (S.D.N.Y. Nov. 14, 2005).

Lexmark International, Inc. v. *Static Control Components, Inc* 253 F.Supp.2d 943 (E.D.Ky. 2003) and 387 F.3d 522 (Fed Cir 6th, 2004).

Los Angeles News Service v. *Reuters Television Int'l Ltd.*, 149 F.3d 987 (9th Cir.1998), 525 U.S. 1141, 119 S.Ct. 1032, 143 L.Ed.2d 41 (1999).

Louis Vuitton v. *Google Inc.* (Paris District Court, February 2005), and on appeal (Paris Court of Appeals, June 2006).

Luck's Music Library v. *Gonzales* 407 F.3d 1262 (2005).

Ludlow Music Inc. v. *Williams* [2002] F.S.R. 57.

Ludlow Music Inc. v. *Williams (No. 2)* [2002] E.M.L.R. 29; [2002] EWHC 638 Ch D.

Macrovision Corp. v. *321 Studios*, Not Reported in F.Supp.2d, 2004 WL 1066323 (S.D.N.Y.) and 2005 WL 678851 (S.D.N.Y.).

Macrovision v. *Sima Products Corporation* WL 1063284 (S.D.N.Y. 20 April 2006); and WL 1472152 (S.D.N.Y. 26 May, 2006).

MAI Systems Corp v. *Peak Computer Inc* 991 F2d 511 (9th Cir. 1993); cert denied 114 S Ct 671 (1994).

Maletta v. *Sony BMG Music Entertainment Corp.*, No. BC343615 (Cal. Super. Ct. Nov. 28, 2005).

Maletta v. *Sony BMG Music Entertainment,* No. 05 CV 10637 (UA) (S.D.N.Y. Dec. 19, 2005).

Marobie-FL Inc v. *National Association of Fire Equipment* Distribs 983 F Supp 1167 (ND Ill 1997).

Mattel Inc v. *Walking Mountain Productions* 353 F.3d 792 (2004).

Mazer v. *Stein* 347 U.S. 201 (1954).

McClurg v. *Kingsland* 1 How. 202 (1843).

McGraw-Hill Companies et al. v. *Google Inc.* Case No. 05 CV 8881-JES (2005), http://www.publishers.org/press/pdf/40%20McGraw-Hill%20v.%20Google.pdf.

Melcon v. *Sony BMG Music Entertainment*, No. C 05 5084 MHP (N.D. Cal. Dec. 8, 2005).

Metro-Goldwyn-Mayer Studios Inc. v. *Grokster Ltd* (2003) 243 F.Supp.2d 1073.

Metro-Goldwyn-Mayer Studios v. *Grokster Ltd.* 259 F.Supp.2d 1029 (2003).

Metro-Goldwyn-Mayer Studios v. *Grokster Ltd.* 380 F.3d 1154 (9th Cir. 2004).

Metro-Goldwyn-Mayer Studios Inc. v. *Grokster Ltd.* 125 S.Ct. 2764 (2005).

Metro-Goldwyn-Mayer Studios, Inc. v. *Grokster Ltd.* 2006 WL 2806882 (United States District Court, Central District of California, 27 September, 2006).

Michaelson v. *Sony BMG Music, Inc.*, No. 05 CV 9575 (NRB) (S.D.N.Y. Nov. 14, 2005).

Millar v. *Kincaid* (1759) 98 ER 210.

Millar v. *Taylor* (1769) 4 Burr. 2303; 98 ER 201.

Morrison Leahy Music Limited v. *Lightbond Limited* [1993] EMLR 144.

Motown Record Company v. *IMesh.com Inc* WL 503720 (2004).

MP3.com, Inc. v. *Cooley Godward LLP*, No. BC 266625 (Filed, L.A. Super. Ct., Jan. 2002).

Newmark, et al., v. *Turner Broadcasting System, Inc* (9 January 2004), http:// www.eff.org/IP/Video/Newmark_v._Turner/20040109_Order.pdf.

Newton v. *Diamond* 204 F. Supp. 2d 1244 (2002).

Newton v. *Diamond* 388 F.3d 1189 (9th Cir. 2004).

Newton v. *Diamond* 125 S.Ct. 2905 (2005).

New York Times Co Inc. v. *Roxbury Interface, Inc.*, 434 F.Supp. 217 (D.N.J.1977).

New York Times Co. Inc. v. *Tasini* 533 U.S. 483 (2001).

Online Policy Group et al. v. *Diebold Inc.* 337 F. Supp. 2d 1195 (2004).

Palmer and Cook v. *First 4 Internet, Sony BMG Music (Canada) Inc and Sony BMG Music Entertainment* (Ontario Superior Court of Justice, 16 January 2006).

Paramount Pictures Corp. v. *Load 'N Go Video* 06 CV 12931, (United States District Court, Southern District of New York, 3 November 2006).

Paramount Pictures Corp. v. *ReplayTV Inc,* No. 2:01CV09358 (Docket) (C.D.Cal. Oct. 31, 2001).

Paramount Pictures Corp. v. *ReplayTV Inc.* 298 F.Supp.2d 921 (C.D.Cal, 2004).

Paramount Pictures Corp. v. *Thompson*, D. Utah, No. 06-0156, complaint filed 2/23/06.

Parke v. *RIAA* ('No Clean Slate lawsuit') 9 September 2003, http://www.eff.org/IP/ P2P/Parke_v._RIAA/Parke_RIAA_Complaint.pdf.

Parker v. *Google, Inc.* 422 F.Supp.2d 492 (2006).

Perfect 10 Inc. v. *Amazon.com Inc.* CV05-4753 AHM (SHx) (US District Court for the Central District of California, 2005).

Perfect 10 Inc. v. *Google Inc.*, 16 F.Supp.2d 828 (2006).

Perquin and UFC Que Cholsir v. *SA Films, Alain Sarde Ste, Universal Pictures Video France* (28 February 2006).

Playboy Enterprises Inc v. *Frena* 839 F. Supp 1552 (MD Fl 1993).

Polydor Limited and Others v. *Brown and Others* [2005] EWHC 3191 (Ch).

Ponting v. *SONYBMG Music Entertainment, LLC*, No. CV-05-08472-JFW(AJWx) (C.D. Cal. Dec. 2, 2005).

Potter v. *Sony BMG Music Entertainment,* No. 05 CV 9607, consolidated as No. 05 CV 9575 (NRB) (S.D.N.Y. Nov. 14, 2005).

Princeton University Press v. *Michigan Document Services* 99 F.3d 1381 (1996).

Progress Software Corp. v. *MySQL AB* 195 F.Supp.2d 328 (D.Mass., 2002).

RealNetworks, Inc. v. *Streambox, Inc.*, No. 2:99CV02070, 2000 WL 127311 (W.D.Wash., Jan. 18, 2000).

Red Hat, Inc. v. *The SCO Group, Inc.*, Not Reported in F.Supp.2d, 2004 WL 883400, (D.Del., Apr. 06, 2004).

Religious Technology Center v. *Netcom* 907 F. Supp 1361 (ND Cal 1995).

RIAA v. *Diamond Multimedia Systems Inc.* 180 F.3d 1072 (1999).

RIAA v. *Verizon Internet Services* 257 F Supp 2d 244 (2003).

RIAA v. *Verizon Internet Services*, 543 U.S. 924, 125 S.Ct. 309 U.S (2004).

Ricciuti v. *Sony BMG Music Entertainment,* No. 05 CV 10190 (BSJ) (S.D.N.Y. Dec. 5, 2005).

Rivas v. *Sony BMG Music Entertainment*, No. 05 CV 9598, consolidated as No. 05 CV 9575 (NRB) (S.D.N.Y. Nov. 14, 2005).

Rogers v. *Koons* 960 F. 2nd 301 (1992).

Schott Musik International GmbH & Co And Others v. *Colossal Records Of Australia Pty Ltd And Others* (1996) 71 FCR 37, 36 IPR 267.

Schott Musik International GmbH & Co And Others v. *Colossal Records Of Australia Pty Ltd And Others* (1997) 75 FCR 321, 38 IPR 1.

SCO Group, Inc. v. *IBM Corp.*, Not Reported in F.Supp.2d, 2005 WL 318784, 2005 Copr.L.Dec. P 28, 957 (D.Utah, Feb. 09, 2005).

SCO Group, Inc. v. *IBM Corp.*, Not Reported in F.Supp.2d, 2005 WL 3776323, 2005 Copr.L.Dec. P 29,027, (D.Utah, Jul. 01, 2005).

SCO Group, Inc. v. *IBM Corp.*, Slip Copy, 2006 WL 2434229, (D.Utah, Aug. 21, 2006).

SCO Group, Inc. v. *Novell, Inc.* Slip Copy, 2006 WL 2403578 (D.Utah, 2006).
Sega Enterprises Ltd v. *MAPHIA* 1997 WL337558 (ND Cal., 8 June 1997).
Shloss v. *Sweeney* C 06-3718 (US District Court for the Northern District of California, 2006).
Slattery v. *Apple Computer Inc.* Not Reported in F.Supp.2d, 2005 WL 2204981 (N.D.Cal.).
Société Civile des Producteurs Phonographiques v. *Antoine G and the Association of Audionautes* (December 2005).
Society of Composers, Authors and Music Publishers of Canada v. *Canadian Association of Internet Providers*, [2004] 2 S.C.R. 427.
Sony Corporation of America v. *Universal City Studios Inc.* 464 US 417 (1984).
Sony Computer Entertainment Inc v. *Ball* [2004] EWHC 1738 (Ch).
Sony Computer Entertainment Inc v. *Owen* [2002] EWHC 45.
Sony Music Productions Pty Ltd v. *Tansing (t/a Apple House Music)* (1993) 27 IPR 640.
Stéphane P and Association UFC v. *Universal Pictures Video France* (22 April 2005).
Stevens v. *Kabushiki Kaisha Sony Computer Entertainment & Ors* [2005] HCATrans 30 (8 February 2005).
Stevens v. *Kabushiki Kaisha Sony Computer Entertainment* (2005) 221 ALR 448.
Stewart v. *Abend* 495 U.S. 207, 228 (1990).
Storage Technology Corporation v. *Custom Hardware Engineering & Consulting, Inc.* 421 F.3d 1307 (Fed. Cir. 2005).
Stynchula v. *Sony Corporation of America*, No. BC343100 (Cal. Super. Ct. Nov. 15, 2005).
Suntrust Bank v. *Houghton Mifflin Company* 136 F. Supp. 2d 1357 (2001).
Suntrust Bank v. *Houghton Mifflin Company*, 268 F.3d 1257 (11th Cir. 2001).
Teleprompter Corp. v. *Columbia Broadcasting System, Inc.*, 415 U.S. 394 (1974).
Telstra Corp Ltd v. *APRA* (1997) 191 CLR 140.
Texas v. *Sony BMG Music Entertainment*, (Dist. Ct., Travis Co, Tex, 2005).
Tonson v. *Collins* (1761) 96 ER 169.
Tracfone Wireless Inc. v. *Sol Wireless Group Inc* 05-23279 (US District Court for the Southern District of Florida, 21 December 2005), http://www.copyright.gov/1201/2006/reply/14granick_WA.pdf.
Tur v. *YouTube Inc.* case number CV 06-4436-GAF (FMO_x) (United States District Court, Central District of California, 14 July 2006).
Twentieth Century Fox Film Corporation et al. v. *Cablevision Systems Corporation et al.* 2007 WL 867093 (S.D.N.Y.), 82 U.S.P.Q.2d 1075 (2007).

UMG Recordings, Inc. v. *Bertelsmann* AG 222 F.R.D. 408 (N.D.Cal., 2004).
UMG Recordings, Inc. v. *MP3.Com, Inc.* 92 F.Supp.2d 349 S.D.N.Y (2000).
Un Nezez v. *Caribbean International News Corporation* 235 F.3d 18 (1st Cir. 2000).
Union Fédérale des Consommateurs – Que Choisir v. *Apple Computer France S.A.R.L. and iTunes S.A.R.L.* (9 February 2005).
United States of America v. *Elcom Ltd* 203 F.Supp.2d 1111 (N.D. Cal. 2002).
Universal City Studios v. *Corley*, 273 F.3d 429 (Fed. Cir. 2nd, 2001).
Universal City Studios v. *Reimerdes* 82 F.Supp.2d 211 (S.D.N.Y. 2000).
Universal City Studios v. *Reimerdes* 111 F.Supp.2d 294 (S.D.N.Y. 2000).
Universal City Studios, Inc. v. *Sony Corporation of America*, 480 F.Supp. 429 (1979).
Universal City Studios, Inc. v. *Sony Corporation of America*, 659 F.2d 963 (1981).
Universal Music Australia Pty Ltd v. *Cooper* [2005] FCA 972.
Universal Music Australia Pty Ltd v. *Miyamoto* [2003] FCA 812 (18 July 2003); [2004] FCA 982 (20 July 2004).
Universal Music Australia Pty Ltd v. *Sharman License Holdings Ltd.* [2005] FCA 1242; (2005) 220 ALR 1.
University of New South Wales v. *Moorhouse* (1975) 133 CLR 1.
Verizon Internet Services v. *RIAA* 351 F.3d 1229 (DC Cir. 2003).
Viacom International Inc. et al. v. *YouTube Inc., YouTube LLC. and Google Inc.* (United States District Court for the Southern District of New York, 13 March 2007).
Wallace v. *Free Software Foundation, Inc* Slip Copy, 2005 WL 3239208 (S.D.Ind., 2005).
Walt Disney Productions v. *Air Pirates*, 581 F.2d 751 (9th Cir. 1978).
Warner Music Australia Pty Ltd v. *Swiftel Communications Pty Ltd* [2005] FMCA 627; and *(No. 2)* [2005] FMCA 706.
White-Smith Music Publishing Co. v. *Apollo Co.*, 209 U.S. 1 (1908).
Williams & Wilkins Co v. *The United States* 420 US 376 (1975).
Xanthakos v. *Sony BMG Music Entertainment, LLC*, No. 05-0009203 (D.C. Super. Ct. Nov. 28, 2005).

LEGISLATION

An Act to Amend the Copyright Act 2005 (C-60)
Audio Home Recording Act 1992 (US)
Benefit Authors without Limiting Advancement or Net Consumer Expectations (BALANCE) Act 2003 (US)
California Business and Professions Code (California)

Child Online Protection Act 1998 (US)
Computer Fraud and Abuse Act 1986 (US)
Constitution Act 1982 (Canada)
Consumer Legal Remedies Act (California)
Consumer Protection Against Computer Spyware Act 2005 (Texas)
Copyright and Related Rights (Amendment) Act 2004 (Ireland)
Copyright Act 1968 (Cth)
Copyright Act 1909 (US)
Copyright Act 1976 (US)
Copyright Amendment Act 1989 (Cth)
Copyright Amendment Act 2006 (Cth)
Copyright Amendment (Digital Agenda) Act 2000 (Cth)
Copyright Amendment (Moral Rights) Act 2000 (Cth)
Digital Media Consumers' Rights Act 2003 (US) HR 107
Digital Millennium Copyright Act 1998 (US)
EC Copyright Term Directive, Council Directive 93/98/EEC of 29 October 1993 harmonizing the term of protection of copyright and certain related rights. Official Journal L 290, 24/11/1993 P. 0009–0013
EC Electronic Commerce Directive 2000/31/EC, passed 8 June 2000
EC Information Society Directive, Council Directive 2001/29/EC of 22 May 2001 on the harmonization of certain aspects of copyright and related rights in the information society
Family Entertainment and Copyright Act 2005 (US)
Family Movie Act 2005 (US)
Inducing Infringement of Copyrights Act (the *Induce Act*) 2004 (US)
Intellectual Property Protection Act 2006 (US)
Lanham Act 1946 (US)
Lucy Maud Montgomery Copyright Term Extension Bill 2003 (Bill C-36)
Performers' Copyright Bill 1975 (Cth)
Public Domain Enhancement Act 2005 (US)
Sherman Act 1890 (US)
Sonny Bono Copyright Term Extension Act 1998 (US)
Status of the Artist Act 1992 (C-33)
Statute of Anne 1710 (UK)
Statute of Monopolies 1624 (UK)
Taxes Consolidation Act 1997 (Ireland)
Trade Practices Act 1974 (Cth)
Uruguay Round Agreements Act 1994 (US)
US Free Trade Agreement Implementation Act 2004 (Cth)
Visual Artists Rights Act 1990 (US)

INTERNATIONAL INSTRUMENTS

Agreement on Trade-Related Aspects of Intellectual Property Rights 1994 (*TRIPS Agreement*), http://www.wto.org/english/tratop_e/trips_e/t_agm0_e.htm.

Australia–United States Free Trade Agreement 2004 (*AUSFTA*), http://www.dfat.gov.au/trade/negotiations/us_fta/final-text/chapter_17.html.

Berne Convention for the Protection of Literary and Artistic Works 1886, http://www.wipo.int/treaties/en/ip/berne/pdf/trtdocs_wo001.pdf.

Draft Treaty on Access to Knowledge (A2K Treaty), http://www.cptech.org/a2k/consolidatedtext-may9.pdf.

Free Trade Area of the Americas, http://www.ftaa-alca.org/.

North-American Free Trade Agreement 1994 (NAFTA), http://www.nafta-sec-alena.org/DefaultSite/index.html.

United States–Singapore Free Trade Agreement 2003, http://www.ustr.gov/new/fta/ Singapore/consolidated_texts.htm.

United States–Chile Free Trade Agreement 2003, http://www.ustr.gov/new/fta/Chile/text/index.htm.

United States–Dominican Republic–Central America Free Trade Agreement, 2005, http://www.ustr.gov/Trade_Agreements/Bilateral/CAFTA/CAFTA DR_Final_ Texts/Section_Index.html.

World Intellectual Property Organization Copyright Treaty 1996, http://www.wipo. int/treaties/en/ip/wct/pdf/trtdocs_wo033.pdf.

World Intellectual Property Organization Phonographs and Phonograms Treaty 1996, http://www.wipo.int/treaties/en/ip/wppt/pdf/trtdocs_wo034.pdf.

Index